LIBRARY OF NEW TESTAMENT STUDIES

452

Formerly the Journal for the Study of the New Testament Supplement series

Editor

Mark Goodacre

Volume One of Luke the Interpreter of Israel

Jesus and the Heritage of Israel
Luke's Narrative Claim upon Israel's Legacy
Edited by David P. Moessner

PAUL AND THE HERITAGE OF ISRAEL

Paul's Claim upon Israel's Legacy
in Luke and Acts in the Light
of the Pauline Letters

Volume Two of
Luke the Interpreter of Israel

Edited by
David P. Moessner
Daniel Marguerat
Mikeal C. Parsons
Michael Wolter

BLOOMSBURY
LONDON • NEW DELHI • NEW YORK • SYDNEY

Bloomsbury T&T Clark
An imprint of Bloomsbury Publishing Plc

50 Bedford Square	1385 Broadway
London	New York
WC1B 3DP	NY 10018
UK	USA

www.bloomsbury.com

Bloomsbury is a registered trade mark of Bloomsbury Publishing Plc

First published 2012
Paperback edition first published 2013

British Library Cataloguing-in-Publication Data
A catalogue record for this book is available from the British Library.

ISBN: HB: 978-0-567-40148-9
PB: 978-0-567-10816-6

Library of Congress Cataloging-in-Publication Data
A catalog record for this book is available from the Library of Congress.

Typeset by Free Range Book Design & Production

CONTENTS

ACKNOWLEDGEMENTS

A significant feature of this volume is the making of seven current, cutting-edge French language essays available to an English-speaking audience. This daunting translation project could not even have been entertained without the enthusiastic support and direction of Dr. Michael Thomas, Divisional Director in the Department of Modern Foreign Languages at Baylor University, who supervised an expert team. The translators included: Dr. James Ernest, Baker Academic; Dr. Theresa Varney Kennedy, Baylor University; Dr. James McConnell, Gardner-Webb Divinity School; Dr. Julien Smith, Valparaiso University; Dr. Alexandre Thiltges, Baylor University, and Timothy Brookins, Eric Gilchrest and Nicholas Zola, all doctoral students in New Testament studies at Baylor University. The initial translation of each article was reviewed by a second (and sometimes third) translator, and when possible also the original author as well as one of the volume's editors (the primary translators are indicated beneath the author's name on the title page of each translated essay [see also the Introduction]). The editors are deeply grateful to Dr. Thomas for his enormous contributions and expertise; indeed, without his supervision, this book could not have been realized.

The editors also express gratitude for the funding of the translations that derived from a number of sources. Mr. Joe Armes, former Regent at Baylor University, generously provided the initial grant that allowed the work to begin. Dr. James Nogalski, Director of Graduate Studies at Baylor University, dedicated portions of several student stipends toward the completion of this work, and Dr. Truell Hyde, Vice-Provost for Research at Baylor, provided a much-needed grant through the Arts & Humanities Faculty Research Program, which enabled us to complete the translation work.

The editors also express thanks to a number of other individuals without whose assistance this project could not have continued: to Ms. Emmanuelle Steffek of Lausanne for her great help in facilitating communication; Josh Stout and Brian Gamel of Baylor University for their assistance in bibliographic references, and to University of Dubuque Theological Seminary students Mark Flynn, Sean Hevener, Andy Phillips, Rob Smith, and Kevin Veldhuisen for their invaluable assistance in research, proof reading, and formatting of the essays. A special debt of gratitude is owed to Ms. Heather Gorman and Mr. Brian Gamel, doctoral students in New Testament at Baylor University, whose facilitation of all things editorial was a marvellous help. Heather compiled the master bibliography, and Brian prepared the indexes for the volume.

Finally, the editors would like to thank David Tiede, one of the leading lights in the inspiration of Luke the Interpreter of Israel series and co-author of the

Introduction and Conclusion of Volume One, *Jesus and the Heritage of Israel.*
In many ways his visionary vigour has continued to propel this project to its
completion and he remains, therefore, in a very real sense, a 'general editor' of
this two-volume enterprise.

The Editors

ABBREVIATIONS

AB	Anchor Bible
ABRL	Anchor Bible Reference Library
ACW	Ancient Christian Writers
AGJU/AGAJU	Arbeiten zur Geschichte des antiken Judentums und des Urchristentums
ANRW	*Aufstieg und Niedergang der römischen Welt: Geschichte und Kultur Roms im Spiegel der neueren Forschung*
ATANT	Abhandlungen zur Theologie des Alten und Neuen Testaments
BETL	Bibliotheca ephemeridum theologicarum lovaniensium
BHG	*Bibliotheca hagiographica Graece*
BHT/BHTh	Beiträge zur historischen Theologie
Bib	*Biblica*
BIS	Biblical Interpretation Series
BiTS	Biblical Tools and Studies
BJRL	*Bulletin of the John Rylands University Library of Manchester*
BTB	*Biblical Theology Bulletin*
BU	Biblische Untersuchungen
BWANT	Beiträge zur Wissenschaft vom Alten und Neuen Testament
BZNW	Beihefte zur Zeitschrift für die neutestamentliche Wissenschaft
CBQ	*Catholic Biblical Quarterly*
CNT	Commentaire du Nouveau Testament
ConBNT/Cb.NT	Coniectanea biblica, New Testament
DBSup/DBS	*Dictionnaire de la Bible, Supplément*
ÉB/ÉtB/Ébib/ÉtBib	Études bibliques
EKKNT	Evangelisch-Katholischer Kommentar zum Neuen Testament
EssBib	Essais Bibliques
ET/ExpT	*Expository Times*
EvT/EvTh	*Evangelische Theologie*
FRLANT	Forschungen zur Religion und Literatur des Alten und Neuen Testaments
FzB/FB	Forschung zur Bibel
GNT	Grundrisse zum Neuen Testament

HBS	Herders Biblische Studien
HBT	*Horizons in Biblical Theology*
HNT	Handbuch zum Neuen Testament
HThK/HTKNT	Herders theologischer Kommentar zum Neuen Testament
HTS/HThS	Harvard Theological Studies
HUT/HUTh	Hermeneutische Untersuchungen zur Theologie
ICC	International Critical Commentary
Int	*Interpretation*
IThS/IthSt	Innsbucher theologische Studien
JBL	*Journal of Biblical Literature*
JHC	*Journal of Higher Criticism*
JR	*Journal of Religion*
JSJSup	Supplements to the *Journal for the Study of Judaism*
JSNT	*Journal for the Study of the New Testament*
JSNTSup	*Journal for the Study of the New Testament*, Supplement Series
JTC	*Journal for Theology and the Church*
JTS/JThSt	*Journal of Theological Studies*
KEK	Kritisch-exegetischer Kommentar über das Neue Testament
LCL	Loeb Classical Library
LD/LeDiv	Lectio divina
LeDi Comm.	Lectio divina, Commentaires
LNTS	Library of New Testament Studies
MdB	Le Monde de la Bible
Neot	*Neotestamentica*
NICNT	New International Commentary on the New Testament
NIGTC	New International Greek Testament Commentary
NovT	*Novum Testamentum*
NovTSup	*Novum Testamentum*, Supplements
NRF	Nouvelle revue française
NTA/NTAbh	Neutestamentliche Abhandlungen
NTD	Das Neue Testament Deutsch
NTGF	The New Testament in the Greek Fathers
NTOA	Novum Testamentum et Orbis Antiquus
NTS	*New Testament Studies*
NTTS	New Testament Tools and Studies
ÖTBK	Ökumenischer Taschenbuchkommentar
PRS/PRSt	*Perspectives in Religious Studies*
QD	Quaestiones disputatae
RB	*Revue biblique*
RHPh/RHPhR	*Revue d'histoire et philosophie religieuses*
RivBib/RivB	*Rivista biblica*
RNT	Regensburger Neues Testament
RSR	*Recherches de science religieuse*

RThPh	*Revue de théologie et de philosophie*
SANT	Studien zum Alten und Neuen Testament
SBAB	Stuttgarter biblische Aufsatzbände
SBLDS	SBL Dissertation Series
SBLMS	SBL Monograph Series
SBLSBS	SBL Sources for Biblical Study
SBLSP	SBL Seminar Papers
SBS	Stuttgarter Bibelstudien
SC	Sources chrétiennes
SECÄ	Studien zur Erforschung des christlichen Ägyptens
SJLA	Studies in Judaism in Late Antiquity
SNTSMS	Society for New Testament Studies Monograph Series
StANT/SANT	Studien zum Alten und Neuen Testament
TANZ	Texte und Arbeiten zum neutestamentlichen Zeitalter
ThB/Tbü	Theologische Bücherei
ThHK/THKNT	Theologischer Handkommentar zum Neuen Testament
ThWB/TDNT	*Theological Dictionary of the New Testament*
TLZ	*Theologische Literaturzeitung*
TZ/ThZ	*Theologische Zeitschrift*
TZTh	*Tübinger Zeitschrift für Theologie*
UTB	Uni-Taschenbücher
WBC	Word Biblical Commentary
WdF	Wege der Forschung
WMANT	Wissenschaftliche Monographien zum Alten und Neuen Testament
WUNT	Wissenschaftliche Untersuchungen zum Neuen Testament
ZBK	Zürcher Bibelkommentare
ZKG	*Zeitschrift für Kirchengeschichte*
ZNW	*Zeitschrift für die neutestamentliche Wissenschaft*
ZTK	*Zeitschrift für Theologie und Kirche*
ZWT/ZwTh	*Zeitschrift für wissenschaftliche Theologie*

CONTRIBUTORS

Timothy Brookins, with **Mikeal Parsons** and **Peter Reynolds**, Baylor University

Simon Butticaz, University of Lausanne

Claire Clivaz, University of Lausanne

Andreas Dettwiler, University of Geneva

Odile Flichy, Centre Sèvres, Facultés Jésuites de Paris

Richard Hays, Duke University Divinity School

Jean-François Landolt, University of Lausanne

Daniel Marguerat, University of Lausanne

David Moessner, University of Dubuque and University of Pretoria

Christopher Mount, DePaul University

Richard Pervo, St. Paul, Minnesota

Yann Redalié, Facoltà Valdese di Teologia, Rome

Jens Schröter, University of Berlin

Gregory Sterling, Notre Dame University

[**Philipp Vielhauer**, (Bonn) 'On the "Paulinism" of Acts', reprinted]

Michael Wolter, University of Bonn

Introduction

The Legacy of Paul in Acts – A 'More Complete and Inhabitable' New Testament?

David P. Moessner, with D. Marguerat,
M. C. Parsons, M. Wolter

A canon which comprised only the four Gospels and the Pauline Epistles would have been at best an edifice of two wings without the central structure, and therefore incomplete and uninhabitable.

Adolf von Harnack, *History of Dogma*
(London: 1896, p. 48 n. 2 [on the role
of Acts in the formation of the
New Testament canon])

One of the inescapable realities of the New Testament is its canonical selecting and sequencing. Though it is obvious that the 'new' is about Jesus of Nazareth, Lord and Son of God, the Christ of Israel, etc., and that its organization and reification into authoritative scriptures of the church in the history of Christianity is inconceivable without the overarching central person and focal point of this Testament, yet at the midpoint of the books of the New Testament is the book of Acts, and at the centre of this book – with nearly three-fourths of its narrative space tangled up with his character – is Paul.[1] And when we ask what role Paul plays when the spotlight of the narrative shifts from the fading light of Stephen to illumine this figure-in-waiting, interpreters of Acts and of Paul are still clamouring for answers and drafting gridlines of understanding. Why does Paul occupy more than half of the 'Act(ion)s of the Apostles', especially when the author Luke never seems to align him squarely as an *apostle* alongside the other apostles? Does Luke really know and depict the Paul of Paul's own letters when, for example, in the Corinthian correspondence or letter to the Galatians his status and authority as an apostle is of great theological consequence?

---

1   Of the 680 numbered pages of the Greek text of the Nestle-Aland 27th edn (German Bible Society, 1993), the precise literary mid-point is the speech and stoning of Stephen, Acts 7 (pp. 337–42), with 'a young man by the name of Saul' waiting in the wings in 7.58.

In 1951 Philipp Vielhauer fired a 'shot across the bow' of New Testament theology, stirring up the controversial relation of Luke to Paul, and fomenting much of the 'troubled waters' of Lukan studies that W. C. van Unnik in the early 1960s would characterize as a 'storm center in contemporary scholarship'. In the twenty-first century the storm has abated perhaps a little but the sea is barely becalmed. Paul's relation to Luke's writings is still disquieting and debated as ever, reeling in new generations of scholars and teachers alike.

Paul and the Heritage of Israel forms the sequel to *Jesus and the Heritage of Israel*, Volume One of Luke the Interpreter of Israel, bringing together fifteen internationally acclaimed scholars in antiquities studies and experts on Paul and Luke, along with the reappearance of Vielhauer's momentous essay. Whereas *Jesus and the Heritage of Israel* provides ample evidence that the evangelist Luke makes his case concerning the significances of Jesus of Nazareth and persuades his audience to those consolidating themes through the narrative text and plotted texture itself, *Paul and the Heritage of Israel* seeks to answer both the 'how' and the 'why' Paul occupies such a central space in the two-volume narrative in illuminating the meaning of Jesus the Christ. Does the dynamic of contour-and-content of the narrative itself provide its own set of hermeneutical passageways and interpretive nodes to answer these questions?

Certainly in the last half of the twentieth century considerable energy was channelled toward Luke's understanding of Paul, whether, for instance, the evangelist properly represented Paul's core convictions as expressed through Paul's 'undisputed' letters. By contrast, in the past two decades the study of Paul in Acts, in the Pauline, Deutero-Pauline, and Pastoral letters has tended to re(con)figure the legacy of this major figure through the lenses of multi-disciplinary approaches to the social and ideological worlds of the interactive networkings of a multi-cultured Greco-Roman milieu. Stemming in large part from the 'postmodern' hermeneutical climate change of the twenty-first century, the focus is now clearly upon the ways Paul was heard, received, read, re-read, and re-interpreted, not only when the apostle was still active, but most especially in those first years and decades following his death when multifaceted efforts to keep his significance alive began to take form and leave their imprint.

All of the following essays except that of Vielhauer reflect this new hermeneutical climate. Many of the contributions originated from deliberations of the international *Society of New Testament Studies* Seminar on 'The Reception of Paul' (2004–2008) or from the Lausanne Conference in 2008 on the 'Pauline Character of Paul in Acts' published as *Reception of Paulinism in Acts/Réception du paulinisme dans les Actes des apôtres* (ed. D. Marguerat; Peeters Press, 2009) and appear here in slightly revised form, in part through the generosity of Peeters Press in permitting several of the essays of the Lausanne conference to be republished in English translation, and to the special skill and largess of the English translating team led by Dr. Michael Thomas of the Modern Foreign Languages Department at Baylor University (see Acknowledgements). Both the 'Reception of Paul Seminar' and the Lausanne conference set out to provoke new approaches to the troubled relation of the Lukan Paul by re-configuring the figure and impact of Paul upon nascent

Christianity within Luke's Acts, within the various Paulines and second-century treatments of Paul, and therefore between the relationships of the two dominant corpuses of the New Testament. The two leading questions of Volume One again drive the investigations: i) Who is 'Israel' and the 'church' for Luke and Luke's Paul? and ii) Who is Jesus of Nazareth and who is Paul in relation to both?

Paul and the Heritage of Israel thus revisits Luke's understanding of Paul, directly or indirectly re-opening all of the conclusions of the popular Vielhauer/Conzelmann/Haenchen era, but with new spectacles from new points of vantage in order to scrutinize yet again one whose stature, in the end, seems impossible to profile, let alone to 'measure':

- In *Part I* of *Paul and the Heritage of Israel* Vielhauer's seminal essay is reprinted in full and serves as a bellwether for five recent attempts to sketch the figure of Paul in the wake of his own reception.
- *Part II* features Lukan trajectories into the thought and influence of Paul, marking implicit as well as explicit comparisons with the Paul of the 'undisputed' and 'Deutero-Pauline' letters, as well as with certain second-century texts that 'remember' Paul.
- *Part III* takes stock of Paul's legacy within specific Deutero-Pauline and Pastoral letters, monitoring the apostle's burgeoning influence in a growing number of 'ecclesiastical' communities within a widening circle of Paul's impact in the Mediterranean basin.

Paul and the Heritage of Israel thus accomplishes what no other single book has done: combining both the 'Paul of Paul' and the 'Paul of Luke' in one seminal volume, while linking the Paul of Acts more fundamentally, more foundationally to Jesus of Nazareth of the Lukan Gospel. Sixteen essays place Luke and Paul in their own and yet shared spaces to design new modules for their joint occupancy of the New Testament.

Does the figure of Paul in Acts, perhaps à la Harnack, indeed make the New Testament more 'complete' and 'inhabitable'?

Part I

RE-FIGURING PAUL

Chapter 1

ON THE "PAULINISM" OF ACTS[1]*

Philipp Vielhauer

The following discussion poses the question whether and to what extent the author of Acts took over and passed on theological ideas of Paul, whether and to what extent he modified them. (I refer to the author of Acts as Luke, for the sake of brevity and in order to identify him with the author of the third gospel. I do not thereby equate him with the physician and companion of Paul whom tradition has identified as the author of the two-volume work, Luke and Acts.) Although one would hardly expect from Acts a compendium of Pauline theology, the question which we put is nonetheless justified, for the author portrays Paul as a missionary and thereby also as a theologian, at least in his speeches, which are generally acknowledged to be compositions of the author and which, according to ancient literary custom, had deliberate and paradigmatic significance.[2] The way in which the author presents Paul's theology will not only disclose his own understanding of Paul, but will also indicate whether or not he and Paul belong together theologically. The question as to the Paulinism of Acts is at the same time the question as to a possible theology of Luke himself. Acts is a richer field for such an inquiry than the Gospel, because in the composition of Acts Luke had to master material which was much less formed and arranged than was the Gospel material; in Acts therefore he was more deeply involved as an author than in the composition of his Gospel. And in Acts it was precisely the Pauline section to which he was most required to give form, for apart from the so-called itinerary, which provides the skeleton for 13:1-14:28; 15:35-21:16, it does not seem possible to demonstrate a source (although in the portrayal of the earliest congregation

---

1   [Editors' Note: This essay is reprinted, with permission of the editors, as it was published in *Studies in Luke-Acts* (FS Paul Schubert; ed. L.E. Keck and J.L. Martyn; Nashville: Abingdon Press, 1966), pp. 33-50. Full bibliographic information on the sources cited in the essay is included in the bibliography at the conclusion of this volume.]

*Translated by Wm. C. Robinson, Jr., and Victor P. Furnish from the article "Zum 'Paulinismus' der Apostelgeschichte," *EvTh* X (1950-51), 1-15, published in the *Perkins School of Theology Journal* XVII (Fall, 1963); used by permission.

2   See, most recently, M. Dibelius, "The Speeches in Acts and Ancient Historiography" (1949), subsequently published in *Studies in the Acts of the Apostles*, German: 1951; English: 1956. Unless otherwise designated, all subsequent references to Dibelius will be to this volume of collected essays, although in each case the original publication date will be indicated.

there are already formed individual accounts, in which one may recognize narrative cycles of the pre-Pauline mission[3] or even a source document.[4])

Since this discussion is focused upon the theology involved, we leave aside the question whether Acts gives an accurate portrayal of the person and history of Paul and of his relationship to the earliest congregation, and also the question (which dominated the work of the Tübingen School) as to the party conflicts within the church which lay behind the discrepancy between the Pauline and Lucan accounts of the same historical events and conditions. We restrict ourselves to the elements of the Lucan portrayal of Paul which characterize him as a theologian; that is, we limit ourselves primarily if not exclusively to his speeches and group the theological statements of the Paul of Acts under four headings: natural theology, law, christology, and eschatology, and compare them with statements on these themes from the letters of Paul.

I

At the high point of his book Luke lets Paul make a speech at the Areopagus in Athens before Stoic and Epicurean philosophers, the only sermon to Gentiles by the missionary to the Gentiles to be found in Acts. In the formal opening of his address the speaker takes his point of departure from an altar inscription, "To an unknown God," and says to his hearers: "What therefore you worship as unknown, this I proclaim to you." (Acts 17:22-23.) Then he speaks of God, the creator and Lord of the world, who needs no temple to honor him because he is without need (vss. 24 f.), of the divine providence which so determines men that they should seek God (vss. 26 f.), and of their kinship to God which excludes the veneration of images (vss. 28 f.). At the conclusion he gives a call to repentance in view of the impending day of judgment "on which God will judge the world in righteousness by a man whom he has appointed, and of this he has given assurance to all men by raising him from the dead" (vss. 30 f.).

In his study "Paul on the Areopagus"[5] Martin Dibelius has carefully analyzed the Areopagus speech as a whole and in its individual motifs, and has come to the convincing conclusions (1) that the speech was conceived as an example of a sermon to Gentiles, (2) that it comes from Luke and not from Paul, and (3) that the speech, looked at from the viewpoint of the study of comparative religion, is a "hellenistic speech about the true knowledge of God,"[6] which becomes a Christian speech only at its conclusion.[7]

---

3   Dibelius, "Style Criticism of the Book of Acts" (1923), pp. 3ff.

4   Cf. Jeremias, „Untersuchungen zum Quellenproblem der Apostelgeschichte," *ZNW,* XXXVI, 1937, pp. 205-21; on this point compare now E. Haenchen, *Die Apostelgeschichte,* 13th ed., 1961, pp. 22-32; 72-80.

5   *Op. cit.,* pp. 26-77.

6   *Ibid.,* p. 57.

7   *Ibid.,* pp. 27, 56.

The speech presupposes on the part of its Gentile hearers a presentiment of the true God and seeks by enlightenment to advance this presentiment to a monotheistic idea of God and to a worship of God without images. It describes God as the creator and Lord of the world (vss. 24 f.); yet the Old Testament idea is hellenized both by the concept "cosmos" and by the motif of God's having no needs, both of which are foreign to the Old Testament and are of Hellenistic, specifically Stoic, origin.[8]

Dibelius' work also made probable a Stoic origin of vss. 26 f.:[9] "And he made from one every nation of men to live on all the face of the earth, having determined allotted periods and the boundaries of their habitation, that they should seek God." This sentence states that men were created as inhabitants of the earth in order that they might seek God;[10] they are inclined thereto by God's providence, which determines for them "times" and "boundaries." Dibelius preferred to understand these terms not "historically," that is, of the nations, their epochs, and their national boundaries, but rather "philosophically," of "the ordered times of the year and the fixed zones of habitation." In opposition to this M. Pohlenz has attempted to support the "historical" understanding, that it is here a question of the differentiation of peoples—their temporal and spatial development, peoples who are here contrasted with the unified origin of the human race expressed in the term "from one" (v. 26), and he has shown that this concept has a Stoic background.[11] Thus the meaning would be: "from the common origin of mankind, regardless of their national differentiations, God has equally implanted the quest for God in the hearts of men who are scattered over the entire face of the globe."[12] This is an element of the Stoic teleological proof of God. This quest for God is a quest for knowledge, and it is understood in Hellenistic terms as an act of thought rather than in Old Testament terms as an act of the will.[13]

In vss. 28 f. the Areopagus speaker bases the possibility of this seeking and finding in humanity's common kinship to God, also a Stoic motif.[14] Quoting from one or two Greek poets,[15] he interprets this kinship as "living, moving, and being in God" and as being "indeed his offspring." And from this divine nature which is man's the speaker deduces the demand for an appropriate knowledge and worship of God, that is, the rejection of the worship of images. The tone of this demand, however, is not of accusation but rather that of enlightenment,[16] for in continuing he refers to the period of image worship emphatically as "times of ignorance" which "God overlooked" (vs. 30), as he also does in the speech

---

8 *Ibid.*, pp. 38-46.
9 *Ibid.*, pp. 28, 35.
10 Pohlenz, "Paulus und die Stoa," *ZNW,* XLII (1949), pp. 83 ff.
11 *Ibid.*, pp. 85-88.
12 *Ibid.*, p. 88.
13 Dibelius, p. 32; Pohlenz, p. 85, n. 35.
14 Dibelius, pp. 47 ff.
15 *Ibid.,* pp. 48 ff.; but cf. Pohlenz, pp. 101 ff.
16 Dibelius, pp. 55 f.

at Lystra (14:16) and with reference to the Jews (3:17; 13:27). The emphasis upon "ignorance" as an excuse is a constant motif of the missionary preaching in Acts.[17]

The conclusion of the speech presents judgment as the motivation to repentance, mentions Jesus (without naming him) and his resurrection as proof of his election (vss. 30 f.), but does not mention the saving significance of his death. Indeed, due to the natural kinship to God and the fact that the knowledge of God is vitiated only through ignorance, this is not necessary. The repentance which is called for consists entirely in the self-consciousness of one's natural kinship to God.[18]

Paul also speaks of the pagan's natural knowledge of God: "for what can be known about God is plain to them, because God has shown it to them. Ever since the creation of the world his invisible nature, namely, his eternal power and deity, has been clearly perceived in the things that have been made" (Rom. 1:19 f.). It has long been recognized and acknowledged that this terminology and viewpoint came from Stoic natural theology. Both for Stoicism and for Paul to know God from nature as creator is at the same time to know oneself, insofar as in this knowledge man understands himself in his relationship to God and in his orientation within the cosmos which is ordered and determined by the divine logos.[19] However in Paul the assertion of the natural knowledge of God is surrounded by statements about God's wrath and human guilt; this knowledge of God has led neither to honoring nor to thanking God (vs. 21), but to "ungodliness" and "wickedness" in "suppressing the truth" (vs. 18) and therefore has called forth the "wrath of God" (vs. 18). Paul states the result of this natural knowledge of God unequivocally: "they are without excuse" (vs. 20).

In the Areopagus speech the worship of images was an indication of "ignorance," but was by no means inexcusable; "not knowing you worship," says Paul on the Areopagus (Acts 17:23), "knowing God they did not honor him as God," says Paul in Romans (1:21), and that is "ungodliness" and "wickedness." But this means that the natural theology has an utterly different function in Rom. 1 and in Acts 17; in the former passage it functions as an aid to the demonstration of human responsibility and is thereafter immediately dropped; in the latter passage it is evaluated positively and employed in missionary pedagogy as a forerunner of faith: the natural knowledge of God needs only to be purified, corrected, and enlarged, but its basic significance is not questioned. "Grace does not destroy nature but presupposes and completes it."

In Paul there is no parallel to the motif of man's kinship to God. Dibelius rightly points out that the Pauline analogue to this is man's nearness to Christ;

---

17   *Ibid.,* Cf. Dibelius' comment on I Timothy 1:13 in *HNT* XIII and Bultmann, *Theology of the New Testament* (1951), I, 66.

18   Dibelius, p. 58.

19   Bultmann, "Anknüpfung und "Widerspruch," *ThZ* II (1946), 401 f.; see also his *Primitive Christianity* (1955), pp. 135 ff.

Paul speaks of fellowship with Christ, not of fellowship with God, and the man who participates in this fellowship is not the natural man but rather the redeemed man.[20] By sin the natural man is essentially separated from God and hostile to God. The connection with God is only established through Christ, through his death on the cross, whereby God judges and pardons the world (II Cor. 5:20 f.; Rom. 3:25 f.). Only "in Christ" is man united with God. It is no accident that in the Areopagus speech the concepts "sin" and "grace" are lacking, not only the words, but also the ideas. Due to its kinship to God the human race is capable of a natural knowledge of God and of ethics (Acts 10:35) and has immediate access to God. The "word of the cross" has no place in the Areopagus speech because it would make no sense there; it would be "folly." The author of this speech has eliminated Christology from Paul's sermon to the Gentiles.

To be sure this speech functions only as preliminary instruction, but at this place in Acts and in the function which the author intends it to fulfill it is a self-contained whole.[21] The basic difference from the Pauline view of Christian and pre-Christian existence cannot be ignored. When the Areopagus speaker refers to the unity of the human race in its natural kinship to God and to its natural knowledge of God, and when he refers to the altar inscription and to the statements of pagan poets to make this point, he thereby lays claim to pagan history, culture, and religion as the prehistory of Christianity. His distance from Paul is just as clear as his nearness to the apologists. Justin, for example, counted the Greek philosophers and the righteous men among the barbarians just as much the forefathers of Christianity as were the patriarchs; however he gave this thesis a christological basis, in that he maintained that these men partook in the logos which is identical with Christ.[22]

II

Acts depicts Paul's attitude toward the ancient religion of the Jews just as positively as the Areopagus speech presents his attitude toward the ancient religion of the Greeks. His attitude toward the law is reflected in Acts less in basic discussions in his speeches than in his practical attitude toward Judaism and Jewish Christianity. This attitude is characterized by the following aspects (of which only those of basic significance will be discussed here) :

1. By his missionary method: beginning at the synagogue; only after a formal rejection by the Jews does he turn directly to the Gentiles;
2. By his submission to the Jerusalem authorities;
3. By the circumcision of Timothy (16:3);

---

20   Dibelius, p. 60.
21   This was not noticed by W. Schmid, *Philologus*, 1942, pp. 79-120, esp. p. 115 f.
22   *Apology* I, 5.4; II, 10; 13.4. Cf. B. Seeberg, *ZKG*, LVIII (1939), 1-81, esp. 53-69; 76-81.

4. By spreading the apostolic decree (16:4) (non-historical);
5. By assuming a vow (18:18);
6. By trips to Jerusalem to participate in Jewish religious festivals (18:21; 20:16). In Rom. 15:25 Paul gives as the reason for his last trip to Jerusalem the collection for the congregation, whereas Acts 24:17 combines both reasons: "to bring my nation alms and offerings." But the account in Acts, having said nothing previously about the collection, thus places the major emphasis upon participation in Jewish worship;
7. By participating, on the advice of James, in a Nazirite vow with four members of the Jerusalem congregation (21:18-28);
8. By stressing when on trial that he is a Pharisee (23:6; 26:5) and that he stands for nothing other than the "hope" of the Jews in the resurrection of the dead.

Acts portrays the Gentile missionary Paul as a Jewish Christian who is utterly loyal to the law. Or more precisely said, it pictures him as a true Jew, since he believes in Jesus as the Messiah in contrast to the Jews who have been hardened, who do not share this faith. This portrayal of Paul in Acts is vigorously challenged as well as untiringly defended. According to Paul's letters, however, the Acts' portrayal of his attitude seems to be quite possible with one or two exceptions; whether it is also historical is another question.

The agreement reached at the Apostolic Council does not contradict Paul's missionary practice of beginning at the synagogue, for the statement (Gal. 2:9) "we should go to the Gentiles and they to the circumcised" marks off mission areas, not religions. Furthermore the synagogues, with their coterie of proselytes and God-fearers, especially women, provided an advantageous basis for the Christian mission. Finally, according to II Cor. 11:24, Paul submitted five times to the synagogue punishment of the lash. In other words, as a Christian he acknowledged the synagogue's jurisdiction over himself. Also as a missionary to Gentiles, in the diaspora he obviously lived as a Jew and, as long as his task permitted, maintained his connection with the synagogue.

This was for him, of course, not a law but one possibility—even though the one lying nearest to hand—among others which he could make use of according to the demand of the hour, as is clear from his statements about his freedom to become as a Jew to the Jews and as one outside the law to those outside the law (I Co. 9:19-23). As a missionary Paul entered into the "various particular natural and historical situations of the people with whom he dealt," surrendered his own "national and religious ties"[23] and, without regard for his own preferences, participated in the varying limitations and freedoms of the people with whom he dealt.[24] This was not an accommodation of kerygma to the varieties of religious knowledge or attitudes among Jews or pagans, but an accommodation of practical attitude,[25] and was based in the freedom which

---

23   Schlier, *ThWB*, II, 497, ll. 37 ff.
24   V. Soden, "Sakrament und Ethik bei Paulus," in *Marburger Theologische Studien* (Rudolf Otto Festschrift), (Gotha, 1931), p. 7.
25   Schlier, *op. cit.,* n. 19.

Christ had given from Jewish law as well as from every law. This freedom was limited by the tie to Christ expressed in the words "under the law of Christ" (I Cor. 9:21), for whom he must "win" Jews and Gentiles and by the principle of "for the sake of the gospel." Where the substance of the gospel is threatened, there is a situation of witness-bearing to one's faith, a situation in which there can be no accommodation (Gal.2) and in which those who teach something else are anathematized (Gal.1:8 f.).

In view of Paul's understanding of freedom one must consider as possible not only his participation in the worship of the synagogue, but also his partici-pation in temple worship, in the observation of Jewish festivals, his assumption of private vows, and his participation in the vows of others as portrayed in Acts 21.

To be sure the motivation of this last episode is highly suspect. This ostenta-tious participation was intended to disprove the accusations of Jews and Jewish Christians, who charged that Paul was teaching apostasy from Moses to all the Jews of the diaspora, that is, that he was teaching them that they should not circumcise their children and that they should not live according to Jewish customs; on the contrary, Paul's participation in the vow was intended to show "that you yourself live in observance of the law" (21:24). True enough, the Jewish accusations are formulated as biased distortions of Paul's teachings; but it was Pauline doctrine that the Mosaic law was not the way of salvation, that circumcision was not a condition of salvation, and that Jewish "customs" were without significance with regard to salvation. To this extent the charge of "apostasy from Moses" was entirely appropriate. To convince the Jew that the charge was unjust would have been extremely difficult for the pioneer of the Gentile church and the author of Galatians and II Corinthians. For Paul Moses was not a prototype but an antitype of the Messiah and a personification of "the dispensation of death" and "of condemnation" (II Cor. 3:4-18); for him the acknowledgment of circumcision meant a nullification of the redemptive act of Christ on the cross (Gal. 5:1-12). Had Paul undertaken to show that such a charge was unjust, he would hardly have succeeded by performing a cultic work of supererogation. Had Paul followed the advice of James, he would not only have been hiding in ambiguity, but he would have been unambigu-ously denying his actual practice and his gospel; that is, this would have been a denial that the cross of Christ alone was of saving significance for Gentiles *and* Jews. It is extremely unlikely that Paul participated in this episode for the reasons given in Acts. It is also difficult to assume that James, who knew Paul, his gospel, and his mission, could have suggested such a deception to Paul.

Now it is clear, on the one hand, that Acts wishes to portray James' advice and Paul's conduct as subjectively honorable and objectively correct and, on the other hand, that Acts looks upon the Jewish charges as slander. This last corresponds with the fact that Acts ascribes the motivation for the Jews' hostility toward Paul primarily to their jealous rivalry or to their disbelief in the messiahship of Jesus, but never to Paul's doctrine of the freedom from law (and thereby also from circumcision). But it was precisely this doctrine which

was the reason for the Jewish hostility, because it nullified the absolute significance of the Jewish people.[26] If the portrayal in Acts is not a biased distortion of
the facts, then it represents the author's own theory of the circumstances, which
he sets forth in good faith. Whether or not the action here attributed to Paul is
historical, the motivation to which Acts ascribes it is due to the author of Acts and
"simply shows that the author wished to represent matters in such a way as if in
all his preaching on the subject of the law the Apostle had never said anything
affecting Judaism in the very least."[27]

It appears to me that this is also the meaning of the remark about the circumcision of Timothy. In my opinion it is wrong to cite I Cor. 9:19-23 to demonstrate
the historicity of this episode. If this passage is not intended to circumscribe
the wide area of matters of indifference, but rather has its point in "for the sake
of the gospel," then it in no sense negates the basic character of the statements
in Galatians on circumcision and its relation to the cross and the sacraments
(Gal.5:2-6; 3:27). Circumcision is never a matter of indifference, but rather is
confession and acknowledgement of the saving significance of the law, is a denial
of baptism, and therefore splits the church: "Now I, Paul, say to you that if you
receive circumcision, Christ will be of no advantage to you." The statement about
the circumcision of Timothy stands in direct contradiction to the theology of Paul,
but it fits Luke's view that the law retains its full validity for Jewish Christians and
that Paul acknowledged this in a conciliatory concession to the Jews.

Paul's statements about his teaching, when on trial, are apologetically formed
and reduce his teaching to the Jewish "hope" of the resurrection of the dead—and
indeed in the sense of a general resurrection (Acts 23:6; 24:15, 21; 26:8); only
Acts 26:23 designates Jesus as "the first to rise from the dead," and at 28:20 it is
perhaps the messianic hope which is meant. These statements obscure the essential
difference from Judaism, its law and its hope, which went with belief in Jesus as
the Messiah. Paul also understands his Christian faith to be in agreement with the
law and the prophets and to that extent as true Judaism. This is evident from the
Abraham-typology (Gal. 3; Rom. 4) and from the parable of the olive tree (Rom.
11). But in Acts the accent is different; the place and function of the "law which
came in beside" (Rom.5:20) in the Pauline conception of redemptive history is not
seen, but rather there is an uninterrupted continuity of redemptive history and the
simple identification of the Jewish and Christian hope—precisely analogous to
the views of the Areopagus speaker on natural and Christian knowledge of God.

Acts permits Paul to express himself thematically on the significance of
the law at only one place; at the conclusion of his speech in the synagogue of
Pisidian Antioch after a long scripture proof for Jesus' messiahship, suffering,
and resurrection, Paul says: "Let it be known to you therefore, brethren, that
through this man forgiveness of sins is proclaimed to you, and by him everyone
that believes is freed from everything from which you could not be freed by the
law of Moses" (Acts 13:38 f.). Clearly Acts intends to let Paul speak in his own

---

26   F. Chr. Baur, *Paul* (German: 1866; English: 1876), I, 197.
27   *Ibid.*, p. 199.

terms; one must however point out striking differences from the statements of the letters of Paul.[28] First of all, justification is equated with the forgiveness of sins and thus is conceived entirely negatively, which Paul never does; again, "forgiveness of sins" does not occur in his major letters, but rather in Col. 1:14 and in Eph.1:7, and is used in Acts 13:38 in the same sense as in the speeches of Peter (Acts 2:38; 3:19; 5:31; 10:43). Furthermore, the forgiveness of sins is tied to the messiahship of Jesus which is based on the resurrection (vs. 37), and also "nothing is said in this connection about the particular significance of his death."[29] Finally, it is here a question only of a partial justification, one which is not by faith alone, but *also* by faith. Harnack was right in saying: "According to Paul the law has absolutely no saving significance, and thus also none for the one who was born a Jew; according to Luke ... justification by faith is so to speak only complementary for Jewish Christians. It is necessary for them because and to the extent that they fall short of the fulfillment of the law or because the law provides no complete justification."[30]

The same concept of law and justification was behind Peter's words, when he pled before the Jerusalem council for the Gentile's freedom from circumcision, that one should not put upon them a yoke "which neither our fathers nor we have been able to bear" (Acts 15:10). Also according to Paul men do not fulfill the law, but it has been done away with not for this reason but rather because Christ has put an end to the law. "It is thus the theology of Luke that we have here."[31]

Luke did know that Paul proclaimed justification by faith, but he did not know its central significance and absolute importance; he thought it was valid primarily for the Gentiles. This understanding of justification is a product of his understanding of the law. In Acts the law, together with the prophets, is sometimes the sacred book of divine prophecies of the Messiah and in this capacity is common possession of Jews and Christians. Sometimes, however, it is a collection of cultic and ritual commands and as such is property of the Jewish people and of the Christians who stemmed from them, but is not obligatory for Gentile Christians, who indeed possess an analogue to the law and the prophets in their natural knowledge of God, and because of their immediacy to God do not need to make the detour by way of Judaism. As a Greek and Gentile Christian Luke had never experienced the law as a way to salvation and therefore did not understand the Pauline antithesis law-Christ. Paul's question regarding the law as a way of salvation, regarding good works as the condition of salvation,—the whole problem of the law—was entirely foreign to Luke. Paul's biographer was no longer troubled by a question which of necessity confronted Paul: "Is the law sin?" Either Luke no longer knew the basic nature of the battle over the law, or else he did not wish to acknowledge it because this battle had long ago been fought out. Luke speaks of the inadequacy of the law, whereas

---

28   Bauernfeind warns against putting this sentence "under the theological microscope," and wants Luke to say only: "Paul preached about justification by faith" *(Die Apostelgeschichte, ThHKNT,* 1939, p. 177). But then the decisive question to ask with respect to the noteworthy performance in vss. 16-37 is how "righteousness" has been understood.

29   De Wette-Overbeck, *Apostelgeschichte,* 1870, p. 205.

30   Harnack, *Neue Untersuchungen zur Apostelgeschichte,* 1911, p. 48.

31   Dibelius, "The Apostolic Council" (1947), p. 95.

Paul speaks of the end of the law, which is Christ (Rom. 10:4). In the doctrine of the law which is in Acts, the "word of the cross" has no place because in Acts it would make no sense. The distinction between Luke and Paul was in Christology.

III

In Acts the contents of Paul's message was in general terms first of all the "kingdom" or "the kingdom of God" (19:8; 20:25; 28:23, 31); then Jesus (19:13; 22:18), "Jesus, whom Paul asserted to be alive" (25:19), "the things concerning me" (23:11), "Jesus and the resurrection" (17:18). In Acts Paul describes the content of his preaching as "the whole counsel of God" (20:27), the gospel of God's grace (20:24), repentance and conversion (26:20; cf. 20:21), and, when on trial, as has already been mentioned, the prediction of the law and the prophets and the hope of the fathers in a resurrection of the dead (23:6; 24:14 f., 26:6 ff.; 28:20).

In Acts the only Pauline statements on christology of any length are made before Jews, in the synagogue in Antioch (13) and before Agrippa (26:22 f.). They consist primarily in the assertion that Jesus is the Messiah who was promised in the Old Testament and expected by the Jews, and in the scriptural proof that his suffering and resurrection were according to the scripture: "... saying nothing but what the prophets and Moses said would come to pass: that the Christ must suffer, and that, by being the first to rise from the dead, he would proclaim light both to the people and to the Gentiles" (26:22 f.). Thus both the Messiah's suffering and resurrection and the justification of the world mission are shown to be according to scripture. The same motifs occur in Acts 13: the suffering and resurrection of Jesus are the fulfillment of "all that was written of him" (vs. 29). The resurrection receives a detailed scripture proof in vss. 34-37 (Ps. 16:10 is the main proof text, and the mode of argument is the same as that in Acts 2:27-31); the Christian mission is also connected to the resurrection (vs. 32). In addition to these parallels Jesus is referred to by name, is designated a descendant of David, is called "Savior" and, according to Ps. 2:7, Son of God (vss. 23, 33).

In Paul's letters there are parallels to these passages at Rom. 1:3 f. and I Cor. 15:3 f.: Jesus is descended from David and installed as Son of God (Rom. 1:3 f.), his appearing is in fulfillment of prophetic writings (vs. 2). In I Corinthians 15:3 f. both death and resurrection are described as according to the scriptures, and also the burial is mentioned. But according to Paul's own statement this passage is an element of tradition from the earliest congregation,[32] and Rom. 1:3 f. is also acknowledged as a pre-Pauline formulation which Paul inserted.[33] Thus it appears that the christological statements of Paul in Acts 13:16-37 and 26:22 f. are neither specifically Pauline nor Lucan but are property of the earliest congregation.

This conclusion is supported by two observations. (1) Some apparent echoes of Pauline passages which are to be found in Acts 13 and 26 are

---

32   Lietzmann, *An die Korinther,* HNT IX, 1931, pp. 76-77; J. Jeremías, *The Eucharistic Words of Jesus* (1955), pp. 127 ff.

33   Bultmann, *Theology of the New Testament,* I, p. 49.

actually not true parallels. Thus the title "Savior" is employed in Acts 13:23 for the earthly Jesus, but is used by Paul in Phil. 3:20 with reference to the returning Lord (cf. Eph. 5:23, with reference to the exalted Lord). In Acts 13:33 Jesus' divine sonship is understood "adoptionistically" whereas Paul understood it metaphysically and never based it on Ps. 2:7. The descriptive phrase "first to rise from the dead" is a strong reminder of Col. 1:18 and I Cor. 15:20, but means something quite different. In Col. 1:18 the resurrection of the first born establishes his dominion over the world, and in I Cor.15:20 it introduces the final drama of the general resurrection of the dead. But in Acts 26:23 it inaugurates the era of the world mission; that is, Acts 26:23 is not a parallel to the cited Pauline passages but rather to Acts 13:31 f.

(2) The structure and content of Paul's speech in Acts 13 is most closely akin to the Petrine speeches in the first part of Acts (the same constitutive elements—kerygma in the form of a brief *vita Jesu,* a scripture proof, and a call to repentance—the same mode of argument, and the same adoptionistic Christology). The introductory part, which is a brief resumé of Israel's history (vss. 16-20), has a parallel in Stephen's speech, and only vss. 38 f. reproduces "Pauline" ideas about justification. Since Luke in composing his speeches made use of preformed material, as Dibelius has shown,[34] the similarity with the speeches of Peter suggests that the Christology of Acts 13 is also that of the earliest congregation, rather than that of Paul.

This Christology is adoptionistic, not a Christology of pre-existence. But it is not this difference in the concept of the person of Christ which separates Acts from Paul, but rather the different concept of his "work," the under-standing of the cross. For Paul the "cross" is judgment upon all mankind and at the same time reconciliation (Rom. 5:6-11; II Cor.5:14-21). With the cross, which Paul understood to involve also the resurrection of Christ, has come the turn of the aeons, the eschaton. In "the word of the cross" it encounters the individual and qualifies his present as "the last hour": "behold, now is the acceptable time; behold, now is the day of salvation!" (II Cor. 6:2). He who believes this proclamation exists "in Christ," belongs to the new world, is "a new creation." This is possible only in the mode of existence in the church, membership in the body of Christ. But in the cross of Christ *salvation is wholly realized.*

According to Acts, specifically in chap. 13, the crucifixion of Jesus is an error of justice and a sin of the Jews, who despite knowledge of holy Scripture did not recognize Jesus' messiahship; but the suffering and death of the Messiah were prophesied, and the Jews unconsciously did their part toward fulfillment of this prophecy. Nothing is said of the saving significance of the cross of Christ; and consequently also nothing of the reality of "in Christ" and of the presence of the whole of salvation. The exalted Messiah demonstrates his power in the mission of the church by directing the mission through the intervention of his Spirit (13:2; 16:6 f.) and the miraculous

---

34   *From Tradition to Gospel* (German: 1933; English: 1934), pp. 15 ff.

effects of his "name." But his power as Messiah is not yet complete; his full messianic dignity will be established only at the parousia (3:19 ff.).[35]

Luke himself is closer to the Christology of the earliest congregation, which is set forth in the speeches of Peter, than he is to the Christology of Paul, which is indicated only in hints. To what extent his own viewpoint accords with the concepts of "the servant of God" and "the author of life/ leader" (Acts 3:13, 26; 4:27, 30; 3:15; 5:31) cannot be determined with certainty. He reproduces them but does not expound them.

IV

After what has already been said about the speeches of Paul the question as to the eschatology of the Paul of Acts has in a large measure been answered. The eschatology disappears. It leads a modest existence on the periphery of his speeches as a hope in the resurrection and as faith in the return of Christ as the judge of the world (17:30 f.), and in this aspect as a motivation of the exhortation to repentance. Eschatology has been removed from the center of Pauline faith to the end and has become a "section on the last things."[36]

But that is Lucan theology. He distinguishes himself thereby not only from Paul but also from the earliest congregation which expected the return of Christ, the resurrection of the dead, and the end of the world in the immediate future, and understood the parousia as the beginning of the new aeon. Paul also lived in the near expectation of the parousia—it motivated his mission and determined his relationship to the world as that of the "as if not" (I Cor. 7:29 ff.)—but the turning point of the world's history has already occurred, the new aeon is already there with the saving act of God in Christ (Gal. 4:4). Paul still awaits the conversion of Israel (Rom. 9-11), the redemption of the "creation" (Rom. 8:19 ff.), and a final cosmic drama with the conquest of hell and of death (I Cor.15), and speaks of "this present evil age" (Gal. 1:4) ; but he never speaks of the "age to come," because the "fullness of time" is already fulfilled. Characteristically, the Pauline "already" and "not yet" are not thought of quantitatively, and their relationship is not understood as a temporal process of gradual realization. It is a question of the paradoxical contemporaneity of the presence and the futurity of salvation, not a question of a temporal but of an ontological dualism. Instructive for this eschatological understanding of history which is Paul's are his statements in I Cor.15:20, 23 f., which define the present as the time of the resurrection of the dead, which began with the resur-rection of Christ: "Christ the first fruits, then at his coming those who belong to Christ, then the end." With this "then" all of world history between Easter and the parousia is majestically ignored; during this interval nothing more of significance can happen, especially no redemptive *history;* the time between

---

35   Harnack, *op. cit.*, p. 75.
36   Cf. Dibelius, "Paul on the Areopagus" (1939), p. 58.

resurrection and return is simply a parenthesis in the life of Christ. With Paul eschatology has become a structural element of Christology.

Luke also held that the new aeon had broken in (Acts 2:16-35; cf. Luke 16:16); that joins Luke to Paul and separates him from the earliest congregation. But the essential has not yet occurred and will take place only at the parousia, which brings the "restoration" (Acts 3:19 ff.); that joins Luke with the earliest congregation and separates him from Paul. The Lucan "already" and "not yet" are understood quantitatively and are conceived in the categories of a temporal dualism which finds its resolution in a temporal process. The time between Pentecost and the parousia is the time of the Spirit and of the progressive evangelization of the world, which is thus an ascending redemptive history.

Pre-Christian time is already characterized in this fashion. In Acts 13:16-22 Paul gives a brief sketch of the history of Israel to David. It is organized under the viewpoint of the steadily enlarging saving acts of God which are continued in the appearance of the Son of David and the Savior, Jesus, "according to promise" (vs. 23). Then follows a report of the gospel history from John the Baptist to the appearances of the risen Christ and the beginning of the mission. Its content is "the good news that what God *promised* to the fathers, this he has *fulfilled* to us their children by causing Jesus to appear" (Acts 13:32 f.).

Here Luke's conception of history as a continuous redemptive historical process is clear. The new aeon is here not because God has set an end to the old aeon in the cross of Christ and has brought forth the new; but rather it has *broken in* because and since God has begun to fulfill his promises, and it becomes actualized further up to the fulfillment. The old and the new aeon are related to each other as are promise and fulfillment, that is, as historical processes. The expectation of the imminent end has disappeared and the failure of the parousia is no longer a problem; Luke replaces the apocalyptic expectation of the earliest congregation and the christological eschatology of Paul by a redemptive historical pattern of promise and fulfillment in which then eschatology *also* receives its appropriate place.

How uneschatologically Luke thinks is apparent not only from the content, but especially from the fact of Acts. The earliest Christian congregations, which expected the imminent end of the world, had no interest in leaving behind to posterity reports on their origin and development. Such an undertaking was possible only for one who expected the world to continue.[37] Collecting, arranging, and chronologically connecting the material in Acts was basically different from the collection of the traditions about Jesus, because the former, in contrast to the latter, did not serve missionary, cultic, and didactic purposes; the establishment of congregations was never the subject of sermons or of catechetical instruction. The purpose of Acts was also not *only* to edify by means of the stories about the faithful, but was primarily to give the historical report— regardless of how far the result was from the examples of antiquity and the claims of modern

---

37   Cf. Dibelius, *A Fresh Approach to the New Testament and Early Christian Literature* (1936), p. 257.

historiography.[38] Luke thought of himself as a historian also in composing the Third Gospel; according to the prologue he was led by historical interest and was historiographically concerned. For him it was a matter of "certainty" (Luke 1:4), the historical reliability of his report. He was led by the same intention also in his portrayal of the apostolic age under the viewpoint of the mission and spread of Christianity. This undertaking was an enormous prolepsis, which antiquated the apologetically intentioned portrayals of church history in the second century even before they appeared, and which drew the author of Acts intellectually closer to Eusebius than to Paul.[39] However, this can be understood only against the background and as a symptom of an uneschatological Christianity which has become secular.

More essential for recognizing the theology of the historian Luke is the fact that he presented his history of the mission as a sequel and second part of the "first book," the Gospel. Without realizing it he thereby called down upon himself the stern reprimand of Overbeck: "Luke took as his subject the one tactlessness of world historical dimensions, the supreme excess of a false viewpoint.... Luke treated historiographie-ally what was not history and what was also not handed down as such."[40] Despite its heated tone, this critical judgment cannot be set aside; Overbeck rightly saw that the congregation's traditions of Jesus were something different from the stories about the apostles, missionaries, and congregations, and that Luke coordinated each to the other in that he made them the objects of historical portrayal. In any case, Acts is not intended as kerygma or as "witness," but as a historically reliable account of the "witnesses of Jesus" and their "witness to Jesus" which they set forth in the power of the Holy Spirit from Jerusalem even to the ends of the earth (Acts 1:8); and by means of this historical reliability Acts intends *also* to make a missionary appeal. When the history of Jesus' "witnesses" gives the continuation of the sacred history of Jesus, then the Lucan conception of redemptive history as history is clearly visible.

To summarize: the author of Acts is in his Christology pre-Pauline, in his natural theology, concept of the law, and eschatology, post-Pauline. He presents no specifically Pauline idea. His "Paulinism" consists in his zeal for the worldwide Gentile mission and in his veneration for the greatest missionary to the Gentiles. The obvious material distance from Paul raises the question whether this distance is not also temporal distance, and whether one may really consider Luke, the physician and travel companion of Paul, as the author of

---

38   W. Nigg fails to recognize this purpose of Luke when he states: "The intention to transmit history to posterity is, however, not present in the author of Acts" *(Die Kirchengeschichtsschreibung,* 1934, p. 2). Ed. Meyer, who approaches Acts with the presuppositions of a historian of antiquity and treats it with the greatest confidence, misunderstands the nature of its accounts and the way in which they are connected *(Ursprung und Anfänge des Christentums,* I, 1921, pp. I ff.; Ill, 1923, pp. 3-208).

39   Although Luke ought by no means to be characterized as a forerunner of Eusebius in the writing of church history.

40   *Christentum und Kultur,* 1919, pp. 78 f.

Acts. But of greater importance than the question of authorship is that of the author's distinctive theological viewpoint and his place in the history of theology.

His own theological position seems to me to lie in the theology of history which has been sketched, and which determines his attitude toward Jews and Gentiles and his portrayal of their being united into a church. It is a theology of history which combines the Old Testament belief in the action of God with his people and the Hellenistic idea of all men's kinship to God in such a fashion that though the former provided the basis it was essentially modified by the latter. The absolute claim of the Jews to be the people of God was replaced by the idea of natural man's immediacy to God, and the significance of Judaism was relativized to that of a venerable *antiqua religio*. The unity of the church composed of Jews and Gentiles is not based in the "body of Christ," but in the given unity of the human race, and this is first actualized in the church. The object of the divine action is the entire human race, and this action is understood as a redemptive history whose beginning is creation, whose end is the "restoration," and whose center is the gospel history as a *stage* along the way of salvation. From this viewpoint the author of the Third Gospel and of the Acts writes an episode of history as redemptive history and therefore also redemptive history as an episode of history.

With the presuppositions of his historiography he no longer stands within earliest Christianity, but in the nascent early catholic church. His concept of history and his view of earliest Christianity are the same as theirs; whether he gave these views to them or received from them is a question whose answer could be attempted only on the broad basis of a New Testament and patristic investigation.[41]

---

41   Overbeck has said some things relevant to this question in an instructive but evidently little noticed essay, "Ueber das Verhältnis Justins des Märtyrers zur Apostelgeschichte," *ZwTh*, 1872, pp. 305-49.

Chapter 2

THE PAUL OF LUKE. A SURVEY OF RESEARCH

Odile Flichy
Trans. James D. Ernest

Work devoted specifically to Paul in the Lukan writings plays a particularly important part within the general framework of the history of research on Acts. Indeed, to the extent that Luke's presentation of the figure of the Apostle decisively influences the interpretation of the whole narrative, studies focusing on that presentation, in all their diversity, make an essential contribution to our understanding of the book of Acts.

I. The Turning Point in Critical Exegesis: Source criticism and the Reopening of the Question of the Historicity of Acts with regard to the Figure of Paul

In the wake of the restoration of philology to a place of honour in the sixteenth-century revival of humanist scholarship, foreshadowed by the emergence of historical criticism in the seventeenth century,[1] the Enlightenment inaugurated a decisive turning in how Acts was read. The onset of critical exegesis called into question the Irenaean and broadly patristic reading according to which Acts, written by Paul's companion Luke, constituted a historical document, a first-hand source, especially for Paul's missionary journeys. Indeed, significant differences were noted between the data of the book of Acts regarding the life and teaching of the apostle and data from Paul's own letters.[2]

Initially this observation simply evoked clarification of the reasons for affirming the historical reliability of Luke's oeuvre. Thus, if the author of Acts never mentions Paul's letters or the persecutions and shipwrecks listed in 2 Cor. 1.8; 4.8-9; 6.4-10; 7.5; 11.24-28, the reason was thought to be that Luke was not constantly with Paul

---

1   By way of example, Grotius offered a linguistic and historical commentary on Acts in 1646. Citing the Greek text, it provides a Latin translation, refers to the Old Testament, Greek literature, and the church fathers, and takes account of textual variants.

2   The documentation following relies on W. W. Gasque, *A History of the Interpretation of the Acts of the Apostles* (Peabody, MA: Hendrickson, 1989); *A History of the Criticism of the Acts of the Apostles* (Grand Rapids: Eerdmans, 1975), pp. 7–54.

and, beyond that, he was not trying to write a history of the life of Paul anyway.[3] In 1810, however, J. G. Eichhorn reached the conclusion (revolutionary at that time!) that Acts does not constitute a historical document: Luke did not use written sources but composed a literary work; the speeches in Acts, which all follow the same pattern, prove the point.[4] Around fifteen years later W. M. Leberrecht de Wette compared the letters and Acts and concluded that the author of Acts was not a companion of Paul and that the information that he provides concerning Paul is both incomplete and partly false.[5]

Indeed, with regard to several major aspects of Paul's life and teaching, the Lukan presentation is irreconcilable with the data from the letters.[6] For example, at the meeting in Jerusalem, minimal dietary rules are imposed on the gentiles, contrary to Paul's intransigence on this point in Gal. 2.1-10. Likewise with regard to Paul's attitude toward the law: in the letters, he proclaims that salvation in Christ abolishes the authority of the law (Rom. 3.20, 21, 28; 4.14; 10.4; Gal. 2.16, 19; 3.10, 11; 5.4; Phil. 3.9); in Acts, he insists on his membership in and loyalty to Judaism (Acts 22.3; 23.1; 24.14; 25.8; 26.5) and circumcises Timothy 'because of the Jews' (16.3). Again, Luke's account of Paul's missionary activity does not speak of letters sent to churches; and Acts reserves the title 'apostle' for the Twelve,[7] while Paul in his letters insistently claims it for himself (1 Cor. 9.1; 15.9; Gal. 1.1).

K. Schrader marked a new stage when, in a volume published in 1836, he considered Acts to be a purely apologetic volume: wishing to defend the church, Luke harmonized Peter and Paul.[8] His statement of the hypothesis is well known: 'Here Peter sounds more like Paul than does Paul himself, and vice versa'.[9] Here is the first appearance of the term 'Paulinism' (*paulisch*). The movement referred to as *Tendenzkritik* made this its war-horse.[10] Because it suggests a possible explanation of the differences noted between Acts and the Pauline letters with regard to the historical Paul, the idea that the Paul of Acts is more of an effect of the author's ecclesiological views than a faithful reflection of actual facts would enjoy

---

3   Cf. J. D. Michaelis, *Introduction to the New Testament* (trans. H. Marsh; 2nd edn; London: Rivington, 1802). Gasque, *History of the Criticism*, pp. 22–23, gives the references.

4   J. G. Eichhorn, *Einleitung in das Neue Testament* (Leipzig: Weidmann, 1810).

5   W. M. L. de Wette, *Lehrbuch der historischen-kritischen Einleitung in die Bibel Alten und Neuen Testaments. Zweiter Teil: Die Einleitung in das Neue Testament enthaltend* (Berlin: Reimer, 1826). In a note, the author suggests comparing Acts 9.26 and 22.17 to Gal. 1.17-18, and Acts 11.30 to Gal. 2.1 (cf. Gasque, *History of the Criticism*, p. 25 n.13).

6   Cf. D. Marguerat, 'Les Actes des Apôtres', in *Introduction au Nouveau Testament: Son histoire, son écriture, sa théologie* (ed. D. Marguerat; MdB, 41; Geneva: Labor et Fides, 2000), pp. 105–28 (121–22).

7   With the exception of Acts 14.4, 14, where the label 'envoys (of God)' attributed to Barnabas and Saul by the inhabitants of Lystra is explained by the context.

8   K. Schrader, *Der Apostel Paulus* (vol. 5; Leipzig: Kollmann, 1836).

9   'Petrus mehr paulisch redet als Paulus hier selbst tut', Schrader, *Apostel Paulus*, p. 516; cf. P. G. Müller, 'Der "Paulinismus" in der Apostelgeschichte: Ein forschungsgeschichtlicher Überblick', in *Paulus in den neutestamentlichen Spätschriften* (ed. K. Kertelge; QD, 89; Freiburg: Herder, 1981), pp. 157–201 (181).

10   Cf. Müller, 'Paulinismus', p. 163.

tremendous success. In retrospect, because of their impact in inspiring further work especially at Tübingen, the first proponents of this movement (among others, J. G. Eichhorn, W. M. de Wette, and K. Schrader), appear as precursors of the so-called Tübingen School, which would exert a major influence on Lukan studies for a number of decades.[11]

II. F. C. Baur, the Tübingen School, and Tendenzkritik: The Paul of Luke Is Not the Paul of History

The incipient debate crystallized around the work of F. C. Baur, published beginning in 1830: this Tübingen theologian would remain the leading figure of the current of *Tendenzkritik*, which would take centre stage in the exegetical scene.[12] Baur sought to explain the orientation of the Lukan narrative by reference to the history of Christian origins; he thus proposed to understand the apologetic outlook of Acts in a historical perspective. In so doing, he offered critical exegesis the means of making a considerable advance on this subject. This advance is due in large part to the methodological principle that henceforth formed the basis for his research: the use of historical criteria to evaluate the differences between the Paul of the letters and the Paul of Luke. On the basis of this approach he would wield decisive influence. Even though his thesis, according to which Luke aimed to reconcile the two opposing groups – one of Jewish origins and the other of gentile origins that together composed the triumphant gentile-Christian church – encountered vigorous criticism because of its Hegelian baggage, his approach opened up another way of reading Acts. Now the background of concrete ecclesial experiences and situations becomes paradigmatic in delineating 'trajectories' and a role for a 'legacy' or inheritance in interpreting a Pauline 'tradition';[13] the influence of this approach upon modern approaches to Acts is manifest.[14] Thus, beyond the conclusions that Baur defended in light of his elevation of the Pauline letters as a norm for reading, the correct insight that guided his research has not lost its legitimacy.

---

11   Gasque (*History of the Interpretation*) considers the dominance of this critical current undeserved and suggests paying more attention to the arguments advanced by advocates for the traditional position concerning the historicity of Acts.

12   F. C. Baur, 'Die Christuspartei in der korinthische Gemeinde, der Gegensatz des petrinischen und paulinischen Christentums in der ältesten Kirche', *TZTh* 5/4 (1831); *Über der Ursprung des Episcopats* (Tübingen: Fues, 1838); *Paulus, der Apostel Jesu Christi* (Tübingen: Fues, 1845).

13   Cf. J. Roloff, *Die Apostelgeschichte* (NTD, 5; Göttingen: Vandenhoeck & Ruprecht, 1981), p. 7.

14   For 'trajectories', see the work of J. R. Robinson and H. Koester, *Trajectories through Early Christianity* (Philadelphia: Fortress, 1971). For legacy, cf. J. C. Beker, *Heirs of Paul: Paul's Legacy in the New Testament and in the Church Today* (Minneapolis: Fortress, 1991); Y. Redalié, *Paul après Paul: Le temps, le salut, la morale selon les épîtres à Timothée et à Tite* (Le Monde de la Bible, 31; Geneva: Labor et Fides, 1994).

Conditioned by his thesis of Luke's 'proto-catholicism', F. C. Baur constructed the figure of Paul as representing the gentile-Christian wing of the church, which became the majority at the end of the first century, over against Peter, the leader of the Jewish-Christian community. For Baur, the observed distance between the Lukan Paul and the historical Paul as known from his letters signals the apologetic intention of the author of Acts and his desire to present a church whose two constituent parts are reconciled. The major difference, in his view, is Luke's insistence on the faithfulness Paul exhibited toward Judaism and on Paul's attachment to the law of Moses. Thus for Baur the Paul of Acts is not the Paul of history. Luke, because of the care he took to safeguard the church's authority by showing the unity of its constituent parts, became the originator of the loss of the Pauline gospel.

Baur's disciples explored the path thus opened. Through their efforts to set forth Luke's 'tendencies' by using the same interpretive lens, they gradually established the idea that Luke, consciously or not, misrepresented or even betrayed the historical facts about Christian origins and the rise of the church. The result: Luke, whether seen as a 'falsifier' or as 'naïve',[15] was completely discredited as a historian from the perspective of source criticism. Aiming principally, as was then thought, at defending the unity of a church torn by internal arguments and at fostering catholicity, Luke accordingly appropriated the Paul of the letters in order to adapt him to his own views, projecting his own ecclesial situation upon the past.

The polemics linked to the labours of the Tübingen School constitute the first important stage in the history of interpretation of the Paul of Acts. Here the terms of the debate opened by the birth of critical exegesis appear in fact as definitively binding: it seems impossible to grasp the identity of the apostle except as either a faithful reflection of the historical Paul or the product of Lukan theology. This polemic reached its zenith in 1950 with the publication of an article by P. Vielhauer [re-printed in this volume as ch. 1] presenting the results of a comparison between the theology of the speeches in Acts and the theology of the letters of Paul.[16] This article had the effect of a veritable thunderclap because of its completely negative evaluation of the historical value of Acts: 'With the presuppositions of his historiography he no longer stands within earliest Christianity, but in the nascent early catholic church.' 'He presents no specifically Pauline idea.'[17] Still, those holding a more conservative position regarding the historical reliability of Acts did not give up on making their voice heard; witness the commentaries of F. F. Bruce[18]

---

15   D. Marguerat, *La première histoire du christianisme* (Paris: Cerf, 1999), p. 15 (ET: *The First Christian Historian: Writing the 'Acts of the Apostles'* [trans. K. McKinney, G. Laughery, and R. Bauckham; SNTSMS, 121; Cambridge: Cambridge University Press, 2002], p. 10).

16   P. Vielhauer, 'Zum "Paulinismus" der Apostelgeschichte', *EvTh* 10 (1950–51), pp. 1–15 (reprinted as 'On the "Paulinism" of Acts', in *Studies in Luke-Acts* [ed. L. Keck and J. Louis Martyn; trans. W. C. Robinson and V. P. Furnish; Nashville: Abingdon, 1966], pp. 33–50, and reprinted, unaltered, with permission of the editors, as ch. 1 in this volume, pp. 3–17).

17   Vielhauer, 'On the "Paulinism" in Acts', p. 17 (this volume).

18   F. F. Bruce, *The Acts of the Apostles: The Greek Text with Introduction and Commentary* (3rd ed.; Grand Rapids: Eerdmans; Leicester, UK: Apollos, 1990).

and J. Munck, for example.[19] W. W. Gasque, according to C. K. Barrett, 'took up arms against' this current,[20] while M. Hengel opposes the radical scepticism of the Tübingen School in a more nuanced way, without supporting the ostracism sometimes inflicted upon the historical method.[21]

Because their arguments presuppose a positivist concept of history, we can hardly accept either side in this debate as tenable today. Nevertheless, the problematic of the relation between history and tradition that grounds the different positions on this subject retains its urgency for contemporary research, because it touches upon the question of the relation of Luke to Pauline tradition. That question is basic for any reading of Acts. [22]

III. M. Dibelius, H. Cadbury, and 'Style criticism': The Paul of History as the Object of Luke's Literary Practice

Around the 1920s, when source criticism[23] passed the baton to form criticism, the work of M. Dibelius[24] in Germany and H. J. Cadbury[25] in the United States sketched new perspectives by subjecting the question of identifying Luke's sources to a style-critical type of literary perspective. Stressing the unique character of the book of Acts among the New Testament writings, they note the limits of a purely historical method that aims at isolating traditional material from the author's literary work and provide the first witness to the fruitfulness of an approach centred on the author's literary activity.

Since his literary analysis leads him to discover all the effort that Luke brings to bear in editing the book of Acts, Martin Dibelius adopts a less radical position on

---

19   J. Munck, *The Acts of the Apostles* (AB, 31; Garden City: Doubleday, 1967).

20   C. K. Barrett, 'The Historicity of Acts', *JThSt* 50 (1995), pp. 515–34 (esp. 522).

21   M. Hengel and A. Schwemer, *Paulus zwischen Damaskus und Antiochien* (WUNT 108; Tübingen: Mohr Siebeck, 1998) (ET, *Paul between Damascus and Antioch* [trans. John Bowden; London: SCM, 1997]).

22   See S. Porter, *The Paul of Acts. Essays in Literary Criticism, Rhetoric and Theology* (WUNT, 115; Tübingen: Mohr Siebeck, 1999) (reprinted as *Paul in Acts* [Library of Pauline Studies; Peabody, MA: Hendrickson, 2001]). His hypothesis that Luke used a written 'we' source – and reproduced its form and theological coherence – is a key element of the thesis of the whole work, which, following the traditional reading of Acts, tries as much as possible to close the gap between the Paul of Acts and the Paul of the Letters.

23   After World War I, the study of oral traditions underlying the written forms of the biblical text, like the study of their *Sitz im Leben*, underwent significant development within the framework of New Testament research.

24   Eleven of Dibelius' main contributions were collected, in 1951, in *Aufsätze zur Apostelgeschichte* (FRLANT 60; 5th ed.; Göttingen: Vandenhoeck & Ruprecht, 1968) (ET: *Studies in the Acts of the Apostles* [ed. H. Greeven; London: SCM, 1956]). The first, titled 'Stilkritisches zur Apostelgeschichte', appeared in Göttingen in 1923 (in *Eucharisterion für H. Gunkel*); Mary Ling's ET is available in Martin Dibelius, *The Books of Acts: Form, Style, and Theology* (ed. K. C. Hanson; Fortress Classics in Biblical Studies; Minneapolis: Fortress, 2004), pp. 32–48. This latter volume is a revision of the 1956 SCM publication.

25   H. J. Cadbury, *The Style and Literary Method of Luke* (HThS, 6; Cambridge: Harvard University Press, 1919–1920).

the historicity of the Paul of Acts.[26] He is certain that Luke is using real information on the life of the apostle. He raises questions, however, regarding the reasons for the selection of the events that the narrative reports. Why doesn't Luke say more? What sources did he have? What were his intentions in using them? He thus reaches the conclusion that Luke's sources for the Paul of history are difficult to identify. The numerous shared features of Paul's and Peter's speeches are so many proofs that the author of Acts was aiming not to write archaeology but rather to establish the figure of Paul as the paradigmatic Christian preacher in the eyes of his community: the community should follow Paul's example in proclaiming the Christian faith to the surrounding gentile world.

Along the same lines, H. J. Cadbury, starting from study of Lukan vocabulary and style, would, beginning in 1928, defend the literary unity of Luke–Acts.[27] He also coedited volumes 4 and 5 of the encyclopedic *The Beginnings of Christianity*, which explored Greek and Jewish historiographical traditions and within this framework emphasized the rhetorical and literary dimension of ancient historiography.[28]

Consequently, the late-twentieth-century consensus regarding the literary unity and historiographical dimension of Luke's work found its first expression in the work of these two authors.

IV. Redaction Criticism: Paul as Decisive Witness to the Beginnings of the Church, Representing Lukan Theology

Research between 1950 and 1970, which remained under the strong influence of M. Dibelius, culminated in the publication of major works still recognized today as landmarks. These include E. Haenchen's commentary, which sees Acts as reflecting gentile Christian theology toward the end of the first century;[29] H. Conzelmann's argument that Luke wrote Acts in response to a crisis stimulated by the delay of the parousia and therefore 'de-eschatologized' history;[30] and the numerous and important publications of J. Dupont in this arena.[31]

---

26   M. Dibelius, 'Paulus in der Apostelgeschichte', in *Aufsätze zur Apostelgeschichte*, pp. 207–14 (ET: 'Paul in the Book of Acts', in *idem, Books of Acts*, pp. 89–94).

27   H. J. Cadbury, *The Making of Luke-Acts* (New York: Macmillan, 1928; Peabody, Mass.: Hendrickson, 2nd edn, 1999).

28   F. J. Foakes-Jackson and K. Lake (eds), *The Beginnings of Christianity* (vol. 1 of *The Acts of the Apostles*; London: Macmillan, 1920–1933). Volume 4 is titled *English translation and Commentary*; Volume 5, *Additional Notes to Commentary*.

29   E. Haenchen, *Die Apostelgeschichte* (KEK, 3; Göttingen: Vandenhoeck & Ruprecht, 1956; 7th ed., 1977) (ET: *The Acts of the Apostles* [trans. Bernard Noble *et al.*; Philadelphia: Westminster; Oxford: Blackwell, 1971]).

30   H. Conzelmann, *Die Mitte der Zeit: Studien zur Theologie des Lukas* (BHTh, 17; Tübingen: Mohr Siebeck, 1954, 1964⁵) (ET: *The Theology of St. Luke* [trans. G. Buswell; Philadelphia: Fortress, 1961]).

31   J. Dupont, *Études sur les Actes des Apôtres* (Paris: Cerf, 1967); *Nouvelles études sur les Actes des Apôtres* (Paris: Cerf, 1984). As Bovon, *Luc le théologien* (MdB, 5; Geneva: Labor et Fides, 2006), p. 96 (ET *Luke the Theologian: Fifty-Five Years of Research (1950-2005)* [Waco,

For Haenchen, the Paul of Luke is not the Paul of the letters but rather the decisive witness to the beginnings of the church, the representative of Luke's theology.[32] The reality to which we are connected by the Paul-centred account in Acts is not the historical Paul but the theologian Luke.

During the 1970s a number of publications moved away from the primary stylistic criticism developed by Dibelius and Haenchen. Now researchers explore a dialectical tension between history and theology to explain the distance between the Paul of Acts and the Paul of the letters and the paradoxical way in which the elevation of Paul as a hero coincides with the 'betrayal' of major aspects of his theology. The normative value attributed to the letters of Paul remains, without critical examination, the unquestioned and unique criterion for evaluation.

The research that developed within this framework proved fruitful, contributing, from its various angles of approach, to the emergence of a new exegetical landscape.[33] It revealed, in particular, the pertinence of the category of 'witness' or 'testimony' for characterizing the Paul of Acts, and by recognizing the value of the nexus between the writer's aim and his reading of history, 'witness' brought to light the identity-forming function attributed by Luke to the apostle.

a. Paul the Witness: A Re-reading of the Historical Role of the Apostle

A first angle of approach remains that of the apologetic history developed at Tübingen beginning with F. C. Baur.

The originality of C. Burchard's work is his claim that the Lukan construction of Paul as 'witness' is not disconnected from historical reality.[34] Although he critiques the hypothesis inherited from *Tendenzkritik* of controversies within the church, he is among those who see an intra-Christian apologetic intention in the presentation of Paul as the 'thirteenth witness' to Christ.[35] As such, Paul is ranked with the Twelve and given, moreover, a unique role in the development of the church: he is the one who took the gospel to the gentiles. This past role, however, now serves a

---

TX: Baylor University Press, 2006], p. 522]) notes: 'Few exegetes have aided the progression toward the understanding of the Lukan hermeneutic as much as Dom J. Dupont.'

32   Haenchen, *Acts,* p. 116.

33   The presentation of this new landscape reprises the basic lines of the typology established by J. Roloff in 'Die Paulus-Darstellung des Lukas: Ihre geschichtlichen Vorausetzungen und ihr theologisches Ziel', *EvTh* 39 (1979), pp. 510–31.

34   C. Burchard, *Der Dreizehnte Zeuge: Traditions- und kompositionsgeschichtliche Untersuchungen zur Lukas' Darstellung der Frühzeit des Paulus* (FRLANT, 103; Göttingen: Vandenhoeck & Ruprecht, 1970).

35   For Haenchen, the apologetic aim is outward-looking: Luke seeks to gain for Christians the *religio licita* status that Rome accorded to Judaism. Jacob Jervell's thesis that Luke is defending Paul against charges that he was a traitor to Judaism (*Luke and the People of God: A New Look at Luke-Acts* [Minneapolis: Augsburg, 1972], pp. 153–83) takes up, in its own way, the Tübingen position. According to R. Maddox (*The Purpose of Luke-Acts* [Göttingen: Vandenhoeck & Ruprecht, 1982]), Luke's purpose is to clear Christians of any responsibility for the Jewish-Christian breach; the story of Paul, the persecuted Christian, merely adds further chapters to the story of Jesus and Stephen.

contemporary end: Luke wrote for the Christians of his own day, following up the story of Jesus with the story of Paul's preaching as witness in order to certify the authenticity of the kerygma now proclaimed by the church.

Along the same lines, K. Löning likewise presents Paul as a legitimizing figure for Christians of gentile origin.[36] For him, it is because of a conflict with the Jewish-Christians of the Lukan community[37] that Luke's treatment of Paul would emphasize his being Christ's witness 'to all humanity' (Acts 22.15), thus stressing the legitimacy of the gentile mission.

b. Paul the Witness: a Christological Figure

By transferring the debate onto theological terrain, and by defending the thesis that Luke's construction of Paul as witness to Christ establishes a christological principle, V. Stolle launched a new line of research. He emphasized what is primarily at stake in a presentation of Paul centred on the figure of a prisoner en route to martyrdom: exhibiting the parallel between the fate of the apostle and that of Christ in order to show how his testimony is rooted in the mission he received from the resurrected Lord. Moreover, Paul's trial has not ended at the close of the book of Acts, so he remains linked to the community's present. By sustaining to the end his presentation of Paul's trial as an occasion for testimony, making his judges into an audience for the message of salvation, Luke, according to Stolle, has established Paul as the model witness to Christ for his readers.[38]

Precisely this close linkage between Paul and Christ is the subject of W. Radl's detailed study of the parallels that the narrative establishes between Jesus and Paul, illuminating the theological significance of Luke's choice of *synkrisis* as a writing strategy.[39] Such a parallel construction already indicates the theological bearing of Luke's two-volume work, namely, that the age of Jesus and the age of the church

---

36   K. Löning, *Die Saulustradition in der Apostelgeschichte* (NTA ,9; Münster: Aschendorff, 1973).

37   This position of K. Löning, in particular, is criticized by V. Stolle (*Der Zeuge* als Angeklagter: Untersuchungen zum Paulusbild des Lukas [BWANT, 102; Stuttgart: Kohlhammer, 1973]). Stolle is convinced that the historical problem of Jewish hostility toward Christianity is resolved in Luke's day and that the Jewish-Christian antagonism in Acts arises from a theological disagreement regarding the interpretation of salvation history.

38   In her little book *Paul the Accused: His Portrait in the Acts of the Apostles* (Zacchaeus Studies, NT; Collegeville: Liturgical Press, Michael Glazier, 1995), M. E. Rosenblatt, like V. Stolle, considers that the chapters dedicated to the Paul's trials are the emblematic presentation of his character. Her choice of a narrative approach, which enables her attention to the movement in the plot and to the evolution of the apostle's role through different stages of his court appearances, gives particular force to her reading. By noting the way the situation reverses between the beginning and the end, and the progressive transformation of Paul from accused to witness, this reading has the advantage of articulating in a dynamic fashion the results of previous research on Paul as witness. The hypothesis that Luke borrows the model of itinerant prophet ensures, moreover, a line of continuity with the portrait thus sketched: like an unjustly accused and persecuted prophet, Paul testifies to the end to his loyalty to Judaism and to the mission he received from Christ.

39   W. Radl, *Paulus und Jesus im lukanischen Doppelwerk: Untersuchungen zu Parallelmotiven im Lukasevangelium und in der Apostelgeschichte* (Bern/Frankfurt: Lang, 1975).

are connected. Nevertheless, for Radl, unlike the writings cited above, a major gap separates the Paul of Acts from the Paul of history. And a corollary to this gap is a complete separation between Christology and history, since, at the end of the work, the figure of Paul disappears, in a way, behind that of Jesus: 'Paul does not simply imitate Jesus but takes on his [Jesus'] own traits'.[40] Here we see the limitation of Radl's research.

J. Roloff rightly raised this exact question, even while noting the importance of this christological aspect: is the Paul of Luke not much more than a timeless 'type'?[41] For his part, he proposes to distinguish the question of the historical conditions in which Luke worked out his image of Paul (i.e., the tradition available to him) from his theological aim. Thus, echoing Burchard's conclusions regarding Luke's interest in the historical role of Paul and refusing to attribute the Paul of Acts solely to Luke's literary artistry, he goes on to acknowledge the stamp of Luke's 'Paulinism' in the identify-forming function that he attributes to the apostle in his narrative. In his own person, indeed, Paul simultaneously invites the Lukan community to find itself in a line of continuity with the history of the people of God and to model its own testimony on the manner in which he testified to his faith in the risen Christ.[42]

Thus, on the threshold of the new turn that would affect studies dedicated to the character of Paul in Acts in the 1980s, a considerable consensus seems to have been achieved regarding the essentially theological dimension of the Lukan hero. In light of the redaction-critical studies, it was largely admitted that Luke's treatment of the historical data reflects the situation of Christianity at the end of the first century more than that of the apostolic generation for which the letters of Paul constitute the only trustworthy evidence. In one sense, historical criticism's case against Luke seems to be closed.

V. The Turn to the New Criticism and the Debate over Paul's Cultural Rootedness

The development of the linguistic sciences and their emergence into the field of biblical studies have introduced new factors into the debate about the Paul of Acts. Thus, under the influence of the movements called New Criticism[43] and Narrative Criticism,[44] linguistic tools hitherto applied only to secular literature were brought

---

40   Radl, *Paulus und Jesus*, p. 385.
41   Roloff, 'Paulus-Darstellung des Lukas', p. 516.
42   Roloff, 'Paulus-Darstellung des Lukas', p. 531.
43   Born at the beginning of the twentieth century and known as 'New Criticism', this new literary-critical school advocated a return to the text, considering it not so much as a 'document that a critic uses to retrieve a great mind or reconstruct the past' but rather as a 'monument that has value in its own right' (J.-L. Ska, 'La "nouvelle critique" et l'exégèse anglo-saxonne', *RSR* 80 [1992], pp. 29–53 [32]: ('The text is no longer a document which the critic uses to recover an important sense or to reconstruct the past; it is a monument which has value in itself.'))
44   The work of R. C. Tannehill (*The Narrative Unity of Luke-Acts: A Literary Interpretation* [2 vols.; Minneapolis: Fortress, 1986–1990]) is one of the first examples of narrative criticism applied to the text of Acts.

to bear on the study of the biblical text.[45] Meanwhile, reflection initiated by P. Veyne,[46] H.-I. Marrou,[47] and M. de Certeau[48] on the status of the historical text called historical positivism into question and thus stimulated a fresh posing of the question of the historicity of the figure of Paul in Acts.[49]

Under the influence of literary criticism, numerous works were devoted to exploring the sociocultural background of Acts and determining its influences on the author of Acts, and particularly how Acts situates the character of Paul.

For some, Luke, who has appropriated Greco-Roman literary conventions and genres,[50] constructs the image of Paul over in the context of a break with Judaism: since so many Jews have refused to accept the Christian message, he has turned away from them to become the apostle to gentiles. Others, however, point to the considerable position occupied by the Jewish Bible in Luke's opus; for them, such a reading of Acts looks too 'Greek'.[51] J. Jervell's[52] new image of a Luke who is close to Judaism caused a considerable stir,[53] as did his hypothesis of a Paul who

---

45   The impact of the publication in 1981 of R. Alter's book *The Art of Biblical Narrative* (New York: Basic Books, 1981) indicates the level of interest shown by the exegetical world in such a literary approach to the study of the Bible.

46   P. Veyne, *Comment on écrit l'histoire: Essai d'épistémologie* (L'univers historique; Paris: Seuil, 1971), p. 1 (ET: *Writing History: Essay on Epistemology* [trans. M. Moore-Rinvolucri; Middletown, CT: Wesleyan University Press, 1984], pp. ix-x).

47   H.-I. Marrou, *De la connaissance historique* (Points, histoire, 21; Paris: Seuil, 1954, 1975).

48   M. de Certeau, *L'écriture de l'histoire* (NRF; Paris: Gallimard, 1975).

49   P. Veyne (*Comment on écrit l'histoire*, 18—19.10), wrote that 'a history, like a novel, explains as it retells'; it is 'a novel that is true' or at least 'a truthful narrative'. In the wake of H. I. Marrou and M. de Certeau, the works of P. Ricoeur likewise mark the renewal of a way of speaking of the notion of 'truth' with reference to history, highlighting the fact that it cannot be separated from the interpretation of the event that is being recounted. See Ricoeur, *Temps et Récit,* vol. 1 (Paris: Seuil, 1983) (ET: *Time and Narrative* [trans. K. McLaughlin and D. Pellauer; Chicago: University of Chicago Press, 1984]).

50   W. S. Kurz, 'Hellenistic Rhetoric in the Christological Proof of Luke-Acts', *CBQ* 42 (1980), pp. 171–95; V. K. Robbins, 'Prefaces in Greco-Roman Biography and Luke-Acts', *PRS* 6 (1979), pp. 94–108 = SBLSP, vol. 2 (1978), pp. 193–207; *idem*, 'The Claims of the Prologues and Greco-Roman Rhetoric: The Prefaces to Luke and Acts in Light of Greco-Roman Rhetorical Strategies', in *Jesus and the Heritage of Israel. Luke's Narrative Claim upon Israel's Legacy,* (vol.1 of Luke the Interpreter of Israel; ed. D. P. Moessner; Harrisburg, Pa.: Trinity Press International, 1999), pp. 63–83; R. I. Pervo, *Profit with Delight: The Literary Genre of the Acts of the Apostles* (Philadelphia: Fortress, 1987).

51   Thus, according to M. Dumais: 'It is wrong to seek models for the narration in Acts only in Greco-Roman literature of the period. Luke is a rich and polyvalent author who, to build his narrative, knows how to draw upon his vast familiarity with the writings of the Old Testament and the Jewish world' ('Les Actes des Apôtres, bilan et orientations', in *De bien des manières: La recherche biblique aux abords du XXIe siècle* [ed. M. Gourgues and L. Laberge; LD, 163; Montreal: Fides, 1995], pp. 307–64 [335]). Dumais is also the author of a work on the midrashic form of Paul's speech at Pisidian Antioch (*Le langage de l'évangélisation: L'annonce missionnaire en milieu juif [Ac 13,16–41]* [Recherches, 16; Tournai: Desclée, 1976]).

52   Jervell, *Luke and the People of God.*

53   The trauma of the Holocaust transformed the literary question of the relation of Luke to the Old Testament into the more ideological question of the attitude of the author of Acts toward Judaism.

remained close to Judaism, remained very observant (as a Pharisee) of the law of Moses, and therefore placed great importance on his mission to the Jews.

Jervell's reversal of perspective forced exegetes to take up again the question of how the Acts narrative articulates Judaism and Christianity and how that picture relates to historical reality. So although the scope of the question of Luke's Paulinism is not as sweeping as that of *Tendenzkritik*, evaluating it remains a priority in Lukan studies.[54]

a. Paul the 'Teacher of Israel': J. Jervell's Thesis

According to the Norwegian exegete, Luke belongs to a community in which the majority is Jewish, and Jews who remain hostile to Christianity have accused this community, represented especially by Paul, of unfaithfulness to the Law. Luke answers this criticism by showing that there is only one people of God: the restored Israel that is the Jewish-Christian community. According to Jervell, Luke knows no mission to the gentiles; the 'nations' (ἔθνη) of Acts are the God-fearers of whom Cornelius is the exemplar. The 'good news' of salvation comes from Israel and the promises of God are accomplished insofar as the nations join themselves to the part of Israel that accepts salvation.

For Jervell, Paul is less a missionary to gentiles (the latter, according to him, consisting solely of God-fearers)[55] than a synagogue-preacher, a 'master of Israel',[56] who has to defend himself against attacks brought against him by Jews who refuse his message. His defence speeches in the course of his trial are aimed precisely at showing that these attacks are unfounded. His Christian faith thus remains in complete continuity with his belonging to Judaism. According to this author, the situation described by the Acts narrative corresponds to the historical reality at the moment when Luke composed his work. He was addressing a Jewish-Christian community that is exposed to Jewish hostility on account of Paul and the verdict of exclusion that he pronounces against unrepentant Israel in Acts 28.[57] Thus the conflict sundering Jews and Christians is an intra-Jewish conflict that does not concern the gentile world except by way of the God-fearers.

Reflecting a time later than that of the events mentioned in the narrative, the story of the Paul of Acts is nevertheless not completely severed from the historical person of the apostle – though, to be sure, Acts reveals an 'unknown'[58]

---

54   Published several years apart, the two articles of P. G. Müller and A. Barbi, both targeting specifically the question of Luke's 'Paulinism', echo this turning in Lukan studies. See Müller, 'Paulinismus'; A. Barbi, 'Il Paolinismo degli Atti', *RivBib* 48 (1986), pp. 471–518.

55   J. Jervell, 'The Church of Jews and God-Fearers', in *Luke-Acts and the Jewish People: Eight Critical Perspectives* (ed. J. B. Tyson; Minneapolis: Augsburg, 1988), pp. 11–20.

56   *Idem*, 'Paulus—der Lehrer Israels: Zu den apologetischen Paulusreden in der Apostelgeschichte', *NovT* 10 (1968), pp. 164–90.

57   *Idem*, 'Paulus in der Apostelgeschichte und die Geschichte des Urchristentums', *NTS* 32 (1986), pp. 378–92.

58   *Idem*, *The Unknown Paul: Essays on Luke-Acts and Early Christian History* (Minneapolis: Augsburg, 1984).

Paul, a Paul whom the letters presuppose but do not bring to light, since their aim is not to speak of the life of Paul.

Since the continuity that Jervell sees between Judaism and Christianity is a matter of imaginative reconstruction of reality and is based on the (positivist) presupposition that the apologetic intent of Acts lines up with historical reality, his thesis cannot be retained as such,[59] especially since it reduces the question of the entry of gentiles into the church to a battle between Jews over groups located at the margins of Judaism. Still, by maintaining the link between the Paul of the letters and the Paul of Acts (holding, for example, that one cannot gain access to the historical Paul without Luke and Acts),[60] Jervell aligns his research with one of the major tendencies of redaction criticism.

From this point forward the debate regarding Luke's Judaism constitutes the background of all research on the Paul of Acts. Even if the character of Paul loses a little bit of the priority that historical research had given it, it nevertheless remains a major element of the case. The work of R. Maddox[61] and R. Brawley,[62] where within the framework of a thematic study of the whole book of Acts an entire chapter is devoted to the character of Paul,[63] confirms this assessment.

b. Paul the Persecuted Witness, Model for the Faith of the Church: R. Maddox

Even while taking into consideration the nuanced presentation in Acts of the Jewish reception of the Christian message, R. Maddox chooses to emphasize Luke's Christian addressees, leaving obscure the aim of the oracle of judgement pronounced against Israel in the final scene (Acts 28.25-29). In fact, his position is the opposite of Jervell's: he considers Luke to be unconcerned with historical reality, giving Paul an essentially symbolic valence. Noting that chs 21–28, which cover Paul's trial process, by themselves occupy space equivalent to all of the other Paul passages, he draws the conclusion that Luke is more interested in Paul as persecuted witness than as missionary.[64] Luke encourages his community to follow Paul's example by pursuing with assurance and confidence its own mission of testimony in the face of hardships and persecution. Paul is a key element, according to Maddox,[65] in the plan of Luke-Acts, which is to bolster the Lukan church in its

---

59   Jervell's thesis provoked numerous reactions and critiques. The volume edited by J. B. Tyson (*Luke-Acts and the Jewish People*) provides a suggestive overview by way of opposing positions, paired in critical conversation.

60   Jervell, *Unknown Paul*, p. 70.

61   Maddox, *Purpose of Luke-Acts*.

62   R. L. Brawley, *Luke-Acts and the Jews: Conflict, Apology, Conciliation* (SBLMS, 33; Atlanta: Scholars Press, 1987).

63   Cf. Maddox, 'The Picture of Paul in Acts', in *Purpose of Luke-Acts*, pp. 66–90; Brawley, *Luke-Acts and the Jews*, pp. 68–83; *idem*, 'Paul in Acts: Aspects of Structure and Characterization', in *SBL Seminar Papers, 1988* (SBLSP, 27; Chico, CA: Scholars Press, 1988), pp. 90–105.

64   In light of its arbitrary character, this conclusion seems indeed debatable: the importance of a section of text does not depend solely on its length.

65   Cf. Maddox, *Purpose of Luke-Acts*, p. 186.

faith tradition by showing it the 'security' (ἀσφάλεια , Luke 1.4) of the Christian message.

c. Paul, Image of Faithfulness to Israel: R. Brawley

R. Brawley finds his place in the line of interpretation inaugurated by Jervell: Luke, in setting out to demonstrate the continuity linking Christianity to Judaism, appeals as much to Jews as to Christians. His thesis, based on study of all the literary devices that Luke uses to legitimate the character of Paul,[66] is that Luke composes a portrait of Paul that is both 'apologetic and irenic'[67] to counter the anti-Paulinism exhibited by both Jews and Christians who are hostile to the universality of his message. According to Brawley, Acts aims to defend the apostle and his gospel: innocent of the charges brought against him and, to the contrary, incarnating the true hope of Israel, Paul is the very image of faithfulness to Judaism. Registering strong disagreement with the idea that the gentile mission is presented as resulting from a break with Judaism, he stresses that Paul does not for a moment give up on his mission to Jews and that they are at no point definitively rejected. The legitimacy of the gentile mission derives precisely from the fact that it fulfils Israel's destiny.

What are we to make of this question? Does the Paul of Acts speak for a break with Judaism or, to the contrary, continuity with Israel? The discussion seems deadlocked: we have, as D. Marguerat observes, 'two absolutely contradictory readings of the Lukan oeuvre that are developed with equal skill'.[68] Noting that both readings are possible, and attributing them to a tension resident in the narrative itself, he proposes to interpret the tension theologically as being inherent in the very mission of Christianity and its original break, as indicated by its universalistic vision of the people of God: for Luke, Jews and Christians coexist in the people of God.

This alternative way of grasping the problem has the advantage of shifting the terms of the discussion, thereby reviving a crucial debate for the interpretation of the Lukan opus and of the character of Paul.

d. Paul Reflects the Sociocultural Reality of the World of Acts

J. C. Lentz infers from the very diversity of hypotheses regarding the role of Paul in Acts that 'attempts to understand the portrayal and how it serves Luke's larger aim are as inconclusive as they are unsatisfying'.[69] He joins others in affirming

---

66   Brawley (*Luke-Acts and the Jews*, pp. 51–67) lists six techniques used to legitimize the character of Paul. Among these, as one example: divine approbation evidenced by the Christophany of Acts 9.

67   Cf. Brawley, *Luke-Acts and the Jews*, p. 83.

68   D. Marguerat, 'Juifs et chrétiens selon Luc-Actes', in *Le Déchirement: Juifs et chrétiens au premier siècle* (ed. D. Marguerat and M. C. de Boer; MdB, 32; Geneva: Labor et Fides, 1996), pp. 151–78 (152).

69   J. C. Lentz, *Luke's Portrait of Paul* (SNTSMS, 77; Cambridge: Cambridge University Press, 1993), p. 1.

the importance of holding together that portrayal's elements of continuity and rupture. Alongside Paul the Jew there is Paul the citizen of Rome and Tarsus, and this bifurcated belonging gives the hero of Acts no ordinary social status. Such is the observation from which his study begins and on the basis of which he establishes his hypothesis, aided by a sociological lens. According to Lentz's hypothesis, Luke presents Paul as 'a man of high social status and moral virtue'[70] in order to offer to the Greco-Roman world as a whole an image of Christianity whose universality would enable it to reach all levels of the social hierarchy.

The sociological approach, brought to bear also by B. J. Malina and J. H. Neyrey, leads these two authors to the same conclusions as Lentz: the character of Paul in Acts reflects the social ideal and the collective culture of the first-century Mediterranean world.

This thesis is persuasive. Its answer to the question as to what extent the character of Paul reflects first-century sociocultural reality brings sociology to the aid of the exegesis of Acts. The historical nature of the quest that it sets forth marks its limits. The coherence that this approach, coming from outside the text, lends to the character of Paul must be confirmed by the narrative itself. Outside of commending Christianity in the eyes of the Roman world, what meaning does this image of the apostle bring to the Acts narrative as a whole? How does it relate to the Pauline tradition? Because it aims less at understanding the figure of Paul than at understanding first-century society, Lentz's work cannot be blamed for not answering this question; but still, the question stands.

VI. The Contribution of Narrative Analysis: the Paul of Acts as a Character Inherited from the Pauline Tradition

The striking development of narrative criticism in the last three decades is one consequence of the introduction of social science into the exegetical arena. Its success, which was foreshadowed by the impact of the publication of R. Alter's major book, *The Art of Biblical Narrative*, is now, in the early years of the twenty-first century, indisputable. One has only to take notice of the numerous publications that draw inspiration from it.[71]

Thus new perspectives have been opened up on the study of the character of Paul in Acts. A particular debt is owed to the work of D. Marguerat for an important advance in the debate regarding the historical value of the Pauline tradition reported in Acts. His contributions have significantly changed the terrain of the debate regarding the relationship of history and Pauline tradition in the Lukan narrative and cast an entirely new light on Luke's historiographical work.[72] Now the point of the narrative is to be found in its very coherence; more specifically, the coherence of Luke's historiographical project, as set forth in his

---

70   Ibid., p. 91.

71   For French-language exegesis, see the RRENAB (Réseau de recherche en narratologie et Bible) online bibliography: http://www2.unil.ch/rrenab/attachments/File/biblio20110331.html

72   Marguerat, *First Christian Historian*, pp. 11–43.

preface to the two-volume opus, is to be verified in his narrative construction of the character of Paul. Nevertheless, highlighting the narrative construction of the character of the apostle does not in any way call into question the very existence of a historical tradition about him.[73] From this point of view we must reject C. Mount's argument that Luke created the character of the apostle to the gentiles from whole cloth in the second century as a way of serving the apologetic needs of Christianity.[74] The author's literary work cannot be purely and simply identified with historical reality. But that is precisely what Mount does when, taking up again the positions of the Tübingen School, he finds in Luke's reconstruction of Paul nothing but the reflection of second-century Christianity's historical situation.

We are now in a position to recognize the legitimacy of the different images the New Testament gives us of the apostle. These images are simultaneously rooted in living memories of the apostle and inextricable from the reception of those memories in the Christian communities.[75] Following D. Marguerat's typology: the Lukan Paul represents the 'biographical' pole of the Pauline inheritance, alongside the 'canonical' pole represented by the authentic letters and the 'doctoral' pole witnessed by the Deutero-Pauline letters (Colossians, Ephesians, the Pastorals).[76] These three poles share a common aim with regard to Paul's identity but, situated on their differing trajectories, they do not give Paul the same standing. Thus the narrative makes Paul neither a legendary character nor a master-teacher whose instruction must be codified in writing. Seeing in him the model witness who announces the word of God, Acts makes him simultaneously a Pauline and Lukan character, signalling a tradition that is still alive in the church. The construction of the Paul of Acts thus appears as the locus where Christian identity, in both its continuity and its discontinuity with Judaism, becomes universal in its faith and in the expression of that faith in the Roman imperial setting.[77]

The fruitfulness of the narrative-critical approach is seen likewise in current explorations of all things related to Luke's 'Paulinism'. The published proceedings of the 2008 Lausanne colloquy on this topic testify to the dynamism of research

73 Cf. O. Flichy, 'Définir un nouveau paradigme', in *idem*, *La figure de Paul dans les Actes des Apôtres: Un phénomène de réception de la tradition paulinienne à la fin du premier siècle* (LD, 214; Paris: Cerf, 2007), pp. 35–49.

74 C. Mount, *Pauline Christianity: Luke-Acts and the Legacy of Paul* (NovTSup, 104; Leiden: Brill, 2002) [Ed. note: for a more recent statement of Mount's position, see ch. 5 of this volume].

75 D. Marguerat, *First Christian Historian*; Flichy, *Figure de Paul*.

76 D. Marguerat, 'L'image de Paul dans les Actes des Apôtres', in *Les Actes des Apôtres: Histoire, récit, théologie; XXᵉ congrès de l'Association catholique française pour l'étude de la Bible (Angers 2003)* (ed. M. Berder; LD, 199; Paris: Cerf, 2005), pp. 121–54.

77 Marguerat, 'Image de Paul', p. 153. On the cultural resonances of the portrait thus tailored by Luke for his ancient readers, cf. S. Butticaz, 'La figure de Paul en fondateur de colonie', in *Et vous, qui dites-vous que je suis? La gestion des personnages dans les récits bibliques* (ed. P. Létourneau and M. Talbot; Montréal: Mediaspaul, 2006), pp. 173–88.

on this topic.[78] In light of the various contributions in that volume, the close links between Luke and the Pauline tradition – and especially between the narrative character of Paul and the Pauline letters, for so long either denied or exaggerated – receive a fresh reevaluation. The search for links is no longer seen as depending on word-for-word borrowings in Acts from expressions in the letters on the model of a strict intertextuality. The contributors to this volume opt, by and large, for a larger idea of 'transtextuality' based on their concern to take into account Luke's manner of taking up Paul's own arguments and reconfiguring them in another historical and cultural context. Thus they honour the dual aspects of continuity and transformation that are entailed in the phenomenon of receiving a tradition. To cite only a few of the contributions to this work, M. Wolter's conclusion to his comparative study of Pauline and Lukan soteriology is that, making allowance for the fact that Luke's theology is expressed in narrative form,[79] 'the Pauline and Lukan conceptions of the death of Jesus are much closer than is generally acknowledged'.[80] Similarly, addressing the thesis that the Paul of the letters and the Lukan Paul are incompatible, J. Schröter establishes that in both corpora the theme of suffering is presented as a matter of paradigmatic Christian testimony.[81] D. Marguerat, in turn, focuses on Paul's ambivalent relationship to Torah in Acts, finding that in Acts 13.38-39 Luke has arranged a 'Paulinization' and that in Acts 21–28 Luke has taken up the Pauline tradition that was operative in his setting to produce a presentation of Paul as faithful to the Law and to Mosaic customs.[82]

The evaluation of Luke's Paulinism, intrinsically linked to his decision to render the Pauline tradition into narrative form, remains a promising path for exploration. One has only to observe, within the framework of the activities of the *RRENAB*,[83] the recent contribution of S. Butticaz on the diverse reception procedures that can be identified in the Lukan opus.[84]

---

78   D. Marguerat (ed.), *Reception of Paulinism in Acts* = *Réception du paulinisme dans les Actes des Apôtres* (BETL, 229; Leuven: Peeters, 2009); [Ed. note: five chapters of this seminal collection are translated into English for this volume: ch. 10 S. Butticaz ≈ ch. 8 of current vol.; C. Clivaz, ch. 12 ≈ ch. 14; ch. 13 J.-F. Landolt ≈ ch. 16; ch. 14 Y. Redalié ≈ ch. 15; ch. 15 A. Dettwiler ≈ ch. 13].

79   This necessity is very pertinently argued in the contribution of S. Butticaz, '"Dieu a-t-il rejeté son peuple?" (Rm 11,1): Le destin d'Israël de Paul aux Actes des apôtres; Gestion narrative d'un héritage théologique', in Marguerat, *Reception of Paulinism*, pp. 207–25 = ET ch. 8 of this volume.

80   M. Wolter, 'Jesu Tod und Sündenvergebung bei Lukas und Paulus', in Marguerat, *Reception of Paulinism*, pp. 15–35.

81   J. Schröter, 'Paulus als Modell Christlicher Zeugenschaft: Apg 9,15f und 28,30 als Rahmen der Lukanischen Paulusdarstellung und Rezeption des "Historischen" Paulus', in Marguerat, *Reception of Paulinism*, pp. 53–80.

82   D. Marguerat, 'Paul et la Torah dans les Actes des Apôtres', in *idem, Reception of Paulinism*, pp. 81–100.

83   Réseau de recherche en Narratologie et Bible (http://www2.unil.ch/rrenab/).

84   S. Butticaz, 'La relecture des *lapsi* pauliniens chez Luc: Esquisse d'une typologie', in *Écriture et réécritures* (5ᵉ colloque international du RRENAB; BETL[Geneva: Peeters, 2010]).

VII. Conclusion

With the birth of critical exegesis, the Christian world faced at the outset the crucial question of the historical reliability of Luke's data vis-à-vis Paul. Exacerbated by the influence of ideas defended at Tübingen and the development of *Tendenzkritik*, even today this issue remains dependent upon the different ways that exegetical currents understand their relation to tradition. The enduring absence of any consensus between and among these currents regarding the interpretation of Acts and the character of Paul is an indicator of the impasse that continues to stymie the discussion. The new direction in reading narrative texts, however, especially in the development of the social sciences, is today an established fact. Reflection on the meaning of 'truth' in history and a better understanding of ancient historiography have made it necessary to redefine the terms of the debate. It is no longer so much a matter of trying to view what Luke does over against the historian's work or the implementation of a particular theology; rather, one inquires into the meaning of these two components of the narrative enterprise and reflects on the ways they connect and are configured in Luke's narrative. In the line of research thus opened, the Paul of Acts is no longer suspected of betraying the Paul of the letters. Of course narrative criticism does not enable pronouncements regarding the narrative's level of historical reliability. But by taking responsibility for the sociocultural rootedness of the text, both from the perspective of the author and from the recipients, narrative criticism has proved its ability to illuminate the particular phenomenon that constitutes, in its diversity and in its singularity, the reception of a tradition.

Chapter 3

THE PAULINISM OF ACTS, INTERTEXTUALLY RECONSIDERED[1]

Richard B. Hays

I. Introduction: Comparing the Theologies of Paul and Acts

Philipp Vielhauer's influential essay 'On the "Paulinism" of Acts' forcefully articulated the case for seeing the theology of Acts as far removed from the thought of the Apostle Paul. Vielhauer's working method was to examine the *speeches* that Luke places in Paul's mouth and to compare their theology to the theology found in Paul's letters. The comparison was carried out in regard to four theological loci: natural theology, law, Christology, and eschatology. In these four areas, Vielhauer found little common ground between Luke and Paul; indeed, he repeatedly concluded that Luke did not know, or did not understand, the distinctive emphases of Pauline theology. 'To summarize: the author of Acts is in his Christology pre-Pauline, in his natural theology, concept of the law, and eschatology, post-Pauline. He presents no specifically Pauline idea... [H]e no longer stands within earliest Christianity, but in the nascent early catholic church.'[2]

In this essay I will propose that, in light of significant advances in NT studies over the past half century, additional evidence ought to be taken into account in forming a fuller picture of the theological relationship between Paul and the author of Acts.[3] Since the original publication of Vielhauer's work in 1950, our understanding of 'Pauline theology' has undergone certain chastenings and adjustments. More recent scholarship, however, has offered us a more complex picture of Paul, particularly with regard to his relationship to Judaism. If indeed Paul's

---

1   A version of this essay was first presented at the 'Reception of Paul Seminar', the SNTS meeting in Aberdeen, Scotland, 2006. I am appreciative of the helpful comments from that session.

2   P. Vielhauer, 'On the "Paulinism" of Acts', p. 17, of ch. 1 of this volume, as reprinted from L. E. Keck and J. L. Martyn, *Studies in Luke-Acts* (Nashville: Abingdon, 1966), pp. 33–50 (48–49); [originally published as 'Zum "Paulinismus" der Apostelgeschichte', *EvT* 10 (1950–51), pp. 1–15]. Vielhauer's essay oddly fails to consider how an author who 'no longer stands within earliest Christianity' could have a 'pre-Pauline' Christology.

3   For critical reassessments of Vielhauer, see, e.g., H. D. Buckwalter, *The Character and Purpose of Luke's Christology* (SNTSMS 89; Cambridge: Cambridge University Press, 1996), pp. 231–72; F. Bovon, 'The Law in Luke-Acts', in *Studies in Early Christianity* (WUNT 161; Tübingen: Mohr Siebeck, 2003), pp. 59–73.

thought remained deeply rooted in a Jewish apocalyptic world view, and if much of his theological reflection was generated and sustained by Israel's scripture – and I would argue that both of these statements are accurate readings of Paul – then Vielhauer's comparison would require fundamental reconsideration.

Furthermore, Vielhauer's method of looking almost exclusively at the content of the *speeches* ascribed in Acts to Paul has the effect of restricting the evidence too narrowly. If our aim is to compare Paul's theology to the theology of *Acts*, it will hardly do to examine only the content of a few speeches; we must consider the whole shape of the Lukan narrative and the theology that comes to expression in and through that narrative. It is perhaps not surprising that an essay written in Germany in 1950 would overlook the significance of *narrative* as a vehicle of theological reflection,[4] and it would be foolish and ungracious of us to chide Vielhauer for failing to employ narrative criticism – as foolish as it would be to chide Luke for failing to apply historical-critical methods in his exegesis of the Psalms. Nonetheless, in our own reading of Acts, we can surely do better.

For example, we cannot simply assume – as Vielhauer does – that Paul's Areopagus speech in Acts 17 gives an adequate summary of Luke's own theology (Vielhauer inexplicably asserts that this speech appears at 'the high point of [Luke's] book';[5] regrettably, this judgement illustrates the severe limitations of Vielhauer's method for interpreting narrative texts). As Beverly Gaventa and other narratively-oriented critics have shown convincingly, the rhetoric of the speeches in Acts is always carefully tailored to the apologetic situation within the unfolding plot of Acts, always keeping in view the symbolic world of the characters being addressed within the narrative setting.[6] Luke's theology, therefore, cannot necessarily be directly extrapolated from any single speech in the story, not even the speeches of 'reliable' characters such as Peter and Paul. One must read the narrative as a whole to see how Luke gradually builds up his picture of the significance of Jesus and the redemptive action of God. Consequently, our ultimate judgement about the 'Paulinism' of the theology of Acts should not depend exclusively on whether Luke's narrative has placed an adequate summary of 'Pauline theology' in the mouth of the character of Paul. We may find influences of and parallels to Pauline thought elsewhere in the narrative.

Indeed, some of the most 'Pauline' theological elements in the story of Acts are actually to be found in the speeches and stories of *Peter*. It has sometimes been argued that the Acts of the Apostles seeks to domesticate Paul by absorbing him into the Petrine theological discourse of early Catholic Christianity.[7] I would like

---

4   On the lengthy history of the neglect of narrative in German theology and biblical scholarship, see H. Frei, *The Eclipse of Biblical Narrative: A Study in Eighteenth and Nineteenth Century Hermeneutics* (New Haven: Yale University Press, 1974).

5   Vielhauer, 'Paulinism', p. 4.

6   See Beverly Roberts Gaventa, 'The Overthrown Enemy: Luke's Portrait of Paul', in *SBL Seminar Papers, 1985* (ed. K. H. Richards; Atlanta, Scholars Press, 1985), pp. 439–49.

7   For a brief survey of this scholarly trend, see Alan J. Thompson, *One Lord, One People: The Unity of the Church in Acts in Its Literary Setting* (LNTS 359; London: T&T Clark, 2008), pp. 3–10; see also, e.g., Ernst Käsemann, 'Paul and Nascent Catholicism', in *Journal for Theology and the Church* 3 (1967), pp. 14–27, esp. pp. 17–18.

to suggest, on the contrary, that *Luke is narrating Peter into the Pauline world view as he understands it*, recruiting Peter as a supporter of the Pauline mission to the gentiles. But to state that claim is to run ahead of our investigation.

I would like to propose an investigative method different from Vielhauer's. Rather than looking only at the Pauline speeches, I suggest that we begin by looking at passages in Acts that quote or clearly allude to the OT. As we do so, our heuristic questions will be as follows: Which OT texts are being cited? Do we find overlap between the passages Luke cites and the texts that Paul refers to in his letters? If so, do Luke and Paul read the texts similarly or divergently? In short, we will be asking about the *intertextuality* of Acts with respect both to the OT and to Paul. Are Luke's intertextual engagements of Israel's story on the same trajectory as Paul's, or not?

A word of explanation about 'intertextuality' is necessary before I begin.[8] I am not asking whether it can be shown that Luke uses Paul's letters as a 'source', or whether we can identify verbatim agreements of Luke's text with Pauline material. It can be shown rather easily that there is very little, if any, such material in Luke-Acts. The question, rather, is whether Luke's readings of the OT live and move and have their being within the same intertextual field as Paul's readings.[9] Are they talking about the same texts, and are they thinking about these texts in similar ways? To put the same question in slightly different terms, do Paul and Luke belong to an interpretive community that shares a recognizably common 'encyclopedia of reception' (to use Umberto Eco's term) for interpreting Israel's scripture?[10] Or do they seem to belong to two different interpretive communities that are receiving these scriptures in notably different ways?

Acts has far too many OT citations to be treated thoroughly in this short essay, and it would in any case be tedious to work through the full list. I propose instead to select a few examples of Acts' OT reading, and to demonstrate that they manifest significant points of contact with the Pauline tradition. One final disclaimer: I am not attempting to show that the author of Luke-Acts was in fact Luke the physician, a companion of Paul on his journeys (in fact, I do not have a settled opinion about this issue). Rather, like Vielhauer, I am interested simply in a theological comparison of the two writers – or, to be more precise, I am interested in a *hermeneutical* comparison of the two writers: how does each one operate as a reader of scripture, and are there any signs of Luke's engagement with Pauline traditions of scriptural exegesis?

---

8   On this topic more generally, see R. B. Hays, S. Alkier, and L. A. Huizenga (eds.), *Reading the Bible Intertextually* (Waco, TX: Baylor University Press, 2009).

9   This way of posing the issue presumes that Luke is not simply compiling traditional sources haphazardly; rather, he is to be understood as a literary artist and theologian who is shaping his material with particular theological and literary aims.

10   As Stefan Alkier explains, 'The *encyclopedia* is the cultural framework in which the text is situated and from which the gaps of the text are filled' (*Reading the Bible Intertexually*, 8).

II. OT Readings in Acts: Some Examples

a. Overlap between Luke and Paul in explicit citations of the OT

We begin with a few cases in which Luke explicitly quotes a text that was previously referenced by Paul in his letters (I use the term 'referenced' to include
both explicit citations and direct allusions, for reasons that will appear in the
discussion of the examples below).

1. Acts 2.17-21/Joel 2.28-32

Peter's Pentecost sermon takes its point of departure from an extensive quotation of the prophet Joel, climaxing in the declaration that '*everyone who calls
on the name of the Lord shall be saved*' (Acts 2.21, citing Joel 2.32 LXX).[11]
We are probably meant to remember this passage at the conclusion of the
sermon when Peter calls his hearers to repent and be baptized in the name
of Jesus in order to receive forgiveness of sins and the Holy Spirit, 'for the
promise is for you, for your children, and for all who are far away, *everyone*
whom the *Lord* our God *calls* to him' (2.38-39). Certainly, the 'promise' refers
to the affirmation in the preceding clause that 'you will receive the gift of
the Holy Spirit' (see also Lk. 24.49). But – in view of the emphasis here on
the universal scope of the promise, and the way that προσκαλέσηται (2.39)
sounds an answering echo to ἐπικαλέσηται (2.21) – it seems likely that, at the
same time, we should also interpret 'the promise' as a reference to the word of
assurance given in Joel's prophecy: 'Everyone who calls on the name of the
Lord shall be saved.'[12] If so, this would provide an artful *inclusio* for Peter's
sermon. Whether that be so or not, it is indisputable that Joel's prophecy of
salvation for those who call upon the name of the Lord stands as the keynote
for Luke's account of the first Christian preaching, and that this prophecy, read
within the wider narrative of Acts, already prefigures the message of salvation
that will go forth to the gentile world.

It is of more than passing interest, then, that Paul employs precisely the same
text in Romans 10 in support of his argument that the gospel is a word of salvation
for Jew and Greek alike. 'For there is no distinction between Jew and Greek; the
same Lord is Lord of all and is generous to all who call on him. For, "*Everyone
who calls on the name of the Lord will be saved*"' (Rom. 10.12-13). In both Acts
2 and Romans 10, Joel 2.32 becomes a major text prefiguring the proclamation of
the gospel. Not incidentally, both texts almost certainly understand 'the Lord' to

---

11   On the whole matter of scriptural interpretation in the Pentecost sermon, see D. P.
Moessner, 'Luke's "Plan of God" from the Greek Psalter: The Rhetorical Thrust of "The Prophets
and the Psalms" in Peter's Speech at Pentecost', in P. Gray and G. R. O'Day (eds.), *Scripture and
Traditions: Essays on Early Judaism and Christianity in Honor of Carl R. Holladay* (NovTSup
129; Leiden: Brill, 2008), pp. 223–38.

12   It is also to be noted that Joel 2.32 LXX ends with these words: καὶ εὐαγγελιζόμενοι
οὓς κύριος προσκέκληται. Undoubtedly, Luke's use of the verb προσκαλέσηται (Acts 2.39)
re-sounds the echo of Joel's prophecy.

be the Lord Jesus. In Romans the link of 10.9 to 10.12-13 makes this identification unambiguous,[13] and in Acts, the connection between 2.21 and 2.36 leads to the same conclusion.[14] Thus, both of our authors are reading Joel's reference to 'the Lord' christologically.

2. Acts 2.34-35/Ps. 110.1

Another key text in Peter's web of OT witnesses in the Pentecost sermon is Ps. 110.1, 'The Lord said to my Lord, "Sit at my right hand, until I make your enemies your footstool"' (Acts 2.34-35).[15] In its context in the sermon, the citation asserts the appropriateness of calling Jesus κύριος (2.36), in view of his resurrection and exaltation to the right hand of God. Paul alludes to the same passage in 1 Cor. 15.25 to affirm the ultimate eschatological triumph of Christ in overcoming even death, so that those who are 'in Christ' will ultimately share in his resurrection. The argumentative purposes of the two citations differ, but in both cases, Psalm 110 is read christologically as an affirmation of Christ's eschatological victory over death. Interestingly, Paul's reference to this Psalm in 1 Corinthians 15 appears with no citation formula, indicating that it is already understood by his readers as part of their symbolic world.[16] Or, to rephrase the point, the christological interpretation of Psalm 110 already belongs to the 'encyclopedia of reception' for Paul's gentile readers in Corinth. (At least, Paul's rhetoric treats it as belonging to that encyclopedia.)[17] Luke's use of the same text in the Pentecost sermon belongs to the same circle of interpretive convention. The fact that this circle includes also the synoptic tradition (Mk 12.35-37 par.), 1 Peter (1 Pet 3.22) and the Letter to the Hebrews (Heb. 1.13) is an interesting fact, whose significance we shall consider in the conclusion of the present essay.

3. Acts 13.47/Isa. 49.6

In Acts 13, Paul's initial 'word of exhortation' in the synagogue at Pisidian Antioch contains a concise summary of Israel's history and a cluster of OT quotations highly reminiscent of Peter's Pentecost sermon (13.32-37, quoting Ps. 2.7, Isa. 55.3 LXX, and Ps. 16.10), as well as a quotation of Hab. 1.5. All

13   C. K. Rowe, 'Romans 10:13: What is the Name of the Lord?' in *HBT* 22/2 (2000), pp. 135–73.

14   For an analysis of Luke's use of *kyrios*, see C. K. Rowe, *Early Narrative Christology: The Lord in the Gospel of Luke* (BZNW 139; Berlin: deGruyter, 2006).

15   On this passage, see D. P. Moessner, '*Two* Lords "at the Right Hand"? The Psalms and an Intertextual Reading of Peter's Pentecost Speech (Acts 2.14-36)', in R. P. Thompson and T. E. Phillips (eds.), *Literary Studies in Luke-Acts: Essays in Honor of Joseph B. Tyson* (Macon, GA: Mercer University Press, 1998), pp. 15–32.

16   For the pervasive influence of Ps. 110 in early Christianity, see David M. Hay, *Glory at the Right Hand: Psalm 110 in Early Christianity* (SBLMS 18; Nasvhille: Abingdon Press, 1973), esp. pp. 35, 39, 50–51.

17   Similarly, Paul's reference to Christ's place 'at the right hand of God' in Rom. 8.34 also suggests an allusion to Ps. 110.1.

of this has the effect of situating Paul's message within the long story of God's elective grace towards Israel, and the accompanying threat of God's judgement ('Beware, therefore, that what the prophets said does not happen to you,' 13.40).

Our immediate concern, however, is with the words spoken by Paul and Barnabas on the following sabbath, when they encounter opposition to their message. They declare that they will leave the synagogue and turn to the gentiles, and they find a scriptural warrant – indeed, a command – for this decision in Isa. 49.6: 'I have set you to be a light for the gentiles, so that you may bring salvation to the ends of the earth' (Acts 13.47). Readers of Acts have known since the first account of Paul's conversion that he is God's chosen instrument 'to bring my name before gentiles and kings and before the people of Israel' (9.15). The explicit citation of Isa. 49.6 in Acts 13 gives a prophetic scriptural grounding for this vocation.[18] Here in Acts 13, Isaiah 49 is interpreted not in a christological sense, but as a commission for the early Christian mission to the gentiles. It is Paul and Barnabas who find themselves addressed by God's word in Isaiah 49: they are the ones sent forth as a light to the nations. Precisely this same passage informs Paul's self-description of his apostolic vocation in Gal. 1.15-16: like the servant figure of Isa. 49.1-6, he was set apart from his mother's womb for the task of proclaiming good news to the nations. The centrality of this text for defining Paul's understanding of his own vocation is shown once again in 2 Cor. 6.2, where – at the climax of a passage declaring his role as an ambassador for Christ – he cites Isa. 49.8: 'At an acceptable time I have listened to you, and on a day of salvation I have helped you.' Clearly this is one point where the portrayal of Paul in Acts corresponds closely to the Paul we encounter in the letters: he is sent by God on a mission to the gentiles, and *Isaiah 49 is the key text, in both cases, for defining and sustaining the mission.* In all the passages just mentioned (Acts 13, Galatians 1, 2 Corinthians 6), Paul draws upon this OT text in the course of defending and justifying the legitimacy of his ministry. It may occasion some surprise that in none of these passages is the servant who brings light to the nations identified as Jesus by either of our authors; rather the interpretation of Isaiah's prophecy is focused on Paul and his missionary associates.[19]

4. Acts 28.25-28/Isa. 6.9-10

The final scripture quotation in Acts appears in Paul's parting admonitory word to the Jewish leaders in Rome who have assembled to hear his message. Luke tells us that some were convinced, but others disbelieved. On their way out the door, they are reminded by Paul of the gloomy prophecy of Isaiah about the people's incapacity to hear the prophetic word and to turn in response to it (Acts 28.25-28, quoting Isa. 6.9-10 in almost verbatim agreement with the LXX). The effect of this citation is once more to link Paul's own prophetic ministry of proclamation to Isaiah's.

---

18   Isaiah 49 also underlies a number of other passages in Luke-Acts that refer to the task of bringing light to the gentiles (e.g. Lk. 2.32, Acts 26.17-18).

19   The christological interpretation of the 'light to the gentiles' motif does appear, however, in Acts 26.23 as well as in Lk. 2.32.

In my view, the citation should *not* be interpreted to mean that Luke finally gives up on the Jewish people and embraces a supersessionist theology, any more than that such a view should be attributed to the prophet Isaiah himself. This is the third time in the narrative of Acts that Paul declares his intention to go to the gentiles (earlier in 13.46-48 and 18.5-6); yet, as many commentators have observed, after each of the first two pronouncements he continues to reach out to the synagogues and the Jewish people, though with results that are at best mixed. Reading the Isaiah citation within its original literary context would lead us rather to suppose that it is a prophetic judgement oracle meant to provoke repentance and faith; and perhaps Paul's citation of it functions in a similar way. If so, Paul's announced intention to take the message of 'the salvation of God' to the gentiles (28.28) should be understood as part of his missionary strategy to make his own people jealous and thus save some of them (Rom. 11.13-14).

In any case, as this link to Romans 11 suggests, we find Paul's passionate treatment of the problem of Israel's unbelief in Romans 9–11 drawing upon precisely this same tradition of Isaiah's proclamation to a people who have 'eyes that would not see and ears that would not hear' (Rom. 11.8). The scriptural citation in Rom. 11.8 is a complicated conflation of three different texts: the phrase πνεῦμα κατανύξεως echoes Isa. 29.10; the idea that God has *given* them this disability 'down to this very day' echoes Deut. 29.3 LXX; and the reference to unseeing eyes and unhearing ears seems to blend Deuteronomy 29 with Isa. 6.9. We cannot here delve into the complexities of this blended citation.[20] The salient point for our present purpose is that Paul addresses the pressing issue of Israel's stubborn rejection of the gospel by evoking the tradition of Isaiah's vocation to preach to a people seemingly incapable of seeing and hearing – precisely the same image with which Luke leaves his readers in Acts 28. Once again here, we find a significant convergence between Luke's portrayal of Paul and Paul's own deployment of scripture to reflect on Jewish response and non-response to the gospel.

Additionally, in Rom. 11.9-10, immediately following his reference to Isaiah 6, Paul amplifies his judgement on Israel by citing Ps. 68.23-24 LXX, the same psalm cited by Luke to describe God's judgement on Judas (Acts 1.20a). Both of these quotations presuppose the common early Christian tradition of reading this psalm as a foreshadowing of Jesus' passion and death – a reading that shows up in Rom. 15.3, John 2.17, and in the tradition attested in all four Gospels that Jesus on the cross was offered vinegar to drink. It is precisely because Jesus is understood to be the speaker of the psalm that the psalm's condemnations of enemies can be applied to those who reject him as Lord. Thus, in Acts 1.20 Luke's loose citation of Ps. 69.26 (=Ps. 68.26 LXX) is an excellent example of the way in which his reading of scripture presupposes the same hermeneutical frame of reference that we find in Paul's use of the same psalm. It is not merely a random prooftext: it can be applied to Judas because of the prior conviction that the psalm is to be interpreted christologically.

---

20   For a full discussion, see J. Ross Wagner, *Heralds of the Good News: Isaiah and Paul 'In Concert' in the Letter to the Romans* (NovTSup 101; Leiden: Brill, 2002).

b. Allusions and Echoes in Acts 10.34-43

We turn now to look all too briefly at the way in which Luke alludes to scriptural texts that he does not quote directly. Even though these passages do not
entail explicit citation, they are no less important for reassessing the Paulinism
of Acts from an intertextual point of view. Precisely where no explicit quotation
is necessary, the shared hermeneutical assumptions may be most powerfully
present. The scope of the present essay allows us to consider only one significant example.

Acts 10.34-43

As suggested by the copious marginal references in Nestle-Aland[27], Peter's
compact sermon to the household of the gentile centurion Cornelius is dense
with scriptural allusions. We cannot now attend to all of these, but I want to call
attention to a few of them that suggest points of contact with Paul's readings
of scripture. In 10.36, Peter declares that God 'sent (ἀπέστειλεν) the word to
the sons of Israel, preaching peace through Jesus Christ (εὐαγγελιζόμενος
εἰρήνην διὰ ᾿Ιησοῦ Χριστοῦ)—this one is Lord of all.' The reference to
'preaching peace' almost surely echoes Isa. 52.7, which Paul quotes explicitly in Rom. 10.15 to describe the role of Christian preachers, who are 'sent
(ἀποσταλῶσιν) ... preaching (εὐαγγελιζομένων) good news'. It should
also be remembered that in Romans 10 Paul has just driven home the point
that the central content of Christian preaching is that Jesus Christ is Lord
(Rom. 10.9-12). Thus, Peter's exclamation in Acts 10.36 that Jesus Christ is
'Lord of all' seems to presuppose precisely the same complex of ideas that
appear in Romans 10, and both of these texts are in turn dependent on Isaiah's
language about the messengers who bring the good news of Israel's redemption from exile.[21] At the same time, I would suggest that the phrase 'preaching
peace through Jesus Christ' is even a clearer echo of Rom. 5:1: 'we have peace
towards God through our Lord Jesus Christ.' In short, Peter's opening words
to Cornelius sound very much as though they could have been lifted out of the
pages of Paul's Letter to the Romans.

The second allusion in Acts 10 to which I would like to draw attention is found
in Peter's announcement that 'God raised him on the third day (ἐν τῇ τρίτῃ
ἡμέρᾳ)' (10.40), a phrase that appears to echo Hos. 6.2. Of course, in Acts 10,
there is no sign of a citation formula, and we might miss the allusion were it not
for Paul's earlier adamant confession that 'he was raised on the third day (τῇ
τρίτῃ ἡμέρᾳ) *in accordance with the Scriptures*' (1 Cor. 15.4). Of course, there is
no reason to think this allusion to Hosea is distinctively Pauline; it appears also in

---

21   The Nestle-Aland[27] text of Acts 10.36 includes a completely conjectural emendation that
would omit the phrase οὗτός ἐστιν πάντων κύριος as a gloss. Such speculations in the absence
of any textual evidence are of doubtful value in a critical edition of the Greek text. However,
by calling attention to the slightly intrusive character of the phrase, this text-critical suggestion
might cause us to consider even more strongly the possibility that its presence here is a sign of
the intertextual influence of Romans 10, where Jesus' Lordship is so prominently featured.

the Matthean and Lukan passion predictions. But it is Paul who draws attention to the conformity of this detail to *scripture*. Interestingly, while Matthew's version of the passion predictions passes over this point in silence, only Luke highlights that the killing and resurrection of Jesus on the third day belongs to that which is 'written about the Son of Man by the prophets' (Lk. 18.31; cf. Lk. 24.46). One wonders whether this is another point – perhaps comparable to the formulation of the Lord's Supper tradition – where Luke shares a common tradition with Paul, a tradition that connects the promise of Jesus' resurrection to Hos. 6.2.

The last scriptural echo in Peter's sermon to Cornelius that is of special interest for our present purposes is considerably less distinct, but nonetheless of some importance. Peter begins his speech by saying, 'I truly understand that God is not one who shows partiality (προσωπολήμπτης), but in every nation the one who fears him and does righteousness is acceptable to him' (10.34-35). The unusual word προσωπολήμπτης seems to echo the language of the scriptural maxim that God 'is not partial and takes no bribe'. (Deut. 10.17, repeated in 2 Chron. 19.7 and slightly elaborated in Sir. 35.12-13 LXX.) But the strongest echo of all, the closest verbal parallel, is to Paul's declaration in Rom. 2.11: οὐ γάρ ἐστιν προσωπολημψία παρὰ τῷ θεῷ. This parallel is of special interest, because in Romans Paul articulates this characterization of God's impartiality precisely in the midst of an argument that God treats *Jews and gentiles alike*. They are equally under judgement for doing evil (2.9) and equally granted 'glory and honor and peace' for doing right (2.10). Indeed, this argument is developed throughout Rom. 2:1-16, and it stands as part of the foundation for Paul's overarching argument that the gospel is 'the power of God for salvation to everyone who believes, *to the Jew first and also to the Greek*' (1.16 and throughout the first four chapters of Romans). In short, the maxim of divine impartiality, which had traditionally been used to underwrite the claim that God does not favour the rich over the poor,[22] that God gives justice to the orphan and the widow, becomes in Paul's hands a theological argument for the acceptance of gentile believers into the people of God through Jesus Christ. And of course, this is precisely the use to which Luke puts the same maxim in the pivotal story of Acts 10. I would submit that once again we might well suppose some intertextual relationship between Acts 10 and Romans 2, even though there is no direct quotation. At the very least, this fundamental element of Luke's theological programme stands within the trajectory launched by Paul's theological justification for the mission to the gentiles.

The Pauline and Lukan use of 'divine impartiality' as a support for acceptance of gentiles is not entirely without foundation in the Torah text from which the maxim originally comes. In Deuteronomy 10, Moses proclaims that though all heaven and earth belong to God, he has 'set his heart in love' on Israel and chosen them out of all the peoples of the earth; nonetheless, God's impartiality means that he also 'loves the stranger' (גֵּר) (10.18). This creates a presumptive obligation for Israel also to 'love the stranger, for you were strangers in the land of Egypt' (10.19). In the LXX, however, Deuteronomy's (גֵּר) is rendered by προσήλυτος. This translation

---

22   As reflected in Jas. 2.1 and 2.9.

creates a linguistic bridge that easily permits a crossing to the Pauline use of 'divine impartiality' as a warrant for the extension of God's grace to gentile *converts* to the faith. Neither Paul nor Luke makes such a connection to Deut. 10.17-19 explicit, but it seems likely that this interpretation belongs to the intertextual field of herme-neutical assumptions underlying both Romans 2 and Acts 10.

One could continue to multiply examples. Again and again, when we scratch the surface of Luke's scriptural citations and allusions, we find a hermeneutical substratum that is shared with Paul. It seems to me that the best explanation for the evidence we have considered is not that Luke is using Paul's letters directly as a source but rather that both of them participate in a common intertextual field, a community of interpretation in which numerous texts from Israel's scriptures have been highlighted, read through the lens of the message of Jesus' death and resurrection, and thereby reinterpreted as witnesses to the gospel and warrants for the emergent mission to the gentile world. The list of interpretive conventions that Paul and Luke share could be extended. For example, both participate in the hermeneutical convention of reading some of Israel's psalms as the speech of Jesus the Messiah (e.g., Acts 2.25-28; Rom. 15.3, 9). Both of them presuppose, perhaps following Deut. 33.2 LXX, that angels were involved in giving the Law at Sinai (Acts 7.38; Gal. 3.19). Both use ὁ δίκαιος – probably on the basis of Hab. 2.3-4 – as an epithet for Jesus the Messiah (as in Acts 3.14; 7.52; 22.14), or so I would contend.[23] And so forth. Rather than continuing to pile up such evidence, however, it may be more fruitful – since this paper constitutes only a preliminary probe of these matters – to take a step back and outline the broad contours of a 'theology' that Acts and Paul share in common, as disclosed by the methodology we have been pursuing here.

III. The Lukanism of Paul? Intertextual Common Ground

a. Shared Theological Themes and Convictions

To be sure, there are many facets of Paul's theology, as reflected in his letters, that appear nowhere in the pages of Acts. If the history of interpretation of the Pauline letters proves nothing else, it shows that Paul was a profound and subtle thinker. His second-order theological reflection is richly detailed and not easily represented through Luke's medium of storytelling. Nonetheless, the intertextual approach that we have begun to explore in this paper does in fact suggest that we may be able to describe the profile of a certain set of theological themes and convictions shared by Paul's letters and the author of Acts. I would summarize this profile in the following list of affirmations.[24]

---

23   For a full statement of this argument, see R. B. Hays, *The Conversion of the Imagination: Paul as Interpreter of Israel's Scripture* (Grand Rapids: Eerdmans, 2005), pp. 119–42.

24   Not everything in the list that follows is directly based on the exegetical observations of the preceding pages of this essay. Where I am filling out the outline with new textual material, I will provide references, without being able to explicate them fully.

1. At the heart of the gospel message stand the crucifixion and resurrection of Jesus. These events happened 'according to the Scriptures'. Vielhauer asserts that in Acts 'Nothing is said of the saving significance of the cross of Christ.'[25] This statement is true, in the sense that Luke gives no explication comparable to Paul's reflections on the death of Jesus as 'judgment upon all mankind and at the same time reconciliation'.[26] And at the same time, Luke emphasizes repentance and forgiveness of sins in a way that finds little parallel in Paul. Yet the two are agreed that the *story* of Jesus' death and resurrection constitutes the heart of the message (in contrast, let us say, to various known or hypothetical 'early Christianities' that concentrate on Jesus as wisdom teacher or on *gnosis* as a means of escape from materiality). And they agree that the cross and resurrection mysteriously constituted God's will, as attested by scripture.

2. Jesus was raised 'on the third day' and he is now exalted, in accordance with Psalm 110.1, to the right hand of God, where his status as Lord is now manifest through the gifts he pours out on his people.

3. Paul was divinely called to a special prophetic role as the proclaimer of God's good news to the gentile world. This role was prefigured in Isaiah's vision of a servant sent as a 'light to the gentiles'.

4. According to Acts, Paul's preaching of the gospel was accompanied by 'signs and wonders' (Acts 14.3, 15.12, 19.11-12), a claim consistent with Paul's own testimony (Rom. 15.18-19, 2 Cor. 12.12). Luke sets these miraculous events in direct parallelism to the works performed by Jesus (Acts 2.22) and through the name of Jesus by the Jerusalem apostles (Acts 4.30, 5.12). These mighty works, as well as the proclamation of the message, were empowered by the Holy Spirit. For both authors, the work of the Holy Spirit is manifest through speaking in tongues, prophecy, healings, and other such signs.

5. Paul's missionary preaching to gentiles, in the narrative of Acts, summoned them to turn from idols 'to the living God' (Acts 14.15, 26.17-20), in accordance with Paul's own summary of his original preaching to the Thessalonians (1 Thess. 1.9-10).

6. Conversion in response to the preaching of the message about Jesus is described, in language derived from Joel 2.32, as 'calling on the name of Lord', and it is an integral part of the message of Paul, as well as of Acts, that *all* who call on the name of the Lord will be saved. The promise of God's mercy is universally inclusive of all who will receive it.

7. For both authors, the scriptural term κύριος applies to Jesus, thus mysteriously fusing his identity with the God of Israel.

8. A corollary of point number 6 is that *gentiles* are to be received fully among the followers of Jesus without having to obey all the commandments of Israel's Law. Paul and Luke are both insistent advocates of a law-free mission to the gentiles and both place the theological justification for this mission at the heart of their writings. Indeed, Luke's narrative enlists *Peter*, particularly in Acts 10–11 and 15, as a star witness in support of this Pauline gospel. The prophecies of Isaiah play an important role in justifying this mission, as does

---

25 Vielhauer, 'Paulinism', p. 14 (45 – Keck and Martyn ed.).
26 Vielhauer, p. 13 (44 – Keck and Martyn ed.).

> the maxim of God's impartiality, rooted in Deuteronony 29, homiletically explicated in Romans 2, and narratively enacted in Acts 10–11.

9. For both of our authors, the unbelief of many in Israel when offered the good news of the gospel constitutes a significant theological challenge. In both cases, this challenge is met through appeal to the prophecies of Isaiah concerning Israel's blindness and deafness. Thus, this anomalous state of affairs is also attributed to the mysterious will and working of God. Paul, more clearly than Luke, envisions an eschatological redemption in which all Israel will be saved; nonetheless, Luke holds open the possibility of a future time when God will restore the kingdom to Israel (Acts 1.6-7, perhaps also 3.21), and he continues to refer to the gospel message as 'the hope of Israel' (28.20; cf. Luke 24.21a).[27]

10. Christ will come again (Acts 1.11; 1 Thess. 4.13-18) in power to bring about the resurrection of the dead (Acts 26.6-8; 1 Cor. 15.20-28), and to act as 'judge of the living and the dead' (Acts 10.42, 17.31; 2 Cor. 5.10; Rom. 14.10b-12).

Much more could be said, but this sketch identifies some of the most important points (I have said nothing at all about matters of biographical detail: Paul as a Pharisee, as persecutor of the church, as one who has always lived with 'a clear conscience before God' [Acts 23.1; Phil. 3.6]).

b. Concluding Reflections

The sketch above does not constitute anything like a full summary of the theology of Paul, or of Luke-Acts. Nor is it my intention to deny that major differences of emphasis and sensibility remain between Paul and Luke. Harmonization of these two major NT witnesses is not the purpose of the present essay. Rather, my ultimate intention is to achieve a more nuanced and rounded picture of each of these figures than Vielhauer's sharply dichotomous essay suggested. Surely a judicious reading of Acts and the Pauline letters will have to acknowledge that there are substantial areas of commonality between them as well as real differences.

In this initial thought-experiment, I have suggested that a study of the ways that Acts and Paul employ scripture might provide a vantage point for observing some of these areas of commonality. In general terms, the consequences of this approach are at least twofold.

1. On the one hand, Vielhauer's judgement that 'Acts is not intended as kerygma or as "witness"'[28] can be regarded only as a historical curiosity, a tendentious offshoot of a certain twentieth-century theological programme hindered by a blind spot for narrative interpretation and overdetermined by existentialist philosophical commitments. Luke is much more deeply immersed in the ongoing story of Israel and in the interpretation of Israel's scriptures than

---

27   See K. Haacker, 'Das Bekenntnis des Paulus zur Hoffnung Israels nach der Apostelgeschichte des Lukas', in *NTS* 31 (1985), pp. 437–51.

28   Vielhauer, 'Paulinism', p. 16 (44 – Keck and Martyn ed.).

Vielhauer believed. In light of the evidence presented even in this brief essay, Vielhauer's judgement that in Acts the 'claim of the Jews to be the people of God was replaced by the idea of natural man's immediacy to God, and the significance of Judaism was relativized to that of a venerable *antiqua religio*' is simply untenable.[29] In a word, then, Luke's theology is more Jewish, more scriptural, and more kerygmatic than Vielhauer recognized – and in all these respects, Luke's thought seems to represent an intelligible trajectory from within a Pauline symbolic world. The theology of Acts can be seen as an organic outgrowth of the Pauline tradition that maintains its roots in at least some of Paul's characteristic themes and concerns.

2. On the other hand, Paul emerges as a more 'Lukan' figure than one would ever guess from reading Vielhauer. Vielhauer has indeed identified certain points where there are real divergences between Luke and Paul. (To take the most striking example, I have a great deal of trouble imagining the author of Galatians acquiescing in the conciliatory gestures narrated in Acts 21.17-26.) Nonetheless, rereading Paul through the intertextual lens of Acts does enable us to see *precisely in his letters* a charismatic Jewish Paul, a figure grounded in apocalyptic hope, exercising a powerful wonder-working ministry (even while also undergoing suffering and rejection for his message), and focused above all on his God-given calling to proclaim the good news of Israel's God to the gentile world. He is at once more deeply Jewish and more theologically consonant with emergent proto-catholic Christianity than Vielhauer's account would suggest. This appears with particular clarity when we attend to his strategies of scriptural interpretation.

3. These comments lead to one final remark. The search for a distinctive 'Paulinism' – along with the tacit presupposition that 'Paulinism' ought to be strongly privileged over other perspectives in the NT – may lead to a significant perspectival distortion in our reading of the material. A careful rereading of Vielhauer will show that he was indeed aware of some of the points of contact that I have described in this essay (for example, the similarities between the Pauline and Petrine sermons in Acts), but that he found them uninteresting because the points of agreement between Paul and Luke were to be found not where Paul speaks with a distinctive voice, but at the points where both of these authors are simply reflecting the common views of 'the earliest congregation'. This was assumed to prove that Luke did not adequately represent 'Paulinism'.

But why think about the question in these terms? Why privilege the solitary religious genius? For example, there is nothing distinctively 'Pauline' about the use of Ps. 110:1 to describe Jesus' exaltation to the right hand of God. This appears to belong to the common stock of hermeneutical property within early Christianity; as we have already noted, a similar reading of the text shows up in the synoptics, 1 Peter, and in Hebrews. But does this make the convergence between Paul and Luke on their use of this motif less significant and interesting? Would it not be equally

---

29 Vielhauer, 'Paulinism', p. 17 (48–49 – Keck and Martyn ed.). Vielhauer's position is also significantly problematized by the recent work of C. Kavin Rowe on Acts 17; see 'The Grammar of Life: The Areopagus Speech and Pagan Tradition', in *NTS* 57 (2011), pp. 31–50.

valuable to seek, as I have sought to do in this paper, to discern the ways in which both Paul and Luke participate in a wider community of intertextual discourse, share certain hermeneutical assumptions, and converge on quite a number of highly significant theological affirmations? To be sure, Luke writes a generation later than Paul's heyday. His concerns differ, and his literary strategy for presenting the gospel through a complex story, narrated καθεξῆς, differs dramatically from the genre of Paul's urgent and highly particular pastoral letters, with their dense theological discourse. But precisely as we observe these differences, we might do well to echo one of Paul's own metaphors for describing the distinct but complementary contributions of different interpreters of the word: Paul planted, Luke watered, but God gave the growth.

Chapter 4

THE DEVELOPMENT OF PAULINE CHRISTIANITY FROM A 'RELIGION OF CONVERSION' TO A 'RELIGION OF TRADITION'[1]

Michael Wolter
Trans. J. M. McConnell and D. P. Moessner

I. The Analytical Categories

The following study presents a potential paradigm for interpreting early Christian history, a model which up to this point has not been applied to the interpretation of the New Testament. This paradigm seeks to answer the question of whether the typological opposition implied in the terms 'religion of conversion' and 'religion of tradition' appropriately characterizes Pauline theology, while at the same time shedding new light on the ways in which Paul's writings were received in the latter decades of the first century, thereby opening up new, previously unidentified insights. This essay, therefore, is more experimental in nature.[2]

To begin with, the principal designations 'religion of conversion' and 'religion of tradition' must be illumined: What meanings are ascribed to them in the following discussion and in what senses do they function as analytical categories?

a. 'Religion of Conversion'

I am using the phrase 'religion of conversion' to describe religious groups that are in the process of emerging. These groups consist *exclusively* of people who have left behind the religious orientation they received in the course of their primary and secondary socialization, and whose identity formation as a new group, or those who are in transition to such a self-definition is accompanied

1   The following essay was originally presented at the 63rd general meeting of the Studiorum Novi Testamenti Societas (SNTS), Lund 2008, in the seminar 'The Reception of Paul'. I would like to thank the seminar participants for their critique and helpful comments. The German original was first published in *Early Christianity* 1 (2010), pp. 15–40.

2   Martin Dibelius has obviously already formulated a concept quite similar to this. In his essay, 'Paulus und die Mystik', originally published in 1941 (and reprinted in Dibelius, M., *Botschaft und Geschichte. II. Zum Urchristentum und zur hellenistischen Religionsgeschichte* [Tübingen: Mohr Siebeck, 1956], pp. 94–116), Dibelius mentions the 'foundational meaning of the process (of conversion) which has always constituted Christian existence, at least so long as Christianity was a religion of conversion'.

by a 'transformation' in their perception of reality and in a new ethos.[3] This applies, of course, to every conversion, even for conversions from within traditional religions (see below). One can therefore only speak of a religion of conversion when a person who becomes a convert to a religious group finds *only* people who have likewise become members of that group through conversion. For this reason, a religion of conversion as such has neither a history nor is it able to avail itself of anything like a social memory. Rather, more typical is that such a group finds itself in the phase of *conceptualization* and ongoing *acculturation* in its view of reality and its social formation. A well of knowledge is beginning to form in such a religion of conversion, a stock of knowledge which transcends any individual understanding and binds all of its members together. Religions of conversion are thus by definition transitory phenomena. According to Victor Turner, a religion of conversion finds itself in the stage of 'liminality' notably 'betwixt and between'.[4] With this state of transition it is also the case that in a religion of conversion the issue of proximity to and distance from mainstream society and to the culture of origin is unclear, and usually becomes a matter of controversy among its members. In this respect it is primarily a question of the ethos by which new religious groupings make their distinctive identities known: none of them can avoid practising something like 'boundary maintenance'. Each group must develop a canon of particularized institutional actions that will function as 'boundary markers' to the outside world and internally as 'identity markers'. But because these groups must in part depend upon and live within the greater society, at least some of the traits of the defining repertoire of the group must also be compatible with the ethos exhibited by that society. From this we can infer generally that the more extensive and peculiar the proportion of distinctive practices is of the particular ethos of the religious group, the more dis-integrated it is from the larger society to which it is related. The opposite is, of course, also true.

I am trying quite consciously to describe this type of religion in an ideal manner as a theoretical construct. I do so because only in this way can one ensure enough space for phenomenological diversity, as well as allow for flexibility in the use of the term. This is the advantage over the term 'conversionist sect', coined by Bryan R. Wilson,[5] which is greatly encumbered by the imprecise concept of 'sect'. Through the acceptance of this concept and its application to the analysis of 1 Peter

---

3   Concerning the concepts 'primary socialization' and 'secondary socialization, cf. P. L. Berger and Th. Luckmann, *The Social Construction of Reality* (Garden City/New York: Doubleday, 1966), pp. 119–35. They use the term 'resocialization' to describe the results of conversion (ibid., pp. 145.148f).

4   V. W. Turner, *The Ritual Process: Structure and Anti-structure* (London: Routledge & Kegan, 1969); *idem*, 'Betwixt and Between: The Liminal Period in Rites de Passage', in *Symposium on New Approaches to the Study of Religion: Proceedings of the 1964 Annual Spring Meeting of the American Ethnological Society* (ed. J. Helm; Seattle: American Ethnological Society, 1964), pp. 4–20.

5   Cf. especially B. R. Wilson, *Magic and the Millennium. A Sociological Study of Religious Movements of Protest among Tribal and Third-World Peoples* (New York: Harper & Row, 1973), pp. 38–41.

by John H. Elliott[6] and that of Ben Witherington on Galatians,[7] it is easy to see that the individual elements of the definition of the term determine the interpretation of the text. The circumstances of those receiving the letters and the perspectives of the letter writers are reconstructed so as to be in agreement with the definition.

A religion of conversion as such not only has no past, but it also has no future. Thus it exists only for a short period of time. It either ceases to exist, or it transforms into what I would like to call a 'religion of tradition'.[8]

b. 'Religion of Tradition'

A 'religion of tradition' differs primarily from a 'religion of conversion' in that in the former there is an awareness of a common history, a reserve of common memories, or even a tradition in the sense of a social memory. The present is no longer perceived as disconnected from the past; instead, the emphasis is on continuity and preservation. It involves a form of the 'culture of memory', the origin of which is the question, 'What dare we not forget?'[9] A 'religion of tradition' is therefore not primarily concerned with conceptualizing a new symbolic world of meaning that affords a cognitive and pragmatic point of reference. Rather, a 'religion of tradition' is occupied with illuminating the present in the light of the wisdom and knowledge handed down as 'tradition' and with developing and expanding this store of tradition, as its own history and culture are engaged with change.

Of course, there can also be conversions to a 'religion of tradition'. In this case, however, it is not as if one enters into a community of other converts; rather, the convert adopts an established culture of memory, including its cognitive and pragmatic traditional knowledge. Or as Philo illustrates, 'He [God] guarantees civic equality to all proselytes, the same as to native Jews (ὅσα καὶ τοῖς αὐτόχθοσι)' (*Spec.* 1.52).

---

6   Cf. J. H. Elliott, *A Home for the Homeless* (London: SCM Press, 1981).

7   B. Witherington III, *Grace in Galatia. A Commentary on St Paul's Letter to the Galatians* (Grand Rapids: Eerdmans, 1998), pp. 272–76.

8   This occurs parallel to the process which Max Weber termed 'routinization of charisma'; cf. M. Weber, *Economy and Society* (London: Routledge, 2008), Chap. III.5; see also, W. Schluchter, 'Einleitung. Max Webers Analyse des antiken Christentums. Grundzüge eines unvollendeten Projekts', in *Max Webers Sicht des antiken Christentums* (ed. W. Schluchter; Frankfurt am Main: Suhrkamp, 1985), pp. 11–71; *idem*, 'Umbildungen des Charismas. Überlegungen zur Herrschaftssoziologie', in *Religion und Lebensführung. Studien zu Max Webers Kultur- und Werttheorie II* (ed. W. Schluchter; Frankfurt am Main: Suhrkamp, 1988), pp. 535–54; W. Gebhardt, 'Charisma und Ordnung. Formen des institutionalisierten Charisma - Überlegungen im Anschluß an Max Weber', in *Charisma. Theorie - Religion - Politik* (ed. W. Gebhardt, A. Zingerle, and M. N. Ebertz; Berlin: W. de Gruyter, 1993), pp. 47–68. Unlike this perspective, what is in view in this essay is not a process of institutionalization, which involves a transition from the extraordinary to the ordinary. It is, rather, specifically the onset and development of a social memory. It should not be questioned, however, that this development is always an aspect of the institutionalization process as described by Max Weber.

9   J. Assmann, *Das kulturelle Gedächtnis* (München: Beck, 1999), p. 30; cf. also *idem*, 'Kollektives Gedächtnis und kulturelle Identität', in *Kultur und Gedächtnis* (ed. J. Assmann and T. Hölscher; Frankfurt am Main: Suhrkamp, 1988), pp. 9–19 (13): 'Cultural memory preserves the group's pool of knowledge, out of which they draw their unity and character.'

II. Pauline Christianity as a Religion of Conversion

It is not difficult to demonstrate that Pauline Christianity may be conceived as a religion of conversion in the sense described above. This judgement applies despite the fact that at least some within the Corinthian community had come to a different conclusion and had further allowed their familiar, everyday world view to determine their lives.[10] In this regard the Jewish-Christian opponents in Galatia were also certainly of a different opinion; obviously they could conceive of non-Jews converting to Jesus Christ only as conversions to the 'religion of tradition' of Judaism.

a. The Break with Cultural Socialization

According to Paul's understanding, however, the situation is unambiguous: commitment to a Christian confession and attachment to a Christian community occurs with a break with one's normal life. Every person who belonged to a Pauline community had undergone his or her cultural socialization within a non-Christian family. Therefore, the life that ensues for one who belongs to Jesus is separated from his or her pre-Christian life by a deep gap. Second Corinthians 5.17: 'if anyone is in Christ, there is a new creation: everything old has passed away; see, everything has become new' (εἴ τις ἐν Χριστῷ, καινὴ κτίσις· τὰ ἀρχαῖα παρῆλθεν, ἰδοὺ γέγονεν καινά) or Rom. 6.11, 'so you also must consider yourselves dead to sin and alive to God in Christ Jesus' (οὕτως καὶ ὑμεῖς λογίζεσθε ἑαυτοὺς εἶναι νεκροὺς μὲν τῇ ἁμαρτίᾳ ζῶντας δὲ τῷ θεῷ ἐν Χριστῷ Ἰησοῦ) as a summation of 6.1-10, presents the clearest evidence for this. Romans 6.17-22; 7.5-6; 1 Cor. 5.7-8; 6.11; Gal. 4.8-9; 1 Thess. 1.9-10 also point in the same direction. According to Rom. 6.2-8, Paul understands baptism as a type of death to the pre-Christian life, and he considers the lives that the baptized now lead (Rom. 6.4) to be in sharp discontinuity with their pre-conversion life.

The same phenomenon can be identified in the parent-child metaphor that Paul uses to describe his relationship to the communities which he founded.[11] Whenever he calls himself 'father' (1 Thess. 2.11) or 'mother' (1 Thess. 2.7) of the community, and those who converted to the Christian faith 'children' (1 Cor. 4.14, 17; 2 Cor. 6.13; 12.14; Gal. 4.19; Phlm. 10; cf. also 1 Cor. 3.1-4; Phil. 2.22), whom he 'fathered' or to whom he 'gave birth' (1 Cor. 4.15; Gal. 4.19; Phlm. 10), the notion that life and identity are imparted to children through their parents is not the only element of the semantic association of these metaphors. Also included is the idea that the beginning of a new life is considered a metaphor for conversion. In Gal. 1.10–2.21 and Phil. 3.3-11 Paul clearly highlights this discontinuity through the example of his own 'biography'.

---

10   This is clearly seen in 1 Cor. 5.1; 6.1-8; 8.1-13; 10.14-22; 11.17-22; cf. also S. J. Chester, *Conversion at Corinth. Perspectives on Conversion in Paul's Theology and the Corinthian Church* (London/New York: T&T Clark, 2003); M. Wolter, *Theologie und Ethos im frühen Christentum* (WUNT, 236; Tübingen: Mohr, 2009), pp. 163–167, 181–196.

11   Cf. C. Gerber, *Paulus und seine 'Kinder'. Studien zur Beziehungsmetaphorik der paulinischen Briefe* (BZNW, 136; Berlin / New York: W. de Gruyter, 2005), esp. pp. 205–214.

This situation was accompanied by the fact that, beyond that which Paul calls 'the gospel' in Rom. 1.3-4 and 1 Cor. 15.3-5, or his summary paraphrase in 1 Thess. 1.9-10, there was no such thing as a common body of knowledge among Christians available to the churches. There was not yet room for the development of a common store of Christian knowledge or a Christian encyclopedia that would also make possible an orientation to the way one is to live in the world. For this situation there are basically two causes which should be mentioned. First, the Christian communities lacked a *common* tradition that could generate an identity, a tradition that creates 'an objective, available system of signs' for individuals experiencing 'an original status of increasing anonymity and provides participation in this sign system by freeing them from these earlier connections of their individual, concrete situations and making available for all who have or will have in the future a system of such signification'.[12]

A second significant influence appears to be that the process of socialization, without which a common body of knowledge for a group or a society cannot develop, was in the beginning for Christians an extraordinary matter and continued to be so during Paul's lifetime. It was worship that brought about an objectification of a corporate Christian identity that 'transcended individual identity'. But whether before or after such corporate experience, those who belonged to Jesus Christ continued to live in the reality of an everyday culture that was based upon a totally different encyclopedia.[13]

b. The Insufficiency of the Inherited Cultural Encyclopedia

Thus for a religion of conversion there is a significant difference between the religious knowledge it possesses and its cultural, everyday knowledge. Or, to express it differently, religious knowledge proves inadequate in interpreting everyday experiences. 1 Thess. 4.13-17 offers a particularly vivid example of a problem based on this scenario: Paul was prompted to write this text because some members of the community in Thessalonica had died in the short time after its founding and after Paul had abruptly left them (cf. 1 Thess. 2.1-12, 17-20; 3.1-8), creating a problematic situation for those left behind. These issues emerged because the community was not able to assimilate the deaths of Christians into their foundational eschatological understanding. On the one hand, at the Lord's return they expected to be carried away and therefore to escape the pressing judgement of destruction immediately following (or perhaps even to take an active part in it). They could not foresee that Christians would die before this occurred. On the other hand, due to their socialization within the Hellenistic culture of that time, they knew that it was impossible for the dead to be raptured. Paul, therefore, finds it necessary to expand the specifically Christian tradition of the community by supplementing it with the assurance of a resurrection of the 'dead in Christ'. In an analogous situation, he encourages the Christians in Corinth, who obviously

---

12   Berger/Luckmann, *Construction* (see n. 3), p. 64.
13   Concerning the problems associated with this situation, cf. Wolter, *Theologie und Ethos* (see n. 10), pp. 153–167.

considered this concept problematic, to incorporate the idea of a bodily resurrection into their cultural encyclopedia. He explains that at the parousia there will certainly be a transformation of the earthly body into a completely different corporeality, due to the fact that it will be given imperishability and immortality (1 Cor. 15.35-54).

Alongside this we can also interpret the Pauline teaching on justification as a conceptualization of a new understanding of reality. This type of formulation is essential whenever a religion of conversion finds it necessary to re-configure its guiding paradigm for the new symbolic world of meaning and thereby clarify the principles through which it differentiates itself from the world view it has left behind.[14] Texts such as Rom. 1.16-17; 3.21-26, 27-30; 10.12-13; 1 Cor. 12.13; Gal. 3.28; 5.6; 6.15 and their surrounding contexts demonstrate that Paul conceived of his teaching on justification as theologically legitimating a foundational paradigm shift (Paul himself calls it a 'new creation' (καινὴ κτίσις [Gal. 6.15]). This shift makes theologically impotent that foundational distinction between Jews and non-Jews within a Jewish comprehension of reality to which Paul owes his own background. One could perhaps even suggest that Paul's stance on justification finds its contextually plausible basis in such liminal situations so as to function as a sort of theory of conversion. It should come as no surprise therefore that Martin Luther experienced this 'theory' in a similar way, as well as many in the ensuing revival of the Reformation.

c. Insecurities over Ethos

Moreover, the nature of Pauline Christianity as a religion of conversion eventually becomes evident through discussions of ethics and conflicts over behaviour as well as by the manner in which Paul deals with them.[15]

From 1 Corinthians 7 it becomes apparent that in a previous letter the Christians in Corinth have asked Paul how they are to deal with sexuality and marriage. This enquiry shows that more than two years after the community had been founded there was still no standard of behaviour tied to the enculturation of Christian belief that they were experiencing daily. The Christian way of life for the community and the ethical options and institutions of their culture that influence sexual behaviour stand in direct opposition to each other, such that the consequences of their Christian stance in the day-to-day ethos of their culture are being openly discussed among the members of the community. This case involves the constellation of issues that can only occur within a religious community founded through conversions, which has yet to develop its own ethos or to pass on its own tradition. Instead, the members of the community are being challenged only with the ethical options they had learned through their primary socialization.

The same can be said concerning the conflicts surrounding conformance to food taboos evident in Rom. 14.1–15.7 and in 1 Cor. 8.1-13; 10.23–11.1, as well

---

14   In addition, cf. the more extensive discussion below on pp. 64–65.

15   For the association to conversion, which Paul takes up in his paraenesis, see also W. Popkes, *Paränese und Neues Testament* (SBS, 168; Stuttgart: Kath. Bibelwerk, 1996), p. 170, who speaks here of a '"paraenesis of life change", in the company of conversion or recourse to it'.

as the manner in which Paul deals with them. In both cases we have essentially the same scenario as in 1 Cor. 7. The difference between the positions of the so-called 'weak' and 'strong' is that the two groups are drawing conflicting conclusions from their conversion to the Christian faith; admittedly in this case the conflicts are in reference to food restrictions, not sexual taboos. Here, too, the options that are being debated emerge out of the cultural context of the communities: in Corinth, may one eat meat offered to idols or not? In Rome, must one abstain from meat and wine, or may one eat anything? Also, in these situations the question is, in what ways must ethical enculturation in a religion of conversion to the Christian faith ultimately take form?

The suggested solutions to the conflicts over the adherence to food taboos that Paul communicates to the communities in Corinth and Rome are no less instructive. They clearly demonstrate that Pauline Christianity can be considered a religion of conversion in precisely the same sense as was proposed above. What characterizes Paul's answers is that he deals with the conflict on an *ecclesial*, not on a *material* basis. Rather than discussing the controversial matter directly, Paul considers how the Christian community is to deal with these kinds of conflicts. The problem per se is pushed into the background, and for Paul the problem would not even be an issue if everyone were in a state of accord. Paul considers the position of the so-called 'strong' theologically correct (cf. 1 Cor. 8.1, 4-6; Rom. 14.14; 15.1); one recognizes, however, from the shape of his answer that he considers the actual matter itself ('may one eat or not?') meaningless, while the point is to portray the *Christian* identity of the community (cf. Rom. 14.5b: 'let each one be convinced in one's own mind' [ἕκαστος ἐν τῷ ἰδίῳ νοῒ πληροφορείσθω]). Because if he were *not* to do so and if he were to declare one of the options debated in each case as ethically binding, he would turn over the Christian identity of the community to a particular ethical tradition already present within the culture. He does not choose this path, however, and insists that the communities construct their identity in such a way as to express their independence from all non-Christian world views. Through Rom. 15.7, 'welcome one another just as Christ has also welcomed you for the glory of God' (προσλαμβάνεσθε ἀλλήλους καθὼς καὶ ὁ Χριστὸς προσελάβετο ὑμᾶς εἰς δόξαν τοῦ θεοῦ), he urges the Christians in Rome to distance themselves from every way of living that has nothing to do with their conversion. He also challenges them to allow their common identity, which they have received through their commitment to the Christian faith, to take precedence over their diverse ethical loyalties.

III. The Development to a Religion of Tradition

One need not prove that Pauline Christianity, as well as ancient Christianity in general, made the transition specifically from a religion of conversion to a religion of tradition. The fact that after 2000 years there are Christian churches and communities whose members profess Jesus Christ and for whom the canon of the New Testament provides access to the beginnings of the history of their identity formation, is proof enough. In this section I want solely to demonstrate that this process itself already begins in the New Testament period.

One of the clearest indications of this is the emergence of the apostolic pseude-pigraphal writings.[16] The literary fiction in the name of personalities from the past assumes an awareness which is marked by continuity, rather than discontinuity. The Christian communities discover not only that they have a past as a Christian community, but also that there is such a thing as a Christian encyclopedia, which they have adopted and which they are to protect as authentic tradition. In this sense the apostolic pseudepigrapha are the appropriate literary means for churches to interpret their own later circumstances through the light and authority of the past. The origin of the truth no longer resides in one's own conversion but rather in the past; correspondingly, the point of the early Christian pseudepigraphal writings is similar to conducting a 'proof from antiquity'.[17]

The significance here is found in the correlation of antiquity and authority, which on the other hand is based on a specific understanding of truth: 'The reliable truth … is provided in full in the beginning and must from that time forward be passed on.'[18]

This understanding of tradition is specifically expressed in a series of texts, from which it becomes clear that the situation of the Christian communities had changed compared to those related to Paul:

2 Thess. 2.15: ἄρα οὖν, ἀδελφοί, στήκετε καὶ κρατεῖτε τὰς παραδόσεις ἃς ἐδιδάχθητε εἴτε διὰ λόγου εἴτε δι' ἐπιστολῆς ἡμῶν.	So then, brothers and sisters, stand firm and hold fast to the traditions that you were taught by us, either by word of mouth or by our letter.
2 Pet. 3.2: … μνησθῆναι τῶν προειρημένων ῥημάτων ὑπὸ τῶν ἁγίων προφητῶν καὶ τῆς τῶν ἀποστόλων ὑμῶν ἐντολῆς τοῦ κυρίου καὶ σωτῆρος.	… that you should remember the words spoken in the past by the holy prophets, and the commandment of the Lord and Saviour spoken through your apostles.
Jude 17: μνήσθητε τῶν ῥημάτων τῶν προειρημένων ὑπὸ τῶν ἀποστόλων τοῦ κυρίου ἡμῶν Ἰησοῦ Χριστοῦ.	But you [beloved] must remember the predictions of the apostles of our Lord Jesus Christ.

The similarity of these texts and their distance from Paul are clear. Past and present are no longer in tension with one another such as 'formerly' but 'now'; they are now tied together in a continuum that is to be preserved. Corresponding to this the addressees of these letters are exhorted to 'hold fast' and 'to remember'. What is decisive for these texts is 'the resolute will to sustain a continuity which is directed

---

16   I consider the following pseudepigraphal: Ephesians, Colossians, 2 Thessalonians, 1 and 2 Timothy, Titus, James, 1 and 2 Peter, and Jude.

17   Cf. P. Pilhofer, *ΠΡΕΣΒΥΤΕΡΟΝ ΚΡΕΙΤΤΟΝ* (WUNT, II/39; Tübingen: Mohr, 1990).

18   N. Brox, 'Zum Problemstand in der Erforschung der altchristlichen Pseudepigraphie', in *Pseudepigraphie in der heidnischen und jüdisch-christlichen Antike* (ed. N. Brox; WdF, 484; Darmstadt: Wiss. Buchgesellschaft, 1977), pp. 311–34.

toward the past';[19] they intend to foster this continuity by holding to the past as normative. What is interesting here is that, unlike that of the historical Paul, Jesus Christ himself is no longer singled out as the standard bearer of their origin. Instead, it is now the word of the *apostle*, the interpretation of Jesus Christ by the apostles. *They* are now the ones who function as the so-called 'original standard bearers',[20] who determine the origin of the truth.

The same difference can be recognized when 1 Cor. 3.11 and Eph. 2.19-20 are compared:

1 Cor. 3.11: θεμέλιον γὰρ ἄλλον οὐδεὶς δύναται θεῖναι παρὰ τὸν κείμενον, ὅς ἐστιν Ἰησοῦς Χριστός.	For no one can lay any foundation other than the one that has been laid; that foundation is Jesus Christ.
Eph. 2.19-20: ἐστὲ ... ἐποικοδομηθέντες ἐπὶ τῷ θεμελίῳ τῶν ἀποστόλων καὶ προφητῶν, ὄντος ἀκρογωνιαίου αὐτοῦ Χριστοῦ Ἰησου.	So then you are ... built upon the foundation of the apostles and prophets, with Christ Jesus himself as the cornerstone.

The distinction is obvious: with Paul, Jesus Christ himself is the foundation of the community, while in Ephesians, it is the 'apostles and prophets'. As in the previous three texts, the apostolic tradition has in similar fashion wedged itself in between Christ and Christians. The difference becomes even more evident when we consider the semantic range of the 'foundation' metaphor. Two distinctive markers stand out. The first is the significance of a foundation as a required component for building a house (it is impossible to imagine a house without a foundation); the second is the temporal priority of the foundation (laying the foundation is the first step in building any house).[21]

This understanding of tradition finds its conceptual consolidation in the idea of a 'deposit' (παραθήκη) which is utilized as a metaphor by the Pastoral Epistles (1 Tim. 6.20; 2 Tim. 1.12, 14; see also the verbal form in 1 Tim. 1.18; 2 Tim. 2.2). Through this image, the entire tradition is characterized as culminating in the repository left behind by Paul, which is to be guarded in every respect.[22]

All these texts portray for us a picture of Christianity that differs funda-

---

19   Ibid., p. 328.

20   Ibid., p. 330.

21   Cf. also H. Merklein, 'Paulinische Theologie in der Rezeption des Kolosser- und Epheserbriefes', in *Paulus in den neutestamentlichen Spätschriften. Zur Paulusrezeption im Neuen Testament* (ed. K. Kertelge; QD, 89; Freiburg: Herder, 1981) pp. 25–69 (33) (ibid., n. 31 justifiably rejecting the attempt to locate the apostles and prophets of Eph. 2.20 in the past); see also G. Sellin, *Der Brief an die Epheser* (KEK, 8; Göttingen: Vandenhoeck & Ruprecht, 2008), p. 237.

22   With the exception of Hermas, Mand. III 2 (παρακαταθήκη which designates the πνεῦμα ἄψευστον given to humanity by God), this term is encountered only here in all of early Christian literature. Regarding the semantic connotations it receives through its various ancient contexts, cf. M. Wolter, *Die Pastoralbriefe als Paulustradition* (FRLANT, 146; Göttingen: Vandenhoeck & Ruprecht, 1988), pp. 115–116.

mentally from the Pauline interpretation of Christian identity. The difference is that whenever Christians look back at the past, they no longer perceive it as discontinuity only but rather as a continuity with the present – to be sure, a continuity which secures for them their own identity. Christian identity is no longer achieved through a break with primary cultural socializations but rather through its own, indeed, Christian socialization. It is this awareness of tradition, so easy to recognize, which renders Ephesians, 2 Thessalonians, and the three Pastoral Epistles *Deutero*-Pauline epistles.

IV. The Reception of Pauline Theology in the Post-Pauline Writings

In this section I would like to relate the early Christian reception of Paul, which is still exhibited in the New Testament, to this schematic cluster. In doing so, I would like to draw attention only to a few select, exemplary texts, through which my own view of the problematic will be confirmed, that the new self-identity of Christianity as a religion of tradition also influenced the reception of Paul. Rather than provide a comprehensive overview, I will limit myself to a few examples.

From a methodological point of view, there are three possible ways to focus the issue, to: (a) concentrate *thematically* on specific theological issues (I will take this approach in the following); (b) consider a specific document from a *literary* standpoint; and (c) interpret certain events and constellations of developments *historically*. Of course, all three levels of interpretation may also be combined. Moreover, one can distinguish between the reception of Pauline theology and the reception of Paul as a historical construct (the so-called 'portrait of Paul').[23] However, we must add a *caveat*: we must not make the mistake of trying to unlock everything in the early Christian reception of Paul through the 'master key' of a religion of conversion to a religion of tradition. This paradigm explains much, but certainly not everything.

a. The Reception of the Pauline Eschatology in the Letter to the Colossians and the Letter to the Ephesians

1. The differentia specifica of the Pauline eschatology is maintained in both letters: 'Hope' (ἐλπίς) functions as the mode or medium of the presence

---

23   The development of Andreas Lindemann's reconstruction is oriented around this contrast. (A. Lindemann, *Paulus im ältesten Christentum. Das Bild des Apostels und die Rezeption der paulinischen Theologie in der frühchristlichen Literatur bis Marcion* [BHT, 58; Tübingen: Mohr, 1979]).

of salvation, because it grants its eschatological signature to present Christian existence. In Paul, the juxtaposition of such texts as Rom. 5.2-5…

²… καυχώμεθα ἐπ' ἐλπίδι τῆς δόξης τοῦ θεοῦ, ³οὐ μόνον δέ, ἀλλὰ καὶ καυχώμεθα ἐν ταῖς θλίψεσιν, εἰδότες ὅτι ἡ θλῖψις ὑπομονὴν κατεργάζεται, ⁴ἡ δὲ ὑπομονὴ δοκιμήν, ἡ δὲ δοκιμὴ ἐλπίδα. ⁵ἡ δὲ ἐλπὶς οὐ καταισχύνει, ὅτι ἡ ἀγάπη τοῦ θεοῦ ἐκκέχυται ἐν ταῖς καρδίαις ἡμῶν διὰ πνεύματος ἁγίου τοῦ δοθέντος ἡμῖν.	… we boast in our **hope** of sharing the glory of God. And not only that, but we also boast in our sufferings, knowing that suffering produces endurance, and endurance produces character, and character produces **hope**, and **hope** does not disappoint us, because God's love has been poured into our hearts through the Holy Spirit that has been given to us.

and Rom. 8.24-25…

²⁴τῇ γὰρ ἐλπίδι ἐσώθημεν· ἐλπὶς δὲ βλεπομένη οὐκ ἔστιν ἐλπίς· ὁ γὰρ βλέπει τίς ἐλπίζει; ²⁵εἰ δὲ ὃ οὐ βλέπομεν ἐλπίζομεν, δι' ὑπομονῆς ἀπεκδεχόμεθα.	For in **hope** we were saved. Now **hope** that is seen is not **hope**. For who **hopes** for what is seen? But if we **hope** for what we do not see, we wait for it with patience.

make clear that salvation, an event which has already occurred, consists of a hope previously not available to Christians and that is currently not available to non-Christians.[24] Paul expresses thereby that there is still something pending (according to Rom. 8.23, 'the redemption of our bodies' (ἀπολύτρωσις τοῦ σώματος ἡμῶν). Yet the presence of hope indicates not merely what the hopeful lack but rather the presence itself of eschatological salvation.

One can still perceive this outline of Paul's eschatology of hope in Colossians and Ephesians. In Eph. 1.18 and 4.4, talk about 'the hope of his/your calling' (ἡ ἐλπὶς τῆς κλήσεως αὐτοῦ/ὑμῶν) corresponds to what the addressees as a result of being 'without Christ' (Eph. 2.12) do not have, and exactly as in 1 Thess. 4.13.[25] Characteristic for Colossians is the christological explanation of hope: 'Christ in you' (Χριστὸς ἐν ὑμῖν) is not only designated as 'the hope of glory' (ἐλπὶς τῆς δόξης), but because Jesus has been exalted to heaven (Col. 3.1c), the author can also steer the readers' view upward and depict hope metonymically as a prize of salvation that is already available in heaven – a prize which is anticipating and revealing, namely, that it will be transformed through real events (3.4).

2. Nevertheless, in the past what has been elaborated primarily is the difference between the eschatological notions of these two letters and Paul's eschatology. It is claimed that in both letters the eschatological reserve which Paul promotes has been 'removed' or has 'dropped out'.[26] What is discussed

24   With this in view, cf. 1 Thess. 4.13. The difference between the Christian community and the λοιποί is that the latter 'have no hope'.

25   See n. 24.

26   For this view cf., e.g., Merklein, 'Paulinische Theologie' (see n. 21), pp. 40–45; see also

is a 'present eschatology',[27] which is characterized by 'emphasizing the final realization of salvation'.[28] Of course, at the same time the fact is not overlooked that both letters are still expecting something in the future, but this expectation is understood to be nothing more than a 'clarification'[29] or a 'revelation of the eschatological realities that already exist in the present'.[30] This is the sense in which Helmut Merklein formulates the distinction to Pauline eschatology:

> With Paul, the present is subsumed to the eschatological events of the future ... In Colossians (and also in Ephesians) it is the reverse that the future is subsumed to the realities of the present. The present determines what the future has still to reveal; the future is an epiphany of the present.[31]

Behind this and other more doxographically aligned descriptions of the distinction between the eschatological concepts of the Pauline letters and Colossians and Ephesians usually are hidden several other questions, which are no less important for the interpretation of the eschatological statements. These questions concern the information contained in the statements, the intent of the statements, the verbal structure of the statements, and their literary context.

When we consider in their contexts the statements in these two letters in which eschatological expectations are expressed, what is striking is that not even in a single passage are eschatological scenarios *described*, in contrast to Paul in Rom. 2.5-10; 1 Cor. 3.12-15; 15.20-28, 51-55; 1 Thess. 4.15-17. Instead, in Colossians and Ephesians, aided always by short, comprehensive, and theologically pointed formulations, what is mentioned are future eschatological summary events. When we line up the corresponding propositional content of the relevant statements, that for which Christians are to hope becomes clear:

'Christ is revealed' (ὁ Χριστὸς φανερωθῇ) (Col. 3.4).
Christians also 'will be revealed with him in glory' (τότε καὶ ὑμεῖς σὺν αὐτῷ φανερωθήσεσθε ἐν δόξῃ) (Col. 3.4).
There will be a judgement, in which 'the wrongdoer will be paid back for whatever wrong has been done' (ὁ γὰρ ἀδικῶν κομίσεται ὃ ἠδίκησεν, καὶ οὐκ ἔστιν προσωπολημψία) (Col. 3.25).
Christians will receive an 'inheritance' (κληρονομία), for which they already possess the Spirit as a 'pledge' (ἀρραβών), and the 'possession' (περιποίησις) of this inheritance consists of 'redemption' (ἀπολύτρωσις) (Eph. 1.13-14).

the summary of the history of scholarship in Th. Witulski, 'Gegenwart und Zukunft in den eschatologischen Konzeptionen des Kolosser- und des Epheserbriefes', *ZNW* 96 (2005), pp. 211–42 (here pp. 211–12).

27   For example, U. Schnelle, *Theologie des Neuen Testaments* (UTB, 2917; Göttingen: Vandenhoeck & Ruprecht, 2007), p. 535, on the Letter to the Ephesians.
28   Ibid. p. 519, on the Letter to the Colossians.
29   Ibid.
30   Witulski, 'Gegenwart und Zukunft' (see n. 26), p. 239.
31   Merklein, 'Paulinische Theologie' (see n. 21).

God will 'in the ages to come ... show the immeasurable riches of his grace in kindness toward us in Christ Jesus' (ἵνα ἐνδείξηται ἐν τοῖς αἰῶσιν τοῖς ἐπερχομένοις τὸ ὑπερβάλλον πλοῦτος τῆς χάριτος αὐτοῦ ἐν χρηστότητι ἐφ᾽ ὑμᾶς ἐν Χριστῷ Ἰησοῦ) (Eph. 2.7).

There will be a 'day of redemption' (ἡμέρα ἀπολυτρώσεως) (Eph. 4.30).

There will be a judgement, in which 'each one', if he or she does good, 'will receive the same again from the Lord' (ἕκαστος ἐάν τι ποιήσῃ ἀγαθόν, τοῦτο κομίσεται παρὰ κυρίου) (Eph. 6.8).

All of these citations have in common that they are lodged within statements concerning the present. Colossians 3.3, 4, 25 and Eph. 4.30; 6.8 are found in contexts of paraenesis, while the statements in Eph. 1.13-14; 2.7 deal with the identity of the addressees. If we differentiate between eschatological *concepts* as such and *discourse* about these concepts in the concrete occasion for the communication (thus between the eschatological *langue* and the eschatological *parole*), then it becomes clear that the occurrence of linguistically diverse eschatological statements in Paul and in both Deutero-Pauline letters can be explained through the transition of Pauline Christianity from a religion of conversion to a religion of tradition. In contrast to Paul, the authors of both letters do not have to *develop* an eschatological knowledge base. They can instead *assume* their addressees possess a store of knowledge concerning eschatological events. For this reason they can, therefore, limit themselves to tersely coded phrases when appealing to this knowledge. In 1 Thess. 4.15-17, Paul still had to describe in detail the events associated with the parousia. The author of Ephesians must only mention the 'day of redemption' (ἡμέρα ἀπολυτρώσεως) – and everyone knows what is being stated. Considered from the opposite direction, one may see an analogous situation in Col. 3.4. There is only one and one reason only why the author does not have to say more than statements such as 'when Christ appears' (ὅταν ὁ χριστὸς φανερωθῇ) or 'then you also shall appear with him in glory' (τότε καὶ ὑμεῖς σὺν αὐτῷ φανερωθήσεσθε ἐν δόξῃ) in order to place his readers within the larger picture he is portraying of the eschatological events; given this connection he can simply assume the availability of a collective Christian body of knowledge. Because in the interim there emerged a Christian tradition and along with it a Christian formation stemming from a corporate encyclopedia, the authors of both letters could limit themselves to the pithy synopses listed above. Thus Pauline eschatology in these letters is received in a way that makes the reformulations of eschatology superfluous in the various levels of expression within the letters. In fact, the authors assume that this eschatology has become an established component of their readers' Christian tradition and, for this reason, the authors need only paraphrase, using a limited number of interpretive catchwords. They no longer have to inform; they need only to remind.

b. The Reception of Pauline Ecclesiology in Ephesians 4.1-6

1. When we in our present context continue our investigation of the image of the Christian community portrayed in the letter of Ephesians and use as a basis the

'religion-of-conversion' or '-tradition' paradigm, we experience somewhat of a surprise. To be sure, in Eph. 2.20 the author possesses an awareness of a Christian tradition. In no place, however, do we find an explicit demand for a continuing alignment with a binding Pauline tradition as in 2 Thess. 2.15, 1 Tim. 6.3-4, and 2 Tim. 1.12-13. There is no insistence, as in the Pastorals, to guard an uninterrupted transmission of the authentic Pauline teaching (cf. 1 Tim. 4.6, 16; 2 Tim. 2.2; Tit. 1.9; 2.1). We discover equally few reminders to 'continue ... in the faith ... without shifting from the hope' as in Col. 1.23. Conversely, the portrayal of Christianity that Ephesians reveals lines up to a greater degree with the character of a religion of conversion. The evidence for this is seen in the author's argument in a repeated use of a 'once–now schema' (Eph. 2.1-6, 11-13; 5.8) or, in a different way, through references to the act of conversion (Eph. 1.13; 2.19; 4.17 ['no longer' {μηκέτι}], 20-24 ['your former way of life' {κατὰ τὴν προτέραν ἀναστροφήν}], 28 [μηκέτι]). But of course one must agree with those interpreters and commentators who suggest that the letter does *not* presuppose an audience of new converts. The auditors of the letter are rather those who have already been socialized in a Christian environment and are part of communities that exist already in their second or even third generation. There are two explanations for this unique tension:

i) The fact that the addressees are not mentioned in the *adscriptio* of the letter indicates that the author was writing to all Christians of his time, not to a single community. Ephesians is thus intended as something akin to a 'catholic' letter.[32] This means, then, that the *ecclesia* in Ephesians is no longer as still in Paul a single, local congregation, but rather a trans-geographical phenomenon. Accordingly it still appears here as only *one* ecclesia. This does not mean, however, that it had become a self-sustaining entity, which existed as an institution independent of the faithful and the baptized. It consists rather of those who belong to it. For semantic reasons Ephesians uses the term 'church' (ἐκκλησία) as synecdoche; it functions as a comprehensive umbrella term, signifying the totality of all believers. For this reason one cannot say,

---

32   Cf. G. Sellin, 'Adresse und Intention des Epheserbriefes', in *Paulus, Apostel Jesu Christi* (Festschrift G. Klein; ed. M. Trowitzsch; Tübingen: Mohr, 1998), pp. 171–86; *idem, Brief an die Epheser* (see n. 21), pp. 65–72. Otherwise, cf. the overview in H. Merkel, 'Der Epheserbrief in der neueren exegetischen Diskussion', in *ANRW* II 25/4 (1987), pp. 3156–246 (3221–22). One must admit that it is possible to reconstruct a coherent original text only through a bit of conjecture (removing [τοῖς οὖσιν]). In this way the original wording would have been: τοῖς ἁγίοις καὶ πιστοῖς ἐν Χριστῷ Ἰησοῦ (see also E. Best, 'Ephesians 1.1 Again', in *Paul and Paulinism* [Festschrift C. K. Barrett; ed. M. D. Hooker; London: SPCK, 1982], pp. 273–79; *idem, Ephesians* [ICC; London/New York: T&T Clark, 1998], pp. 99–100, with previous proponents of this position, p. 100. n. 8). Tertullian's statement in *Adv. Marc.* 5.17 ('We have it from the true tradition of the church that this letter was sent to the Ephesians, not to the Laodiceans; Marcion, however, at one time was very much wanting to alter its title by inserting a different one' [i.e., to Laodicea] [trans. eds] [*Ecclesiae quidem veritate epistolam istam ad Ephesios habemus emissam, non ad Laodicenos; sed Marcion et titulum aliquando interpolare gestit*]), however, makes it clear that neither he himself nor Marcion read the destination in the text of the letter. The issue here concerns only which address was in the *titulus* (thus in the superscription); Tertullian is arguing over the authority of the ecclesial consensus, not the wording of the text.

as does Jürgen Roloff, that the church in Ephesians is found 'between Christ and the faithful' and that 'ecclesiology ... has become a presupposition of soteriology'.[33] The 'church' is in fact identical to the community of those who are 'saved by grace' (2.5, 8), and soteriology, therefore, always takes precedence over ecclesiology in Ephesians as well.

ii) The second explanation is related to the first. Although one may not overlook the fact that the author of Ephesians is firmly anchored in the Pauline tradition,[34] this author does not presume that the communities to which he is writing are also familiar with this tradition. This separates Ephesians from the Pastoral Epistles and 2 Thessalonians. For this reason the Pauline self-presentation is not found in the beginning of the letter. Instead, the author waits until ch. 3, describing instead the identity of the addressees in chs 1–2, before he follows Paul's introduction with instructions for the ethical formation of this identity in chs 4–6. The 'Pauline' self-presentation in 3.1-13 and the intercessory prayer in 3.14-21 therefore function to ensconce the historical Paul as authorization of the pseudonymous Paul and to build upon him as an epistolary authority. The author of Ephesians desires that his auditors accept Paul as an authority who has something significant to tell them; and this concern is also based on his conviction that Paul's theology is applicable for all Christians in his time, and indeed for all Christianity (hence the missing addressees and the universal-ecclesiological orientation).

2. The author proceeds in two steps to advance Pauline theology from a context of a religion of conversion to that of a religion of tradition. He first seizes upon one of the historical Paul's most important theological concerns, the removal of differences caused by diverging contexts for Christian faith and Christian baptism (Rom. 10.12; 1 Cor. 1.23-24; 12.13; Gal. 3.28; 5.6; 6.15) and the emphasis on the 'one-ness' of the Christian community (Rom. 12.4, 5; 1 Cor. 10.17; 12.9, 11-14; Gal. 3.28). He does so in this instance by treating Eph. 2.11-14 as a phenomenon of a religion of conversion. The author does not describe the specific history of a particular community's conversion but rather the ideal foundational story of the gentile church as a whole. Gentile conversion occurred in the time of the 'apostles and prophets', who function as a 'foundation' upon which all of the Christian faith was 'built' (2. 20). This diachronically profiled 'one-ness' of the ecclesia (cf. the 'once-now' schema in vv. 11-13) is then, after the intervening chapter about Paul in Eph. 3, taken up at the beginning of the paraenetic section in 4.3-6 and reformulated synchronically:

---

33   J. Roloff, *Die Kirche im Neuen Testament* (GNT, 10; Göttingen: Vandenhoeck & Ruprecht, 1993), p. 237; here in reference to H. Merklein, *Christus und die Kirche. Die theologische Grundstruktur des Epheserbriefes nach Eph. 2.11-18* (SBS, 66; Stuttgart: Kath. Bibelwerk, 1973), p. 81.

34   The evidence for this has already been discussed many times and need not, therefore, be repeated here; cf., e.g., Lindemann, *Paulus im ältesten Christentum* (see n. 23), pp. 122–130; M. Gese, *Das Vermächtnis des Apostels. Die Rezeption der paulinischen Theologie im Epheserbrief* (WUNT, II/99; Tübingen: Mohr, 1997).

Eph. 4.3-6: ³σπουδάζοντες τηρεῖν τὴν ἑνότητα τοῦ πνεύματος ἐν τῷ συνδέσμῳ τῆς εἰρήνης· ⁴ἕνα σῶμα καὶ ἕν πνεῦμα, καθὼς καὶ ἐκλήθητε ἐν μιᾷ ἐλπίδι τῆς κλήσεως ὑμῶν· ⁵εἷς κύριος, μία πίστις, ἕν βάπτιμσα, ⁶εἷς θεὸς καὶ πατὴρ πάντων, ὁ ἐπὶ πάντων καὶ διὰ πάντων καὶ ἐν πᾶσιν.

... making every effort to maintain the unity of the Spirit in the bond of peace. There is one body and one Spirit, just as you were called to the one hope of your calling, one Lord, one faith, one baptism, one God and Father of all, who is above all and through all and in all.

It is obvious what is happening here.[35] The author of Ephesians is updating a central concern of Pauline theology – those things that unite, which bind Christians together, must prevail over all differences – in the post-Paul era and is reformulating it in light of the fact that in the meantime Christianity has become a religion of tradition. That which the author of Ephesians calls 'ecclesia' Christianity exists in the second half of the first century already as a trans-local phenomenon, for there were 'congregations' in many localities. But it is precisely here where the problem took root. These 'local congregations' all had an individual character, because they were shaped by differing traditions; they practised different 'customs' (cf. already 1 Cor. 11.16!). Given this background one can interpret the identity-forming attributes catalogued in Eph. 4.4-6 as a first attempt at designating ecumenical 'identity markers', which define the unity of Christianity. By doing so the author gives new voice to Pauline theology in a changed historical context. The point of reference, however, is no longer, as with Paul, the tensions between the common Christian identity of the members of the community and their differing contextual identities (as is normally the case in a religion of conversion); rather it involves the differences which occur now within the universal ecclesia between the individual congregations, which are due to their own particular enculturation and institutionalization.

c. The Reception of Paul's Teaching on Justification in Ephesians 2.8-10 and Titus 3.4-7

1. One can describe Paul's teaching on justification as a semantic field that exhibits a particular terminological topography. At the centre one finds the terms for righteousness (δικαιοῦν, δικαιοσύνη, δίκαιος, δικαίωσις) precisely in the midst of the discussion of faith (πίστις/πιστεύειν). While the discussion of faith originally belonged to the constitutive elements that Paul ascribed to his communities (cf. 1 Thess. 1.3, 8; 2.13; 3.2, 5, 6, 7, 10; 4.14; 5.8), it is not until Paul addresses the Galatian controversy that the sayings about righteousness are added. This occurred on the basis of Gen. 15.6 (LXX) ('[Abram] believed God; and it was reckoned to him as righteousness'). This connection first appears in Gal. 2.16; 3.8, 24, and then in Phil. 3.9, as well as in Rom. 1.17; 3.22, 26, 28, 30; 5.1; 9.30; 10.4, 6, 10. As a negatively stated proposition, this statement of the substantive relationship between the two is placed as a foil at the centre, namely that 'righteousness' can 'not' be

---

35   In the following I am indebted to K. M. Fischer, *Tendenz und Absicht des Epheserbriefes* (FRLANT, 111; Göttingen: Vandenhoeck & Ruprecht, 1973).

attained 'through works of the Law' (οὐ δικαιοῦται ἄνθρωπος ἐξ ἔργων νόμου), ['no one can be justified through works of the Law'] (Gal. 2.16a; see also 2.16c; 3.11; Rom. 3.20, 21, 28; see also Phil. 3.9). Two further sub-points become attached to this: concerning the first, the reference to 'sin' grounds the explanation that no one is justified through works of the law (for the first time, Gal. 3.22; then Rom. 3.20; 7.7-25). The other point is the *abolition of the difference between Jew and non-Jew* – to be sure, either through the inclusivity of faith (Rom. 1.16; 3.27-30; 10.11-12; Gal. 2.15-16) or through the universality of sin (Rom. 1.18–3.20; esp. 3.9). This abrogation is aligned with the assertion that the doing of the law cannot result in justification in so far as 'law' here always refers to Torah, and it is precisely the doing or the not doing of the Torah that marks the difference between a Jew and a non-Jew. Just so in this way can the Pauline teaching about justification function in the manner outlined above,[36] namely, as a theological construct of a 'new creation' (καινὴ κτίσις) (Gal. 6.15); that is to say, functioning as a theory of a religion of conversion which Paul conceptualizes over against a Jewish world view.

2. When we now consider Eph. 2.8-10 and Tit. 3.4-7, it immediately becomes clear how selectively the authors of both letters have reconfigured the semantic field of the Pauline teaching on justification:

Eph. 2.8-10: [8]Τῇ γὰρ χάριτί ἐστε σεσωσμένοι διὰ πίστεως· καὶ τοῦτο οὐκ ἐξ ὑμῶν, θεοῦ τὸ δῶρον· [9]οὐκ ἐξ ἔργων, ἵνα μή τις καυχήσηται. [10]αὐτοῦ γάρ ἐσμεν ποίημα, κτισθέντες ἐν Χριστῷ Ἰησοῦ ἐπὶ ἔργοις ἀγαθοῖς οἷς προητοίμασεν ὁ θεὸς, ἵνα ἐν αὐτοῖς περιπατήσωμεν.

For by grace you have been saved **through faith,** and this is not your own doing; it is the gift of God – **not the result of works,** so that no one may boast. For we are what he has made us, created in Christ Jesus for good works, which God prepared beforehand to be our way of life.

Tit. 3.4-7: [4]ὅτε δὲ ἡ χρηστότης καὶ ἡ φιλανθρωπία ἐπεφάνη τοῦ σωτῆρος ἡμῶν θεοῦ – [5]οὐκ ἐξ ἔργων τῶν ἐν δικαιοσύνῃ ἃ ἐποιήσαμεν ἡμεῖς ἀλλὰ κατὰ τὸ αὐτοῦ ἔλεος ἔσωσεν ἡμᾶς διὰ λουτροῦ παλιγγενεσίας καὶ ἀνακαινώσεως πνεύματος ἁγίου, [6]οὗ ἐξέχεεν ἐφ᾽ ἡμᾶς πλουσίως διὰ Ἰησοῦ Χριστοῦ τοῦ σωτῆρος ἡμῶν, [7] ἵνα δικαιωθέντες τῇ ἐκείνου χάριτι κληρονόμοι γενηθῶμεν κατ᾽ ἐλπίδα ζωῆς αἰωνίου.

But when the goodness and loving kindness of God our Saviour appeared, he saved us, **not because of any works of righteousness** that we had done, but according to his mercy, through the water of rebirth and renewal by the Holy Spirit. This Spirit he poured out on us richly through Jesus Christ our Saviour, so that, **having been justified** by his grace, we might become heirs according to the hope of eternal life.

Ephesians 2.8-9 reads as if it were a 'short paraphrase of Rom. 3(,21-30)'.[37] Besides the comparison of 'faith' (πίστις) and 'works' (ἔργα), the author traces salvation back to God's grace (χάρις) (cf. Rom. 3.24), takes up the Pauline 'as a gift' (δωρεάν) (Rom. 3.24), in δῶρον and also emphasizes that, through the rescue

36   See above p. 64.
37   Sellin, *Brief an die Epheser* (see n. 21), p. 184.

through faith and not out of works, 'boasting' (καυχᾶσθαι) becomes impossible (Rom. 3.27). 'Those who are justified' (δικαιούμενοι) (Rom. 3.24) is replaced by 'those who are saved/rescued' (σεσῳσμένοι) (Eph. 2.8). The difference between the two texts is, however, clear. It is seen primarily in the negations and the contrasts. 'Not through/out of works' (οὐκ ἐξ ἔργων) augments 'not your own doing' (οὐκ ἐξ ὑμῶν), and 'we' and 'God' will be contrasted with each other. The ἔργα νόμου are generalized ethically as '(good) works' (cf. 2.10). The forbidden 'boasting' (καυχᾶσθαι) is to be understood not as in Rom. 2.17 – to which Paul makes a connection in 3.27 (Israel boasts of its special relationship to God in contrast to others) – but rather in the sense of 1 Cor. 1.29 – the universal nature of πᾶσα σάρξ here corresponds to that of τις in Eph. 2.9. Moreover, it is the 'works' of the intended auditors which can become the grounds for 'boasting'. Both the correlation of the Pauline teaching on justification with the abolition of the difference between Jews and gentiles (3.29-30),[38] as well as the connection of these ideas in Paul to the universal nature of sin (3.22-23), are now missing. The contrast between 'faith' and 'works' (πίστις and ἔργα) instead becomes a means of presenting a Christian anthropology.

The treatment in Tit. 3.4-7 (cf. vv. 5, 7) of δικαιοσύνη and δικαιοῦσθαι is different from that in Eph. 2.8-10. The chief difference is that baptism, described as 'a washing of regeneration' (λουτρὸν παλιγγενεσίας) (Tit. 3.5) takes the place of faith. Otherwise, in this text, as in Eph. 2.8-10, nothing of the Jew-Gentile theme has been retained, and likewise the term 'works' (ἔργα) is spoken of in the same 'ethical' manner as in Eph. 2.9. The author even assumes that the auditors have performed 'works of righteousness' (v. 5), and an analogous evaluation of 'works' is undoubtedly also presupposed in 2 Tim. 1.9 ('who saved us and called us *not according to our works*' (οὐ κατὰ τὰ ἔργα ἡμῶν).

That the Pauline teaching on justification has undergone realignment in both texts is obvious, even as it has often been so depicted in the literature and as the object of regret. Ferdinand Hahn sees in Eph. 2.8-10 'the overarching Pauline conception as broken',[39] and Helmut Köster, in reference to the Pastoral Epistles, even speaks of a 'selling out of the Pauline theology under adverse conditions'.[40] In my opinion, however, one does much more justice to the reception of Paul in these texts when they are interpreted as hermeneutical attempts to advance and to re-contextualize Paul's theology of justification. The advantage of this interpretation is that it also explains the development of a theological profile into the contours of

38   Similarly, cf. also M. Theobald, 'Der Kanon von der Rechtfertigung (Gal. 2.16; Rom. 3.28) - Eigentum des Paulus oder Gemeingut der Kirche?', in *Worum geht es in der Rechtfertigungslehre?* (ed. Th. Söding; QD, 180; Freiburg: Herder, 1999), pp. 131–92 (176).

39   F. Hahn, 'Taufe und Rechtfertigung. Ein Beitrag zur paulinischen Theologie in ihrer Vor- und Nachgeschichte', in *Studien zum Neuen Testament. II. Bekenntnisbildung und Theologie in urchristlicher Zeit* (WUNT, 192; ed. F. Hahn; Tübingen: Mohr, 2006), pp. 241–70 (250): What is missing is 'the antithesis to works of the law, as οὐκ ἐξ ἔργων circumscribes only οὐκ ἐξ ὑμῶν; above all the question no longer concerns *iustificatio sola fide*'.

40   H. Köster, 'GNOMAI DIAPHOROI: The Origin and Nature of Diversification in the History of Early Christianity', in: J. M. Robinson and H. Koester, *Trajectories through Early Christianity* (Philadelphia: Fortress, 1971), pp. 114–157 (156).

a religion of tradition, as clearly both letters assume a Christianity that is no longer a religion of conversion. The abandonment of the distinction between Jews and gentiles, an area of Paul's theology which required some strenuous revisioning on his part, had already for quite some time become a non-issue and could therefore be dropped altogether. Corresponding to this, it was possible, if not even necessary, to separate 'works' from Torah and to reframe this term in a more generic ethical sense. More than that, the teaching on justification was no longer needed to legitimate theologically the fundamental paradigm shift, because, with its assistance, Paul had established an understanding of reality that had already during the longer interim period become an integral component of the Christian encyclopedia.

V. A View Ahead

A summary would be inappropriate, since it was not my intent to present conclusive results. My concern was limited much more to bringing to discussion a new model of interpretation and to showcase the heuristic potential of this approach for probing the reception of Paul in early Christianity, selecting a few examples.

If we were to broaden the perspective still more and take into view not only the reception of Pauline theology but carry it over also to the problems of explaining the historical occurrences and constellations of developments,[41] then one could also inquire whether the conflict between the author of the *Pastoral Epistles* and the opponents with whom he contends, a conflict of two contrasting concepts of Christianity, could be explained as two divergent 'patterns of religion'. One must not overlook the fact that the author of the three letters understands Christianity as a religion of tradition, while the opponents perceive it as a religion of conversion. When we orient ourselves to the way, on the one hand, in which the author presents his own concept of a Christian ethos[42] and, on the other, the behaviour of the opponents,[43] we see that the opponents appear in his community, proposing an identity that is aimed at an uncompromising disintegration of society. The Pastoral Epistles proclaim a markedly *inclusive* ethos and precisely in this way make apparent their interest in an integration of the Christian community within their societal context. At the same time, a distinctively *exclusive* ethos on the side of the opponents is evident.[44] Their promotion of it has obviously been successful; the author of the Pastoral Epistles considers this ethos a threat to continuing their link to the origins of the tradition which had first established their identity. One can perhaps go even further in viewing the opponents with whom the Pastoral

41 Cf. the possibilities listed on p. 58.

42 Here, cf. primarily 1 Tim. 2.1-2, 8-15; 3.1-7, 8-13; 5.1-2, 3-16; 6.1-2; Tit. 1.7-9; 2.1-10; 3.1-2.

43 This occurs at least in 1 Tim. 4.3 ('They forbid marriage and demand abstinence from foods'); 6.20-21 ('contradictions of what is falsely called knowledge'); 2 Tim. 2.18 ('claiming that the resurrection has already taken place').

44 On this distinction see pp. 54f.

Epistles disagree as in the vein of those who represent the first intra-Christian renewal movement, which would be followed later by many others.

And finally, a look at the Lukan two-volume work in light of our topic should not be missed. In the following, I assume that its author accompanied Paul, making this apparent through the so-called 'we passages'.[45] But even if we do not make this assumption, we can presume that Luke was theologically enculturated or formed within the Pauline tradition. He owes much, so to speak, to Paul. This corresponds also to the fact that he projects a picture of the Pauline mission that is organized with a high degree of historical plausibility. Paul calls for 'conversion' (μετάνοια, μετανοεῖν; Acts 17.30; 20.21; 26.20), and Luke relates the story of the proclamation of Christ as the story of the separation of Christianity from Judaism. It is telling that Luke, with the exception of the account of Stephen, narrates the material on Paul that treats only such episodes of division. The series begins in Acts 8.1 with the separation from Jerusalem. It continues in Pisidian Antioch (Acts 13.44-46, 50-51), in Corinth (Acts 18.4-7), in Ephesus (Acts 19.8-9), and finally once again in Jerusalem (Acts 21.27–26.32). One could perhaps also add those texts in which Luke relates that Paul had also to flee from a city simply because his life was threatened by the local Jewish population; this is the case in Damascus (Acts 9.23-25), in Jerusalem (Acts 9.28-30), in Iconium (Acts 14.4-7), and in Beroea (Acts 17.10-14).

These observations give reason to consider whether we should not reverse the literary perspective on the Lukan writings: in the past they were viewed from the standpoint of the other Gospels, and the distinctive quality of Luke's presentation was attributed to his story of Jesus that, though similar to the accounts of the other Gospels, was extended nevertheless through the Acts of the Apostles during the time of the proclamation of Christ by those who had witnessed the resurrection. This development prompted Franz Overbeck to his well-known judgement: 'This is the one tactless maneuver of worldwide proportions, of the greatest excess of misplaced priorities that Luke has passed off as a legitimate subject.'[46] It is surely correct that Luke wrote and published his account of Jesus before his narrative of the history of the proclamation of Christ by the witnesses to the resurrection. On the other hand, there is not a little to be said for the idea that, from a conceptual point of view, Luke proceeded in exactly the opposite manner. He lengthened the narrative of the parting of Christianity and Judaism, a period of history which he experienced and described in Acts, by pushing back *the beginning* of the narrative. And he did so not only through the narrative of the times he recounts, but by going back to the previous epochs of Israel's history. This is seen most clearly in Lk. 1–2, as well as in the speeches of Stephen in Jerusalem and Paul in Pisidian Antioch (Acts 7.2-53; 13.16-41). According to Paul's argumentation in his inaugural speech in Pisidian

---

45   Here, cf. M. Wolter, *Das Lukasevangelium* (HNT, 5; Tübingen: Mohr, 2008), pp. 8–9. 'Luke' is thus intimately familiar with the Pauline mission and theology, as has oftentimes been assumed in the past (cf. also D. Marguerat [ed.], *The Reception of Paulinism in Acts*, [BETL, 229; Leuven: Peters, 2009]).

46   F. Overbeck, *Christentum und Kultur. Gedanken und Anmerkungen zur modernen Theologie* (Basel: Schwabe, 1919 = Darmstadt: Wiss. Buchgesellschaft, 1963), pp. 78–79.

Antioch, the history of Christianity begins with the election of the patriarchs (cf. esp. Acts 13.17). Luke wishes to narrate the account of the parting of Christianity and Judaism as an epoch of the history of Israel. The theological interest closely tied to Luke's agenda becomes immediately transparent when we refer back to the description of the paradigm that has formed the basis of our analysis: Luke's desire is to furnish Christianity with a history and a tradition. He wants to prove that Christianity, far from being a new religion of conversion, has from its very inception been and always remained a religion of tradition.

Chapter 5

PAUL AFTER PAUL: A (HI)STORY OF RECEPTION

Daniel Marguerat
Trans. Michael D. Thomas and Julien C. H. Smith

The question of the reception of Paul is as old as historical criticism. I express it as follows: how can we understand and connect the different facets of Paul's extraordinary image, which Paul enjoyed within early Christianity? What paradigm should be applied in order to interconnect the Deutero-Pauline epistles (Colossians, Ephesians, 2 Thessalonians), the Pastorals (1–2 Timothy, Titus), the Acts of the Apostles, and the *Apocryphal Acts of Paul?*[1]

Each of these texts creates, in effect, a specific construct of Paul's image. The Deutero-Paulines, as well as the Pastorals, explicitly take up the thematic and biographical motifs of the apostle's letters. Acts differs from them in presenting Paul, not as a writer, but rather a missionary founder of churches. As for the *Apocryphal Acts of Paul*, dating from the end of the second century, they do equal justice both to the image of the missionary and to that of the writer (third letter to the Corinthians). The way in which I define my subject indicates that on the literary level I adopt the position which consistently seems to me to be the most illuminating, even if it is the object of debate: the Deutero-Paulines and the Pastorals are part of an 'after Paul' legacy, whoever the responsible authors (a secretary? the Pauline school?) of this post-Pauline tradition may be. I therefore treat these letters as originating not from the hand of the apostle, but rather as appropriating the legacy of Pauline thought.

I will begin by posing the problem of the reception of Paul with respect to the relationship between Acts and the Pauline correspondence (I.), then propose a model of the reception of Paul (II.), and apply this model to three common themes shared by Paul and by the writings belonging to his heritage (III.): first, the status of the apostle (III.a.); second, the suffering of the apostle (III.b.); and third, Paul's teachings (III.c.). Finally, I will close with a brief conclusion (IV.).

---

1   This article is the *Presidential Address* which I delivered at the 62nd assembly of the SNTS at Sibiu, August 1, 2007. An earlier version of the thesis I am proposing here was presented at the University of Manchester as a part of the *Manson Memorial Lecture*, October 26, 2006. I thank the colleagues who, on these two occasions, gave me a number of interesting suggestions.

I. The Paul of the epistles and the Paul of Acts: Between Incompatibility and Harmonization

The question of the connection between the image of Paul drawn from his writings and the image which emerges from Acts has been scrutinized since the Tübingen school. The question of connectedness continues to give rise to the clash of two theses: from one point of view, the two images of Paul are declared irreconcilable (the thesis of incompatibility), while from the other perspective, they are harmonized.

The divergences between the given facts of the letters and those of Acts are well known; I will but recall them briefly. They appear on the level of the *informative*: Paul acknowledges himself as a mediocre orator (1 Cor. 2.4; 2 Cor. 10.10) while Luke credits him with brilliant discourses like those of ancient orators (Acts 13; 14; 17; 20; 22; 26).[2] The Jerusalem assembly, which must settle the discord between Paul's mission to non-Jews and the Jewish Christians of Jerusalem, concludes in Acts with the imposition of four practices from which non-Jews must abstain (Acts 15.20, 29), while Paul boasts in Gal. 2.5-10 that nothing was imposed upon him except collecting the offering for Jerusalem. Paul protests that some Christians have returned to the practice of circumcision (Gal. 5.1-12), but in Acts 16.3 he circumcises Timothy. One notices, moreover, troubling *silences*: why does the author of Acts mention neither the theological conflicts which Paul had to face in his communities, nor his epistolary activity? Why does Luke refuse to the man of Tarsus the title of 'apostle', which plays nonetheless such a fundamental role in Paul's self-understanding (Gal. 1.1; 1 Cor. 9.1; 15.9)? On the *theological* level, the disagreements become obvious. It is well known that Paul's essential theological struggle revolves around the issue of the Torah: for the apostle, salvation in Jesus Christ is a salvation 'apart from the works of the law' (Rom. 3.20), and one reads in Galatians that Paul does not admit the slightest compromise on this score; this polemic is absent in Acts, which shows Paul displaying an unfailing attachment to the customs of the fathers (Acts 28.17b). Even more, the crystallization of Pauline theology of the cross is met with, in the discourses of Acts, a focus upon the *kerygma* of the resurrection of Christ: the discord between Jews and Christians in Acts is not centred on the cross, as it is for Paul, but rather with the resurrection of Jesus (Acts 2.22-36; 3.15-21; 13.26-39; 23.6-9; 26.6-8).

The thesis of incompatibility found its classic expression in a famous article by Philipp Vielhauer in 1950.[3] The author vehemently argues the idea that Luke, in Acts, contravenes the teaching of Paul, in part by defending a natural theology in Paul's discourse in Athens (Acts 17.22-31), and in part by abandoning the Pauline position on the Torah in the name of a Christian-Jewish continuity, leaving out

---

2   J. C. Lentz, *Luke's Portrait of Paul* (SNTSMS, 77; Cambridge: Cambridge University Press, 1993).

3   P. Vielhauer, 'Zum "Paulinismus" der Apostelgeschichte', in *Aufsätze zum Neuen Testament* (ThB, 31; München: Kaiser, 1965), pp. 9–27 (ET: P. Vielhauer, 'On the "Paulinism" of Acts', in *Studies in Luke Acts* [ed. L. Keck and J. Louis Martyn; W. C. Robinson and V. P. Furnish (trans.); Nashville: Abingdon, 1966], pp. 33–50 [reprinted as ch. 1 of this volume]).

the Christology of the cross, and attesting a collapsed eschatology. In brief, he concludes, 'the author of Acts is pre-Pauline in his Christology, and post-Pauline in his natural theology, concept of the law, and eschatology. One finds in him not a single specifically Pauline idea'.[4] Here we see Luke expelled from the Pauline school for reporting so poorly! Now in its entirety, Vielhauer's position proves to be untenable. It is incorrect to say that Acts 17 defends a natural theology; the failure of pagan knowledge of God is also affirmed there as much as in Rom. 1.18-32: God brings to an end, says the Lukan Paul at Athens, to the 'times of ignorance' (χρόνους τῆς ἀγνοίας, Acts 17.30a) in announcing the necessity of conversion to the One whom he has designated as Judge of the world (17.30b); the necessary *metanoia* injects the idea of a moment of change, which breaks with natural theology. Moreover, to oppose the circumcision of Timothy (Acts 16.3) with the non-circumcision of Titus does not take into account the fact that Titus is a gentile, while Timothy has a Jewish mother; this corresponds to the position that the apostle assumes in 1 Cor. 9.20-21: 'I became as a Jew for the Jews ... for those without the law as one without the law': Paul puts forward an explicitly differentiated position with respect to religious status. Moreover, to view the Pauline version of the Jerusalem assembly (Gal. 2.5-10) as contradictory to that of Luke (Acts 15.5-21) does not take into account the different literary genres: Paul is arguing a case, while Luke is describing a practice.[5]

One must add that, methodologically, the specific aim of each writer must be kept in view. Luke describes Paul as debating with outsiders, in the synagogue or with a gentile audience; in his correspondence, the apostle takes a position within an internal debate, thus arguing as an insider. Luke's Paul proclaims the gospel; the Paul of the epistles exposits it. One might equally expect that a biographical writing would mention traits of the apostle which he himself might omit or mention only briefly; such is the case with his acts of healing, to which I will return later. The methodological deficiency of Vielhauer's position is that it overlays two literary genres and considers Paul's letters to be the norm to which Acts should conform; in brief, his thesis of Lukan infidelity to the Pauline tradition is no longer defensible. One could demonstrate, moreover, that the stark contrast between Luke and Paul constructed by Vielhauer is deeply permeated with the theological controversy between Barth and Brunner during the 1930s, and that Vielhauer thinks he must reiterate the 'no' signified by Barth to Brunner concerning the relationship between nature and grace.[6]

---

4   Vielhauer, 'Zum "Paulinismus" der Apostelgeschichte', p. 26 (ET: Vielhauer, 'On the "Paulinism" of Acts', 49).

5   This argument is explored in the Greco-Roman literature by Hillard et al. T. Hillard, A. Nobbs and B. Winter, 'Acts and the Pauline Corpus I; Ancient Literary Parallels' in *The Book of Acts in Its First Century Setting* (ed. B. W. Winter and A. D. Clarke; vol. 1; Grand Rapids: Eerdmans, 1993), pp. 183–213.

6   E. Brunner, *Natur und Gnade* (Tübingen: Mohr, 1934); K. Barth, *Nein! Antwort an Emil Brunner* (TEH, 14; München: C. Kaiser, 1934); (ET: E. Bruner and K. Barth, *Natural Theology: Comprising "Nature and Grace"* [trans. P. Fraenkel; London: The Centenary Press, 1946]); I am indebted to M. Wolter for these references.

At the other extreme, harmonizing the contents of the epistles and Acts is equally unsatisfying.[7] If one may argue correctly for the complementarity of the contents of the apostle's writings and those of Luke, the positions set forth in various places regarding the Torah may not be forced to fit each other. Vielhauer is correct: the acuity of the debate regarding the validity of the law is no longer Luke's concern. The Christology of Acts is not at all that of Paul, which is focused on the cross. The thesis of harmonization, in my view, is no more defensible than the thesis of incompatibility in the final analysis.

What can we do, other than leave behind the alternatives of incompatibility or a harmonization? A differentiated approach to the reception of Paul must be permitted.

II. A Typology of the Reception of Paul

What information did the author of Acts have at his disposal in order to write his work? In my view, it hardly appears possible to defend the idea that the author was a companion of Paul, given that the Christianity reflected in Acts is closer to that of the Pastorals, dating from the 80s. It has been demonstrated numerous times that the farewell discourse to the Ephesian elders (Acts 20.18-35) bears witness to a situation analogous to that issue addressed by the Pastorals: the announcement of internal tensions, the questioning of Paul's integrity, and the polemic against false preaching.[8] To maintain the notion of an eyewitness only aggravates the problem: how could a witness who listened daily to Paul omit his epistolary activity, or deny him the title of apostle, for which he fought?

We must therefore ask ourselves yet again what information Luke had at his disposal. The model of harmonization and that of incompatibility share a common presupposition: Luke knew of the letters of Paul, yet for unexplained reasons does not cite them. Can one be so sure? Can we be certain that Luke knew of the Pauline correspondence? The intense work currently focusing on Christian apocryphal literature leads us, in effect, to examine again the means by which the tradition was transmitted. The existence of numerous apocryphal gospels or apocryphal acts of the apostles leads us to the realization that outside and alongside the tradition which was fixed in the canonical texts, a number of both oral and partially written traditions, later gathered up into the apocrypha, were circulating in the communities. Today, we know with greater clarity that the redaction of canonical texts did not by any means exhaust the tradition of Jesus and the apostles. Many other traditions, and

---

7   F. F. Bruce, 'Is the Paul of Acts the Real Paul?', *BJRL* 58 (1976), pp. 282–305; C. J. Hemer, *The Book of Acts in the Setting of Hellenistic History* (WUNT, 49; Tübingen: Mohr, 1989); S. E. Porter, *The Paul of Acts. Essays in Literary Criticism, Rhetoric, and Theology* (WUNT, 115; Tübingen: Mohr Siebeck, 1999); A. Mittelstaedt, *Lukas als Historiker. Zur Datierung des lukanischen Doppelwerkes* (TANZ, 43; Tübingen: Franke, 2006).

8   J. Dupont, *Le discours de Milet. Testament pastoral de saint Paul (Actes 20,18-36)* (LD, 32; Paris: Cerf, 1962); B. Roberts Gaventa, 'Theology and Ecclesiology in the Miletus Speech: Reflections on Content and Context', *NTS* 50 (2004), pp. 36–52.

the communities giving life to these traditions – passed on orally or promulgated by prophets and teachers – composed the network of Christianity during the first two centuries.

What transpired after the death of Paul, around the year 60? The circulation of his letters is already attested during his life (2 Cor. 10.10). His writings were progressively collected and assembled, the first indications of a canon of Pauline letters dating from the end of the first century. *First Clement*, Ignatius of Antioch, and Polycarp of Smyrna, make clear their awareness of his writings, but without any interest in the person of the apostle.[9] Between 60 and 100, what else took place? Paul's heritage was preserved by other means, along other paths than the collection of his writings. It is in my view an anachronism to imagine Luke writing a history of Paul with the letters of the apostle in front of him. Between Acts and the canon of Pauline letters a historical stage is neglected: the complex and multiform phenomenon of the reception of Paul.

a. The Three Poles of the Reception of Paul

To speak of 'reception' signals a change of paradigm for the proponents of the theories of incompatibility and harmonization. The phenomenon of reception implies that a dialectic of identity and displacement characterizes the relationship between an original thought and its subsequent resumption. The diversity of forms which the Pauline tradition took conforms to this observation. On one hand, some letters imitate the apostle's style and present a teaching in his name: these are the Deutero-Pauline letters and the Pastorals. On the other hand, the memory of the apostle is magnified by the recollection of his actions: this is the case with Acts and the *Acts of Paul*. François Bovon defended the thesis that the reception of the apostle, in the first century, had taken two forms: on one hand, Paul survived in the letters as a 'document'; on the other, in biographical writings as a 'monument'.[10] The proposition is interesting, but it calls for a correction: Colossians and Ephesians, as well as 2 Timothy, continue the epistolary activity of Paul, but at the same time do so without neglecting the biographical dimension of his persona, noting his life of suffering (Col. 1.1-11; 1.24–2.4; Eph. 3; 2 Tim. 1.12–2.7; 4.6-8).

Pursuing this insight, I would say that the reception of Paul is organized around three poles: *documentary, biographical,* and *doctoral.* The 'documentary' pole remembers Paul as a writer: his writings are collected, copied, reconfigured in certain cases, and assembled in a collection which is integrated within the New Testament canon. From the 'biographical' pole, Paul is celebrated as herald of the gospel, the missionary to the nations, of whom one narrates the salient facts (as Luke does in Acts); a hagiography is in the works here, of which the *Acts of Paul*

---

9   A. Lindemann, *Paulus. Apostel und Lehrer der Kirche. Studien zu Paulus und zum frühen Paulusverständnis* (Tübingen: Mohr Siebeck, 1999), pp. 294–322.

10   F. Bovon, 'Paul comme Document et Paul comme Monument' in *Chrétiens en conflit. L'Épître de Paul aux Galates* (ed. J. Allaz *et al.*; Essais bibliques, 13; Genève: Labor et Fides, 1987), pp. 54–65 (ET: F. Bovon, 'Paul as Document and Paul as Monument' in *New Testament and Christian Apocrypha: Collected Studies II* [ed. F. Bovon and G. Snyder; Tübingen: Mohr Siebeck, 2009], pp. 307–17).

is the first installment a century later. From the 'doctoral' pole, Paul is invoked as doctor of the church: one imitates his sentences in pseudepigraphical letters; one extends his teaching in the areas of ecclesiology and ethics, one writes in his name; these are the Deutero-Paulines and Pastorals.

It is essential to recognize that these three types of reception are parallel and simultaneous, unfolding between 60 and 100. They represent three modes of responding to the absence of the apostle, be it in establishing the memory of his life ('biographical' heritage), be it in preserving his writings ('documentary' heritage), or be it in instituting him as theological icon that guarantees orthodox interpretation ('doctoral' heritage; cf. Col. 2.5). Each of these strategies of managing the Pauline heritage selects the traits of the apostle's persona most amenable to its view and confers upon this persona a specific status. The persona of the apostle is thus constructed along three parallel paths. Here I must stress that the canon of Pauline epistles does not constitute the common documentary basis, the backdrop against which the entire reception of the apostle would be constructed. The documentary reception constitutes in itself a stream of the reception of Paul's persona, a specific stream which preserves his status as a polemical writer. Once again, it is anachronistic to think that, since we have his correspondence before our eyes today, his letters constituted the sole means by which he was known in the first century. All that we know of the rarity of writing in Antiquity should lead us to think the contrary: the memory of the apostle was preserved primarily through oral tradition preserved in the communities which he had founded. Only literate persons had access to texts. In no way was the social memory of the apostle transmitted through purely literary channels.

The consequences of the paradigm that I am proposing are important for the construction of Paul's image. The 'doctoral' pole traces the literary activity of the apostle and is based upon his writings; this activity of reading and rereading can be pinpointed among the effects of an intertextual conversation between pseudepigraphical and proto-pauline letters.[11] The same does not apply to the 'biographical' pole, as rendered by Luke's silence with regard to Paul's writings: the author's knowledge of Paul is not a literary one. Luke works with the memory of Paul's life and teaching, such as it was preserved by his circle, where twenty years later, Paul's debate concerning the Torah has lost its urgency. The memory of it was preserved (Acts 15.1-35; 16.1-6; 21.17-26), but the discussion as such is absent from Acts – not because Luke would have read Paul poorly, but because he depends upon another source of information. By contrast, the memory of the communities founded by the apostle to the gentiles furnishes Luke with abundant narrative material absent from the letters. It is therefore inadequate to measure the Lukan historiographical reliability by a norm constituted by the corpus of Pauline writings, precisely because these writings in and of themselves did not constitute the norm of Pauline tradition.

---

11   A. Merz, *Die fiktive Selbstauslegung des Paulus. Intertextuelle Studien zur Intention und Rezeption der Pastoralbriefe* (NTOA, 52; Göttingen/Fribourg: Vandenhoeck und Ruprecht/ Academic Press, 2004).

b. Paul the Healer

An example: the image of Paul the healer. The book of Acts recounts five miraculous acts (13.9-11; 14.8-10; 16.16-18; 28.7-8), as well as the resurrection of a dead person (20.7-12) and a summary of healings (19.11-12). The Tübingen School highlighted the technique of *syncrisis* between Peter and Paul systematically constructed in Acts, concluding that Luke would have distributed between Peter and Paul the same qualities in order to model the portrait of the one upon the other. Jacob Jervell had good reason to protest, invoking the therapeutic activity of Paul attested by his letters.[12] He drew attention to the 'signs of the apostle' (σημεῖα τοῦ ἀποστόλου) demanded by the apostle in 2 Cor. 12.12. The modality of the 'signs of the apostle' is explained by the triad 'deeds of power, wonders and signs' that one recognizes in Acts.[13] In Rom. 15.18b-19, the apostle synthesizes his ministry using the same terms: Christ worked through him 'to win obedience from the gentiles, by word and deed, by the power of signs and wonders (σημείων καὶ τεράτων)'. To the Thessalonians, he speaks of the gospel which 'came to you not in word only, but also in power and in the Holy Spirit' (1 Thess. 1.5).

In brief, that which Paul touches upon so discreetly, the 'biographical' memory has preserved for us. Acts inscribes it upon the heart of a correlative schematic – Jesus-Peter-Paul – while the *Acts of Paul*, in their rereading of the canonical Acts, gives way to amplification in a legendary mode; fundamentally, however, which is to say in describing Paul as a healer, these writings have invented nothing. Furthermore, they permit us to comprehend better the 'Paul effect' in the communities he founded, and which welcomed him, following the example of the Galatians, as 'an angel of God' (Gal. 4.14).

c. Points of Contact

The terminological points of contact between Acts and Pauline language are not numerous.[14] The same verb πορθεῖν designates Paul's opposition to the Christian movement (Gal. 1.13; Acts 9.21) as well as the formula ζηλωτὴς ὑπάρχων (Gal. 1.14; Acts 22.3). In the episode of the flight from Damascus, one reads the same expressions, 'through an opening in the wall' (διὰ τοῦ τείχους) and 'lowering' (χαλάω) in 2 Cor. 11.33 and Acts 9.25. These points of contact may be explained easily by the diffusion of the Pauline legend: as one perceives it in the reading of Phil. 3.6, Paul himself contributed to the diffusion of his portrayal as a repentant perse-cutor. These terminological contacts relating to his teaching, present in the discourse between Peter and Cornelius (Acts 10.43) and in Paul's speech in Pisidian Antioch (13.38-39), will be treated below under III.c; it is not a matter of citation, but rather of a utilization of the *logia* of the apostle in circulation among Pauline communities.

---

12   J. Jervell, *The Unknown Paul. Essays on Luke-Acts and Early Christian History* (Minneapolis: Augsburg, 1984), pp. 76–95.

13   Acts 2.22; 8.13. See also 2.19, 43; 4.30; 5.12; 6.8; 7.36; 14.3; 15.12.

14   Cf. W. O. Walker, 'Acts and the Pauline Corpus Reconsidered', *JSNT* 24 (1985), pp. 3–23 or S. E. Porter and C. E. Evans (eds), *The Pauline Writings* (The Biblical Seminar, 34; Sheffield : Sheffield Academic Press, 1995), pp. 55–74.

Let me illustrate my thesis on these two points of narrative contact between Acts and the Pauline letters: the result of the Jerusalem assembly and the flight from Damascus.

Even as Paul assesses the Jerusalem assembly for the benefit of the Galatians – 'we did not submit to them even for a moment, so that the truth of the gospel might always remain with you' (Gal. 2.5) – the account in Acts sets up the four required abstinences of the apostolic decree (Acts 15.20, 29): idolatry, immorality (πορνεία), eating strangled meat, and drinking blood are forbidden to gentile Christians. Once again the basic contradiction between Paul's text and the Lukan text has led most often to the suspicion that Luke has inserted here a late and local decree adopted by Jewish-Christian communities; possibly Luke himself actually recorded such a pronouncement. Most importantly, in my view, he thereby gives an account of the actual practice of Paul. When Paul demands, in Corinth (1 Corinthians 8) or in Rome (Romans 14), that the strong have regard for the weak, he pleads, in effect, *soteriologically* for the freedom of the strong, but *pragmatically* recommends their abstinence: 'If your brother or sister is being injured by what you eat, you are no longer walking in love. Do not let what you eat cause the ruin of one for whom Christ died' (Rom. 14.15). Does not one discover in the apostolic decree this echo of the apostle, at the same time theologically firm and ethically supple, in the name of *agape*?[15] One conceives that in the rhetorical strategy of Galatians 2, Paul defends the soteriological principle and not its ethical modulations; these have been retained in the memory of the apostle recorded by Luke.

The second point of narrative contact is the famous incident of the flight in the basket down the wall of Damascus. The hostility which forced the apostle to flee is attributed by Paul to the ethnarch under King Aretas (2 Cor. 11.32-33), by Luke to the Jews (Acts 9.25). The two versions are thus not in agreement. The proposals in the history of exegesis which attribute to Luke a distorted re-reading of the episode of 2 Corinthians 11 are by no means absent. But it is more plausible that such a spectacular anecdote had given rise, in the oral tradition, to multiple variants; the author of Acts has thus drawn his version, without a doubt choosing the one most amenable to his purpose, in order to be able to present the Jews in the role of persecutors of Paul, himself only recently converted from his activity of persecuting Christians (9.26-30).[16] Here again, the tradition upon which the author of Acts draws is inspired primarily not by the writings of the apostle, but by the history of his life.

It is correct, of course, to question the historical plausibility of such a paradigm. Could such a great admirer of Paul as the author of Acts have ignored the existence of letters attributed to his hero? The existence, within the Pauline communities, of copies of certain letters could hardly have passed unnoticed. Therefore, we cannot affirm with certainty that Luke was unaware of them; but with regard to Luke's

15   K. Loening, 'Das Evangelium und die Kulturen. Heilsgeschichtliche und kulturelle Aspekte kirchlicher Realität in der Apostelgeschichte' in *ANRW* II/25.3 (Berlin: de Gruyter, 1985), pp. 2604–46 (2623–25).

16   See D. Marguerat, *Les Actes des apôtres (1-12)* (CNT, 5a; Genève: Labor et Fides, 2007), pp. 340–41.

work, one may observe that he ignored them. Their absence in Acts does not prove the literary ignorance of the author, but rather signals that within the traditional milieu to which he belonged, the letters did not control the memory of the apostle. To insist that an 'authentic' knowledge of Paul is mediated exclusively through his letters, while at the same time blatantly ignoring the traces of his actions left in history, is a prejudice which dates back to the Enlightenment.

E. J. Goodspeed, in his time, launched the idea that the canon of Pauline letters had been assembled by an anonymous admirer of Paul, the interest in such a collection having been sparked by the reading of the recently published Acts, and that this person had collected his letters from within the communities founded by the apostle.[17] Taking into account the long and complex process which presided over the establishment of the Pauline canon and the reconfiguration of certain of his letters, this romantic idea should be abandoned; but the intuition which guided it may be retained: at the time Luke wrote, the canon of Pauline letters was neither truly assembled nor completed – since the redaction of the Pastorals was still in progress – nor, above all, consolidated into a referential corpus of the apostle's memory.[18]

I will now illustrate this differentiated management of the Pauline heritage by demonstrating how the presence of motifs from the 'biographical' pole and the 'doctoral' pole develop the possibilities present in the apostle's letters. In other words, I wish to show how the choice of different motifs from one or the other of the poles of Pauline reception corresponds to the possibilities present in Paul's letters, yet these motifs developed in diverse ways in service of the needs of the tradition.

III. A Differentiated Reception of Paul

How was Paul's persona constructed in the writings which I associate with the biographical and doctoral poles? And can one identify in Paul's letters the traditional source of the motifs retained in this construction differentiated according to his writings? I repeat: in my view, that which distinguishes the biographical stream from the doctoral stream is that the 'doctoral' writings yield themselves to a re-reading of the proto-Pauline letters, while the 'biographical' writings derive from a memory of the apostle which had not been normalized by the writings from Paul's own hand.

a. Paul's Status

What status is accorded to Paul from the point of view of the history of salvation? In Acts, the situation is clear. Luke's account testifies to the distinct interest in the person of Paul, which dominates the narration of ch. 13. Paul is the σκεῦος ἐκλογῆς (9.15), the instrument chosen by God to proclaim the gospel outside

---

17   E. J. Goodspeed, *New Solutions of the New Testament Problems* (Chicago: The University of Chicago Press, 1927).

18   C. K. Barrett, 'Acts and the Pauline Corpus', *ET* 78 (1976), pp. 2–5.

of its originating space, Judaism. Luke sees in him the providential man through whom the testimony of the resurrection will reach to the ἐσχάτου τῆς γῆς (1.8). The progressive concentration of the narrative on the person of Paul is the result of a narrative strategy: introduced surreptitiously into the account on the occasion of the martyrdom of Stephen (7.58–8.3), converted (9.1-31), active in Antioch (11.25-26), Saul/Paul is the companion of Barnabas in Acts 13–14, then he plays the primary role in the second missionary voyage of Acts 15–21; from ch. 22 onwards he figures solely as an accused witness, proclaiming the gospel before Jerusalem and the officials of the empire. Luke has skillfully fashioned a picture of the rise to power of his hero from Acts 7–28.[19]

But it must be immediately added that the plot of Acts sets up a series of characters prior to him: Paul is preceded. He is neither the first, nor – as is too frequently said – the partner in a tale of two personalities, Peter and Paul. Luke, for whom the argument of continuity provides a theological structure, has put in place – between the time of the twelve apostles in Jerusalem (Acts 1–6) and the time of Paul (Acts 13–28) – a series of intermediary figures: Stephen, who provokes the crisis with Judaism in Jerusalem (6.8–7.60), Philip, who evangelizes outside of Judea (8.5-40), Barnabas, who introduces Paul to the community in Jerusalem (9.27) and is his associate in the evangelization of Antioch (11.25-26). This narrative succession inserts Paul in a chain of witnesses which prevent the reader from isolating him. Even more importantly, Paul does not inaugurate the mission to non-Jews; this privilege is attributed to Peter in the famous encounter with Cornelius, which sanctions the abandonment of the ancient barrier between pure and impure (10.1–11.18). This narrative device is significant: the programmatic beginning of the evangelization of non-Jews, to which God pushes Peter, is inserted between the account of Paul's conversion at Damascus (Acts 9) and the start of his mission (Acts 13); Paul merely continues what Peter began and was put into place before him by the Hellenistic Christians who had found refuge in Antioch (11.19-20). This secondary status of Paul with respect to the Twelve is verified in the surprising refusal by Luke to accord him the title of ἀπόστολος, reserved for the companions of Jesus (1.21-22).[20] Can one imagine that a reader of the letters would dare to deny such apostolic standing to Paul? The final image of a Paul in Rome, welcoming and preaching to 'all who came to him' (28.30), Jews and non-Jews, puts into concrete form the relationship constituted within Acts by the man of Tarsus, between Israel and the Church – a link which Luke reaffirms despite the notice of Israel's rejection of the gospel at the end of the book (28.26-27).

In the Deutero-Paulines, Paul is also a figure of inclusiveness, no longer between Israel and the Church, but between Jews and pagans. The slogan of Gal. 3.28, but also Rom. 3.22-23 and 10.12-13 must have resonated within Pauline tradition. In Colossians, Paul appears as the herald *par excellence* of the word of God (1.25),

---

19   D. Marguerat, 'L'image de Paul dans les Actes des Apôtres,' in *Les Actes des Apôtres. Histoire, récit, théologie* (ed. M. Berder; LD, 199; Paris: Cerf, 2005), pp. 121–54.

20   I consider the exception of 14.4, 14, where ἀπόστολος designates, in the plural, Barnabas and Paul, to be a lapse, signalling that the author is conscious of the apostolic title accorded to Paul, yet decides not to attribute it to him.

a word identified with the gospel (1.5) and interpreted as a 'mystery' (μυστήριον, 1.26); this mystery, hidden since the ages and now made manifest, and of which Paul is the privileged recipient, is not simply 'Christ', but rather 'Christ among you' (ἐν ὑμῖν, 1.27).[21] The category of the μυστήριον, fundamental in Colossians (1.26, 27; 2.2; 4.3), finds its ultimate concrete expression in the presence of the gospel among the nations, of which the existence of the Colossian church is a sign. The letter to the Ephesians brings to the μυστήριον its ecclesiological interpretation. The mystery, which was made known to Paul through revelation (3.3), is always the 'mystery of Christ', but its contents are described in 3.6: 'the Gentiles have become fellow heirs, members of the same body, and sharers in the promise in Christ Jesus through the gospel'. Ephesians thus brings out the ecclesiological implications of 'Christ among you' of Colossians: it concerns the creation of the new person distinct from Jews and pagans, and the reconciliation of the two with God in one body by means of the cross (2.15-16 condenses 2.11-22). The 'mystery' is thus none other than the ecclesiological and missiological interpretation of the Pauline gospel. What is significant here is that Paul is not just the recipient of the revelation, but also its divinely authorized herald. He becomes an integral part of the gospel which he announces, since for him it concerns the accomplishment (πληρῶσαι) of the word of God (Col. 1.25). Paul belongs henceforth to the μυστήριον.[22]

This picture changes noticeably in the Pastorals. Paul is the sole author of the letters (contrasted with Col. 1.1) and the sole apostle named in the letters. Paul is the 'chief' (πρῶτος, 1 Tim. 1.15), the *first* among saved sinners, the 'model' (ὑποτύπωσις, 2 Tim. 1.13) of all those who come to faith. He is at the heart of the 'good treasure' (καλή παραθήκη, 2 Tim. 1.14), which Timothy is charged to preserve. Paul thus exhorts Timothy to keep his teaching, his sound doctrine, governing the life of the Church following the model of the Greco-Roman *oikos*: 1 Timothy and Titus are witnesses to this type of household organization, distributing to each category of person (bishop, deacon, elder, widow, slave) his or her place, behaviour, and role. Paul is presented here as the founder and organizer of the Church. The priority he is credited with as πρῶτός (1 Tim. 1.15) is at the same time a temporal priority in the order of conversion, as well as a theological priority inasmuch as it forms a model for believers to come. There is a blatant contradiction with the declaration of 1 Cor. 15.8-9, in which the apostle degrades himself in the face of the first beneficiaries of the paschal appearances, in portraying himself as the ἔσχατον πάντων, the 'last of all', the 'least', the ἐλάχιστος; it is Cephas, in fact, who is recognized as having the status of πρῶτος (1 Cor. 15.5). In reality, however, a tension dominates the passage, since Paul affirms in v. 10: 'On the contrary, I

---

21   This is my translation. The phrase ἐν ὑμῖν can also be translated 'within you'.

22   '"Paul" himself now belongs to the contents of the proclamation, and thus belongs to the "mysterium"' (H. Merklein, 'Paulinische Theologie in der Rezeption des Kolosser- und Epheserbriefes' in *Paulus in den neutestamentlichen Spätschriften* [K. Kertelge {ed.}; QD, 89; Freiburg: Herder, 1981], pp. 25–69 [29]). A difference between Colossians and Ephesians is perceived in the measure to which the Paul of Colossians is solely authorized to proclaim the mystery (Col. 4.4); no reference being made to the common apostolic tradition. By contrast, the μυστήριον in Eph. 3:5 is revealed 'to his holy apostles and prophets by the Spirit'.

worked harder than any of them (περισσότερον αὐτῶν πάντων ἐκοπίασα).'
There is a tension between the posteriority of Paul (the ἔσχατον πάντων) and his
claim of a more efficacious grace having been given to him. Paul never presents
himself as the first in a line, and Ephesians portrays him as 'the very least of all the
saints' (Eph. 3.8). The argument of preeminence, well known to have been widely
diffused throughout popular philosophy, is thus inverted between 1 Cor. 15.5 and
1 Tim. 1.15, just as the Petrine priority of 1 Corinthians 15 is transposed upon Paul
in 1 Timothy.[23] It appears to me that the Pastorals radicalize the Pauline paradox of
1 Corinthians 15. In simplifying it from the 'more than' (περισσότερον) of 1 Cor.
15.10, which becomes the dominant element, they thus construct the type of 'first
sinner'/'first saved'. The theological foundation is certainly maintained: in any case
the action comes from God, in 1 Corinthians (cf. 15.10a) as in 1 Timothy (cf. the
divine passive ἠλεήθην, 'I received mercy' in 1.13, 16).

Second Timothy, which occupies a singular place at the heart of the Pastorals,
distinguishes itself by a biographical anchorage that certifies Paul's teaching, in
contrast to 1 Timothy and Titus. Its image of the author, imprisoned and preaching
in Rome (2 Tim. 1.17), recalls the final scene of Acts 28.30-31 in order to present
the situation in which the letter speaks; it thus clearly envisions the time after Paul.
The apostle's forced inactivity explains the unstable situation of the Church, in
which former collaborators work without remaining reliable; it is in this fragile
period of succession that 2 Timothy intervenes. The network of Paul's collaborators
is extensively named (1.5, 15-18; 2.17; 3.12-13; 4.9-21). Those who abandoned
him (1.15; 4.9-10) are contrasted with those who have remained faithful to him
(1.16; 4.11). The Pauline tradition here mixes the data from the epistles and from
Acts with its own data, with a concern to draw together the 'doctoral' pole and the
'biographical' pole.[24]

From the integration of Paul into a chain of witnesses (Acts) to the position
of the founder of the Church (Pastorals), one sees an evolutionary line forming
whereby Paul receives a progressively more hieratic status. The Deutero-Paulines,
which attribute to the apostle the function of mediating a 'mystery' (Colossians/
Ephesians), occupy a median position in this development. This is accentuated even
more if one moves on to the *Acts of Paul*, a writing attributed by Tertullian to an
elder who was an admirer of Paul (though a poorly inspired author, according to
Tertullian; cf. *De Baptismo* 17.5). This text helps us to see the superimposition of
the figure of Christ onto that of the apostle.

There is no lack of examples. Led to the theatre to be burned, Thecla looks
around for Paul and sees 'the Lord sitting in the form of Paul'; the moment she
fixes her eyes upon him, he departs into heaven (*Acts of Paul* 3.21 [*NT Apocrypha*,
ed. Schneemelcher, trans. R. McL. Wilson]). Paul had been previously driven from

23   With M. Wolter, *Die Pastoralbriefe als Paulustradition* (FRLANT, 146; Göttingen:
Vandenhoeck und Ruprecht, 1988), pp. 51–56.
24   Is this conjunction of poles an indication that 2 Timothy was drafted before the other
Pastorals in a time when the memory of Paul was yet vital, or (rather) the sign that the writing of
2 Timothy testifies to a late inclination to harmonization between the different poles of Pauline
reception?

the city, and it is Christ who borrows his appearance in order to reassure Thecla before the ordeal. Later, when Paul is imprisoned before being handed over to wild beasts, he prays to God to be delivered. A miracle occurs: the doors of the prison open, the guards are asleep, and here 'a young man resembling the body of Paul, lighting [the way] not with a lantern, but with the radiance of his body, preceded them until they reached the sea' (9.20). It is Christ in the guise of Paul who guides them to deliverance.

Let us note how subtle the process is. Jesus is not confused with Paul but bears his traits. The conviction that the Lord intervenes through him is so strong that it generates an unclear image: is it Paul who acts, or rather Jesus? We perceive here the emergence of a stage of veneration of the apostle attained towards the middle of the second century: Paul is no longer the disciple, the apostle, but the saint, the blessed; his image rejoins that of Christ to the point of temporarily fusing with it. By successive shifts, Christ is absorbed by the divine sphere, and the apostle tends to identify with the Saviour. In terms of the biographical itinerary of the *Acts of Paul*, the apostle is decapitated by order of Nero. After his execution, he appears before the emperor and his court: 'Caesar, behold, here is Paul, the soldier of God; I am not dead but live' (14.6 [trans. J. K. Elliot]). Paul's return to life duplicates the miracle of Easter, and his resurrection becomes a proof which confounds the incredulous pagans. From his status as mediator, the apostle has become a source of revelation.

Finally, this growing concentration on the uniqueness of Paul suggests to me that the different roles accorded to the apostle correspond to the diverse 'faces' of Paul's own self comprehension. Each pole of Pauline reception made concrete a potential that is present in the writings of the apostle. The placement of Paul in a chain of witnesses (Acts) and his secondary status with respect to the apostolic foundation (Ephesians) corresponds to the position of the apostle in 1 Cor. 15.5-11, where he aligns himself in last place after Cephas, after the circle of the Twelve and a series of witnesses, as the last of the apostles. Paul declares himself to have been preceded by an apostolic tradition. But when the Pastorals construct the figure of the founder of the Church, they validate a tradition which developed out of other declarations by Paul: those in which he declares himself to be the beneficiary of a revelation which owes nothing to human mediation, a direct revelation from Jesus Christ (Gal. 1.11-12); those in which Paul presents himself as father (1 Thess. 2.11) or mother (1 Thess. 2.7) of the community; those in which he declares himself the 'good aroma of Christ' (2 Cor. 2.15) for the Church. At the same time, in this conflict with the Christians of Galatia, Paul does not hesitate to refute all possibility of 'another gospel', one other than the one he proclaims and which is confused with 'the gospel of Christ' (Gal. 1.6-7). The image of Paul contained in his letters is neither smooth, nor uniform. One encounters in it this ambivalence of Paul being at once situated in a tradition which precedes him and at the same depicted as the origin of a movement which arises from his gospel. The history of reception amplified this ambivalence even as it constructed equally divergent images of the apostle.

b. The Suffering of the Apostle

The Christological foundation given to the suffering of the apostle, and thereby to the suffering of the community, is a fundamental theological structure of Paul's theology. This foundation is made concrete by the category of 'sharing'/'solidarity' (κοινωνία): 'to know Christ and the power of his resurrection and the sharing (κοινωνίαν) of his sufferings by becoming like him (συμμορφιζόμενος) in his death' (Phil. 3.10). The participial phrase, συμμορφιζόμενος τῷ θανάτῳ αὐτοῦ, offers commentary on sharing in the sufferings of Christ; the present tense signals that it does not apply to baptism, but rather to the trials of the apostolic life. Thus the apostolic condition is the place of a double experiment, at once of the power of the resurrection (under the eschatological horizon – Phil. 3.11) and of the conformity to the suffering destiny of Christ. The same semantic field of death/resurrection appears in 2 Cor. 13.4, in which the structural parallelism aligns the destiny of the apostle with that of Jesus:

> For he was crucified in weakness, but lives by the power of God. For we are weak in him, but in dealing with you we will live with him by the power of God.[25]

The same category of κοινωνια is applied to the suffering of believers. The Christians of Corinth were 'sharers (κοινωνοί)' in the sufferings (2 Cor. 1.7); they endured 'the same sufferings' (2 Cor. 1.6). The apostolic suffering constitutes the horizon of understanding for the community's own suffering, in the same way that the suffering of Christ constitutes the horizon of understanding for the suffering of the apostle.[26] This double correlation of community/apostle and apostle/Christ is explicit in the verses that refer to 'imitation': 'And you became imitators of us and of the Lord' (1 Thess. 1.6 [NRSV]; see 1 Cor. 1.11).

What is to become of this Christological foundation of the apostolic suffering in Pauline reception?

Let us look at the Deutero-Paulines. In its construction of the image of Paul the prisoner, the letter to the Ephesians retained the image of the suffering of the apostle 'for the sake of you Gentiles' (Eph. 3.1). But the Christological dimension is to be found, rather, in the famous formula of Col. 1.24: 'I am now rejoicing in my sufferings for your sake, and in my flesh I am completing what is lacking in Christ's afflictions for the sake of his body, that is, the church.' The well-known difficulty with this verse arises from the fact that it seems to postulate an insufficiency with the salvific work of Christ, which contradicts the Christological hymn of 1.15-20.

---

25 This conformity to the suffering of Christ returns under a changed terminology: the παθήματα τοῦ Χριστοῦ are profusely assigned to the apostle (2 Cor. 1.5); he bears in his body the νέκρωσιν τοῦ Ἰησοῦ (2 Cor. 4.10); he bears the στίγματα τοῦ Ἰησοῦ (Gal. 6.17). These genitives possess a qualitative value: it is the participation in the suffering of Jesus which is the irrefutable marker of the apostolate and which guarantees its authenticity (2 Corinthians 10–13). This communion with the destiny of the Crucified One assures within the life of the community the salvific dimension of the cross: 'So death is at work in us, but life in you' (2 Cor. 4.12).

26 M. Wolter, 'Der Apostel und seine Gemeinden als Teilhaber am Leidensgeschick Jesu Christi: Beobachtungen zur paulinischen Theologie', *NTS* 36 (1990), pp. 535–57 (551).

Without wishing to explore the complex problem of this verse, at the same time semantic and theological, I will limit myself to two remarks in order to justify my reading of Col. 1.24:

Νῦν χαίρω ἐν τοῖς παθήμασιν
ὑπὲρ ὑμῶν
καὶ ἀνταναπληρῶ τὰ ὑστερήματα τῶν θλίψεων τοῦ Χριστοῦ ἐν τῇ σαρκί μου
ὑπὲρ τοῦ σώματος αὐτοῦ, ὅ ἐστιν ἡ ἐκκλησία

On the one hand, this verse is composed of two parallel phrases: one is concerned with the sufferings 'for your sake', the other with the afflictions 'for the sake of his body, that is, the church'. We are thus outside the ecclesiology of Paul, which understands the local community as a concretization of the body of Christ. This leads us, however, to conclude that the lack of these afflictions does not characterize the engagement of the apostle Paul as witness of Jesus in the world for the church of the Colossians only, but rather for the universal Church conceived as a cosmic entity. On the other hand, the syntactical order places ἐν τῇ σαρκί μου after τὰ ὑστερήματα τῶν θλίψεων τοῦ Χριστοῦ. The deficit does not affect Christ's afflictions themselves, but rather their presence in Paul's flesh; it is in Paul's story that they still have to be accomplished.[27] Moreover, θλῖψις, according to Paul, always designates the tribulations of the apostle and of his churches. In brief, Colossians takes over the Pauline structure of apostolic engagement as participation in the sufferings of Christ, but gives to it an extension which corresponds to the universal dimension of its ecclesiology.

In the Pastorals, 2 Timothy alone creates the image of a suffering Paul. From the outset, Timothy is exhorted as a co-sufferer with Paul for the gospel (2 Tim. 1.8); he is thus invited to engage in a life of trials, for which the model is the apostle (1.12). But the most interesting passage is 2.11b-13, which establishes a correlation between the destiny of suffering and the eschatological sanction he will receive. This is a traditional piece, formed out of elements which are themselves already composite; through its structure it recalls the sentence from Q 12.8-9, and by the use of συναπεθάνομεν, it echoes Rom. 6.8: 'If we have died with him (συναπεθάνομεν), we will also live with him (συζήσομεν); if we endure, we will also reign with him (συμβασιλεύσομεν); if we deny him, he will also deny us...'

The Pauline *koinonia* is present in the constructions with the prefix συν-, but how does it relate to the Christological foundation? The context of 2.8-13 indicates that the interpretive key to this credo resides in Paul's situation: his suffering permits the salvation of the elect (2.10). The reference to salvation history has thus changed: the suffering has become the passion of Paul for the Church; it permits the verification of the eschatological correlation of the solidarity. It is the apostle's committed existence that lends credibility to our passage, and one notices here the

---

27   Here I take up the reading proposed by J.-N. Aletti, *Saint Paul. Épître aux Colossiens* (EtB, 20; Paris: Gabalda, 1993), pp. 134–37.

point at which the paradigmatic status conferred upon the apostle exercises strong influence on Christology.[28]

Up to this point we have noticed that Colossians 1 maintains the Christological foundation of the apostle's suffering, while 2 Timothy 2 evokes it without working it out theologically. What is the situation in the Acts of the Apostles? Paul's destiny of suffering is revealed from the very beginning, at the moment of his conversion in Damascus: he is the instrument chosen to 'bear the name' of Christ and to commit himself the path of trials: 'I myself will show him how much he must suffer (παθεῖν) for the sake of my name' (Acts 9.16). Significantly, his conversion is followed immediately (εὐθέως – 9.20) by his preaching activity in the synagogues of Damascus, to which the Jews react by plotting his death (9.23). His flight from Damascus leads him to Jerusalem, where once again, a plot by Hellenistic Jews threatens his life (9.29). The sequence of 9.1-30 is programmatic of Paul's destiny, which passes from the status of persecutor of Christ to that of persecuted witness of Christ. The episode of Antioch of Pisidia (13.13-52) presents the scenario repeated throughout the Pauline mission: an initially favourable reception to his preaching in the synagogue is followed by a second hearing, in which Paul is violently rejected. Luke has reproduced this scenario with a regularity that borders on monotony: at Iconium (14.1-7), at Thessalonica (17.1-9), at Berea (17.10-14), at Corinth (18.1-10), at Ephesus (19.8-10) the schema repeats itself: Paul reaps the hostility of a large part of the synagogue (synthesized under the name οἱ Ἰουδαῖοι), while arousing the interest of the God-fearers and the Greeks. The hostility is not exclusively Jewish, as is to be seen by the riot of the silversmiths of Ephesus (19.21-40). The difficulties encountered are not only proper to Paul; they also affect his collaborators, Silas, Jason, Sosthenes, or Alexander: all of them participate in Paul's distress.

At first glance, the Christological foundation of these trials appears to be absent, because it is not formulated. Methodologically, it is not recommended that one analyze a narrative theology in the same way that one would an argumentative theology. Luke does not make explicit in Acts the Christological foundation, but rather gives it meaning narratively; our attention must therefore do justice to the tools at the narrator's disposal to accomplish this task. I recall that Vielhauer based his analysis only upon the discourses in Acts, neglecting the narrative frame; this methodological error further contributed to the one-sidedness of his reading. The process which the author of Acts sets into motion may be perceived in the final sequence of the book, chs 21–28, in which Paul is no longer the missionary founder of communities, but rather a witness on trial.[29] Following his arrest in Jerusalem (Acts 21) until his arrival in Rome (Acts 28), Paul is the imprisoned witness called to defend his own innocence. The author of Acts has multiplied the apologies of Paul: before the people of Jerusalem (Acts 22), before the Sanhedrin (Acts 23), before Felix (Acts 24), before Agrippa and his court (Acts 26), before the Jewish delegation to Rome (Acts 28). Now, throughout this sequence, he has also multiplied

---

28   On this text, see Y. Redalié, *Paul après Paul. Le temps, le salut, la morale selon les épîtres à Timothée et à Tite* (MdB, 31; Genève: Labor et Fides, 1994), pp. 193–99.

29   M.-E. Rosenblatt, *Paul the Accused. His Portrait in the Acts of the Apostles* (Collegeville: Liturgical Press, 1995).

analogies with the passion of Jesus. Paul finds himself alone, facing the people who want his death (21.36; 22.22), just as Jesus found himself alone. Paul appears before the Sanhedrin, before the Roman authorities, and before King Agrippa (Acts 21.40–26.32), just as Jesus appeared before the Sanhedrin, before Pilate, and before King Herod (Lk. 22.66–23.25). Paul, like Jesus, is accused of propagating a teaching that incites the people, and one which has spread widely (Acts 24.5; Lk. 23.5). On three occasions, Pilate finds Jesus innocent (οὐδὲν εὑρίσκω αἴτιον, Lk. 23.4; οὐδὲν ἄξιον θανάτου, 23.15; οὐδὲν αἴτιον θανάτου, 23.22); on three occasions, a Roman authority affirms Paul's innocence (μηδὲν δὲ ἄξιον θανάτου ἢ δεσμῶν, Acts 23.29; μηδὲν ἄξιον αὐτὸν θανάτου, Acts 25.25; ἀπολελύσθαι ἐδύνατο, Acts 26.32). The cry of the crowd clamouring for the death of Paul (αἶρε αὐτόν, Acts 21.36; αἶρε ἀπὸ τῆς γῆς τὸν τοιοῦτον, Acts 22.22) echoes the cry of the crowd at the Passion (αἶρε τοῦτον, Lk. 23.18).

Luke has utilized a narrative device which, through an intertextual echo internal to his work, triggers in the reader a memory of the gospel. The *synkrisis* between Jesus and Paul makes it understood that the destiny of the witness duplicates that of his master. Thus, contrary to appearances, the Christological foundation of Paul's suffering is preserved in this testimony of the 'biographical' pole, namely Acts. The narration suggests it rather than describing it, and it is up to the reader to make the connection between these two parts of Luke's work, Acts and the Gospel.[30]

As for the *Acts of Paul*, the superimposition of the figure of the apostle upon that of Christ, already discussed earlier, verifies this. The announcement of the apostle's martyrdom is made by Christ himself: 'Paul, I am going to be crucified once again' (*Acts of Paul* 13.2; author's trans.). The *koinonia* tends towards identification. The devotion owed to the apostle erases the distance between the Lord and his servant.

c. Teaching: Luke and Paul

I return, in this final section, to the face-to-face meeting with which I began: Luke and Paul. How can one identify the reception of Pauline theology in the Lukan image of Paul? How should one evaluate the Paulinism in the theology that Luke attributes to Paul in Acts? My line of thinking began by rejecting an immediate face-to-face connection between the letters of the apostle and the text of Acts, in order to envision Luke constructing his portrait of Paul on the basis of narrative traditions about his life. I see Luke as an investigator, a reporter, a curious individual collecting, throughout the course of his numerous voyages, the memory of the founding apostle preserved in the communities. It would not surprise me if Luke belonged to a movement of evangelists perpetuating not only the memory, but also the missionary practice of their hero. The question that surfaces at this point is how to know what access to Paul's theology Luke had at his disposal.

---

30   I have developed elsewhere the idea that the unity of Luke-Acts is realized as a result of work suggested by the narrator but which is actualized by the reader: 'Luc-Actes: une unité à construire' in *The Unity of Luke-Acts* (ed. J. Verheyden; BETL, 142; Leuven: Leuven University Press, 1999), pp. 57–81; see also D. Marguerat, *The First Christian Historian. Writing the "Acts of the Apostles"* (SNTSMS, 121; Cambridge: Cambridge University Press, 2002), pp. 43–64.

The terminological contacts with his letters, one remembers, are not numerous. Besides the terms already noted,[31] several Pauline theological formulae arise during Peter's discourse with Cornelius (10.34b-35, 43b) concerning the impartial God and the pardon granted by faith in Christ, and in Paul's homily at Antioch of Pisidia (13.38b-39) concerning the Law's incapacity to save.[32] Pauline formulae are thus present, but without the wording of the letters; this is too meagre to speak of intertextuality. I see in this that Luke is not a reader of letters, but rather that he depends upon a summary, a sort of *epitome* of Paul's theology, from which he draws adequate formulae. This is the same Luke who adequately summarizes the first preaching of the converted Paul at Damascus with the words 'to proclaim Jesus is the *Son of God*' (9.20; author's trans.). The project of Luke's Paulinism should thus be re-opened on this basis. By way of conclusion, let me sketch this evaluation of Acts as reception of Paul in three areas: soteriology, the relationship to Israel, and Christology.

Concerning *soteriology*: the declaration of Acts 13.38 regarding the pardon of 'all those sins from which you could not be freed by the Law of Moses' shows that Luke upholds the disqualification of the Torah as a way to salvation; Acts 15.9-11 confirms this. Acts 10.34-35 and 10.43 attest that salvation by faith is accorded to whoever believes, regardless of religious status. One knows that the verb form of justification is nowhere more present in the NT than in Luke-Acts (7 occurrences of δικαιόω: Lk. 7.29; 7.35 [par. Mt. 11.19]; 10.29; 16.15; 18.14; Acts 13.38, 39). But it is most important to take note of the passages about the impossibility of justification by the Law and about the impartiality of God that have been inserted in Acts in strategic places: on one hand, Peter's discourse with Cornelius (10.34-43), on the other hand, Paul's programmatic homily at Antioch of Pisidia (13.16-41); they are in each case followed by their ecclesiological consequences, in which one finds the typical Pauline articulation between justification and ecclesiology. Upholding the Mosaic *ethos* by the Lukan Paul (Acts 28.17) and his attachment to the customs of his ancestors bear witness to the fact that the Torah assumes here the function of identification. It marks the continuity between Israel and the Church; and for Luke, Christianity is unimaginable without this visible continuity. The role allotted to the Law is for the purpose of identification; it no longer has theological relevance.

Concerning the *relationship to Israel*, I do not consider the Lukan position to be significantly different from that which Paul defends in Romans 9–11. It is a matter of stating differently an idea that was previously expressed. That the promises of salvation are destined to the elect and that Jesus is the saviour of Israel (Acts 13.23) are the constant affirmation of the discourses in Acts addressed to Jews (cf. Rom. 9.4-5). That Israel has rejected the Messiah that God destined for it (Rom. 10.1-4) is confirmed in the final scene of Acts by citing Isa. 6.9-10 (Acts 28.26-27). That salvation destined 'to the Jew, then to the Greek' is translated

---

31   See above, pp. 76–77.

32   Acts 10.34b-35 approximates Rom. 2.10-11, but ἐργαζόμενος δικαιοσύνην is not Pauline. In Acts 10.43b, only the final formula finds an analogy in Rom. 1.16; 3.22; 10.11. Acts 13.38b-39 can be seen as parallel to Gal. 2.16, with the exception of the negative οὐκ ἐξ ἔργων νόμου.

into the narrative scenario of the Pauline mission, which always begins with Paul visiting the synagogue. On the one hand, however, Luke is silent concerning the eschatological salvation of Israel (cf. Rom. 11.25-26); on the other hand, he thinks about the relationship to Israel in the context of a separation unfolding between the Church and the Synagogue, which is not the situation of Paul. This does not prevent Luke from hoping for a Christianity in which both Jewish Christians and gentile Christians may be found, as in the image of Paul at the end of Acts, receiving 'all who came to him' (Acts 28.30).

Without a doubt, on the level of *Christology*, the differences between Luke and Paul are the most spectacular. It is not only the sacrificial dimension that Luke hesitates to assign to the death of Jesus, but a redemptive value: it is the entire life of Jesus, and not the instant of his death, in which Luke recognizes a dimension of redemption (Acts 2.22; 3.26; 10.36-39; 13.23-26). His comprehension of the cross is dominated by the formula of contrast, which opposes the murderous action of humans with the resurrecting activity of God: 'The God of our ancestors raised up Jesus, whom you had killed by hanging him on a tree' (Acts 5.30; cf. 2.23-24; 3.13-15; 10.39-40; 13.28-30). This redemptive value, recognized in the sending of Jesus and in the insistence on the role of human guilt in his death, appears to me to reflect not Paul, but that which is known of the theology of the Hellenists, such as it appears in the discourse of Stephen in Acts 7 (see especially 7.51-53).[33] One would find here the confirmation that the reception of Paul according to Luke is combined with the heritage of Hellenistic Jewish-Christianity.[34]

IV. Conclusion

My concluding reflections are threefold.

a. My proposal to consider the reception of Paul around these three poles should permit the modulation of the relationship with the writings of Paul, depending on whether one is situated in the realm of intertextuality ('doctoral' pole) or of the construction of a biographical memory. It should absolve Acts from the undue burden of having to justify the Pauline label before the tribunal of the apostle's writings; these have not constituted the norm of knowing Paul.

b. Our acquaintance with the historical Paul should not make us hesitate to take seriously the biographical memory such as it is preserved in Acts. The influence of Paul derived from a practice and from a discourse; the biographical memory

---

33   The understanding of the cross by Hellenistic Christians of Antioch is rather marked by a theology of providence and martyrdom (D. Boyarin, *Dying for God. Martyrdom and the Making of Christianity and Judaism* [Stanford: Stanford University Press, 1999]). I owe this reference to F. Bovon, 'La mort de Jésus en Luc-Actes. La perspective sotériologique' in *"Christ est mort pour nous." Études sémiotiques, féministes et sotériologiques en l'honneur d'Olivette Genest* (ed. A. Gignac and A. Fortin; Sciences bibliques - Études/Instruments, 14; Montréal: Médiaspaul, 2005), pp. 370–71.

34   J. Pichler, *Paulusrezeption in der Apostelgeschichte* (Innsbrucker Theologische Studien, 50; Innsbruck, Tyrolia, 1997), pp. 314–54.

has preserved for us the recollection of his missionary practice rather than of his discourse.

c. Every phenomenon of reception implies coherence *and* displacement, continuity *and* discontinuity with respect to the original. At what point did the reception of Paul abandon coherence to break with its model, if not in fact betray it? Every exegete must also respond to this question.[35] I offer an invitation to do so, under two conditions: on the one hand, verifying our understanding of who Paul was, while, on the other, recognizing the necessity and legitimacy of the phenomenon of reception.

35   On this subject, read the clarifying proposals of U. Luz, 'Rechtfertigung bei den Paulusschülern' in *Rechtfertigung. Festschrift E. Käsemann* (Tübingen: Mohr Siebeck, 1976), pp. 365–83.

Chapter 6

PAUL'S PLACE IN EARLY CHRISTIANITY

Christopher Mount

I. Constructing Early Christianity

About 185 CE Irenaeus produced a five-volume treatise, *Against Heresies*, in which he compared the perverse speculations of heretics to the teachings of the apostles preserved by the Church. To defend his construction of a normative Christianity, Irenaeus was the first church father to compare the Paul of a collection of Pauline letters with the Paul of the Acts of the Apostles:

> If, then, any one shall, from the Acts of the Apostles, carefully scrutinize the time concerning which it is written that [Paul] went up to Jerusalem on account of the fore mentioned question, he will find those years mentioned by Paul [in Galatians] coinciding with it. Thus the statement of Paul harmonizes with, and is, as it were, identical with, the testimony of Luke regarding the apostles.[1]

Luke was according to Irenaeus a companion of Paul and the one responsible for recording the gospel preached by Paul. The Paul of the New Testament was thereby created, and this Paul along with the Jesus of four apostolic Gospels established for Irenaeus the historical foundation for the Church and the gospel. 'For the Lord of all gave to His apostles the power of the Gospel, through whom also we have known the truth.'[2]

This late second-century comparison between the representation of Paul in a collection of Pauline letters and the representation of Paul in the Acts of the Apostles established a canon, an apostolic tradition, and a history of the Church that continue to shape subsequent reconstructions of early Christianity. In 1950 Philipp Vielhauer

---

1   *Haer.* 3.13.3 (*ANF* 1:437). *Si quis igitur diligenter ex Actibus apostolorum scrutetur tempus de quo scriptum est ascendisse Hierosolymam propter praedictam quaestionem, inueniet eos qui praedicti sunt a Paulo annos concurrentes. Sic est consonans et uelut eadem tam Pauli adnuntiatio quam et Lucae de apostolis testificatio.* Text from the critical edition by Adelin Rousseau and Louis Doutreleau, *Irénée de Lyon. Contre les hérésies. Livre III* (2 vols.; Sources Chrétiennes; Paris: Les Éditions du Cerf, 1974).

2   *Haer.* 3. preface (*ANF* 1:414). *Etenim Dominus omnium dedit apostolis suis potestatem Euangelii, per quos et ueritatem.*

raised once again the question of the theological ideas of the author of Acts in relation to the ideas of Paul.

> The following discussion poses the question whether and to what extent the author of Acts took over and passed on theological ideas of Paul, whether and to what extent he modified them. (I refer to the author of Acts as Luke, for the sake of brevity and in order to identify him with the author of the Third Gospel. I do not hereby equate him with the physician and companion of Paul whom tradition has identified as the author of the two-volume work, Luke and Acts.)[3]

The parenthetical qualification situates Vielhauer's investigation within the tradition of Irenaeus's construction of Christian origins and the canon. To be sure, what in Irenaeus's comparison of the Paul of the letters to the Paul of Acts was construed as one and the same (mediated by 'Luke the companion of Paul') has become difference for Vielhauer, but the frame of Irenaeus's canon still determines Vielhauer's construction of early Christian history and the questions he asks about Paul's theological ideas. Vielhauer summarizes his comparison of Paul in Acts to the undisputed Pauline letters with an assessment of the place of the author of Luke-Acts in the development of early Christianity: '[T]he author of Acts is in his Christology pre-Pauline, in his natural theology, concept of law, and eschatology, post-Pauline.'[4] He goes on to conclude:

> With the presuppositions of his historiography [the author of the Third Gospel and the Acts] no longer stands within earliest Christianity, but in the nascent early catholic church. His concept of history and his view of earliest Christianity are the same as theirs; whether he gave these views to them or received from them is a question whose answer could be attempted only on the broad basis of a New Testament and patristic investigation.[5]

With this conclusion and final query Irenaeus's opponents, along with what they have to say about Paul and the gospel, have become merely an unexpressed periphery around 'the earliest congregation', 'Paul', and the emergence of the 'nascent early catholic church' assumed in Vielhauer's comparison.[6] Despite what

---

3   Philipp Vielhauer, 'On the "Paulinism" of Acts' in *Studies in Luke-Acts* (ed. Leander E. Keck and J. Louis Martyn; Philadelphia: Fortress Press, 1980), p. 33 [reprinted as ch. 1 of this volume, pp. 3–17]. On the theology of 'Luke' see also Hans Conzelmann, *The Theology of St. Luke* (trans. Geoffrey Buswell; Philadelphia: Fortress Press, 1982); Ernst Haenchen, *The Acts of the Apostles: A Commentary* (trans. Bernard Noble, Gerald Shinn, Hugh Anderson, and R. McL. Wilson; Oxford: Basil Blackwell, 1971).

4   'On the "Paulinism" of Acts', p. 48 [this volume, p. 17].

5   'On the "Paulinism" of Acts', p. 49 [this volume, p. 17].

6   This unexpressed periphery is easily ignored because it has materially largely disappeared. In Vielhauer's introduction to the history of early Christian literature, the apocryphal Gospels are allotted approximately 80 pages and the apocryphal acts approximately 25 pages. In contrast the New Testament writings are allotted almost 600 pages (*Geschichte der urchristlichen Literatur: Einleitung in das Neue Testament, die Apokryphen und die Apostolischen Väter* [Berlin: Walter de Gruyter, 1975]). The selective forces created by Irenaeus's canon are all too easily overlooked. For

is already an implied negative assessment of the tradition about Luke in his opening sentences (the author of Luke-Acts is not Luke the companion of Paul, a tradition constructed by Irenaeus's theological interests to unite representations of Paul in the letters and in Acts), Vielhauer does not go beyond Irenaeus's correlation of these texts with the history of early Christianity.[7] Irenaeus's construction of centre and periphery remains unchallenged. The Pauline letters alongside the Acts of the Apostles still occupy a privileged position for understanding the history of early Christianity.

Vielhauer's comparison of these New Testament representations of Paul belongs to a discourse about the history of early Christianity that began in the second century and continues to the present, a discourse that correlates a history of early Christianity with a canon of Pauline texts framed by the Acts of the Apostles. An answer to Vielhauer's final query, a question posed in such a way as to give prominence to the New Testament in the investigation of early Christianity, can only be answered in light of an evaluation of the construction of early Christianity that has been built on the canonically determined comparison of representations of Paul established by Irenaeus. An answer requires a consideration of the construction of Paul's place in early Christianity both as an ancient project and as a modern project.

---

example, as part of an argument to defend the basic reliability of the tradition about the Gospels and Acts reported by Irenaeus, Martin Hengel rejects the idea that the process of canonization by the 'mainstream' church imposed order on what was previously 'an almost "chaotic" diversity'. He goes on to comment: 'Here no sufficiently clear distinction is made between *textual criticism*, which is founded on the uniquely broad manuscript tradition of the text in antiquity, and the modern *literary criticism*, which investigates behind the text that has been handed down and thus seeks to clarify the origin of the works of the New Testament literature which came into being before the manuscript tradition which has come down to us, but as a rule works in a much more hypothetical way than textual criticism, which is based solely on textual evidence and above all on manuscripts' (*The Four Gospels and the One Gospel of Jesus Christ: An Investigation of the Collection and Origin of the Canonical Gospels* [trans. John Bowden; Harrisburg: Trinity Press International, 2000], p. 30). The selected nature of this 'uniquely broad manuscript tradition' is evident in the fate of Marcion's canon. None of the texts in Marcion's canon can be reconstructed from the manuscript tradition. Kurt and Barbara Aland comment, 'These insights gained from the history of the canon are fundamental and of vital significance for the history of the text—New Testament textual criticism has traditionally neglected the findings of early Church history, but only to its own injury, because the transmission of the New Testament text is certainly an integral part of that history' (*The Text of the New Testament: An Introduction to the Critical Editions and to the Theory and Practice of Modern Textual Criticism* [2nd ed.; trans. Erroll F. Rhodes; Leiden: Brill and Grand Rapids: Eerdmans, 1989], p. 49). On the apologetic interests served by comparisons involving early Christianity, see Jonathan Z. Smith, *Drudgery Divine: On the Comparison of Early Christianities and the Religions of Late Antiquity* (Chicago: University of Chicago Press, 1990), pp. 36–53.

7   On Vielhauer's assessment of the author, see also *Geschichte der urchristlichen Literatur*, p. 406: 'Daß der Verfasser der Apg und des Lk kein Reisegefährte des Paulus gewesen sein kann, haben wir gesehen ... Es kann also auch nicht Lukas, der Arzt (Kol 4,14), gewesen sein.'

II. Irenaeus

In *Against Heresies* Irenaeus assigns a history to various teachings and practices associated with followers of Jesus. The ideas and practices of the heretics 'spring from Simon, the father of all heretics'.[8] The proclamation of the true gospel forms the tradition 'which originates from the apostles, and which is preserved by means of the successions of presbyters in the Churches'.[9] Irenaeus of course was not the first to construct a history of Christian origins that went beyond a life of Jesus to define the gospel. Marcion preceded him by several decades, as did the author of Luke-Acts.[10] However, Irenaeus was the first to use what came to be the core of the New Testament – four Gospels, the so-called Acts of the Apostles, and a collection of Pauline letters that included the Pastorals – for such a history. In Book 3 of *Against Heresies* the key text for Irenaeus's defence of a canon of four Gospels alongside a collection of Pauline letters is the Acts of the Apostles, a text that prior to Irenaeus was of little significance but after Irenaeus became the anchor for the emerging canon of a Jesus of four (apostolic) Gospels and a Paul of thirteen (or fourteen) letters alongside the Paul of Acts.[11] For Irenaeus the Acts of the Apostles demonstrates that all the apostles proclaimed the same gospel. Therefore, a collection of four apostolic Gospels (against the perverse Gospels of the heretics, *Haer.* 3.11.9) belongs alongside a collection of Pauline letters (against those who rejected Paul, *Haer.* 3.15.1) as the apostolic deposit of truth preserved and correctly interpreted by bishops such as Irenaeus himself.

In support of this claim Irenaeus created a history of the apostles by recasting pieces of tradition into a new framework that is both canonical and historical.

---

8   *Haer.* 3. preface (*ANF* 1:414): *a Simone patre omnium haereticorum.* See also *Haer.* 1.23.

9   *Haer.* 3.2.2 (*ANF* 1:415): *quae est ab apostolis, quae per successiones presbyterorum in Ecclesiis custoditur.*

10   The earliest 'Christian histories' were lives of Jesus. Compare Adela Yarbro Collins, 'Is Mark's Gospel a Life of Jesus? The Question of Genre' in *The Beginnings of the Gospel: Probings of Mark in Context* (Minneapolis: Fortress Press, 1992), pp. 1–38. For the authors of the Gospels of Mark, Matthew, John, Thomas, Peter et al., Christian identity is sufficiently determined by the words and actions of Jesus. Luke-Acts is conceptually quite different from these narratives. C. K. Barrett comments on Luke-Acts: 'Luke had to write this book in such a way as to show that the story of the Church was not an independent or spontaneous movement, but the outcome of the life of Jesus' (*Luke the Historian in Recent Study* [London: Epworth Press, 1961], p. 60). This necessity is just what the authors of other accounts of Jesus' words and deeds did not feel. The necessity felt by the author of Luke-Acts to connect the life of Jesus to a history of the church places the author of Luke-Acts conceptually closer to Marcion than to the authors of the other three Gospels in the New Testament. The development in imagining Christian origins that the text of Luke-Acts represents over the texts attributed to Matthew, Mark, and John is too often obscured by the tendency to date Luke-Acts to the first century. See, for example, Hengel, *The Four Gospels and the One Gospel of Jesus Christ*, pp. 186–89.

11   See Christopher Mount, *Pauline Christianity: Luke-Acts and the Legacy of Paul* (NovTSup, 104; Leiden: Brill, 2002), pp. 11–44.

For after our Lord rose from the dead, [the apostles] were invested with power from on high when the Holy Spirit came down [upon them], were filled from all [His gifts], and had perfect knowledge: they departed to the ends of the earth, preaching the glad tidings of the good things [sent] from God to us, and proclaiming the peace of heaven to men, who indeed do all equally and individually possess the Gospel of God. Matthew also issued a written Gospel among the Hebrews in their own dialect, while Peter and Paul were preaching at Rome, and laying the foundations of the Church. After their departure, Mark, the disciple and interpreter of Peter, did also hand down to us in writing what had been preached by Peter. Luke also, the companion of Paul, recorded in a book the Gospel preached by him. Afterwards, John, the disciple of the Lord, who also had leaned upon His breast, did himself publish a Gospel during his residence at Ephesus in Asia.[12]

Irenaeus has taken what he received from Papias about Matthew and Mark and from other sources about John, and he has combined these traditions with his reading of the narrative of Acts and his own deductions about the author of Luke-Acts to establish not just apostolic authorship of these texts but a history of the spread of the gospel from Palestine to Rome.[13] This history becomes the foundation for 'the tradition of the apostles manifested throughout the whole world'.[14] Irenaeus connects his historical account of the composition of the four Gospels to a tradition of apostolic succession at Rome.[15]

Since, however, it would be very tedious, in such a volume as this, to reckon up the successions of all the Churches [this from an author who has spent chapters reciting the tedious details of heresy], we do put to confusion all those who, in whatever manner, whether by an evil self-pleasing, by vainglory, or by blindness and perverse

---

12   *Haer.* 3.1.1 (*ANF* 1:414). Eusebius, *Hist. eccl.* 5.8, quotes part of this passage: ὁ μὲν δὴ Ματθαῖος ἐν τοῖς Ἑβραίοις τῇ ἰδίᾳ αὐτῶν διαλέκτῳ καὶ γραφὴν ἐξήνεγκεν εὐαγγελίου, τοῦ Πέτρου καὶ τοῦ Παύλου ἐν Ῥώμῃ εὐαγγελιζομένων καὶ θεμελιούντων τὴν ἐκκλησίαν· μετὰ δὲ τὴν τούτων ἔξοδον Μάρκος, ὁ μαθητὴς καὶ ἑρμηνευτὴς Πέτρου, καὶ αὐτὸς τὰ ὑπὸ Πέτρου κηρυσσόμενα ἐγγράφως ἡμῖν παραδέδωκεν· καὶ Λουκᾶς δέ, ὁ ἀκόλουθος Παύλου, τὸ ὑπ᾽ ἐκείνου κηρυσσόμενον εὐαγγέλιον ἐν βίβλῳ κατέθετο. ἔπειτα Ἰωάννης, ὁ μαθητὴς τοῦ κυρίου, ὁ καὶ ἐπὶ τὸ στῆθος αὐτοῦ ἀναπεσών, καὶ αὐτὸς ἐξέδωκεν τὸ εὐαγγέλιον, ἐν Ἐφέσῳ τῆς Ἀσίας διατρίβων.

13   See Mount, *Pauline Christianity*, pp. 29–44.

14   *Haer.* 3.3.1 (*ANF* 1:415).

15   Hengel argues that the source of Irenaeus's information on the composition of the Gospels in *Haer.* 3.1.1 is the Roman archive. He comments, 'In other words Irenaeus, or probably the Roman archive, is amazingly well informed about the circumstances and chronological order of the composition of the Gospels' (*The Four Gospels and the One Gospel of Jesus Christ*, p. 39). Hengel cites with approval Claus-Jürgen Thornton, *Der Zeuge des Zeugen: Lukas als Historiker der Paulusreisen* (WUNT, 56; Tübingen: Mohr [Siebeck], 1991). Because Hengel accepts Irenaeus's report in 3.1.1 as ancient, essentially reliable tradition about the Church's four Gospels, he misinterprets evidence for the fluid situation with respect to Gospels prior to Irenaeus. Concerning Eusebius's report in *Hist. eccl.* 6.12.2-6 about Serapion and the Gospel of Peter, Hengel can only express surprise: '[Serapion's] generosity in initially allowing [the Gospel of Peter] to be read in worship is amazing' (*The Four Gospels and the One Gospel of Jesus Christ*, p. 13). In book 3 of *Against Heresies* Irenaeus is creating a history and a canon that did not previously exist.

opinion, assemble in unauthorized meetings; we do this, I say, by indicating that tradition derived from the apostles, of the very great, the very ancient, and universally known Church founded and organized at Rome by the two most glorious apostles, Peter and Paul.[16]

The perversity of those who assemble in unauthorized meetings is thus precisely defined in relation to a theory of Christian history and canon proposed by Irenaeus at the end of the second century.

The tradition of Peter and Paul at Rome is not the perspective of the texts and traditions that Irenaeus incorporated into his Gospel canon and apostolic history. Papias neither places Peter and Mark at Rome nor does he provide any geographical or temporal information about Matthew.[17] The author of Luke-Acts does not bring Peter to Rome.[18] The text Irenaeus attributes to Matthew leaves Peter on a mountain in Galilee; the Gospel according to John ends with Peter alongside the Sea of Galilee.[19]

Rather, this tradition of Peter and Paul at Rome aligns Irenaeus with those leaders in early Christianity who found value in what Walter Bauer identified as the slogan of the 'orthodox' at Rome in early Christianity.[20] What before Irenaeus was a tradition of the martyrdom of these two apostles at Rome used by leaders at Rome to legitimate their status as successors of the apostles becomes for Irenaeus an anchor for a canon of texts. The tradition of bishops at Rome reported in *Haer.* 3.3 anchors Irenaeus's history of the composition of the four Gospels reported in 3.1 to the authority of the Church to speak for the apostles (3.2.2). The apostolic tradition passed on to the Church by the preaching of Peter and Paul at Rome, defended by the succession of bishops at Rome, and preserved in these four Gospels stands against the heretical Gospels read in 'unauthorized meetings'.[21]

The theological proof for this creative recasting of traditional information about Matthew, Mark, and John in relation to what Irenaeus has to say about Paul, Luke, and the Acts of the Apostles is given by Irenaeus in 3.11.8:

> It is not possible that the Gospels can be either more or fewer in number than they are. For, since there are four zones of the world in which we live, and four principal winds, while the Church is scattered throughout all the world, and the pillar

---

16   *Haer.* 3.3.2 (*ANF* 1:415): *maximae et antiquissimae et omnibus cognitae, a gloriosissimis duobus apostolis Petro et Paulo Romae fundatae et constitutae Ecclesiae.*

17   See Eusebius, *Hist. eccl.* 3.39.

18   Moreover, in Lk. 1.1-4 (compare Acts 1.1-2) the author fails to make the one claim that would be most important for an account of events of the past: he does not claim to be an eyewitness. The author does not claim to be the narrator of the second part of Acts, nor a companion of Paul. On the importance of the claim of a historian to be an eyewitness, compare Josephus, *Jewish War*, 1.1-3.

19   None of Paul's letters place Peter in Rome, but see 1 Pet. 5.13.

20   Walter Bauer, *Orthodoxy and Heresy in Earliest Christianity* (trans. Philadelphia Seminar on Christian Origins; Philadelphia: Fortress Press, 1971), pp. 111-13.

21   See *Haer.* 3.11.9; on Marcion see also 3.13.

and ground of the Church is the Gospel and the spirit of life; it is fitting that she should have four pillars, breathing out immortality on every side, and vivifying men afresh.[22]

Irenaeus thus produced the historical, canonical, and theological innovation that would establish the Paul of the New Testament at the centre of the history of early Christianity.

Irenaeus used the second half of Luke-Acts, which he called the Acts of the Apostles, as proof of the unity of all the apostles and thus of the harmony of his canon of four Gospels alongside the Pauline letters. Two comparisons involving Paul were important to establish the reliability of Acts. First, Irenaeus compares Paul in Acts to the Paul of one of the letters in what was the Marcionite collection of ten Pauline letters, Galatians.[23] Paul's account of his trip to Jerusalem for the council matches the report of the trip in the Acts of the Apostles. The two representations of Paul match up to 'what really happened'.[24]

A second comparison was more important and involved the identity of the author of Luke-Acts in relation to a collection of Pauline letters that included the Pastoral letters. To establish that the author was a reliable companion of Paul, Irenaeus identifies the 'we' narrator of Acts with a certain Luke of his collection of Pauline letters.

But that this Luke was inseparable from Paul, and his fellow-labourer in the Gospel, he himself clearly evinces, not as a matter of boasting, but as bound to do so by the truth itself. For he says that when Barnabas, and John who was called Mark, had parted company from Paul, and sailed to Cyprus, 'we came to Troas' …

As Luke was present at all these occurrences, he carefully noted them down in writing, so that he cannot be convicted of falsehood or boastfulness, because all these particulars proved both that he was senior to all those who now teach otherwise, and that he was not ignorant of the truth. That he was not merely a follower, but also a fellow-labourer of the apostles, but especially of Paul, Paul has himself declared also in the Epistles, saying: 'Demas has forsaken me … and is departed to Thesssalonica; Crescens to Galatia, Titus to Dalmatia. Only Luke is with me'. From this he shows that he was always attached to and inseparable from him. And again he says, in the Epistle to the Colossians: 'Luke, the beloved physician, greets you'. But surely if Luke, who always preached in company with Paul, and is called by him 'the beloved', and with him performed the work of an evangelist, and was entrusted to hand down to us a Gospel, learned nothing different from him [Paul], as

22   *ANF* 1:428. *Neque autem plura numero quam haec sunt neque rursus pauciora capit esse Euangelia. Quoniam enim quattuor regiones mundi sunt in quo sumus et quattuor principales spiritus et disseminata est Ecclesai super omnem terram, columna autem et firmamentum Ecclesiae est Euangelium et Spiritus uitae, consequens est quattuor habere eam columnas undique flantes incorruptibilitatem et uiuificantes homines.*

23   *Haer.* 3.13.3 (quoted above).

24   Compare Rolf Noormann, *Irenäus als Paulusinterpret: Zur Rezeption und Wirkung der paulinischen und deuteropaulinischen Briefe im Werk des Irenäus von Lyon* (WUNT, 2.Reihe, 66; Tübingen: Mohr [Siebeck], 1994), pp. 47–52.

has been pointed out from his words, how can these men, who were never attached to Paul, boast that they have learned hidden and unspeakable mysteries?[25]

Therefore, the representation of Paul in the Acts of the Apostles not only matches up with the representation of Paul in the letters but also is the work of an eyewitness of the apostles. Against those who would either reject Paul or accept only Paul, Luke the author of the Acts of the Apostles demonstrates that Paul proclaimed the same gospel proclaimed by all the other apostles. Paul belongs in the company of all the apostles, who are represented by the Gospels of Matthew, Mark, Luke, and John (*Haer.* 3.15.1). Irenaeus thus creates a canonical 'Paul' and 'Luke' for one form of Christianity at the end of the second century.

In short, Irenaeus's canon of four Gospels alongside a collection of Pauline letters and the Acts of the Apostles is held together by a comparison of the representation of Paul in these texts. This comparison, to adapt the words of J. Z. Smith, has been carried out with 'an overwhelming concern for assigning value, rather than intellectual significance, to the results of comparison'.[26] Irenaeus asserts the sameness of the Paul in these texts and rejects the comparisons of the Marcionites (promoting Paul at the expense of all the other apostles) and those who did not accept Paul (*Haer.* 3.11.9; 3.13; 3.14.1). The Paul constructed by Irenaeus not only established an apostolic history for the Church but also defined Christianity in relation to Judaism and heresy.[27] This definition of Christianity established the Acts of the Apostles and a specific collection of Pauline letters as the centre for constructing Paul's place in early Christianity and relegated 'heresy' to the periphery.

III. Luke-Acts

Irenaeus's juxtaposition of four Gospels with a collection of Pauline letters is neither an obvious outcome of the history of early Christianity nor an innovation that can be entirely attributed to Irenaeus. The structure of Irenaeus's canon of four Gospels and Pauline letters is a development from Marcion's decision to establish a canon of texts as a correlate of a history of early Christianity. This canon and history defined

---

25 *Haer.* 3.14.1. *Quoniam non solum prosecutor sed et cooperarius fuerit apostolorum, maxime autem Pauli, et ipse autem Paulus manifestauit in epistolis dicens.* See 2 Tim. 4.9-11. See also *Haer.* 3.10.1: 'Luke also, the follower and disciple of the apostles' (*ANF* 1:423; *Lucas autem, sector et discipulus apostolorum*). Irenaeus is creating a link between the authorial persona of Lk. 1.1-4 and the 'we' narrator of Acts in terms of a certain Luke mentioned in Paul's letters. Irenaeus is either making these connections on the basis of an otherwise unknown Luke to whom the Third Gospel is attributed or is supplying the name himself on the basis of a comparison of Acts with a collection of Pauline letters that includes the Pastorals. See Mount, *Pauline Christianity*, pp. 39–44.

26 Smith is here commenting on the comparison of Christianity to the religions of late antiquity (*Drudgery Divine*, p. 46).

27 Eusebius explicitly develops the history of the Church along these lines.

the gospel against what for him was heresy.[28] Marcion's canon consisted of one Gospel (apparently a form of the first volume of Luke-Acts that differed from the one used by Irenaeus – see *Haer.* 3.14.4) and a collection of ten Pauline letters. Marcion's claim that only Paul preached the true gospel was tied to his comparison of Christianity to Judaism. The god of the Christians was not the creator god of the Jews. All the other apostles corrupted the true gospel preached by Paul with teachings from the god of the Jews. Marcion's canon thereby elevated Paul at the expense of the other apostles and replaced the Jewish scriptures. The emergence of canon in early Christianity was thus connected to an explicit attempt to define Paul's place in a history of Christianity. For Marcion Paul's place was defined by a negative comparison with Judaism. Irenaeus's canonical Paul was a response to Marcion's canon and apostolic history.

The innovative character of the historical claims made by Irenaeus about Paul is evident in relation to the very texts and traditions Irenaeus used against his opponents.[29] Papias wrote a decade or so before Marcion and supplied Irenaeus with information about Matthew and Mark. As far as can be determined from the fragments of his writings that have survived, Papias presented himself as an authoritative investigator into apostolic tradition. In the preface to his *Interpretations of the Sayings of the Lord* he takes a critical stance toward previous written accounts about Jesus and proposes to remedy deficiencies in them.[30] Unfortunately, the quotations

---

28   For Marcion's role in the formation of the New Testament, see Hans von Campenhausen, *The Formation of the Christian Bible* (trans. J. A. Baker; Philadelphia: Fortress Press, 1972), pp. 147–209.

29   The readiness with which scholars continue to read Irenaeus's canon back into the history of early Christianity before Marcion is testimony to the persuasiveness of Irenaeus's construction of early Christianity preserved in the New Testament, a persuasiveness made more powerful by the effective elimination of the voices of dissent. Hengel, for example, still treats Marcion as a corrupter of 'the εὐαγγέλιον τετράμορφον in one collection in the mainstream church' (*The Four Gospels and the One Gospel of Jesus Christ*, p. 55). The close connection between scholarly restatements of Irenaeus's theory of Christian origins and Irenaeus's apologetic for the religious truth of the gospel is evident in an article by Ben Witherington III, 'Why the "Lost Gospels" Lost Out', *Christianity Today* (June 2004), pp. 26–32. He comments, 'The issue of canon—what books constitute the final authority for Christians—is no small matter. If the critics are correct, then Christianity must indeed be radically reinterpreted, just as they suggest. If they are wrong, traditional Christians have their work cut out for them, because many seekers remain skeptical of claims to biblical authority' (p. 26). Accompanying this article is the following timeline: '110 Papias gives anecdotal information about the four Gospels' [!]; 'c. 130 Four Gospels and 13 of Paul's letters accepted as authoritative in some parts of the church'; 'c. 140 Marcion publishes his truncated "New Testament," inciting the orthodox to establish a New Testament canon'; 'c. 180 Irenaeus the first to mention the four Gospels in the current order'. The *Oxford Dictionary of the Christian Church* (1997) is cited as the basis for the timeline. The tradition established by Irenaeus continues to be useful in contemporary Christian apologetics.

30   According to Eusebius, *Hist. eccl.* 3.39: 'This, too, the presbyter used to say. "Mark, who had been Peter's interpreter, wrote down carefully, but not in order, all that he remembered of the Lord's sayings and doings. For he had not heard the Lord or been one of His followers, but later, as I said, one of Peter's. Peter used to adapt his teachings to the occasion, without making a systematic arrangement of the Lord's sayings, so that Mark was quite justified in writing down some things just as he remembered them. For he had one purpose only—to leave out nothing

of Papias preserved by Eusebius are notoriously difficult to understand, in no small part because Eusebius has imposed his own interests to define the canon on these excerpts in a way that obscures the sense intended by Papias.[31] In any case, Papias appears to be making the claim that his own collection of the sayings of the Lord is superior to that available through certain texts that he connects to Matthew and Mark.

> I shall not hesitate to furnish you, along with the interpretations, with all that in days gone by I carefully learnt from the presbyters and have carefully recalled, for I can guarantee its truth. Unlike most people, I felt at home not with those who had a great deal to say, but with those who taught the truth; not with those who appeal to commandments from other sources but with those who appeal to the commandments given by the Lord to faith and coming to us from truth itself. And whenever anyone came who had been a follower of the presbyters, I inquired into the words of the presbyters, what Andrew or Peter had said, or Philip or Thomas or James or John or Matthew, or any other disciple of the Lord, and what Aristion and the presbyter John, disciples of the Lord, were still saying. For I did not imagine that things out of books would help me as much as the utterances of a living and abiding voice. (Eusebius, *Hist. eccl.* 3.39)

Papias speaks in the first person as an investigator of apostolic traditions passed on by word of mouth. He conceives of his work as preserving the living and abiding voice of Jesus. This apostolic tradition of the words of Jesus has only minimally been organized into an apostolic history in terms of a list of authoritative names. Paul does not figure in this list as an authoritative conveyer of the commandments given by the Lord. Moreover, the written texts of Matthew and Mark carry no authority *as books*. Indeed, Papias suggests his work is better because it is based on what all the apostles said. This persona of an authoritative 'I' investigating apostolic tradition was also adopted by Marcion. Marcion, however, was a collector of texts and proposed a much more comprehensive history for the texts than can be observed in what remains of the writings of Papias.

The author of Luke-Acts like Papias also speaks in the first person as an investigator into apostolic traditions and intends to replace inadequate accounts with a single account (see Lk. 1.1-4; Acts 1.1-2). Unlike Papias but like Marcion, the author of Luke-Acts recognizes the need for apostolic traditions to be grounded in an explicit apostolic history, and Paul figures into this history as a character in a

---

that he had heard, and to make no misstatement about it." Such is Papias' account of Mark. Of Matthew he has this to say: Matthew compiled the *Sayings* in the Aramaic language, and everyone translated them as well as he could.'

Translations by G. A. Williamson, revised by Andrew Louth, *Eusebius. The History of the Church from Christ to Constantine* (London: Penguin Books, 1989).

31 Immediately after excerpting what Papias has to report about Mark and Matthew, Eusebius goes on to say: 'Papias also makes use of evidence drawn from 1 John and 1 Peter ...' (κέχρηται δ' ὁ αὐτὸς μαρτυρίαις ἀπὸ τῆς Ἰωάννου προτέρας ἐπιστολῆς καὶ ἀπὸ τῆς Πέτρου ὁμοίως). Eusebius selected excerpts from Papias to support his own understanding of the canon, not to clarify what Papias had to say about his own work two centuries earlier.

narrative, though not as a voice speaking through a collection of letters. The abiding voice of Jesus needs to be channelled through a history of Christian origins (see Acts 1.1-2).[32]

The 'I' of a Christian intellectual investigating apostolic traditions belongs to the second century. Efforts to construct an explicit Christian history as a correlate to apostolic tradition began to emerge in the second century as part of a larger project to define Christianity in relation to Judaism and paganism.[33] In this project representations of Paul played an important role. To construct a history of Christianity both the author of Luke-Acts and Marcion correlated a single text about Jesus with a representation of Paul. Both therefore oriented their work over against other written accounts of Jesus' life.[34] Marcion connected Jesus and Paul through a canon of written texts set over against Judaism. The author of Luke-Acts, on the other hand, connected Jesus and Paul not through a canonical collection of texts but through a narrative placing Jesus, the twelve apostles, and Paul in a history of the spread of Christianity in the Roman Empire. Both Marcion and the author of Luke-Acts construct the history of early Christianity as authoritative investigators into the traditions of the apostles. Marcion used the tools of a literary critic; the author of Luke-Acts the tools of a historiographer.

In Lk. 1.1-4 the author of Luke-Acts announces his task as a historian to be the narration of fulfilled events.[35] 'Concerning the events that have been fulfilled among us' (περὶ τῶν πεπληροφορημένων ἐν ἡμῖν πραγμάτων) anticipates the words of the resurrected Jesus in Lk. 24.44, 'it is necessary that all that has been written in the law of Moses and the prophets and the psalms concerning me be fulfilled' (δεῖ πληρωθῆναι πάντα τὰ γεγραμμένα ἐν τῷ νόμῳ Μωυσέως καὶ τοῖς προφήταις καὶ ψαλμοῖς περὶ ἐμοῦ), and the words of James concerning the gentile mission in Acts 15.15, 'and the words of the prophets agree with this' (καὶ τούτῳ συμφωνοῦσιν οἱ λόγοι τῶν προφητῶν).[36] The author thereby announces that the events of Christian origins belong to a history of Christianity as a religion.[37]

---

32   The need for such channelling is implicit in Papias' listing of specific followers of Jesus and the apostles.

33   On this larger project see Arthur J. Droge, *Homer or Moses? Early Christian Interpretations of the History of Culture* (HUT, 26; Tübingen: Mohr [Siebeck], 1989). What might be labelled 'proto-apostolic histories' of the type implied by Papias' list of authoritative individuals are present in lists of names of Jesus' followers in Mk 3.13-19; Mt. 10.1-4; Lk. 6.12-16 (cf. Acts 1.12-26); John 1.

34   In Lk. 1.1-4 (see also Acts 1.1-2; compare with the more inclusive ending added to the Gospel of John, Jn 21.25) the author of Luke-Acts establishes an entirely negative comparison with other attempts to construct Christian origins around the life of Jesus. Thus, Justin's 'memoirs of the apostles' (for example, *1 Apol.* 66) are a rejection of these second-century attempts to produce a single authoritative text about Jesus.

35   See Vielhauer, 'On the "Paulinism" of Acts', pp. 47–49 [this volume, pp. 17–18].

36   See also the words of Paul in Acts 13.32. On the theme of divine necessity in Acts see Mark Reasoner, 'The Theme of Acts: Institutional History or Divine Necessity in History?', *JBL* 118 (1999), pp. 635–59.

37   See Hubert Cancik, 'The History of Culture, Religion, and Institutions in Ancient Historiography: Philological Observations concerning Luke's History', *JBL* 116 (1997), pp. 673–95. See also Vielhauer's comment on the historiography of the author of Luke-Acts: '... the significance

Historiography and the ethnography of religion were closely connected in the Greek tradition of writing history.[38] The fifth-century BCE historian Herodotus wrote a history of the Persian wars 'in the hope of thereby preserving from decay the remembrance of what men have done, and of preventing the great and wonderful actions of the Greeks and Barbarians from losing their due meed of glory'.[39] The result was not just a history of events but a comparison of Greek and Barbarian cultures. As part of this project of cultural comparison Herodotus proposed a theoretical model of cross-cultural identifications explained by diffusion.[40] For example, on the relation of Greek and Egyptian gods:

> The Egyptians were also the first to introduce solemn assemblies, processions, and litanies to the gods; of all which the Greeks were taught the use by them. It seems to me a sufficient proof of this, that in Egypt these practices have been established from remote antiquity, while in Greece they are only recently known. The Egyptians do not hold a single solemn assembly, but several in the course of the year. Of these the chief, which is better attended than any other, is held at the city of Bubastis in honor of Artemis. (2.58-59)

> The Bubastis of the Egyptians is the same as the Artemis of the Greeks. (2.137)

Using the same theoretical model of cross-cultural identifications and diffusion, the author of Luke-Acts makes several important comparisons involving Paul to construct Christianity as a religion in the Greco-Roman world.[41]

The author of Luke-Acts explicitly compares to Judaism and paganism the message preached by Jesus, the Twelve, and Paul that defines the origin of Christianity. This comparison to Judaism and paganism involves both a claim of similarity and difference. 'This is what was said through the prophet Joel', announces Peter on the day of Pentecost with reference to the manifestations of the spirit (Acts 2.16).[42] 'Fulfilment' is more than a theological category in the history of Luke-Acts. Fulfilment is a cultural claim: the god of the Christians is the god of the Jews now acting in history in a new but previously anticipated way. Thus, the Paul of Acts begins his preaching in every city in

---

of Judaism was relativized to that of a venerable *antiqua religio*' ('On the "Paulinism" of Acts', p. 49 [this volume, p. 17]. Reasoner's criticisms of Cancik establish too sharp a distinction between divine necessity and institutional history ('The Theme of Acts', pp. 635–59). For the author of Luke-Acts, the church as an institution is a divine necessity.

38   Cancik, 'The History of Culture, Religion, and Institutions in Ancient Historiography', pp. 682–94. See also the detailed discussion of Gregory E. Sterling, *Historiography and Self-Definition: Josephos, Luke-Acts and Apologetic Historiography* (NovTSup, 64; Leiden: Brill, 1992), pp. 1–310.

39   Herodotus, *The Persian Wars* (trans. George Rawlinson; New York: Random House, 1942), 3. The following translations are taken from this edition.

40   See Smith, *Drudgery Divine*, pp. 45–56; *idem*, *Map Is Not Territory: Studies in the History of Religions* (SJLA, 23; Leiden: Brill, 1978), pp. 243–49.

41   On Christians in the narrative of Acts, see Acts 11.26; 26.28.

42   See also Lk. 24.44-49; Acts 15.15.

the synagogue.[43] A similar cultural claim is also made in relation to paganism. 'What you worship as unknown, this I proclaim to you' the Paul of Acts declaims to the Athenians (Acts 17.23). He goes on to assert, 'In him we live and move and exist, as also some of your poets have said: "For we too are his offspring"' (Acts 17.28; see Lk. 3.38).[44] The god of the Christians is also the god worshipped in ignorance by pagans in the past. The Christ-cult proclaimed by Paul is the fulfilment of pagan culture.[45] Nevertheless, this Christ-cult departs from Judaism and paganism over the issue of temple worship. The controversy in Acts 19.23-40 in relation to a pagan temple anticipates the uproar in Jerusalem in 21.27–22.30 in relation to the Jewish temple: Paul's announcement of Jesus historically relativizes temple worship.[46] In what might be characterized as the author's history of religions of antiquity, temple worship represents a cultural misunderstanding of the deity, whether Jewish or pagan. This misunderstanding at its worst is connected to mob action. In Luke-Acts Paul speaks for a culturally enlightened worship of a god who does not dwell in temples. The Paul of Acts is a literary construct that serves the interests of the author to define Christianity as a religion for an educated, enlightened audience.[47] The author has created a cultural map to place Christianity in the Greco-Roman world. As part of this literary construct Paul belongs to a history that is defined by the life of Jesus (who is an educated, enlightened Jew; compare Lk. 4.16-30 with Mk 6.1-6) and his twelve apostles.[48] The Jesus of volume one of the author's work becomes the presupposition for the Christ-cult proclaimed by Paul in volume two. The Paul of Acts is not, however, defined by an authoritative collection of letters.[49] Nor is the Paul of Acts defined in relation to an apostolic collection of Gospels.

In short, the author of Luke-Acts, Marcion, and Irenaeus all constructed histories of Jesus, the apostles, and Paul that placed the message proclaimed by Paul alongside one or more written accounts of the life of Jesus. Paul became a character in the attempts of second-century Christian intellectuals to imagine an apostolic past.

---

43 See for example Acts 17.1-3, which contrasts with how Paul describes the background of the participants in the Christ-cult in 1 Thess. 1.9-10. A community of Jews would not be characterized as former worshippers of idols.

44 To the extent that the poets were considered to be inspired by the Muses, the author of Luke-Acts is appealing to 'inspired' texts of pagan culture in the same way he has appealed to 'inspired' texts of Jewish culture.

45 Vielhauer, 'On the "Paulinism" of Acts', p. 37; see also pp. 48–49 [this volume pp. 5–6].

46 Compare Acts 7.1-53.

47 See Mount, *Pauline Christianity*, pp. 103–104.

48 The status of Jesus in Mark as a fatherless, uneducated artisan has been transformed in Luke-Acts to the status of an educated, respected teacher whose connection to the community is established by his father.

49 See comments below on Steve Walton, *Leadership and Lifestyle: The Portrait of Paul in the Miletus Speech and 1 Thessalonians* (SNTSMS, 108; Cambridge: Cambridge University Press, 2000).

IV. Paul and Magic

The form of early Christianity associated with Paul can be characterized as a spirit-possession cult.[50] Paul established communities of those possessed by the spirit of Jesus. Paul can speak of an individual having the spirit of Christ (for example Rom. 8.9 – εἰ δέ τις πνεῦμα Χριστοῦ οὐκ ἔχει οὗτος οὐκ ἔστιν αὐτοῦ)[51] or Christ being in an individual (for example Rom. 8.10-11 – εἰ δὲ Χριστὸς ἐν ὑμῖν).[52] In much the same way, other early Christian texts describe individuals as having a demon (for example Mk 3.22 – ἔλεγον ὅτι Βεελζεβοὺλ ἔχει),[53] or a hostile spirit can be said to be in someone (for example Mk 1.23 – καὶ εὐθὺς ἦν ἐν τῇ συναγωγῇ αὐτῶν ἄνθρωπος ἐν πνεύματι ἀκαθάρτῳ).[54] In the context of such beliefs about spirit possession, certain behaviours were identified as possession phenomena.[55] Just as possession by hostile spirits can be manifested by speech (for example Mk 1.24 – τί ἡμῖν καὶ σοί, Ἰησοῦ Ναζαρηνέ;),[56] so too the spirit that possesses members of Paul's communities is thought to enable the speech of those in the community (see especially 1 Corinthians 14 on prophesying and speaking in tongues). The power to do miracles/magic and exorcisms is also identified as possession phenomena: for example Mk 3.22 – ἔλεγον ὅτι Βεελζεβοὺλ ἔχει καὶ ὅτι ἐν τῷ ἄρχοντι τῶν δαιμονίων ἐκβάλλει τὰ δαιμόνια;[57] Gal. 3.5 – ὁ οὖν ἐπιχορηγῶν ὑμῖν τὸ

---

50   See Christopher Mount, '1 Corinthians 11:3-16: Spirit Possession and Authority in a Non-Pauline Interpolation', *JBL* (2005), pp. 313–40. For a useful model of spirit possession, see I. M. Lewis, *Ecstatic Religion: A Study of Shamanism and Spirit Possession*, (3rd ed.; London and New York: Routledge, 2003); see also John Ashton, *The Religion of Paul the Apostle* (New Haven and London: Yale University Press, 2000). Alan F. Segal has discussed Paul's religious experiences under the category of Jewish mysticism (*Paul the Convert: The Apostolate and Apostasy of Saul the Pharisee* [New Haven and London: Yale University Press, 1990], pp. 34–71). See also Colleen Shantz, *Paul in Ecstasy: The Neurobiology of the Apostle's Life and Thought* (Cambridge: Cambridge University Press, 2009). On spirit possession and magic in the Jesus tradition, see Morton Smith, *Jesus the Magician* (San Francisco: Harper & Row, 1978). Stevan L. Davies comments on spirit possession in Paul in the context of possession phenomena associated with Jesus (*Jesus the Healer: Possession, Trance, and the Origins of Christianity* [New York: Continuum, 1995], pp. 176–87). On trance experiences in the narrative of Acts see John J. Pilch, *Visions and Healing in the Acts of the Apostles: How the Early Believers Experienced God* (Collegeville, MN: Liturgical Press, 2004).

51   'If anyone does not have the spirit of Christ, this person does not belong to him.'

52   'If Christ is in you.' The plural ὑμῖν refers to the community of possessed *individuals* – see v. 9. See also, for example, 1 Thess. 4.8; Gal. 3.5.

53   'They were saying, "He has Beelzebul."' Compare Jn 10.20.

54   'And just then there was in their synagogue a man possessed by an unclean spirit' – an unclean spirit that can be forced to leave (ἐξελθε ἐξ αὐτοῦ, v. 25). Compare Lk. 4.33: ἄνθρωπος ἔχων πνεῦμα δαιμονίου ἀκαθάρτου. See also Mk 5.1-13, a story in which spirits relocate their residence.

55   Lewis puts well the prerequisite for the analysis of spirit possession as a social phenomenon: 'Let those who believe in spirits and possession speak for themselves!' (*Ecstatic Religion*, p. 25).

56   'Leave us alone, Jesus of Nazareth!' Compare Mk 5.5; see also Lucian, *The Lover of Lies*, 16.

57   'They were saying, "He has Beelzebul and by the ruler of the demons he casts out demons".'

πνεῦμα καὶ ἐνεργῶν δυνάμεις ἐν ὑμῖν.[58] For Paul this possessing spirit produces a transformation of moral behaviour (see for example Gal. 5.16-25 – λέγω δέ, πνεύματι περιπατεῖτε καὶ ἐπιθυμίαν σαρκὸς οὐ μὴ τελέσητε)[59] in the context of a spiritual battle that protects the members of the community from the power of Satan (see 1 Cor. 5.1-13). Such possession phenomena may have involved trance (for example visions, 2 Cor. 12.1-3; speaking in tongues, 1 Cor. 14.2, 23; perhaps prophesying, 1 Cor. 14.30; ascents to heaven, 2 Cor. 12.1-10) but not necessarily (for example 1 Cor. 12.28: ἀντιλήμψεις, 'helpful deeds'; κυβερνήσεις, 'administrative roles'). Whether or not such possession phenomena occurred in a trance, the essential point in characterizing Paul's communities as spirit-possession cults is their belief that individuals within the community had come under the control of a spirit. In this discourse of spirit possession, those who believed acted as ones possessed by a deity.[60] First Corinthians 14.26-33 describes the meeting of such a possession cult.

Through Paul's itinerant performances of the power of spirit possession, he offered those who believed an opportunity to participate in such performances. For his pagan audiences, to turn from idols to serve the living God is to be possessed by the deity that works miracles through Paul – that is, to be possessed by Jesus.[61] At least some of the pagans who form Paul's earliest communities have likely abandoned participation in possession phenomena associated with pagan gods.[62] In

58   'The one who gives you the spirit and works miracles among you.' See also Rom. 15.19; 1 Cor. 12.9-11.

59   'I say, walk by the spirit and do not satisfy your physical desires.' See also Rom. 8.9-17.

60   Compare Gal. 2.20, ζῶ δὲ οὐκέτι ἐγώ, ζῇ δὲ ἐν ἐμοὶ Χριστός ('I no longer live, but Christ lives in me'); see Lewis, *Ecstatic Religion*, p. 57 (citing K. Stewart, 'Spirit-possession in native America', *Southwestern Journal of Anthropology* 2 [1946], p. 325); Davies, *Jesus the Healer*, pp. 22–42.

61   Compare 1 Thess. 1.5 (τὸ εὐαγγέλιον ἡμῶν οὐκ ἐγενήθη εἰς ὑμᾶς ἐν λόγῳ μόνον ἀλλὰ καὶ ἐν δυνάμει καὶ ἐν πνεύματι ἁγίῳ – 'our gospel did not come to you by word only but also by power and by holy spirit') with 1 Thess. 1.9 (πῶς ἐπεστρέψατε πρὸς τὸν θεὸν ἀπὸ τῶν εἰδώλων δουλεύειν θεῷ ζῶντι καὶ ἀληθινῷ – 'how you turned to God from idols to serve the living and true God'); 1 Thess. 4.8 (τὸν θεὸν τὸν καὶ διδόντα τὸ πνεῦμα αὐτοῦ τὸ ἅγιον εἰς ὑμᾶς – 'the god who gives his holy spirit to you'; see also Gal. 3.5); Rom. 8.9-11.

62   1 Cor. 12.2-3 contrasts pagans carried away by mute [!] idols and those who speak possessed by the spirit of Jesus. ὅτι ὅτε ἔθνη ἦτε πρὸς τὸ εἴδωλα τὰ ἄφωνα ὡς ἂν ἤγεσθε ἀπαγόμενοι ('that when you were pagans, how you were led astray to mute idols, being carried away') – ὡς repeats ὅτι; ἂν with imperfect is iterative; see BDAG s.v. ἄγω. This contrast is between possession phenomena of pagan religion and the possession phenomena of Christ-cults associated with Paul. The utterance of 12.3 is speech under the control of a possessing spirit. Compare the cautious comments by Conzelmann, *1 Corinthians*, pp. 204–206. Compare also 1 Cor. 14.23 – οὐκ ἐροῦσιν ὅτι μαίνεσθε ('Will they not say that you are mad?'), a question probably intended to characterize possession phenomena within Paul's communities as different from pagan possession phenomena. See Christopher Mount, 'Religious Experience, the Religion of Paul, and Women in Pauline Churches', in *Women and Gender in Ancient Religions: Interdisciplinary Approaches* (Stephen P. Ahearne-Kroll, Paul A. Holloway and James A. Kelhoffer, eds.; WUNT, 263; Tübingen: Mohr Siebeck, 2010), pp. 323–47. Followers of the deities Dionysus (Bacchus) and Cybele for example were well-known for the possession phenomena by which the adherents to the deities acted out their possession by the deities.

these Christ-cults Paul's power to work signs and wonders through spirit possession is replicated in the power this possessing spirit offers to these earliest followers of this new deity.[63] The possession phenomena described in detail in 1 Corinthians 12 and 14 are not an aberration nor unique to Corinth.[64] Such phenomena are constitutive of the Christ-cults associated with Paul. Paul's narration in Galatians of his trips to Jerusalem as an apostle possessed by Jesus (Gal. 1.16, 'revealed his son in me'; 2.2, 20), the account to which Irenaeus appeals to establish that the Paul of the letters and the Paul of Acts are one and the same, subverts the construction of apostolic tradition and ecclesiastical authority created by Irenaeus's canon organized around the Acts of the Apostles. Possession by Jesus not apostolic tradition determined the truth of the gospel (Gal. 2.1-20). In the New Testament, on the other hand, the place of Paul in the development of early Christianity is redefined in relation to apostolic tradition as an expression of ecclesiastical authority.

The close connection between magic and spirit possession in the Greco-Roman world created an interpretive problem for what happened within the church and what happened outside the church. At the beginning of the second century Christianity began to come under increasing scrutiny by educated pagans. Tacitus, Pliny, and Suetonius characterized Christianity as superstition.[65] Celsus, the first

---

Performances associated with spirit possession were also characteristic of oracles. Alexander's oracle for Glycon for example was established on the basis of a performance of possession (Lucian, *Alexander the False Prophet*, 12). The practice of so-called magic often involved possession by a deity (a familiar) by whose power the magician invoked spells. Spells also existed to cause an individual to become possessed by a deity to function as an oracle. The Mithras liturgy invokes a spell that sends the individual's soul on a heavenly journey that leads to a commingling of the soul and the deity (PGM IV.710; compare IV.625-630) and produces a revelation. Paul's performance of signs and wonders through the power of a spirit at his disposal would have been right at home in the cities of the Roman Empire, and his offer of this spirit to his audience would have appealed to anyone persuaded by his performance that this spirit offered relief from the perceived troubles of their daily lives.

63   See for example 1 Thess. 1.5; 2 Cor. 12.12, τὰ μὲν σημεῖα τοῦ ἀποστόλου κατειργάσθη ἐν ὑμῖν ἐν πάσῃ ὑπομονῇ, σημείοις τε καὶ τέρασιν καὶ δυνάμεσιν ('the signs of an apostle were performed among you, signs and wonders and miracles'); Rom. 15.18-19, κατειργάσατο Χριστὸς δι᾽ ἐμοῦ εἰς ὑπακοὴν ἐθνῶν, λόγῳ καὶ ἔργῳ, ἐν δυνάμει σημείων καὶ τεράτων, ἐν δυνάμει πνεύματος θεοῦ ('[what] Christ accomplished through me for obedience of the gentiles, by word and deed, by power of signs and wonders, by power of the spirit of God'); Gal. 3.5; 1 Cor. 12.4-11, including ἐνεργήματα δυνάμεων ('workings of miracles'). Signs and wonders were the currency to be spent to found oracles (Lucian, *Alexander the False Prophet*, 12), to establish the reputation of wandering representatives of various deities (for example Apollonius of Tyana, as reported by Philostratus; Jesus of Nazareth as reported by various Christian Gospels), and to spread the fame of temples themselves (the power of whose gods was proclaimed for example through the dedication to the temple of the deity of various objects in response to miraculous deliverances and healings thought to have been accomplished by the deity).

64   See for example 1 Thess. 5.19, τὸ πνεῦμα μὴ σβέννυτε ('do not suppress the spirit'); compare also Gal. 3.5; Rom. 15.18-19.

65   Tacitus, *Ann.* 15.44.3-8 (*repressaque in praesens exitiabilis superstitio* – 'and the pernicious superstition was checked for a moment' [John Jackson, LCL]); Pliny, *Ep.* 96 (*Nihil aliud inveni quam superstitionem pravam et immodicam* – 'I found nothing but a degenerate sort of cult carried to extravagant lengths' [Betty Radice, LCL]); Suetonius, *Nero* 16.2 (*afflicti suppliciis Christiani, genus hominum superstitionis novae ac maleficae* – 'Punishment was inflicted on the

pagan to produce an extended critique of Christianity, accused its founder of being a magician.[66]

These problems of interpretation and authority associated with miracle and spirit possession were taken up by the author of Luke-Acts in his project to define Christianity in the Greco-Roman world.[67] In Luke-Acts Paul is a spokesman for a religion that stands over against magic (Jewish or pagan – Acts 13.4-12; Acts 19.11-20) and that subordinates spirit possession to the authority of the word proclaimed by the apostles.[68] Paul's stand against magic is anticipated in the narrative of Acts by the story in Acts 8, in which spirit possession and miracle associated with the apostles is distinguished from magic and the possession of a familiar sought by individuals such as Simon.[69] This story is perhaps one of the earliest in the developing Simon legend used by Irenaeus. The powers of Philip, a preacher of Christ (8.5) and worker of 'signs' (σημεῖα, 8.6), are contrasted with the powers of Simon the 'worker of magic' (μαγεύων, 8.9), who proclaims himself (8.9) and works μαγείαι (8.11) in Samaria. In this version of the competition of miracle workers/magicians, even Simon is persuaded by Philip's miracles and is baptized.

This account of the competition between Philip and Simon has been joined in the narrative of Acts to the arrival of Peter's authority in Samaria to place the stamp of the apostolic church upon the spread of the message to Samaria. Peter with John travels to Samaria and the believers receive the spirit through the laying on of hands (8.17). No visible manifestations of the spirit's presence are reported in Acts 8, but Acts 2 has already located possession phenomena under the authority of the apostolic proclamation of the word (2.32-36; cf. 1.8). Nevertheless, Simon recognizes the potential for magical power from this spirit and seeks to gain the power from the apostles with money. In what foreshadows the fate of 'magicians' at the hands of ecclesiastical authority, Peter curses Simon (compare Acts 5.1-11, the fate of Ananias and Sapphira at the hands of Peter as representative of the authority of the apostles). Philip is then transported by the spirit to another location. In this episode as throughout Acts spirit possession functions under the authority of the apostolic preaching of the word. This apostolic authority is defined in terms of a succession from Jesus to the Twelve (see especially 1.8, 15-26; compare Lk. 1.1-4).[70] The point of the story in Acts 8 is that proper exercise of the powers of

---

Christians, a class of men given to a new and mischievous superstition' [J. C. Rolfe, LCL]). See Smith, *Jesus the Magician*, pp. 50–53.

66   See Robert L. Wilken, *The Christians As the Romans Saw Them* (New Haven and London: Yale University Press, 1984), pp. 1–30, 94–125.

67   See Acts 26.19-29.

68   Note the implied inadequacy of Apollos as 'burning with enthusiasm' (ζέων τῷ πνεύματι) in relation to the message of Paul. The deficiency in Apollos's message is connected by the author to John the Baptist and corrected by Priscilla and Aquila (18.24-28) and by Paul (19.1-10).

69   This competition between miracle and magic represented by Peter and Simon is developed elaborately in the Acts of Peter. On the problem of magic in Acts see Hans-Josef Klauck, *Magic and Paganism in Early Christianity: The World of the Acts of the Apostles* (trans. Brian McNeil; Edinburgh: T&T Clark, 2000), pp. 119–21.

70   Spirit possession in Acts 10.44-48 (as a sign of the spread of the gospel to the gentiles) is subject to apostolic authorization in 11.1-18 and 15.1-35. Compare 19.1-7, where Paul is operat-

the spirit and miracles occurs within the church under the authority of the apostles. Spirit possession and acts of power outside of the church fall into the realm of magic.

Paul is brought into this construction in Acts 9, 13, and 19. Paul's conversion in Acts 9.1-31 is carefully narrated to subordinate Paul's vision and possession by the spirit (9.17) to the authority of the church (9.6: ἀλλὰ ἀνάστηθι καὶ εἴσελθε εἰς τὴν πόλιν καὶ λαληθήσεταί σοι ὅ τί σε δεῖ ποιεῖν – 'Get up and enter the city, and you will be told what to do', commands Jesus in Paul's vision). Unlike Paul's claims in Gal. 1.15-17, in Acts 9 Paul's commission and spirit possession are mediated by human agents acting on behalf of the church. Paul's authority is derivative of the authority of the apostolic church. In 13.4-12 and 19.11-20 he acts as a representative of this institutional authority as he combats magic. Whatever the author may have known about spirit possession in Christ-cults associated with Paul has been reinterpreted in favour of the author's construction of the authority of (the 'historical') Jesus and the Twelve for the proclamation of the word. Spirit possession has been thoroughly institutionalized in the portrayal of Christianity as a respectable religion in the Greco-Roman world.

The Pastoral Epistles take up the problem of authority and spirit possession as well. Using the literary device of pseudonomy, the author of the Pastorals constructs a representation of Paul in which spirit possession is subordinated to the authority of the church as an institution presided over by a male hierarchy and construed as the bulwark of the truth (1 Tim. 3.25; compare 4.14). The authority of the spirit-possessed believer is limited to prophetic powers bestowed by the laying on of hands by the male leadership of the church (1 Tim. 4.14; cf. 4.1). In the Pastoral letters women (possessed by the spirit? – compare 1 Cor. 14.33b-36 as a gloss to control the possession phenomena of 1 Corinthians 12 and 14[71]) are a threat to proper social order (εὐσέβεια), and community gatherings are characterized by the ordered reading of scripture (compare 1 Tim. 4.13 with 1 Cor. 14.26-31). The Paul of the New Testament has been moved from a periphery characterized by magic and 'uncontrolled' spirit possession to the centre of respectability for religious institutions in the Greco-Roman world.[72]

The problematic relation between the spirit and miracle in the church, on the one hand, and magic and familiars outside the church, on the other, can be seen in two passages from Irenaeus. In the first, Irenaeus characterizes the 'magic' of certain 'heretics':

Thus, then, the mystic priests belonging to this sect [the followers of Simon] both lead profligate lives and practise magical arts, each one to the extent of his ability. They use exorcisms and incantations. Love-potions, too, and charms, as well as

ing under the authority of the council of 15.1-35 (see 16.4). On the role of glossolalia in the gentile mission see Philip F. Esler, 'Glossolalia and the Admission of Gentiles into the Early Christian Community', *Biblical Theology Bulletin* 22 (1992), pp. 136–42.

71   See Mount, 'Religious Experience', pp. 323–47 (341–45).

72   On such respectability see Livy's account of the Bacchanalian affair of 186 BCE (*History of Rome* 39.8-19).

those beings who are called 'Paredri' (familiars) and 'Oniropompi' (dream-senders), and whatever other curious arts can be had recourse to, are eagerly pressed into their service. (*Haer.* 1.23.4 [*ANF* 1:348])

A second passage puts a different spin on such phenomena as they occur within the church as defined by Irenaeus:

In like manner we do also hear many brethren in the Church, who possess prophetic gifts, and who through the Spirit speak all kinds of languages, and bring to light for the general benefit the hidden things of men, and declare the mysteries of God. (*Haer.* 5.6.1 [*ANF* 1:531])[73]

For Irenaeus the spirit is a gift of God if properly bounded within the church that possesses the apostolic deposit of truth;[74] spirit possession outside the properly defined apostolic church is the domain of magicians and heretics.

In the second century, phenomena associated with spirit possession surfaced in Phrygia.[75] The fourth-century church historian Eusebius preserves sources that suggest the way certain like-minded Christian leaders and intellectuals attempted to control this 'outbreak' of 'heretical' spirit possession. According to Eusebius and his sources, genuine possession phenomena belongs under the control of the church as an institution presided over by a male hierarchy preserving the apostolic deposit of truth. There is a sharp distinction between possession phenomena that occur within the church under the control of its leaders and possession phenomena that occur outside the church as a challenge to its leaders. In *Hist. eccl.* 5.3 Eusebius comments:

It was at that very time, in Phrygia, that Montanus, Alcibiades, Theodotus, and their followers began to acquire a widespread reputation for prophecy; for numerous other manifestation of the miraculous gift of God, still occurring in various churches, led many to believe that these men too were prophets. When there was a difference of opinion about them [that is, those manifesting possession phenomena], the Gallic Christians again submitted their own careful and most orthodox conclusions on the question ...

73   Cited by Eusebius, *Hist. eccl.* 5.7, against possession phenomena outside the church associated with Montanism.

74   Irenaeus can thus find a place in the church for what has been called Montanism. Irenaeus comments on the rejection of such phenomena in *Haer.* 3.11.9: 'These things being so, all who destroy the form of the Gospel are vain, unlearned, and also audacious ... . [Some] set aside at once both the Gospel and the prophetic Spirit. Wretched men indeed! who wish to be pseudo-prophets, forsooth, but who set aside the gift of prophecy from the Church; acting like those who, on account of such as come in hypocrisy, hold themselves aloof from the communion of the brethren. We must conclude, moreover, that these men cannot admit the Apostle Paul either. For, in his Epistle to the Corinthians, he speaks expressly of prophetical gifts, and recognizes men and women prophesying in the Church. Sinning, therefore, in all these particulars, against the Spirit of God, they fall into the irremissible sin.' (*ANF* 1:429)

75   The movement was variously labelled but is widely known as 'Montanism' after one of its early leaders. The leadership of this movement included the female prophet Maximilla.

Eusebius claims spirit possession was at home in the church in the second century (he cites Irenaeus to support this claim) just to the extent that differences of opinion about possession phenomena are resolved by careful intellectual inquiry and a consensus of an apostolic orthodoxy. In other words, the manifestations of spirit possession are subject to the consensus of a community of churches and their leaders (who do not necessarily manifest possession phenomena) enforcing ecclesiastical order. Eusebius quotes a letter by Serapion on this point:

> In order that you may know this, that the working of the so-called New Prophecy of this fraudulent organization is held in detestation by the whole brotherhood throughout the world, I am sending you the writings of Claudius Apolinarius, Bishop of Hierapolis in Asia, of most blessed memory. (*Hist. eccl.* 5.19)

Manifestations of spirit possession are subject to the glosses of those writing in service of the true Church, and the genuine succession of prophecy has been institutionalized by a carefully defined ecclesiastical consensus.[76] This consensus of Christianity is a fiction created by Irenaeus's canon and apostolic history constructed to define and marginalize heresy.

V. Paul and the New Testament

The effect of the spell cast by Irenaeus's account of the origins of Christianity – an account in which four Gospels, the Acts of the Apostles and the Pastoral letters establish a fictional history of Paul's place in early Christianity – is evident in the way comparisons between the representations of Paul in the New Testament continue to be carried out. For example, one goal of Steve Walton's monograph *Leadership and Lifestyle: The Portrait of Paul in the Miletus Speech and 1 Thessalonians* is to provide evidence that what he calls the 'Vielhauer/Haenchen view' – that the Paul of Acts and the Paul of the letters are at variance – is overstated.[77] Walton evaluates lexical similarities between Paul's speech in Acts 20.17-35 and 1 Thessalonians on the basis of narrowly defined comparisons. His statistics for the use of key words follow a set formula: word x occurs in the New Testament y times.[78] From this information, Walton draws conclusions based on

---

76   Compare *Hist. eccl.* 5.16 ('[Those possessed by a spirit] were taught by this arrogant spirit to denigrate the entire Catholic Church throughout the world, because the spirit of pseudo-prophecy received neither honour nor admission into it; for the Asian believers repeatedly and in many parts of Asia had met for this purpose, and after investigating the recent utterances pronounced them profane and ejected the heresy. Then at last its devotees were turned out of the Church and excommunicated') and *Hist. eccl.* 5.17 ('For the prophetic gift must continue in the true Church until the final coming').

77   *Leadership and Lifestyle*, p. 213. See Christopher Mount, review of Steve Walton, *Leadership and Lifestyle: The Portrait of Paul in the Miletus Speech and 1 Thessalonians*, *JR* 82 (2002), pp. 100–101.

78   Walton places key words or phrases and synonyms at the top of his hierarchy of connections

how many times the word occurs in Paul's letters (particularly 1 Thessalonians) and Acts (particularly the Miletus speech) in relation to the frequency of the occurrence of the word in the New Testament as a whole. At times, Walton refers to the LXX, but in general he ignores texts outside the New Testament (Christian, Jewish, or pagan). This self-contained lexical environment of the New Testament is a product of Irenaeus's late second-century construction of Christian origins in which comparisons between the representation of Paul in Acts and in his letters establish a self-contained universe determining the relationship of these texts. For example, according to Walton νουθετέω (Acts 20.21) is a 'clearly Pauline' word based on his observation that the word is used six times in Paul and once in Acts but nowhere else in the New Testament. He concludes, 'The occurrence of as clearly Pauline a word as νουθετέω in a Pauline speech points to some understanding by Luke of the vocabulary that Paul used.'[79] The plausibility of such a conclusion rests on the assumption that the New Testament creates a meaningful world to correlate texts and early Christian history. In another comparison Walton analyzes Paul's use of ἐπιστρέφω in 1 Thess. 1.9 in relation to the use of μετάνοια in Acts 20.21 and adopts the Irenaean perspective of sameness in the representations of Paul's religion in the New Testament: 'The equivalence of μετάνοια and ἐπιστρέφω in the two places may be taken as highly likely, given the relative rarity of the terms in the Pauline corpus. Further, both verses speak of the converts having turned to God.'[80] The comparative conclusion of 'equivalence' obscures the difference between the two portrayals of Paul. From what have the converts turned to God? In 1 Thessalonians, the converts have turned from idols to serve the living God, a characterization that defines the converts as gentiles, not Jews or supposed 'God-fearers' connected to the synagogue.[81] In Acts repentance to God is the message proclaimed by both Peter (2.38; 3.19) and Paul (17.30), a message directed at both Jews and gentiles based on their kinship to God (17.29). Such repentance is the proper response of those who, whether Jew or gentile, whether serving God in the temple at Jerusalem or at the altar of the unknown god, return to the living God who is not served in temples. Pagan idolatry does not stand in contrast to Jewish devotion to the one true God. Instead, paganism and Judaism together form the prehistory of Christianity.[82]

Why did converts become participants in Christ-cults associated with Paul? According to Paul, his performance of power and spirit possession was persuasive. Paul was a spirit-possessed worker of wonders (1 Thess. 1.5; see also 1 Cor. 2.1-5; 2 Cor. 12.15; Gal. 3.1-5; Rom. 15.18-19). According to Acts, Paul's followers at Thessalonica were convinced by his preaching in the Jewish synagogues from the Jewish scriptures (Acts 17.1-5; see also 13.13-43; 17.10-12; 18.1-5, 24-28; 28.23). Repentance (Acts 20.21) is the proper response for entry into the religion

---

(*Leadership and Lifestyle*, pp. 44–45).

79   *Leadership and Lifestyle*, pp. 161–62.

80   *Leadership and Lifestyle*, p. 176.

81   For Paul's communities as gentile communities see also Rom. 15.14-19; 1 Cor. 10.14-22; Gal. 1.16; 2.1-10; 3.1-29; Phil 3.3-4.

82   See Vielhauer, 'On the "Paulinism" of Acts', pp. 35–37 [this volume pp. 8–9].

proclaimed by Paul and the other apostles in Acts, a version of Christianity in which miracle is subordinate to proclamation, lest the religion be confused with magic. Only the Irenaean framework for the canon and history of Christianity lends plausibility to Walton's conclusion that ἐπιστρέφω in 1 Thess. 1.9 is equivalent to the use of μετάνοια in Acts 20:21.

Walton's comparison of the representation of Paul in the undisputed Pauline letters and in Acts can be characterized as a literary comparison. David Wenham, 'Acts and the Pauline Corpus: II. The Evidence of Parallels', carries out a historical comparison.[83] That is, he compares the events suggested by the representation of Paul in the undisputed letters to the events represented by Acts. His statement of method is worth citing in full.

> In comparing Acts and the Pauline letters it is possible, on the one hand, to ask broad questions about the portrayal of Paul and his theology in the two traditions. The danger with this approach is that it can be relatively subjective: Luke's portrayal of Paul and Paul's own portrayal of himself can both be construed in all sorts of different ways, and have been so construed. It is possible, on the other hand, to attempt a more detailed historical examination of possible parallels of points of contact and points of tension. This approach also has its dangers, since the details must ultimately be seen not in isolation but in their broad context, and yet it may be preferable to start with some of the detailed groundwork before proceeding to more ambitious analyses. This chapter attempts to do some of that groundwork, going through the Acts narrative, examining possible points of contact and conflict with the Pauline letters, and setting out some of the evidence, issues and options that face the scholar.[84]

This statement of method raises at least one important question. Why are theological comparisons relatively more subjective than a more detailed historical examination? According to Wenham, there is no fixed point to anchor a theological comparison (he presumably leaves aside Irenaeus's assertion that such an anchor is found in the gospel preserved by the Church). Theology can be construed in all sorts of different ways. Historical details, however, have such an anchor, apparently in 'what really happened'. How though is what really happened – history – determined by Wenham?

The language of his historical comparisons is telling. 'The evidence of Acts and the epistles on this period is thoroughly compatible' (p. 217). 'There is nothing here to contradict the Acts account' (p. 220). 'However, it would be absurd literalism to take Paul's remark in Galatians 1:16 to mean that he had nothing to do with any Christians in Damascus when he was converted' (p. 220). 'The references in Acts 9 to Paul's stay in Damascus do not necessarily imply that his stay in the city was very short' (p. 223). 'But it is entirely possible—even probable—that the converted

---

83   In *The Book of Acts in Its Ancient Literary Setting* (ed. Bruce W. Winter and Andrew D. Clarke; vol. 1 of *The Book of Acts in Its First Century Setting*, ed. Bruce W. Winter; Grand Rapids: Eerdmans, 1993), pp. 215–58.

84   'Acts and the Pauline Corpus', p. 216, perhaps with reference to the type of theological comparison carried out by Haenchen and Vielhauer.

Paul will have witnessed to Jews in Damascus on his return from Arabia (if not also while in Arabia), and it is quite likely that they will have responded with hostility' (p. 223). 'However, it is quite possible ...' (p. 224). 'It is also quite possible ...' (p. 224). 'Acts' description of the resulting plot against Paul is not unlikely' (p. 225). 'But there is no significant, proved discrepancy between Acts and the Pauline epistles, and Luke's additions to the Galatians account are historically possible' (p. 226). (How, one might wonder, could a significant discrepancy between Acts and the Pauline epistles ever be proved using this methodology?) 'A plausible reconstruction of events on the basis of the Lukan and Pauline evidence ...' (p. 239). He concludes his comparison of the Paul in Acts with the Paul of the epistles (p. 258): 'Those scholars who consider the picture of Paul in Acts to be historically misleading must appeal to general impressions rather than to proven discrepancies with the epistles. Other scholars will judge that the cumulative evidence suggests that Acts is a well-informed historical narrative.'

What is historically possible, plausible, probable, likely, or certain for Wenham is determined by the canonical history established at the end of the second century by Irenaeus. Wenham is only able to consider such comparisons as less subjective because he has suppressed that 'what really happened' is a reconstruction of history based on the Irenaean construction of Christian origins.[85]

Ernst Haenchen came to quite different conclusions about the similarities and differences between Paul in Acts and Paul in his letters than do Walton and Wenham. Nevertheless, Haenchen assumes the same essential connection between the Acts of the Apostles and the letters of Paul established by Irenaeus's canon and account of Christian origins. On the question of sources for the narrative about Paul in Acts, Haenchen comments:

> When, years after Paul had run his course, Luke set about the task of describing the era of primitive Christianity, various possibilities of collecting the required material lay open to him. He could himself, for example, look up the most important Pauline communities—say Philippi, Corinth, Ephesus, Antioch. He might even visit Jerusalem. But it was also possible for him to ask other Christians traveling to these places to glean for him whatever was still known of the old times (if he was preparing Acts about the year 75, twenty years would not yet have elapsed since Paul's death, and perhaps forty from the foundation of the community in Antioch). Lastly, he could have written to the congregations in question and asked them for information.[86]

On what grounds is this optimistic assessment of information available to the author about Paul plausible?[87] The grounds are the same as those Wenham uses to judge

---

85   With reference to the appointing of elders in Acts 14.23 Wenham comments, 'The church of 1 Cor. may look like an unstructured, charismatic church, but it was founded shortly after that in Thessalonica, and is likely also to have had leaders' ('Acts and the Pauline Corpus', p. 244, n. 67) – lest phenomena associated with spirit possession lead to the wrong impression of 'what really happened' at Corinth.

86   *Acts*, 86.

87   See Bauer's assessment of Paul's legacy at Ephesus (*Orthodoxy and Heresy in Earliest*

what is possible, plausible, likely, and certain in his comparison of representations of Paul in Acts and in the letters: Irenaeus's construction of a historical framework for understanding how Paul and his churches fit smoothly into the development of Christianity. As a result of this framework Haenchen dates Luke-Acts much earlier than is warranted by the authorial persona in Lk. 1.1-4 and Acts 1.1-2 and by the author's decision to correlate a life of Jesus with an account of the history of the church. Although Haenchen, like Vielhauer, rejects the Irenaean tradition of Luke the companion of Paul as the author of Acts, Irenaeus's framework for the history of early Christianity remains in place.[88]

Vielhauer likewise occupies Irenaeus's construction of a historical framework for understanding Paul's place in early Christianity. Vielhauer's comparisons in 'On the "Paulinism" of Acts' assign certain theological ideas to entities and individuals in early Christianity: 'the earliest congregation', 'Paul', 'Luke', and 'the nascent early catholic church'.[89] Constructing differences of theology as temporal and linear allows him to imagine Christianity as a set of ideas developing over time from 'the earliest congregation' to 'the nascent early catholic church'. This development recreates the Irenaean centre and periphery. The ideas of Paul and 'Luke' by implication belong to the centre of this development. The periphery is ill defined. Vielhauer's imagination of how theological ideas can be compared and correlated with actual churches operates within the drastically reduced universe of Irenaeus's polemic against heresy.

The differences Vielhauer identifies between the theology of 'Luke' and the theology of Paul are interpreted Christologically, and for Vielhauer Christology is an idea, and so 'the earliest congregation', 'Paul', 'Luke', and 'the nascent early catholic church' are largely place holders for ideas in the history of Christianity, ideas which for Irenaeus contrast explicitly with heresy on the periphery of the Church. But for Paul, 'Christology' is a possession experience that determines his authority over against other apostles (Gal. 2.11-14).[90] The difference between Paul and Luke is not indicative of development in a line from the 'earliest congregation' to the 'nascent early catholic church' somehow defined by the theology of Paul and Luke. For Vielhauer as for Irenaeus, the history of early Christianity is a history of ideas. And these ideas create a centre and periphery in which the New Testament occupies the centre so that the development from earliest Christianity to the nascent catholic church can be imagined as one of ideas defined by the New Testament.

Christianity, pp. 82–84). On information available to the author about Paul, see Mount, *Pauline Christianity*, pp. 105–162.

88 See *Acts*, 112–16, for Haenchen's comments on the author's relation to Paul.

89 See for example p. 46 [this volume p. 15]: 'Luke also held that the new aeon had broken in … that joins Luke to Paul and separates him from the earliest congregation. But the essential has not yet occurred and will take place only at the parousia, which brings the "restoration" … that joins Luke with the earliest congregation and separates him from Paul.'

90 Vielhauer mentions 'spirit' in relation to the theology of mission in Acts (see pp. 45–46 [this volume pp. 14–15]).

VI. Canon and History

Vielhauer's final question –

> With the presuppositions of his historiography [the author of the Third Gospel and the Acts] no longer stands within earliest Christianity, but in the nascent early catholic church. His concept of history and his view of earliest Christianity are the same as theirs; whether he gave these views to them or received from them is a question whose answer could be attempted only on the broad basis of a New Testament and patristic investigation.

– is predicated on a persistent fiction about Paul's place in early Christianity. Vielhauer's 'Paul', 'earliest Christianity', and 'nascent early catholic church' are historical fictions created around the Paul of the New Testament. The Paul of the New Testament emerged in the second century when Paul became a character in competing constructions of the history of Christianity. The constructions of Christianity offered by the author of Luke-Acts, Marcion, and Irenaeus were also claims to authority among Christian intellectuals in the second century. Irenaeus's version of apostolic history and canon became normative in the New Testament. As a result, the importance of the Acts of the Apostles and a collection of Paul's letters for understanding early Christianity has been exaggerated, and modern comparisons of the representation of Paul in the New Testament continue to be carried out within the historical fiction established by Irenaeus. Representations of Paul in Acts and in the Pauline letters continue to be shuffled around, but the framework used to reassemble these pieces persists. The juxtaposition of the (undisputed) Pauline letters, the Paul of Acts, and the Pastoral letters is a late-second-century contrivance intended to produce a particular interpretation of early Christianity. To advance the interpretation of comparisons of the Paul of the letters and the Paul of Acts, reconstructions of the history of early Christianity need to be freed from the Irenaean construct of centre and periphery around a canon framed by the Acts of the Apostles.

Part II

THE FIGURE AND LEGACY OF PAUL IN THE BOOK OF ACTS

Chapter 7

LUKE'S 'WITNESS OF WITNESSES': PAUL AS DEFINER AND DEFENDER OF THE TRADITION OF THE APOSTLES – 'FROM THE BEGINNING'[1]

David P. Moessner

Any testimony, the further off it is from the original truth, the less force and proof it has ... the more hands the tradition has successively passed through, the less strength and evidence does it receive from them.

[John Locke, *Essay concerning Human Understanding*, IV.16.10][2]

Luke completes his two-volume work in the last decades of the first century CE when the first generation of disciples who had been with Jesus for much of his public ministry have died or are no longer able to give credible witness to their experiences of Christ. At a time when apostolic traditions are proliferating,[3] when Paul's letters are circulating in varying collections and continuing to stir controversy,[4] Luke promotes Paul's emphasis on the rejection and exaltation of Israel's Messiah as *the authoritative* interpretation of *the apostles* among the nascent 'churches' of a growing catholic network.

This thesis is demonstrated by showing how Luke utilizes rhetorical 'methods of elaboration' (ἐξεργασίαι) intrinsic to the conventions of Hellenistic historiographic 'narrative arrangement' (οἰκονομία) to portray Paul as Messiah's chief 'witness'. Because of space restrictions, our treatment of Luke's rhetorical strategies must be more illustrative than thorough. Yet we aim to show that through, I. 'arranging' his material on a 'topic' or 'event' (πραγματικὸς τόπος) to create a 'sequence' (τάξις) according to the criteria of 'disposition' or 'division' (διαίρεσις), Luke establishes 'the continuity of the narrative' (τὸ τῆς διηγήσεως

---

1   A shorter version of this paper was first presented in the 'Acts and Hellenistic Historiography' Seminar of the SNTS in Berlin, August 2010. I am appreciative of the helpful critique.

2   Cited in C. A. J. Coady, *Testimony. A Philosophical Study* (Oxford: Clarendon Press, 1992), p. 199.

3   Note the five volumes of Jesus (and apostle) 'traditions' (λογίων κυριακῶν ἐξηγήσεως) that Papias is able to compile based on what he calls 'the living and enduring voice' (39.4) at the turn of the century or first decades of the second century (Eusebius, *Eccl. Hist*. III.39).

4   2 Pet. 3.16 gives evidence that Paul's letters are being read severally together and, though difficult to comprehend and used to 'distort' the faith, they are, at the time of this writing, being regarded as substantive renderings of the Christ events as are 'the rest of the scriptures'.

συνεχές); and by, II. 'linking' his two volumes together through a 'recapitulatory' 'preface' (προοίμιον), re-configures his first volume on 'all that Jesus began to do and to teach' as the defining template for all that Jesus continues to do and teach through his 'witnesses'; and thus by, III. binding Paul to 'the beginning' (ἡ ἀρχή) of volume two, enfolds Paul into 'the beginning' (ἡ ἀρχή) of Messiah Jesus and 'the Twelve' such that Paul becomes the incomparable, indispensable 'witness' to 'the beginning of the gospel' and, indeed, himself becomes *definitive* of the tradition of 'the Twelve'.

To be sure, identifying Paul as a prime 'witness' of or for 'the gospel' in Luke's second volume is hardly a novel idea. German scholarship in particular of the late-twentieth century drew attention to this signature role and characterization of Paul in Acts in a number of primarily redaction and composition critical studies.[5] Especially, the work of C. Burchard[6] and of V. Stolle[7] should be highlighted. For Burchard, Luke portrays Paul in the critical role of spanning the apostolic kerygma with an equally authentic kerygma for the church's own day toward the end of the first century when the active witness of both the Twelve and of the historical Paul have been eclipsed. As the 'thirteenth witness' to Christ, Paul is given the distinctive task of spreading the apostles' gospel to the gentile world, thus aligning Paul, on the one side, with the authority of the Twelve as apostolic witness by Christ's command, but also, on the other, of establishing for him this unparalleled role in the history of the church's developing testimony.[8] Stolle, on the other hand, showcased the emblematic shape of Paul's 'witness', especially as the second book ends with Paul still suffering, on trial, and whose enduring testimony beckons the church to follow suit.[9] Paul in effect has become the model witness for all Christian readers.[10]

The role of 'witness' for Paul appears to establish an enduring legacy for the one who, ironically, is never singled out as 'apostle' in the Acts. What is distinctive about the following portrayal of Paul as Luke's 'witness of witnesses' is, 1) the elaboration of the standard tropes of rhetoric that Luke engages to

---

5   See especially in this volume (ch. 2), O. Flichy's perceptive tracing of the modern portrayals of Paul as developments from and foils to the influential approach of the 'Tübingen School'.

6   C. Burchard, *Der Dreizehnte Zeuge: Traditions- und kompositionsgeschichtliche Untersuchungen zur Lukas' Darstellung der Frühzeit des Paulus* (FRLANT, 103; Göttingen: Vandenhoeck & Ruprecht, 1970).

7   V. Stolle, *Der Zeuge als Angeklagter: Untersuchungen zum Paulusbild des Lukas* (BWANT, 102; Stuttgart: Kohlhammer, 1973).

8   Similarly, K. Löning (*Die Saulustradition in der Apostelgeschichte* [NTA, 9; Münster: Aschendorff, 1973]) presents Paul as a legitimizing figure for Christians of gentile origin and thus for 'all humanity' in the midst of intra-ecclesiastical tension between Jewish and non-Jewish believers.

9   See also, e.g., W. Radl, *Paulus und Jesus im lukanischen Doppelwerk: Untersuchungen zu Parallelmotiven im Lukasevangelium und in der Apostelgeschichte* (Bern/Frankfurt: Lang, 1975).

10   Cf., e.g., M. E. Rosenblatt, *Paul the Accused: His Portrait in the Acts of the Apostles* (Zacchaeus Studies, NT; Collegeville: Liturgical Press, Michael Glazier, 1995), who traces even more than Stolle how the narrative is extended from Paul the 'accused' to Paul the enduring and model 'witness' on trial at the lengthy end of the narrative.

display the inimitable role that Paul plays in authenticating and extending *the apostolic kerygma of Jesus* to succeeding generations, 2) Luke's interweaving the call of the servant in Isaiah as '*hypotext*'[11] for the calling of Paul as 'witness' to God's eschatological reign over the whole world, and thereby, 3) demonstrating the conclusive 'end' and 'ending' of the two volumes when Paul reaches Rome. Consequently, more than 'the Twelve', it is Paul who bequeaths the Jesus shape of the gospel to the emerging church catholic.

I. 'The Beginning' as Determining the 'Continuity of the Narrative'

a. Polybius of Megalopolis on the 'Economy' of the 'Continuity' of 'Narrative Arrangement'

If by re-conceptualizing poetic *mimēsis* Aristotle conceived a powerful counter-vision to his mentor's attack on the poets' 'license' (and licentiousness!),[12] nevertheless, his attempt in his *Poetics* to erect an unbreachable divide between dramatic prose composition (ποίησις) and *diēgētic* historiography (ἱστόρια) must be deemed a failure. Long before the fourth century, the composed orality of Homeric epic had pervaded the earliest attempts at writing, whether of the pioneering historical accounts of the Ionic logographers or of the later written versions of sophistic oratorical performance so creatively eschewed in Plato's prose 'dialogue'.[13]

This growing interdependence of oral and written expression means, then – to employ Aristotle's wider notion of 'thought' (διάνοια) – that an author's overall purpose for impacting an audience and the selection of a written genre appropriate to that impact had become the basis for the coherence of a text, its unity as a 'work',

---

11 See esp. G. Genette, *Narrative Discourse Revisited* (Ithaca, NY: Cornell University Press, 1988); for the notion of meta-narrative or 'megatext' in which earlier classical narratives (here, e.g., Isaiah) are 'future reflexive' of later events so as to form a 'narrative continuum' in which the later narrator 'in the present has been a narratee in the past' (e.g., 'just as it stands written'), see A. A. Lamari, 'Knowing a Story's End: Future Reflexive in the Tragic Narrative of the Argive Expedition Against Thebes', in *Narratology and Interpretation. The Content of Narrative Form in Ancient Literature* (Trends in Classics – Supplementary Volumes, 4; J. Grethlein, A. Rengakos [eds]; Berlin: W. de Gruyter, 2009), pp. 399–419 (404).

12 Cf., e.g., G. F. Else, *Plato and Aristotle on Poetry* (P. Burian [ed.]; Chapel Hill: University of North Carolina Press, 1986); L. Golden, *Aristotle on Tragic and Comic Mimesis* (American Philological Association American Classical Studies, 29; Atlanta: Scholars Press, 1992), pp. 41–62; W. Trimpi, *Muses of One Mind. The Literary Analysis of Experience and Its Continuity* (Princeton: Princeton University Press, 1983), pp. 17–21, 273–75; K. Eden, *Poetic and Legal Fiction in the Aristotelian Tradition* (Princeton: Princeton University Press, 1986), pp. 25–61; D. A. Russell, *Criticism in Antiquity* (Berkeley: University of California Press, 1981), pp. 102–08: 'His [Aristotle's] assertion that poetry is about "generalitities" (ta katholou), while history is about particular acts of individual people, implies a rebuttal of Plato's denial of the poets' claim to possess or impart knowledge' (108).

13 The extent to which writing was primarily an aide to persuasive speech is striking in Plato's dialogue *Phaedrus*, where Socrates casually refers to a taxonomy of 'souls and corresponding discourses' [271d, e].

and not some rarefied notion of strict causality of the poets over against the 'loose' time frame of the historians.[14] In fact, it is not long after the time of Aristotle before writers of history like Polybius (*c*.202–120 BCE), Diodorus Siculus (fl. Julian period) or Dionysius of Halicarnassus (fl. Augustan period) – each thoroughly immersed in the culture of suasive speech – will conceive their own narrative histories as persuasive, *diēgētic* ποίησις.[15]

This carefully coordinated correspondence between genre and audience impact was, of course, a function of the evolving tropes in this culture of 'rhetoric' that was emerging as a discrete 'school' discipline. Evidence indicates that well before the time of Polybius, a rather sophisticated system of 'arrangement' (οἰκονομία) had developed in an effort to influence or persuade audiences to particular under-standings. A triadic synergy of authorial purpose (τέλος/συντέλεια), realized through discrete forms of the text (ποίησις/σύνταξις) as 'managed' (οἰκονομέω) through 'methods of elaboration' (ἐξεργασίαι), leading to audience approbation of the author's 'understanding' or 'thought' (ἐπιστήμη, διάνοια) is typical of the discussions of *diēgētic* logic and epistemology in the Hellenistic period. Limits of space allow only brief sketches of 'the continuity of narrative arrangement' in the second-century historian Polybius.

While Polybius does not refer to his narrative composing as poetic *mimēsis* à la Aristotle, yet he is the first (extant) composer of multi-volume narrative (διήγησις) to appeal to his narrative organization as an 'arrangement' (οἰκονομία) specifically designed to lead his audience to the proper (sc., authorially intended!) understanding of the events which he recounts. Similar, then, to Aristotle's formu-lation, the historian should portray events of a specific time period as they are known to have occurred in order to provide a reliable picture of 'all the events in their contiguous relationships that happened to one or more persons' (ὅσα ἐν τούτῳ συνέβη περὶ ἕνα ἢ πλείους, ὧν ἕκαστον ὡς ἔτυχεν ἔχει πρὸς ἄλληλα, *Poetics* 23.22-23). But contrary to Aristotle, Polybius will compose his narrative history like a well-constructed epic, as 'converging to the same goal' (*History* I.3.4 [πρὸς ἕν γίνεσθαι τέλος τὴν ἀναφορὰν ἁπάντων]; cf. *Poetics* 23.26 [πρὸς τὸ αὐτὸ συντείνουσαι τέλος]). For it is his bold assertion that never before in the history of the world had events coalesced in this most unusual way to link the world as one and thus produce a 'common history' (καθόλου πραγμάτων, I.4.2[16]). Polybius must, he contends, construct a narrative

14   Cf. Russell (*Criticism in Antiquity*), p. 17: 'the Aristotelian insight that imaginative litera-ture uses discourse in a fundamentally different ("mimetic") way from oratory is either forgotten or set aside'; M. Heath, *Unity in Greek Poetics* (Oxford: Clarendon, 1989), p. 151: 'Aristotle seems to have regarded chronological closure as the equivalent in history to the unified action of epic and drama, the structural *sine qua non* of good order. Later rhetorical theory does not follow him in this.'

15   See, e.g., Dionysius of Halicarnassus, *Pompeius*, §3 in *The Critical Essays* 2.370-85 (LCL; Cambridge, MA: Harvard University Press, 1985).

16   See A. C. Scafuro, 'Universal History and the Genres of Greek Historiography'(unpub-lished doctoral dissertation, Yale University, 1983), pp. 102–15; Polybius refers to his work as *ta katholou*, in contrast to historians who concentrate on limited geographical areas of (a) specific nation(s), who thus write *kata meros*, e.g., *History* I.4.2; III.23.3; V.31.3; VII.7.6; VIII.2.11; XVI.14.1; XXIX.12. Scafuro contends that 'rather than invent a new name—one that represented

that reflects this unity through its own 'narrative arrangement of continuity' (τὸ συνεχὲς τῆς διηγήσεως).[17]

Hence for Polybius, a specific formal 'arrangement' which includes the 'ordering' or 'disposition' of the subject matter is requisite to the particular impact, both noetic and empathic, that the author wishes to convey of his/her own overall grasp and comprehension to the audience. Since 'Fortune' had orchestrated an unprecedented interweaving of events, his history writing must reflect these phenomena through its own 'narrative continuity' (I.5.5).[18] Even through forty long volumes Polybius must create a narrative 'road' that will lead all those who take the journey to comprehend this unparalleled convergence of peoples and affairs. Rather than the tightly-knit 'necessary or probable causality' of the one-action plot of tragedy or epic, the unity of Polybius' composition will be established through a 'continuity of narrative performance' (τὸ συνεχές)[19] which leads the audience to this 'one result' (τέλος).

b. *Diodorus Siculus and Linking, Recapitulatory 'Prooimia'*

To be sure, by the first century BCE rhetoric had become an all-encompassing heuristic for compositional performance, whether of speaking or writing.[20] In this milieu the first-century BCE historian Diodorus Siculus[21] provides some of the most detailed descriptions of how a single plot (τὸ συνεχές) for a multi-volume work should be properly 'partitioned' or 'divided' (διαίρεσις) in crafting a 'sequence' (τάξις) of 'narrative continuity' (τὸ τῆς διηγήσεως συνεχές). What is particularly instructive is Diodorus' notion of a 'complete' or 'completed' volume (αὐτοτελεῖς) that will ensure the cognitive and affective impact that the author is deliberately designing for the targeted audience(s). 'Complete' volumes consist of the full scope of the nexuses of cause and effect of important events of a given period surrounding a ruler or actions of a city/state, which in turn are related to other key movements and developments within the larger work. A volume 'complete in itself' enables readers to 'remember' what is presented because the chains of earlier

---

the fact that its universality was "horizontal" (synchronic) rather than "vertical" (diachronic)—he [Polybius] kept the old names of *koinē historia* and *hē katholou'* (111).

17   All translations are my own, unless otherwise specified; see esp. *History* I.13.9: 'With such an approach there will be no break in the continuity of the narrative (τὸν τρόπον συνεχοῦς γινομένης τῆς διηγήσεως ... ῥηθήσεσθαι) ... this <u>arrangement</u> rendering what follows as <u>intelligible and easy for students</u>' (τοῖς τε φιλομαθοῦσιν ἐκ τῆς τοιαύτης οἰκονομίας εὐμαθῆ καὶ ῥάδιαν) [Greek text from the LCL 1.32 (1922)].

18   Cf., ibid., I.5.5: ὁ συνεχὴς λόγος ('the message/text that continues on ...'), i.e., to its overall goal (τέλος/συντέλεια).

19   Cf., e.g., *Histories* IV.1.8; VI.2.1.

20   See esp. R. L. Enos, *Greek Rhetoric Before Aristotle* (Prospect Heights, IL: Waveland Press, 1993), pp. 91–140.

21   For the relation of Diodorus to previous Hellenistic historians, see esp. Scafuro, 'Universal History ...', pp. 116–54, 205–62; K. S. Sacks, *Diodorus Siculus and the First Century* (Princeton: Princeton Univ., 1990); G. Wirth, *Diodor und das Ende des Hellenismus. Mutmassungen zu einem fast unbekannten Historiker* (Oesterreichische Akademie der Wissenschaften, 600; Wien: Verlag der Oestereichischen Akademie der Wissenschaften, 1993).

causes developed through medial influences and leading to specific outcomes are 'clear' (σαφῆ) and 'uninterrupted for the readers' (τὴν ἱστορίαν εὐμνημόνευτον καὶ σαφῆ γενέσθαι τοῖς ἀναγινώσκουσιν) (XVI.1.1).

But how does an author sustain a 'continuity' of the narrative when the work consists of multiple volumes? How can an audience possibly follow from one volume to the next?

One of the 'methods of elaboration' (ἐξεργασίαι) of historiographic synchronic networking that Diodorus utilizes is 'linking transitions' at the beginnings and endings of each volume, including a 'recapitulatory *prooimion*' for the sequel volume. To make absolutely certain that his audience does not miss the emplotted significations of the 'continuous thread of the narrative', Diodorus inserts at the beginning of each new book a summary capsulation of the previous volume, along with a listing of the main events that will develop out of this prior emplotment.[22] Even beyond that, because of the complex webbings of cause and effect, it is not unusual for him at the end of a volume to include 'metonymic prompts'. By such *aide-mémoire* Diodorus nudges the reader to recall that what the author-narrator had projected must take place, has in fact developed through the linear and lateral connections configured throughout the sequel volume.

For instance, in declaring that he is on task by closing Book XV (XV.95.4) with the events that led up to King Philip, Diodorus announces that Book XVI will begin (ἄρξομαι) with Philip's accession to the throne and incorporate '*all the achievements of this king to his death* (τελευτή), *including in its compass* (συμπεριλαμβάνοντες) *those other events as well which have occurred in the known portions of the world*'. At the same time, Diodorus is echoing the beginning of volume XV where he had announced his scope as *beginning* with the war of the Persians against Evagoras in Cyprus and *ending* with the year preceding the reign of Philip, son of Amyntas (XV.1.6).

Consequently it is no surprise when, at the beginning of the next volume, Book XVI (1.3-6), Diodorus declares, '*Now that I have reached the actions of Philip son of Amyntas, I shall endeavor to include the deeds performed by this king within the compass* (περιλαβεῖν) *of the present Book*.' Even more telling, Diodorus proceeds to summarize the main achievements of Philip by previewing *the scope* and *culminating events* of this new book (e.g., '*he took over the supremacy of all Hellas with the consent of the states*' [XVI.1.4], resulting in '*the greatest of dominions in Europe*' [XVI.1.3], and '*left armies so numerous and powerful that his son Alexander had no need to apply for allies*' [XVI.1.5], etc.). The reader is thus clued in from the very beginning what to expect by way of 'continuity' and 'culmination' for that book. Thus, in order to meet audience expectations, Book XVI must show 'through a continuous thread of the narrative' (XVI.1.6) how and/or why Philip was able to accomplish all of this.

Or again, at the conclusion of Book XVI (95.1), Diodorus summons the line of XVI.1.3, that 'Philip … had made himself the greatest of the kings in Europe',

---

22   *Library of History* II.1.1-3; III.1.1-3; IV.1.5-7; V.2.1; VI.1.1-3; [VII–X]; XI.1.1; XII.2.2-3; XIII.1.1-3; XIV.2.4; XV.1.6; XVI.1.3-6 [cf. XV.95.4!]; XVII.1.1-2; XVIII.1.5-6; XIX.1.9-10; XX.2.3; [XXI–XL]; [] indicate fragmentary books without extant linking passages.

before summing up the causes he purports to have illumined through his narration: more than any previous ruler, Philip excelled in an 'adroitness and cordiality of diplomacy' (XVI.95.2). But this primary characterization stands in stark contrast to the Lacedaemonians whose moral decline and unscrupulous diplomacy, portrayed in Book XV, propelled them into an irreversible forfeiting of their hegemony. The moral point is clear enough. Not only has the continuity of Books XV and XVI driven home Diodorus' intended lesson, but also an overarching 'moral' trajectory for Diodorus' 'universal history' is once again reinforced through the more encompassing narrative vehicle. Predictably enough, Book XVII begins, '*In this Book, by writing down the continuing strands of the narrative* (τὰς συνεχεῖς), *we shall begin the events from the accession of Alexander as king, including the deeds of this king down to his death, and we shall write down also those events which took place together with them* (τὰ ἅμα τούτοις συντελεσθέντα) *in the known parts of the inhabited world*' (XVII.1.2).

To sum up, Diodorus develops intricate interconnections for ensuring audience comprehension, including metonymic prompts to configure new events and circumstances into the more encompassing plot. Or as he himself boasts at the *archē* of Book XVII, 'This is the best procedure, we maintain, that events be remembered, since the narrative is arranged by subject matter and adheres to the continuity from the beginnings to the very end' (τὰς πράξεις εὐμνημονεύτους ἔσεσθαι κεφαλαιωδῶς τεθείσας καὶ συνεχὲς ἐχούσας ταῖς ἀρχαῖς τὸ τέλος) (XVII.1.2)!

c. Polybius, Diodorus, and Dionysius of Halicarnassus on 'the Beginning' of the 'Continuity of the Narrative'

Another essential component or 'method of elaboration' of sustaining 'threads of continuity' through 'disposition'/'division'/'partitioning' is the determination of a *'beginning' point* which will characterize the overall shape and outcome of the narrative 'continuity'. Already Polybius seems to have inherited from the previous generation of history writers an operative assumption that without a clearly marked 'beginning', it is impossible to communicate the meaning of individual events as well as significances of the larger whole that the author wishes to convey. Polybius goes so far as to say:

> **V.32.1-5** For those in ancient times (οἱ ἀρχαῖοι), saying that *the beginning* (τὴν ἀρχήν) is half the whole, would advise that in different matters the greatest effort should be made to make a good beginning (ὑπὲρ τοῦ καλῶς ἄρξασθαι) ... One might rather confidently even declare that *the beginning* (τὴν ἀρχήν) is not merely half of the whole, but *extends all the way to the end* (πρὸς τὸ τέλος διατείνειν). For how is it possible to begin something well (ἄρξασθαί τινος καλῶς οἷόν) without at the same time *encompassing within one's own mind the overarching goal of the entire enterprise* (τε μὴ προπεριλαβόντα τῷ νῷ τὴν συντέλειαν τῆς ἐπιβολῆς), nor knowing its scope nor its relation to other affairs nor the reason for the undertaking in the first place! (μηδὲ γινώσκοντα ποῦ καὶ πρὸς τί καὶ τίνος χάριν ἐπιβάλλεται τοῦτο ποιεῖν)? Or again, how is it possible in any suitable fashion to draw together the events under one heading (συγκεφαλαιώσασθαι πράγματα δεόντως) without

at the same time carrying them along from their beginning (μὴ συναναφέροντα τὴν ἀρχήν), *and understanding from where, how, and why the final situation of the events was brought about* (πόθεν ἢ πῶς ἢ διὰ τί πρὸς τὰς ἐνεστώσας ἀφῖκται πράξεις)? Therefore we should know that *beginnings* (τὰς ἀρχάς) do not only extend half way, but extend to the end, and both *speakers/performers* (τοὺς λέγοντας) and auditors (τοὺς ἀκούοντας) [of a general history] *should take the greatest pains to relate them to their whole(s)* (πλείστην περὶ ταύτας ποιητέον σπουδὴν ... πειρασόμεθα).

It is no exaggeration to say that Polybius views 'the beginning' (ἡ ἀρχή) as decisive in determining the 'character of the whole' (σύνταξις), the larger 'purpose' or 'goal' of the work (τὸ τέλος), and even the 'scope' of the 'plotted continuity' (συντέλεια) – especially as it is determinative in tracing 'cause and effect' for the audience. Without a clearly tagged 'beginning', the audience is lost.

We have already discovered that Diodorus[23] defines 'complete' history narratives as those that develop 'beginning' events through medial occurrences that 'thicken' or lead to 'concluding' events bringing the author's grasp of a larger set of 'cause and effect nexuses' to an 'end' which the audiences can 'follow'. Moreover, Diodorus can also tie a 'beginning point' (ἡ ἀρχή) of a larger work to individual 'beginning points' for each additional volume. Only when the *archē* for each sequel volume organizes the continuity of the developing events surrounding a ruler or actions of a city/state for a limited period can the auditor make sense and follow the author's intended valuation of those events within the narrative's more extensive whole. As a corollary, therefore, an ἀρχή for each volume is an indispensable anchor by which all subsequent causes and effects of particular sequences are to be gauged and compared with the movement of the larger whole.

In Dionysius of Halicarnassus we reach a flowering of ancient criticism[24] in the Hellenistic Greek traditions of speech-making and of narrative historiography[25] that extends into the Augustan period.[26] We shall focus on Dionysius's extensive criticism regarding the proper 'beginning' to a narrative accounting of events, especially as he wields the critic's knife to the corpus of Thucydides' *Peloponnesian War*.

In his most mature critical essay, *On Thucydides*, Dionysius applies the threefold schema of narrative criticism to Thucydides' 'arrangement'/'management' (οἰκονομία) of larger narrative blocks and finds it rhetorically inadequate to

---

23   See note 21.

24   Cf. varying assessments: e.g., S. F. Bonner, *The Literary Treatises of Dionysius of Halicarnassus. A Study in the Development of Critical Method* (Cambridge Classical Studies, V; Cambridge: Cambridge University, 1939), p. 40: 'The rhetorician makes no distinction; all writers for him form a single quarry from which he may draw material for the all-important study of effective public speaking'; D. A. Russell, *Criticism in Antiquity*, p. 54: 'Dionysius comes closer to modern ideas of a literary critic than any earlier writer.'

25   See esp. E. Gabba, *Dionysius and the History of Archaic Rome* (Berkeley: University of California Press, 1991).

26   Cf. G. M. A. Grube, 'Dionysius of Halicarnassus on Thucydides', *The Phoenix* 4 (1950), pp. 95–110 (95): 'We have far more of his [Dionysius'] work than we have from the hand of any Greek critic after Aristotle. Only the writings of Cicero and Quintilian compare with his in bulk.'

the task.[27] Instead of persuading his audience to the proper moral lessons and actions that the Peloponnesian war should make abundantly evident, Dionysius's own 'read' of Thucydides is that he composes a bewildering 'continuity of the emplotted narrative' (τὸ διηνεκὲς τῆς ἀπαγγελίας), especially as he selects both an improper 'beginning' and 'ending' to this larger work. However one judges Dionysius' conclusions, the Halicarnassan taps into the now well-developed criticism of faulty sequence (τάξις) due to infelicitous 'division' or 'partitioning' (διαίρεσις) of the entire narrative:

De Thuc. 9 Wishing to follow a new path, untraveled by others, he [Thucydides] *divided* (ἐμέρισε) his history by summers and winters. This decision produced an outcome contrary to his expectations: the seasonal *division by time periods* (ἡ διαίρεσις τῶν χρόνων) did not lead to greater *clarity* (σαφεστέρα) but to *greater difficulty in following the narrative* (δυσπαρακολουθητοτέρα). It is rather amazing how he failed to realize that *a narrative* (ἡ διήγησις) that is broken up into small sections, which *taken together* are to describe *the many events* (πολλὰ πράγματα) that took place in many different places, will not catch that 'pure light' that 'shines from afar'[28] as becomes obvious from [the following of] the events themselves. As an example from the third book ... he *begins to write* (ἀρξάμενος γράφειν) about the Mytileneans, but before *completing this whole section of the narrative* (ὅλην ἐκπληρῶσαι τὴν διήγησιν), he withdraws to the affairs of the Lacedaemonians. And he does not even round these events off before relating the siege of Plataea. What is more, even this he leaves *unfinished* (ἀτελῆ) in order to recount the Mytilenean War. Then from there *he switches his narrative* (ἄγει τὴν διήγησιν) to the affairs of Corcyra ... . He then leaves this account, too, half-finished (ἡμιτελῆ) ... . What more do I need to say? The *whole* (ὅλη) of the book is chopped up in this way, and *the continuity of the plotted narrative* (τὸ διηνεκὲς τῆς ἀπαγγελίας) is destroyed. As we would now expect, we wander around here and there, *finding it difficult to follow the events that have been described* (δυσκόλως τοῖς δηλουμένοις παρακολουθοῦμεν), *because our mind is confused by the scattering of the events* (ταραττομένης ἐν τῷ διασπᾶσθαι τὰ πράγματα τῆς διανοίας) and cannot easily or *reliably* (ἀκριβῶς) remember *the half-completed references* (τὰς ἡμιτελεῖς ... ἀναφερούσης) which it has heard. Rather, *a history narrative should be a flowing and uninterrupted written account* (τὴν ἱστορικὴν πραγματείαν εἰρομένην εἶναι καὶ ἀπερίσπαστον), especially when it is concerned with a considerable number of events that are difficult to learn about.[29]

Dionysius faults Thucydides for the confused sequence of his narrative that prevents any clear understanding of the lasting significance of the events. The readers cannot 'follow' (παρακολουθέω) the events (πράγματα) and therefore cannot '*reliably*', '*with proper understanding*' (ἀκριβῶς) construe sufficient 'clarity' (σαφήνεια) to

27   For greater detail, see D. P. Moessner, 'The triadic synergy of Hellenistic poetics in the narrative epistemology of Dionysius of Halicarnassus and the authorial intent of the evangelist Luke (Luke 1:1-4; Acts 1:1-8)', *Neotestamentica* 42 (2008), pp. 289-303.

28   Allusion to Pindar, *Pythian Odes*, iii.75 (so S. Usher, trans., *Dionysius of Halicarnassus, Critical Essays* [LCL; Cambridge, MA: Harvard University, 1974] 1.483).

29   Greek text from LCL.

determine their relative importance. Because the interconnections of the 'subject matter' – the relation of each part to other parts in the whole of the narrative – are puzzling, so is any adequate grasp of their meaning as intended by the author. The blame for this falls squarely upon Thucydides himself who should have 'divided up' his subject matter in ways that would render those relationships clear.

Dionysius moves quickly to link Thucydides' inadequate 'partitioning' to his unfortunate choices of 'beginning' and 'ending' points:

> **De Thuc. 10** Some critics also find fault with the *sequence* (τὴν τάξιν) of his [Thucydides'] narrative, complaining that he neither chose the right *beginning* (ἀρχή) for it nor a proper *ending* (τέλος). They say that by no means the least important aspect of *good arrangement* (οἰκονομίας ἀγαθῆς) is that a work should have as its *beginning* (ἀρχήν) the point where nothing necessarily be perceived as preceding it, and that the account should *end* (τέλει) where it appears that nothing further need follow. Because of these considerations, they claim that he [Thucydides] has not paid proper attention to either of these aspects. The historian himself has provided them sufficient grounds for this charge. For after he states right from the start that the Peloponnesian War was of far greater magnitude … than any war that preceded it, he begins to conclude his *prooimion* by wanting first to state the *causes* (τὰς αἰτίας) [of the War] *from which he had determined its beginning* (ἀφ' ὧν τὴν ἀρχὴν ἔλαβε). He lays out two, the true cause, which is not generally spread about (the growth of the Athenian war machine), and that which is not true, the one fabricated by the Lacedaemonians (the sending of the allied forces to aid the Corcyreans against the Corinthians). Indeed, *he does not begin his narrative* (τὴν ἀρχὴν πεποίηται τῆς διηγήσεως) from the true cause, the one which he himself believes, but from that other point.

As we have observed already in Polybius and Diodorus, 'beginning points' organize basic *causes* (αἰτία) which justify the telling and hence the arranging of the plot in the first place. Emplotment without proper causal connections is epistemologically impotent in effecting the desired responses from the audience. In Dionysius's view, Thucydides' audience cannot connect causal consequences of later events to a definitive seminal event and, consequently, also to the fundamental forces that had first coalesced to produce that *beginning* (ἡ ἀρχή).

Dionysius proceeds to quote verbatim several of the paragraphs from Thucydides' text mentioned above, including the description of the Athenians' intolerable building up of armaments, to demonstrate to his own readers how much more effective Thucydides would have been if he had followed true rhetorical wisdom:

> **De Thuc. 11** For he ought to *have stated at the beginning* (ἀρξάμενον) of his inquiry into *the true causes of the war* (τὰς αἰτίας τοῦ πολέμου … ἀποδοῦναι) the cause which he considered to be the true one: for not only is it a natural requirement that *prior events should begin before later ones* (τὰ πρότερα τῶν ὑστέρων ἄρχειν), and true causes be stated before false ones, but also *the beginning of his narrative would have been far more rhetorically productive if he had adhered to such arrangement* (τῆς διηγήσεως εἰσβολὴ κρείττων ἂν ἐγίνετο μακρῷ τοιαύτης οἰκονομίας τυχοῦσα).

Thucydides not only 'begins' his narrative at the wrong point, he also does not know how to 'end' it!

> **De Thuc. 12** His history *does not come to a head at the proper point of completion* (ἔδει κεφάλαια τετελευτηκέναι). For although the war lasted twenty-seven years and he lived the whole time right up to *its conclusion* (τῆς καταλύσεως), he carried his history down only to the twenty-second year by extending the eighth book through the Battle of Cynossema, even though he says in the prooimion that he intends to cover *all* (πάντα) the events which *taken together made up the war* (κατὰ τόνδε τὸν πόλεμον).[30]

By presenting an inadequate scope, Thucydides' conclusion is in-conclusive. The notion of 'narrative wholeness' is striking here, especially as Dionysius describes all the events between the proper 'beginning' and 'ending' points as those 'which taken together made up the war'. When the 'continuity' does not comprehend sufficient *pragmata* to build to a climax through a properly sequenced beginning, middle, and end,[31] the overall impact is destroyed. Hence without *all* the events properly related to the 'whole' of the war, the entire narrative history is unsuitably 'arranged' and therefore rhetorically defective.

With both *archē* and *telos* inappropriately selected, the 'arrangement' is doomed from the start. In the final analysis, poor audience 'management' is the reason Dionysius alleges for Thucydides' weak 'economy'. As we have seen previously, the triadic synergy of the Hellenistic narrative hermeneutic also figures prominently in Dionysius' rhetorical judgements.

d. Conclusion

In Hellenistic narrative composition of sequences of events, a 'beginning point' (ἡ ἀρχή), is crucial in determining *for the audience* the quality and completeness (αὐτοτελεῖς) of the whole, the purpose (τέλος), and even the 'scope of the plotted continuity' (τὸ συνεχὲς μέχρι τῆς τελευτῆς) of the *diēgētic* performance (σύνταξις).

II. 'The from the Beginning Eyewitnesses and Attendants' as Defining Apostolic 'Witness' to 'All that Jesus Began to Do and to Teach' (Lk. 1.2→Acts 1.1)

Luke intends to 'arrange a narrative' that will give his audience 'a firm grasp' of the overarching significance (ἀνατάξασθαι διήγησιν ... ἀκριβῶς καθεξῆς

---

30 Usher in his LCL translation of 1.493 [n. 29] appears not to render κατὰ τόνδε correctly in a distributive sense: 'having expressed his intention in his introduction to *include all the events of the war*' (emphasis mine).

31 Note again how Aristotle's prescription (*Poetics* 7 and 18) for the proper magnitude of 'beginning', 'middle', and 'end' which together emplot a 'new state of affairs' (καταλῦσις/ μεταβολή) is operative.

σοι γράψαι ... ἵνα ἐπιγνῷς περὶ ... λόγων τὴν ἀσφάλειαν) of the 'good news' of the Kingdom of God. This 'reign' embraces the far corners of the world through an enthroned-crucified Messiah of Israel and extends as far as the heart of (the) empire.[32] As a Hellenistic historian,[33] Luke provides a formal 'continuity' of his narrative 'thought' by crystallizing a divine control or 'steering' of world history in a formulation borrowed in part from Isaiah, namely, 'the plan/will (βουλή) of God'.[34] This comprehensive scheme is 'written' in the scriptures and divine oracles of Israel's founding documents and has become in fact a worldwide reality of cosmic or eschatological propor-tions through the events of Messiah Jesus and 'his witnesses'. Luke draws this profile in a volume devoted to the rejection and enthronement of the one who enacts a 'turning point' or 'change of fortune' for Israel and the nations (cf. Lk. 24.44-49), and Luke re-formats the traditions of 'all that Jesus began to do and to teach' by extending them through the 'continuity' of 'his witnesses' who enact this scriptural script to the ends of the earth (Acts 1.1-8).[35] Chief among them, without peer, is Paul, and by featuring this most controverted 'apostle' in his sequel, Luke ensconces Paul at the centre of the gospel. As a result of this narrative-rhetorical strategy, Luke re-constitutes Paul's legacy, inscribing him into the very 'warp and woof' of the scriptures' witness to Israel's salvation through 'the Messiah of God'.[36]

---

32   Cf., e.g., Acts 26.26b.

33   See esp. J. Frey, C. K. Rothschild, J. Schröter (eds), *Die Apostelgeschichte im Kontext antiker und frühchristlicher Historiographie* (BZNW, 162; Berlin: de Gruyter, 2009); cf. L.C.A. Alexander, 'The Preface to Acts and the Historians' in *Acts in its Ancient Literary Context. A Classicist Looks at the Acts of the Apostles* (LNTS, 298; London: T&T Clark, 2005), pp. 21–42.

34   Lk. 7.30; Acts 2.23; 4.28; [5.38]; 13.36; 20.27; [27.42-43]; see esp. Isa. 44.26 where the 'word of his servant and will/counsel of his [servant's!] messengers' (ῥῆμα παιδὸς αὐτοῦ καὶ τὴν βουλὴν τῶν ἀγγέλλων αὐτου) is linked with Cyrus's anointed task (45.1) to re-establish Jerusalem and the Temple in fulfilling the 'will' (πάντα τὰ θελήματά μου ποιήσει) of the 'Lord God'; cf. βουλή in Isa. 46.10; 55.8.

35   J. Schröter ('Zur Stellung der Apostelgeschichte im Kontext der antiken Historiographie', in *Apostelgeschichte im Kontext*, pp. 27–47) comes, independently, to the same thematic unity of one historiographical work: 'Luke orders the events involving the impact of the witnesses in such a way that the impression emerges that the first phase of the exaltation of Jesus is actually an introduction to the continuation of the history of Christianity that culminates in the unimpeded proclamation of Paul in Rome' (47); S. Mason, *Josephus and the New Testament* (Peabody, MA: Hendrickson Publishers, 2nd edn, 2003), esp. pp. 251–95: 'Josephus's work is of the same ... genre as Luke-Acts: they are both histories ... which we may loosely call Hellenistic' (252); for 'witness' more generally in the NT, cf. A. Trites, *The New Testament Concept of Witness* (SNTSMS, 31; Cambridge: Cambridge University Press, 1977), esp. pp. 136–42.

36   Cf. Lk. 9.20; 24.44-49; Acts 26.22-23. C. Mount ('Luke-Acts and the Investigation of Apostolic Tradition: From a Life of Jesus to a History of Christianity', in *Die Apostelgeschichte im Kontext*, pp. 380–92) argues for a similar circumscribing of the tradition in Paul through the narrative of Acts, though he places Acts in the second century; see now ch. 5 of this volume for his most recent refinement of his position.

a. Secondary Prefaces and the 'Continuity of the Narrative'

Curiously, Luke begins his second volume with a 'linking, recapitulatory *prooimion*' which, like Diodorus, discloses the 'continuity of the narrative' even as it re-formats the entire work.[37] Unlike Diodorus, however, Luke re-configures *chronologically* one resurrection day (Lk. 24.1-51) into forty days of teaching and appearances of the crucified-resurrected Christ (Acts 1.3-14). Specifically, Lk. 3.21–24.53 corresponds to (≈) Acts 1.1-2; Lk. 24.13-43 ≈ Acts 1.3; Lk. 24.36-49 ≈ Acts 1.4-5; Lk. 24.50-51 ≈ Acts 1.6-11; and Lk. 24.52-53 ≈ Acts 1.12-14. The result is that this particular *intra*textuality of Lk. 24.13-53 and Acts 1.1-14 weaves the 'continuous thread of the narrative' of 'book' two with the 'apostolic' *'witness'* of the 'opening of the scriptures' to 'Israel and the nations' enabled by the 'power' of the 'Holy Spirit' as disclosed by the resurrected-crucified Messiah himself:

1. In Lk. 24.13-35 and 24.36-49 the resurrected-crucified one reveals his presence to the Emmaus disciples and to the larger group of apostles and acquaintances of the 'upper room',[38] respectively, by *'opening* the scriptures' *at table* with them. 'Were not our hearts burning within us ... as he was opening to us the Scriptures ... And they gave him a piece of broiled fish. And taking it as they looked on, he ate it ... Then he opened their mind to comprehend the Scriptures' (24.32, 42-43, 45).[39]

2. Already within the first period of the secondary preface a *metaleptic* prompt ('until the day he was taken up') directs Luke's audience back to the end of volume one where, *at table*, Jesus charges the eleven to 'stay in this city [Jerusalem] until you are clothed with *power* from the exalted place' (Acts 1.2→Lk. 24.49b). Apparently their eating and drinking with him is not only garnished with a future, but their 'recognition' of Jesus must now also entail the empowering presence of the 'Holy Spirit'.

3. This 'opening' of the mind at table that enables the 'opening' of the scriptures with a proper hermeneutic is summed up in Jesus' explanation to his 'apostles' of his role within the 'Reign' or 'Kingdom of God': As the one who 'had suffered' he was now 'alive', revealing his identity to them through 'many convincing proofs'. The role of Jesus' *apostles* apparently is far from over as they are instructed over a 'forty-day' period (Acts 1.3). Will their role in this 'Kingdom' also entail 'suffering'?

---

37   Cf. M. C. Parsons, *Acts* (Paideia Commentaries on the NT; Grand Rapids, MI: Baker Academic, 2008), pp. 12–15, 26–28 [based on historiographical and rhetorical parallels, no pre-canonical narrative unity]; M. Wolter, 'Die Proömien des lukanischen Doppelwerks (Lk1,1-4 und Apg 1,1-2)', in *Die Apostelgeschichte im Kontext*, pp. 476–94 [no prospective content in the Acts *prooimion*, yet clearly one work signified]; L. Alexander, 'Preface to Acts and the Historians', p. 38: 'it is precisely the unrhetorical, recapitulatory prefaces of Diodorus' earlier books that Acts recalls ... . the effect of the recapitulation is to place the current work in a sequence within the author's total *oeuvre*'.

38   Acts 1.12.

39   For a treatment of the passages 'opened' in Acts, see, e.g., D. P. Moessner, 'The "script" of the Scriptures in Acts: suffering as God's "plan" (βουλή) for the world for the "release of sins" in *History, Literature, and Society in the Book of Acts* (B. Witherington [ed.]; Cambridge: Cambridge University Press, 1996), pp. 218–50.

4. Luke focalizes 'the forty days' in a typical setting[40] with a specific charge. In so doing he performs a striking rhetorical manoeuvre: (narrator's voice ...) 'While eating with them he charged them not to depart from Jerusalem but (... narrator's voice continuing ...) to await the promise which *you* heard from *me* (Jesus' voice!), namely, that John baptized with water, but not after many of these days you shall be baptized by the Holy Spirit' (... Jesus' voice) (1.4-5). 'Power from the exalted place' must now be interpreted as being 'baptized by/ in the Holy Spirit not after many days' (Lk. 24.49→Acts 1.4b-5). In contrast to John who 'baptized with water', the characteristic mark of the apostles' *witness* will be a baptism *by* the Holy Spirit. Hence this interruption by the main character of book one not only establishes a *material* continuity between the two volumes through Jesus' disclosures at table; Luke also forges a *formal* link by Jesus continuing *to act and to speak*. Jesus has in fact 'interrupted' the narrator's speech to address his audience directly in the command to await the power of the Holy Spirit. Jesus' own *teaching voice* binds the two volumes for Luke's audience who hear the 'living' voice of Jesus continuing 'to do and to teach'. The 'end' of the Gospel volume must now be viewed as a telescoped summary of the beginning of the second or sequel volume.

5. The apostles' new recognition of Jesus is first forged to the 'fulfillment of all that stands *written*' about Jesus as 'the Christ' (Lk. 24.44-49). Their 'mind' has first to be opened to comprehend (24.45) that the whole of Israel's scriptures focuses upon Jesus as 'the Christ who suffers, rises from the dead on the third day, and in/by his name a release of sins is proclaimed into all the nations' (24.46-47). This 'topic' of scripture forms their new identity as 'witnesses' (μάρτυρες, 24.48) 'of the things' they have witnessed in Jesus of Nazareth. What is to be proclaimed 'into all the nations, beginning (ἀρξάμενοι) from Jerusalem' (24.47), is this new comprehension, this sweeping hermeneutic of Moses, the prophets, and the Psalms that finds its *telos* in Jesus as the Christ (cf. Lk. 22.37b: τὸ περὶ ἐμοῦ τέλος ἔχει). It would appear that the 'opening of the scriptures' to all the peoples of the world forms the crux of what it means to be 'witnesses of these things' (24.48) and would thus stitch the connecting thread of the 'continuity of the narrative'.

6. The apostles' question regarding the 'restoration of the kingdom to Israel' (Acts 1.6-8) transforms this last gathering with the risen-crucified one into a new comprehension (μετάνοια) of 'witness' vis-à-vis 'the kingdom of God'. Rather than Israel's kingdom of God's rule first being re-constituted so that the nations might participate in the witness to Israel's glory,[41] on the contrary, Israel's witness to God's rule must first be taken to all the nations of the earth through the authenticated, representative 'witness' of the *twelve* apostles. It is no accident that the first emplotted episode of book two commences with the restoration of 'the Twelve' witnesses-apostles to fulfil their 'place of apostolic service'[42] rather than the restoration of the *ethnos* Israel (Acts 1.15-26).[43]

---

40   Note the use of the present participle: συναλιζόμενος, Acts 1.4.

41   See Lk. 2.32 where Simeon, endowed with the Holy Spirit, already prophesies of this different type of 'witness'.

42   τὸν τόπον τῆς διακονίας ταύτης καὶ ἀποστολῆς, Acts 1.25.

43   Curiously in his short depiction of the 'Jews' as a distinct 'people'/'nation' (ἔθνος), Diodorus finds it important to include the number of their tribes as *twelve* (regarded by them as

Now Peter, who had previously 'denied' any association with Jesus,[44] 'turns around' (ἐπιστρέφω, Lk. 22.32) and 'opens the scriptures' to the gathered post-resurrection disciples to interpret the plot of the arresting party of Jesus – led by 'one of the twelve' – as already predicted 'about Jesus' in the Psalms ([LXX] Pss. 68 and 108 in Acts 1.20-21; cf. Lk. 24.44b: 'it must be fulfilled in the Psalms about me' [δεῖ πληρωθῆναι ... ἐν ... ψαλμοῖς περὶ ἐμοῦ]).

Thus, the final message of Jesus before his 'taking up' (cf. Lk. 9.51→Acts 1.11) – the *prooemial* voice of the 'Lord' (Acts 1.6, 11; cf. Lk. 24.3) – continues to sew the narrative thread by outlining the intended scope or 'goal' of their witness. Their sending 'into all the nations' is to extend from Jerusalem into all of Judea and Samaria in passage to 'the end of the earth' (ἕως ἐσχάτου τῆς γῆς, Acts 1.8; cf. Isa. 49.6). It would appear that the *goal* of the narrative continuity (τέλος) will be reached in a *culminating event* (τελευτή) in which it has become comprehensible and clear to the reader that this 'end of the earth' has been breached by the 'opening of the scriptures'.

b. The 'Beginning' (Archē) and the 'Beginnings' (Archai) of Luke-Acts

Most significantly, Luke in his recapitulatory, linking preface anchors this 'new' scriptural notion of 'witness' to a definitive 'beginning' (ἡ ἀρχή).

'Until the day in which he was taken up' (Acts 1.2) is laced with the command Jesus gives 'through the Holy Spirit to the apostles *whom he had chosen*' (οὓς ἐξελέξατο). This *metalepsis*[45] echoes Lk. 6.13 ('choosing from among them [the disciples] twelve whom he also named apostles' [ἐκλεξάμενος ἀπ' αὐτῶν δώδεκα οὓς καὶ ἀποστόλους ὠνόμασεν]), thus taking the audience back to the first volume. Jesus' choice of them from the beginning was now coming to a new rationale. 'The Holy Spirit' also anticipates forward involvement of the Spirit's presence at Pentecost (Acts 2.33), when the 'exalted Jesus' – 'because he has received the Holy Spirit' – 'begins to pour forth *the promise from the Father*', tying Acts 2 to 1.2 and again back to the table scene and 'promise of my Father' (Lk. 24.49).

Like a 'hinge', Acts 1.2 pulls the sending out of 'witnesses' at the beginning of the sequel back to 'those who from the beginning were eyewitnesses and attendants of the message' (οἱ ἀπ' ἀρχῆς αὐτόπται καὶ ὑπηρέται γενόμενοι τοῦ λόγου, Lk. 1.2) so that this witness continue 'of all that Jesus began to do and to teach' (ἤρξατο ὁ Ἰησοῦς ποιεῖν τε καὶ διδάσκειν, Acts 1.1). By historiographical conventions such as *metaleptic*, intratextual cross-referencing and synchronic overlapping, Luke dovetails the 'tradition' (καθὼς παρέδοσαν ἡμῖν) of the 'acts of the apostles' into the 'the beginning' (ἡ ἀρχή) of the whole work:

a 'perfect' number and corresponding to the number of months of the year) (*Library of History* XL.3.1-8).

44   Lk. 22.54-62.

45   See, e.g., I. de Jong, 'Metalepsis in Ancient Greek Literature', in J. Grethlein, A. Rengakos (eds), *Narratology and Interpretation*, pp. 87–115.

1. First, Jesus' words in Acts 1.4b-5 echo John the Baptist's words in Lk. 3.16: 'the promise of my Father which you heard from me. For (ὅτι) John baptized with water but you shall be baptized with the Holy Spirit not after many of these days'→ 'I myself am baptizing you with water, but one who is coming who is mightier than I … he will baptize you with Holy Spirit and fire.' Not only then does Jesus' voice take over the continuing narrator's voice and point back to his own words in Lk. 24.49 ('await the promise of my Father'), but these words also vault the audience back to the *beginning* of John the Baptist's ministry. What significance does John's baptism have for the notion of 'witness'?

2. John's words come just before the narrator summarizes the Baptist's entire calling as the one who, fulfilling the role of the prophet called in Isaiah 40, 'was proclaiming good news' (εὐηγγελίζετο, Lk. 3.18; cf. Isa. 40.9 – ὁ εὐαγγελιζόμενος). But hardly do these words stick before the narrator flashes forward to John's imprisonment by Herod (Lk. 3.19-20). As the clanging doors of the prison gates are still reverberating in the audience's ears (3.20), they see the Holy Spirit alight upon Jesus 'as a dove' and hear the voice from heaven proclaim Jesus to be 'My beloved Son, in you I take pleasure' (3.21-22; cf. Isa. 42.1).

3. Moreover, John's 'baptism' forms the decisive touchstone for authentic witness. Not only is the restoration of the apostolic ministry/service dictated by scripture, as we have seen above, but Judas' place in the apostolic ministry 'must' be replaced by 'one of these men who accompanied us the whole time that Jesus went in and out among us, *beginning from the baptism of John* (ἀρξάμενος ἀπὸ τοῦ βαπτίσματος Ἰωάννου), one of these must become a witness *with us* to the resurrection' (Acts 1.21-22). '*From the baptism of John*' thus coordinates *the beginning* of Jesus' calling and witness (Lk. 3.21-22) with the calling and witness of the apostles to function as a semaphore for the ἀρχή of the two volumes. Like Polybius and Diodorus, the secondary ἀρχή derives its significance from the primary ἀρχή, when Jesus himself was 'anointed with the Holy Spirit and power'.

4. Curiously this 'baptism' will be summoned by Peter in his 'word' to Cornelius' household as *seminal to Jesus' entire public activity*:

> The word/message (τὸν λόγον) which God sent to the sons and daughters of Israel by proclaiming the good news of peace (εὐαγγελιζόμενος εἰρήνην)[46] through Jesus the Messiah … you know, the event throughout the whole of Judea, *beginning* (ἀρξάμενος) from Galilee *after the baptism which John proclaimed* (μετὰ τὸ βάπτισμα ὃ ἐκήρυξεν Ἰωάννης) … how God anointed him with Holy Spirit and power … and we are *witnesses* (μάρτυρες) to all these things which he did in the region of the Jews and in Jerusalem (Acts 10.36-38).

Thus again 'witness' is tied to 'all that Jesus began to do and to teach' *as defined by* Jesus' anointing by the Holy Spirit and *as declared in advance by John*.

---

46   Cf., e.g., Isa. 52.7.

But more than that, Peter narrows the role of 'witness' 'from the beginning' of Jesus' public activity *only* to those to whom the resurrected-crucified one 'had become manifest after he had risen from the dead' – in fact, neither to 'all the people' nor to any who happened to follow Jesus but only to 'those witnesses who had been *chosen beforehand* by God, namely, to those who *had eaten and drunk with him* after he had risen up from the dead'! (Acts 10.40b-41) Thus again, Peter takes Luke's audience back to Acts 1.4b-5 and Lk. 24.36-47 *at table*, while the reference to 'God choosing in advance' harks back to Jesus' 'choosing' twelve 'apostles' early on for their special role (Lk. 6.13). Acts 1.1-2 is therefore functioning again as a linchpin to hold both volumes together along the axis of 'witness' to Israel's Messiah Jesus.

5. But if there still be any doubt about the significance of 'the beginning' and 'witness' defined, 'from/after the baptism of John', Peter's defence before the 'circumcision party' of his lodging with Cornelius re-sounds even more distinctly Jesus' words in the secondary preface (Acts 1.4b-5). Peter declares to those who were critical of his behaviour in Caesarea, that 'just as the Holy Spirit' began to fall upon Cornelius and his household, 'I remembered the *word of the Lord* how he had said, "*John baptized with water, but you shall be baptized with Holy Spirit*"' (11.16). This 'word' can be none other than the voice-over of Acts 1.4b-5 which Peter restates verbatim, minus the adverbial phrase 'not after many of these days'. Moreover, this 'word of the Lord/ Jesus' is linked to a 'beginning', a second 'beginning' which, like Diodorus, refers to the 'continuity' of the sequel volume and is organically related to 'the beginning' (ἡ ἀρχή) and hence 'continuity' of the whole work. For now Peter refers back to Pentecost precisely as the fulfilment of the 'promise of the Father' which Jesus had uttered as the risen-crucified one before he 'was taken into heaven': '*As I had begun to speak, the Holy Spirit fell upon them just as indeed upon us in the beginning*' (ἐν ἀρχῇ). Peter's interlocutors respond, interestingly, with, '*Then indeed to the nations God has given a change of mind*' (μετάνοια) *which leads to life*' (Acts 11.18b→Lk. 24.47).

'A change of mind … into the nations' must again refer to Jesus' charge *at table* to 'await the promise of my Father' when they will become empowered to be 'witnesses to those things' of the suffering, raised up Messiah now *read* in the scriptures (Lk. 24.46-47→Acts 1.4b-8). It is precisely at Pentecost when 'every nation under heaven', symbolically present in the Jewish pilgrims, 'hear in their own tongues the marvels of the works of God' through Galilean Jews who, 'filled with the Holy Spirit, began to speak other languages just as the Spirit was giving them to utter' (Acts 2.5-12). 'Beginning from Jerusalem', Peter declares that their group had in fact become 'witnesses (μάρτυρες) of this Jesus whom God had raised' and who was now commanding that they 'change their mind (μετανοέω) … and receive the gift of the Holy Spirit' (Acts 2.32-33, 37-39).

c. Conclusion

'*From/after the baptism of John*' thus coordinates *the beginning* of Jesus' calling and witness with the calling and witness of the apostles to function as a semaphore for the *the beginning* (ἡ ἀρχή) of the two volumes. Like Polybius and Diodorus, the secondary ἀρχή derives its significance from the primary ἀρχή when Jesus himself was 'anointed with the Holy Spirit and power'. In this way, then, 'the beginning' (ἡ ἀρχή) of Jesus becomes a prerequisite of *witness* for those appointed *to witness* to the coming of the Holy Spirit upon the 'unclean gentiles' (cf. Lk. 3.22; Acts 10.38; 11.15-18; 15.7). At the heart of this witness is Jesus' eating and drinking with 'unclean' 'tax collectors and sinners' (Lk. 5.30; 7.34; 15.2; 19.7). As Peter acknowledges to his 'circumcision' critics, 'If therefore God gave them [gentiles] the same gift as he had also given to us who had come to believe in the Lord Jesus Christ, who was I to be able to hinder God?'! (11.17). Witness <u>to</u> and witness <u>from</u> Jesus' 'eating and drinking' has in fact become a *sine qua non* to becoming a 'witness to the resurrection', whether 'in Jerusalem and in all of Judea, in Samaria, and even to the edge of the earth' (Acts 1.8; 10.42).

III. From Leading the Witnesses to Leading 'Witness': Paul as the Definer and Defender of 'the from the Beginning' 'Witness' of the Apostles to 'All that Jesus Began to Do and to Teach'

The *Thesis* Re-stated: *Luke entangles Paul into the 'beginning' of the entire two-volume work both formally and materially through plotted 'arrangement' in such a way that the audience cannot comprehend the 'continuity' and 'goal' of both 'books' apart from Paul's seminal role.*

a. Links to 'the Beginning'

1. As chief Anti-'Witness', Saul unleashes a massive persecution upon the 'church which is in Jerusalem' (ἡ ἐκκλήσια ἡ ἐν Ἱεροσόλυμα, Acts 8.1): In a most ironic twist, Saul/Paul is con-scripted into the suffering of Jesus Messiah that epitomizes 'the Twelve' 'apostles' from the 'days of beginnings' (e.g., 3.18; 4.27-31; 5.41), thereby to become the 'witness' par excellence to the suffering required 'for the sake of my [Jesus'] name' (Acts 9.16; cf. 14.22 – δεῖ ... εἰσελθεῖν εἰς τὴν βασιλείαν τοῦ θεοῦ). 'Saul' is introduced as 'a young man' 'coaching' 'the witnesses' (οἱ μάρτυρες, Acts 7.58) who were perpetrating the 'violent death' of Stephen. But Stephen, 'full of the Holy Spirit', has just 'seen the glory of God and Jesus standing at the right hand of God' and cries out this vision to his persecutors in words reminiscent of the anointing of Jesus at his 'baptism from John': 'I see the heavens opened up' (Acts 7.56a→Lk. 3.21b). Before those of 'the Sanhedrin who are *sitting* in judgment' (Acts 6.15), Stephen sees 'the son of humankind *standing* at the right hand of God', recalling Daniel 7 and the 'one like a son of humankind' of the persecuted 'saints of the Most High' who is exonerated by the *standing* heavenly council, even as this figure is *enthroned* in the presence of the 'Ancient of Days' (Acts 7.55-58→Dan. 7.13-14—αὐτῷ ἐδόθη ... ἡ βασιλεία).[47]

Stephen before the Temple authorities has just delivered a reading of the scriptures of the whole of Israel's history that crescendoes in the Deuteronomistic

---

47　Theodotion; LXX – ἐδόθη αὐτῷ ἐξουσία.

pronouncement of judgement against the 'stiff-necked' leaders of the cult. Like their forebears, they have 'always resisted the Holy Spirit ... by killing those who announced the coming of the *just one*' and now whose 'betrayers and murderers' they have 'become' (Acts 7.51-53).[48] Saul is the leading 'witness' of this opposition and thus chief anti-'witness' to Stephen's opening of the scriptures as 'concerning' a suffering, raised-up messiah (cf. Luke 24.45-46→Acts 7.51-53). His leading role against Stephen sparks 'a great persecution against the church *which was in Jerusalem*', and with Saul 'going from house to house, expunging the church, and, rounding up both men and women, he was delivering them over to prison' (παρεδίδου, Acts 8.3→Lk. 22.21 – ὁ παραδιδούς). As a result, the church is forced to 'scatter into Judea and Samaria', but Luke's narrator adds that while they were fleeing, 'they were proclaiming *the message* of good news' (εὐαγγελιζόμενοι τὸν λόγον, 8.4, cf. Lk. 1.2 – ... καὶ ὑπηρέται γενόμενοι τοῦ λόγου), 'except, that is, the apostles' who remained in Jerusalem (Acts 8.1b). Ironically, Saul's persecution leads to preaching in those regions commanded by the risen Jesus in Acts 1.8, albeit without the apostles and to 'Jews' only.

2. Saul's/Paul's calling on the road to Damascus and the resulting 'turn about' reverses and dovetails his course into 'the way' defined already by 'the Twelve' and reiterated with differing accents by Stephen:

i) Stephen's death and the ensuing persecution form a major 'complication' to the 'continuity of the narrative'. Now for the first time the 'people' of Israel (λαός) turn against and begin to oppose 'the way' of 'the disciples' of Jesus. Instead of thousands of them 'changing their mind' or 'believing in' Messiah Jesus (Acts 2.42, 47; 4.4; 5.14; 6.7), they are now stirred up by 'false witnesses' (μάρτυρες ψευδεῖς) and join in the attempt to silence Stephen (6.11-13). Now instead of persecution originating solely from the Temple authorities and the Sanhedrin, the 'disciples' are also opposed by their own kinfolk.

ii) When it first appears that the apostles Peter and John will finally begin to fulfil the crucified-risen one's command in Acts 1.8 to be witnesses in Samaria to the change of mind through opening the scriptures (8.25: διαμαρτυράμενοι καὶ λαλήσαντες τὸν λόγον τοῦ κυρίου) – but only after Philip's [one of the 'seven'] first encounters [8.5-40] – Saul is still on the scene in Jerusalem and Judea as counter-witness (οἱ μάρτυρες, 7.58; cf. 1 Cor. 15.15! – ψευδομάρτυρες τοῦ θεοῦ), 'breathing his threats' and 'binding' 'disciples' 'of the way' *back to* Jerusalem (Acts 9.1-3; cf. 4.29). Thus when as late as 9.32-42 Peter has remained in Judea and must be given a special revelation to comprehend that the 'nations' were not 'unclean' with respect to 'the word', it becomes clear that Luke has quite intentionally sandwiched the calling of the one sent to *both* the 'people' of Israel *and* the nations (Acts 9.15 in 9.3-30) between the coerced sending of the apostles to Samaria, on the one side (8.4-25), and the divine summoning of Peter to the gentile Cornelius, on the

---

48   For the Deuteronomistic dynamic explanation of Israel's history in Luke-Acts, see D. P. Moessner, *Lord of the Banquet. The Literary and Theological Significance of the Lukan Travel Narrative* (Minneapolis: Fortress, 1989; Harrisburg, Pa.: Trinity Press International, 1998 pb. edn), esp. pp. 91–257.

other (9.31–11.18).[49] Does this signify that it will be Saul/Paul – and not the twelve apostles – who will be a witness to this gospel both to the people of the Jews and of the nations?

3. Already when Paul leaves Damascus to return to Jerusalem he has been transformed from prime 'God-antagonist' (θεομάχοι, 5.39) to primary protagonist of 'the way' of 'the Lord Jesus Christ':

> The significance of Paul 'not being able to see anything' and 'not eating or drinking' anything (Acts 9.8-9) to subsequently 'looking up', 'seeing' with new eyes ('something like scales falling off') and 'being filled by the Holy Spirit', 'is baptized', and 'taking food becomes strengthened' is now striking (9.17-18): He may already be 'seeing' what Peter has not yet grasped. What is more, his calling switches from 'scattering' to 'gathering' as he forms a group of 'his disciples' in Damascus (οἱ μαθηταὶ αὐτοῦ, Acts 9.25) and thus, other than Jesus himself among his following, Saul is the only character in Luke-Acts etched with the authority of teaching his own 'disciples'. Ironically Gamaliel's warning to the Sanhedrin comes true for his student Saul (cf. 22.3): Saul goes from a 'fighter against God' to a 'chosen instrument' (Isa. 54.16) of the 'Lord Jesus', from a ravager of the 'plan' (βουλή) of God to its principal ambassador (Acts 5.39→9.15).

To fellow Jews in the Damascus synagogues he powerfully 'demonstrates' – from the scriptures – that 'Jesus is the Son of God' (Acts 9.20), 'the Messiah' (9.20-22). His fate in a leading city of Syria (cf. Lk. 2.2) followed by the same treatment in Jerusalem takes on an 'uncanny' similarity to the corporate servant's reception by Israel (Isa. 49.5-6). The message is roundly rejected but the hostility appears to be funnelled to one individual within the group who is most representative of the servant's mission: 'the Jews were plotting to kill him' [Paul in Damascus] (Acts 9.23b); 'the Hellenists were attempting to kill him' [Paul in Jerusalem] (9.29b). It is particularly ironic in the latter instance that Paul's cohort of antagonists who had erupted so violently against Stephen now joins forces to 'scatter' Paul into the diaspora (Acts 9.29-30;[50] cf. 6.9-15).

4. But before he is 'led by the brothers and sisters' to Caesarea (Acts 9.30a), Saul is further authenticated 'in the way' of apostolic suffering by Barnabas, who is 'of'/'from the apostles' (ἀπὸ τῶν ἀποστόλων, 4.36) of the beginning days (cf. Acts 11.15; 15.7):

> Barnabas forges Paul to 'the beginning' in two distinct ways:
> i) When Saul returns to Jerusalem from Damascus for the first time since he had been the leader of the violence, the 'disciples' there naturally 'are afraid of him, because they could not believe that he had become a disciple' (Acts 9.26). It takes one 'called Barnabas' – 'from the apostolic leadership' – known as a 'one who

---

49   Note how Peter's activity, culminating within the confines of Judea in his lodging with the ritually unclean Jewish tanner (Acts 9.36-43), functions as a foil for his resistance to 'visit' the 'unclean' gentile Cornelius.

50   Cf. διασπείρω in Acts 8.1, 4; 11.19.

encourages others',[51] to convince the believers in Jerusalem that Saul is no longer dangerous but in fact quite the opposite. The authentication must come through the 'apostles' themselves, and the proof given to them of Paul's radical reversal are the remarkable parallels to their own connection to the risen Christ: 'He had seen the Lord on the way', and that 'he [the Lord] had spoken to him [Saul]' and that as a result, Saul had now become a fearless proclaimer 'in the name of Jesus' (Acts 9.27b→Lk. 24.13-35, 36-49). Barnabas becomes the human agent who vouchsafes Saul's/Paul's 'change of mind' and 'joins' him to 'the disciples' and 'the apostles' in Jerusalem (cf. Ananias, 9.13-18, 21!). The 'way' of the disciples *from the begin-ning*' (Lk. 24.44-49→Acts 1.1-8) has become the 'way' of Paul. And like 'the Twelve', now this calling of Messiah has become the way of 'how much he *must suffer* for the sake of my name' (Acts 9.16→Lk. 18.31-34; 22.31-34).

ii) Not only to the disciples and the apostles, but also to the peculiar identity of the emerging authority of 'the church which is in Jerusalem' (ἡ ἐκκλήσια ἡ οὖσα ἐν Ἰερουσαλήμ, 11.22→8.1) must Saul's/Paul's newfound status and unlikely 'calling' be authorized. Again it is Barnabas who provides the key link. After some period has passed in which those scattered from the persecution against Stephen have been preaching in Judea and Samaria (8.1) and in Phoenicia, Cyprus, and Antioch (11.19), and presumably, Peter has been summoned through special revelation to Cornelius' house (10.1–11.18), Barnabas is sent by 'the church which was in Jerusalem' to Antioch to find out whether the rumour of the large number of gentiles now coming to the faith was true and how legitimate this development was.

Parallel then to Barnabas' 'certification' of Paul's calling, Barnabas is now to give his word on the legitimacy of non-Jewish 'Greeks' 'turning to the Lord' [Jesus] (Acts 11.21b). The net result of 'the grace of God' that Barnabas encountered (Acts 11.23) is that he goes and retrieves Saul from Tarsus so that that two of them can 'gather' the whole church of those of Jewish and gentile backgrounds and 'teach them' there in Antioch 'for a whole year' (11.26a). Apparently the social dynamic of this new mixture spawns a new name for 'the disciples', namely, 'Christians' (11.26b). In any case, what is remarkable is that by the end of Acts 11, Saul is already an official representative of the 'disciples' in Antioch to send relief to the church in Jerusalem, the latter group described now for the first time as having its own 'elders' (πρεσβύτεροι) (11.29-30; cf. 4.5, 8, 23; 6.12; 23.14; 24.1; 25.15).

In sum, well before Luke turns the spotlight on Paul's mission into the Diaspora in chs 13–19, the author of the two-volume work through his narrative plotting has grafted Paul's significance into *the beginning* of the apostolic ministry as commis-sioned by the crucified-risen Jesus himself. The structuring of the formal and material intratextual interactions of both volumes suggests a fundamental parallel between the twelve apostles and Saul: both had spent a significant amount of time in either mis-understanding or in outright opposition to a messiah who must be rejected by his own people and be raised up. Both have been charged by the risen-crucified one to 'turn around' from their disobedience and to 'change their whole way of thinking' about the scriptures' presentation of a suffering-exalted Messiah and the reality that this Messiah is Jesus (cf. Lk. 22.21-27, 31-34; 24.13-35, 44-49

---

51   Hebraism/Septuagintism: 'son of encouragement'/'consolation'.

with Acts 9.1-16). It would appear that Luke has taken advantage of this basic parallelism to insert Paul into the beginning core of apostolic witness, even though Paul
does not technically qualify for appointment as a 'twelfth' or 'thirteenth' apostle
(see further below).

*b. Speeches (λόγοι) as Medial Links that 'Carry' the 'Continuity of the
Narrative' and 'Motivate' the Plot to Its 'Purpose'/'End' (τέλος)*

*1. Paul's Preaching the Message to Jews Followed by Gentiles Sets the
Standard for Apostolic Mission*

Acts 13.13-52 – Paul's 'Word'

Acts 13.4-12 and 13.13-52 as 'type scenes' re-draw the lines of 'the continuity
of the narrative' for the reader as Paul takes over the narrative space. In Cyprus,
the 'prophet', who is Jewish, remains under the authority of 'the devil', while the
gentile, who is Roman, 'turns from darkness to light'. Paul's 'opening of the scriptures' in the synagogue as he first arrives in Pisidian Antioch sets the pattern that
will be repeated over and over throughout the rest of his Mediterranean itinerary
(Acts 14.1–20.38).

The climax of Paul's opening of the scriptures divides his audience of 'Israelites'
(Acts 13.16b→13.45). As will happen in other cities, the response can be positive
at first but then precipitously turn to violent rejection. Acts 13.13-52 provides a
graphic two-stage type-profile of a first meeting (13.15-43) followed by a subsequent encounter of opposition[52] (13.44-52):

> i) By Paul repeating 'the word' of Peter, Luke reconfigures Paul's preaching as the
> 'Apostolic Word':
>
> Paul builds in his opening of the Psalms and Isaiah to declare that the promised
> Saviour from the line of David was in fact present to grant release of sins (13.26-
> 38). Indeed, Paul's exposition of the scriptures was in reality the 'the word of
> this salvation' (ὁ λόγος τῆς σωτηρίας, 13.26b), 'the word of the Lord' (τὸν
> λόγον τοῦ κυρίου, 13.44b; cf. 2.41 – 'his [Peter's] word' [τὸν λόγον αὐτοῦ])
> 'through this one [hung on a tree – resurrected Jesus] proclaiming to you a
> release of sins' (ἄφεσις ἁμαρτιῶν) (13.38, 44).
>
> a.) As in the 'speech' at Pentecost, Paul combines texts from the prophets and Psalms
> to present both Jesus' rejection by his own people *and* his raising up from the dead
> as fulfilments of the divine plan (βουλή) pre-scribed in scripture. In both 'words',
> David's role as anticipating and fulfilling his own part in the 'plan' is highlighted.
> Psalm 15 (LXX) depicts David as a 'suffering righteous' servant whose persecution
> and opposition from his own people leads him to see a 'Lord at his right hand'. In
> Peter's word, 'this Lord' is no less than the 'my Lord' who according to Ps. 109
> (LXX) is 'from David's womb' (ἐκ γαστρὸς ... ἐγέννησά σε) and is exalted at

---

52   For further detail, see D. P. Moessner, '"Completed End(s)ings" of Historiographical
Narrative: Diodorus Siculus and the End(ing) of Acts', in *Die Apostelgeschichte und hellenis-
tische Geschichtsschreibung. Festschrift für Dr. Plümacher* (C. Breytenbach and J. Schröter [eds];
AGAJU, 57; Leiden: Brill, 2004), pp. 193–221, esp. pp. 217–21.

the 'right hand of the Lord God' (Acts 2.22-28, 29-34; cf. Ps. 109.1, 5). David thus pre-patterns and predicts his offspring messiah who will also be rejected by his own people but will also be the one raised out of the dead to the 'exalted place' to bring God's plan of salvation for Israel and the nations to its intended goal. Likewise Paul emphasizes that David was especially chosen by God to advance his 'plan' and 'will' to lead to Israel a 'savior Jesus'. This 'plan' is announced in the prophets and Psalms and realized again precisely by a violent demise facilitated by the anointed servant's own people and carried out by the Romans. Again a psalm text is combined with one of the prophets to argue that God's embattled 'son' (Ps. 2) is to 'inherit the nations' as the χριστός (Ps. 2.8b; cf. Isa. 54.17, 3), while bringing the 'sure and faithful decrees' to David (Isa. 55.3) of a 'covenant to the nations' to its realization. Psalm 15 once again enriches the comprehension of this 'plan' by linking the 'anointed son's' violent treatment to his freedom from 'decomposing in the grave'. David's preview of the 'Lord always before me', where 'delights are at his right hand forever as the ways that bring life' (Ps. 15.8, 11), is David's *inheritance through the Lord's deliverance*. 'For when David had served the plan of God with respect to his own generation, he died and was added to his fathers and saw corruption, but he whom God raised did not see corruption ... Let it be known therefore ... that *through this one release of sins is being proclaimed to you*' (διὰ τούτου ὑμῖν ἄφεσις ἁμαρτιῶν καταγγέλλεται, 13.36-38a→2.38 – ἐπὶ τῷ ὀνόματι Ἰησοῦ χριστοῦ εἰς ἄφεσιν τῶν ἁμαρτιῶν ὑμῶν). Paul's reading of the law of Moses, the prophets, and the Psalms is *the interpretation given by the risen Christ* himself (Luke 24.44-47).

b.) Luke has his audience understand that Paul regarded *John the Baptist's preaching* as 'proclaiming in advance the baptism of a change of mind' (βάπτισμα μετανοίας) as characteristic of the greater one's coming (13.24-25). Though the term 'beginning' is not used, the role of John is still to prepare the way for the beginning or '*entrance* (εἴσοδος) of Savior Jesus' (13.24a).

c.) Luke has Paul acknowledge the group of those who 'had journeyed with Jesus from Galilee to Jerusalem' and received appearances from the 'raised Jesus' 'over many days' as 'his *witnesses* to the people' (13.31). But Paul continues to announce the same fulfilments of 'all that stands written', the same 'promise of good news that was given to the patriarchs' that the first 'witnesses' proclaim. There is no hint that what Paul preaches from scripture as fulfilled is any different from their basic 'word of salvation/of the Lord'.

ii) The pattern of Jewish rejection of Paul and his turning to the gentiles fulfils a servant mission in Isaiah 40–55:

On the next Sabbath when 'jealous Jews' begin to 'speak against'[53] and to 'revile' what Paul and Barnabas were contending from the scriptures (13.45), Paul *and* Barnabas counter by claiming for themselves the mission of the servant of Isaiah! Since the audience 'judges itself unworthy of the eternal life' offered 'through this one' [resurrected Jesus] (13.39), 'look, we are turning to the nations/gentiles' (στρεφόμεθα εἰς τὰ ἔθνη) (13.46). Paul cites Isa. 49.6 explicitly as the rationale for his 'turning' (Acts 13.47→Acts 1.8). From the context of Paul's speaking, the 'you' (σε) of the abbreviated citation must refer to Paul

---

53   Note the echo and ironic fulfilment of Simeon's prophecy for Paul's calling (Lk. 2.34; cf. 2.29-32).

and Barnabas and others of their mission. 'The Lord' who 'commands' must now refer primarily to the 'Lord Jesus', the resurrected *prooemial* voice of Acts 1.8, and the 'you', the 'servant', can refer therefore only to the smaller group within Israel whose mission to Israel also issues in the 'light of the nations/gentiles' through the 'salvation' which the servant extends 'to the end of the earth' (τοῦ εἶναί σε εἰς σωτηρίαν ἕως ἐσχάτου τῆς γῆς). Isaiah 49.1-6 choreographs Paul's mission. Paul and colleagues identify themselves as the corporate servant, and the 'Lord Jesus', the suffering raised up 'son' of God, son of David (13.33), is the individual servant who, through them, proclaims light to Israel and *the nations* (cf. Isa. 55.3[54] in Acts 13.34b!).

As if on cue, 'the nations/gentiles rejoice' at this good news (13.48a; cf. Isa. 42.10, 12; 45.24, 26), as the 'word of the Lord begins to spread throughout the whole region' (Acts 13.49). The members of the 'Israelites' who turn against Paul and Barnabas also incite 'leading members' of the gentiles/nations, women and men, to riot against them ('And as many shall be astounded over you, so shall your presence be dishonored, and your reputation shall be shamed among the sons and daughters of humankind', Isa. 52.14). Again, there is no surprise when the narrator concludes, 'And the disciples were being filled with joy and with the Holy Spirit' (Acts 13.52).

2. Peter's Corroborating 'Word'

Acts 15.1-35 (15.7-11 ≈ 11.1-18 ≈ 10.1-48)

At the 'apostolic assembly' of Acts 15, one of the 'elders', James, delivers a clinching judgement regarding the status of 'those from the nations who are turning to God' (τοῖς ἀπὸ τῶν ἐθνῶν ἐπιστρέφουσιν ἐπὶ τὸν θεόν) (15.19). But it is the *apostle* Peter who passes the *apostolic mantle of witness* to the nations to the non-apostle[55] Paul (and Barnabas), by first addressing the gathering:

> You yourselves know that from the days of the beginnings (ἀφ' ἡμερῶν ἀρχαίων) God chose among you that through my mouth the nations (τὰ ἔθνη) should hear the message of the good news and come to believe. And God who knows the heart bore witness (ἐμαρτύρησεν) to them by giving to them the Holy Spirit just as also He gave to us. And by cleansing (καθαρίσας) their heart through faith, He made no discrimination between us and them ... Rather, we believe that it is through the grace of the Lord Jesus that we are saved just in the same way that they are (Acts 15.7b-9, 11).

The echo of Acts 1.8 as well as the voice from heaven 'not to call what God has cleansed (ἐκαθάρισεν) unclean' (Acts 11.9b→10.15) ring together as one. Now

---

54   See, e.g., O. Eissfeldt, 'The Promises of Grace to David in Isaiah 55:1-5', in *Israel's Prophetic Heritage* (B. W. Anderson and W. Harrelson [eds]; FS J. Muilenburg; New York: Harper & Brothers, 1962), pp. 196–207: 'there can be no doubt that Israel is here given the same promise which is found elsewhere in Isa. 40-55, particularly in the "Servant Songs"' (206).

55   The two uses of ἀπόστολος for Paul (and Barnabas) (Acts 14.4,14) refer to their being sent out by the (Antioch) church in the more generic sense of 'one who is sent' (cf. Lk. 11.49 with Acts 13.1-3).

Peter has merged the days *'in the beginning'* (ἐν ἀρχῇ) of the falling of the Spirit upon themselves at Pentecost with *'from those days of* [characterized by] *beginnings'* of the falling of the Spirit upon the nations through Peter's preaching.[56] Now instead of the Jewish believers' receiving the Spirit as paradigmatic for the salvation of the gentile nations, Peter flips the encounter around to make the receipt of the Spirit by Cornelius' household the touchstone for the 'grace of the Lord Jesus' among the Jewish believers. Peter has himself undergone a 'turning' almost as radical as the 'turning of the nations'. He had had to learn that his prior designation of the nations as 'unclean' was, in God's mind, 'discrimination' against them in defiance of the risen Christ's command to be his witnesses to them (Acts 1.8).

The result of the assembly was a ringing endorsement of Paul's (and Barnabas') calling to 'proclaim the good news' among the nations:

i) The primary locus of the debate is fixed in Antioch, the church which had commissioned Paul and Barnabas for 'the work to which I [the Holy Spirit] have called them' (Acts 13.2). It is only after 'certain ones' from Jerusalem had gone down to Antioch and begun teaching the church there – 'unless you practice circumcision according to the custom of Moses, you cannot be saved' (οὐ δύνασθε σωθῆναι) (Acts 15.1) – that the debate heats up and requires adjudication in Jerusalem by the 'apostles and elders' (15.2b).

ii) After 'Paul and Barnabas, along with some others are appointed to go up' (15.2b), 'they were passing through both Phoenicia and Samaria, explaining in detail to them the turning of the nations/gentiles (τὴν ἐπιστροφὴν τῶν ἐθνῶν, 15.3). This news is greeted by 'the brothers and sisters' there with 'great joy' (15.3b). The commission of the resurrected Christ of Acts 1.8 to be witnesses in Samaria appears – in large measure – to be fulfilled. No resistance to the 'turning of the nations' is narrated by Luke.

iii) The ecclesial letter issued by the 'apostles, elders, and the whole church' to broadcast the outcome of the assembly serves as both 'rite-' and 'right of passage' for Paul (and Barnabas). After their initial welcome in Jerusalem, Paul and Barnabas 'report all the things that God had been doing with them' (Acts 15.4). But unlike Samaria, the only reaction described by those in Judea and Jerusalem is the protest by 'certain believers of the party of the Pharisees' (15.5).

Yet, the response at the end of the assembly is for 'the apostles, elders, and the whole of the church' to produce a resolute affirmation of Paul's (and Barnabas') calling (13.1-3). Not only are Barnabas and Paul commended 'unanimously (ὁμοθυμαδόν) ... as beloved brothers who have given over their lives for the sake of the name of our Lord Jesus Christ', they are also sent back with 'two or three witnesses',[57] Judas and Silas, 'who will tell you these same things by mouth. For

---

56 'From those beginning days'; see further, D. P. Moessner, '"Managing the Audience". The Rhetoric of Authorial Intent and Audience Comprehension in the Narrative Epistemology of Polybius of Megalopolis, Diodorus Siculus, and Luke the Evangelist', in *The Word Leaps the Gap: Essays on Scripture and Theology in Honor of Richard B. Hays* (J. R. Wagner, C. K. Rowe, and A. K. Grieb [eds]; Grand Rapids: Eerdmans, 2008), pp. 179–97, esp. pp. 194–96.

57 Cf. Deut. 19.15-16.

it seemed good to the Holy Spirit and to us ...' (Acts 15.25-28). The same Spirit who had sent out Barnabas and Paul is now appealed to as corroborating their witness. The events of Acts 13–14 are fully sanctioned; truly God has 'opened the door of faith to those of the nations' (cf. Acts 14.27b). The apostolic word to Peter (Acts 1.8→10.15→11.9b) and the 'opening of the scriptures' by the elder James (Acts 15.15-21), have both motivated and re-configured the 'continuity of the narrative' toward its goal. The non-apostle Paul's 'rite of passage' in Acts 13.1-3 in executing the *prooemial* voice's charge 'to the nations' in Acts 1.8 has been granted a resounding 'right of passage' back 'to the nations'. Paul had entered Jerusalem through *Samaria and Judea* and now from Antioch returns back 'to the nations' 'to visit the brothers and sisters in every city where we have already proclaimed the word of the Lord' (Acts 15.36–16.5→Acts 13–14).[58] Thus Luke, by carefully coordinating chronological and syn-chronological connectors, crafts a convincing transfer of the apostolic authority of the Holy Spirit from Peter (and Cornelius) to Paul (and Silas).[59] From Acts 16.6 on, in fact, Peter and the rest of the twelve apostles disappear from the 'narrative continuity' all-together.

c. Medial Synchronological Links Leading to the 'End' (τέλος) of the Two-volume Work

1. Paul, not the 'Twelve Apostles' nor the group led by the 'Seven', fulfils Messiah Jesus' Mandate of Apostolic Witness in Acts 1.8

Acts 22.4-21 and 26.9-23 as Re-configured Repetitions ('Relectures') of Acts 9.3-30

Once Paul is fully integrated into 'the beginning' and legitimated as the definitive spokesperson for the apostolic 'word', all of Luke's focus is upon Paul's culminating witness in the centre of empire that controls 'the edge/end of the earth' (Isa. 45.22; 49.6). The two repetitions of Paul's calling overlap as *medial*, synchronic connectors to re-configure the growing impact of Paul arising from his own sending as the 'rising action' progresses from *the beginning* to its *goal*:

> Acts 22.4-21 adds critical information to link the events of Paul's first foray into Jerusalem (Acts 9.26-30) to his final arrest there (21.15-36). Now according to Paul's version of Ananias' visitation, Ananias related that God 'had selected' (προ–

---

58   As if to add further corroboration, Luke has Paul take Silas – one of the confirming witnesses sent by the assembly (Acts 15.27) to replace Barnabas as Paul's leading co-proclaimer (15.40) – to proceed to the very regions addressed by the letter from the assembly (15.23b, 41).

59   Paul's insistence in Gal. 2.1-10 that he did not back down one iota in defending his 'gospel' among the 'pillars' of Jerusalem is better explained when the Acts 15 passage through the 'continuity of the narrative' is seen as corroborating his calling to proclaim the same 'grace of our Lord Jesus Christ' to the gentiles as to the Jews which is granted through faith(-fulness). The provisions of the 'apostolic decree' (cf. Acts 16.4) do not define the basis or even the contingencies by which 'we are saved just in the same they are' (15.11b), but rather the *conditions* by which the two saved parties can live 'all together as one' (ὁμοθυμαδόν) in fulfilling God's decrees for all human beings everywhere as outlined by Moses ('who ... in every city ... is read every Sabbath in the synagogues', Acts 15.21; cf. 1 Cor. 6.9–8.13).

εχειρίσατο) Paul to 'know his will (γνῶναι θέλημα αὐτοῦ) and to see and hear the just one' (τὸν δίκαιον, cf. Isa. 53.12) and, on the basis of this 'seeing and hearing', to be a 'witness for him to all humankind' (μάρτυς ... ὧν ἑώρακας καὶ ἤκουσας, Acts 22.15). What Paul has just seen and heard, of course, is that as he persecutes those of the way (e.g., 'the blood of your witness (μάρτυς) Stephen', 22.20), he is also persecuting the risen Jesus, the 'just one' himself. But now, in addition, Luke informs his audience that when Paul's life was in danger in Jerusalem (9.29-30), Paul was sent out of Jerusalem from a vision in the Temple (similar to Isaiah [Isa. 6]) in which he, again, 'saw' and 'heard' the 'just one', now saying to him, 'They will not accept your testimony (μαρτυρία) about me ... Get going, because I am sending you into the nations afar' (εἰς ἔθνη μακράν) (Acts 22.17-21).

i) Thus, like Peter and the apostles, Paul receives from the same *prooemial* voice of the risen Christ a command to be 'a witness of these things into all the nations, *beginning from Jerusalem*' (Luke 24.47b-48). Early in his calling, therefore, Paul's own suffering is forged to that of the 'just one' in a corporate solidarity of rejection reminiscent of the servant – sc., characteristics of an individual within a smaller group of Israel – in Isa. 40–55. As we have seen in Acts 13 (vv. 14–20), Paul's mission *into* the nations is characterized repeatedly by his witness vigorously opposed first in the synagogues before – similar to the servant – he 'turns' to the gentiles within those cities/nations.[60]

ii) Even more importantly, the 'shutting of the Temple doors' now takes on special significance (Acts 21.30). The prophecy of the risen 'just one' in the Temple vision had now been decisively fulfilled (Acts 22.18 ≈ 9.28-29). Paul has in the interim taken his witness three times to Jerusalem;[61] now in this final visit he is arrested in the Temple precincts and nearly loses his life to the *laos* of Israel – similar to the treatment of Stephen. Not only do the *laos* of Israel as a whole, gathered for Pentecost, spontaneously solidify to charge Paul of violating the sanctity of the Temple (Acts 21.27-30); but even the 'myriads' of Jews 'who have come to believe' have become convinced that Paul is a traitor to the scriptures and customs of Israel such that his life is now 'negotiable'! (21.20-26). When the Temple doors are 'immediately shut' behind Paul as he is dragged out and nearly beaten to death (21.30), this development is a 'concluding' and 'conclusive' event of causes and influences traced throughout the 'continuity of the narrative'. The chief enemy *of* the way has become the chief enemy *in* the way of the 'the people, the law, and this place' (21.28a). As 'the Lord' will soon tell Paul – again in a vision – that because he has 'born testimony concerning me in Jerusalem', what remains is 'the necessity to bear witness also in Rome' (δεῖ καὶ εἰς Ῥώμην μαρτυρῆσαι) (23.11). From this point on it appears that only 'the door of faith to the nations' (14.27) remains open.

iii) Acts 26.9-23 portrays Paul before 'many nations' and 'kings' who 'marvel' and 'shut their mouths' at his report (cf. Isa. 52.15a). The narrator casts Paul's

---

60   For a tracing of this pattern of 'debate on the scriptures' in the synagogue, see D. P. Moessner, 'The script of the Scriptures', pp. 245–48 (n. 39).

61   Acts 11.30; 15.3-29; 18.22; on the role of Jerusalem in Luke-Acts, see M. C. Parsons, *Luke. Storyteller, Interpreter, Evangelist* (Peabody, MA: Hendrickson, 2007), pp. 86–95: 'an ending to the story of Jesus and ... the beginning of the church's end-time witness, which included ... the gentile mission' (95).

defence before Agrippa and Festus with all the pomp and circumstance of a pre-trial hearing to build up to his 'imperial majesty' (Acts 25.25). The 'king' Agrippa and his wife Bernice and military tribunes and the leading 'lights' of Caesarea enter ceremoniously to 'examine' Paul and provide the substance for 'his excellency' Festus 'to write' 'the lord' Caesar (Acts 25.26; cf. 25.13; Lk. 1.3-4). King Agrippa marvels at Paul's fantastic story from 'the prophets' that would lure him, while the governor Festus 'shuts his mouth' over the incredulity of a mind run mad! (26.24-29; cf. v. 13). 'For they to whom no account had been brought shall see, and they who had previously not heard, shall seriously consider it' (Isa. 52.15b). What is more, Paul sums up his entire calling in the lights and shades of the servant mission and, in essence, declares that his mission has brought Acts 1.8 to fulfilment. Now the 'Lord' 'Jesus' himself 'of the heavenly vision' tells Paul he is to be a 'servant and witness (ὑπηρέτης καὶ μάρτυς) of the things you have just seen and of those in which I will appear to you, rescuing you from the people and from the nations into which I am sending you in order that they should open their eyes and turn (ἐπιστρέψαι) from darkness to light, from the authority of Satan to God, to receive a release of sins ... ' (26.16-18). Great opposition has sparked light.

Moreover, Paul looks back upon his entire sending and pronounces it successful: he has (1) 'first to those in Damascus and then those in Jerusalem and then to all the region of Judea' (which includes Samaria)[62] 'and to those of the nations/gentiles, (2) been proclaiming a change of mind and a turning to God' (ἀπήγγελλουν μετανοεῖν καὶ ἐπιστρέφειν ἐπὶ τὸν θεόν) (26.20; cf. Lk. 24.47; Acts 1.8). 'For these reasons (ἕνεκα τούτων) the Jews seized me in the Temple, trying to kill me' (Acts 26.21). All along this course he has opened the scriptures, 'bearing witness (μαρτυρόμενος) ... and saying nothing except what the prophets and Moses said would take place, namely, that there would be a suffering Christ (εἰ παθητὸς ὁ χριστός), and that he [the Christ], being the first from the resurrection of the dead, would himself proclaim light to both the people and to the nations' (φῶς μέλλει καταγγέλλειν τῷ τε λαῷ καὶ τοῖς ἔθνεσιν) (26.22b-23; cf. Lk. 24.44-46). Wherever Paul has spoken, it has actually been the anointed Christ who, like the anointed servant (Isa. 42.1-4), has been proclaiming light to Israel and the nations.

To sum up, the nexuses of cause and consequence have been elaborated from the *beginning* of Paul's calling through *middle* developments of rising opposition to a *bursting forth* in arrest and violent attack by his own people. Like Diodorus,[63] Luke has even grounded this historiographical causation in the mythic stories/scriptures of Israel's divine origin and prophetic calling which Luke depicts, cites, and echoes as coming to fruition.

---

62   To a Roman audience as in Acts 26, the geographical 'region of Judea' would encompass the Roman province 'Judaea' which included Samaria, if not even a greater portion of 'Palestine'.

63   In *Library of History* I.3.2 Diodorus criticizes other historians for regarding mythic origins of ethnic groups/nations as secondary and unreliable material for writing their history rather than illuminative of a group's values and founding principles, even when the events described are not credible.

2. When Paul Reaches Rome,[64] the 'Goal'/'End' (τέλος) of the Two-volume Work Has Been Achieved

Acts 28.17-31

As Diodorus confides early on to his audience (I.4.6) that 'the plan for his narrative has reached its goal' (ἡ ... ὑπόθεσις ἔχει τέλος), Luke has also begun by promising a 'secure grasp' of 'the events brought to fruition' through following the sequence of Luke's new narrative configuration (Lk. 1.3-4). Acts 28 formally and 'finally' secures that grasp through a concluding event 'from which' – to use Aristotle's definition of an 'end' – 'nothing of necessity must follow'.[65] By the time the narrator finishes his comments in Acts 28.30-31, the goal (τέλος) of the narrative has been reached, and Luke has opened up a new era to his readers in which the 'continuity of the narrative' no longer holds since the church finds itself in a new setting of mission among the nations, 'welcoming all' (ἀπεδέχετο πάντας) (cf. Lk. 20.24 [καιροὶ ἐθνῶν]).

Structurally, the encounter of Paul in Rome with the 'leading members of the Jews' in a follow-up session resembles the dual exhortation of Paul in the synagogue of Pisidian Antioch (Acts 13). In both instances, the Jewish 'brothers' initially evince a sincere desire to engage Paul's ideas (Acts 28.22; cf. 13.15, 42-43). In both settings, Paul 'exhorts from' or 'lays out' the scriptures, 'persuading them about Jesus from the law of Moses and from the prophets' (28.23, 25-28; cf. 13.15b, 17-31, 32-41). And in both, there is a mixed reaction, some 'are persuaded', others are not (28.24; cf. 13.43).

But here the similarities end. In the contrasting description of the 'second session' of Acts 28 lies a telling clue. The outraged reaction is absent. Instead of some Jews taking umbrage at Paul's words, the Jews agree harmoniously to be 'disharmonious' in their understanding of this Jesus and the 'Kingdom of God' (28.25; cf. v. 23). No opposition is expressed directly against Paul. Contrary to the chronic pattern, Paul himself has escaped controversy. From that point on, in fact, Paul 'welcomes' and 'proclaims to *all* (ἀπεδέχετο πάντας), who enter to see him, bearing witness to the Kingdom of God and the things concerning the Lord Jesus Christ' (28.30b-

---

64   For the ending of Acts and bibliography, see esp. D. Marguerat, 'The Enigma of the Silent Closing of Acts (28, 16-31)', in *Jesus and the Heritage of Israel, Luke's Narrative Claim Upon Israel's Legacy* (vol. 1 of Luke the Interpreter of Israel; D. P. Moessner [ed.]; Harrisburg, Pa.: Trinity Press International, 1999), pp. 284–304 (cf. n. 52); ibid., *The First Christian Historian. Writing the 'Acts of the Apostles'* (SNTSMS, 121; Cambridge: Cambridge University Press, 2002), esp. pp. 147–54, 205–30. For views on the significance of 'Israel' at the end of Acts, see the articles by M. Wolter, R. C. Tannehill, I. H. Marshall, and the 'wrap-up' by D. P. Moessner and D. L. Tiede in *Jesus and the Heritage of Israel*, pp. 307–68; cf. J. B. Tyson (ed.), *Luke-Acts and the Jewish People. Eight Critical Perspectives* (Minneapolis: Augsburg, 1988).

65   *Poetics* 7 (1450b).28-29: 'An end (τελευτή), by contrast [to a beginning], is that which itself naturally occurs, whether necessarily or usually (ἢ ἐξ ἀνάγκης ἢ ὡς ἐπὶ τὸ πολύ), after a preceding event, but need not be followed by anything else' (trans. S. Halliwell; LCL, 199 [1995], p. 55). Aristotle grounds his definitions of 'beginning', 'middle', and 'ending' in analogy to a 'holistic organism' like a beautiful animal whose structure must be perceived by the viewer *as a whole* (*Poetics* 7[1450b].30–1451a.1-15); cf. Diodorus' comparison of a *unified universal history* to a living organism (XX.1.5).

31a). Both Jews and the nations can respond to Paul's opening of the scriptures (cf. 15.11). No longer is a distinction to be made between bearing witness *first* to the Jews before also including the gentiles. Acts 1.8 has been fulfilled. The dynamic of the servant mission that Acts 1.8 legitimated and the risen Christ enacted is no longer in force. The reader who has followed the narrative thread throughout the sequence of Acts recognizes that, in Rome, that line has been snapped:

i) The utter refusal by the 'leading members' of the Jewish people in Jerusalem to engage Paul's witness (Acts 21) has consummated and concluded 'to the Jews first' and opens the period that Jesus himself had called 'the times of opportunities for the nations/gentiles' (Lk. 21.24). Jesus had linked Jerusalem's coming destruction and deportation 'into all the nations' – εἰς τὰ ἔθνη πάντα (cf. Lk. 24.47!) with their refusal to receive his and his emissaries' 'testimony/witness' (μαρτύριον) during a period when Jesus *himself* would speak through and for them (Lk. 21.5-24: ἐγώ ... δώσω ὑμῖν στόμα [15]). With the Temple doors shut against Paul and Paul 'in chains for the hope of Israel', that specially 'sent' 'testimony' is over. In Rome, that conclusion is announced.

ii) Even though the Jewish gathering is divided – similar to the usual pattern – Paul invokes the Holy Spirit *not* as empowering the 'change of mind', but as speaking, in advance, a word of warning to the Israel present for their failure in 'turning' to the Lord, for their growing inability to 'change their mind'. Rather than Paul ignite the rage of Israel, Paul turns the threat of God's judgement upon them. Isaiah's calling from the Temple (Isaiah 6) to be 'sent' to Israel with the message of 'turning' has now arrived at an unprecedented stage in the lacklustre response of 'this people' as a whole. Now the Spirit speaks to 'your fathers' a lament of unrequited response (cf. 13.17, 26!), 'lest they should turn (ἐπιστρέψωσιν) and I would heal them' (28.26-27). First Jesus, now Paul offers a solemn assessment of the dullness of Israel's heart; it has hardened beyond the rhythm of 'life as usual' (cf. Lk. 19.41-44; 21.20-36). Paul's sweeping, stereotyped allegation seems out of line; after all, 'some Jews were persuaded' – unless, of course, the *telos* of the narrative continuity has been reached.

iii) For the first and only time, the announcement of God's 'saving act' in the 'Lord Jesus Christ' is 'sent' *only* 'to those of the nations' (τοῖς ἔθνεσιν ἀπεστάλη) (Acts 28.28). Jesus the 'servant' (παῖς) had been 'sent' *first* to Israel (Acts 3.26) as the 'anointed one' (10.36-38) who fulfils 'all that stands written' (13.26-29), Peter and John had been 'sent' to Samaria (8.14), and Paul had been 'sent' to Israel and the nations (26.17; 13.26-46→18.6). *Now* the 'sending' is to the nations. 'They indeed will hearken' (28.28b). The narrative thread is broken.

iv) The city of Rome is the symbolic centre of the great power controlling 'the end of the earth', used in God's comprehensive 'plan' both as blessing and as judgement upon Israel.[66] Like Cyrus in Isaiah 45 who controls the 'nations at the end(s) of the earth' and obliterates any opposition, so Rome's power is pervasive and settles all disputes among the nations. Yet also like Cyrus, Rome's power enables Paul's servant mission to progress and succeed to the end of its God-ordained course. Without the intervening force of Rome, Paul's 'testimony' to 'all' in the capital

---

66   Cf. Isa. 5.26 where Assyria represents God's judgement upon Israel issuing 'from the end of the earth' (ἀπ' ἄκρου τῆς γῆς), and Jer. 6.22–Babylonia (ἀπ' ἐσχάτου τῆς γῆς).

city would, historically speaking, have been impossible. Diodorus himself credits the vast power of Rome for his ability to access written records pertaining to the whole world: 'For the supremacy of this city [Rome], a supremacy so powerful that it extends to the corners of the inhabited world (διατείνουσα τῇ δυνάμει πρὸς τὰ πέρατα τῆς οἰκουμένης), has provided us ... with copious resources in the most accessible form' (I.4.3). Thus, when Paul reaches Rome, the Roman Empire has fulfilled Cyrus' projected impact upon Israel, when 'you nations who are at the end of the earth' may now 'turn and be saved' (Isa. 45.22: ἐπιστράφητε πρός με καὶ σωθήσεσθε οἱ ἀπ' ἐσχάτου τῆς γῆς). The fact that Rome was associated with 'the end of the earth' in at least one Jewish, pre-Christian text, *Ps. Sol.* 8.15, only adds further credence to Luke's correlation of Paul's 'witness' to the 'witness' of Isaiah's 'servant'. Like Diodorus, then, Luke con-figures the leading collateral forces within a larger providential plan[67] to exhibit the consequences of cause upon 'the way', as well as to re-configure Israel's mythic origins/scriptures which prefigure and 'motivate' that plan.

v) Finally, Luke closes volume two as he began. Like Diodorus, Luke re-sounds his programmatic beginning. Paul's 'bearing witness (διαμαρτύρομαι) to the Kingdom of God' and 'the matters concerning the Lord Jesus Christ, with entirely unhindered openness' for 'two full years' (Acts 28.23, 30-31) culminates Jesus' plain speech about the Kingdom. Rather than ponder times and seasons that are 'set' and known only by 'the Father', Jesus spends a discrete period of time teaching from the scriptures about his own 'suffering', his 'living status', and the coming 'power' of the Holy Spirit as the essence of 'the Kingdom of God' (Acts 1.3-5). Rather than speak about a 'kingdom' 're-constituted *to* and *for* Israel', Jesus speaks about Israel's 'witness' to and for that Kingdom which has been re-constituted through 'the matters concerning the Lord Jesus Christ' and the 'power' of his 'witnesses'. The culminating event (τελευτή) in which the 'witness' of the 'opening of the scriptures' is open to all the world, even to its 'ends', has taken place. In the 'unconfined' quarters of confinement in Rome, Luke *ends* his work with Paul indeed *defining and defending that witness*.[68]

---

67   See n. 33; cf. *Library of History* I.1.3-5 where Diodorus insists on the unified plotting of his universal history because of the interweavings of Providence through Fate of all the happenings of the known world into an intended pattern; see further, J. T. Squires, *The Plan of God in Luke-Acts* (SNTSMS, 76; Cambridge: Cambridge University Press, 1993), esp. pp. 15–52.

68   Cf. the title of C.-J. Thornton's work, *Der Zeuge des Zeugen. Lukas als Historiker der Paulus Reisen* (WUNT, 56; Tübingen: Mohr/Siebeck, 1991), in which Luke functions as a writing witness to Paul *the* witness.

Chapter 8

'HAS GOD REJECTED HIS PEOPLE?' (ROMANS 11.1).
THE SALVATION OF ISRAEL IN ACTS: NARRATIVE CLAIM OF A
PAULINE LEGACY

Simon Butticaz
Trans. Nicholas J. Zola

I. The Paulinism of Acts: A Brief Look Back

a. Paulinism and 'Early Catholicism'

Although independent in its beginnings, the question of the Paulinism of the New Testament writings and Apostolic Fathers rapidly became associated with the historical research devoted to the emergence and development of early Christianity that was begun at the threshold of the nineteenth century.[1] Concerned with specifying the historical and institutional evolution of nascent Christianity, many scholars soon developed an explanatory model that met with resounding success: the model of proto-catholic decline. It was Ferdinand Christian Baur, the leading scholar of the famous Tübingen School, who set the tone in several of his works.[2] Applying the Hegelian model of the dialectical development of history to the formation of primitive Christianity, Baur concluded that early church history was characterized by a powerful and dynamic synthesis of two opposing currents: the Jewish-Christianity of Peter and the gentile-Christianity of Paul. It was within this school of thought that it would first become necessary to consider the Paulinism of Luke.[3] Soon it was believed that the *auctor ad Theophilum*, anxious to promote and defend a unified Christianity under the leadership of a centralizing episcopate, refashioned the Pauline image and theology toward *his own* conciliatory and harmonistic leanings. In short, the Paul of Acts, stripped of his gospel concerning

---

1   On the history of research devoted to Paulinism, consult P. G. Müller, 'Der "Paulinismus" in der Apostelgeschichte: Ein forschungsgeschichtlicher Überblick', *Paulus in den neutestamentlichen Spätschriften* (ed. K. Kertelge; QD, 89; Freiburg: Herder, 1981), pp. 157–201. See also J. Pichler, *Paulusrezeption in der Apostelgeschichte: Untersuchungen zur Rede im pisidischen Antiochien* (IThSt, 50; Innsbruck: Tyrolia-Verlag, 1997).

2   F. C. Baur, *Paulus, der Apostel Jesu Christi: Sein Leben und Wirken, seine Briefe und seine Lehre: Ein Beitrag zu einer kritischen Geschichte des Urchristenthums* (Stuttgart: Becher & Müller, 1845); *Idem, Das Christentum und die christliche Kirche der drei ersten Jahrhunderte* (Tübingen: Fues, 2nd edn 1860).

3   Cf. P. G. Müller, 'Der "Paulinismus" in der Apostelgeschichte', pp. 182ff.

God's justification, was recycled in the service of a Petrine theology with strong Jewish-Christian accents. In its place, the author of Acts did not hesitate to put on the lips of James and Peter the central *theologoumena* of the Pauline epistles: criticism of the Law and justification by faith. In sum, the book of Acts appears to have been the founding document of a unified, 'catholic' church, a document designed to neutralize the centrifugal forces plaguing the numerous trajectories of nascent Christianity. It was for this ideological purpose that the Lukan figure of Paul was 'sacrificed'.[4]

This monumental thesis argued by Ferdinand Christian Baur and his successors, although temporarily eclipsed by the advent of dialectical theology, was taken up once again following World War II by such equally prestigious figures as Philipp Vielhauer, Ernst Käsemann, and Willi Marxsen. One of the major results of Baur and his school was the annexation of Paulinism into the hypothesis of the proto-catholicism of emergent Christianity. From that moment and for a long time thereafter, the term 'Paulinism' was diverted for making negative value judgements on the early promoters of this 'early catholicism'. Paulinism became synonymous with the 'diversion', 'distortion' or 'betrayal' of the 'true' Pauline gospel.[5]

b. The Devastating Rupture of Philipp Vielhauer

The 1950s marked a revival of interest for Paulinism and the theses developed by the Tübingen School. It is to Philipp Vielhauer and his programmatic article 'Zum "Paulinismus" der Apostelgeschichte' that we owe the most consummate and emblematic expression of this resurgence. Listing four themes that summarize the principal assertions of Paul in his speeches in Acts – natural theology, the Law, Christology, and eschatology – Vielhauer tested their affinity with the corpus of Pauline epistles.[6] His conclusion was monolithic and seemingly irrefutable: 'He [Luke] presents no specifically Pauline idea. His "Paulinism" consists in his zeal for the worldwide Gentile mission and in his veneration for the greatest missionary to the Gentiles.'[7] In short, pre-Pauline in matters of Christology, the author of Acts is partial to post-Pauline traditions for the three other theological themes under consideration.[8] The traditional argument of a rupture between the Paul of the epistles and the Paul of Acts had been launched and would relentlessly fuel the debate to come.[9]

4   Ibid., p. 183: 'Paulinism, understood as the misappropriation of the Paul of the letters, was the sacrifice that Luke was willing to perform in order to reconstruct Catholicism. But at the same time, the dynamic of the true Paul was also lost within the church.'

5   Cf. J. Pichler, *Paulusrezeption in der Apostelgeschichte*, p. 33.

6   P. Vielhauer, 'Zum "Paulisnismus" der Apostelgeschichte', *Aufsätze zum Neuen Testament* (Tbü, 31; München: Kaiser, 1965), pp. 9–27 (10ff.) [ET: Philipp Vielhauer, 'On the "Paulinism" of Acts', in *Studies in Luke-Acts: Essays Presented in Honor of Paul Schubert* (ed. L. E. Keck and J. L. Martyn; trans. W.C. Robinson, Jr. and V.P. Furnish; London: SPCK, 1968), pp. 34–49].

7   Ibid., p. 26 [ET p. 48].

8   Ibid., p. 26 [ET p. 49]: 'The author of Acts is in his Christology pre-Pauline, in his natural theology, concept of the law, and eschatology, post-Pauline' (ET p. 48].

9   In this vein, we can point out the monograph of C. Mount, *Pauline Christianity: Luke-Acts and the Legacy of Paul* (NovTSup, 104; Leiden: Brill, 2002).

c. Jacob Jervell and the 'Unknown Paul'

In reaction to this 'clap of thunder'[10] sparked by Philipp Vielhauer's provocative essay, several contributions emerged espousing the continuity of Paul and Luke. Most often, these exegetical appeals revived the patristic theory of Luke the physician, companion of Paul.[11] On the other side of the research spectrum, I would like to mention first Jacob Jervell's proposal, which is as audacious as it is creative.[12] Accustomed to the swing of the pendulum,[13] the Norwegian exegete embarked on a path hitherto untrodden. He probed the shadowy regions of the Pauline epistles in order to exhume an unknown profile of the apostle to the gentiles. Pointing out the two dominant facets of the Lukan portrait of Paul – Paul as an observant Christian Pharisee (Acts 21.23-26; 23.6; etc.) and Paul as miracle worker (Acts 13.8-12; 14.8-10; 16.16-18; 19.11; 20.7-12; 28.8-10) – Jervell compared them to the data provided by the Pauline epistles. The results of this comparative work were astounding: Luke appears to have retained two aspects of the historical Paul camouflaged in the latter's epistles and hitherto neglected by exegetical research. In other words, far from distorting the figure of the historical Paul, the author to Theophilus has delivered us two otherwise unknown facets thereof![14] Although radical and somewhat hypothetical, Jervell's rejoinder is correct on one point: its refusal to reduce all the substance of the historical Paul into the thin body of his writings. That being said, even if Jervell's hypothesis proves attractive for recognizing Paul as a healer, it hardly presents a convincing picture of Paul as a Jew, a practising Pharisee – and this even after his conversion. In the case of Paul's Judaism, the Pauline image promoted in the Acts of the Apostles seems more dependent on Luke's agenda concerning identity in his historical narrative:[15] through Paul's Judaism in Acts, it is the impossibility of imagining 'the Christian identity ... outside of the bond with Israel'[16] that the *auctor ad Theophilum* seems to uphold.

Along this same line of inquiry into Pauline-Lukan continuity, we can also place the collection of essays on the Paul of Acts published in 1999 by Stanley

---

10   O. Flichy, 'État des recherches actuelles sur les Actes des Apôtres', *Les Actes des Apôtres: Histoire, récit, théologie: XXe congrès de l'Association Catholique Française pour l'Étude de la Bible (Angers, 2003)* (ed. M. Berder ; LD, 199; Paris: Cerf, 2005), pp. 13–42 (15).

11   Cf. Irenaeus, *Adv. Haer.* 3.3.1; 14.1; *Muratorian Canon* 2-8; Tertullian, *Marc.* 4.2.4-5.

12   J. Jervell, 'Paul in the Acts of the Apostles: Tradition, History, Theology', in *Les Actes des Apôtres: Traditions, rédactions, théologie* (ed. J. Kremer; BETL, 48; Leuven: Leuven University Press, 1979), pp. 297–306; *Idem*, 'Der unbekannte Paulus', in *Die paulinische Literatur und Theologie/The Pauline Literature and Theology* (ed. S. Pedersen; Århus: Forlaget Aros; 1980), pp. 29–49; *Idem*, 'Paulus in der Apostelgeschichte und die Geschichte des Urchristentums', *NTS* 32 (1986), pp. 378–92.

13   It is also to Jacob Jervell that we owe the radical reversal of perspective that has arisen in the research devoted to the image of Judaism in Luke: *Luke and the People of God: A New Look at Luke-Acts* (Minneapolis: Augsburg, 1972).

14   J. Jervell, 'Paul in the Acts of the Apostles', p. 303: 'We are now dealing with elements lying in the shadow in Paul's letters, but placed in the sun by Luke.'

15   See in this sense D. Marguerat, 'L'image de Paul dans les Actes des Apôtres', in *Les Actes des Apôtres: Histoire, récit, théologie; XXᵉ congrès de l'Association catholique française pour l'étude de la Bible (Angers 2003)* (ed. M. Berder; LD, 199; Paris: Cerf, 2005), pp. 121–54.

16   Ibid., 138.

E. Porter.[17] Less iconoclastic and more methodical than Jervell, Porter, in his final chapter, examines point by point the criticisms made by Ernst Haenchen and Philipp Vielhauer accusing Luke of biographical and theological infidelity vis-à-vis the Pauline epistles. At the end of this meticulous inventory, Porter arrives at the conclusion that the differences alleged by the Haenchen-Vielhauer tandem are not relevant. On the contrary, there is every indication that 'the author of the book of Acts had some form of close contact with Paul and his beliefs'.[18] As for the aforementioned differences, he attributes them to two plausible factors: first, to the inevitable idiosyncrasies characteristic of two established authors; and second, to the different literary genres and their specific intentions of communication. The genius of Stanley Porter is his foresight to seek Luke's continuity with Paul within the inevitable displacement between them.

d. Locating the Paulinism of Acts between Continuity and Distance

Modern research now appears to be firmly engaged in a third direction: locating the Paulinism of Luke between irrefutable proximity and noteworthy distance. In other words, the exegetes are increasingly convinced that neither the model of proto-catholic decline nor the model of harmonized continuity satisfactorily handles the Lukan reception of Paul.[19] This modern-day paradigm shift also translates into the terminological world: it is no longer a question of the 'distortion' or 'falsification' of the Pauline tradition, but of its 'legacy'[20] and 'creative treatment'.[21]

In two recent contributions, Daniel Marguerat[22] has offered a vigorous plea for abandoning the rigid dichotomy formerly cultivated in scholarship,[23] commending in its place the concept of 'legacy' developed by J. C. Beker. As justification for this approach, Marguerat points to the variety of forms that the reception of Paul took on in early Christian literature. That is, the complex phenomenon of the receptions of the apostle Paul bears witness to this creative rewriting and recording of the Pauline

---

17   *The Paul of Acts: Essays in Literary Criticism, Rhetoric, and Theology* (WUNT 115; Tübingen: Mohr Siebeck, 1999).

18   Ibid., 206.

19   See, for example, W. O. Walker, 'Acts and the Pauline Corpus Reconsidered', *JSNT* 24 (1985), pp. 3–23.

20   A term introduced into the discussion of Pauline reception by J. C. Beker, *Heirs of Paul: Paul's Legacy in the New Testament and in the Church Today* (Minneapolis: Fortress Press, 1991).

21   J. Schröter, 'Kirche im Anschluss an Paulus: Aspekte der Paulusrezeption in der Apostelgeschichte und in den Pastoralbriefen', *ZNW* 98 (2007), pp. 77–104 (97): 'It is much more significant to recognize the Lukan interpretation of Paul as a *creative treatment* of the inheritance of Paul in a new configuration within the story of early Christianity' (emphasis added).

22   D. Marguerat, "L'image de Paul dans les Actes des Apôtres", *Les Actes des Apôtres*; *idem*, 'Paul après Paul: Une histoire de réception', *NTS* 54 (2008), pp. 317–37 [= ch. 3 of this volume].

23   D. Marguerat, 'Paul après Paul', p. 320 [ET=ch. 3 of this volume, p. 73]: 'What can we do, other than leave behind the alternatives of incompatibility or of harmonization?'

tradition. Extending the dual typology laid out by François Bovon,[24] Marguerat[25] identifies three ways of rephrasing 'Paul after Paul': the 'documentary' pole (Paul and his epistolary corpus), the 'biographical' pole (Paul, herald of the gospel), and the 'doctoral' pole (Paul, doctor of the church). Each trajectory rendered the Pauline legacy at the close of the first century in a singular and creative manner. Luke's composition is in line with the biographical pole, whereas the Deutero-Pauline writings (Colossians, Ephesians, 2 Thessalonians) are on the doctoral trajectory of this Pauline reception model. In other words, the author of Acts appears to have selected a unique facet of the Pauline portrait – Paul the missionary and founder of communities – and ignored the other components. He did not compose this profile on the basis of the Pauline correspondence but rather on the narrative memory circulating in the communities founded by the apostle of the gentiles. In short, it is an image of the apostle independent of the one mediated by scripture.

All typology inevitably involves both advantages and risks. The three-way reception of the Pauline tradition outlined by Daniel Marguerat possesses an undeniable heuristic potential to detect the diverse forms adopted by the reception of Paul and to explain their troubling silences. For example, if Luke does not take Paul's epistolary activity into account, it is because he is not advancing a literary memory, but a biographical legacy. He is not dependent on the body of Paul's letters, but on the narrative recollections preserved by the communities in Paul's missionary sphere. The explanation is attractive and the model works. There is another undeniable advantage of this typology: its refusal to gauge all the receptions of Paul against a single standard – the canon of his letters. The historical Paul is not identical to the 'canonical' Paul; even the 'canonical' Paul is a constructed image, a creative phenomenon of reception.[26] That being said, the proposed typology need not drive us to trace overly rigid boundaries between these trajectories of reception. That there were various and diverse shifts within the rereading of Paul is beyond discussion. That the historical reception of Paul has tended to focus at times on the biographical Paul, or on the doctoral Paul, or on the canonical Paul is equally probable. However, these three modes of reception should not be compartmentalized in a strict fashion: they often interact with each other, giving rise to combinations that are as varied as they are novel. I will offer two examples:

24   F. Bovon, 'Paul comme Document et Paul comme Monument', in *Chrétiens en conflit. L'Épître de Paul aux Galates* (ed. J. Allaz *et al.*; Essais Bibliques, 13; Genève: Labor et Fides, 1987), pp. 54–65. ET = 'Paul as Document and Paul as Monument', in *New Testament and Christian Apocrypha: Collected Studies II* (ed. F. Bovon and G. Snyder; Tübingen: Mohr Siebeck, 2009), pp. 307–17.

25   D. Marguerat, 'L'image de Paul', pp. 132-35; *idem*, 'Paul après Paul', pp. 320–23 [= ET this volume pp. 74–75]. See also S. Vollenweider, 'Paul entre exégèse et histoire de la réception', in *Paul, une théologie en construction* (ed. A. Dettwiler, J.-D. Kaestli, and D. Marguerat; MdB 51; Genève: Labor et Fides, 2004), pp. 441–59 (452–54).

26   D. Marguerat, 'L'image de Paul', p. 133: '... the canon of the Pauline epistles does not constitute the documentary base or the backdrop on which the reception of the apostle is to be erected'. In this sense see also O. Flichy, *La figure de Paul dans les Actes des Apôtres. Un phénomène de réception de la tradition paulinienne à la fin du premier siècle* (LD, 214; Paris, Cerf, 2007), p. 39.

the Deutero-Pauline letters (Colossians and Ephesians) and the book of the Acts of the Apostles.

Colossians and Ephesians erect Paul, the apostle of the gentiles, as a *monument* that forms an integral part of the proclaimed 'mystery' (Col. 1.25-27; Eph. 3.3-5, 9).[27] It is in him, in his preaching (Col. 1.25; 4.3; Eph. 3.7-8) and his life of suffering (Col. 1.24; 2.1; 4.3, 10; Eph. 3.1, 13; 4.1; 6.20), that this mystery is fulfilled (cf. Col. 1.25: πληρῶσαι). Moreover, Paul himself is the revelatory channel (Eph. 3.3).[28] Yet, the content of this 'mystery' is none other than the *Pauline* gospel of Christ in its missiological (Colossians)[29] and ecclesiological (Ephesians)[30] effects. Furthermore, in these two pseudepigraphical letters it is the Pauline *theologoumena* that serve as an interpretive screen for traditions of various origins.[31] Is it possible to discriminate here between the Pauline biographical memory (Paul the suffering preacher) and theological figure (Paul the leading thinker)?

Concerning the second volume of Luke, the assessment is similar: separating the narrative image of Paul from his theological legacy is a delicate and controversial enterprise. Admittedly, the Acts of Luke do not explicitly claim the apostle of the gentiles as a source, do not reflect his literary activity, and conspicuously disregard certain classic themes of his theology. Nevertheless, the theological and literary contacts between Paul and Luke are not non-existent (especially in Acts 13, 15, or 17)[32] and the importance of Paul the theologian should not be underestimated. Jens Schröter concludes after a recent study on the Paul of Acts and the Paul of the Pastorals, 'Luke, as also occurs in the Pastorals, closely associates Paul's ministry and teaching. Furthermore, in both cases a profile of Paul the "theologian" is formulated.'[33] In conclusion, the typology put together by D. Marguerat should be promoted in two respects, without, however, leading to an inflexible use. It enables

---

27   Well demonstrated by H. Merklein, 'Paulinische Theologie in der Rezeption des Kolosser- und Epheserbriefes', *Paulus in den neutestamentlichen Spätschriften*, pp. 28–37.

28   A. Dettwiler, 'L'épître aux Colossiens', in *Introduction au Nouveau Testament. Son histoire, son écriture, sa théologie* (ed. D. Marguerat; MdB 41; Genève: Labor et Fides, 2001), pp. 265–77 (269): 'Now Paul himself belongs to the content of the preaching and becomes a constitutive element of the "mystery"; the figure of Paul has thus become an integral part of the process of revelation.'

29   Well formulated by A. Dettwiler, 'L'épître aux Colossiens', p. 269: 'The term "mystery" denotes not only the content of the Pauline gospel (the cross and resurrection of Christ as the decisive event of salvation); it also includes the universal proclamation of the gospel effected by Paul.'

30   H. Merklein, 'Paulinische Theologie', pp. 28–29. D. Marguerat, 'Paul après Paul', p. 328, provides a good summary [this volume pp. 80–81]: 'The "mystery" is thus nothing other than the ecclesiological and missiological interpretation of the Pauline gospel.'

31   H. Merklein, 'Paulinische Theologie', pp. 37–62.

32   A. Lindemann has compiled an inventory of Pauline literary influences that can be observed in the Acts of Luke and concludes his comparative inquiry as follows: 'In my opinion, the question of whether Luke knew Paul's letters can be answered with a cautious "yes" …. Thus it seems that Luke apparently used Rom. and 2 Cor (10-13?), perhaps Gal as well, as "historical" sources for his presentation.' (*Paulus im ältesten Christentum. Das Bild des Apostels und die Rezeption der paulinischen Theologie in der frühchristlichen Literatur bis Marcion* [BHT, 58; Tübingen, Mohr Siebeck, 1979], pp. 163–173 [171]).

33   J. Schröter, *Kirche im Anschluss an Paulus*, pp. 96–101 (103).

us to seize, in effect, the many processes that make up the Pauline memory in the first century and invites us to bid farewell to the illusory idea of an 'original' and 'normative' Paul. At the same time, a typology is never a mimetic representation of reality, but rather a heuristic and ideal-typical model. Therefore it should be engaged with care.

The variegated history of Paul's receptions, receptions energetically engaged in adopting and adapting, also invite us to reflect on its terms: *How* did Paul's inheritors handle a tradition that was diverse from its beginning? *What means* did they employ to rewrite Paul after Paul? How do we define precisely the phenomenon of *reception*? The administration of a legacy?[34] A transformative rereading?[35] Literary mimesis?[36] Intertextual echoes?[37] The borrowing of genre? To answer these questions, we would like to make a brief methodological excursus, in order to clarify the overly-vague concept of 'reception'.

II. Finding a Conceptual Model for the Phenomenon of Reception

a. Beyond the Model of Source Criticism

Long ago, Pauline reception was examined in terms of source criticism.[38] In other words, it was the objective and material evidence, the heterogeneous borrowing, that was tracked in the post-Pauline writings.[39] Run through the gamut of verbal similarities, structural affinities, and semantic relationships, each later tradition was deemed either familiar with or ignorant of the Pauline correspondence. Although linguistic convergences may certainly indicate literary dependence, reception can equally manifest itself in other ways – without a trace of lexical or structural heterogeneity.[40] For this reason it is advantageous to introduce into this methodological

---

34   J. C. Beker, *Heirs of Paul,* pp. 48–64.

35   D. Marguerat, 'Les "Actes de Paul". Une relecture des Actes canoniques', *La première histoire du christianisme (Les Actes des apôtres)* (LD, 180; Paris: Cerf – Labor et Fides, 2003²), pp. 375–97. ET = *The First Christian Historian: Writing the 'Acts of the Apostles'*, (trans. K. McKinney, G. Laughery, and R. Bauckham; SNTSMS, 121; Cambridge: Cambridge University Press, 2002).

36   D. M. Reis, 'Following in Paul's Footstep: Mimèsis and Power in Ignatius of Antioch', in *Trajectories through the New Testament and the Apostolic Fathers* (ed. A. F. Gregory and C. M. Tuckett; Oxford: Oxford University Press, 2005), pp. 287–305.

37   A. Merz, *Die fiktive Selbstauslegung des Paulus. Intertextuelle Studien zur Intention und Rezeption der Pastoralbriefe* (NTOA, 52; Göttingen: Vandenhoeck und Ruprecht, 2004).

38   See, for example, A. Lindemann, *Paulus im ältesten Christentum*, pp. 15–19.

39   See on this subject the criteria enumerated by J. Pichler, 'Das theologische Anliegen der Paulusrezeption im lukanischen Werk', in *The Unity of Luke-Acts* (ed. J. Verheyden; BETL, 142; Leuven: Leuven University Press, 1999), pp. 731–33. He himself borrows them from two studies by G. Lohfink ('Die Vermittlung des Paulinismus zu den Pastoralbriefen', in *Studien zum Neuen Testament* [SBAB, 5; Stuttgart: Katholisches Bibelwerk, 1989], pp. 267–89 ; 'Paulinische Theologie in der Rezeption der Pastoralbriefe', in *Paulus in den neutestamentlichen Spätschriften* [ed. K. Kertelge; QD, 89; Freiburg: Herder, 1981], pp. 70–121).

40   This was duly recognized by W. O. Walker, 'Acts and the Pauline Corpus Reconsidered', pp. 3–23 (especially p. 10).

discussion today's well-received notion of 'intertextuality'. We will find here a fruitful model for redefining what we mean by the term 'reception'.

b. Introducing Intertextuality into the Discussion: The Example of Annette Merz

The most systematic and sizable application of intertextuality to the question of Paul's reception was carried out by Annette Merz in her doctoral thesis published in 2004.[41] After defining her methodology, she analyzes the *dual intertextual locales* of the Pastorals: they function as a reception of the Pauline letters on the one hand, and as a 'pretext' for the letters of Ignatius of Antioch and Polycarp of Smyrna on the other. Without discussing the results of this intertextual approach to the Pastorals here, we simply want to summarize the methodological foundations established by Merz in this study. Distinguishing intertextuality from its cousin, source criticism, she situates the former in the articulation of the authorial intent and the reader response, between a theory of textual production and an esthetic of reception. To identify the intertextual echoes belonging to the Pastorals, Annette Merz relies on the criteria developed by Manfred Pfister for evaluating the intensity and intentionality of intertextual phenomena:[42] (1) referentiality; (2) communicativity; (3) autoreflexivity; (4) structurality; (5) selectivity; (6) dialogism. We would like to consider the sixth criterion, dialogism.

Dialogism understands intertextuality as an *expressly dialogical* phenomenon, characterized by an energetic exchange of adoptions and revisions between the text being reread and the text engaged in the rereading.[43] This highlights an aspect of intertextuality that is too often neglected – since literary critics are content simply to inventory the *affinities* of language and form between text and intertext – and one particularly fruitful for essaying the reception of Paul after Paul. The management of the Pauline legacy in the first and second centuries is characterized by this subtle dialectic of continuity *and* displacement. Regarding the Pauline reception of Acts, however, we must take two supplementary steps: first, by introducing the concept of 'hypertextuality' forged by Gérard Genette; then, by reflecting on the genre of the Lukan composition.

c. Redefining the Pauline-Lukan Dependence in Terms of Hypertextuality

In his taxonomy of intertextual relations, Gérard Genette employs the term 'hypertextuality' to characterize any derivative or ancillary relationship, other than commentary, between a text engaged in rereading (the hypertext) and a text being reread (the hypotext). This derivation by imitation or transformation does not necessarily imply the mention or explicit borrowing of the source text.[44] For

---

41   A. Merz, *Die fiktive Selbstauslegung des Paulus*.

42   Ibid., pp. 105–113.

43   Ibid., p. 109: 'A complete affirmation is weaker than an antithetical reference. The most acute is a "differentiated dialectic of connecting and distancing as the optimum dialogism".'

44   G. Genette, *Palimpsestes. La littérature au second degré* (Poétique; Paris: Seuil, 1982), p. 12: 'It [the hypertextual derivation] can be of a different order, such that B makes no mention

example, the *Aeneid* is the hypertextual rereading of Homer's *Odyssey*. Yet the Homeric hypotext is neither cited nor its primacy explicitly disclosed. This intertextual derivation at the origin of the *Aeneid* is precisely the fruit of a *transformative rewriting*: Virgil follows the epic genre and central framework of the Ulysses saga, all while recounting the adventures of a different hero and a different people. In sum, a similar process of transformation between a text and its intertext inevitably implies a dialectic of continuity and novelty, of borrowing and distancing. This concept of intertextuality strikes us, more than any other notion, as particularly adequate to evaluate the dialectical nature of the Lukan reception of Paul. In fact, the absence of Pauline vocabulary in Luke can be perfectly explained by this same phenomenon of hypertextuality. Additionally, Luke's selection of *narrative* for the genre of Acts is assuredly a significant dimension of this *transformative rereading*. Therefore we would next like to consider this point.

d. Luke-Acts: A Sonderfall?[45]

Unlike Paul and the authors of the Deutero-Paulines, Luke did not opt for the epistolary or discursive medium. His mode of expression is narrative, story. For evidence that this is a conscious, and therefore deliberate, choice of communication on the part of the author of Luke-Acts, we may turn to the oft-discussed prologue of Lk. 1.1-4. The only technical term Luke employs to describe the literary works of his predecessors, and following them his own authorial contribution, is the word *diēgēsis* (Lk. 1.1: διήγησις).[46] A quick survey of its various occurrences in ancient literature permits us to specify its meaning:[47] a *diēgēsis* refers to a macro-narrative (historical or not), as compared to a *diēgēma*, which is equivalent to a narrative scene, or a *chreia*, which corresponds to an anecdote. More precisely, a *diēgēsis* is understood as an ordered account, presupposing a thoughtful and meaningful arrangement of multiple literary units.[48] This is exactly what Luke makes explicit in v. 3 with the expression καθεξῆς γράψαι.[49]

---

of A, but could not exist as such without A, which B shows at the end of an operation that I will describe, again provisionally, as transformation, and which, consequently, B evokes more or less clearly, without necessarily speaking of or citing it.'

45   K. Löning, 'Paulinismus in der Apostelgeschichte', *Paulus in den neutestamentlichen Spätschriften*, p. 209: '... because within the spectrum of Pauline and deutero-Pauline literature the Lukan two-volume work is already a special case due to its form, so that the task of theological comparison proves to be especially difficult'.

46   See in this sense H. J. Cadbury, *The Making of Luke-Acts* (London: Macmillan, 1927), p. 299: 'The form of his work is narrative, and narrative carries with it the intention of supplying information'; R. C. Tannehill, *The Narrative Unity of Luke-Acts. A Literary Interpretation* (vol. 1; Philadelphia, PA: Fortress Press, 1986), p. 10.

47   Aelius Theon, *Progymnasmata* 78.16-17; Polybius, *Histories* 3.36.1; 38.4; 39.1; 2 Macc. 2.32; 6:17; Josephus, *War* 7.3.2; 8.8.1; *Ant.* 1.2.3; 4.8.4; 9.10.2; etc.; Lucian, *Quomodo Historia conscribenda sit* 55; etc.

48   J. A. Fitzmyer, *The Gospel according to Luke* (AB 28; vol. 1; Garden City, N.Y.: Doubleday, 1981), p. 292: 'Etymologically, it [*diēgēsis*] would denote a composition that "leads through to an end", a comprehensive story which aims at being something more than a mere collection of notes or a compilation of anecdotes.'

49   H. J. Cadbury, in *The Beginnings of Christianity*, vol. 2 (ed. F. J. Jackson and K. Lake;

The fact that Luke has turned to the macro-genre of narrative, rather than writing letters, is not an insignificant move.[50] On the contrary, this choice of form is crucial for appreciating the Lukan rereading of Paul.[51] The leap from discourse to narrative certainly invalidates any investigation focused only on tracking verbal affinities from one work to the other. Luke's theology cannot be condensed into discursive statements – hence the poverty of the Pauline lexicon in Luke – but is communicated through a *diēgēsis*, a narrative discourse of traditions that he has inherited. To sound out his theology, we must investigate first and foremost the narrative construction of his work.[52] Among the many receptions of Paul in the first century, Luke's composition thus constitutes a *Sonderfall*: the author of Acts has effected a *narrative transformation* of the Pauline legacy. In other words, the fidelity of Luke's Pauline message, along with its inevitable displacement, does not come across on the level of the discursive statements, but does resurface in the argumentative structures that underlie his narrative.

For the remainder of this study, we propose to demonstrate how Luke has narratively transposed the major points of Paul's theological reflection *devoted to the fate of Israel* (Romans 9–11). As we have established, it would be erroneous to seek in Luke a speech that summarizes the Pauline arguments and terminology found in Romans 9–11. By opting for a narrative, the author of Acts has thus 'narratively' implemented Paul's theological legacy on the subject of Israel. We will demonstrate this narrativization of Pauline thought on the basis of four theological affirmations that are central to chs 9–11 of Romans: a. the election of a remnant of Israel; b. 'the Jew first, then the Greek'; c. the hardening of Israel and the universal expansion of salvation: a causal link?; d. missionary eschatology. We will conclude this discussion by also noting a significant shift occasioned by this narrative rewriting of the Pauline legacy.

vol. 2 of *The Acts of the Apostles*; London: Macmillan, 1934), p. 495.

50   Indeed, genre is not simply the outer layer of a 'pure' work, it is a condition of existence (D. Maingueneau, *Le discours littéraire. Paratopie et scène d'énonciation* [Paris: Armand Colin, 2004], p. 175).

51   See, in this sense, D. Marguerat, 'L'image de Paul dans les Actes des Apôtres', p. 135, especially n. 1; S. E. Porter, *The Paul of Acts*, p. 206.

52   This was argued with force and conviction by B. R. Gaventa, 'Toward a Theology of Acts. Reading and Rereading', *Int* 42 (1988), pp. 146–57. Against this see H. Conzelmann, *The Theology of St. Luke* (trans. Geoffrey Buswell; New York: Harper, 1961), who for his part disassociated kerygma and historical narrative, barring the way for an assessment of Luke's *narrative theology*: 'Whereas in Mark the narrative itself provides a broad unfolding of the kerygma, Luke defines the narrative as the historical foundation, which is added as a secondary factor to the kerygma, a knowledge of which he takes for granted (Luke i, 4). The factual record is therefore not itself the kerygma, but it provides the historical basis for it' (p. 11).

*III. The Fate of Israel from Paul to the Acts of the Apostles: Between
Theological Continuity and Historical Drift*

a. The Elect 'Remnant' of Israel

The problem underlying chs 9–11 of Romans initially surfaces in chapter 3 of the
same letter. The sorrow and anguish that trouble Paul regarding his brothers (9.2-3)
first find mention here: 'What then? If some were unfaithful, will their faithlessness
nullify the faithfulness of God?' (3.3). This is the burning question that plagues the
apostle and to which he will risk a response. How is it possible to uphold Israel's
countless historic privileges in light of its rejection of Jesus the Messiah? Paul finds
a satisfactory answer in the 'holy remnant' concept of Old Testament theology. So
Paul's initial line of argument through chs 9–11 retraces the rationale of election
that presided in Israel's past, the rationale of a remnant saved by grace. Initiated
with Abraham, this division between children of the promise and children of the
flesh has perpetuated itself across the entire history of the chosen people, passing
through Isaac and Esau (9.7b-13) all to the way to Paul himself (11.1-2). In sum,
faced with the unfaithfulness of one part of Israel, Paul will not allow for the failure
of the divine Word: the history of God with his people is not one of failed promises,
but one of partial success! In other words, the people of the promise is indeed Israel,
God's 'remnant' saved by grace – in a word: Jewish-Christians.

Although in a different historical situation, faced with a largely gentile-Christian
church and excluded from the synagogue, Luke does not argue differently.[53] For
him, it is certainly no longer a question of current events that drives him, but the
necessary continuity between nascent Christianity and the Jewish faith from which
it sprung. Nonetheless, his argumentation follows the same route as Paul's in
Romans: the church has not replaced the Jewish people by embodying the 'verus'
Israel, but lies in its historical *and* empirical continuity. To achieve this, the author
to Theophilus tells the tale of a permanent division among the Jewish hearers of
the Christian message. From the day of Pentecost (Acts 2.12-13) to Paul's arrival
in Rome (Acts 28.24-25), the story of the Jewish mission is a story of division, a
story of 'the falling and rising of many in Israel' (Lk. 2.34b).[54]

Thus, neither Paul nor Luke conceives of the church as a new or true Israel
called to station itself in place of the Jewish people. Both reserve the honorific
title of Israel/Israelites for Jews alone.[55] What Paul argues with the help of several

---

53   *Contra* J. Jervell, 'Paul in the Acts of the Apostles', p. 305: 'They [Paul and Luke] have
not the same solution. To Paul Israel will be saved in the future (Rom. 11); for Luke Israel is saved
now or in the past, namely in the church.'

54   This was first argued by J. Jervell, 'The Divided People of God. The Restoration of
Israel and Salvation for the Gentiles', *Luke and the People of God*, pp. 41–74; also see P. G.
Müller, 'Die jüdische Entscheidung gegen Jesus nach der Apostelgeschichte', *Les Actes des
Apôtres: Traditions, rédaction, théologie*, pp. 523–31 (529): 'The structure of the narrative pro-
gression (6.8-7.60) makes the primary, ambivalent impact of the proclamation of the gospel in a
Jewish milieu clear.'

55   In this sense, see P. G. Müller, 'Die jüdische Entscheidung gegen Jesus', pp. 524–526.
Against this see H. Conzelmann, *The Theology of St. Luke*, p. 146: 'Both statements are the

scriptural examples (Isaac, Esau, himself, Elijah and the seven thousand men that God has kept for himself), Luke recounts via narrative: the story of Israel is a story of division into a 'remnant' that is loved and the 'others'[56] that are hated (cf. Rom. 11.5-8). This Lukan narrativization of Israel's elective history comes across particularly in two forms: the schism that afflicts the Jewish hearers of the Christian mission on the one hand,[57] and the massive Jewish conversions that populate the account on the other.[58] In sum, for Luke as for Paul, the story of God with his people is not the story of a monumental failure; the church does not rise on the ashes of the chosen people, but emerges from their historical *and* empirical extension. Moreover, like Paul himself in Rom. 11.1, Luke does not hesitate to make the apostle of the gentiles the *emblem* of this rationale of election that runs through the history of Israel.[59] Indeed, the conversion of Saul recounted three times in Acts (9, 22, and 26) does not divest him of his Jewishness, but reorients it.[60] *In Paul himself, the saved 'remnant' of Israel emerges.*

b. 'The Jew first, then the Greek'

The affirmation of the priority of the Jews over the gentiles is an element that runs through the letter to the Romans (1.16; 2.9-10). It is the expression of a strong theological conviction: Israel occupies a privileged position in salvation history. It is not simply a question of a temporal antecedent in the order of the Christian mission, but truly a matter of historio-salvific privilege. It is, moreover, what Paul will repeat explicitly in Rom. 3.1-2 and especially in the exordium of 9.4-5: Israel has inherited a brilliant history to which God is intimately tied. The proof is in God's gifts and calling (cf. 11.29). This insistence on the preeminence of Israel woven through the letter to the Romans is not an accidental theme. It reflects the great anxiety that drives Paul: has unfaithful Israel, the children of the flesh, been dismissed from this history of promises? Would God annul his decrees for Israel because of Israel's disobedience? Riding a fine line, Paul still cannot bring himself to sign the eviction notice of the Jewish people out of salvation history. Proof lies in the aporetic wording with which he signs off his long and chaotic argumentation: 'As regards the gospel, they are enemies for your sake; but as regards election they are beloved for the sake of the patriarchs' (11.28). As Daniel Marguerat rightly puts it, 'If the history of grace is now woven in with the Christians, it is not to the point

---

outcome of the view that the Church represents the continuity of redemptive history, and to this degree is "Israel".'

56 Οἱ λοιποί (Rom. 11.7). The use of this expression to describe the unbelievers is found twice in Luke (Lk. 8.10-11; Acts 5.13). On this point see J. Gnilka, *Die Verstockung Israels. Isaias 6,9-10 in der Theologie der Synoptiker* (SANT, 3; München: Kösel-Verlag, 1961), p. 123.

57 Schisms that occur between the people and the Jewish authorities may be found in Acts 4.1-4; 4.18, 21b; 5.26b, 33; schisms that occur within the synagogue community may be found in Acts 13.43, 45; 14.1-2; 17.4-5, 10-13; 18.4-6; 19.8-9; 28.21-22, 24-25.

58 Acts 1.15; 2.41; 4.4, 33; 5.14; 6.1, 7; 9.31, 42; 12.24; 13.43; 14.1; 17.10-12; 21.20.

59 On this point see D. Marguerat, 'L'image de Paul dans les Actes des Apôtres', pp. 136–39.

60 Ibid., p. 137.

that God's relationship with Israel is emptied of the mercy that sustained it.'[61] It is the mystery of salvation history!

Several commentators have noted Luke's proximity on this point.[62] Of all the New Testament writers, it is Luke who offers the closest parallels to the Pauline formula 'the Jew first, then the Greek'. Whether in Acts 3.26 or in Acts 13.46, the πρῶτον placed in the mouth of Peter and Paul is undeniably consonant with the Pauline agenda of salvation history (see equally Acts 2.39; 5.31). Moreover, the author of Acts does not limit himself to this meagre lexical connection. As we have already said, his theology is not primarily discursive, but narrative. Thus Luke offers from this πρῶτον a narrative translation in the recurring scenario of the Pauline mission:[63] invariably, after arriving in a new city, the apostle to the gentiles begins his missionary activity with the Jewish synagogue. This scenario, established at the beginning of Paul's kerygmatic activity (Acts 13), prevails all the way to its close, at his arrival in Rome (Acts 28).[64]

c. The Hardening of Israel and the Universal Expansion of Salvation: A Causal Link?

There is a third affirmation that brings Luke closer to Paul: the causal link woven between the refusal of the Jews and the proclamation of the gospel to the gentiles. This causal relationship was vigorously and forcefully denied by Jacob Jervell,[65] who alleged that in Luke the opposite is true: it is the conversion of Israel that is responsible for the offer of salvation to non-Jews. On this point, Jervell exaggerates. Here, too, Luke appears to be the faithful preserver of the epistolary Paul. Let us see why.

In response to the hardening of his relatives according to the flesh, Paul identifies two motifs of consolation: the first, as we have said, consists of affirming the election of a remnant, tangible proof of the success of salvation history; as for the second motif of consolation, it relates directly to the hardening of the Jewish people. For Paul, this serves a salvific plan of grafting the wild olive shoot onto the holy root (cf. Rom. 11.17). In other words, Israel's blindness is not in vain, but participates in the divine project of *universally* manifesting the richness of the divine glory (cf. 9.23). The scriptural example extracted from the exodus event is very clarifying in this regard (9.17): the hardening of Pharaoh was not an end in itself, since it ultimately led to the proclamation of God's name in all the earth (ἐν

---

61   D. Marguerat, *Paul de Tarse. Un homme aux prises avec Dieu* (Poliez-le-Grand: Ed. du Moulin, 1999), p. 74.

62   See especially E. Plümacher, 'Rom. in der Apostelgeschichte', in *Geschichte und Geschichten. Aufsätze zur Apostelgeschichte und zu den Johannesakten* (ed. J. Schröter and R. Brucker; WUNT, 170; Tübingen: Mohr Siebeck, 2004), p. 154.

63   In this sense, see D. Marguerat, 'Paul après Paul: une histoire de réception', pp. 317–37 [this volume pp. 87–88].

64   Cf. J. Gnilka, *Die Verstockung Israels*, p. 143.

65   J. Jervell, 'The Divided People of God', p. 55: 'One usually understands the situation to imply that only when the Jews have rejected the gospel is the way opened to Gentiles. It is more correct to say that only when Israel has accepted the gospel can the way to Gentiles be opened.'

πάσῃ τῇ γῇ). If Israel is temporarily 'disobedient and rebellious' (10.21), it is for the benefit of the gentiles!

Luke also appears to trace this same line from cause to effect.[66] The scenario of the Pauline mission of Acts just mentioned is its narrative crystallization: inaugurating his evangelizing activity by frequenting the synagogue, Paul is systematically banned; Pisidian Antioch, Iconium, Thessalonica, Beroea, Corinth, Ephesus, and Rome all endlessly repeat the same pattern of expulsion, from which follows the reorientation of the Pauline mission to a non-Jewish audience and to gentile settings for teaching (Acts 18.7; 19.9). Three episodes are particularly revealing to this effect: Pisidian Antioch (13.13-52), Corinth (18.1-11), and Rome (28.16-28). All three contain a clear affirmation of this gentile approach taken by the Christian mission following Jewish hostility (13.46-47; 18.6; 28.25-28). Although salvation has been universal *de jure* since the beginning of the Lukan Gospel (Luke 2.32; 3.6), salvation is now *de facto* extended to the gentiles following its rejection by its natural benefactors. On this point, Luke stands incontestably in line with the theology of Paul.

d. Missionary Eschatology

Contrary to the scathing verdict of Philipp Vielhauer, who judged Lukan eschatology to be incompatible with Paul's theology, we would like to highlight a significant point of convergence: both promote a missionary eschatology – that is, both transpose eschatology into the realm of mission history.[67] This aspect of the Pauline eschatology comes up explicitly in Rom. 10.18 and 11.25: the proclamation of the gospel, according to Paul, has a universal range that encompasses the entire *oikoumenē* and results in the entry of the gentiles into the holy people prior to the advent of the Parousia.[68] As for apocalyptic reversal of the hardening of Israel, it will not take place until the 'full number of the gentiles' is integrated (Rom. 11.25). Remarkably, these two aspects of Pauline eschatology – the mission to the ends of the earth and the entry of the gentiles into the chosen people – are strongly featured and articulated in Luke's narrative. Without question, the universal aspect of the Christian witness is clearly depicted from the very beginning of Acts: 'You will be my witnesses in Jerusalem, in all of Judea and Samaria, and to the end(s) of the earth' (Acts 1.8). The expression 'to the end(s) of the earth' (ἕως ἐσχάτου τῆς γῆς) is not unlike the phrase used in Rom. 10.18, 'to the corners/ends of the inhabited world/earth': εἰς τὰ πέρατα τῆς οἰκουμένης. As the overwhelming majority of scholars have noted, the story of Acts delivers the narrative substance

---

66   Duly noted by M. P. Bonz, 'Luke's Revision of Paul's Reflection in Romans 9–11', in *Early Christian Voices in Texts, Traditions and Symbols* (Festschrift F. Bovon; ed. D. H. Warren *et al.*; BIS, 66; Leiden: Brill, 2003), pp. 143–51 (149).

67   In this sense, see V. Fusco, '"Point of View" and "Implicit Reader" in two Eschatological Texts. Lk 19,11-28; Acts 1,6-8', in *The Four Gospels 1992* (Festschrift. F. Neirynck; ed. F. van Segbroeck *et al.*; BETL, 100; vol. 2; Leuven: Leuven University Press, 1992), pp. 1677–1696 (1694).

68   Cf. ibid., 1694: 'He [Paul] knows that the parousia will be preceded by the entry of "the full number of the Gentiles" (Rom 11,25), so that the temporal span becomes a spatial span, the eschatological tension becomes a missionary tension.'

(at least in part; cf. Acts 28.22: πανταχοῦ) of this geographical and missionary eschatology that is supposed to occur between the Ascension and the Parousia of Christ.[69] It is an eschatology whose ultimate aim is in fact *the entry of the gentiles into the people of God*, if we consider the parallel evidence of Luke 24.47-48 and Acts 1.8. The ends of the earth have an undeniable ethno-religious connotation for Luke (cf. also Acts 13.47). These 'times of the gentiles', a source of eschatological tension between the resurrection and the Parousia, had in fact already appeared on the lips of Jesus in the Gospel (Luke 21.24). There remains a burning question to which the Paul of Romans responds by resorting to a logical pirouette: what of the final salvation of 'unbelieving' Israel? It is with this issue that we wish to conclude our study.

e. Does Salvation Await 'Unbelieving' Israel?

Juggling between the irrevocable election of Israel and his gospel of justification by faith alone, Paul emerges with an aporia: Israel is at the same time loved by God and an enemy of God (cf. Rom. 11.28). Only by resorting to the apocalyptic category of 'mystery' (μυστήριον) can he overcome, or we might say override, this paradoxical predicament: founding his knowledge on a prophetic revelation, Paul announces the ephemeral nature of Israel's hardening and its eschatological salvation (Rom. 11.25-26). So, 'all Israel will be saved', not just the Jewish-Christians, but the others as well!

What about Luke's position? Does the author to Theophilus likewise maintain a final redemption of the 'rebellious' people? This is a particularly complex issue in the modern exegesis of Acts. The vast majority of scholars have answered in the negative.[70] Acts 28.25-27 appears to be the final judgement against the Jews who oppose the gospel.[71] No reversal of their plight is to be expected on the horizon of history. Narratively-speaking, these *ultima verba* placed in the mouth of Paul in Rome have the condemning effect of a verdict without appeal, closing off a string of similar pronouncements encountered earlier in the story (13.46-47 and 18.6).[72] On this point, it is necessary

---

69   I am borrowing, and extending, an expression from D. Marguerat, *Les Actes des apôtres (1–12)* (CNT, 5a; Genève: Labor et Fides, 2007), p. 42.

70   For example: E. Haenchen, *Die Apostelgeschichte* (KEK, 3; Göttingen: Vandenhoeck & Ruprecht, 7th edn), pp. 112–13: '*Luke no longer hopes, like Paul, for the conversion of Israel. Stiff-necked Israel is itself addressed for the final time in Rome*—and then turned over to judgment: "This salvation has now been sent to the gentiles; they will hearken"! —this is the last word of Paul in the Acts of the Apostles (Acts 28.28)' (emphasis original); D. Marguerat, 'Paul après Paul: une histoire de réception', p. 336 [this volume p. 88]: '... Luke is silent concerning the eschatological salvation of Israel (cf. Rom. 11.25-26).'

71   Cf. J. Gnilka, 'Die Verstockung Israels', pp. 150–54; M. P. Bonz, 'Luke's revision of Paul's Reflection', p. 151: 'With this pronouncement, Luke's narrative essentially ends, making Paul's words of judgment against Jewish unbelief no longer interim reflection but the final word—and not only Paul's final word, but God's final word as well.'

72   In my *Diploma of Specialization* devoted to Acts 28.16-31, I showed that this Isaianic citation goes beyond the strict setting of the episode in Rome and takes on a general applicability in Acts to the Jewish people as a whole: S. Butticaz, *La finale des Actes entre parole et silence*

to concede a *shift in emphasis* on the part of the author of Acts. Unlike the epistolary Paul, for whom the mission to Israel is still alive, Luke cannot hide the rupture that has already occurred between Judaism and Christianity, which drastically reduces any chance of an eschatological reversal. A page in salvation history seems to have turned. That being said, this position deserves to be nuanced, if one considers the many pronouncements of salvation for Israel that are peppered throughout the diptych of Luke-Acts: Luke 13.34-35; 21.24; Acts 3.21.[73] Acts 28.27b could indeed fall along this same trajectory.[74] In sum, the pronouncements should not be overdrawn, but neither should they be underestimated.

IV. Summary and Conclusion

Faced with the difficult and highly debated issue of the re-readings of Paul, we began by embracing the 'paradigm shift' widely accepted in current scholarship. The reception of Paul in Acts must certainly be evaluated in terms of continuity *and* displacement. We likewise voiced our support for the recent attempts to reconsider the Pauline-Lukan dependence in terms of intertextuality rather than source criticism. In particular it was Gérard Genette's idea of *hypertextual derivation* between a source text and a text engaged in rereading that seemed to us to redefine the concept of reception. Still, we also felt it necessary to go a step further, given the genre of the Lukan composition. The current investigation into the rereading of the Pauline tradition cannot afford to ignore the *formal change* effected by the author of Acts from a theology focused on discursive statements and phrases to one intimately tied to storytelling. Thus, anyone who probes the speeches in Acts in order to unearth possible Pauline traits, as Philipp Vielhauer once did, commits a grave error in reading. The genre effectively functions as a reading pact between the author and the reader that serves to guide the reception of the text in question. Having undertaken these methodological considerations, we tested their effectiveness on the burning question concerning the fate of Israel, seeking to identify the similarities and differences between Paul and Luke. This inquiry allowed us to detect Luke's intense effort to *translate narratively* the major axes of Paul's argumentation in Romans 9–11. Although discreet in his lexicographical

---

[Ac 28, 16-31]. Récits de fondation, mimèsis littéraire et rhétorique du silence (mémoire de DEA ; Lausanne, 2005), pp. 16–19.

73   P. G. Müller, 'Die jüdische Entscheidung gegen Jesus', pp. 527ff; F. Mussner, 'Die Idee der Apokatastasis in der Apostelgeschichte', *Lex Tua Veritas* (Festschrift H. Junker; Trier: Paulinus, 1961), pp. 233ff; V. Fusco, 'Luke-Acts and the Future of Israel', *NovT* 38 (1996), pp.10–15.

74   See in this sense F. Bovon, '"Il a bien parlé à vos pères, le Saint-Esprit, par le prophète Esaïe" (Actes 28,25)', *L'œuvre de Luc* (LD, 130; Paris: Cerf, 1987), pp. 145–53 (150); A. Deutschmann, *Synagoge und Gemeindebildung. Christliche Gemeinde und Israel am Beispiel von Apg 13, 42-52* (BU, 30; Regensburg: Pustet, 2001), pp. 200–13, 257–60; M. Karrer, '"Und ich werde sie heilen". Das Verstockungsmotiv aus Jes 6,9f. in Apg 28,26f.', in *Kirche und Volk Gottes* (Festschrift J. Roloff; Neukirchen-Vluyn: Neukirchener, 2000), pp. 255–71.

borrowings, Luke proves to be very faithful in terms of rephrasing the Pauline legacy for a new historical situation. That being said, this faithfulness does not prevent him from thinking differently on certain aspects: the Pauline hope for the salvation of all Israel is reduced to a bare minimum in Luke. All intertextual reception is expressly *dialogical*, built on a subtle exchange of adoption and adaptation.[75] In this respect, the author of Acts has not failed.

75   Cf. W. O. Walker, 'Acts and the Pauline Corpus Reconsidered', p. 14.

Chapter 9

(NOT) APPEALING TO THE EMPEROR: ACTS (AND *THE ACTS OF PAUL*)

Richard I. Pervo

I. Introduction[1]

From the perspective of the Greek elite, general contrasts between the first and the second centuries CE are possible. The first century reveals near hostility to the empire from Dio of Prusa, the victim of exile, and a certain reservation, exemplified by Plutarch.[2] Second-century writers, on the other hand, manifest little hostility to Roman rule, although they do not tend to identify themselves with it.[3] Discovery of the causes of this shift do not require the acuity traditionally attributed to rocket scientists. In the last third of the first century Rome experienced a period of instability, the Greek East's recovery from the ravages of Republican rule and Civil War was underway but not yet vibrant, and the imperial officials had just begun the process of introducing Eastern provincials into official positions.

Since Christianity lacked writers of elite background and accomplishment until *c.*150, and later, Christian literature is not often comparable to the works of well-educated and highly placed Greeks. Attempts have been made to date Acts, to select a random example, on the grounds that its view of the government is earlier than those of Revelation or, alternatively, prior to the 'Neronian persecution' for similar reasons.[4] Consistent application of these criteria would require dating the *Acts of Paul* prior to the canonical Acts.[5] Attitude toward the ruling power is not a very

1   I am grateful to Thomas Phillips, Mark Reasoner, and Glenn Snyder for their assistance.

2   These comments follow S. Swain's careful study, *Hellenism and Empire. Language, Classicism, and Power in the Greek World, AD 50-250* (Oxford: Clarendon, 1996). On Plutarch see pp. 135–86; for Dio 187–241.

3   Swain analyzes the writings of Arrian, Appian, Aristides, Lucian, Pausanias, Philostratus, and Cassius Dio, pp. 242–408.

4   The former argument is offered by G. Sterling, *Historiography and Self-Definition. Josephos, Luke-Acts and Apologetic Historiography* (NovTSup, 64; Leiden: Brill, 1992), p. 330 (who dates Acts *c.*90–93), the latter by C. J. Hemer, *The Book of Acts in the Setting of Hellenistic History* (ed. C. J. Gempf; Winona Lake, Ind.: Eisenbrauns, 1990), p. 377.

5   For a study of *APL* 14 from a historical perspective see W. Rordorf, 'Die neronische Christenverfolgung im Spiegel der Apokryphen Paulusakten', *NTS* 28 (1981–1982), 365–74; repr. in idem, *Lex Orandi—Lex Credendi. Gesammelte Aufsätze zum 60. Geburtstag* (Paradosis, 36;

useful tool for dating any of the Acts. Persecuting powers may evoke some fear, but they are not likely to generate much love from their targets. Those for whom the *Acta Alexandrinorum* speak, for example, view themselves as the persecuted victims of Roman emperors aided and duped by some well-positioned Jews.[6] This perspective, which has more than a little in common with that of the canonical Acts, cannot be attributed to a specific date.

To be fair and balanced, Christians who oppose the empire can be found in more or less every century through the Middle Ages, at least. For the vast majority of the early followers of Jesus, the Roman Empire was, not unlike the weather, a source of possible generous benefactions, cruel disasters, and, in most years, something in between. Until 250 CE, Emperors were not the primary enemies of the Christians. Nero was the chief exception, but a place on Nero's enemies' list was a valuable credential, and much the same could be said of Domitian. Local officials, institutions, and populaces constituted the biggest threats.[7] Even Christian texts tend to present governors as moderate officials who wish to avoid condemning the accused, from whom, according to our rather unfair and imbalanced sources, they received only occasional help – until the Decian Persecution.

In the first three centuries of Christian history, no unqualifiedly pro-imperial writers can be identified. The closest one comes to an exception is Paul. It is necessary to speak of balance sheets – lists of pros and cons. In some cases the pros are neglected or even denied, but they are always there. The same may be said of the cons, although they can almost always be identified. Proper analysis requires making explicit lists of each. Actual analysis has tended to prepare arguments based upon one of the two, which is then used to discredit the other column, unless that column is simply ignored. In studies of Lucan thought the dominant approach has been to lean toward the pro side.[8] Good reasons for this orientation existed, since it reflects the impression regularly gained by generations of readers. Nonetheless, the con column always exists and demands examination. Recent literature has sought to redress the balance.[9] The project

Fribourg: Universitätsverlag, 1993), pp. 368–77. His arguments are more nuanced than those cited in the previous n.

6   The standard edition is H. Musurillo, *The Acts of the Pagan Martyrs* (Oxford: Clarendon Press, 1954). The dramatic dates range from Augustus to Commodus.

7   See T. D. Barnes, *Early Christian Hagiography and Roman History* (Tübingen: Mohr Siebeck, 2010), p. 49.

8   A noticeable exception was R. J. Cassidy, *Society and Politics in the Acts of the Apostles* (Maryknoll, N.Y.: Orbis, 1987). He was not alone, as shown by the earlier *idem* and Philip J. Sharper, eds. *Political Issues in Luke-Acts* (Maryknoll, N.Y.: Orbis, 1983).

9   For surveys of the subject see S. Walton, 'The State They Were In: Luke's View of the Roman Empire', in *Rome in the Bible and the Early Church* (ed. Peter Oakes; Grand Rapids: Baker, 2002), pp. 1–41; A. Neagoe, *The Trial of the Gospel: An Apologetic Reading of Luke's Trial Narratives* (SNTSMS, 116; Cambridge: Cambridge University Press, 2002), pp. 175–87. Other recent studies include J. Sobrino, *No Salvation Outside the Poor: Utopian-Prophetic Essays* (Maryknoll, N.Y.: Orbis, 2008); B. S. Billings, '"At the Age of 12": The Boy Jesus in the Temple (Luke 2.41-52), the Emperor Augustus, and the Social Setting of the Third Gospel', *JTS* 60 (2009), pp. 70–89; J. Howell, 'The Imperial Authority and Benefaction of Centurions and Acts 10.34-43', *JSNT* 31 (2008),

is commendable. Scholarship advances through the issuance of challenges to prevailing assumptions.

II. The Loyalist Tradition: Romans 13.1-7 and Its Successors

'[N]o other paragraph in [Romans] 12.1-16.23 has commanded the sustained attention of interpreters in the last two Millennia of Romans Conversations.'[10] Romans 13.1-7 became one of Paul's most imitated bits of advice.[11] None of the undisputed letters discuss what believers owe to the government. Israelites had long lived under foreign monarchs. That experience provides the background. Specifically, the Wisdom tradition, with its knowledge of the vicissitudes of court life, offered a repertory of prudent counsel on the matter. Romans 13.1-7 reflects this tradition in a naïve and utopian manner – interlaced with bureaucratic jargon[12] – that is apparent not only in many of its antecedents but most convincingly in its successors, none of which assert without qualification the divine source and support of and for all authority. In due course Christians will pledge obedience to all lawful directives while shifting their emphasis from obedience to prayer for the authorities, with particular reference to petition that the emperors do the right thing. In Paul's defence it must be said that one of his objects in writing Romans was to show that he was a conservative, 'bourgeois', male Jew, despite his deviant theology. Although this little paragraph has been responsible for a great deal of harm,[13]

---

pp. 25–51; C. K. Rowe, 'Luke-Acts and the Imperial Cult: A Way Through the Conundrum?' *JSNT* 27 (2005), pp. 279–300; *idem, World Upside Down: Reading Acts in the Graeco-Roman Age* (Oxford: Oxford University Press, 2009); and K. Yamazaki-Ransom, *The Roman Empire in Luke's Narrative* (LNTS, 404; New York: T&T Clark, 2010).

10   M. A. Reasoner, *Romans in Full Circle: A History of Interpretation* (Louisville: Westminster John Knox, 2005), p. 129. Reasoner immediately adds that the situation is changing. Pp. 129–142 include discussions of the passage by interpreters from Origen through Barth and beyond.

11   Works consulted include R. Jewett, *Romans* (Hermeneia; Minneapolis: Fortress, 2007), pp. 780–803, who provides a substantial data on all issues touching Rom. 13.1-7; J. D. G. Dunn, *Romans 9-16* (Word 38b; Dallas: Word, 1988), pp. 757–74; C. E. B. Cranfield, *The Epistle to the Romans* (ICC; 2 vols; Edinburgh: T&T Clark, 1979), pp. 2:651–73; C. Morrison, *The Powers that Be: Earthly Rulers and Demonic Powers in Romans 13.1-7* (SBT, 29. Naperville, Ill.: Allenson, 1960); A. von Harnack, *The Mission and Expansion of Christianity in the First Three Centuries* (trans. J. Moffatt; 2 vols; New York: G. P. Putnam's Sons, 1908), pp. 1:297–98); and C. Spicq, *Les épitres pastorales* (EB; 2 vols; Paris: Galbalda, 4th edn, 1969), pp. 1:358–66.

12   For evidence see A. Strobel, 'Zum Verständnis von Röm 13', *ZNW* 47 (1956), pp. 67–93, and 'Furcht, wem Furcht gebührt. Zum profangriechischen Hintergrund von Röm 13, 1-7', *ZNW* 55 (1964), pp. 58–62. A survey of the reception of Rom. 13.1-7 in early Christianity provides solid evidence against the view that the 'powers' in question are spiritual rather than earthly. That interpretation is venerable, for Irenaeus felt obliged to refute it (*Adv. Haer.* 5.24.1).

13   I remember that, as recently as 1965, students at a large, conservative Protestant seminary were told that it was wrong to engage in peaceful protests against segregation on the grounds of Rom. 13.1-7. To oppose a government was to align oneself against God. (This was after the passage of the Civil Rights Act!)

it should also be said that Paul did not intend to hand down an eternal decree engraved on tablets of imperishable stone.[14]

The Israelite tradition held that monarchs rule at God's pleasure.[15] This was a two-edged sword. Paul does not even consider the possibility of lawless or corrupt officials, an oversight that cannot be attributed to want of evidence. Although tradition affirmed that all authority derived from God,[16] the major focus of texts from the Second Temple era was prayer and sacrifice for the ruler. Royal sacrifices date back to the Persian period (2 Esd. 6.9-10; Bar. 1.11) and continued to the destruction of the second Temple.[17] Since synagogues are locations where prayer is offered for the ruler, destruction of these facilities amounts to impiety, argues Philo (*Flaccus* 49).[18] For Jews this protestation, while sincere,[19] had an apologetic dimension, for these prayers were a substitute for participation in the Imperial Cult. Christians, too, came to focus upon prayer for the emperor rather than exhortation to submit to God-given authority.

Although sentiments in agreement with and quite likely inspired by Rom. 13.1-7 are not infrequent, the phrase '… for there is no authority except from God, and those authorities that exist have been instituted by God',[20] did not reappear in the NT texts 1 Pet. 2.13-17, 1 Tim. 2.1-3, and Titus 3.1-3, 8. Selwyn viewed their common features as evidence for the presence of a catechetical source.[21] An intertextual relationship is more likely, especially for the Pastorals, where use of Pauline letters is widely acknowledged.[22] The case of 1 Peter is subject to debate,[23] but it is quite probable that Romans 13 is also in the background there.[24] The possible use of Romans 13 in 1 Peter and its probable use in *1 Clement* mitigate against the hypothesis that Rom. 13.1-7 is an interpolation, since most likely *1 Clement* and

14   E. Käsemann, *An Die Römer* (HNT, 8a; Tübingen: Mohr Siebeck, 1973), pp. 334–44, is quite emphatic on this point, with which the vast majority of modern commentators are in agreement.

15   D. Winston, *The Wisdom of Solomon* (AB, 43; Garden City, NY: Doubleday, 1979), p. 152.

16   Cf. 2 Sam. 12.8; Jer. 27.5-6; Dan, 2.21, 37-38; 4.17, 25, 32; 5.21; Wis. 6.3; 1 Enoch 46.5. Josephus, *B. J.* 2.140 (Essene).

17   On these sacrifices see E. Schürer, *A History of the Jewish People in the Time of Jesus Christ* (Rev. and ed. G. Vermes, F. Millar, *et al.*; 3 vols; Edinburgh: T&T Clark, 1973–87), pp. 1:379–80. Texts include 1 Macc. 7.33; *Aristeas* 45; Josephus *c. Ap.* 2.77; *B.J.* 2.197, 409.

18   For data and references see P. W. van der Horst, *Philo's Flaccus. The First Pogrom* (Atlanta: Society of Biblical Literature, 2003), pp. 147–48.

19   *Pirke Abot* 3:2.

20   οὐ γὰρ ἔστιν ἐξουσία εἰ μὴ ὑπὸ θεοῦ, αἱ δὲ οὖσαι ὑπο θεοῦ τεταγμέναι εἰσίν. Words utilizing the stem *tag-* (*'order'*, *'arrange'*) appear four times in seven verses.

21   E. G. Selwyn, *The First Epistle of St. Peter* (London: Macmillan, 2nd edn, 1947), pp. 426–29. See Table XI, p. 427.

22   Notice, e.g., Tit. 3.1 in relation to Rom. 13.1.

23   On the debate see R. Pervo, *The Making of Paul: Constructions of the Apostle in Early Christianity* (Minneapolis: Fortress, 2010), pp. 125–26.

24   P. J. Achtemeier, *1 Peter* (Hermeneia; Minneapolis: Fortress, 1996), pp. 180–82, stresses the differences in meaning between Romans and 1 Peter. Such differences do not disprove a literary relationship, as the receptor text often utilizes its source for the purpose of altering its meaning.

possibly 1 Peter refer to an edition of Romans that was independent of a collection of Pauline letters. The governing premise is that an interpolation would have been introduced in a 'conservative' edition of the Pauline corpus.[25]

First Clement 60.4–61.1 is an example of prayer for the rulers:

> Give harmony and peace to us and to all who dwell on the earth, just as you did to our ancestors when they reverently called upon you ... while we render obedience to your almighty and most excellent name, and to our rulers and governors (ἄρχουσιν καὶ ἡγουμένους) on earth. You, Master, have given them the power of sovereignty (τὴν ἐξουσίαν τῆς βασιλείας) through your majestic and inexpressible might, so that we, acknowledging the glory and honor that you have given them, may be subject to them (δόξαν καὶ τιμὴν ὑποτάσσεσθαι αὐτοῖς), resisting your will in nothing. Grant to them, Lord, health, peace, harmony, and stability, so that they may blamelessly administer the government that you have given them. (Holmes)[26]

This prayer, presumably based upon Jewish antecedents,[27] states that God is the source of political power and that this is the grounds for human obedience, but the object of prayer is that rulers do the right thing. The wording includes echoes of Romans 13,[28] but the notion of unqualified obedience is mitigated. The Roman community had experienced persecution.

Polycarp, *Phil.* 12.3, like 1 Timothy, which derives from a similar environment,[29] is an exhortation to pray 'for all the saints ... for kings and magistrates and rulers' (*pro regibus et potestatibus et principibus*) and for persecutors.

---

25   For references and arguments supporting the interpolation hypothesis see, for earlier material, J. C. O'Neill, *Paul's Letter to the Romans* (Hammondsworth: Penguin, 1975), p. 207–8, and W. O. Walker, Jr., *Interpolations in the Pauline Letters* (JSNTS, 213; London: Sheffield Academic Press, 2001), pp. 221–31, and Jewett, *Romans*, pp. 782–84. One pillar of the argument supported by O'Neill is that no one cites the passage before Irenaeus (c. 180). This is quite the opposite of my proposal, which appeals to early allusion. (O'Neill's authorities refer to explicit citation; I argue from allusion.) O'Neill claims that the passage is a collection of Stoic injunctions. The initial phrase 'every soul' (*pasa psychē*) is Septuagintal language, indicating Jewish mediation, at least. Stoics, moreover, were not the political pushovers that O'Neill implies, as the first century provides a number of Stoics who resisted the Principate to the death. See R. MacMullen, *Enemies of the Roman Order* (Cambridge: Harvard University Press, 1966), pp. 46–94.

26   M. W. Holmes (trans.), *The Apostolic Fathers. Greek Texts and English Translations* (Grand Rapids: Baker, 3rd edn, 2007), p. 127.

27   On Jewish prayer for rulers see M. Dibelius and H. Conzelmann, *The Pastoral Epistles* (trans. P. Buttolph and A. Yarbro; Hermeneia; Philadelphia: Fortress, 1972), pp. 37–38.

28   So A. Lindemann, *Die Clemensbriefe* (HNT, 17; Tübingen: Mohr/Siebeck, 1992), p. 174. One could argue that the verbal overlap points back to hypothetical common sources, but Romans 13 is a source known to the author. On Christian prayer for rulers see Lindemann's excursus, pp. 175–76.

29   See H. von Campenhausen, *Aus der Frühzeit des Christentums: Studien zur Kirchengeschichte des ersten und zweiten Jahrhunderts* (Tübingen: Mohr Siebeck, 1963), pp. 197–252. Campenhausen has convinced few, but he has demonstrated that Polycarp and the Pastorals come from a very similar milieux.

In the *Martyrdom of Polycarp* (10.2) the bishop, in response to the proconsul's demand that he make a convincing argument to the *demos*, said, 'You I might have considered worthy of a reply, for we have been taught to pay proper respect to rulers and authorities appointed by God (δεδιδάγμεθα γὰρ ἀρχαῖς καὶ ἐξουσίαις ὑπὸ τοῦ θεοῦ τε τεταγμέναις τιμὴν), as long as it does us no harm... .' (Holmes). Lightfoot confidently identifies the agent of 'taught' as Rom. 13.1-7 and 1 Pet. 2.13.[30] This may well be the case, but an important qualification ('no harm')[31] has been added, and, rather than speak of obedience and subjection, the obligation is characterized as 'respect'. The passage leaves open the possibility that not all rulers and authorities have been appointed by God. Polycarp is, of course, about to be executed at the behest of a Roman, a circumstance that may have motivated his deviation from Pauline purity. In short Paul did not take up the issue of a conflict between God's message/messenger and the civil law/ruler.

The apologetic tradition was well aware of such conflicts and continued the practice of describing Christians as good subjects who supported the authorities by their prayers. Justin (*1 Apol.* 17) states that Christians willingly pay taxes, citing Mk. 12.13-17. Believers pray that the emperors may enjoy good mental health, a not utterly unwelcome but not particularly flattering petition. Athenagoras (*Legatio* 37) states that the faithful pray for the imperial family, alluding to 1 Tim. 2.2. The ruler cult provides the context for Theophilus of Antioch (*Ad Autolycum* 1.11). Christians honour the emperor by praying for him. There are evident allusions to Rom. 13.1, 1 Pet. 2.15, 17, and 1 Tim. 2.2. Tertullian opposed any act that might reduce the chance of persecution, but he said that believers pray for the well-being of the emperors (*pro salute imperatorum, Apol* 30), fleshing this out in 39.2: 'We pray also for Emperors, for their ministers and those in authority, for the security of the world, for peace on earth, for postponement of the end.'[32] The liturgical tradition (e.g. *Apostolic Constitutions* 8.12) attests the continuation of the practice.[33]

Strictly construed, Paul's views in Rom. 13.1-7 are as radical as any noted in the following section. While the 'loyalist' posture was generally predominant in emerging orthodoxy, its actual formulation presented a rather qualified picture.

III. Luke and Empire

Insofar as competition involves flattery, it also generates a certain ambiguity. Christianity would not have dared to compare its programme to the *Pax*

---

30   J. B. Lightfoot, *The Apostolic Fathers* (5 vols; New York: Macmillan, 1889–90), pt. 2, pp. 3:381.

31   The most obvious referent for 'harm' is the imperial cult.

32   Tertullian, *Apology* (trans T. R. Glover; LCL; Cambridge: Harvard University Press, 1931), p. 175. See also *Ad Scap.* 2.

33   For an apt analogy from polytheist religion is the general prayer in Apuleius' *Met.* 11.17, where an officer of the Isis cult prays 'for the great princeps, the Senate, the Knights and the entire Roman people' (*principi magno senatuique et equiti totoque Romano populo*). Since the worship of Isis had had its difficulties at Rome, an apologetic interest is possible.

Romana if that condition did not go beyond destroying in order to save, as Tacitus says in words attributed to a British rebel.[34] Competition more or less demands a pro to balance each con, even if our side does a better job of arranging things, yielding bigger cons. The shadow of this straddle extends across most of Luke's proposed anti-imperialism. It is most striking in Luke 1–2, with the virile nationalism of the *Benedictus* (Lk. 1.68-79), the revolutionary rhetoric of the *Magnificat* (Lk. 1.46-55), and the announcement of a new emperor's arrival, with its explicit claim of a peace-bringing saviour (Lk. 2.11-14). Despite the recognition that the distinctly non-revolutionary theology of the Pastoral Epistles also appropriates the language of the imperial cult[35] (a sterling example of the ambiguity generated by imitation) and the particular status of Luke 1–2, which are generally recognized as the latest parts of the Gospel and are occasionally viewed as a subsequent addition to it,[36] these claims cannot be brusquely dismissed. Luke thought that God could do better than the Roman Empire, which was not, for that reason, wicked. This belief, which few would have disputed, then or later, belongs on the con side of the ledger. The same material that makes Jesus a rival of Augustus (and Trajan) is also willing to see emperor and empire as tools of Providence: Lk. 2.1-7.

The term 'imperial decree' (δόγμα Καίσαρος) used in Lk. 2.1 appears in Acts 17.7, in the plural, without a proper name, in an accusation by Thessalonian agitators. 'Caesar', in the sense of 'the emperor', occurs also in Acts 25.8, 10, 11, and 21; 27.24; and 28.19. Non-believers used the word in 25.12 and 26.32. 'Lord' is used as an imperial title in 25.26.[37] The Greek equivalent to 'Augustus', *Sebastos*, appears in 25.21, 25, the latter on the lips of Paul. 'King' is always used of client kings, except in the noteworthy case of 17.7: '*... Jason and some believers* are all acting contrary to the decrees of the emperor, saying that there is another king named Jesus' (καὶ οὗτοι πάντες ἀπέναντι τῶν δογμάτων Καίσαρος πράσσουσιν βασιλέα ἕτερον λέγοντες εἶναι Ἰησοῦν). The implication of 'another king' is that Caesar is the legitimate monarch. Similar to this is 16.21: '*Paul and Silas in Philippi* are advocating customs [ἔθη] that are not lawful for us as Romans to adopt or observe.'[38]

For the readers of Acts both statements are manifestly false; they are the (somehow) unison speech of mobs viciously intent upon lynch justice.[39] The

---

34   Auferre, trucidare, rapere falsis nominibus imperium, atque ubi solitudinem faciunt, pacem appellant. (*Agricola* 30.)

35   See R. Pervo, *The Making of Paul: Constructions of the Apostle in Early Christianity* (Minneapolis: Fortress, 2010), p. 92.

36   Latest: R. E. Brown, *The Birth of the Messiah*. (ABRL; New York: Doubleday, 2nd edn, 1993), pp. 238–39. Subsequent addition: J. B. Tyson, *Marcion and Luke-Acts: A Defining Struggle* (Columbia: University of South Carolina Press, 2006).

37   On this see R. Pervo, *Dating Acts: Between the Evangelists and the Apologists* (Santa Rosa, Calif.: Polebridge, 2006), p. 316.

38   Statistics for *API* 14: 'Caesar', *c.* fifteen times; 'Lord Caesar', two times; 'king' (of the emperor), no examples.

39   Modern readers may note that 'Messiah' (17.3) could be rendered 'king', but that interpretation will not fit the dramatic setting.

narrator's views are placed on the lips of Paul: 'I have in no way committed an offense against the law of the Jews, or against the temple, or against the emperor' (25.8). The last of these three denials appears gratuitous, as he has not been charged with a crime against the emperor. In the context it serves the immediate purpose of reminding the dramatic audience that the judge and court are Roman and a long-range goal of rebutting any charges of *laesa maiestas*.

IV. Not Praying for the Emperor

Twelve professed Christians from the small African town of Scillium were tried on 17 July 180.[40] Their spokesperson rejected both the emperor and 'the empire of this world' (6). They also rejected a request to swear by the genius of the emperor *and to offer prayers for his welfare.* The second refusal is rather remarkable, as it denies what believers elsewhere have been told and have claimed to do for at least two generations.[41]

When asked about the books in his case (*capsa*), the leader Speratus said, 'Books and letters of a just man named Pau' (12).[42] One would like to know more details about these documents, notably where they had learned from Paul to reject imperial authority. Romans 13.1-7 would be a weak proof text in this context, while 1 Tim 2.1-2 enjoins prayer for the emperor. The *Acts of the Scillitan Martyrs* represents a radical stance toward the empire like that found in the text to which the discussion now turns.

V. Acts of Paul *14*

'The Paul of the [*Martyrdom* chapter of the *Acts of Paul*], in contrast to the historical Paul, is quite unmindful of the Emperor's criminal jurisdiction and refuses any recognition of his earthly power and authority.'[43] Just so. At some variance with the canonical Acts is the portrait painted in *Acts of Paul* 14, the martyrdom. It is quite possible that this story existed independently before its incorporation into the *Acts of Paul*, but it has been edited.[44] As it stands, the chapter begins with a strong contrast to Acts, from which it also borrows. Paul arrives in Rome as a free person and rents a facility in which he preaches to all comers.[45] The

---

40   For the Latin text of the *Acts of the Scillitan Martyrs* with a facing English translation, see H. Musurillo, *The Acts of the Christian Martyrs* (Oxford: Clarendon, 1972), pp. 86–88. See the discussion in R. Pervo, *Making of Paul*, pp. 1–2.

41   See above.

42   *libri et epistulae Pauli viri iusti.*

43   H. W. Tajra, *The Martyrdom of St. Paul: Historical and Judicial Context, Traditions, and Legends* (WUNT, 67; Tübingen: Mohr Siebeck, 1994), p. 129.

44   For some proposals on the editing of this chapter see G. E. Snyder, 'Remembering the *Acts of Paul*', (unpublished dissertation, Harvard, 2010), pp. 10–66.

45   As in the canonical book, the narrator of the *Acts of Paul* both acknowledges the prior existence of believers in Rome and writes as if Paul were the founder of the community.

narrator clearly marks the story as picking up where Acts left off (28.30-31), despite the alteration of the circumstances of Acts.[46]

Two major factors distinguish this chapter from the other sections of the *Acts of Paul*. Since martyrdoms were excised from the various acts and used for liturgical purposes, they were subject to substantial editing, including censorship.[47] That the inflammatory anti-imperial stance of *API* 14 survived censorship is remarkable.[48] It would seem that not all monks were politically correct. In any case, the politics of ch. 14 stand out. On two earlier occasions in the extant text Paul confronted Roman officials, both proconsuls. The section 3.14-21 describes his encounter with the Proconsul Castellius in Iconium. Paul's arrest there was due to the unprincipled machinations of the distressed Thamyris, alienated fiancé of Thecla. Thamyris, not without reason, blames his predicament upon Paul. Castellius engages in due process (3.16), admires Paul's message,[49] but finally caves in to the pressure of the mob and from general abhorrence at the hideous behaviour of the insolent Thecla. Absent the insolent young woman, the pattern is like canonical Acts.

Circumstances are similar in Ephesus (9.12-27). Paul was seized in a citizens' arrest. After the conventional 'You can destroy my body but you have no power over my soul' introduction[50] (9.13), the apostle delivers a sermon. Hieronymus, the wimpy governor, emulates Pontius Pilate, as it were, and leaves the judgement to the crowd, with a predictable result: condemnation to the beasts. By 9.27, I am happy to report, Hieronymus, injured in the divine judgement against the prospective execution, has repented of his wrongdoing, and been healed.

In both cases the governors regard Paul as a philosopher worthy of audition – the apostle was sufficiently astute to omit from his defence speech the necessity of celibacy – and seek to exercise due process, but ultimately yield to mob pressure. This is not especially flattering to the officials, but it labels the mob as the principal enemy. Representation of this sort is not unlike what often occurs in Acts and is not atypical of the second century, although it must be recognized that this depiction goes back to the story of Jesus' execution. In *API* 14.3, to the contrary, the Roman mob intervenes to *halt* the persecution.

Caesar thereupon ordered that all the prisoners be burned at the stake, excepting Paul, who was to be decapitated, in accordance with Roman law. This did not silence Paul, who continued to share the message with Longinus the prefect and Cestus the centurion.[51] Because of the machinations of the evil one many Christians

46　The opening utilization of 2 Tim. 4.10-11 indicates that the author also wished to co-ordinate with the Pastoral Epistles. Apocryphal authors could have as much interest in harmonizing various early Christian texts as those considered more Orthodox.

47　Although many parts of the various Apocryphal Acts survive in but a single ms., the final sections are usually attested in multiple mss and versions.

48　Nero was a stock tyrant and fair game, but hostility to the empire is not limited to this negative example.

49　3.20, evoking Herod, as reported in Mark 6.20.

50　See the Martyrdoms of Carpus et al., 11, 13; Justin, 17, 23; Polycarp 11.2.

51　The names vary in the mss.

were being executed at Rome [by Nero?] without trial,[52] so many in fact that the citizenry gathered in front of the palace shouting, 'Enough, Caesar. These are our people! You are ruining Roman power!' He desisted on the grounds that no Christian should be touched until he had investigated the facts of the case.[53]

The other substantial contrast to the (extant) earlier portions of the *Acts of Paul* is that the apostle does not just say no to sex. Whereas celibacy has sometimes seemed to be the essential element of his Gospel ('God's message about self-control and resurrection,' 3.5), in this chapter the dominant theme is militant opposition to the transitory kingdoms of this world. The absence of demands for sexual renunciation and the presence of incendiary politics are strong indicators that *APl* 14 was not a concoction by the author of other chapters, but an adaptation from a source.[54]

As the chapter stands, the narrative borrows the precipitating incident from the canonical Acts while fashioning an internal connection. The precipitating incident that ignites the Neronian persecution was the death and revival of one Patroclus, who fell from a window while listening to Paul. Arguments for dependence upon Acts are nearly insuperable.[55] As might be expected, the *Acts of Paul* makes a number of improvements to the story. The major difference is its narrative function. Like Jesus (Lazarus, John 11), Paul will be killed for bringing life. That line cannot, however, be pursued, for several reasons, one of which is that Nero is pleased with rather than vexed by Patroclus' restoration.

Parallels with the story of Thecla are clear. Both young persons heard Paul while seated in a window; both accepted his message and shared it to the disapproval of their superiors, and, although this is scarcely unusual, both were delivered from certain death by miracle. Such correspondences offer pleasure to those who recognize them – the vast majority of the audience in this case – and serve somewhat subtly to unify the narrative. Sex is evidently present, although as a love that dare not speak its name. The youth's name, Patroclus (viewed in post-Homeric Greece as Achilles' lover),[56] his role, cupbearer to Nero, i.e., a Ganymede to the empire's Zeus,[57] and the emperor's grief at the report of his death (14.2) strongly imply that Nero has been deprived of a sexual object, as Thamyris was deprived of his fiancée, Thecla.[58] This leads to the

---

52   There are textual problems here.

53   The text is evidently corrupt.

54   Similar observations may be made about the tradition of the Passion of Jesus.

55   See François Bovon, 'La vie des Apôtres: traditions bibliques et narrations apocryphes', in *Les Actes des apôtres: christianisme et monde païen* (ed. F. Bovon; Geneva: Labor et Fi'des, 1981), p. 150; D. R. MacDonald, 'Luke's Eutychus and Homer's Elpenor: Acts 20:7-12 and *Odyssey*, 10-12', *JHC* 1 (1994), pp. 5–24; and R. Pervo, 'A Hard Act to Follow: *The Acts of Paul* and the Canonical Acts', *JHC* 2 (1995), pp. 3–32 (10–12).

56   Aeschylus, fr. 134a.

57   It was widely believed that Zeus kidnapped Ganymede for sexual purposes, e.g., Theognis 1345–48. See Wilhelm H. Roscher, 'Ganymedes', *Ausführliches Lexicon der Griechischen und Römischen Mythologie* (Leipzig: Teubner, 1886–1890), pp. 1:1595–1603.

58   The *Martyrium beati Apostoli Pauli*, known from its alleged author as 'Ps.-Linus', prefaces *deliciosus*, thus making sexual relationship explicit.

hypothesis that the editor of the *Acts of Paul* was responsible for the episode about Patroclus, since celibacy and its consequences for the plot are otherwise absent in ch. 14.[59]

Be that as it may, Patroclus shares his faith with his lord. Nero continues their conversation:[60]

'Who brought you back to life?'
Uplifted by the enthusiasm of his belief, the youth said, 'Christ Jesus the king of the ages.'
Upset, Caesar said, 'Is he therefore going to rule the ages and abolish every kingdom?'
'Yes. He will destroy all kingdoms. He alone will be eternal and no kingdom will elude him.'
Nero struck him on the face, saying,[61] 'Patroclus, are you also a soldier of that king?'
'Yes, Lord Caesar, for he raised me after I had died.' Then Barsabas 'Flatfoot' Justus,[62] Orion the Cappadocian, and Festus the Galatian, Nero's leading men, said, 'We too serve in the army of the king of the ages.'

Patroclus receives pertinent assistance from Nero, who introduces both the idea that King Christ Jesus will destroy every kingdom and also the military image for the new religion.[63] The names of his principal assistants, Barsabas Justus, Orion the Cappadocian, and Festus the Galatian, attest to the author's dim knowledge of and concern for the prosopography of Nero's court, which, however else it may be denounced, was not composed of characters culled, *mutatis mutandis*, from a casting call for an ancient equivalent to 'The Beverly Hillbillies'.[64]

A roundup of the soldiers of Christ promptly followed. Nero, who evidently preferred to do his own investigating, went to have a look at the catch.
Among the many taken into custody was Paul. The other prisoners paid careful attention to him. Observing this, Caesar concluded that he was in charge of the soldiers and addressed him, 'Agent of the great king, albeit my prisoner, why did you come up with the idea of surreptitiously entering Roman territory and recruiting from my dominion?'

---

59   Tajra, *Maryrdom*, p. 128 assumes that ch. 14 demanded celibacy and that the conversion of Patroclus would have entailed the renunciation of sex. On Patroclus see the following. Tajra gives no evidence for his views.

60   The translation is a draft prepared for the Anchor Commentary on the *Acts of Paul* now in progress.

61   Cf. John 18.22.

62   For the name see Acts 1.23.

63   A. von Harnack, *Militia Christi, The Christian Religion and the Military in the First Three Centuries* (trans. D. M. Gracie; Philadelphia: Fortress, 1981), p. 44 says, 'One could almost describe this language as seditious…'

64   The localities specified are evidence for the provenance of this chapter, at least. D. MacDonald, *The Legend and the Apostle: The Battle for Paul in Story and Canon* (Philadelphia: Westminster Press, 1983), pp. 36–37, notes that a Barsabas Justus was the subject of a story attributed by Papias to the daughters of Philip (Frg. 3.9). For comparable geographical observations see the *Acts of Peter* 3-4.

Inspired, Paul responded, with the entire audience in mind, 'Caesar, we do not recruit from your dominion alone, but from every inhabited place, for we have been directed to exclude no one who wishes to enlist in the service of my king. If enrolling in his service should actually appeal to you, neither wealth nor the splendours of present existence will avail you, but if you submit[65] and entreat him, you will experience deliverance. For on a single day he will destroy the world.' (14.3)

Paul had been arrested in a general sweep and revealed as important because of the respect he received from other prisoners. With confident sarcasm,[66] the emperor asks why Paul had engaged in his covert subversion. Happily accepting the status of a soldier of the great king, the apostle explains that he is an equal-opportunity recruiter and offers Nero the gospel in a nutshell, the halves of which are promise and threat.[67]

Not long thereafter, Longinus, a prefect, and the centurion Cestus, asked the now condemned[68] Paul:

'Where do you get this king from, in whom you so trust that even death will not change your mind?' Paul shared the message with them, 'Gentlemen, living in ignorance and deceit, change your minds and be saved from the conflagration that will inundate the world.[69] We are not enrolled, as you imagine, in the service of a terrestrial king, but one from heaven, the living God, who because of the lawless things done in this world is coming as judge. Blessed are those who will have trust in him and live forever, when he comes to purify the world with fire!'
They thereupon begged him, 'Please, please help us and we shall let you go.'
'I am no deserter from Christ, but a loyal soldier of the living God.' (14.4)

Dennis MacDonald summarizes it: 'That story depicts Nero as the archetypal antichrist, and the empire as the diabolical counterpart to the kingdom of God. No one serves two masters in the story.'[70] Although the military imagery is metaphorical here, it is corporate and, pardon the term, militant.[71] This imagery has a long and diverse history.[72] In the Qumran *War Scroll* and related texts the

---

65   The concrete sense 'fall down' is also quite possible.

66   Cf. Pilate's *titulus* for Jesus' cross, John 19.19.

67   Rulers ever so much less tyrannical and oppressive would take exception to such speech.

68   The sentence of beheading presumes Roman citizenship. The author probably obtained that information from Acts.

69   On the theme of 'the fire next time' see Rordorf, 'Die neronische Christenverfolgung', pp. 371–74.

70   MacDonald, *The Legend*, 66.

71   J. Bolyki, identifies fourteen occurrences of 'soldier' and related terms in the chapter in his interesting study: 'Events after the Martyrdom: Missionary Transformation of an Apocalyptical Metaphor in Martyrium Pauli', in *The Apocryphal Acts of Paul and Thecla* (ed. Jan Bremer; SECA, 2; Kampen: Kok Pharos, 1996), pp. 92–106.

72   Note, in particular, Harnack, *Militia Christi*, pp. 27–64; E. J. Cadoux, *The Early Christian Attitude to War* (New York: Gordon, 1919; repr. 1975); the bibliography listed in Gracie's introduction to Dibelius and Conzelmann, *The Pastoral Epistles*, pp. 32–33; Otto Bauernfeind, στρατευομαι κτλ, *TDNT* 7:701-13; C. Spicq, *Les épitres pastorales*, pp. 1:350–51,

language is concrete, but depicts spiritual warfare.[73] The enemy, as in the *Acts of Paul*, is the Roman Empire.

Philosophers compared life to military service to stress that it was a serious business, requiring order, obedience and discipline.[74] This imagery is congenial to the diatribe,[75] and is generally comparable to the use of tropes from athletic competition.[76] (The imagery of armour in Eph. 6.10-17, differs. Although parenetic, it is individualistic and oriented to spiritual warfare.)[77] The theme of the Christian life as military service,[78] *militia Christi*, thrived in the Deutero-Pauline world,[79] with inspiration from the undisputed letters.[80]

On the subject of inspiration, it appears that a leading source of the military imagery in this chapter was the Pastoral Epistles! The closest parallels to this imagery appear in 1 Tim. 1.18-19 and 2 Tim. 2.3-7.[81] The christological language of *APl* 14 also displays affinities, e.g. with 1 Tim. 1.17: 'To the King of the ages, immortal, invisible, the only God, be honor and glory forever and ever' (although the epithet is applied to Christ in *APl* 14.2, God in the PE).

If this hypothesis has validity, it shows that dialogue with the Pastorals extends across a range of the *Acts of Paul*, i.e., beyond the story of Thecla. More than this, it reveals the author or editor of this chapter to have been quite clever. Whereas one can set in opposing columns the sentiments expressed in the Pastorals and those found in the Thecla stories, in this case the author uses the theme of *militia Christi* to oppose the quiet resignation of 2 Timothy with a militant rejection of imperial authority and might. One could even claim that such manly and robust imagery is much better suited to the strident words and action of the *Acts of Paul* than to the passive and pacifistic, ruler admiring, and authority idolizing Pastoral Epistles.[82]

It also challenges the canonical Acts. As noted above, *APl* 14 carefully locates itself as a continuation of Acts. In Acts 27.24, at the climax of the storm that would wreck the ship, Paul delivered, despite the desperate circumstances, a pep talk, in the course of which he reported that a heavenly messenger had assured him that he must appear before Caesar, the implication of which was that he would survive

2:739–44; and, for artistic and other references. F. Cumont, *Oriental Religions in Roman Paganism* (London: G. Routledge & Sons, 2nd edn, 1911), p. 213 n.6.

73   The texts are 1QM, 1Q33, 4Q 491-7, 4Q471; 4Q285; 11Q14.

74   The usage is as old as Plato: *Apol*. 28.

75   Note *1 Clem*. 37.1-4, which does not neglect to emphasize order and obedience.

76   Cf. 1 Cor. 9.7, a list of professions, evidently imitated in 2 Tim. 2.3-7.

77   M. Dibelius, *An die Kolosser Epheser. An Philemon* (HNT, 12; Tübingen: Mohr Siebeck, 2nd edn, 1927), pp. 74–75; G. W. Clarke, *The Octavius of Marcus Minucius Felix* (ACW, 39; New York: Newman Press, 1974), p. 365 n. 622.

78   The metaphorical usage should be distinguished from the question of Christians serving in the armed forces. On this see J. Helgeland, 'Christians and the Roman Army from Marcus Aurelius to Constantine', in *ANRW* II.23.1 (1979), pp. 724–834; W. Rordorf, 'Tertullians Beurteilung des Soldatenstandes', in *Lex orandi, lex credenda: gesammelte Aufsätze zum 60. Geburtstag* (Freiburg: Universitätsverlag, 1993), pp. 263–99, with bibliography (263 n.1).

79   E.g., *1 Clem*. 37, 1 Tim. 1.18-19; 6.12; 2 Tim. 2.3-7; Ign. *Pol*. 6.2.

80   E.g. 1 Cor. 9.7; 2 Cor. 10.1-6; Phlm. 2.

81   Note also Ign *Pol*. 6.2, which speaks of potential deserters.

82   See the summary in Tajra, *Martyrdom*, pp. 120–21.

the present ordeal, and that, as a bonus, so to speak, God was throwing in the lives of everyone aboard. The author of the *Acts of Paul* would not have been the only person disappointed by the narrator's perfidious failure to relate that appearance. Since it is a thoroughly reasonable position to hold that Luke chose not to narrate a trial because it led to Paul's execution, it is also reasonable to hypothesize that the author of the *Acts of Paul* rejected what he would have viewed as an egregious sellout and supplied his readers with a fine and edifying conclusion to the story of Paul.

The postulation of these two targets, Luke and the Pastorals, does not indicate that those two texts stem from the same era. A good deal of evidence does, however, support that hypothesis.[83] Many of those who wish to date the Pastorals *c.*100 will be willing to assign Acts to a slightly earlier time, *c.*90–95, but they will then be obliged to pull Polycarp – not to mention Ignatius – into the same framework.[84]

VI. Squaring the Circle

The more or less indisputable intertextual relationship between the *Acts of Paul* and the *Acts of Peter* is quite complex. The Martyrdom of the *Acts of Peter* appears to have been influenced by the *Acts of Paul*, quite probably modelled upon it.[85] On the basis of that hypothesis, one notable change, as Ann Graham Brock has argued, is the relatively innocuous political stance of the *Acts of Peter* in contrast to the *Acts of Paul*.[86] Whether the hypothesis is accepted, the contrast between the two underlines the radical character of the *Acts of Paul*.

A homily of the fifth or sixth century honoring Thecla,[87] which makes some modifications in the tradition found in the *Acts of Paul*, reports: 'The judges were afraid of the penalties against her, but she trampled down all such penalties through her will which cried, "Rulers are not a terror to good conduct, but to bad."'[88]

---

83   See Pervo, *Dating Acts*, pp. 299–301 and 201–308 *passim*.

84   Ignatius, who was martyred *c.*130, wrote a letter to Polycarp. The latter's letter to the Philippians has so much in common with the Pastorals that Polycarp has been proposed as their author. See Pervo, *Dating Acts*, pp. 305–7. On the date of Ignatius see Pervo, *The Making of Paul*, pp. 134–35.

85   See *Semeia* 80 (1997), *The Apocryphal Acts of the Apostles in Intertextual Perspectives*. The most interesting shared item is the *Quo Vadis* story. The account in *APtr* 35(7) seems primary in comparison to *APl* 13, but it is arguable that the *APtr* presents an artistic improvement. (Note that *APtr* 35 uses the term 'deserter', which is primary to *APl* (14.4).)

86   A. G. Brock, 'Political Authority and Cultural Accommodation: Social Diversity in the *Acts of Paul* and the *Acts of Peter*', in *The Apocryphal Acts of the Apostles* (ed. F. Bovon, A. G. Brock, and C. R. Matthews; Cambridge: Harvard University Press, 1999), pp. 145–69, (145–52).

87   Sources of this sermon are PG 50, cols. 745–48 and Michel Aubineau, 'Le panégyrique de Thècle, attribué à Jean Chrysostome (*BHG* 1720): la fin retrouvée d'un texte motile', *Analecta Bollandiana* 93 (1975), pp. 349–62 (351–52).

88   See D. R. MacDonald and A. D. Scrimgeour. 'Pseudo-Chrysostom's *Panegyric to Thecla*: The Heroine of the *Acts of Paul* in Homily and Art', *Semeia* 38 (1986), pp. 151–59, for a full discussion and translation. This excerpt comes from p. 156.

This thought (or statement) cites Rom. 13.3 and might be seen as proof that the rebellious teen had been drawn into the loyalist camp. In this context, however, the words evidently represent the boldness of the accused righteous victim in the face of tyranny.[89] Rather than affirm that the law-abiding have nothing to fear from authorities, it asserts innocence, come what may. Thecla did know how to listen to Paul, orally and in writing.

VII. Conclusion

One purpose of this paper has been an attempt to demonstrate that attitude toward the Roman Empire, by which one must mean 'attitudes', is not a valid criterion for dating texts. The chronological table that begins with radical apocalyptic, *c.*30 CE, and ends with the church as chaplain to the establishment, *c.*330 CE, is utter nonsense. The millenarian Orosius, for example, belonged to the early *fifth* century.

Although I called for evaluations that included both pros and cons, I have not followed my advice, as one purpose of this endeavour is to set a standard for the 'con' side. The *API* 14 is, without qualification or reservation, anti-imperial. If one wants to tell the story of Paul's execution in a manner unflattering to the empire, this is the touchstone. That does not mean that all anti-imperial statements must meet the standard, but it does cast a long shadow.

Luke's orientation is that of a reformer.[90] The conservative argument 'If it ain't broke, don't fix it' presumes that it ain't broke (although possibly showing a few cracks). The radical position is 'knock the obnoxious structure down and start from scratch'. Reformers want to fix it. Unlike Palestinian and Diaspora Jews, who might well resent foreign rule of the homeland, or Greeks like Plutarch, who could look nostalgically back to the era of Greek independence (when their forebears held high offices), it is unlikely that the author of Acts felt a powerful tug of anti-Roman patriotism. The Way he envisioned was amenable to Greco-Roman culture and to imperial rule, but it was neither married to it nor overly concerned with defending it, although it could help make some improvements. Various Greeks and Romans of status and culture might well have asked Dio and Plutarch for their views on Roman rule and received answers of varying candour. It is almost impossible to conceive of such persons posing that question to the author of Acts. We care what Luke thought about the empire and rightly debate the matter. We shall also do well not to forget that, in Luke's day, no one who counted even cared.

89   On this theme see R. Pervo, *Acts. A Commentary* (Hermeneia; Minneapolis: Fortress, 2009), pp. 118–19.
90   R. Pervo, *Acts*, p. 25.

Chapter 10

IN PAUL'S DEFENCE: THE CONTRIBUTION OF CRAMER'S CATENA TO THE EARLY RECEPTION OF PAUL IN ACTS

Timothy Brookins, Mikeal Parsons and Peter Reynolds[1]

I. Introduction

It is a commonplace among many Acts scholars to speak of the idyllic portrait of the early church and its leaders. For example, J. C. Lentz argues that Luke portrays Paul as a Roman citizen of high social standing and concludes, 'By the end of Acts, the Paul who is described is, frankly, too good to be true'.[2] Early interpreters of the Acts of the Apostles, however, apparently would disagree with this assessment. There is strong evidence that some of the early interpreters sought to clarify any detail in Luke's portrait of Paul that could be viewed negatively in any way. J. A. Cramer's catena on Acts contains a largely ignored treasure trove of early interpretations of Paul, many of which remain untranslated. We have found in these texts an attempt to disabuse their audiences of misconceptions about St. Paul, which may arise from a particular reading of the book of Acts, and to exonerate Paul from any apparent infelicity or wrongdoing.

II. Cramer's Catenae

John Anthony Cramer's *Catenae Graecorum Patrum in Novum Testamentum* (1838) preserves a wealth of patristic commentary which together covers nearly every verse of the New Testament. As seen in the title, *catena* is the Latin word for

---

1   The following persons, at various times, contributed to the translations of the scholia contained in this essay: Brian Gamel, Heather Gorman, Chris Kuhl, Peter Rice, Josh Stout, and Nick Zola. Gratitude is expressed to each for allowing us to incorporate their work into this article. We also wish to thank Professor Chris De Wit for giving permission to use some of the material from an earlier article, 'In Defense of Peter and Paul: The Contribution of Cramer's Catena to the Early Reception of Canonical Acts', published in the *Journal of Early Christian History* 1.1 (2011) [formerly *Acta Patristica et Byzantina* 22.1].

2   J. C. Lentz, *Luke's Portrait of Paul* (SNTSMS, 77; Cambridge: Cambridge University Press, 1993), p. 171. See also J. Fitzmyer, *To Advance the Gospel: New Testament Studies* (New York: Crossroads Publishing, 1981), p. 251; and L. T. Johnson, *Acts of the Apostles* (ed. D.J. Harrison; Collegeville, Minn.: Liturgical Press, 1992), p. 270.

'chain', used to describe commentary excerpted from various authors, usually in short chunks, and linked together to form a running commentary of scripture.[3] In most catenae these excerpts, known as *scholia*, are attributed to a particular writer with a prefixed heading – e.g., the name of the writer in the genitive case, or an abbreviated form of his name. The first known compiler of such a collection was Procopus of Gaza (d. 538), whose catena consisted of commentary from the Greek fathers on the Octateuch (the Pentateuch plus Joshua, Judges, and Ruth). From Procopus until the invention of the printing press, the use of catenae remained a popular and highly effective way of preserving valuable exegetical nuggets out of the commentaries of the great fathers of the church. Extant in Greek, Latin, and Syriac, the catenae are responsible for preserving countless pages of patristic commentary that would otherwise have sunk into oblivion.[4]

For some books of the Bible, we have several catenae, as in the case of Acts.[5] The Acts catena found in Cramer (vol. 3) has been transcribed from the twelfth-century manuscript *Oxon. Novi Coll. 58*.[6] Cramer notes, however, that this manuscript is based on an eleventh-century exemplar known as *Coislin 25*. This manuscript includes, in addition to the catena on Acts: the Chief Acts of Pamphilus, the Journeys of Paul, the catena on the Catholic Epistles, the Martyrdom of Paul, and a final note naming 'Andrew, the merciful and humble presbyter' (Ἀνδρέου δὲ τοῦ ελεεινοῦ καὶ ταπεινοῦ πρεσβυτέρου) as the compiler. Although Cramer's manuscript (*Oxon.* 58) lacks the account of Pamphilus and the note about the compiler, given its similarities with *Coislin* 25, Cramer reasonably concludes that the latter is the exemplar and that Andrew the Presbyter is also the compiler of our text. This Andrew is thought to be the same Andrew who was archbishop of Caesarea of Cappadocia in the first half of the seventh century, and who is identified as one of the three compilers of the manuscript used for Cramer's catena on the Apocalypse (Ἀνδρεα τῷ μακαριστάτῳ ἀρχιεπισκόπῳ Καισαρείας Καππαδοκίας, 'Andrew the most blessed archbishop of Caesarea of Cappadocia').[7] Accordingly, all of the scholia in the Acts catena derive from the seventh century or earlier.

---

3   Though the word 'catena' is commonly used in this technical sense today, it does not appear in reference to works of this kind until 1484, with the publication of the *Catena Aurea* of Thomas Aquinas.

4   For instance, the Acts material from Ammonius in *Patrologia graeca* (*PG* 85:1361–1610) was drawn from Cramer's catenae.

5   For the various Acts catenae, see R. Devreese, 'Chaines exégétiques grecques', *DBSup* 1 (1928), pp.1205–06.

6   Though Cramer had dated it to the fourteenth century (J. A. Cramer, ed, *Catenae Graecorum Patrum in Novum Testamentum* [Volume 3; *In Acta SS. Apostolorum*] 1967], p.iii). On the current dating, see R. Devreese, 'Chaines exégétiques', pp. 1205–06; and P. R. Jones, *The Epistle of Jude as Expounded by the Fathers—Clement of Alexandria, Didymus of Alexandria, the Scholia of Cramer's Catena, Pseudo-Oecumenius, and Bede* (Lewiston: The Edwin Mellen Press, 2001), pp. 5–6.

7   See Karl Staab, 'Die griechischen Katenenkommentare zu den katholischen Briefen', *Bib* 5 (1924), pp. 296–353 (346–47); cf. P. F. Stuehrenberg, 'The Study of Acts before the Reformation: A Bibliographic Introduction', *NovT* 29 (1987), pp. 100–36 (112–13).

In Cramer's text, scholia are usually prefixed with the name of the commentator in the genitive case. John Chrysostom, cited most often, seems to have formed the backbone of the Acts catena.[8] After Chrysostom, Ammonius is cited most frequently, by a slim margin over Severus. All three of these authors, each included below, are cited dozens of times in Cramer. Amid the roughly thirty other commentators represented there appear several scores of unattributed scholia, some bearing the lemma Ἐξ ἀνεπιγράφου ('from an anonymous author'), and others to which no lemma has been attached at all.

It is difficult to determine why no name is prefixed to many of these. Possibly, they appeared this way in Cramer's manuscript.[9] This, at least, is the impression one gets by surveying his index and list of variants: it may be supposed that it is the variant readings from *Coislin* 25 that have provided the headless scholia in his text with their correct attributions found in his index.[10] But it is equally possible that the occasional lack of headings is ascribable to errors in transcription. For it is unclear why some 'anonymous' scholia would be designated as such in the manuscript while others would not; these could have been omitted accidentally by Cramer, or by an assistant (he does not claim to have transcribed the manuscript himself). Indeed, on account of negligence, attribution in Cramer's volumes has elsewhere proved less than perfect. Even where names are attached to scholia, there is sufficient reason to doubt that they are always accurate. Another Acts catena (*Barb.* 582) attributes to Maximus a scholion that Cramer's manuscript attributes to Didymus.[11] Where the error lies in that case we cannot be sure. Nevertheless, we know from Claude Jenkins' work on the 1 Corinthians catena that Cramer's attributions are frequently at odds with his manuscript, and that these errors are ascribable to the collator. Cramer did not always make his own collations, and the collator he employed for that volume turns out to have been careless, if not entirely inadequate for the task. In Jenkins'[12] close examination of the relevant manuscript (Paris, grec 227), he found 'no less than fifteen passages assigned in the MS to Chrysostom, but in Cramer to Origen'.[13] Since Origen's commentary on 1 Corinthians is attested

---

8   *Coislin* 25 is prefixed with the title: Ἑρμενεία τῶν Πράξεων τοῦ Χρυσοστόμου καὶ ἑτέρων διαφόρων.

9   To which we have not had access.

10   The following scholia, for example, are headless in Cramer's text, but attributed to Chrysostom in the index and in *Coislin* 25: 386.6-14 (= *In Acta Apostolorum* 60.355); 409.26 (= *In Acta Apostolorum* 60.374); 414.24 (= *In Acta Apostolorum* 60.380-381); 364.3-16 (= *In Acta Apostolorum* 60.333); 365.27 (*In Principium Actorum* 51.99.57-59). It should be noted, however, that Cramer has relied on the work of another for his manuscript's variants with *Coislin* 25 (Cramer, *Catenae* 1987, p. xii).

We are aware of at least one further case where a headless scholion can be attributed. As we discuss below, while scholion 366.1-20 lacks a heading in Cramer's text and is accordingly listed in his index under 'scholia quibus nullum nomen praefigitur' ('scholia to which no name is prefixed'), we have discovered that this scholion is actually to be identified with a portion of Chrysostom's homily on Acts 22 (*PG* 60:334-36).

11   Cramer, *Catenae*, p. 153.20-33; so Devreese 'Chaines exégétiques', pp. 1205–1206.

12   C. Jenkins, 'The Origen-Citations in Cramer's Catena on 1 Corinthians', *JTS* 6 (1904) pp. 113–16 (115).

13   He further notes that errors extend beyond the names to the text itself.

independent of Cramer's catena, fortunately these errors were amendable. We do not have that luxury where we rely entirely on the catenae for our material. In any case, if we do have errors or omissions in attribution, what we have said may suggest that we have less reason to believe that they are ascribable to the mistakes of medieval scholiasts and copyists, than to the oversight of Cramer or his assistants. Such problems can ultimately be corrected.

Much of Cramer's work has never been translated in print, particularly the material unattested elsewhere. In the case of Acts, Chrysostom's complete homilies, which are attested independent of the catena, are translated in the *Nicene and Post Nicene Fathers* (1999).[14] Translations of a few otherwise unattested scholia can be found scattered throughout the *Ancient Christian Commentary on Acts*. From other volumes of Cramer, select translations have appeared sporadically.[15] But large portions of Cramer are yet to be translated from Greek. With the exception of the headless scholion in Cramer 366.1-20 which is correctly ascribed to John Chrysostom,[16] to date we have found none of the following selections in modern translation, English or otherwise.

III. Select Scholia from Cramer's Acts Catena

a. Anonymous on Acts 15.39 (Cramer 258.35-259.6)

{Ἐξ ἀνεπιγράφου.} Ὁ παροξυσμὸς τῶν Ἀποστόλων οὐ μάχης (35)
(259.) ἕνεκεν ἀλλ' οἰκονομίας γέγονεν· ἐπειδὴ γὰρ ὁ Παῦλος ἔμελλεν
συνέκδημον λαμβάνειν τὸν Τιμόθεον, εἰκότως τὸ Πνεῦμα τὸ Ἅγιον
τῷ Βαρνάβα τὸν Μάρκον παρέδωκεν· ὅτι δὲ καὶ Παῦλος αὐτὸν
ἠγάπα, ἄκουσον αὐτοῦ γράφοντος τῷ Τιμοθέῳ· "Μάρκον ἀναλα—

---

14   Nevertheless, this translation is based on a poorly preserved and highly confused Greek text. As Stevens notes in the preface to the American edition: 'The imperfect state of the original text of the Homilies on Acts is a serious embarrassment, alike to translator and editor, in this part of the work. Often the reports of the discourses are in hopeless confusion, and it is impossible to determine confidently the meaning of what has been reported, much less of what the preacher originally said.'

15   Other portions of Cramer's NT catenae that have appeared in print include the following. The Origen extracts from the 1 Corinthians catena were published in a series of articles at the beginning of the last century (Jenkins, 'Origen on I Corinthians', *JTS* 9 [1908], pp. 231–247; 353–372; 500–514); Bart Ehrman has translated the Gospel excerpts from Didymus the Blind, whose extant commentary derives almost entirely from the catenae (*Didymus the Blind and the Text of the Gospels* [The New Testament in the Greek Fathers 1; Atlanta: Scholars Press, 1986]); the Jude portion of the catena on the Catholic Epistles, found in the same manuscript as that of Acts, was recently translated into English for the first time by P. R. Jones (*The Epistle of Jude as Expounded by the Fathers—Clement of Alexandria , Didymus of Alexandria, the Scholia of Cramer's Catena, Pseudo-Oecumenius and Bede* [Texts and studies in religion, 89; Lampeter: Edwin Mellen Press, 2001]. Select translations from various volumes of Cramer can be found throughout the *Ancient Christian Commentary* series.

16   This, though, is only a partial exception, since the Greek text from which the NPNF worked differs substantially from ours; see n. 37.

"βῶν ἄγε μετὰ σεαυτοῦ· ἔστι γάρ μοι εὔχρηστος εἰς διακονίαν·" (5)
οἶμαι δὲ τοῦτο γράφειν αὐτὸν, δι'[17] ἀμφοτέρων κηδευθῆναι βουλό–
μενος.

Of an anonymous author. A 'sharp disagreement' between the apostles did not arise because of a quarrel, but because of divine dispensation.[18] For since Paul intended to take Timothy as his companion, naturally, the Holy Spirit gave Mark over to Barnabas. But we know that Paul also loved Mark; listen to what he writes to Timothy: 'Take Mark and bring him with you; for he is quite useful to me for ministry' (2 Tim. 4.11). I believe he wrote this because he wanted to be assisted by both of them.

b. Ammonius[19] on Acts 15.39 (Cramer 259.8-260.12)

{Ἀμμωνίου.} Διὰ τοὺς κεκαυτηριασμένους τὴν συνείδησιν, ὡς
διὰ συντόμου ἀπολογητέον περὶ τῶν Ἀποστόλων Βαρνάβα καὶ
Παύλου· οἱ ἐπὶ τοσοῦτον ἐπέτειναν τὴν φιλονεικίαν, ὅτι καὶ ἐχω– (10)
ρίσθησάν, φησιν. ὁ Μάρκος ἔδοξεν ἡμαρτηκέναι ἀπολιπὼν αὐτούς·
ὁ Παῦλος πρὸς τὸ σωφρονισθῆναι αὐτὸν ὠργίζετο, καὶ ἤθελεν
αὐτὸν πρὸς ὀλίγον λυπῆσαι· ἵνα αἰσθόμενος ἐκεῖνος μετανοήσῃ,
καὶ λοιπὸν ὑποταγῇ τῷ μὴ ποιεῖν τὸ θέλημα τὸ ἑαυτοῦ, ἀλλὰ
παρὰ τὴν ἑαυτοῦ θέλησιν ἀκολουθεῖν πρὸς τὸ ἔργον τῆς διακονίας· (15)
οὕτως ἐποίησε καὶ ἐπὶ τοῦ Κορινθίου· ἐκβαλὼν αὐτὸν τῆς ἐκκλη–
σίας, καὶ αὐτὸς ὑπὲρ αὐτοῦ παρακαλῶν, ἡνίκα μετεμελήθη· οὕτως
οὖν ἤθελε καὶ τὸν Μάρκον δαμάσαι. ὁ δὲ Βαρνάβας ἁπλούστερος
ὢν, συνεχώρησεν αὐτῷ μᾶλλον καὶ δίχα ἐκπλήξεως τὸ ἁμάρτημα·
ὃν ὁ Παῦλος παρεκάλει λέγων, μὴ οὕτως ὡς ἔτυχε τὸν δραπετεύ– (20)
σαντα τῆς συνοδίας προσλαβεῖν, ἀλλ' ἀποστραφῆναι αὐτὸν, διότι
οὐκ αὐτοὺς ἐνύβρισε τοῦτο ποιήσας, ἀλλὰ τῆς διακονίας κατα–
φρονήσας, τὸν Θεὸν ἐξουδένωσε. τούτῳ οὖν τῷ σκοπῷ ἀντέλεγεν ὁ
Παῦλος τῷ Βαρνάβα· ἀμέλει οὐδὲ ὠργίζετο, ἀλλὰ παρεκάλει
αὐτὸν, ὡς φησὶν ἡ γραφὴ, "Παῦλος δὲ ἠξίου·" οὐκοῦν ὁ μὲν Βαρ– (25)
νάβας χρηστότητα εἶχε πρὸς τοὺς ὑπηκόους ἕτοιμον, ὁ δὲ Παῦλος
ἀποτομίαν, πρὸς καιρὸν ἀποδίδους τοὺς καταφρονητὰς τῷ διαβόλῳ
εἰς ὄλεθρον τῆς σαρκός, ἵνα μεταμεληθῶσιν. οὐκοῦν ἀμφότεροι
κατὰ τὸν οἰκεῖον σκοπὸν καλῶς ἔπραξαν· ἀπεχωρίσθησαν δὲ καὶ

---

17   For οἶμαι δὲ τοῦτο γράφειν αὐτὸν, δι' *Coislin* has οἶδε γράφειν τοῦτο αὐτὸ δι'.

18   Cf. Augustine, *City of God* 16.21: 'When Abraham and Lot departed from one another and settled in separate homes, it was not because of the disgrace of discord (*non foeditate discordiae*), but because of the need to support their households' (author's translation).

19   Cramer's Acts catena attributes well over a hundred scholia to Ammonius. His precise identity is uncertain, however. He is typically identified with Ammonius of Alexandria, a fifth-century presbyter to whom several fragmented commentaries are attributed (including commentaries on the Psalms, Daniel, Luke, 1 Corinthians, Acts, and 1 Peter).

Cramer's catenae are the source for all of the Ammonius material in *PG* (80:1361-1610). For more on his identity, see M. Geerard, *Clavis Patrum Graecorum* (Corpus Christianorum , 1974-83; vol.3; p.5504); H. Rahner, 'Ammonios v. Alexandrien', *LTK* 1 (1957), p. 441.

διὰ τοῦτο ἀπ᾽ ἀλλήλων· ἐπείπερ οὐκ ἦσαν μιᾶς ἕξεως ἀμφότεροι· (30)
καὶ ἠδύνατο καὶ οὕτως, διὰ τῆς ἄγαν ἀνεξικακίας μὴ θέλων κρίνειν
ἄλλον, δυσωπῆσαι τοὺς πιστούς· καὶ ὁ Παῦλος διὰ τοῦ ἐπιστατι–
κοῦ ἑαυτοῦ καὶ ζηλοτυπικοῦ, σῶσαι καὶ σωφρονίσαι τοὺς ἀμελεῖς·
οὕτω γὰρ διδάσκει λέγων· "ἔλεγξον, ἐπιτίμησον, παρακάλεσον·"
οὐχ ὡς μὴ δυνάμενοι δὲ φέρειν ἀλλήλων τὰ ἐλαττώματα ἀπέστη– (35)
(260.) σαν· ὅπουγε πολὺν συνέζησαν χρόνον, συγκαμόντες ἀλλήλοις
καὶ συγκινδυνεύοντες· ἀλλ᾽ ἵνα μή τις τὸ ἀνώμαλον τῆς αὐτῶν ὁρῶν
πολιτείας σκανδαλισθῇ[20] πρὸς ἕνα, ἢ τὸν Παῦλον ὀργίλον καλῶν, ἢ
τὸν Βαρνάβαν καταφρονητὴν καὶ ἑαυτοῦ γινόμενον· μὴ θέλοντα δὲ
τοὺς ἁμαρτάνοντας ἐπιστομίζειν, ἀλλὰ παρορῶντα τοὺς τῆς ἑαυ– (5)
τῶν ἀμελοῦντας σωτηρίας· ἐθνικοῖς μάλιστα μέλλοντες εὐαγγελί–
ζεσθαι, τοῖς μηδεμίαν ἔχουσι διάκρισιν καλοῦ καὶ κακοῦ· καὶ
πολλάκις ἐκ τοῦ διαφόρου τῆς αὐτῶν πολιτείας, ὡς ἀσύμφωνον
ἐχόντων ἕξιν, ἀσύμφωνον καὶ τὸ παρ᾽ αὐτῶν εὐαγγελιζόμενον μυ–
στήριον ὑποπτεύοντες εἶναι· ὅπερ μᾶλλον ὑπονοήσαντες, ἀπέστη– (10)
σαν ἀπ᾽ ἀλλήλων· οὕτως εὖ ἔχειν κρίναντες πρὸς τὴν τοῦ λόγου
διακονίαν.

Of Ammonius.[21] On account of those who are 'seared in their own conscience' (1 Tim. 4.2), briefly a defence should be made[22] concerning the apostles Barnabas and Paul. The author says that Barnabas and Paul increased strife to such a degree that they departed from one another. Mark made up his mind to go astray by abandoning them. Paul became indignant in order that Mark might be brought to his senses; and he was wanting him to experience some grief for a little while, in order that, upon feeling grief to the full, he might repent, and might in the future resign himself not to making his own plan, but might against his own plan resign himself to following the work of the ministry. Thus Paul also did in the case of the Corinthian man – having driven him out from the church, and exhorting them on the man's account, at which time the man repented.[23] Therefore, he wanted to discipline Mark also in this way. But Barnabas, being simple, instead waived Mark's sin even without any consternation.[24] Paul was exhorting Barnabas, saying, under present circumstances,[25] not to take him back who had fled companionship, but to turn him away, because he had not insulted *them* in doing this, but rather, by despising the ministry, had rejected *God*. Paul was opposing Barnabas with this aim. He was actually[26] not angry with him, but was exhorting him; as the scripture says, 'And Paul thought it right'. Accordingly, Barnabas was keeping indulgence ready for the

20   TLG's text rightly reads σκανδαλισθῇ.

21   *Coislin* 25 has Ἀμμωνίου Πρεσβυτέρου.

22   ἀπολογητέον. Ammonius is fond of the verbal adjective; cf. n. 40.

23   ἐκβαλὼν αὐτὸν τῆς ἐκκλησίας, καὶ αὐτὸς ὑπὲρ αὐτοῦ παρακαλῶν, ἡνίκα μετεμελήθη. An allusion to the problem in 1 Cor. 5.1-13 and its resolution as indicated in 2 Cor. 2.5-11.

24   It is difficult to tell whether the consternation is Mark's or whether it is Barnabas'.

25   ἔτυχε. When impersonal, 'at any time, place, etc.', lit. 'as it happened'; thus, our rendering, 'under present circumstances'.

26   ἀμέλει. Impersonal used adverbially, 'doubtless', 'of course', 'actually'.

obedient, but Paul was keeping severity, at the right time giving back the despisers to the devil for destruction of the flesh[27] in order that they might repent. Doubtless, both men acted well in accordance with their own aims. However, they were also separated from one another on account of this difference, seeing that they were not both of one disposition. And even in this way – through too much longsuffering, not wanting to condemn another person – one could[28] win over the believers; as well, Paul could, through his own administration and zeal, save the heedless and return them to their senses. For thus he teaches, saying, 'Convict, rebuke, exhort' (2 Tim. 4.2). And they did not depart from one another as if unable to bear one another's weaknesses – seeing that they had spent much time together, laboured together, and so often risked their necks together – but rather in order that someone, seeing the inconsistency of their way of life, may not take offence at one of them, either calling Paul irascible, or calling Barnabas one who has become a despiser even of himself, and one not wanting to keep in check those doing wrong but rather condoning those who are heedless of their salvation. And, most of all, since they were about to preach to the heathen, who have no discernment of good and evil; and the heathen, perhaps from the difference of their way of life, suspecting the mystery preached by Paul and Barnabas also to be discordant, on account of the fact that their disposition was discordant – rather, having considered all of *this*,[29] Paul and Barnabas withdrew from one another, having thus judged it to be good for the ministry of the word.

c. Ammonius on Acts 16.7-8 (Cramer 264.26-31)

{Ἀμμωνίου.} Σημειωτέον ὅτι οὐδὲν ἐποίουν ἰδίᾳ αὐθεντίᾳ οἱ
Ἀπόστολοι· ἀλλὰ πάντα ἃ ἐποίουν, ὑπὸ τοῦ Πνεύματος νυττόμενοι
ἐποίουν ἢ οὐκ ἐποίουν· ὥστε οὖν οὐκ ἀκίνδυνον μέμφεσθαι τὰ ὑπὸ
τῶν Ἀποστόλων γινόμενα, ἢ πολυπραγμονεῖν τὰ ὑπὸ τοῦ Πνεύμα–
τος διατυπούμενα· οὐ δεῖ οὖν ζητεῖν, διατί ἄρα οὐκ ἐπέτρεψε τὸ (30)
Πνεῦμα τῷ Παύλῳ κηρύξαι ἐν Ἀσίᾳ.
    Καὶ ὅραμα διὰ νυκτὸς ὤφθη τῷ Παύλῳ· ἀνὴρ Μα–
(265.) κεδών τις ἦν ἑστώς, καὶ παρακαλῶν αὐτὸν καὶ λέγων,
διαβὰς εἰς Μακεδονίαν, βοήθησον ἡμῖν.

Of Ammonius. One should note[30] that the apostles were doing nothing by their own authority. But all the things that they were doing, they were doing or not doing in accordance as they were pricked by the Spirit. Therefore, it is not without peril to

---

27   ἀποδίδους τοὺς καταφρονητὰς τῷ διαβόλῳ εἰς ὄλεθρον τῆς σαρκὸς. An allusion to 1 Cor. 5.5.

28   ἠδύνατο. Barnabas is the implied subject. Σῶσαι is then the complement to another, implied ἠδύνατο, which takes ὁ Παῦλος as its subject. Ammonius is therefore saying that it is possible to accomplish essentially the same end through either Barnabas' or Paul's method.

29   ὅπερ – the antecedent is ἐθνικοῖς μάλιστα μέλλοντες εὐαγγελίζεσθαι ... ἀσύμφωνον ἐχόντων ἕξιν, ἀσύμφωνον καὶ τὸ παρ᾽ αὐτῶν εὐαγγελιζόμενον μυστήριον ὑποπτεύοντες εἶναι.

30   A distinctive of Ammonius in the Acts catena, the verbal adjective σημειωτέον frequently introduces his scholia (e.g., Cramer 247.7-12; 252.10-18; 254.32-34; 256.3-5; 262.16-20).

find fault with the things done by the apostles – or rather, to meddle in the things perfectly designed by the Spirit. One must therefore not question why the Spirit did not permit Paul to preach in Asia.

d. Ammonius on Acts 16.33-34[31] (Cramer 278.12-19)

{Ἀμμωνίου.} Ἰδοὺ πάλιν καὶ ὧδε προλαμβάνει ἡ κατήχησις
τὸ βάπτισμα· διὸ τὸν τέλειον ἄνδρα, Ἕλληνα ὄντα καὶ ἔξω ἔχοντα,
οὐκ ὀφείλει βαπτίζειν τις, ἐν ᾧ μὴ δύναται ἀκοῦσαι λόγον κατη–
χητικὸν καὶ καταδέξασθαι, μάλιστα εἰ μηδέποτε ἐμυήθη λόγων (15)
θείων· βλέπε δὲ ὅτι διὰ τὴν ἀνάγκην εὐθὺς μετὰ τὴν κατήχησιν
ἐπηκολούθησε τὸ βάπτισμα· δέος γὰρ ἦν, μὴ διωχθέντος τοῦ δυ–
ναμένου βαπτίσαι, μείνῃ ἀμέτοχος τῆς ζωῆς ὁ βουλόμενος, διὰ τὸ
μὴ εἶναι τὸν τοῦτο ποιοῦντα.

Of Ammonius. See once again, here also[32] catechesis precedes baptism. Wherefore, one is not obligated to baptize the 'perfect man',[33] who is a Greek and is beyond (the need for baptism),[34] in whom it is impossible to hear and receive the word of instruction, especially if he was never initiated into the mysteries of divine words. But notice that baptism, by necessity, followed immediately after catechesis. For there was fear lest, should the one who was able to perform the baptism be persecuted, the one wanting to be baptized might remain without a share in life, since the one who might have performed it no longer lived.

e. Maximus[35] on Acts 22.27 (Cramer 365.11-18)

{Μαξίμου.} Τί δήποτε ὁ Ἀπόστολος Παῦλος Ῥωμαῖον ἑαυτὸν
ἀποκαλεῖ· καὶ πρὸς χιλίαρχον διαλεγόμενος ἔφη· "ὅτι ἐγὼ δὲ
"καὶ γεγέννημαι;" οἱ κατὰ πᾶσαν χώραν, ὡς δή τι μέγα τὸ

---

31   Cramer's text of Acts 16:34 reads ἀναγαγὼν δὲ for the NA[27]'s ἀναγαγὼν τε.

32   Ammonius previously discussed the priority of catechesis in his comments on 16.14 (Cramer, *Catenae*, 266.31-277.20).

33   Ammonius seems to be alluding, tongue in cheek, to the concept of the philosophical 'wise man', whose attainment of consistent exercise of virtue earned him the title 'perfect'. The logic here runs as follows: instruction should always precede baptism; the so-called 'perfect' man has no need for instruction; therefore the 'perfect' man should not receive baptism. Cf. Philo, *All. Leg.* 1.94: 'It is not necessary to give instructions or prohibitions or recommendations to the perfect man, made according to the image of God, for the perfect man needs none of these things' (author's translation).

34   This is our best guess for ἔξω ἔχοντα in the context (ἔχω with adverb = 'be').

35   Maximus the Confessor (b.580–d.662) was the leading defender of orthodoxy in the face of Monothelitism. Although he had at one time served in the imperial court, he later fell out of favour with the emperor because of his refusal to make peace with the Monothelite factions. According to tradition, he was twice banished for his refusal to sign the Type, and had his tongue and right hand removed. He died during his second banishment in 662. Although Maximus is not alone in feeling the need to justify Paul's claiming Roman citizenship, his own experience of trial and torture before political powers gave him a unique perspective.

Ῥωμαῖοι καλεῖσθαι νομίζοντες, παρέχοντες δόσεις ἀπεγράφοντο
Ῥωμαῖοι, καὶ ἔτρεχεν εἰς τὸ γένος τὸ ὄνομα· ἐπεὶ οὖν οἱ γονεῖς (15)
τοῦ Ἀποστόλου ὄντες ἐν Ταρσῷ ἀπεγράφησαν εἰς τὸ καλεῖσθαι
Ῥωμαῖοι, εἰκότως ὁ Ἀπόστολος ὡς ἐξ αὐτῶν γεννηθεὶς λέγει·
"ὅτι ἐγὼ δὲ καὶ γεγέννημαι."

Of Maximus. Why, do you suppose, does the apostle Paul call himself a Roman? He said to the tribune, 'I was even born a citizen' (Acts 22.28). Those throughout the whole land, since they thought that it was truly something great to be called Romans, were being registered as Roman citizens by giving gifts, and the title 'Roman' was advancing among the people of their nations.[36] Therefore, since the apostle's parents, while in Tarsus, were registered as Roman citizens, naturally, the apostle, since he was born from them, says, 'I was born a citizen'.

f. Scholion[37] on Acts 23.1-2[38] (Cramer 366.1-20)

(366.) Τινὲς φασὶν ὅτι οὐκ ᾔδει ὅτι ἐστὶν ἀρχιερεύς· τί οὖν ἀπολο-
γεῖται ὡς κακηγορίας οὔσης, καὶ ἐπάγει, "ἄρχοντα τοῦ λαοῦ σου
"οὐκ ἐρεῖς κακῶς;" εἰ γὰρ μὴ ἄρχων ἦν, ἄλλον ἀπλῶς ὑβρίζειν
ἔδει· αὐτός φησι, "λοιδορούμενοι εὐλογοῦμεν· διωκόμενοι ἀνεχό-
μεθα·" ἐνταῦθα δὲ τοὐναντίον· καὶ οὐ λοιδορεῖται μόνον ἀλλὰ (5)
καὶ ἐπαρᾶται· παρρησίας μᾶλλόν ἐστι τὰ ῥήματα ἢ θυμοῦ· οὐκ
ἐβούλετο εὐκαταφρόνητος φανῆναι τῷ χιλιάρχῳ· εἰ γὰρ αὐτὸς
μὲν ἐφείσατο μαστίξαι, ὡς δὴ τοῖς Ἰουδαίοις ἐκδίδοσθαι μέλλοντα,
τὸ ὑπὸ τῶν οἰκετῶν τύπτεσθαι, μᾶλλον ἂν ἐκεῖνο θρασύτερον εἰρ-
γάσατο· διὰ τοῦτο οὐ πρὸς τὸν παῖδα ἀποτείνεται, ἀλλὰ πρὸς (10)
αὐτὸν τὸν ἐπιτάξαντα· τὸ δὲ "τοῖχε κεκονιαμένε, καὶ σὺ κάθη
"κρίνων με κατὰ τὸν νόμον;" ἀντὶ τοῦ ὑπεύθυνος ὤν· ὡσανεὶ

36   Literally 'the name ran (ἔτρεχεν) into the race (τὸ γένος)'.
37   This scholion, which both text and index of Cramer leave unattributed, turns out to be a variant version of an excerpt from Chrysostom's *Homilies on the Acts of the Apostles* (Homily 48). The highly confused text history of Chrysostom's *Homilies* is yet to be resolved in an adequate critical edition, and the confusion is amply reflected here. Apparently Chrysostom's Acts sermons were largely extemporized, only to be copied by an unskilled editor from a tachygrapher's transcript; the poorly transcribed text was then never subjected to Chrysostom's own revision. A later and smoother Byzantine recension comprises the material for the most recent and accessible critical edition to date, that of Migne (*PG* 60), from which TLG derives its text. The older, more difficult text is preserved in several other manuscripts, as well as in the catenae; the catena text is certainly the more difficult of the two, in both its syntax and its logic. Both the catena and the Migne text differ from that on which the NPNF translation is based. The first complete English translation of Chrysostom's *Commentary* (1851) worked from one of the earliest known critical editions (Saville, 1610). Although subsequently revised for NPNF, the translation was left 'substantially unchanged' (NPNF, p. iii).
    For the state of the evidence and a plea for a new critical edition, see A. M. Devine, 'Manuscripts of John Chrysostom's 'Commentary on the Acts of the Apostles': A Preliminary Study for a Critical Edition', *Ancient World* 20 (1989), pp. 111–25.
38   Cramer's biblical text reads ἐκέλευσε for the NA[27]'s ἐπέταξεν Acts 23.2); εἶπεν for the NA[27]'s εἶπαν (Acts 23.4); and adds ὅτι before NA[27]'s quotation of Exod. 22.27 (Acts 23.5).

ἔλεγε, καὶ μυρίων πληγῶν ἄξιος ὤν. Καὶ μετ᾽ ὀλίγα—Σφόδρα
πείθομαι μὴ εἰδέναι αὐτὸν ὅτι ἀρχιερεύς ἐστι· διὰ μακροῦ μὲν
ἐπανελθόντα χρόνου, μὴ συγγενόμενον δὲ Ἰουδαίοις, ὁρῶντα δὲ αὐ— (15)
τὸν ἐν τῷ μέσῳ μετὰ πολλῶν καὶ ἑτέρων· οὐκέτι γὰρ δῆλος ἦν ὁ
ἀρχιερεύς, πολλῶν ὄντων καὶ διαφόρων. Καὶ μετ᾽ ὀλίγα—Οὐδὲ
ὕβρις ἦν τὸ παρ᾽ αὐτοῦ εἰρημένον, εἰ μὴ καὶ τὰ τοῦ Χριστοῦ ὕβριν
εἴποι τις, ὅταν λέγῃ· "οὐαὶ ὑμῖν γραμματεῖς καὶ Φαρισαῖοι, ὅτι
"παρομοιάζετε τάφοις[39] κεκονιαμένοις." (20)

Some say he didn't know that it was the high priest. Why, then, does he defend
himself as if it were slander and go on to say, 'You shall not speak ill of the ruler
of the people'? (Acts 23.4)[40] This is because, even if he were not the ruler, Paul
must simply have insulted someone else.[41] He says, 'Being reviled, we bless; being
persecuted, we endure' (1 Cor. 4.12). But here he does the opposite; and not only is
he being reviled, but he also curses! His words are more of boldness than of anger.
He did not want to appear contemptible to the commander. For if the commander
himself had refrained from scourging Paul when he was about to be handed over
to the Jews, his being beaten by the slaves would have served to make him all the
bolder. For this reason, Paul did not lash out against the slave, but against the one
who gave the slave the order. The statement, 'Whitewashed wall, and do you sit
judging me according to the law?' (Acts 23.3) meaning,[42] 'you are liable', as if he
were saying, 'you are worthy of countless blows' ...[43] I am very much convinced
that Paul did not know that it was the high priest, since he had returned after a
long absence, was not having continuous association with Jews, and was seeing
him amid a crowd of many others. For the high priest was no longer conspicuous,
as there were many and diverse people present. And no insolence did he speak,
unless someone should also say that the words of Christ were insolence,[44] when
he said, 'Woe to you, scribes and Pharisees, for you are like whitewashed tombs'
(Mt. 23.27).[45]

---

39   *Coislin* 25 has τοίχοις for τάφοις in its text, but the latter in the margin.
40   Cf. Exod. 22.28. Here, the semi-colon indicating the question in the Greek text should
be moved outside of the quotation.
41   In other words, even if the person Paul insulted was not a ruler, Paul's words were
clearly directed against *someone*.
42   ἀντι. In the sense of 'corresponding to'.
43   The ellipsis stands in for Καὶ μετ᾽ ὀλίγα ('after a little'), an expression apparently
inserted by the scholiast to indicate that he has omitted material from the original. The phrase
recurs in line 17.
44   εἰ μὴ καὶ τὰ τοῦ Χριστοῦ ὕβριν εἴποι τις, ὅταν λέγῃ. This line of argument is
common in patristic exegetical argumentation: 'If *x* is the case, then Christ is guilty of the same.
We know that Christ could not be guilty of this. Therefore *x* cannot be the case.' See, for another
example, Augustine, *City of God* 1.12 on Lk. 12.4.
45   οὐαὶ ὑμῖν γραμματεῖς καὶ Φαρισαῖοι, ὅτι παρομοιάζετε τάφοις κεκονιαμένοις. A
quotation of Mt. 23.27, omitting the ὑποκριταί that should follow Φαρισαῖοι.

g. *Anonymous on Acts 23.3-5 (Cramer 366.28-367.2)*

{Ἐξ ἀνεπιγράφου.} Εἴ τις⁴⁶ ἀμφιβάλλει εἰ καλῶς ἐλέχθη τὰ
προκείμενα, ἀκουέτω, ὡς εἰ μὲν λοιδορῆσαι σπεύδων τοῦτο ἐποίη–
σεν, οὐ δεόντως· εἰ δὲ χάριν ἐλέγξαι ὑπόκρισιν, καὶ τοῦ κολάσεως (30)
ὀφειλέτην εἶναι τὸν ὄντα μὲν κακόν, πλαττόμενον δὲ τὸ καλὸν ἐπὶ
ἀπάτῃ πολλῶν, προσηκόντως εἴρηται· διὸ οὐδὲ ἀρχιερέα εἰδέναι
λέγει, εἴγε ἀρχιερέως μὲν ἔργον τὸ καὶ σῴζειν τὸ ὑποτεταγμένον
(367.) ποίμνιον· οὗτος δὲ καὶ ἐπέτριβε καὶ ἐλυμαίνετο, ἀφιστῶν τῆς
δεδομένης σωτηρίας παρὰ Θεοῦ.

Of an anonymous author. If anyone doubts whether Paul made the preceding
remarks rightly, let him listen. If, on the one hand, Paul did this because he was
eager to revile the high priest, then he spoke unfittingly. But if, on the other hand,
he spoke in this way in order to expose the high priest's outward display of grace as
hypocrisy, and in order that this one – who was evil but who was fabricating good so
that many people were deceived – become a debtor of punishment, then it has been
spoken fittingly. Therefore, he says that he did not know the high priest, inasmuch
as saving the flock that is subject to him is the work of a high priest, while this 'high
priest' was both exasperating his flock and bringing it to ruin, having defected from
the salvation that has been given by God.

h. *Severus on Acts 23.3-5 (Cramer 367.3-14)*

{Σευηριανοῦ.}⁴⁷ Διατί τοῖχον κεκονιαμένον καλεῖ; ἐπειδὴ λαμπρὰν
μὲν εἶχε τὴν ὄψιν, ὡς νόμου ἔκδικος, καὶ νόμῳ δικάζων, ἡ δὲ διά–
νοια ἀνομίας πεπλήρωτο· ἐλέγχει αὐτοῦ τὸ σχῆμα ἐκ τῆς ἔξωθεν (5)
διαθέσεως· οἱ δὲ παρεστῶτες ἔλεγον· "τὸν ἀρχιερέα τοῦ Θεοῦ
"λοιδορεῖς;" ὁ δὲ ἅγιος Παῦλος βουληθεὶς δεῖξαι, ὅτι δεῖ καὶ
θυμὸν δίκαιον περιστέλλειν, καὶ ἀγανάκτησιν δικαίαν καλύπτειν·
ὥσπερ μεταμεληθεὶς λέγει· "οὐκ ἤδειν," καὶ τὰ ἑξῆς· οὐκ ἤδεις
ὅτι ἱερεύς ἐστι; πῶς οὖν ἔλεγες, "καὶ σὺ κάθῃ κρίνων με κατὰ (10)
"τὸν νόμον;" ἀλλὰ προσποιεῖται ἄγνοιαν, οὐ βλάπτουσαν ἀλλ'
οἰκονομοῦσαν· ἔστι γὰρ καὶ μεταχειρισμῷ χρήσασθαι ἰσχυροτέρῳ
παρρησίας· πολλάκις μὲν παρρησία ἄκαιρος ἔβλαψε τὴν ἀλήθειαν·
μεταχειρισμὸς δὲ εὔκαιρος κατόρθωσε τὸ προκείμενον.

---

46   *Coislin* 25 has the adverbial accusative τι. Possibly, the meaning would then be, 'If he
doubts at all whether...'

47   *Coislin* has Σευήρου ἐπισκόπου Γαβάλων while TLG has Σευηριανοῦ. Severus,
however, was bishop of Antioch, while Severianus was bishop of Gabala. So, if Cramer has correctly recorded the variant in Coislin, then the Coislin text is almost certainly incorrect. Perhaps
the Coislin text should be taken as agreeing with the text found in TLG (which is a transcription of
Oxon. 58, the same manuscript that Cramer used) since it seems far more likely that Σευηριανοῦ
might be mistaken for Σευήρου, than Γαβάλων be mistaken for Ἀντιοχείας.

Of Severus. Why does he call him a whitewashed wall? Because, although the high priest could see clearly as a legal representative of the law, and one who judges by the law, his understanding was full of lawlessness.[48] He exposes his character by his outward disposition, for those present were saying, 'Do you revile the high priest of God?' (Acts 23.4). But Saint Paul, since he wanted to show that it is necessary to conceal just rage and to hide righteous indignation, as if repenting says, 'I did not know ...' (Acts 23.5). You did not know that he was a priest? How, then, did you say, 'and do you sit in judgement of me according to the law?' (Acts 23.3). But he pretends ignorance, not out of malice but rather expedience. For to modify one's statement[49] is often more effective than boldness. Often ill-timed boldness hinders the truth, but well-timed retraction corrects the matter at hand.

IV. Summarizing the Arguments of the Catena

All seven passages reflect, in one way or another, attempts to defend the actions of Paul, recorded in the canonical Acts.[50]

Several times, the scholia address the issue of whether or not the apostles were guilty of creating strife and dissension. The anonymous writer of scholion a. attributes the disagreement between Barnabas and Paul over Mark (Acts 15.39) to 'divine dispensation' in order that both Paul and Barnabas would have assistance. Further, drawing on 2 Tim. 4.11, the writer reminds the reader that Paul also loved Mark. Ammonius (scholion b.) offers a fuller account of the disagreement between Barnabas and Paul, claiming that 'both men acted well in accordance with their own aims'. Paul wished to 'convict, rebuke, and exhort' in order 'to bring Mark to his senses'. Barnabas, on the other hand, 'waived Mark's sin' in order to keep 'indulgence ready for the obedient'. Ultimately the separation of Paul and Barnabas was not the result of their discordant disposition, but rather because they 'judged it to be good for the ministry of the word'.

In two other places, Ammonius seeks to justify Paul's action. In scholion c., Ammonius defends the decision that Paul not go to Asia by claiming that 'the apostles were doing nothing by their own authority'; rather they were only doing (or not doing) what was ordered by the Spirit. Ammonius admonishes his readers 'not to meddle in the things perfectly designed by the Spirit'. Elsewhere (scholion d.), Ammonius defends Paul's actions in baptizing the Philippian jailor and his family (Acts 16.33-34) before they have received full catechism (the accepted practice in Ammonius' day) because of the fear that 'the one who was able to perform baptism' (Paul) might be persecuted and martyred, leaving the one desiring baptism 'without

---

48   Possibly an allusion to Eph. 4.18.

49   The word μεταχειρισμὸς is quite rare, occurring only nine times in the TLG corpus. It seems clear that the author has chosen his words carefully. An English equivalent is, however, difficult.

50   Such a practice was not uncommon in early Christianity; see e.g., George Rice, 'Western Non-Interpolations: A Defense of the Apostolate', *Luke-Acts: New Perspectives from the Society of Biblical Literature Seminar* (ed. Charles Talbert; New York: Crossroad, 1984), pp. 1–16.

a share in life'. In such circumstances, baptism might follow immediately whatever instruction could be delivered, however briefly.

In another place, an effort is made to defend Paul against charges of cultural assimilation. According to Maximus (scholion e.), Paul's claim to be a Roman citizen was not rooted in the deplorable practice of 'buying citizenship' but rather was simply the result of being born to parents who were registered in Tarsus as Roman citizens.

Elsewhere, we see the questionable actions and words of Paul toward others being defended. Several writers rush to the defence of Paul in his encounter with the high priest recorded in Acts 23, although they do not necessarily agree on the intent of Paul's rebuke ('Whitewashed wall, and do you sit judging me according to the law?'). The writer of scholion f., whom we have identified as Chrysostom,[51] suggests that Paul 'did not know it was the high priest, since he had returned after a long absence, was not having continuous association with Jews, and was seeing him amid a crowd of many others'. Chrysostom reasons that Paul was further emboldened by the fact that the commander had not scourged Paul, and Paul who 'did not want to appear contemptible to the commander' responds boldly against the one who ordered him struck. Even so, Chrysostom argues, one could not accuse Paul of insolence unless one were willing to accuse Christ himself of insolence for calling the Pharisees 'whitewashed tombs'! The anonymous writer of scholion g. and Severus (scholion h.) take a different tack, arguing that Paul does, indeed, know the high priest. Paul speaks, not simply to revile the high priest, but to 'expose the high priest's outward display as hypocrisy' (Cramer 366.30-31) and because 'his understanding was full of lawlessness' (Cramer 367.4-5).

V. Conclusion

This essay is an exercise in 'rescue and recovery', attempting to bring to light some of the largely overlooked interpretations of Paul in Acts, preserved in J. Cramer's catena. These interpretations aim to clarify, illuminate, and ultimately defend the actions of Paul, as recorded in the book of Acts. They extend and expand the 'idealized' portrait of Paul beyond that which is already found in the canonical Acts. As such, they represent an important aspect of the early reception of Paul, which we all ignore to our own peril and loss.

---

51   See note 37.

Part III

THE PAULINE FIGURE OF ACTS WITHIN THE PAULINE LEGACY

Chapter 11

PAUL THE FOUNDER OF THE CHURCH: REFLECTIONS ON THE RECEPTION OF PAUL IN THE ACTS OF THE APOSTLES AND THE PASTORAL EPISTLES[1]

Jens Schröter

I. Introduction

The Acts of the Apostles and the Pastoral Epistles belong to a trajectory of early Christianity committed to the heritage of Paul's mission and theology. This development, occasionally designated somewhat ambiguously as the *Pauline school*, was quite diverse within early Christianity. The Deutero-Pauline letters (2 Thessalonians; Colossians; Ephesians; 1 and 2 Timothy; Titus) already give evidence that Paul's missionary activity and his theological thinking have been affiliated and perpetuated in various ways. As for the claim that all these different writings belonged to one and the same 'school' – even located at a particular place in Asia Minor (Ephesus?), as is sometimes assumed – not much can be said. Rather, Paul's heritage was developed in these letters in different ways and thereby became edifying for the emerging church.

The Acts of the Apostles differs from these letters principally in that Acts does not refer to Paul as a letter writer, but instead portrays Paul as a missionary, founder of communities, and orator. As will be argued below, this is a striking disparity to the reception of Paul in the Pastoral Epistles. On the other hand, one encounters another distinctive reception of Paul in 1 Clement and the letters of Ignatius. In these writings Paul is invoked in certain places in order to strengthen the arguments developed in these letters. The focus, however, on Paul's person or his influence does not reach the intensity of the Deutero-Pauline letters or the Acts of the Apostles.[2] The *Acts of Paul* then depict his entire career from the perspective of the second century in a comprehensive way and diverge – as do, in their own

---

1   This paper was originally presented at the seminar 'The Reception of Paul' at the 61st General Meeting of Studiorum Novi Testamenti Societas, 25th–29th of July 2006 in Aberdeen. I would like to thank the participants for their suggestions during the discussion, in particular Michael Wolter (Bonn) for his detailed critical response, which has enriched the revision of this paper considerably.

2   Cf. A. Lindemann, 'Paul's Influence on "Clement" and Ignatius', in *The New Testament and the Apostolic Fathers. II. Trajectories through the New Testament and the Apostolic Fathers* (ed. A. F. Gregory and C. M. Tuckett; Oxford: University Press, 2006), pp. 9–24.

way, the Pastoral Epistles – from the image generated by the Acts of the Apostles.[3] The Acts of the Apostles and the Pastoral Epistles must therefore be considered as developments within a broader spectrum of connections to Paul in the late first and the second century, reaching an initial highpoint in the history of Christian theology at the end of the second century in the writings of Irenaeus of Lyon.

Upon careful consideration, some similarities between the Acts of the Apostles and the Pastoral Epistles can be detected which have already been observed in earlier scholarship. These include analogies in vocabulary and style, common themes, such as the shape of Christian life and the suffering of Paul, the reference to πρεσβύτεροι and ἐπίσκοποι as leaders of the Christian community, as well as the mention of locations of the first missionary journey, which do not appear in the genuine letters of Paul. These correspondences have occasionally been explained through the hypothesis of a common author of Luke-Acts and the Pastorals.[4] In this case, the Pastorals form the third part of a composition which ends with an account of Paul entrusting two of his co-workers with the preservation of his doctrine and eventually taking leave in 2 Timothy through a 'farewell discourse'.[5]

However, closer scrutiny demonstrates that the assumption of common authorship proves untenable. The similarities in content are of a general nature and become more specific only when the Miletus speech is compared to 2 Timothy. Moreover, such a hypothesis creates other problems:[6] Why should Luke now depict Paul as a letter writer, given that this was not mentioned in the account of his apostolic career? Why would the author create a contradiction by stating that Timothy was present on the journey from Ephesus to Greece (cf. Acts 20.4) and that he remained in Ephesus (cf. 1 Tim. 1.3)? Why should the same author allow Paul to compose two different 'testaments', an oral one for the elders in Ephesus, and a literary one for Timothy? Moreover, it seems difficult to imagine Luke composing a fictional letter from Paul to Titus, who is never mentioned in the Acts of the Apostles.

Given that it seems rather improbable, therefore, that the author of Luke-Acts also wrote the Pastorals, it is nevertheless evident that both of these works are

---

3   A more recent survey about the *Acts of Paul* is provided by H.-J. Klauck, *Apokryphe Apostelakten: Eine Einführung* (Stuttgart: Katholisches Bibelwerk, 2005), pp. 61–92. Cf. also H.-C. Brennecke, 'Die Anfänge einer Paulusverehrung', in *Biographie und Persönlichkeit des Paulus* (eds E.-M. Becker and P. Pilhofer; WUNT, 187; Tübingen: Mohr, 2005), pp. 295–305.

4   Cf. e.g. S. G. Wilson, *Luke and the Pastoral Epistles* (London: SPCK, 1979); A. Strobel, 'Schreiben des Lukas? Zum sprachlichen Problem der Pastoralbriefe', *NTS* 15 (1968/9), pp. 191–210; J. D. Quinn, 'The Last Volume of Luke: The Relation of Luke-Acts', in *Perspectives on Luke-Acts* (ed. C. H. Talbert; Danville / Edinburgh: Association of Baptist Professors of Religion, 1978), pp. 62–75. More recently R. Riesner, 'Once More: Luke-Acts and the Pastoral Epistles', in *History and Exegesis* (ed. Sang-Won (Aaron) Son; Essays in Honor of Dr. E. Earle Ellis for his 80th Birthday; New York / London: T&T Clark, 2006), pp. 239–58, who considers the hypothesis of common authorship worthy of discussion.

5   Cf. A. Weiser, *Der Zweite Brief an Timotheus* (EKK, 26/1; Düsseldorf: Patmos / Zürich: Benziger / Neukirchen-Vluyn: Neukirchener, 2003), p. 35, for the genre of 2 Timothy ('apostolisches Mahnschreiben'.

6   Cf. also L. T. Johnson, *The First and Second Letters to Timothy* (AncB, 35A; New York: Doubleday, 2001), pp. 88–89.

related to each other in that they were composed at the end of the first century and focus on Paul's teachings, in order to apply them to the contemporary historical situation at the end of the first or the beginning of the second century. These writings, therefore, provide insight into circumstances and controversies within the church after its first encounters with Jesus and Paul. As will be argued below, the Acts of the Apostles and the Pastoral Epistles respond to these situations each in its own way, by depicting Paul as the decisive figure upon whose activity and theology the characteristic shape of the church is based. Before turning to a comparison of the texts, however, it is necessary to address the methodology applied to these documents.

In recent research on the Acts of the Apostles, one notices a tendency to dismantle the hypothesis that there is a fundamental contradiction between Luke and Paul, a hypothesis developed particularly in German scholarly circles after the time of Martin Dibelius. This older approach was characterized by the view that Luke only preserved a few clichés and stereotyped phrases of Paul's theology, but had abandoned their very substance and instead generated a picture of Paul as a great preacher and missionary for the gentiles.[7] When one recognizes that the alleged fundamental differences between Paul's speeches in Acts 13 and 17 on the one hand and his own letters on the other are not sustainable, this assumption then becomes questionable. As more recent investigations have shown, the distinctions between Paul's theology in the Acts of the Apostles and his own letters have been improperly interpreted as principal contradictions.[8] Instead, it is more appropriate to understand them as an application of Paul's teachings to a specific historical situation. Given this interpretation the question has also been raised anew of whether Luke had direct knowledge of Paul's theology, or perhaps even knew some of his letters.

Due to this assumption, Jürgen Roloff's claim, argued in a seminal article on the portrait of Paul in Acts, must be scrutinized. Roloff saw a decisive difference between Paul's portrait in the Acts of the Apostles and those in the Pastoral Epistles in that the latter are based on Paul's authority as a teacher, while for Luke 'the specific Pauline teaching tradition does not play a decisive role for the solution of the continuity problem'.[9] Roloff's position, namely that the 'remembrance of Paul's activity' and 'commitment to Paul's authoritative teaching' are in opposition is, however, hardly convincing. In the end, as will be shown in detail below, Luke generates an image of Paul as influenced by hostilities and imprisonments and by no means exclusively a picture of a successful missionary. The assumption of a 'heroic image of Paul' in Acts must therefore be corrected.

---

7   Thus programmatically P. Vielhauer, 'Zum "Paulinismus" der Apostelgeschichte', in *idem, Aufsätze zum Neuen Testament* (München: Kaiser, 1965), pp. 9–27. A more balanced view is to be found in J. Roloff, 'Die Paulus-Darstellung des Lukas': Ihre geschichtlichen Voraussetzungen und ihr theologisches Ziel', *EvTh* 39 (1979), pp. 510–31, esp. pp. 511, 519.

8   Cf. e.g. S. E. Porter, *The Paul of Acts: Essays in Literary Criticism, Rhetoric, and Theology* (WUNT, 115; Tübingen: Mohr, 1999), pp. 187–206.

9   Roloff, 'Paulus-Darstellung' (see n. 7), pp. 521–22.

Concerning the Pastoral Epistles, a perspective prevalent for decades has likewise been questioned in recent discussion. In earlier research it was a common-place to insist on regarding the three documents as a corpus of three interrelated letters, each of which involves both a fictive author and addressee; the three letters should therefore be analyzed as a single entity.[10] In reconsidering this assumption, the authenticity of the Pastoral Epistles as well as the references to specific situations in each of the three letters became again a subject of discussion.[11] Consequently, a more nuanced assessment of the Pastoral Epistles could emerge, one that would replace a long-prevailing consensus.[12]

From this discussion, for the argument developed here the following aspects should be noted: the arguments for pseudepigraphical authorship of the Pastoral Epistles as pointed out by critical research are still valid.[13] Besides the frequently noted evidence of the presupposed (or claimed) structure and organization of the Christian community and the profile of the opponents, other strong arguments for non-Pauline origin of the Pastorals include the designation of Paul's gospel as παραθήκη, which must be preserved by his co-workers and the commu-nities, as well as the description of Paul as the first converted sinner and model for suffering, lacking, however, the Christological foundation of Paul's genuine letters.[14] In addition, the distinct Christology of these letters as well as the well-known difficulties to incorporate them into a biography of Paul point towards their pseudepigraphal authorship. A plausible conclusion, therefore, is that the Pastorals, together with the other Deutero-Pauline letters and the Acts of the Apostles, belong to an early stage of the *reception* of Paul's missionary activity and theology.[15] Regarding their close relationship in language and content, it is also obvious that the Pastorals share a common theological perspective and were perhaps even composed by one author.

---

10   Cf. e.g. P. Trummer, 'Corpus Paulinum – Corpus Pastorale: Zur Ortung der Paulustradition in den Pastoralbriefen', in *Paulus in den neutestamentlichen Spätschriften: Zur Paulusrezeption im Neuen Testament* (ed. K. Kertelge; QD, 89; Freiburg: Herder, 1981), pp. 122–45.

11   Johnson's commentary argues for Pauline authorship and provides a distinct place for each of the three letters within the Pauline biography. An origin of the Pastorals as post-Pauline, written by different authors – during a period of about 60 years! – is assumed by W. A. Richards, *Difference and Distance in Post-Pauline Christianity: An Epistolary Analysis of the Pastorals* (Studies in Biblical Literature, 44; New York: Peter Lang, 2002). For the hypothesis of the Pastoral letters as composed by using fragments of genuine Pauline letters, see: J. D. Miller, *The Pastoral Letters as Composite Documents* (MSSNTS, 93; Cambridge: University Press, 1997).

12   Cf. the overview on recent commentaries by J. Herzer, 'Abschied vom Konsens? Die Pseudepigraphie der Pastoralbriefe als Herausforderung an die neutestamentliche Wissenschaft', *ThLZ* 129 (2004), pp. 1267–82.

13   Cf. the summary of J. Roloff, 'Pastoralbriefe', *TRE* 26 (2000), pp. 50–68.

14   1 Tim. 1.12-17; 2 Tim. 2.3; 3.10f. See also below, section III.

15   Under these assumptions they were examined more recently by A. Merz within the con-text of early Christian theology: A. Merz, *Die fiktive Selbstauslegung des Paulus: Intertextuelle Studien zur Intention und Rezeption der Pastoralbriefe* (NTOA, 52; Göttingen: Vandenhoeck & Ruprecht, 2004).

By way of their fictive integration into the last period of Paul's activity the Pastorals react to certain situations in Pauline communities by maintaining Paul's presence in a post-Pauline period of time through fictional letters to his co-workers.[16] This becomes obvious when one considers the fact that 1 Timothy and Titus answer the assumed situations of harassment of the congregations by heretical teachings by providing rules for organization and life of the communities, authorized by Paul himself. The locations Ephesus and Crete, in contrast to the described situations of sender and addressee, are not necessarily fictional, but refer to a specific situation within the Pauline mission field.[17] The purpose of 2 Timothy, however, is to conclude these instructions with a testament and to have Paul leave Timothy by corroborating his instructions with the reminder to preserve his heritage.[18] Eventually, by connecting the Pastorals to Paul's genuine letters, their function changed in that they have now influenced the understanding of the Pauline corpus as a whole.[19]

For the argument developed in this article it must be concluded, therefore, that the theme emphasized in the Acts of the Apostles narratively – the commitment of the church to Paul's activity and teaching – is accomplished in the Pastoral Epistles by the composition of three letters, each making its own contribution to a portrait of Paul as the authoritative figure for the communities addressed. The difference in genre – a historiographical account on the one hand, three personal letters on the other – thus proves to be an essential aspect of the reception of Paul in each case.

Concerning the relationship of the Acts of the Apostles and the Pastoral Epistles within the history of reception of Paul in early Christianity, in what follows three aspects of the respective images of Paul will be compared: First, I will investigate in a general way the significance of Paul's person with special attention to the biographical portrayals (II.). Next, this will be substantiated by looking at the topic of suffering (III.), then at Paul's teaching (IV.). Special attention will be devoted to the comparison of Paul's farewell address in Miletus (Acts 20.18-35) with 2 Timothy. It is striking that in both portrayals a testament of Paul is provided, although at different stages of his biography. The relation to Paul's theology as it appears in the genuine letters will be considered within those passages in which

---

16   For the meaning of the *topos* 'presence of the Apostle' in the Pastoral Epistles, cf. W. Stenger, 'Timotheus und Titus als literarische Gestalten: Beobachtungen zu Form und Funktion der Pastoralbriefe', *Kairos NF* 16 (1974), pp. 252–67.

17   This is the common perspective in research. Cf. eg. J. Roloff, *Der Erste Brief an Timotheus* (EKK, 15; Zürich: Benzinger / Neukirchen-Vluyn: Neukirchener, 1988), pp. 42–43.

18   It is impossible to establish a definite sequence from the letters themselves, like Richards, *Difference and Distance* (see n. 11) rightly explicates. As is well known, the sequence is difficult to determine, especially with regard to 1 Timothy and Titus. If one assumes with Richards that different authors composed the letters, it is plausible to understand 2 Timothy as the first letter written and 1 Timothy as the last. If, however, the letters were written by the same author, they would fill in the last period of Paul's missionary activity, while 2 Timothy would have to be moved to the end.

19   This applies of course only to those collections which comprise the Pastoral Epistles. That collections of Pauline letters without the Pastorals existed can be inferred from P[46] and the collection used by Marcion, from which they were obviously missing.

the specific treatment of Paul's teachings in the post-Pauline writings can be highlighted. A summary will then conclude the study (V.)

II. The Significance of Paul's Person

At a first glance it is already striking that the importance of Paul is depicted in specific ways in the Acts of the Apostles and the Pastorals. In the former he is integrated into the circle of other witnesses for the risen Jesus. The propagation of the testimony to Christ begins with the circle of the Twelve and the Hellenists, whom Paul joins after his conversion and his designation as Christ's 'chosen instrument' (Acts 9.15). Also, the central theological insight, that the people of God is open to all who fear God and do justice (10.35), has already been formulated before Paul himself enters the scene as an active participant in the course of events.

At first Paul appears with Barnabas, who, according to Luke, establishes contact with the community in Jerusalem (9.27). Later he becomes a leading figure in the community of Antioch and introduces Paul there (11.22-26). At Barnabas' side Paul becomes his own man during the missionary journey, starting in Antioch and continuing on to Cyprus and to the interior of Asia Minor (Acts 13–14). As a result of this journey, it is stated that God has opened a door of faith for the gentiles (14.27). At the apostolic meeting in Jerusalem immediately following the journey, this is interpreted as part of the broader concept of the mission to the gentiles, based on Peter's vision related in Acts 10.[20] Paul's own mission, which began after the Jerusalem council, is embedded therefore in Acts into a broader narrative concept. It constitutes a special part of Luke's portrait of Paul and leads him to various cities in the Aegean region. Eventually, it is completed in his farewell speech in Miletus, through which he prepares the communities for the time following his departure (20.18-35). This speech, however, is not Paul's final word in the Acts of the Apostles. He will provide this after his imprisonments and interrogations in Jerusalem and Caesarea and his coming to Rome. Paul's final speech in Acts, which takes place in this city, is composed as a scriptural reference concerning the hardening of the Jews who oppose the Christian gospel. The conclusion drawn by Paul is that, according to God's plan of history, salvation is now sent to the gentiles (28.25-28).

According to Luke, Paul's specific role within God's plan of history is to bear the name of Jesus before gentiles, kings, and the sons of Israel, and to suffer for this name. This commission,[21] formulated in 9.15f, is made effective by Paul, who introduces Christ's name mainly to the Jews outside of Palestine. Through this course of action gentiles also come into contact with the word of God and the proclamation of Christ; some of them – predominately the so-called 'God-fearers' – even convert

---

20   The emphasis is striking: Peter explains in detail the decision made by God 'in the early days' (15.7-11), which includes the decisive argument against the requirement of circumcision. Barnabas and Paul's report, considerably shorter and communicated in indirect speech, then indicates the practical experience of the realization of God's plan.

21   In Paul's autobiographical speeches in Acts 22 and 26 only being sent to the gentiles (22.21; 26.17-18) is mentioned.

to it. Roman authorities and King Agrippa also become aware of the Christian message. The Paul of Acts, therefore, is responsible for a specific part of God's plan of history, which is completed in Rome with Paul's final words mentioned above.

The Acts of the Apostles portrays Paul's missionary activity and theology as a continuation of a development that originated with the circle of Twelve, the Hellenists, and even with Jesus himself. The author's main concern in his two-part work is to describe the events that 'have been fulfilled among us' (Lk. 1.1). Therefore, Paul must bear witness to the name of Jesus first to Jews, then later to gentiles as well. This theme is developed gradually. In the beginning Jesus himself confronts Israel with God's kingdom, which is closely connected to his own activity. After his resurrection and exaltation, reported at the end of the first and the beginning of the second part of Luke's two-volume work, the course of events continues under new circumstances.[22] By describing some events in analogous ways – e.g. the court cases against Jesus, Stephen, and Paul – one surmises that they are part of a broader course of events guided by God himself.

Within this broader horizon the literary function of Paul is to connect the origin of the church with Jesus, the Twelve and the Hellenist, to the gentiles, and to determine the status of the gentile Christian church with respect to both Jews and gentiles. Therefore, the description of Paul's career is consciously concluded with his arrival in Rome, his last words on the hardening of the Jews, and the sending of salvation to the gentiles. The last image of the Paul of Acts is that of one who for two years preaches the kingdom of God unhindered.

The image of Paul in the Pastoral Epistles differs from this portrayal. First, Paul's conversion as reported in 1 Tim. 1.12-17 is comparable to the account in Acts 9 (cf. also chapters 22 and 26). In contradiction to Paul's own references to this event, it is represented in both texts as the conversion of a former enemy of God. In Paul's own understanding, however, his pre-Christian career was not a negative phase *as such*, but only from the perspective of his encounter with Christ.[23] Unlike in the Acts of the Apostles, in 1 Timothy Paul does not become a member of a circle of early Christian witnesses. He is rather introduced programmatically as the first (πρῶτος) of the saved sinners, who then became the 'prototype' (ὑποτύπωσις) of all those who will come to faith.[24] Therefore it is of crucial importance that Paul is the *first* converted sinner, and thus has priority in the experience of salvation. Given this concept, 1 Tim. 1.15f contradicts 1 Cor. 15.5-9, in which Paul as 'the last of the apostles' (ὁ ἐλάχιστος τῶν ἀποστόλων) stands vis-à-vis Cephas as the 'first' (πρῶτος).[25] This corresponds to the fact that in the Pastoral Epistles an apostle besides Paul

22   Cf. A. Prieur, *Die Verkündigung der Gottesherrschaft: Exegetische Studien zum lukani-schen Verständnis von βασιλεία τοῦ θεοῦ* (WUNT, II/89; Tübingen: Mohr, 1996).

23   Cf. M. Wolter, 'Paulus, der bekehrte Gottesfeind: Zum Verständnis von 1. Tim 1:13', *NT* 31 (1989), pp. 48–66, esp. pp. 60–66.

24   For the interpretation of the entire passage, cf. M. Wolter, *Die Pastoralbriefe als Paulustradition* (FRLANT, 146; Göttingen: Vandenhoeck & Ruprecht, 1988), pp. 27–64. For the two terms mentioned, esp. pp. 50–59 as well as Roloff, *1 Tim* (see n. 17), pp. 96–98.

25   Likewise Johnson, *Letters* (see n. 6), p. 180, who is forced to harmonize 1 Timothy and 1 Corinthians 15, because he cannot maintain his view under the assumption of the authenticity of 1 Timothy.

is never mentioned, not even Barnabas, although the author knows about Paul's missionary activity in Antioch, Iconium, and Lystra (2 Tim. 3.11). Rather, Paul is depicted as the only apostle, entrusted with the gospel as the 'sound teaching'[26] or as a deposit (παραθήκη), which must be preserved.[27] Other names occurring in these letters always refer to persons from Paul's immediate sphere of influence and serve to substantiate his image developed in these letters.

However, there are differences within the Pastoral Epistles. 2 Timothy displays by far the most intensive involvement of Paul in a network of co-workers, renegades, and enemies. Thus in 4.9-21 a great number of persons is mentioned, some of them also appearing in other letters within the Pauline corpus or in the Acts of the Apostles, others occurring only in 2 Timothy. Some are even mentioned in other early Christian sources.[28] Demas, Luke, and Mark occur in the salutatory list of Philemon and Colossians; Mark is also mentioned in 1 Tim. 1.20 as well as in the Acts of the Apostles and in 1 Peter. Titus is found in 2 Corinthians and in the letter of Titus, Tychicus in Col. 4.7; Eph. 4.21; Tit. 3.12 as well as in Acts 20.4. A person with the name 'Alexander' is mentioned in 1 Tim. 1.20 as well as in Acts 19.33. Prisca and Aquila also occur in the Acts of the Apostles and are mentioned by Paul in 1 Cor. 16.19, as well as in Rom. 16.3. An 'Erastus' is mentioned in Acts 19.22 and in Rom. 16.23, Trophimus in Acts 20.4; 21.29.[29] Alexander and Hymenaeus are connected to 1 Timothy, Titus and Tychicus to the letter of Titus. Crescens is mentioned only in 2 Timothy (4.10), in addition to Lois and Eunice (1.5), Phygelus and Hermogenes (1.15), the household of Onesiphorus (1.16; 4.16), Philetus (2.17), and Carpus (4.13). Of the names mentioned in 4.21, three occur again in other early Christian writings: Linus is listed by Irenaeus and Eusebius as the first bishop of Rome; Claudia occurs as his mother in the bishop's list in the Apostolic Constitutions; and Eubulus is mentioned in the prescript of the so-called 'Third letter to the Corinthians' in the *Acts of Paul*.

These personal data reveal a close connection of 2 Timothy to other Pauline traditions. Thus, the following characteristics can be observed. According to the remarks in 1.15 and 4.16 Paul has been left by everyone and therefore finds himself alone. The first passage alludes to former followers in the province of Asia, the latter to his πρώτη ἀπολογία. Both references may refer to the same incident, namely a difficult predicament, but probably also to an arrest in Ephesus, to which Paul himself alludes in 1 Cor. 15.32 and 2 Cor. 1.8. 2 Timothy emphasizes Paul's isolation, in which he suddenly finds himself due to the lack of solidarity of almost all of his former companions. Some of these disloyal persons are mentioned explicitly: Phygelus, Hermogenes (1.15) and Demas (4.10). They are contrasted with the positive examples of Onesiphorus and his house, Luke

---

26　1 Tim. 1.10; 2 Tim. 4.3; Tit. 1.9: ὑγιαίνουσα διδασκαλία. Cf. 1 Tim 6.3; 2 Tim. 1.13: ὑγιαίνοντες λόγοι.

27　1 Tim. 6.20; 2 Tim. 1.12, 14.

28　Cf. also the excursus in Weiser, *Der Zweite Brief an Timotheus* (see n. 5), pp. 328–39.

29　Whether Alexander and Erastus are one and the same person, as well as whether 2 Timothy identifies him with another person of this name mentioned elsewhere, are still open questions.

as the only faithful person staying in Rome with Paul, and Mark, who is 'useful in my ministry'.

Furthermore, it is significant that the persons from the Pauline circle reside at various places that obviously belong to the Pauline missionary field. This applies to Crescens in Galatia, Titus in Dalmatia, Tychicus in Ephesus, and Timothy himself. The location of the latter is not mentioned explicitly in 2 Timothy, but from 1.18 (Timothy himself knows better than Paul of Prisca's and Aquila's work in Ephesus) and 4.19 (Timothy is asked to greet Prisca and Aquila as well as the house of Onesiphorus) it can be concluded that Ephesus is presupposed as Timothy's location. Details about Erastus and Trophimus also belong to this context. The former stays in Corinth, the latter in Miletus. But it is not explicitly mentioned that they went or stayed there in order to continue Paul's work. In Trophimus' case it is even explicitly stated that his co-operation with Paul is hindered by disease. Through the references to these persons, the author generates an image of Paul's co-workers as spread all over Paul's missionary area.

Thus, in 2 Timothy a situation is created that is constructed from various traditions about Paul. The author combines these traditions in order to generate the image of Paul as being almost completely out on a limb[30] during his imprisonment and calls upon Timothy as his 'beloved child' (1.2), who should preserve the 'good treasure' and be steadfast in suffering. By taking the last image of the Acts of the Apostles – Paul as imprisoned, but at the same time an unrestricted preacher of the kingdom of God – as its point of departure, 2 Timothy looks at the time after Paul whereas in Acts the period of Paul's proclamation and founding of communities is predominant. This new period is characterized by faithful and unfaithful companions of Paul located at different places. In light of this 'unstable' situation Paul's admonition to preserve his gospel as παραθήκη gains its specific importance.

In 1 Timothy and Titus the situation depicted in 2 Timothy is reiterated with some modifications. As already mentioned above, the remarks concerning persons around Paul are of less importance. In Titus 3.12f names of four men are given (Artemas, Tychicus, Zenas, and Apollos) whom Paul wants to send to Timothy or whom Timothy shall equip for their journeys. But for the situation presupposed in the letter personal data are generally considerably less important than in 2 Timothy. In the greeting list in 3.15, as well as in the reference to opponents in 1.10-16, names are completely omitted. In 1 Timothy not a single person from Paul's circle is mentioned. The only exception is 1.20, in which there is a short reference to Hymenaeus and Alexander, mentioned also in 2 Timothy 2.17 and 4.14; these two have 'suffered shipwreck in their faith' and Paul has therefore handed them over to Satan.

The specific concept of 2 Timothy – Paul instructs his co-workers to preserve his gospel – is developed in 1 Timothy and Titus through other emphases. Unlike in 2 Timothy, in 1 Timothy Paul does not appear as suffering and abandoned, but rather as the prototype of the converted sinner in whom God's saving activity can be realized archetypically. Moreover, the confrontation with competing teachers

---

30   This aspect is underlined by Col. 4.4, in which, of the two co-workers Demas and Luke, only the latter is still with Paul.

is much more strongly emphasized; two of his opponents, perhaps even former community leaders, were handed over by Paul to Satan. The letter to Titus depicts its own fictional situation – Paul writes to Titus, who sojourns in Crete and urges him to come soon to Nicopolis, where Paul himself is – a remark which evidently connects to information about Paul's sojourn at Crete (cf. Acts 27.9-13) and presupposes a Christian community there. Paul's personal situation is not at stake here. Instead, as in 1 Timothy, the issue of leadership within the Christian community is a burning issue which, in turn, is not mentioned in 2 Timothy.

In comparison with the Acts of the Apostles, Paul's career in the Pastorals reveals the following characteristics. In the Acts of the Apostles, the final image is of Paul under house arrest, yet freely preaching the gospel. In this way the fulfilment of his role in God's plan of history is emphasized in that he has proclaimed the Christian message to Jews and gentiles, and carried the name of Jesus before political rulers. Through the Jews' refusal of the testimony to Christ and the gentiles' acceptance of this message a specific situation has emerged. It is Paul's task to explain this development as having been announced in the scriptures as God's hardening of his people and the sending of salvation to the gentiles. What this means for the church's position within pagan society at the end of the first century is, however, not explained in detail in the Acts of the Apostles.

2 Timothy bridges this gap and reacts to the actual situation in Ephesus and the province of Asia with the composition of a fictional letter from Paul from his imprisonment in Rome. It takes up various traditions about Pauline co-workers and opponents from the Aegean region as well as traditions of Paul's previous missionary activity in the interior of Asia Minor. It is not by accident that analogies can be found to the only speech of Paul in the Acts of the Apostles which points *beyond* Paul's own time and views the situation of the Christian community in the time after Paul, namely Paul's address in Miletus. These analogies include the reference to Paul's suffering as well as the announcement of dangers to come for the community from outside as well as from inside. It is not necessary to assume direct knowledge of the Acts of the Apostles by the author of 2 Timothy (or the Pastorals). Rather, the same topic is treated in both writings in its own way. It is obvious, however, that in 2 Timothy traditions are treated which concern the locations of places of Paul's mission, persons from the Pauline circle, as well as information about his imprisonment in Rome, which are also to be found in Acts of the Apostles. A further analogy is that Paul looks at the time after his departure in the farewell speech in Miletus as well as in 2 Timothy.

In 1 Timothy and Titus Paul's specific circumstances play a less important role. Rather, in both letters Paul appears as the organizer of the life of the communities by means of fictional letters to his co-workers. The presupposed biographical situations are, however, prior to that of 2 Timothy. 1 Timothy explicitly mentions that Timothy has been left behind in Ephesus, which is also implied in 2 Timothy. This situation is integrated into the Pauline biography in a way which competes with Acts 20.4. Paul is depicted in 1 Timothy as a prototype of the saved sinner, which thus excludes other apostles and missionaries who would have proclaimed the gospel before him. The letter to Titus by analogy describes the situation of

Titus as left behind in Crete. This can be harmonized with the Acts of the Apostles only by reference to a sojourn in Crete, but in Acts Titus is not mentioned anyway.[31] Unlike 2 Timothy, 1 Timothy and Titus do not depict Paul's missionary activity as completed. Instead, each letter looks forward to Paul rejoining Timothy and Titus,[32] and 1 Tim. 3.15 even mentions a possible delay of Paul's arrival. By means of these fictional data a longer period of time is envisioned, which is then concluded by Paul's 'testament' in 2 Timothy. Therefore, the author insinuates that the instructions given by 'Paul' in these letters are authoritative for the Christian community. Paul's current location – and therefore the place of composition of the letters – remains unstated. The reason for that is obvious: the organization of the life of the communities in a dangerous situation is at stake in these letters, not (yet) Paul's personal circumstances.

Accordingly, compared to the Acts of the Apostles, the perspective in the Pastoral Epistles has shifted to the post-Pauline period. The Pastorals take the last period of Paul's missionary activity as an occasion for him to formulate rules for the Christian communities in a fictional period before the Miletus speech, rules which go beyond what is explicated in that speech and in its analogy, the 'testamentary letter' of 2 Timothy. The 'literal figures' Timothy and Titus[33] thus serve to bridge the gap of time between the 'historical' Paul and the actual situation of the Christian communities and in this way ensure continuity with Paul. The disparity with the reception of Paul in the Acts of Apostles can also be seen in Timothy's commitment to Paul's teaching and activity; it is placed at the end of the Pastorals, as his 'testament', whereas Paul's last word in the Acts of the Apostles concerns the hardening of the Jews and the salvation sent to the gentiles.

Hence, both the Acts of the Apostles and the Pastoral Epistles take up specific aspects of Paul's self-understanding developed in his genuine letters and on this basis elaborate their own portraits of Paul. In 1 Cor. 15.5-11, mentioned above, Paul presents himself at the end of a long line of witnesses of Jesus' resurrection, beginning with Cephas and the Twelve. In this group, he is the 'least of the apostles', not even worthy to be called an 'apostle' (v. 9). This is also the case in Galatians, in which Paul traces his apostolic authority back to God's revelation and emphasizes his independence from the Jerusalem 'pillars'. He explicitly mentions those who have already been apostles before him (Gal. 1.17), and highlights the equivalence of his εὐαγγέλιον τῆς ἀκροβυστίας with Peter's εὐαγγέλιον τῆς περιτομῆς. At the same time, Paul can present himself as the decisive, irreplaceable mediator of God's revelation in Jesus Christ to 'his' communities (first and foremost in 2 Corinthians). This self-understanding is expressed in metaphors such as 'father', 'bride's attendant', 'aroma of Christ', or with the image of the apostle as an ambassador of peace. These descriptions of his own role within the salvation process

31   These discrepancies highlight that the focus in 1 Timothy and Titus is to integrate the letters into Paul's biography, although chronological and factual differences to other traditions have to be stated. If this originates from competing distinct Pauline traditions remains an unanswered question.

32   1 Tim. 3.14; 4.13; Tit. 3.12.

33   Cf. the title of Stenger's contribution (see n. 16).

become especially intensified in those cases in which his apostolic authority is called into question.[34]

The image of Paul developed in the Acts of Apostles, namely as one who has been integrated into the early Christian testimony as a whole and whose significance is considered within this background does not directly contradict the self-understanding of Paul. The characteristics of his theology, however, are modified in that it now appears as an organic continuation of the development of Christian theology from its very beginning. When, on the other hand, the Pastoral Epistles depict Paul as the only apostle who at the end of his missionary career calls for the preservation of his teaching as the καλὴ παραθήκη and regulates the life of the Christian communities according to the model of the ancient οἶκος,[35] they merely emphasize what has been already expressed by Paul himself, namely the commitment of the gospel to his very own apostolic – and therefore authoritative – shape. Therefore, the Pastorals also do not contradict Paul's own apostolic self-understanding, but rather remember him in situations characterized by conflicts with heretics. Because there is now a special need to define the place of the church within pagan society, the affiliation with Paul's apostolic authority becomes important. Eventually, the Acts of the Apostles and the Pastorals in the post-Pauline time period emphasize each in its own way characteristics that were already implied in Paul's self-conception in the genuine letters. In both approaches he is presented as the authoritative figure whose activity is connected to crucial events for the development of the emerging church of the late-first and early second century.

III. The suffering Paul

In the research of years past one of the characteristics of the portrait of Paul in the Acts of the Apostles that was often mentioned but seldom developed has drawn more recent attention. According to Acts 9.15-16 (cf. also 21.13), already mentioned above, it is Paul's commission to bear witness for the name of Jesus as well as to suffer for this very name. This suffering is even the explanation (γάρ) for Luke's depiction of Paul as Christ's 'chosen vessel' (σκεῦος ἐκλογῆς). Obviously, suffering is an integral part of Paul's task to bear witness to the name of Jesus. As the further development shows, this facet of Luke's image of Paul is at least as significant as Paul's role in representing the emerging church, which consists mainly of pagan Christians, in its commitment to the history of Israel as well as in its departing from Judaism. In more recent times, the suffering Paul has been

---

34   For the metaphors used by Paul to describe his role in relation to his communities, cf. C. Gerber, *Paulus und seine 'Kinder': Studien zur Beziehungsmetaphorik der paulinischen Briefe* (BZNW, 136; Berlin / New York: Walter de Gruyter, 2005). For the use of the topos in 2 Corinthians cf. also J. Schröter, 'Gottes Versöhnungstat und das Wirken des Paulus. Zur Gestaltwerdung des Evangeliums nach 2Kor 5,18-21', in *Unterwegs mit Paulus* (ed. J. Hainz; O. Kuss zum 100. Geburtstag; Regensburg: Pustet, 2006), pp. 87–107.

35   Cf. J. Roloff, *Die Kirche im Neuen Testament* (GNT, 10; Göttingen: Vandenhoeck & Ruprecht, 1993), pp. 250–67.

acknowledged as an important characteristic of Luke's portrait both in regard to its legal historical basis[36] and to its meaning for Luke's reception of Paul.[37] In what follows I will focus on the second aspect.

In the Acts of the Apostles Paul frequently appears as a persecuted, accused, and imprisoned witness of Christ. This begins early on with the attempts of the Jews from Damascus and Jerusalem to put him to death because of his testimony to Jesus immediately after his conversion (9.22-25, 29). This recurs during the first missionary journey, when Jews from Pisidian Antioch and Iconium persecute Paul and even succeed in stoning him in Lystra (13.50; 14.2, 19). After their return to Pisidian Antioch Barnabas and Paul conclude from these experiences that entrance into the kingdom of God has to be preceded by the endurance of many sufferings.[38] On his independent missionary journey Paul is persecuted by Jews and gentiles, and he is accused before the local administration; in Philippi one finds the owners of a pagan maid with a spirit of divination, who drag Paul and Silas before the ἄρχοντες and στρατηγοί. In Thessalonica and Corinth there are Jews who take him to court before the πολιτάρχαι and the ἀνθύπατος Gallio; in Ephesus a disturbance among the pagan urban population emerges because of his proclamation, which can only be quelled by the town clerk.

A closer look reveals a telling feature for the interpretation of Luke's portrait of Paul. Both in Thessalonica and in Ephesus the riots are triggered by Paul's preaching, but members of the local congregation are immediately affected, not Paul and his companions: Jason and some brothers in Thessalonica; Paul's companions Gaius and Aristarchus as well as the Jew, Alexander, in Ephesus. In this way Luke describes situations in which the Christian community is faced with hostility from Jews and gentiles, even if Paul himself is not any longer present. Paul and Barnabas' experiences in Antioch, Iconium, and Lystra (Acts 14.22), the places which are also mentioned in 2 Tim. 3.11, were already being interpreted as descriptions of the general situation of the Christian communities. Afterwards, Luke draws attention to the situation of the communities even in post-Pauline time, which is explicitly envisioned in Paul's farewell speech at Miletus.

Finally, the extensive descriptions of Paul's imprisonments, accusations, and interrogations before the proconsuls Felix and Festus, Paul's apologetic speeches before Jews in Jerusalem and King Agrippa in Caesarea, as well as his journey to Rome as a prisoner must be mentioned. The importance of this final part of Acts becomes obvious due to the fact that it is the longest and most detailed description of Paul's career in Acts. Even in the description of his missionary activity Paul is

---

36   Cf. H. Omerzu, *Der Prozess des Paulus: Eine exegetische und rechtshistorische Untersuchung der Apostelgeschichte* (BZNW, 115; Berlin / New York: Walter de Gruyter, 2002); H. W. Tajra, *The Trial of St. Paul: A Juridical Exegesis of the Second Half of the Acts of the Apostles* (WUNT II, 235; Tübingen: Mohr 1989).

37   Cf. Roloff, 'Paulus-Darstellung' (see n. 7), pp. 529–31, as well as M.-E. Rosenblatt, *Paul the Accused: His Portrait in the Acts of the Apostles* (Zacchaeus Studies New Testament; Collegeville: Liturgical, 1995); M. L. Skinner, *Locating Paul: Places of Custody as Narrative Settings in Acts 21–28* (SBL Academia Biblica, 13; Atlanta: Society of Biblical Literature, 2003).

38   Acts 14.22: διὰ πολλῶν θλίψεων δεῖ ἡμᾶς εἰσελθεῖν εἰς τὴν βασιλείαν τοῦ θεοῦ. Carl Holladay has called the seminar's attention to the importance of this passage.

by no means merely a successful orator and founder of communities, but at the same time the prosecuted and accused witness of Christ. The testimony to the name of Jesus and the suffering for his name are therefore remarkably interconnected; Paul is integrated narratively into the destiny of Jesus, which becomes apparent especially through the allusions to the passion of Jesus.[39] Through the figure of Paul, therefore, Luke shows that bearing witness for Jesus means to live in a hostile situation in which one has to be aware of antagonism and persecution from either gentiles or Jews at any time. Paul, who brought the Christian gospel to the gentiles, thus gains paradigmatic meaning for the life of the Christian communities founded by him.

In the Pastoral Epistles the topic of Paul's suffering only appears in 2 Timothy.[40] As in the Acts of the Apostles the image of the suffering Paul plays an important role here as well. This becomes obvious through the occasion of Paul's isolation, left by all his companions and accompanied only by Luke, mentioned above. Moreover, 2 Timothy ties in with a situation which is also presupposed in Philemon and Philippians, as well as in Colossians and Ephesians: the imprisoned Paul, suffering for the sake of the gospel. In 2 Tim 1.18 Paul is called a δέσμιος of the Lord, who admonishes Timothy to suffer with him for the gospel.[41] This instruction to Timothy, appearing at the beginning of the letter, is the specific manner to bear witness for Christ. Therefore, the admonition to rekindle the grace of God which had been bestowed upon him by the laying on of hands (1.6) can be further developed by the demand to suffer with Paul (1.8). The term συγκακοπαθεῖν thus stands in semantic opposition to ἐπαισχύνειν, which otherwise is used in ancient Christian literature in contrast to ὁμολογεῖν (Mk 8.38) or δοξάξειν (1 Pet. 4.16).[42] Objects of shame are thereby the Son of Man (Mk 8.38), the gospel (Rom. 1.16), or the name 'Christian' (1 Pet 4.16). Accordingly, in 2 Tim. 1.8 'suffering with' is the specific form of preserving the gospel which Paul expects from Timothy and for which, according to 1.12, he himself serves as role model.[43]

Gerhard Lohfink has pointed out that the readiness to suffer is a characteristic trait of the attitude required of Timothy in the whole course of 2 Timothy; this can be demonstrated by an analysis of longer parts of the letter.[44] In each of 1.15–2.13, 3.1-17, and 4.1-8, a negative situation is presupposed: Paul's loneliness (1.15-18); vicious people (3.1-9); and heretics (4.3f). These situations are constantly contrasted with a converse, introduced by σὺ οὖν (2.1) or σὺ δέ (3.10; 4.5). In this

---

39   For a comparative analysis of the court cases against Jesus and Paul see E. Heusler, *Kapitalprozesse im lukanischen Doppelwerk: Die Verfahren gegen Jesus und Paulus in exegetischer und rechtshistorischer Analyse* (NTA NF, 38; Münster: Aschendorff, 2000).

40   Cf. G. Lohfink, 'Paulinische Theologie in der Rezeption der Pastoralbriefe', in *Paulus in den neutestamentlichen Schriften* (see n. 10), pp. 70–121, esp. pp. 86–93. Lohfink is of the opinion that the topic of the apostle's suffering is a very important one in the Pastoral Epistles (87). His references, however, out of necessity are taken exclusively from 2 Timothy and not from 'the Pastorals' in general.

41   2 Tim. 1.8: συγκακοπάθησον τῷ εὐαγγελίῳ κατὰ δύναμιν θεοῦ.

42   Cf. Weiser, *Der Zweite Brief an Timotheus* (see n. 5), p. 111.

43   Cf. 2 Tim. 2.15: Timothy should be an ἐργάτης ἀνεπαίσχυντος.

44   Lohfink, 'Paulinische Theologie' (see n. 40), pp. 90f.

way Timothy is committed to communion with Paul in teaching and suffering. In 2.3 the verb συγκακοπαθεῖν appears again, and in 3.10f the reference to Timothy's loyalty in persecutions and suffering which Paul endured in Iconium, Lystra, and Derbe is mentioned.[45] Eventually, in 4.5 the word κακοπαθεῖν occurs, because Paul here refers to his imminent death and looks to the future in which Timothy is committed to perpetuate his work.

The close connection between teaching and suffering includes an aspect which already appears in Paul's genuine letters.[46] For Paul the intrinsic structure of his ministry for Christ is prefigured in God's activity through Christ. Therefore, Paul can maintain that in the proclamation of the crucified Christ form and content must correspond with each other. An example of this is the weakness of the minister of the gospel (1 Cor. 2.1-5). In 2 Cor. 4.7-12 Paul develops this topic in an intensive manner by revealing that he carries in his body the death of Jesus, so that the life of Jesus is also made visible in his body (v. 10).[47] In this passage the experiences of persecution and tribulation – as listed e.g. in 2 Cor. 6.4; 11.23-28 – as well as the fact that he nonetheless is able to continue his apostolic ministry for Christ – are interpreted christologically by referring to the death and resurrection of Jesus Christ. These have an influence on Paul's own body as well as within the Corinthian community. Finally, in Phil. 3.10, Paul describes the communion within the suffering of Christ and speaks of becoming at one with Christ's death, which would lead also to participation in the resurrection from the dead. By way of his very own participation in the suffering of Christ his Christian communities also become part of this process and share this communion with Christ. In 1 Thess. 1.6 Paul can therefore praise the community of Thessalonica for having become his and the Lord's μιμηταί by receiving the word (the gospel) under many difficulties and with the joy of the Holy Spirit. In 2 Cor. 1.5-7, in an analogous way he speaks of the affliction and consolation of Christ as establishing a communion between himself and the Christian communities.

The structure of Paul's argument is therefore always that he himself as the messenger of Christ participates in Christ's suffering. This corresponds on the one hand to his preservation by God and on the other to the future resurrection. In this way Paul mediates the saving effects of the Christ event. Through participation in Paul's – and thereby in Christ's – sufferings, the communities also become part of that process. They are therefore μιμηταί of Paul and the Lord and become τύποι for others (1 Thess. 1.7). When Paul therefore admonishes his Christian communities to become *his* μιμηταί, or praises them to have already done so, this implies

---

45   Here reference is made to those places at which, according to the Acts of the Apostles, Timothy was not even present. Perhaps this is so because the author knew traditions about events occurred at these places which he could use to depict Timothy as Paul's successor in his way of suffering.

46   Cf. M. Wolter, 'Paulus und seine Gemeinden als Teilhaber am Leidensgeschick Jesu Christi', *NTS* 36 (1990), pp. 535–57.

47   Cf. J. Schröter, 'Der Apostolat des Paulus als Zugang zu seiner Theologie: Eine Auslegung von 2 Kor 4,7-12', in *The Corinthian Correspondence* (ed. R. Bieringer; BEThL, 125; Leuven: Peeters, 1996), pp. 679–92.

at the same time that they have become μιμηταί of Christ.[48] The τύπος-μιμητής-schema therefore results in a characteristic category for describing the process of mediation of the Christ event through Paul's ministry.

With the issue of suffering for the Christian message, the author of 2 Timothy thus takes up a genuine topic of Paul's thinking. The foundation for the treatment of the topic within the letter is provided in 2 Tim 2.8-13, in which the admonition to suffer with Christ is explained by taking up certain key words of Paul's own vocabulary.[49] In vv. 8-10 the content of the Christian gospel for which Paul suffers is explained with a reference to Rom. 1.3f. This is followed in vv. 11b-13 by four parallel conditional clauses in which a specific human behaviour is contrasted with its eschatological reward. In the first two clauses two statements referring to 'us' are contrasted, whereas in the final clauses two statements referring to 'our' behaviour and a correlation with Christ are mentioned. The last phrase is additionally substantiated by a causal clause. The scheme is therefore as follows:

εἰ γὰρ συναπεθάνομεν, καὶ συζήσομεν·
εἰ ὑπομένομεν, καὶ συμβασιλεύσομεν·
εἰ ἀρνησόμεθα, κἀκεῖνος ἀρνήσεται ἡμᾶς·
εἰ ἀπιστοῦμεν, ἐκεῖνος πιστὸς μένει,
    ἀρνήσασθαι γὰρ ἑαυτὸν οὐ δύναται.

The first phrase contrasts dying with Christ and living with him in the future. This can be found analogously in, e.g., Rom. 6.5, 8 and 2 Cor. 5.14f. It therefore appears as a central topic in Paul's own letters. The second phrase contrasts ὑπομένειν and συμβασιλεύειν. Both phrases specify dying with Christ and living with him in the future as perseverance in a contentious situation. Here, this indicates that Christian existence is motivated by Jesus' experience and defined as perseverance in affliction, which will lead to eschatological salvation.

The next two statements contrast 'our' behaviour with that of Christ himself: 'Our' denial of Christ will correspond to Christ's denial of 'us'. Thus, the verb ἀρνῆσθαι semantically corresponds to the ἐπαισχύνειν in 1.8, 12 and to the ἀνεπαίσχυντος in 2.15.[50] Being ἄπιστος, however, is in opposition to Christ's being πιστός, and is explained with the remark that he cannot deny himself. In this case, therefore, 'our' negative behaviour does not correspond to an analogous behaviour on the part of Christ, but rather is contrasted with a positive answer. The structure of the previous sentences is therefore interrupted with the effect that the entire passage ends with a comforting command to endure in afflictions.

---

48   Explicitly mentioned in 1 Thess. 1.6f; 1 Cor. 11.1. In 1 Cor. 4.16; Phil. 3.17, however, Paul only notes that the congregations should become *his* μιμηταί. Indeed, Paul is able to serve as τύπος for the Christian communities, because he himself is a μιμητής of Christ as the τύπος.

49   Cf. J. Roloff, 'Der Weg als Lebensnorm (2 Tim 2,8-13): Ein Beitrag zur Christologie der Pastoralbriefe', in *Anfänge der Christologie* (eds. C. Breytenbach and H. Paulsen; FS F. Hahn; Göttingen: Vandenhoeck & Ruprecht, 1991), pp. 155–67.

50   This semantic relationship is also witnessed by analogy in the synoptic tradition, formulated in Q 12.8f with ἀρνῆσθαι, but in Mk 8.38 with ἐπαισχύνειν.

The function of this passage within 2 Timothy is to establish a connection between gospel and suffering on a christological-eschatological basis and in this way to undergird the admonition to Timothy to suffer with Paul. The reason this relationship is emphasized is probably due to the fact that the addressees lived in a pagan environment, in which affliction was present both inside and outside. The plausibility of this is demonstrated on the one hand by the remark in 3.12 that all who want to live their life in Christ Jesus will be persecuted. On the other hand there are the allusions to heresies, vicious persons, and the turning away from the 'sound teaching' in order to turn towards teachers whose teaching is merely pleasing to the ear.[51] The author of 2 Timothy addresses this situation with the idea of the personal mediation of Paul's gospel as παραθή κη, whose preservation includes suffering with Paul.

Against this background it becomes obvious why 2 Tim. 3.11 mentions those places in which – at least according to the Acts of the Apostles – Timothy had not yet been a companion of Paul. Paul's suffering at these places – where Paul, according to 2 Timothy, was still alone – from which the Lord has saved him is characterized in this way as a 'prototype experience' of the Christian exist-ence.[52] According to 2 Timothy, Timothy himself now becomes the prototype of this existence because he has followed Paul in doctrine, suffering, and perse-cution (3.10). In this way Timothy becomes a literary figure through whom Paul's activity can be communicated in the period following Paul and thereby warrants its authenticity. Paul's disciple Timothy hence takes over the purpose that is mediated by the narrative itself in the Acts of the Apostles.[53]

It must be concluded, therefore, that the topic of Paul's suffering plays a central role in the Acts of the Apostles, as well as in 2 Timothy. In the former the figure of Paul, afflicted by Jews and gentiles, serves as a paradigm for the situation of the Christian communities in the time after his departure. Therefore, unlike in 2 Timothy, the relation of suffering and gospel and its Christological foundation is not an issue. The situation of temptation and harassment of the Christian communities, according to the Acts of the Apostles, is a consequence of the fact that the Christians are undeservedly suspected as unfaithful towards Jewish traditions and as politically subversive troublemakers. But in Acts this is not correlated to the Christological structure of the gospel as the message of cross and resurrection. Therefore, in the Miletus speech, the Paul of Acts admonishes the elders to be alert in view of imminent danger and points to his own efforts for each and every member of the Christian community (20.31).

2 Timothy, on the other hand, reflects the situation of the persecuted Christian community in a Christological way by referring to the structure of dying with Christ and living with him in the future as the foundation for the

---

51   Cf. the phrase κνήθησθαι τὴν ἀκοήν in 2 Tim 4.3.

52   This becomes apparent in the sentence following immediately in 3.12: 'So, *all*, who want to live a godly life in Christ Jesus, will be persecuted.'

53   The literary function of Paul's disciples Timothy and Titus in the Pastoral Epistles, neither of whom are to be seen as historic figures nor as 'church leaders', has convincingly been depicted by Stenger, 'Timotheus und Titus' (see n. 16).

admonition to perseverance and to bear witness to Jesus Christ. Unlike in Paul's genuine letters, however, a direct connection between the suffering of Christ and the suffering of Paul or Timothy is not established. The specific Pauline interpretation of suffering as participation in the παθήματα Χριστοῦ, mediated by Paul himself to the communities, does not, therefore, appear either in Acts or in 2 Timothy. This is a significant shift, rooted in the emphasis on Paul's paradigmatic role in the period following Paul's work.

IV. The Teaching of Paul

Here at the beginning of this section once again some basic observations concerning the Acts of the Apostles shall be mentioned. As noted above, in contrast to the differences between the theology of Paul's letters and the portrait of Paul in the Acts of the Apostles as maintained in previous research, currently more attention is being paid to the way in which Luke treats central topics of Paul's theology. This does not lead to a harmonization of the 'Lukan Paul' and the Paul of the letters. Rather, the view that Luke has replaced Paul's theology with 'early Catholicism' has been supplanted by a new position that argues that Pauline topics are being considered from a new perspective at the end of the first century.

It has frequently been noticed that in Paul's first speech in the Acts of the Apostles in Pisidian Antioch (Acts 13.16b-41) characteristic topics from his own letters already appear.[54] To these belong the statement about the enthronement of Jesus as Son of God after his resurrection (13.33), formulated through a quotation of Ps. 2.7 and related to Rom. 1.4, as well as the passages about forgiveness of sins and justification by faith which cannot be achieved by the law of Moses (13.38f). The latter is emphasized by the declaratory statement γνωστὸν οὖν ἔστω ὑμῖν, which appears only at one other place in a speech of Paul, namely in 28.28 as introduction to the proclamation that the gentiles, in contrast to the hardened Jews, will listen to the gospel.[55] The common characteristic in these statements is that both of them reflect a central theme of Paul's theology: God's justification by faith, not by works of the law – in light of the situation of a predominantly pagan-Christian church, which is legitimated by the connection of the Christian message to the scriptures of Israel. This topic is prominent until the end of Acts and leads to a solution of the Israel problem similar to that developed by Paul himself in Romans 9–11.[56] But unlike Paul, Luke does not depict the law as a curse from which Christ has

---

54   Cf. e.g. J. Pichler, *Paulusrezeption in der Apostelgeschichte: Untersuchungen zur Rede im pisidischen Antiochien* (IThS, 50; Innsbruck / Vienna: Tyrolia, 1997).

55   Cf. also 2.14; 4.10, where Peter speaks.

56   This has been frequently emphasized in recent discussion. Cf., e.g., E. Plümacher, 'Rom. in der Apostelgeschichte', in *idem, Geschichte und Geschichten: Aufsätze zur Apostelgeschichte und zu den Johannesakten* (eds. J. Schröter and R. Bruckner; WUNT, 170; Tübingen: Mohr, 2004), pp. 135–169.

ransomed the Jews (Gal. 3.10), but as an institution which has no relevance for the life of Jews and gentiles in the Christian communities, because it does not lead to justification anyway and has been difficult to maintain, even for the Jews themselves (Acts 15.10).

This example shows that there are of course differences between Paul's theology in his genuine letters and its reception by Luke. To discredit the latter as, for example, 'flattening', 'cliché', or even to deny Luke's acquaintance with central topics of Paul's theology, however, would certainly be inappropriate. Rather, Luke's portrait of Paul has to be regarded as a creative treatment of Paul's heritage in a new situation within early Christian history.

This observation also applies to the Areopagus speech, Paul's second great missionary speech in the Acts of the Apostles. In this case, the Lukan Paul delivers a speech before pagan philosophers, in which he explains that the God of Israel is the only true and living God.[57] It would be inappropriate, however, to interpret this as 'knowledge of God by nature' by the gentiles, through which Luke would replace the Pauline doctrine of justification.[58] Rather, one must take into account that the Areopagus speech is a missionary speech to gentiles and aims at a conversion towards the true and living God and Jesus as the future judge. This is precisely that for which Paul had praised the Thessalonians in 1 Thess. 1.9f.[59] Moreover, Luke does not deal here with a 'theologia naturalis'. The Lukan Paul leaves no doubt that the gentiles are unaware that their 'gods' are idols, made from gold, silver or stone,[60] and that only a conversion to the only true God and to Jesus Christ, who has been enthroned by him as judge, leads to salvation. Therefore, in this speech Luke also generates an image of Paul as a missionary to the gentiles that does not contradict Paul's own theology, but rather transforms it in a way to serve Luke's own purposes.

The Miletus speech is particularly suitable for a comparison of the Paul of Acts with the Paul of the Pastorals. In this regard, the relationships to 2 Timothy are especially revealing. I will not deal here with the question of whether this speech shows an unusual affinity to genuine Pauline traditions – especially to 1 Thessalonians – and should therefore be regarded as further evidence for Luke's

---

57 Cf. J. Schröter, 'Konstruktion von Geschichte und die Anfänge des Christentums: Reflexionen zur christlichen Geschichtsdeutung aus neutestamentlicher Perspektive', in *Konstruktion von Wirklichkeit: Beiträge aus geschichtstheoretischer, philosophischer und theologischer Perspektive* (eds J. Schröter and A. Eddelbüttel; TBT, 127; Berlin / New York: Walter de Gruyter, 2004), pp. 202–19, esp. pp. 213–17; Porter, *Paul of Acts* (see n. 8), pp. 141–50.

58 Cf. Vielhauer, 'Paulinismus' (see n. 7), pp. 12f.

59 The relationship of 1 Thess. 1.9f to Tit. 2.11-14 must be noted here. Both passages describe the turning away from impiousness and worldly lusts and the turning towards hope for the ἐπιφάνεια of the σωτήρ Jesus Christ as consequences of the pedagogical function of God's saving grace. I am indebted to Michael Wolter for this idea; Wolter characterizes the passage in Titus as the 'elaboration of a conversion-theological statement in the context of a tradition-based religion'.

60 The latter is not made explicit in the speech itself, but in the description of Paul's arrival in Athens in 17.16; Paul loses his temper because the town is κατείδωλον.

access to such traditions.[61] In any case, such a connection is much less obvious than in the Pauline speeches mentioned above.[62]

The similarities between the Miletus speech and 2 Timothy have already been mentioned.[63] In a slight variation of the hypothesis of identical authorship of the Acts of the Apostles and the Pastoral Epistles, mentioned at the beginning of this article, it has occasionally even been assumed that the author of the original Miletus speech, which was later taken up by Luke, was also the author of the Pastorals.[64] Even if one does not want to go that far the agreements are striking.

First, the texts agree in that both provide fictional 'testaments' of Paul, in which he looks back to his missionary activity and forward to the future. In the face of his imminent death he considers different segments of his biography – at the end of his Aegean mission and during his imprisonment in Rome – interpreted through the metaphor of the 'completed race'.[65] Although on the literary level the Christian community of Ephesus, which is represented by the elders and by Timothy, is the direct addressee of Paul's 'testament', it has fundamental meaning for the time after his departure and death.[66]

Moreover, in both texts Paul emphasizes right at the beginning his own suffering as part of his ministry for the Lord and for the gospel. The ἐπιβουλαὶ τῶν Ἰουδαίων mentioned in Acts 20.19, which Paul had to sustain during his

---

61   This is the hypothesis of S. Walton, *Leadership and Lifestyle: The Portrait of Paul in the Miletus Speech and 1 Thessalonians* (MSSNTS, 108; Cambridge: University Press, 2000). Before him, L. Aejmelaus had already opted for a reception of the Pauline letters in the Miletus speech and had paid special attention to 1 Thessalonians as well.

62   Both Aejmelaeus and Walton try to provide evidence for the Pauline character of the Miletus speech by analyzing terminological relations of the Acts of the Apostles to the Pauline letters, especially 1 Thessalonians. But they mostly deal with unspecific terms and phrases, which in many cases are used differently by Luke and Paul. A connection between Luke and Paul presumably lies on a thematic level rather than in an alleged reception of common traditions or in a direct reception of the Pauline letters by Luke.

63   Cf. e.g. Wolter, *Pastoralbriefe* (see n. 24), pp. 223–25; R. Pesch, *Die Apostelgeschichte (Apg 13–28)* (EKK, 5/2; Zürich: Benziger / Neukirchen-Vluyn: Neukirchener, 1986), pp. 206f; J. Roloff, *Die Apostelgeschichte* (NTD, 5; Göttingen: Vandenhoeck & Ruprecht, 1981), p. 302; C. K. Barrett, *The Acts of the Apostles II. Volume II: Introduction and Commentary on Acts XV–XXVIII* (ICC; Edinburgh: Clark, 1998), pp. 964f; W. Eckey, *Die Apostelgeschichte: Der Weg des Evangeliums von Jerusalem nach Rom. II. Apg 15,36-28,31*, (Neukirchen-Vluyn: Neukirchener, 2000), p. 470. Cf. also Walton, *Leadership* (see n. 61), pp. 192–98. Walton discusses the arguments of Schmitals (see n. 64) and concludes that the Miletus speech is closer to the Pauline tradition, especially to 1 Thessalonians, than to the Deutero-Pauline letters.

64   So W. Schmitals, 'Apg 20,17-38 und das Problem einer "Paulusquelle"', *Der Treue Gottes trauen* (eds. C. Busmann and W. Radl; FS G. Schneider; Freiburg: Herder, 1991), pp. 307–21, esp. p. 320.

65   Acts 20.24: τελειώσω (τελειῶσαι) τὸν δρόμον μου; 2 Tim. 4.7: τὸν δρόμον τετέλεκα. The metaphor of running a race for living one's life is widespread. Paul himself uses it in 1 Cor. 9.24-27. Therefore, it would have been plausible to refer to it in connection with Paul's reminiscence of his work. There is no need to assume a closer, even literary dependence.

66   Cf. B. R. Gaventa, 'Theology and Ecclesiology in the Miletus Speech: Reflections on Content and Context', *NTS* 50 (2004), pp. 36–52, who emphasizes this aspect with regard to the Miletus speech.

missionary activity, have their counterpart in the διωγμοὶ καὶ παθήματα in Iconium, Lystra, and Derbe, mentioned in 2 Tim. 3.11. The reflection on Paul's missionary activity in the Miletus speech is more elaborate and detailed than in 2 Timothy; Paul's teaching in public as well as in private houses before Jews and gentiles is explicitly mentioned. According to the assumed situation, the present text refers only to the future δεσμὰ καὶ θλίψεις of Paul's last imprisonment (Acts 20.23), whereas this situation in 2 Timothy is described as already having been fulfilled (1.8, 16). Accordingly, in the Miletus speech Paul's testimony for which he had suffered and on which the Christian community is founded is of primary importance, whereas in 2 Timothy it is the gospel for which he presently suffers.

The pivotal difference, however, is that in the Acts of the Apostles no connection is established between the suffering of Paul and that of the elders and bishops of the Christian communities. This corresponds to the result in 1 Timothy and Titus in which elders, bishops, and deacons are instructed by Paul as 'office holders' of the Christian communities,[67] although a relationship established by common suffering for the gospel is missing, even between Paul and Timothy or Titus. In 2 Timothy, as mentioned above, this is different. No community leaders are mentioned here; instead, Timothy takes over Paul's role and is supposed to prevent his gospel from misrepresentations and to suffer with him. The reason for this difference was already highlighted above; in the Acts of the Apostles Paul's missionary activity is treated narratively and thereby gains paradigmatic meaning. In the Pastorals this role is developed by way of the double fiction of the letters; the co-workers Timothy and Titus, addressed by Paul himself, are models for the preservation of his teaching and his missionary activity and thus convey the 'presence of the apostolic authority in the manifold activities of the post-apostolic church and [...] the apostolic teaching as the "healthy teaching" of the post-apostolic church'.[68]

Finally, a further common feature is the emphasis on a future situation characterized by external and internal threats. But no specific content of the heretical teaching comes into focus. Instead, the emphasis is on general warnings against other teachers who will attack the community like 'savage wolves' (Acts 20.29), teach pleasing things (2 Tim. 4.3), and come up with a teaching characterized as βέβηλοι κενοφωνίαι (2 Tim. 2.16). The only concrete details of their heretical doctrine one receives are found in 2 Tim. 2.18; some former members of the community assume that the resurrection has already taken place. In this statement it is possible to detect a controversy about the right interpretation of Paul's heritage, because it is precisely this view which is held in Col. 3.1 and Eph. 2.4-6.[69] In general, however, in 2 Timothy as well as in the Acts of the Apostles, a principal polemic against other teachings predominates, teachings that would endanger

---

67   πρεσβύτεροι: 1 Tim. 5.1f, 17, 19; Tit. 1.5; ἐπίσκοποι: 1 Tim. 3.2 (v.1: ἐπισκοπή); Tit. 1.7; διάκονοι: only 1 Tim. 3.8, 12; 4.6.

68   Stenger, 'Timotheus und Titus' (see n. 16), p. 267.

69   There is no need to assume an actual conflict within the Christian community in 2 Timothy. The portrayal of this controversy might instead belong to an 'historicizing tendency' of the letter. I owe this remark to Michael Wolter as well.

the Christian communities.[70] Therefore, no distinctive heresy, such as a kind of 'Gnosticism', is attacked here. Rather, it is the need to save the communities from any confusion that could arise from different interpretations of the Christian message. The admonitions to watchfulness (Acts 20.31), avoidance of controversy (2 Tim. 2.14: μὴ λογομαχεῖν; 2.23f), and a godly life (2 Tim. 3.12: εὐσεβῶς ζῆν) are therefore of primary importance.

In 1 Timothy and Titus the conflicts with heresies become more detailed. In both letters this situation is opposed through organizational structures, through which the communities' existence within a pagan society can be stabilized. Here, genuine Pauline ideas are transformed into these new contexts. One notices, for example, the topic of relationship to public authorities that is treated in Rom. 13 and 1 Tim. 2.2. The use of ἐπίσκοποι and διάκονοι is a terminological connection; these also appear in a genuine letter of Paul (Phil. 1.1). At the same time, these examples reveal essential differences between the Paul of the genuine and the pseudepigraphical letters. Whereas in Romans 13 the principal acceptance of the administrative function of public authorities is emphasized, 1 Timothy requires prayers for the authorities that will ensure a 'peaceful life' of the community in εὐσέβεια and σεμνότης.[71] The author, therefore, clearly takes up an early Christian tradition of prayer.[72] With regard to the community structures it is significant that Paul – unlike 1 Timothy and Titus, as well as Acts – obviously does not yet presuppose the function of 'elders', which exists along with bishops and deacons. This points to a further developed and advanced situation regarding the organization of Christian communities in the Pastorals and the Acts of the Apostles.[73]

Furthermore, in the Pastorals, Paul's gospel is described by the quotation of early Christian traditions. This is the case, for example, in 1 Tim. 1.15; 2.15; 3.16; 2 Tim. 2.11b-13 and Tit. 3.4-7.[74] Phrases such as ἐγηγερμένον ἐκ νεκρῶν, ἐκ σπέρματος Δαυίδ (2 Tim. 2.8); ὃς ἔδωκεν ἑαυτὸν ὑπὲρ ἡμῶν ἵνα λυτρώσηται ἡμᾶς ἀπὸ πάσης ἀνομίας (Tit. 2.14) or οὐκ ἐξ ἔργων τῶν ἐν δικαιοσύνῃ ἃ ἐποιήσαμεν ἡμεῖς ἀλλὰ κατὰ τὸ αὐτοῦ ἔλεος ἔσωσεν ἡμᾶς (Tit. 3.15) are similar to Paul's genuine letters. These phrases, however, are not specific themes of Paul's theology; they belong, rather, to common early Christian traditions. On the other hand, the idea of rebirth in Tit. 3.5, as well as the concept of the epiphany of the saviour Jesus Christ, who serves as mediator between God and humankind and through whom God saves humanity, appears in all three Pastoral letters; this represents a departure from Paul's theology.

---

70   So in 2 Timothy. Cf. especially the passages 2.14–3.9; 4.3f.

71   That this does not simply apply to a 'civic life', but to 'the inner fortitude and the content of piety', was shown by M. Reiser. Cf. *idem*, 'Bürgerliches Christentum in den Pastoralbriefen?', *Bib.* 74 (1993), pp. 27–44, esp. p. 35.

72   Roloff, *Der Erste Brief an Timotheus* (see n. 17), p. 109.

73   Cf. the excursus in Roloff, *Der Erste Brief an Timotheus* (see n. 17), pp. 169–89. I will not consider here the relationship of 1 Tim. 2.11-14 and 1 Cor. 14.33b-35, because I regard the passage in 1 Corinthians 14 as secondary, and thus not originating with Paul himself.

74   By phrases like πιστὸς ὁ λόγος (1 Tim. 1.15; 3.1; 4.9; 2 Tim. 2.11; Tit. 3,8) as well as ὁμολογουμένως (1 Tim. 3.16), traditional Christian confessions are highlighted.

In the Acts of the Apostles and the Pastoral Epistles, therefore, Paul's teaching is treated in different ways. By composing the speeches in Acts 13 and 17 Luke emphasizes that for him certain aspects of Paul's theology are fundamental for the self-understanding of the church: Jesus' declaration as Son of God; justification by faith in Jesus; the inferior role of the law; and the necessity of conversion to the God of Israel and to the man who has been enthroned as judge. In the Pastorals particular themes from Paul's letters appear, which are treated in specific ways and are connected to early Christian traditions. In both cases, therefore, one can observe the reuse and reinterpretation of Pauline themes in new situations. In the Acts of the Apostles, Paul's role as a missionary before Jews and gentiles is emphasized, whereas the Pastoral Epistles stress his importance as a 'mediating authority' of the παραθήκη, which needs to be preserved in the emerging church.

V. Conclusion

For the Acts of the Apostles as well as for the Pastoral Epistles Paul's missionary activity is constitutive and essential for the church the authors of these texts have in mind. The most striking difference in their receptions of Paul is first of all due to their respective genres. The Acts of the Apostles narrates the story of Paul's career, starting with his conversion on the road to Damascus and ending with his imprisonment in Rome. The Pastoral Epistles, however, develop their subject matter by means of a literary double fiction. This means, on the one hand, that the Acts of the Apostles integrates Paul's missionary activity and theology into the early theology of Christian history in a much more comprehensive way than the Pastorals. On the other hand, the Pastorals are able to ensure continuity with the Pauline heritage by means of his co-workers Timothy and Titus; the Acts of the Apostles, however, connects to Paul's missionary activity by means of communicating his activity and fate to Christian communities.

A second difference results from the respective contexts: in the Pastoral Epistles, at the very end of his missionary activity, Paul inculcates the preservation of his teaching as καλὴ παραθήκη or ὑγιαίνουσα διδασκαλία, in light of external and internal threats. The Pastorals, therefore, expand the Pauline tradition, as developed in the Acts of the Apostles, in that 'their' Paul establishes rules for the Christian communities in his mission field and departs in 2 Timothy with a testamentary letter.[75] In the Acts of the Apostles this aspect is subordinated to the emphasis on Paul's historical function to fulfil God's plan to bring the salvation to the gentiles. This is evident by the fact that Paul's farewell speech in Acts is not delivered at the very end of the story (in Rome), but has already occurred at an earlier point before Paul leaves his mission field in Asia Minor and the Aegean region. Paul's final word in Rome, nevertheless, fulfils the same role as that of 2 Timothy. This final word therefore in a way presents

---

75   It should again be emphasized that this does not mean that a knowledge of the Acts of the Apostles on the part of the author of the Pastorals is assumed. However, both authors obviously rely on common Pauline traditions.

a second 'testament' of Paul, aimed now at providing a fundamental theological explanation of his role in this history.

Moreover, a comparison of the reception of Paul in the Acts of the Apostles with the Pastoral Epistles leads to the following results. Paul's integration into the group of early Christian witnesses for Christ is of essential importance for his portrait in the Acts of the Apostles. Paul's specific function is determined in 9.15f, namely bearing witness before gentiles, kings, and Jews as well as suffering for the name of Jesus. In this way he must realize God's eternal plan to bring salvation also to the gentiles. In the Pastoral Epistles such a comprehensive integration of Paul's career does not appear. Rather, with the exception of the allusion to his conversion in 1 Tim 1.12-17, these letters concentrate on the last period of Paul's missionary activity.[76] Consequently, Paul is depicted as the only apostle to whom the gospel has been entrusted and who hands it over as a 'deposit' and a 'sound teaching' to his co-workers Timothy and Titus. Thus, 1 and 2 Timothy diverge from each other in respect to their portrait of Paul. While 2 Timothy generates the image of a suffering Paul who requests Timothy to suffer with him for the sake of the gospel, 1 Timothy develops the image of the first converted sinner who experienced God's saving grace in a prototypical manner. In this way certain aspects of Paul's self-conception are taken up and treated in specific ways.

The topic of Paul's suffering is of chief importance for the Acts of the Apostles and 2 Timothy. As the examples mentioned above have shown, this also represents the continuation of a certain theme of Paul's genuine letters. Thus, by taking up the idea of the gospel as mediated through Paul's suffering, 2 Timothy stands in closer relation to Paul himself than Acts, in which Paul's suffering is treated narratively as mediating between Jesus' fate (and that of Stephen) and the conditions endured by the communities founded by Paul. Paul, therefore, opposed by Jews and gentiles, becomes a model for what the Christian communities are facing in the period after Paul. In 2 Timothy Paul's own idea that his suffering is immediately connected to that of Christ is modified, in that suffering for the gospel is now mediated from Paul to Timothy, who in this way becomes a guarantor for the preservation of Paul's heritage and the personal relationship between Paul and the communities.

As far as Paul's teaching is concerned, in the speeches in Acts 13 and 17 several themes from Paul's own letters are adopted as part of the historical development towards a church consisting of Jews and gentiles, whereas the Pastoral Epistles integrate these themes into the concept of church organization, which is based on the οἶκος-model. Therefore, Roloff's claim, that Luke – in contrast to the Pastoral Epistles – was only interested in Paul's ministry, not in his teaching, is in need of revision. For Luke as well as for the Pastoral Epistles Paul's ministry and his teaching are closely connected. Moreover, in both cases a profile of Paul the 'theologian' is developed. Paul's theology therefore becomes part of the wider context of early Christian theology, although its concrete shape remains more distinct in Acts than in the Pastoral Epistles. This could be due to the fact that in contrast to the Pastorals the Acts of the Apostles

---

76   The reference to persecutions and suffering in Antioch, Iconium, and Lystra (2 Tim. 3.11) underscores this result, in that not only Paul but also Barnabas is mentioned.

does not rely exclusively on Paul, but refers also to Peter as another guarantor for early Christian traditions.

It can be concluded, therefore, that the reception of Paul in the writings analyzed here is a multifaceted phenomenon, the importance of which cannot be encompassed as a tendency of an 'early Catholicism', deficient in comparison to Paul's own theology. The remaining contribution of this reception for the early history of Christianity and its theological development is rather to preserve various facets of Paul's activity and theology and to make it suitable for new contexts. In this way the emerging church's affiliation with Paul is developed. The Acts of the Apostles and the Pastorals are thus connected in that they depict Paul in specific ways as the missionary and theologian upon whom the characteristic form of the Christian church is founded. In the Acts of the Apostles it is Paul who realizes that the gentiles have been accepted into God's people, fulfilling a development that had its beginnings with Jesus and continued with the apostles and other witnesses of the risen Jesus. In the Pastoral Epistles Paul is the first of converted sinners, who was entrusted with the gospel as a 'word that is trustworthy', suffered for it, and handed it over to his co-workers as παραθήκη and ὑγιαίνουσα διδασκαλία.

In the discussion concerning the reception of the Pauline heritage these writings therefore pose the question of how the preservation of Pauline intentions can be correlated to new situations for which they have to be made applicable.

Chapter 12

FROM THE 'LEAST OF ALL THE SAINTS' TO THE 'APOSTLE OF JESUS CHRIST': THE TRANSFORMATION OF PAUL IN THE FIRST CENTURY[1]

Gregory E. Sterling

The relationship between Paul and beginnings of Christianity has been a point of extended discussion in the last two hundred years. Ferdinand Christian Baur delivered one of the most famous judgements about Christian origins. He wrote: 'That Christianity, in the universal historical importance which it achieved, was the work of the Apostle Paul is undeniably a matter of historical fact.' He did, however, recognize that the process was not entirely straightforward: 'but in what manner he brought this about, how we are to conceive of his relations with the other Apostles, whether it was in harmony with them or in contradiction and opposition to them ... this still requires a more thorough and searching inquiry'.[2]

Baur's view was not new. At the end of the first century CE, two early Christian authors came to the conclusion that the church as they knew it was largely the result of the labours or thought of Paul.[3] One of these authors lived within the circle of

1   This essay was first presented as a paper to the Reception of Paul Seminar of the Studiorum Novi Testamenti Societas at the general meeting of 2005. I am grateful to Daniel Marguerat and David Moessner for the invitation to present the paper and to the members of the seminar for their helpful comments, especially to Jens Schröter who served as my respondent. The paper first appeared in revised form as 'From Apostle to the Gentiles to Apostle of the Church: Images of Paul at the End of the First Century', *ZNW* 99 (2008), pp. 74–98. I want to express my appreciation to Michael Wolter and the publishing house of Walter De Gruyter for permission to publish it here in a revised form.

2   F. C. Baur, *Paul: The Apostle of Jesus Christ, His Life and Work, His Epistles and Doctrine, A Contribution to a Critical History of Primitive Christianity* (2 vols.; London: Williams and Norgate, 2nd edn, 1875–76), 1:3–4. For a more recent and nuanced assessment see J. D. G. Dunn, *Beginning from Jerusalem, Vol. 2: Christianity in the Making* (Grand Rapids: Eerdmans, 2009), pp. 539–41.

3   I consider the author of Ephesians to be someone other than the author of Acts. Some have argued for the identity of the two, e.g., R. P. Martin, 'An Epistle in Search of a Life-Setting', *ET* 79 (1968), pp. 296–302 and *idem, New Testament Foundations: A Guide for Christian Students* (Grand Rapids: Eerdmans, 1975–78), 2:230–33, suggested that Luke gave Ephesians its final form. This is problematic on several counts: it assumes that Luke is the author of Acts (an assumption that I am not willing to grant) and, while it accounts for the similarities between the two, it does not account for the significant differences. On the relationship between Ephesians and Acts see C. L. Mitton, *The Epistle to the Ephesians: Its Authorship, Origin and Purpose* (Oxford:

Pauline disciples and the other did not. One elected to write a pseudepigraphon in the form of a letter modelled and based on letters in the Pauline tradition, the other chose to compose an extended narrative in two scrolls that included a *vita* of Paul in the latter half of the second scroll.[4] One created an image of Paul along the lines of a *vita contemplativa*, the other along the lines of a *vita activa*.[5] The portraits are thus strikingly similar in some ways and dissimilar in others.

The distinct portraits of Paul in the two works is a result of multiple factors. The conventions of the literary traditions of an epistle and a narrative require different strategies. It is not possible to develop a full sketch of an individual within the epistolary framework of the Pauline tradition, at least Paul did not do so nor did any of his disciples who wrote in his name. The task of the pseudepigrapher was to create an implied author who could speak to a situation that the historical Paul did not. The statements about the implied author thus constitute the basis for the image of Paul. If the pseudepigrapher has created an image that is suitable for the occasion, we should be able to move from the image of Paul as the implied author to the occasion of the letter. In this way we gain some understanding both of how a Paulinist conceived of the apostle and of the occasion for the letter. The situation with Acts is completely different. From Herodotus onwards,[6] authors in the Greek historiographical tradition frequently wrote with a biographical orientation. It is certainly true of a number of Hellenistic-Jewish historians,[7] including Josephus who regularly sketched characters in his *Antiquitates Judaicae*.[8] The author of Luke-Acts followed this tradition with two significant *bioi*, Jesus and Paul, and built a number of other parts of the narrative around key figures, e.g., John the Baptist, Peter. The biographical orientation of this narrative permitted a far fuller portrait than the pseudepigraphal letter.

Clarendon, 1951), pp. 198–220, who examined specific points of contact. For a broader thematic comparison see E. Käsemann, 'Ephesians and Acts', in *Studies in Luke-Acts* (ed. L. E. Keck and J. L. Martin; Philadelphia: Fortress, 1980), pp. 288–97.

4   G. Schulze, 'Das Paulusbild des Lukas. Ein historisch-exegetischer Versuch asl Beitrag zur Erforschung der lukanischen Theologie' (unpublished dissertation, Kiel, 1960), p. 24, has a wonderful summary of Acts that plays off of M. Kähler's famous description of Mark: Acts is 'ein Paulusbuch mit sehr breiter Einführung'. This is cited by A. Lindemann, *Paulus im ältesten Christentum : Das Bild des Apostels und die Rezeption der paulinishcen Theologie in der früh-christlichen Literatur bis Marcion* (BHTh, 58; Tübingen: J. C. B. Mohr [Paul Siebeck], 1979), p. 49 n. 2.

5   I do not want to push the distinction too hard since Ephesians recognized Paul's role as a missionary, e.g., 3.8-9.

6   On the place of biographical treatments in Herodotus see J. Cobet, *Herodots Exkurse und die Frage der Einheit seines Werkes* (Historia Einzelschriften, 17; Wiesbaden: Steiner, 1971), pp. 158–76 and K. H. Waters, *Herodotus the Historian: His Problems, Methods and Originality* (Norman: University of Oklahoma Press, 1985), pp. 136–51. On the relationship between biography and history more broadly see P. Stadter, 'Biography and History', in *A Companion to Greek and Roman Historiography* (ed. J. Marincola; Blackwell Companions to the Ancient World; 2 vols.; Oxford: Blackwell, 2007), 2:528–40.

7   E.g., Artapanus Frg. 1 concentrated on Abraham, Frg. 2 on Joseph, and Frg. 3 on Moses.

8   These have been studied in detail by L. H. Feldman, *Josephus' Interpretation of the Bible* (Hellenistic Culture and Society, 27; Berkeley: University of California Press, 1998) and *idem, Studies in Josephus' Rewritten Bible* (JSJSup, 58; Leiden/New York: E. J. Brill, 1998).

The differences, however, extend beyond the constraints of the literary traditions: each of these authors valued a different aspect of the Pauline tradition. It
is their valuation of the tradition that we need to address. We will do so by using
Ephesians as our *point d'appui*. There are three texts in Ephesians that create the
basic image of the implied author.[9] We will examine each of these and compare the
image of Paul in them with the corresponding image of Paul in Acts.[10] I will not try
to address the full scope of the Acts portrait, but use it as a counterpoint. While it
would be possible to extend such a comparison to the Pastorals or the *Acts of Paul*
as two other examples of epistolary and narrative portraits from a common milieu,
it would take us well into the second century. I will work from the assumption that
the author of Ephesians knew and used Colossians as a basic source for the writing
of the letter.[11] The relationship between the two plays an important role in the three
texts that we will examine. This will permit us to assess the ways in which the
author of Ephesians shaped the inherited tradition.

9   There are a number of important studies on the image of Paul in Ephesians. These include:
K. M. Fischer, *Tendenz und Absicht des Epheserbrief* (FRLANT, 111; Göttingen: Vandenhoeck &
Ruprecht, 1973), pp. 95–108; E. Dassmann, *Der Stachel im Fleisch. Paulus in der frühchristlichen
Literatur bis Irenäus* (Münster: Aschendorff, 1978), pp. 45–57, esp. 51–55; Lindemann, *Paulus im
ältesten Christentum*, pp. 40–42; *idem, Paulus, Apostel und Lehrer der Kirche: Studien zu Paulus
und zum frühen Paulusverständnis* (Tübingen: J. C. B. Mohr [Paul Siebeck], 1999), pp. 211–27;
J. Gnilka, 'Das Paulusbild im Kolosser- und Epheserbrief', in *Kontinuität und Einheit* (Festschrift
F. Mußner; Freiburg: Herder, 1981), pp. 179–93; and J. Blasi, *Making Charisma: The Social
Construction of Paul's Public Image* (New Brunswick: Transaction, 1991), pp. 91–97.
10   There is a huge bibliography on the portrait of Paul in Acts. The most significant
recent works include: C. Burchard, 'Paulus in der Apostelgeschichte', *TLZ* 100 (1975), pp.
880–95; Lindemann, *Paulus im ältesten Christentum*, pp. 49–68; J. Jervell, 'Paul in the Acts
of the Apostles: Tradition, History, Theology', in *Les Actes des Apôtres: Traditions, redactions,
théologie* (ed. J. Kremer; BEThL, 58; Leuven: Leuven University Press, 1979), pp. 299–306; J. C.
Lentz, *Luke's Portrait of Paul* (SNTSMS, 77; Cambridge/New York: Cambridge University Press,
1993); M.-E. Rosenblatt, *Paul the Accused: His Portrait in the Acts of the Apostles* (Collegeville:
Liturgical Press, 1995); Blasi, *The Social Constructions of Paul's Public Image*, pp. 75–88; S.
E. Porter, *The Paul of Acts: Essays in Literary Criticism, Rhetoric, and Theology* (WUNT, 115;
Tübingen: J. C. B. Mohr [Paul Siebeck], 1999); and C. Mount, *Pauline Christianity: Luke-Acts
and the Legacy of Paul* (NovTSup, 104; Leiden/Boston/Köln: E. J. Brill, 2002).
11   There is an extensive bibliography on the relationship between Colossians and
Ephesians. The most important works in my judgement are E. Percy, *Die Probleme der Kolosser-
und Epheserbriefe* (Acta reg. societatis humaniorum litterarum Lundensis, 39; Lund: G. C. K.
Gleerup, 1946); Mitton, *The Epistle to the Ephesians*, pp. 55–97; and M. Gese, *Das Vermächtnis
des Apostels: Die Rezeption der paulinishcen Theologie im Epheserbrief* (WUNT, 2.99; Tübingen:
J. C. B. Mohr [Paul Siebeck], 1997), pp. 39–54. For a recent challenge of the *communis opinio*
see E. Best, 'Who used Whom? The Relationship of Ephesians and Colossians', *NTS* 43 (1997),
pp. 72–96.

I. Apostle or Chosen Vessel?

a. Ephesians

The first text is the letter opening. Ephesians begins with the familiar elements of the Pauline epistolary tradition.[12]

Colossians 1.1-2	Ephesians 1.1-2
[1]Paul, an apostle of Christ Jesus	[1]Paul, an apostle of Christ Jesus
by God's will,	by God's will,
and Timothy our brother	
[2]to the saints in Colossae	to the saints who are in Ephesus
and the faithful brothers and sisters	and the faithful
in Christ:	in Christ Jesus:
Grace to you	[2]Grace to you
and peace from God our Father.	and peace from God our Father.
	and the Lord Jesus Christ.[13]

There are several noteworthy features of this opening.[14] The author follows Colossians rather carefully in the opening lines. Both the author of Ephesians and the author of Colossians kept the pattern of the Deutero-Pauline literature in designating Paul an apostle. Paul used the designation in four of his seven letters.[15] All of the Deutero-Pauline letters use the designation with the exception of 2 Thessalonians that modelled itself on 1 Thessalonians where Paul did not use it.[16] The author qualified Paul's apostleship with a phrase taken from Colossians and shared with both of the Corinthian letters, 'by God's will' (διὰ θελήματος θεοῦ).

---

12   Taking the letters in chronological order compare 1 Thess. 1.1; Gal. 1.1-5; 1 Cor. 1.1-3; Phil. 1.1-2; Phlm. 1-3; 2 Cor. 1.1-2; and Rom. 1.1-7 among the authentic Pauline letters. Compare 2 Thess. 1.1-2; Col. 1.1-2; Eph. 1.1-2; 1 Tim. 1.1-12; Tit. 1.1-4; and 2 Tim. 1.1-2, among the Deutero-Pauline letters.

13   All translations are my own.

14   The most helpful analysis of the openings of Pauline letters is F. Schnider and W. Stenger, *Studien zum neutestamentliochen Briefformular* (NTTS, 11; Leiden: E. J. Brill, 1987), pp. 4–14. Unfortunately, they do not address the omission of the co-sender in Ephesians (see below).

15   He used it in Gal. 1.1, ἀπόστολος; 1 Cor. 1.1, κλητὸς ἀπόστολος Χριστοῦ Ἰησοῦ; 2 Cor. 1.1, ἀπόστολος Χριστοῦ Ἰησοῦ; and Rom. 1.1, δοῦλος Χριστοῦ Ἰησοῦ, κλητὸς ἀπόστολος. 1 Thess. 1.1 lacks any self-defining noun. Phil. 1.1 uses δοῦλος and Phlm. 1 uses δέσμιος.

16   With the noted exception of 2 Thessalonians, all of the Deutero-Pauline letters use the expression ἀπόστολος Χριστοῦ Ἰησοῦ (Col. 1.1; 1 Tim. 1.1; 2 Tim. 1.1) except for Titus that is closer to the fuller expression in Romans, δοῦλος θεοῦ ἀπόστολος δὲ Ἰησοῦ Χριστοῦ (Tit. 1.1).

Paul regularly offered some qualifying phrase when he mentioned his apostleship,[17] and the authors of the Deutero-Pauline letters followed suit.[18]

The first difference between Ephesians and Colossians is striking: the author of Ephesians did not mention a co-sender. This is very unusual in the Pauline tradition. Paul included co-senders in every letter except Romans.[19] In the case of Romans, he wrote to introduce himself to a community that he did not found. In the Deutero-Pauline corpus, only Ephesians and the Pastorals omit a co-sender.[20] The Pastorals did not need a co-sender because of the nature of the letters: they present themselves as letters from Paul to one of his trusted lieutenants. The situation in Ephesians is quite different. The omission placed the focus entirely on Paul and created an exclusive relationship between Paul and the readers/hearers. The exclusivity of this relationship gave additional weight to Paul's status as an apostle. As Rudolf Schnackenburg wrote: 'Everyone else must retreat behind his outstanding figure.'[21]

b. Acts

It is well known that the author of Luke-Acts (whom we will call 'Luke' by convention), avoided the term 'apostle' (ἀπόστολος) for Paul. Luke did not have a preferred term for Paul. When he introduced him formally to the narrative in the first rehearsal of his call/conversion,[22] he had God order Ananias: 'Go, for he (Paul) is a vessel whom I have chosen (σκεῦος ἐκλογῆς) to bear my name before Gentiles, kings, and the children of Israel.'[23] This statement summarizes the function of Paul in Acts. The inclusion of three different audiences for Paul – Gentiles, kings, and the children of Israel – elevates his position in the narrative. The broad scope of his mission suggests that he is *sui generis* as the phrase 'chosen vessel' (σκεῦος ἐκλογῆς) suggests. He is the only figure in Acts to receive the designation.

The historian's reluctance to use the term 'apostle' (ἀπόστολος) is associated with his peculiar understanding of it.[24] He first used the term in the gospel when Jesus selected the twelve 'whom he named apostles'. The third evangelist is the

---

17   Gal. 1.1 and Rom. 1.1-6 have more elaborate qualifications than do 1 Cor. 1.1 and 2 Cor. 1.1.

18   Col. 1.1 and 2 Tim. 1.1 have διὰ θελήματος θεοῦ. The Pastorals have other significant expansions.

19   1 Thess. 1.1; Gal. 1.2 (unnamed); 1 Cor. 1.1; Phil. 1.1; Phlm. 1; 2 Cor. 1.1. Cf. Rom. 1.6.

20   2 Thess. 1.1; Col. 1.1. Cf. 1 Tim. 1.1; Tit. 1.3; 2 Tim. 1.1.

21   R. Schnackenburg, *Ephesians: A Commentary* (Edinburgh: T&T Clark, 1991), p. 42. So also J. Gnilka, *Der Epheserbrief* (HThK, 10.2; Freiburg: Herder, 1971), p. 54 and A. T. Lincoln, *Ephesians* (WBC, 42; Nashville: Thomas Nelson, 1990), p. 5. E. Best, *Ephesians* (ICC; Edinburgh: T&T Clark, 1998), pp. 97–98, argued that this was an indication that the author of Ephesians did not use the preface in Colossians, a position that I find untenable given the extensive agreements between the letters as a whole. Lindemann, *Paulus im ältesten Christentum*, p. 41, missed the significance of Eph. 1.1 when he said that Ephesians did not place any special emphasis on Paul's apostleship.

22   Saul is mentioned in passing earlier at Acts 7.58.

23   Acts 9.15. Compare 2 Cor. 4.7, where Paul uses the same term in a metaphorical expression: 'we have this treasure in clay jars' (ἔχομεν δὲ τὸν θησαυρὸν ἐν ὀστρακίνοις σκεύεσιν).

24   For a summary see the dated but still useful work of W. Schmitals, *The Office of the Apostle in the Early Church* (trans. J. E. Steely; Nashville/New York: Abingdon, 1969), pp. 247–50.

only Synoptic author to add the qualifying relative clause.[25] Luke thought of an apostle as an eye-witness of Jesus' ministry, death, and resurrection. He stated this explicitly when the community replaced Judas with Matthias.[26] They are the 'eye-witnesses' (αὐτόπται) in the preface to the double-work[27] and are regularly called 'witnesses' (μάρτυρες) in Acts.[28] In the speech attributed to Paul at Psidian Antioch, the Tarsus native referred to the witnesses and excluded himself. Speaking of the resurrection of Christ, he said: 'who appeared for many days to those who had accompanied him from Galilee to Jerusalem, who are his witnesses (μάρτυρες) to the people'.[29] The historian is not, however, consistent; in at least two other contexts, he referred to Paul as a 'witness' (μάρτυς) of what he had seen.[30] Like the 'apostles', Paul saw the risen Christ. In this way, he was fully their equal and could be counted among the witnesses. He was not, however, with Jesus in Galilee and could not be counted among the Twelve. He is therefore a 'witness' (μάρτυς), but not one of the 'witnesses' (μάρτυρες) from Galilee.

The ambiguity evident in the use of 'witness' (μάρτυς), may help us understand Luke's use of the term 'apostle' (ἀπόστολος). The historian called Paul an 'apostle' (ἀπόστολος) twice on his first journey. Paul's preaching at Iconium led to the split among the populace: 'The crowd of the city was divided. Some sided with the Jews, but others with the apostles (ἀπόστολοι).' The apostles were presumably Paul and Barnabas, an assumption that is supported by the reference to their activities in Lystra: 'when the apostles (ἀπόστολοι), Barnabas and Paul, heard these things, they tore their clothes ...'.[31] Why did the historian call them 'apostles' (ἀπόστολοι) here and nowhere else? Was he following a source that called Paul and Barnabas 'apostles' (ἀπόστολοι) and failed to redact it properly?[32] Did he think of Barnabas and Paul as emissaries of the church at Antioch and use the term in this broader sense and not as a *terminus technicus,* perhaps playing with deliberate ambiguity?[33]

---

25   Mt. 10.1//Mk. 3.14//Lk. 6.13. There is good support for the same clause in a number of manuscripts of Mk. 3.14; however, this is probably an interpolation resulting from harmonization. The UBS committee was of the same judgement. Cf. B. M. Metzger, *A Textual Commentary on the Greek New Testament* (Stuttgart: United Bible Societies, 2nd edn, 2000), p. 69.

26   Acts 1.21-22.

27   Lk. 1.2.

28   Acts 1.8; 2.32; 3.15; 5.32; 10.39, 41; 13.31. Cf. also Acts 4.33.

29   Acts 13.31.

30   Acts 22.15; 26.16. Cf. also Acts 22.18.

31   Acts 14.4, 14.

32   There is a common tradition in German scholarship that argues that the term was in a source in v. 14 and that Luke has introduced it in v. 4 under the influence of v. 14: E. Haenchen, *The Acts of the Apostles: A Commentary* (trans. B. Noble, G. Shinn, and H. Anderson; revised by R. McL. Wilson; Philadelphia: Fortress, 1971 [German 1965]), pp. 420 and 428; H. Conzelmann, *Acts of the Apostles* (trans. J. Liburg; A. T. Kraabel, and D. H. Juel; Hermeneia; Philadelphia: Fortress, 1987 [German 1972]), p. 108; and G. Schneider, *Die Apostelgeschichte* (HThK, 5.1-2; Freiburg: Herder, 1980–1982), 2:151–52. For American examples see J. A. Fitzmyer, *The Acts of the Apostles* (AB, 31; New York: Doubleday, 1998), pp. 525–26 and R. I. Pervo, *Acts* (Hermeneia; Minneapolis: Fortress, 2009), 350, who suggests that the author was consciously playing with the meanings of the term that he found in his source.

33   For a parallel see 2 Cor. 8.23. This position is held by Lindemann, *Paulus im ältesten*

Or did he use the term 'apostle' more broadly than the phrase 'the Twelve'?[34] Each of these suggestions (and others) has significant problems. It is not clear that Luke had a source for the first journey (it does not have parallels in the letters of Paul as the second and third journeys of Acts do).[35] Even if he had an Antiochene or another source, why did he leave the term here? He does not use it elsewhere in Acts for Paul. Did it only appear here, was he simply sloppy, or deliberately ambiguous? If he used it as a non-technical term, this is the only non-technical use in Acts. How did the author think of Barnabas whom he consistently distinguished from the apostles?[36] I think it best to conclude that the author was not entirely consistent with either the term 'apostle' (ἀπόστολος) or 'witness' (μάρτυς). He used them in technical ways, but was also aware that others used them differently. The case was particularly problematic for Paul whom he knew did not technically qualify as an apostle, but whom he regarded as the key figure in the church of his day. The inconsistency in language reflects the tension between the author's restricted technical usages and the need to bestow a status on Paul that is not inferior to those for whom the technical usages applied. It is worth remembering that Paul was himself aware of his unusual position[37] and that the author of Ephesians echoed this as well.[38] This raises the question of the relationship between Paul and the apostles.

Christentum, p. 62 and I. H. Marshall, *The Acts of the Apostles* (ICC; Edinburgh: T&T Clark, 1994–1998), 1:671–72.

34   So J. Jervell, *Die Apostelgeschichte* (KEK, 3; Göttingen: Vandenhoeck & Ruprecht, 17th edn, 1998), pp. 370–71.

35   I am not convinced that there are any parallels to the first journey. There are some parallels for the European (second) journey (I will list the places in sequence and the references with the parallels marked by //): Syria and Cilicia, Gal. 1.21//Acts 15.26-41, esp. 41; Derbe and Lystra, Acts 16.1-5; Phyrgia and Galatia, Gal. 4.13//Acts 16.6; Mysia, Acts 16.7-8; Troas, Acts 16.8-10; Samothrace, Acts 16.11; Neapolis, Acts 16.11; Philippi, 1 Thess. 2.2//Phil. 4.15//Acts 16.12-40; Amphipolis and Apollonia, Acts 17.1; Thessalonica, 1 Thess. 2.1-12//Phil. 4.15//Acts 17.1-9; Beroea, Acts 17.10-14; Athens, 1 Thess. 3.1-6//Acts 17.15-34; Corinth, 1 Cor. 3.6; 4.15// Acts 18.1-7; Cenchrea, Acts 18.18; Ephesus, Acts 18.19-21; Caesarea, Acts 18.22. There are well-known parallels to the Jerusalem conference that I situate between the European journey and the collection journey: Jerusalem, Gal. 2.1-10//Acts 18.22; 15.1-29; Antioch, Gal. 2.11-14// Acts 18.22; 15.36-39. There are also parallels with the collection journey: Galatia and Phrygia, Acts 18.23; Ephesus, 1 Cor. 16.8//Acts 19.1-40; Corinth, 2 Cor. 13.1-2 (cf. also 2 Cor. 1.15-16; 2.1-2, 5-8; 7.11-12; 12.14, 19-21); Ephesus, 2 Cor. 2.3-4, 9; 7.8-13; Macedonia, 2 Cor. 7.5-7//Acts 20.1; Illyricum, Rom. 15.19; Corinth/Greece, Rom. 15.26; 16.1//Acts 20.2; Macedonia/Philippi, Acts 20.3-6a; Troas, Acts 20.6b-12; Assos, Mitylene, Chios, Samos, Acts 20.13-15; Miletus, Acts 20.16-38; Cos, Rhodes, Patara, Acts 21.1-2; Tyre, Acts 21.3-6; Ptolemais, Acts 21.7; Caesarea, Acts 21.8-14; Jerusalem, Rom. 15.25//Acts 21.15.

36   Acts 4.36-37; 9.27; 15.1-35 and 16.4.

37   1 Cor. 15.8.

38   Eph. 3.8. On this text see Fischer, *Tendenz und Absicht des Epheserbrief*, pp. 94–98.

II. Paul and the Apostles

a. Ephesians

The relationship surfaces a couple of times in Ephesians including in the second text that we will consider, the aside on the revelation of the mystery to Paul (3.1-13).[39] This text is a digression that is marked by an *inclusio* formed by the repetition of 'for this reason' (τούτου χάριν) in vv. 1 and 14. The digression proper therefore consists of vv. 2-13 which comprise three sentences in Greek (vv. 2-7, 8-12, 13).[40] There are, however, two basic conceptual units that are set off by references to Paul's ministry. The first *inclusio* is unambiguous: verses 2 and 7 repeat the same language.

V. 2   ... surely you have heard of the administration
of the grace of God that was given to me for you

V. 7   ... of which I became a minister
according to the gift *of the grace of God that was given to me*
by the working of his power ...

The second *inclusio* is marked by a common reference to the humility of Paul in his ministry, although it does not share a verbal repetition.

V. 8a ... to me, the least of all the saints, was this grace given ...

V. 13 Wherefore I pray that you will not weaken over my difficulties
on your behalf; they are your glory.

39   Paul is presented as a prisoner on behalf of the gentiles in 3.1 and 4.1. The author alludes to his sufferings in 3.13 as well. I have chosen not to develop this extensively for this essay since the view of Paul as a suffering apostle is not unique; it is shared with Colossians (see below for a brief treatment). On this motif see Percy, *Die Probleme der Kolosser- und Epheserbriefe*, p. 351; Fischer, *Tendenz und Absicht des Epheserbrief*, pp. 104–08; and Gnilka, 'Das Paulusbild im Kolosser- und Epheserbrief', pp. 190–93. For an alternative eschatological interpretation see G. H. P. Thompson, 'Eph 3,3 and 2 Tim 2,10 in Light of Col 1,24', *ET* 71 (1959–1960), pp. 187–89.

40   There are a number of important treatments of this text. See P. Benoit, 'Ephesians (Épître aux)', *DBS* 7 (1966), pp. 195–211, esp. 208–09; H. Merklein, *Das kirchliche Amt nach dem Epheserbrief* (StANT, 33; München: Kösel, 1973), pp. 159–71; H. E. Lona, *Die Eschatologie im Kolosser- und Epheserbrief* (FB, 48; Würzburg: Echter Verlag, 1984), pp. 277–308; C. Reynier, *Évangile et mystère: Les enjeux théologiques de l'épître aux Ephesians* (LD, 149; Paris: Éditions du Cerf, 1992), pp. 15–81, esp. 43–79, where he provides a summary of structural analyses along with his own; and M.-É. Boismard, *L'Enigme de la letter aux Éphésians* (EtB, 39; Paris: J. Gabalda, 1999), pp. 102–07, who argues that vv. 8-13 come from an authentic letter and that vv. 2-7 are from a reviser based on Col. 1.23-29; Ch. Karakolis, '"A Mystery Hidden to be Revealed?" Philological and Theological Correlations between Eph 3 and 1', in *Ethik als angewandte Ekklesiologie. Der Brief an die Epheser* (ed. M. Wolter; Monographische Reihe von 'Benedictina'. Bibl.-Ökumen, 17; Rome: Benedictina, 2005), pp. 65–108, who argues that Eph. 3.14-21 is parallel with 1.15-23 and 3.1-13 with 1.1-14.

The reference to 'grace' (χάρις) in vv. 2, 7, and 8 (and only in these verses in this section) provides a link between the two sets of brackets.

The two sets of brackets (vv. 2 and 7 and vv. 8a and 13) embrace two accounts of the revelation of God's mystery. In the first account (vv. 3-6), the revelation of the mystery occurred in two phases. In phase one, Paul received the mystery that the gentiles were fellow heirs, fellow members of the body, and fellow partners in the promise. God gave this to him by revelation and he wrote it down for the benefit of the readers (vv. 3-4). In phase two, the same process took place for the apostles and prophets (vv. 5-6). There is thus a double disclosure of the mystery: first to Paul and then to the apostles. In both cases, the disclosure was to human beings. In the second account (vv. 8b-12), God disclosed his mystery to the cosmic powers through the church. This disclosure was made through the ministry of Paul who brought the gentiles into the church, thereby disclosing God's eternal purpose to the cosmic forces. The first unit thus records the revelation of the mystery to humans – first Paul and then the apostles – and the second to the cosmic powers.

In both cases, a contrast is drawn between a mystery hidden in the past but disclosed in the present. The contrast follows an established pattern that is attested in other Pauline and Deutero-Pauline texts.[41] The synopsis in the appendix sets out the texts for the sake of convenience. The common elements in the contrast (set in bold) are a reference to a mystery,[42] its hidden or concealed nature,[43] the groups from whom it is hidden,[44] a temporal reference indicating that the situation has changed,[45] the revelation,[46] the group(s) to whom the present revelation has been made,[47] and the agency by which the revelation came.[48] The fact that the pattern appears at least three times in the Pauline and Deutero-Pauline corpus outside of Ephesians and on two other

---

41   There are several studies that have explored this pattern, e.g., N. A. Dahl, 'Formgeschichte Beobactungen zur Christusverkündigung in der Gemeindepredigt' (FS R. Bultmann; BZNW, 21; Berlin: Walter de Gruyter, 1954), pp. 3–9, esp. 4–5, who identified two forms: the Pauline and Deutero-Pauline (1 Cor. 2.6-10; Col. 1.26; Eph. 3.4-7, 8-11; Rom. 16:25-27) and the Pastorals and non-Pauline corpus (2 Tim. 1.9-11; Tit. 1.2; 1 Pet. 1.18-21; 1 Jn. 1.1-3; Ignatius, *Magn.* 6.1; Hermas, *Sim.* 9.12); D. Lührmann, *Das Offenbarungs-Verständnis bei Paulus und in paulinischen Gemeinden* (WMANT, 16; Neukirchen-Vlyn: Neukirchener Verlag, 1965), pp. 125–33; Merklein, *Das kirchliche Amt nach dem Epheserbrief*, pp. 167–70; and M. Wolter, 'Verborgene Weisheit und Heil für die Heiden. Zur Traditionsgeschichte und Intention des "Revelationsschemas"' *ZThK* 84 (1987), pp. 297–319.

42   1 Cor. 2.7, wisdom hidden in a mystery; Col. 1.26; Eph. 3.4, 9; Rom. 16.25.

43   The verb varies: ἀποκρύπτω (1 Cor. 2.7; Col. 1.26; Eph. 3.9), οὐκ γνωρίζω (Eph. 3.5), and σιγάω (Rom. 16.25).

44   1 Cor. 2.8-9 and Col. 1.26 have it concealed from both cosmic powers and humans; Eph. 3.5, from humans; and Eph. 3.9, from cosmic powers.

45   In all of the texts except 1 Cor. 2.10, the temporal adverb νῦν appears.

46   The verbs vary: ἀποκαλύπτω (1 Cor. 2.10; Eph. 3.5), φανερόω (Col. 1.26 and Rom. 16.26), and γνωρίζω (Eph. 3.10).

47   1 Cor. 2.10, to us; Col. 1.26, to the holy ones=saints; Eph. 3.5, to his holy apostles and prophets; Eph. 3.9-10, to the rulers and authorities.

48   This is included in four of the five texts: 1 Cor. 2.10 and Eph. 3.5, through the Spirit; Eph. 3.6, through the gospel; Eph. 3.10, through the church; and Rom. 16.26, through the prophetic writings.

occasions where there is not a reference to a mystery suggests that it was an established form.[49]

Why has Ephesians presented two accounts of the revelation (vv. 3-7 and 8-13)? Perhaps it would be helpful to remind ourselves of the relationship of Ephesians to Colossians at this point.[50] We will print the texts in a synoptic fashion for ease of reference. When the words are identical, we will set them in bold. When Ephesians is dependent on Colossians, but the material is out of sequence, I will set the material in Colossians in italics.

Colossians 1.24-29	Ephesians 3.1-13
[24]I now rejoice	[1]For this reason I Paul,
in my sufferings	the prisoner of Christ (Jesus)
on your behalf,	**on your behalf,** the gentiles–
and in my flesh	
I am filling up what is lacking	
in the afflictions of Christ	
on behalf of his body,	
that is the church.	
[25]*of which I became a minister*	
	[2]surely you have heard
according to **the administration**	of **the administration**
of God	of the grace **of God**
that was given to me for you	**that was given to me for you,**
to complete the Word of God,	
	[3](how) by revelation
	the mystery was made known to me,
	as I wrote above in brief
	[4]so that you could, by reading,
	grasp my understanding
[26]*the* **mystery**	of **the mystery** of Christ.
that was hidden for aeons	
and for **generations,**	[5]In other **generations** it
	was not revealed
	to human beings,
but has **now** *been disclosed*	as it has **now** been revealed
to his holy *ones ...*	**to his holy** apostles
	and prophets by the Spirit:
	[6]that the gentiles may be fellow heirs,
	fellow members of the body,
	and fellow participants in the promise

---

49   Cf. also Tit. 2.2-3 and 2 Tim. 1.9-10 for a similar pattern, but without reference to a μυστήριον.

50   Ephesians follows the basic order of Colossians. In this case Col. 1.21-23//Eph. 2.11-22; Col. 1.24-29//Eph. 3.1-13; and Col. 2.1-10//Eph. 3.14-21.

	in Christ Jesus
	through the gospel.
25I became a minister of the church	**7I became a minister** of the gospel
according to the administration	**according to the** gift of the grace
of God	**of God**
that was given to me	**that was given to me**
	by the working
	of his power.
for you,	
	8Even though I am the least
	of all the saints,
	this grace was given
to make the word of God known–	to announce to the gentiles
	the measureless riches of Christ
	9and to bring to light (for everyone)
26the mystery	the administration of **the mystery**
that was hidden	**that was hidden**
for aeons	**from the aeons**
and for generations,	
	in God who created everything,
but **now** has been disclosed	**10so that it may now** be made known
to his saints.	to the rulers and authorities
	in the heavenly places
	through the church,
	namely the richly diverse
	wisdom of God.
	11This was in accordance
	with the eternal purpose
27To these God wished to reveal	
the extent of the riches of the glory	
of this mystery	
among the gentiles,	
that is **Christ** among you,	that he enacted in **Christ** Jesus
	our Lord,
the hope of glory.	
	12in whom we have boldness
	and confident access
	through faith in him.
28We announce him	
by admonishing every person	
and teaching every person	
with all wisdom,	
so that we may present every person	
perfect in Christ.	

	[13] Wherefore I pray
	that you will not weaken
[29]It is for this goal that I labour,	
contending	over my difficulties on your behalf;
with all of his energy	
that works powerfully in me.	
	they are your glory.

The synopsis makes it clear that Colossians 1.24-29 was the inspiration for Ephesians 3.1-13. There are, however, a number of issues that need to be addressed. We have already noted that Ephesians has two revelation schemas (vv. 3-7 and 8-13), whereas Colossians has only one. While it has been common to assume that Ephesians drew from Colossians for the first revelation schema (vv. 3-7), it is more likely that it served as the principal basis for the second revelation schema (vv. 8-13).[51] I say this for several reasons. Colossians 1.25 and 1.29 form frames for the conclusions of the two revelations in Eph. 3.7 and 13; this makes it natural to think of the material in Eph. 3.7-13 as coming from Col. 1.25-29. More specifically, Eph. 3.7 picks up directly from Col. 1.25, suggesting that this is the beginning point. It is relatively easy to find parallels for the remainder of the section (Col. 1.25-29//Eph. 3.7-13), note especially Col. 1.26 and Eph. 3.9-10. The parallels are closer and more frequent than they are in the first revelation scheme (compare Col. 1.25-29 and Eph. 3.3-5). This suggests that we should understand Col. 1.25-29 to be parallel with Eph. 3.7-13.

There are, however, some parallels between Eph. 3.3-5 and Col. 1.25-26 (set off in italics in the synopsis). These are close enough to suggest that Ephesians drew its inspiration for the revelation formula in vv. 2-7 from Colossians as well as the later formula in vv. 7-10. This is clear from the verbal echoes between Col. 1.25//Eph. 3.2 and Col. 1.26//Eph. 3.4-5.[52] This means that while the basic parallel is between Col. 1.25-29 and Eph. 3.7-13, the revelation formula in Eph. 3.2-7 was created on the basis of the later parallel.

Why did the author of Ephesians double the revelation scheme? We ought to note that the repetition in Eph. 3.4-5 and 3.7-10 is not a redundancy, i.e., the author of Ephesians did not simply repeat the revelation formula. On the contrary, there is a careful distinction between the two revelation accounts. The formula in Colossians suggests that the mystery was hidden 'for aeons' (ἀπὸ τῶν αἰώνων) and 'for generations' (ἀπὸ τῶν γενεῶν). While it is likely that the Colossians only intended to suggest a temporal period ('for ages and generations'),[53] the

---

51   The assumption is generally that Col. 1.24-29 served as the basis for the first revelation schema, e.g., Mitton, *The Epistle to the Ephesians*, pp. 291 and 293; Merklein, *Das kirchliche Amt nach dem Epheserbrief*, pp. 159–71; Boismard, *L'Enigme de la letter aux Éphésians*, pp. 102–07.

52   Several have recognized the repetition, e.g., Benoit, 'Éphésians', pp. 208–09 and Merklein, *Das kirchliche Amt nach dem Epheserbrief*, pp. 37, 166. They have not, however, picked up on the significance of the doubling.

53   This is a relatively standard reading of Col. 1.26, e.g., E. Lohse, *Colossians and Philemon* (trans. W. R. Poehlmann and R. J. Karris; Hermeneia; Philadelphia: Fortress, 1971

author of Ephesians understood the former to refer to different groups of recipients ('aeons'=supernatural beings and 'generations'=human beings) and split them into two distinct revelation schemas. The author consistently redacted the text in Colossians to eliminate the aeons from the first revelation schema and humans from the second revelation schema. Notice again the language of the revelation in each of the two disclosures. I will set the key agreements in bold and the omission in italics.

The Revelation to His Holy Apostles and Prophets

Colossians 1.26	Ephesians 3.4-5
	[4]so that you could, by reading,
	grasp my understanding
[26]**the mystery**	of **the mystery** of Christ.
that was hidden for aeons	
and for **generations,**	[5]In other **generations**
	it was not revealed
	to human beings,
but has **now** been disclosed	as it has **now** been made known
to his holy ones	**to his holy** apostles
	and prophets by the Spirit

There is no reference to the aeons, only to humans.

The Revelation to the Supernatural Powers

Colossians 1.25-26	Ephesians 3.7-10
[25]**I became a minister** of the church	[7]**I became a minister** of the gospel
according to the administration	**according to the** gift of the grace
of God	**of God**
that was given to me	**that was given to me**
	by the working
	of his power.
for you,	
	[8]Even though I am the least
	of all the saints,
	this grace was given
to make the word of God known–	to announce to the gentiles
	the measureless riches of Christ
	[9]and to bring to light for everyone
[26]**the mystery**	the administration of **the mystery**
that was hidden	**that was hidden**
for aeons (ἀπὸ τῶν αἰώνων)	**from the aeons** (ἀπὸ τῶν αἰώνων)
and for generations,	

[German 1968]), pp. 74–75 and P. T. O'Brien, *Colossians, Philemon* (WBC, 44; Waco: Word, 1982), p. 84.

	in God who created everything,
but **now** has been disclosed	[10]so that it may **now** be made known
to his holy ones.	to the rulers and authorities
	in the heavenly places
	through the church,
	namely the richly diverse
	wisdom of God.

The reverse has now taken place: there is no reference to the generations of humans, only to the supernatural powers.[54] The author of Ephesians has thus taken the two groups from whom the revelation was concealed in Colossians and made them into two separate revelations.

This is not all. The author of Ephesians has taken the reference of the recipients of the revelation in Colossians, 'to his holy ones' (τοῖς ἁγίοις αὐτοῦ) and made them 'to his holy apostles and prophets by the Spirit' (τοῖς ἁγίοις ἀποστόλοις αὐτοῦ καὶ προφήταις ἐν πνεύματι). It was not enough to indicate that Christians had come to understand that the gentiles should be included in the church; it was important to emphasize that this revelation came through the apostles and prophets. Why? If we are correct that the author of Ephesians is drawing from Colossians, then it appears that the author has inserted 'apostles' (ἀποστόλοις) into 'to his holy ones' (τοῖς ἁγίοις αὐτοῦ) and added 'and his prophets by the Spirit' (καὶ προφήταις ἐν πνεύματι) to bring this in line with the earlier statement in 2.20 where he said that gentile Christians 'had been built on the foundation of the apostles and the prophets, with Christ Jesus himself as the cornerstone' (ἐποικοδομηθέντες ἐπὶ τῷ θεμελίῳ τῶν ἀποστόλων καὶ προφητῶν, ὄντος ἀκρογωνιαίου αὐτοῦ Χριστοῦ Ἰησοῦ). The basis for their place as a foundation is now given as the revelation that they received. I take the adjective 'holy' (ἅγιοι) to refer to both the apostles and prophets since they are governed by one article and understand the final prepositional phrase 'by the Spirit' (ἐν πνεύματι) to indicate instrumentality since this is a common feature in the revelation-schema.[55] The effect that this has is to emphasize the importance of the apostles and prophets as the recipients of the revelation on which the church rests.

There is yet another twist that needs to be noted. The author of Ephesians has reversed the order of the groups from whom the mystery was hidden: in Colossians

54   On this second revelation see N. A. Dahl, *Studies in Ephesians: Introductory Questions, Text- & Edition-Critical Issues, Interpretations of Texts and Themes* (ed. D. Hellholm, V. Blombvist, and T. Rornberg; WUNT, 131; Tübingen: Mohr Siebeck, 2000), pp. 349–63.

55   So also Gnilka, *Der Epheserbrief*, p. 167; *idem*, 'Das Paulusbild im Kolosser- und Epheserbrief', p. 184; Lona, *Die Eschatologie bei Kolosser- und Epheserbrief*, pp. 285–86; Best, *Ephesians*, pp. 306–08; H. Hoehner, *Ephesians: An Exegetical Commentary* (Grand Rapids: Baker Academic, 2002), pp. 441–44. Others understand 'holy' to refer to the apostles and 'by the Spirit' to refer to the prophets, e.g., Merklein, *Das kirchliche Amt nach dem Epheserbrief*, pp. 187–88; Schnackenburg, *Ephesians*, p. 133; and apparently P. Pokorny, *Der Brief des Paulus an die Epheser* (ThHK, 10.2; Leipsig: Evangelische Verlagsanstalt, 1992), pp. 142–43, who does not make his view on 'holy' explicit. Lincoln, *Ephesians*, pp. 178–80, argues that 'his holy' refers only to the apostles, but that 'by the Spirit' modifies the verb.

the mystery was hidden 'for aeons' and 'for generations'; in Ephesians, the revelation came first to humans and then to the aeons. It is possible that the order in Ephesians was a result of the fact that the revelation in Colossians was disclosed to humans (Col. 1.26). The author of Ephesians might have followed suit and delayed the revelation to the supernatural powers. There is, however, another possibility that helps us understand both the change in order and the emphasis on the apostles.

As we noted above, the first disclosure (Eph. 3.3-6) has two phases: vv. 3-4 mention the revelation of the mystery to Paul; vv. 4-6 present the revelation to the holy apostles and prophets. The revelation to Paul does not follow the standard pattern that we observed above; it only emphasizes the revelation, not the hidden nature of the past mystery. The revelation to 'the holy apostles and prophets' has the formal contrasts that we expect to find in the literary pattern. Compare the following:

The Revelation to Paul

The Elements	The Hidden Past	The Revealed Present
Mystery		the mystery
Time		
Revelation		was made known by revelation
Group		to me
Agent		

The Revelation to the Holy Apostles and Prophets

The Elements	The Hidden Past	The Revealed Present
Mystery		
Time	in other generations	as now
Revelation	was not made known	was revealed
Group(s)	to humans	to his holy apostles and prophets
Agent		by the Spirit

The revelation to Paul (vv. 3-4) is thus the unique element and is the contribution of the author. The author probably has in mind Paul's call in Gal. 1.15-16: 'when God, who set me apart before birth and called me by his grace, was pleased to reveal his Son in me so that I would announce him among the gentiles'.[56] The revelation to preach to the gentiles was part of Paul's call. The author of Ephesians has picked up on this and accentuated the mission that came with the call (Gal. 1.16b, 'so that I would announce him among the gentiles') more than the personal encounter that Paul had with Jesus Christ (Gal. 1.16a, 'to reveal his Son in me' [ἀποκαλύψαι τὸν υἱὸν ἐν ἐμοί]). More importantly, the author has situated Paul's call before the

---

56   Cf. also Gal. 1.12 and 2.2. Paul alludes to the mission to the gentiles indirectly in 1 Cor. 15.9-11.

revelation to the apostles and prophets; this is hardly an accident.[57] I do not think that the author was confused chronologically; rather he is making a theological and ecclesiological claim. His argument is that Paul has pride of place in the revelation of God's mystery.

Why make this claim? The most likely explanation is that the author knew two different traditions about the revelation that the church included the gentiles: one was the tradition that associated the gentile mission with the apostles who were Jesus' associates (see below) and the other was the tradition that associated the gentile mission with the Apostle to the gentiles.[58] While the author of Ephesians knew both traditions, he subordinated the tradition that associated the revelation with the apostles and early Christian prophets to the tradition that associated it with Paul.

The last point that we need to consider in order to understand the sequence is the alteration in the mystery itself. As we have just noted, the author accentuated Paul's vocation in Gal. 1.16 rather than his personal experience. The same is true of his redaction of the mystery taken from Colossians: the author of Ephesians has transformed the mystery from the experience of Christ in Colossians ('Christ among you' [1.27]) to the inclusion of the gentiles. The author made the point explicit in vv. 6 and 8, especially the former ('that the gentiles may be fellow heirs, fellow members of the body, and fellow participants in the promise'). In this way, salvation history has replaced personal religious experience. It is only when God's eternal purpose became a historical reality that the cosmic powers became aware of it. The sequence now makes sense. It begins with the key recipient of God's revelation and broadens it to include the apostles and prophets. When this revelation had become a historical reality, the cosmic powers became aware of it.

The reader has a place in this schema. According to the author of Ephesians, Paul wrote the mystery down so that the readers could share in his understanding (vv. 3-4). What is meant by the reference in v. 3, 'as I wrote above in brief'? There have been a number of suggestions including an allusion to a fictional letter that Paul previously wrote to the Ephesians,[59] an introduction to the Pauline corpus as a whole,[60] a reference to a specific text such as Romans 16.25-27,[61] or, more likely, a reflection back on earlier sections in Ephesians, especially 2.11-22.[62] The author

---

57   I am thus distinguishing between Paul and the 'holy apostles and prophets'. While the author of Ephesians considered Paul to be an apostle, here he has in mind the original twelve. Cf. also Eph. 2.20 (contrast 1 Cor. 3.9-11); Rev. 21.14.

58   E. Best, 'The Revelation to Evangelize the Gentiles', *JThS NS* 35 (1984), pp. 1–31, has a helpful overview of the evidence.

59   Lindemann, *Paulus, Apostel und Lehrer der Kirche*, pp. 220–21.

60   E. J. Goodspeed, *The Meaning of Ephesians* (Chicago: University of Chicago Press, 1933), pp. 41–42, who suggested that Ephesians was an introduction to the Pauline corpus, and Mitton, *The Epistle to the Ephesians*, pp. 233–36, who qualified Goodspeed's hypothesis by suggesting that it referred only to those sections of Paul's letters that dealt with the mystery.

61   So L. Davies, 'I Wrote Afore in Few Words (Eph 3,3)', *ET* 46 (1934–1935), p. 568. He assumes that Romans 16 was added by Paul to Romans and was addressed to the Ephesians. He also assumes that Ephesians is authentic. Both of these assumptions are problematic.

62   This is the view of the majority of modern scholars, e.g., Percy, *Die Probleme der*

apparently thought that his interpretation of the Pauline tradition in this text was part of the revelation vouchsafed to Paul. This is an important hint for understanding the occasion of the letter (see under conclusions).

b. Acts

The portrait in Acts has some of the same dynamic tensions that we have just seen, but reaches different solutions for them. Luke gave pride of place for the gentile mission to Peter. He made the Cornelius story a major unit within the narrative by devoting more space to it than any other narrative[63] and by relating it three times,[64] one of only two episodes to receive such attention.[65] The other event that received the same level of attention is the conversion/call of Paul.[66] The two events have one thing in common: they both deal with the mission to the gentiles. The author goes out of his way to emphasize the importance of this mission.[67]

The question that intrigues me is why Luke chose to situate the conversion of Paul prior to Peter's mission to Cornelius. The two narratives are among the five major narratives in the central part of Acts (8.4–12.25) that radiate out from the persecution that culminated in the death of Stephen (6.1–8.3). Each of the major narratives is anchored in the Stephen episode in some way: the ministry of Philip, who was one of the seven;[68] the conversion of Paul, who was one of the persecutors;[69] the activities of Peter, who moved beyond Jerusalem as others began preaching in the surrounding communities;[70] the mission in Antioch led by those who fled the persecution;[71] and the death of James and arrest of Peter, a second example of martyrdom that forms an *inclusio* with the Stephen episode.[72]

These narratives serve as a bridge between the development of Christianity in Jerusalem (1.3–8.3) and the expansion of Christianity to the ends of the earth (13.1–28.31). The author makes the transitional nature of these chapters evident by echoing the language of Acts 1.8 ('you will be my witnesses both in Jerusalem,

---

Kolosser- und Epheserbrief, p. 350; Gnilka, *Der Epheserbrief*, p. 164; Merklein, *Das kirchliche Amt nach dem Epheserbrief*, pp. 215–17; C. Caragounis, *The Ephesian Mysterion: Meaning and Content* (CB.NT, 8; Lund: G. C. K. Gleerup, 1977), pp. 99–100; Lincoln, *Ephesians*, p. 174; Schnackenburg, *Ephesians*, p. 132; Best, *Ephesians*, pp. 302–03; and Hoehner, *Ephesians*, pp. 427–28.

63   Acts 10.1–11.18 has sixty-six verses, more than any other single narrative in Acts. On this see E. M. Humphrey, 'Collision of Modes?–Vision and Determining Argument in Acts 10:1-11:18', *Semeia* 71 (1995), pp. 65–84 and Pervo, *Acts*, p. 264.

64   Acts 10.1-48; 11.1-18; 15.7-11.

65   Luke does repeat some items three times, e.g., there are three prison liberations (5.19-20; 12.6-12; 16.25-40); however, these are three separate incidents rather than repetitions of the same event.

66   Acts 9.1-19a; 22.1-21; 26.1-23, esp. 12-18.

67   So also Haenchen, *The Acts of the Apostles*, pp. 327–28; Schneider, *Die Apostelgeschichte*, 2.22-23.

68   Acts 6.5 and 8.5-40.

69   Acts 7.58; 8.1-3 and 9.1-30; 11.25-30; and 12.24-25.

70   Acts 8.1 and 9.32–11.18.

71   Acts 8.1-3 and 11.19-26.

72   Acts 7.54-60 and 12.1-23.

and in all of Judea and Samaria, and to the ends of the earth') at key junctures: 8.1 repeats 'Judea and Samaria' and 13.47 echoes 'the ends of the earth'. The chapters open with the move away from Jerusalem and conclude before Paul begins his mission. They explain how Christianity moved from an exclusively Jewish base in Jerusalem to a predominately gentile base that culminated in Paul's arrival in Rome. The speech of Stephen sets up this section by arguing that God is not confined to the temple, but has always dealt with people away from Jerusalem. This is why the speech relates events in the LXX that are outside of *Eretz Israel* and Jerusalem in particular. Stephen's speech is thus the theological justification for the movement away from Jerusalem.[73]

The question is why did the author arrange the five narratives that radiate out from Stephen's death in the present sequence? The first four narratives are not presented in strict chronological order by the author, but as independent episodes that sprang from a common beginning.[74] The clearest evidence of this is the statement in Acts 11.19 that recalls 8.4. It is not clear whether the founding of the community in Antioch (11.19-26) preceded, followed, or occurred at roughly the same time as Philip's mission among the Samaritans and conversion of the Ethiopian eunuch (8.4-40) or the founding of the community in Caesarea (10.1–11.18). The most that we can say historically is that a mixed community of Jews and gentiles developed in Caesarea and Antioch. It may well be that our two accounts rest on local traditions. This leads us to ask why the narrator has situated the conversion of Paul where it is.

It is not clear that it belongs here historically;[75] there are, however, several reasons why the author might have placed it here. Hans Conzelmann captured the most obvious reason in his inimitably succinct way: 'Before the first conversion of a Gentile the agent for the great mission to the Gentiles is prepared, whereby once again the meaning of both the preceding and the following episodes is clarified.'[76] The preceding episode is explained by virtue of the fact that the gospel will now go 'to the ends of the earth'. The following episode is explained in several ways. The first step was for Paul to return to Jerusalem where Luke has Barnabas introduce him to the apostles – this before Peter went to Caesarea.[77] Luke says: 'he was with them, going in and out of Jerusalem boldly preaching in the name of Jesus' (9.28).

---

73   See G. E. Sterling in the first volume of this series, '"Opening the Scriptures": The Legitimation of the Jewish Diaspora and the Early Christian Mission', in *Jesus and the Heritage of Israel* (vol. 1 Luke the Interpreter of Israel; ed. D. P. Moessner; Harrisburg, Pa.: Trinity Press International, 1999), pp. 199–225.

74   Acts 8.1-3 relates the persecution that sent Philip away from Jerusalem. Acts 9.1 returns to Paul's persecution in 8.3. Peter's movements in 9.32–11.18 appear to extend from his trip to Samaria in 8.14-25 which is a direct result of the persecution. Acts 11.19-26 explicitly links the establishment of the church in Antioch with the persecution in 8.1-3.

75   For some of the historical difficulties about the sequence of Paul's movements in these chapters of Acts see K. Lake, 'The Conversion of Paul and the Events Immediately Following It', in *The Beginnings of Christianity* (ed. F. J. Foakes Jackson and K. Lake; 5 vols.; reprint, Grand Rapids: Baker, 1979), 5:188–95.

76   Conzelmann, *Acts of the Apostles*, p. 71.

77   Acts 9.26-30.

The image of Paul mixing freely with the apostles put their seal of approval on him. This is the last time in Acts that the apostles appear as the sole authorities in Jerusalem. James and the elders come to prominence after this. In this final scene of the apostles as the exclusive authority, Paul is placed alongside them.[78] As Andreas Lindemann put it: 'In Acts it is certainly correct that in Jerusalem Paul is not acknowledged as one of the apostles; but neither is he subordinated to them.'[79] It is only after this has been established that Luke narrated the conversion of Cornelius. He thus does not deny the pride of place to Peter as the first to convert a gentile, but makes sure that the *missionnaire extraordinaire* is in place before this conversion takes place.

This suggests that Acts draws the same basic portrait of Paul as Ephesians. There are, however, some important differences. We have already seen that Ephesians did not distinguish between Paul's call to be an apostle and the revelation that he was to preach to the gentiles.[80] The relationship is not as tightly bound in Acts where the relationship between Paul's conversion and call differs in the three accounts: in chapter nine, the Lord did not disclose his mission to Paul but to Ananias who, presumably, relayed it to Paul;[81] in chapter twenty-two, the Lord disclosed his mission to him in a vision in the temple after he returned to Jerusalem;[82] whereas in chapter twenty-six, the Lord disclosed his mission to him during his call.[83] Whether these are the result of different sources or different emphases that spring from the specific contexts, they indicate that Luke did not always associate Paul's vocation with his call. In fact it is only in Acts 26 where this takes place.[84]

There is another important and related difference. As we suggested above, the author of Acts wanted to mould the traditions into a unified stream, a desire that led to some tensions with the Pauline tradition. The most famous case is the number of visits Paul made to Jerusalem. The following chart sets out the visits that Paul made to Jerusalem according to his own statements and the visits that he made according to Acts.

Occasion	Paul	Acts
Education		22.3
Persecutor		7.58; 8.3; 9.1-2
Ministry after conversion	Gal. 1.18-19	9.26-29; 22.17-21; 26.20
Famine Relief fund from Antioch		11.30; 12.25
Jerusalem Conference	Gal. 2.1-10	18.22; 15.1-29
Delivery of Collection	Rom. 15.25	21.15

---

78   See the helpful comments of Haenchen, *Acts of the Apostles*, p. 336.

79   Lindemann, *Paulus im ältesten Christentum*, pp. 66–67.

80   See Eph. 3.6-7 and 8.

81   Acts 9.15-16.

82   Acts 22.17-21.

83   Acts 26.15-19.

84   There is a large bibliography on these three narratives. For a recent summary of the scholarly discussion see J. B. Miller, *Convinced That God Had Called Us: Dreams, Visions, and the Perception of God's Will in Luke-Acts* (BIS, 85; Leiden: E. J. Brill, 2007), pp. 186–202.

Luke has Paul in Jerusalem more frequently than the letters of Paul suggest: Paul is educated in Jerusalem, resident in Jerusalem during the early days of the church, and brought the famine-relief fund from Antioch to Jerusalem. Without debating the historicity of these events, it is safe to say that while Paul minimized his relationship to Jerusalem, Luke maximized it. Luke's effort to situate Paul in Jerusalem is a result of his effort to harmonize paradoxical events. On the one hand, Paul was nurtured in Jerusalem and consistently returned to it in a show of solidarity; on the other hand the decisive events of his life occurred away from it suggesting that he was not defined by Jerusalem. Further, he was called before the gentile mission began and it was his mission to the gentiles that served as the catalyst for the Jerusalem council. There is a sense in which the council was an attempt to come to terms with the Pauline mission. At the same time, the council ensured harmony between the mission and the Jerusalem church, a harmony that Paul accepted.

Can this pattern be situated within a larger framework? Luke understood Christianity in terms of a succession that began with Jesus, continued through the twelve apostles, and reached an apex in Paul. The succession scheme is clear enough that Charles Talbert made a case that the two-volume work was modelled on the pattern of successive biography that was prominent in philosophical schools.[85] For example, Sotion, an Alexandrian Peripatetic, wrote a thirteen volume *Succession of the Philosophers* (Διαδοχὴ τῶν φιλοσόφων). Diogenes Laertius provides a better-known example of this type of work. While the difference between the full narratives of Luke and of Acts rather than the simple pattern of lists of who studied with whom make me sceptical that Luke-Acts belongs to the biographical tradition, Talbert is correct in recognizing the use of the succession pattern. He was by no means the first to recognize this pattern. It is not an accident that Irenaeus rescued Acts from the oblivion of the second century and assigned it an important position in his reconstruction of Christian origins.[86] The bishop of Lyons argued that the rule of faith came from the apostles to the bishops who were their successors. This put a premium on the fourfold Gospel (as he understood it) and Acts. He wrote about those who used Luke but refused to recognize Paul: 'they should either reject the other words of the Gospel which we have come to know through Luke alone, and not make use of them; or else, if they do receive all these, they must necessarily admit also that testimony concerning Paul…'.[87] He added a strong statement about Acts: 'It may be, indeed, that it was with this view that God set forth very many Gospel truths, through Luke's instrumentality, which all should esteem it necessary to use in order that all persons, following his subsequent testimony which treats upon the acts and doctrine of the apostles, and holding the unadulterated rule of truth, may

---

85   C. H. Talbert, *Literary Patterns, Theological Themes and the Genre of Luke-Acts* (SBLMS, 20; Missoula, Montana: Scholars Press, 1974), and *idem*, *Reading Luke-Acts: A Literary and Theological Commentary on the Third Gospel* (New York: Crossroad, 1982), pp. 2–6.

86   See the excellent treatment of Mount, *Pauline Christianity*, pp. 11–58, esp. 11–44. He summarized his reading of Irenaeus in these words: 'The narrative of Acts, read by Irenaeus as an account of the origin of a unified apostolic tradition, demonstrates that from the beginning all the apostles preached the same Gospel and thus support Irenaeus' claim for the unity and perfection of his fourfold gospel canon alongside the gospel preached by Paul in his letters.'

87   Irenaeus, *Adv. haer.* 3.15.1.

be saved.'[88] Eusebius of Caesarea later used the same scheme, only in a more direct and expansive capacity in the *Historia ecclesiastica*.[89] In Luke's scheme, Paul is the final figure in the succession. The apostles served as a bridge between Jesus, the founder of Christianity, and Paul, the architect and contractor who built the church.

III. The Definitive Voice

a. Ephesians

This leads to the third and final text in Ephesians that presents the implied author, the postscript. It is closely modelled on a parallel text in Colossians, although unsurprisingly goes its own way. I have set the two out in a synopsis and placed the identical words in bold.

Colossians 4.7-18	Ephesians 6.21-24
	[21]So that you also may know
[7]As for **my circumstances,**	**my circumstances**
	and what I am doing
Tychicus, the beloved brother	**Tychicus, the beloved brother**
and faithful minister	**and faithful minister**
and fellow servant	
in the Lord,	**in the Lord,**
will make everything known to you.	**will make everything known to you.**
[8]**I sent him to you for this reason**	[22]**I sent him to you for this reason**
so that you may know	**so that you may know**
our circumstances,	**our circumstances,**
and he may encourage your hearts,	**and he may encourage your hearts.**
[9]along with Onesimus,	
the faithful and beloved brother,	
who is one of you.	
They will make	
all the circumstances here known to you.	
[10]Aristarchus, my fellow prisoner,	
sends his greetings,	
as does Mark, Barnabas' cousin–	
concerning whom	
you have received directions:	
if he comes to you,	
welcome him–	

---

88   Irenaeus, *Adv. haer.* 3.15.1.

89   He announced it as one of his major themes in *Hist. eccl.* 1.1 and repeated it in 1.4. Eusebius worked largely with episcopal succession, much in the same way that Irenaeus conceived of it (*Adv. haer.* 3.3.1), except that the Caesarean emphasized the most important Eastern churches rather than Rome.

[11]and Jesus who is known as Justus.	
These are the only ones	
from the circumcised	
who are my fellow workers	
for the kingdom of God,	
as such they have been	
an encouragement to me.	
[12]Epaphras sends his greetings,	
who is one of you,	
a servant of Christ [Jesus]	
who is always contending on your behalf	
in his prayers	
so that you may stand perfect	
and fully assured	
in all of God's will.	
[13]For I testify	
that he has worked hard	
on behalf of you,	
those in Laodicea,	
and those in Hierapolis.	
[14]Luke, the beloved doctor,	
sends his greetings	
and Demas.	
[15]Greet	
those in Laodicea,	
Nymphas,	
and the church in her house.	
[16]When this letter is read	
in your presence	
make arrangements	
so that it is read	
in the church in Laodicea	
and that you also read	
the letter from Laodicea.	
[17]Tell Archippus:	
'Pay attention to your ministry	
that you received in the Lord	
to fulfill it.'	
[18]The greeting is mine,	
with my own hand.	
Remember my bonds.	
	[23]Peace to the brothers and sisters
	and love with faith
	from God the father

	and the Lord Jesus Christ.
May grace be with you.	[24]**May grace be with** all
	who love our Lord Jesus Christ
	without fail.

There are several notable features about this closing statement. First, there is significant verbal agreement between Colossians and Ephesians, enough verbal agreement to require – in my opinion – that we consider the literary dependence of Ephesians on Colossians as certain.[90] Second, Ephesians has omitted all of the greetings in Colossians. This has the same impact that the omission of a co-sender had at the beginning of the letter: it places the focus entirely on Paul. While this may be due – in part – to the nature of the letter as a treatise rather than a genuine letter, the effect on the image of Paul should not be missed: it projects an exclusive relationship between Paul and the reader. Finally, Ephesians expanded the simple grace benediction of Colossians by combining a peace wish[91] and a fuller grace benediction,[92] standard features of Pauline and Deutero-Pauline letters. The author kept them in their standard sequence: the peace wish, when it appears, always precedes the grace benediction.[93]

The simplicity and brevity of the postscript to Ephesians is noteworthy. It maintains some of the standard features of the Pauline epistolary tradition. The reference to Tychicus, via Colossians, provides a touch of verisimilitude.[94] The absence of any travel plans points to the reality that readers can not expect to interact with a living Paul in the future; Paul must be mediated through the reading of his letters. Paul is therefore not a personal presence, but a voice offering an understanding of the church at the end of the first century.[95]

b. Acts

Acts also has a brief, even abrupt ending: 'He lived for two full years in his own rented residence. He received all who came to him, proclaiming the kingdom of God and teaching about the Lord Jesus Christ with all boldness and without

---

90   Best, 'Who used Whom?', pp. 77–79, challenges the standard view that the author of Ephesians used Colossians.

91   The following Pauline letters have peace wishes: 1 Thess. 5.23; Gal. 6.16; Phil. 4.9; 2 Cor. 13.11b; Rom. 15.33. Only 1 Cor. and Phlm. lack a peace wish. The following Deutero-Pauline letters have peace wishes: 2 Thess. 3.16 and Eph. 6.23. Colossians and the Pastorals lack a peace wish.

92   All Pauline letters have grace benedictions: 1 Thess. 5.28; Gal. 6.18; 1 Cor. 16.23-24; Phil. 4.23; Phlm. 25; 2 Cor. 13.13; Rom. 16.20. The same is true for the Deutero-Pauline letters: 2 Thess. 3.18; Col. 4.18; Eph. 6.24; 1 Tim. 6.21; Tit. 3.15; 2 Tim. 4.22.

93   1 Thess. 5.23, 28; Gal. 6.16, 18; Phil. 4.9, 23; 2 Cor. 13.11b, 13; Rom. 15.33; 16.20. Cf. also 2 Thess. 3.16, 18 in the Deutero-Pauline tradition.

94   W. L. Knox suggested that this was a veiled reference to Tychicus as the author. C. L. Mitton suggested that Tychicus was an old man who was known to both the author and the community and that he gave his blessing to the writing of Ephesians in Paul's name (*The Epistle to the Ephesians*, pp. 268–69).

95   So also Gnilka, *Der Epheserbrief*, p. 320 and Lincoln, *Ephesians*, p. 464.

interference.'[96] Several questions remain open for readers. Why did not Luke narrate Paul's death? What happened to the Jewish community in Rome? Was there a permanent rupture? How can we make sense of the image of Paul when his end is left open? The openness is not an accident, it is deliberate. The author has indicated that Paul would die in Rome,[97] but has chosen not to narrate the event. Instead he has told us how long he lived there preaching: two years. The life of Paul is over but his preaching or mission is not: it lives on in the church that he helped to create. In this way, the author has maintained the same portrait that dominated the narrative from chapter thirteen onwards, a battered Paul fearlessly proclaiming the kingdom. It is also the same image that we have in Ephesians. In both texts, Paul is a prisoner who continues to preach: in Ephesians through the written word and in Acts through oral proclamation. The point in both texts, however, is the same: the attempt to silence the voice of Paul has only kept it alive. It is his vision of the church that we should embrace (Ephesians) or his mission that we should imitate (Acts).

IV. Conclusions

We began by suggesting that there is a relationship between the image of Paul in the pseudepigraphon that we know as Ephesians and the occasion of the letter. It is time to return to that suggestion as we consider the nature of the two portraits. The basic image of Paul in Ephesians is shaped by the revelation that he received and the letter that he allegedly wrote. While the author is aware of Paul's career, it is not the activities of Paul that interest him but the Apostle's thought. This is why he gives Paul pride of place in terms of the revelation and why in both chapters three and six he suggests to the readers that our access to Paul is through his letters. This agrees with the nature of Ephesians itself. Ephesians is largely an interpretation of letters in the Pauline tradition.[98] The interpretation is fresh and creative; as we noted earlier, the author considered it part of the revelation. How does Ephesians' recasting of Pauline letters align with the image of Paul as the recipient of revelation and letter writer?

I suggest that the author reflected on the church at the end of the first century. The church as he knew it was largely Pauline. There was, however, something different about the church as the author knew it and the churches that Paul established and nourished. By the time of the author, the Jewish-Gentile controversy was largely over.[99] Paul had defeated his opponents, even

---

96   Acts 28.30-31. The best treatment of the ending of Acts in my judgement is D. Marguerat, 'The Enigma of the Silent Closing of Acts (28:16-31)', in *Jesus and the Heritage of Israel*, pp. 284–304, esp. 302–04.

97   See Acts 20.38; 21.11.

98   The two most helpful treatments are Mitton, *The Epistle to the Ephesians*, pp. 55–158 and Gese, *Das Vermächtnis des Apostels*, pp. 39–85.

99   For a survey of work on this issue with a fresh take that suggests that Eph. 2.11-22 should be read against the background of Jewish perspectives on ethnic reconciliation see T. L. N. Yee, *Jews, Gentile and Ethnic Reconciliation: Paul's Jewish Identity and Ephesians* (SNTSMS, 130; Cambridge: Cambridge University Press, 2005).

if those who sided with him did not fully understand him. The author was aware of the nature of Paul's letters: they were occasional missives to local communities for specific reasons. The question that the author of Ephesians asked was what would a Pauline theology look like that addressed the whole church that Paul helped to create? Ephesians is the answer. It is an attempt to reflect on Paul's thought and that of some of his disciples in an effort to offer an understanding of the one church. Paul is no longer the Apostle to the gentiles, he is the Apostle to the Church. He may have been 'the least of all the saints' at one time, but now he is the preeminent vessel to whom God granted the revelation of the unified church. Ephesians is both a celebration of Paul's accomplishments and thought as well as an authoritative statement that should help the church understand its past and present. It is in this sense that Paul's life is presented as a *vita contemplativa*.

Acts is far less cerebral. Like Ephesians, Acts recognizes that Paul was the defining point. The author had Paul say in his speech to the elders of Ephesus: 'I know that after my departure, savage wolves will come to you and not spare the flock ...'[100] In spite of the awareness that heresy lay beyond Paul, the author did not develop a theology in the way that the author of Ephesians did. Unlike the author of Ephesians who knew a significant number of Paul's letters, it is not clear that the author of Acts knew them, at least Acts does not contain convincing traces of them.[101] Acts gave its readers a hero rather than a theologian. The life of Paul was a *vita activa*. Like Ephesians, the author of Acts did recognize that God gave Paul this ministry to the gentiles, a ministry of grace for which he was willing to give his life.[102] In this way Acts is a narrative parallel to the theological construct of Ephesians.[103]

Together the two portraits form a striking pair: one accentuated Paul's career and the other his thought. Both regarded Paul as a pivotal figure. While the images that they gave of Paul did not match the image that Baur gave centuries later, they anticipated his recognition of Paul's importance by eighteen centuries.

---

100   Acts 2.29.

101   J. Knox, 'Acts and the Pauline Letter Corpus', in *Studies in Luke-Acts*, pp. 279–87, argued that Luke deliberately omitted any reference to Paul's letters because of their use by the Marcionites, a view that assumes a date that is too late for Acts in my judgement. For a recent attempt to work through the evidence see D. Wenham, 'Acts and the Pauline Corpus. II. The Evidence of the Parallels', in: *The Book of Acts in its First Century Setting, Volume 1: The Book of Acts in Its Ancient Literary Setting* (ed. B. W. Winter and A. D. Clarke; Grand Rapids: Eerdmans, 1993), pp. 215–58.

102   Compare Acts 20.24 and Eph. 3.2, 7.

103   Compare the formulation of Käsemann, 'Ephesians and Acts', p. 292: 'According to (Eph) 2:20 the apostles function as the foundation of a unified Christianity, whose truth and rightness in turn are demonstrated by referring to these witnesses. The whole portrait of Acts is nothing less than the visualization of such theologoumena in narrative form.'

Appendix 1

The Revelation of the Mystery

1 Corinthians 2.7-10	Colossians 1.26	Ephesians 3.4-6	Ephesians 3.9-10	Romans 16.25-27
[7]But we speak God's wisdom			[9]and to bring to light	[25]To the one who is able
			[for everyone]	to strengthen you
				according to my gospel
				and the preaching of Jesus Christ
			the administration	according to the revelation
in a mystery,	[26]the mystery	In the mystery of Christ	of the mystery	of the mystery
		[5]that in other generations		that for long aeons
a wisdom that is hidden	that was hidden	was not made known	that was hidden	was kept secret,
that God foreordained				
before the aeons				
for our glory				
[8]None of the rulers				
of this aeon have known it.	for aeons		from the aeons	
			in God who created everything,	
For had they known,				
They would not have crucified				
The Lord of glory.				
[9]But as it is written,				
'What eye has not seen	and for generations,	to human beings,		
and ear has not heard				
and what has not entered				
a human heart',				
these things God prepared				
for those who love him,				

Corinthians 2.7-10	Colossians 1.26	Ephesians 3.4-6	Ephesians 3.9-10	Romans 16.25-27
to us God revealed em	but has now been disclosed	as it has now been revealed	[10] so that it may now be known	[26]but has now been disclosed,
	to his holy ones ...	to his holy apostles	to the rulers and authorities	
		and prophets		
			in the heavenly places	
hrough		by	through	and through
he Spirit;		the Spirit:	the church,	the prophetic writings
or the Spirit searches verything,				
ven the deep things f God.				
		[6]that the gentiles	namely the richly diverse	
		may be fellow heirs,	wisdom of God ...	
		fellow members of the body,		
		and fellow participants		
		in the promise		
		in Christ Jesus		
		through the gospel ...		
				has been made known
				to the gentiles
				according to the command
				of the eternal God
				for the obedience of faith–
				[27]to the only wise God
				through Jesus Christ,
				to whom be the glory forever,
				Amen.

Chapter 13

AUCTORITAS PAULI ACCORDING TO THE DEUTERO-PAULINE LITERATURE AND THE ACTS OF THE APOSTLES

Andreas Dettwiler
Trans. Eric Gilchrest and Nicholas J. Zola

I. By Way of Introduction: Presuppositions and Approach

In studying the Deutero-Pauline literature, the astute reader quickly realizes that the issue of authority is fundamental to understanding these texts. Deutero-Pauline writings utilize a range of strategies for assigning authority that function not only to clarify Paul's role, but also to legitimize the author's own approach. It will be expedient to consider the historical and hermeneutical issues involved with the literary device of pseudepigraphy. Accordingly it will be helpful to adopt the question of authority as the key to reading these texts.

The authoritative dimension remains in large part beneath the different post-apostolic images of Paul and yet is highly determinative of them. More specifically, our approach will be as follows: in each section we will begin with the epistolary reception of Paul, focusing on Colossians and Ephesians, in order to put this 'backbone' of the Pauline school[1] into dialogue with the Lukan image of Paul. Needless to say, this approach is not intended to summon Luke[2] before the court of Colossians and Ephesians, a constellation of texts which, a few decades ago, would have signalled the worst for the 'Paulinism' of Luke. Fortunately, we are now beyond this kind of theological interrogation.[3] It is also needless to mention that the chosen approach is not in any way striving toward a harmonized or unified

---

1   On the subject of the hypothesis of one or more 'Pauline schools', cf. among others P. Müller, *Anfänge der Paulusschule. Dargestellt am zweiten Thessalonicherbrief und am Kolosserbrief* (ATANT, 74; Zürich: TVZ, 1988); T. Schmeller, *Schulen im Neuen Testament? Zur Stellung des Urchristentums in der Bildungswelt seiner Zeit. Mit einem Beitrag von Christian Cebuli zur johanneischen Schule* (HBS, 30; Freiburg: Herder, 2001); A. Dettwiler, 'L'école paulinienne: évaluation d'une hypothèse', in *Paul, une théologie en construction* (ed. A. Dettwiler, J.-D. Kaestli, and D. Marguerat; MdB, 51; Genève: Labor et Fides, 2004), pp. 419–40.

2   Here and throughout we are using the term 'Luke' conventionally to designate the author of the work *ad Theophilum* without expressing an opinion on the historical identity of the author.

3   Cf. rightly K. Löning, 'Paulinismus in der Apostelgeschichte', in *Paulus in den neutestamentlichen Spätschriften: Zur Paulusrezeption im Neuen Testament* (ed. K. Kertelge; QD, 89; Freiburg: Herder, 1981), pp. 202–34 (209, 219).

perception of the post-apostolic image of Paul. The fact that we are dealing here with two starkly different types of reception – epistolary, on the one hand, and historiographic, on the other – already calls for prudence and nuance. Finally, it is hardly also necessary to point out that our approach is experimental and that we have no intention of capturing the phenomenon in all of its complexity. Jürgen Roloff, a seasoned Lukan scholar, wrote the following words some thirty years ago: 'The Lukan portrait of Paul is certainly a very complex phenomenon, and it is expected that any treatment of the subject will only perceive a part of the references and associations interwoven within.'[4] Our work is no exception, even more so because our contribution will focus primarily on the Deutero-Pauline literature and will have a highly synthetic orientation.

II. Pauline Authority in the Epistolary and Historiographical Receptions of the New Testament – A Phenomenological Approach

a. An Uncontested Authority

It is striking to see how Colossians and Ephesians describe Paul as an uncontested authority. Compared to the undisputed Pauline literature – particularly the Corinthian and Galatian correspondences – which exhibit a Paul who is almost constantly concerned with intensely and controversially reasserting his apostolic authority, the Deutero-Pauline writings convey the image of an uncontested Paul. The first clue: Colossians and Ephesians use the title of apostle (Col. 1.1, and again, in the same way, Eph. 1.1: Παῦλος ἀπόστολος Χριστοῦ Ἰησοῦ διὰ θελήματος θεοῦ κτλ.) without any intention of polemical demarcation. The second clue: clearly the two epistolary self-commendations of Colossians (1.24–2.5) and Ephesians (3.1-13) – foundational texts for the construction of Paul's image in these two letters[5] – have the general pragmatic function of rendering the author present among the recipient community, by demonstrating his irreproachable *ethos*. However, a detailed analysis shows that these two key passages have no real biographical aim. Therefore, the Paul of Colossians, and even more noticeably the Paul of Ephesians, seems to have become a figure detached from any historical contingency or individuality. These letters are not concerned with Paul's

---

4   J. Roloff, 'Die Paulus-Darstellung des Lukas. Ihre geschichtlichen Voraussetzungen und ihr theologisches Ziel', *EvTh* 39 (1979), pp. 510–31 (516).

5   For the literary genre of 'authorial self-commendation' or 'epistolary self-presentation' see the study by F. Schnider and W. Stenger, *Studien zum Neutestamentlichen Briefformular* (NTTS, 11; Leiden: Brill, 1987), pp. 50–68; the authors speak of 'briefliche Selbstempfehlung', while M. Wolter, *Der Brief an die Kolosser. Der Brief an Philemon* (ÖTBK, 12; Gütersloh and Würzburg: Gütersloher Verlag and Echter Verlag, 1993), pp. 98–99, prefers the term 'briefliche Selbstvorstellung'. K. Berger, 'Hellenistische Gattungen im Neuen Testament', in *ANRW* II/25.2 (1984), pp. 1031–1432 and 1831–85 (1353–54); and *idem, Formgeschichte des Neuen Testaments* (Heidelberg: Quelle und Meyer, 1984), p. 268, speaks of 'Apostolikon', defining it as follows: '[…] epistolary self-introduction of the apostle, to which belongs not only his *name*, but also the *description of his function*, a short report of his *message* and his *self-understanding*'. The terminological nuances are negligible.

psychological or historical individuality, but his function or, if one prefers, his theological work in the revelation of the 'mystery' (μυστήριον) on behalf of the world. We can speak here of a kind of 'iconization' of the figure of Paul, without necessarily confusing it with the process of 'legendarization'. Michael Gese has convincingly shown that the image of Paul in Ephesians resists either 'heroization' or 'legendarization', and thus also resists the utilization of Paul as a simple figure with whom to identify (whether ethical or otherwise).[6]

A few brief remarks should suffice to illustrate this point. The limited biographical information, imported from undisputed Pauline writings, are dissociated from the person of Paul and accentuated in a new way: the *imitatio Pauli* – a *topos* already well known in the undisputed Pauline letters (cf., for example, 1 Cor. 4.16; 11.1; Gal. 4.12; Phil. 3.17)[7] – is transformed into the *imitatio Dei* (Eph. 5.1, Γίνεσθε οὖν μιμηταὶ τοῦ θεοῦ ὡς τέκνα ἀγαπητά); believers are no longer 'children' of Paul (cf. 1 Cor. 4.14) but of God (Eph. 5.1); the Pauline self-designation 'slave of Christ' is generalized and applied to all believers (δοῦλοι Χριστοῦ, Eph. 6.6). Finally, we note that Paul certainly remains a 'prisoner of Christ' (ἐγὼ Παῦλος ὁ δέσμιος τοῦ Χριστοῦ, Eph. 3.1; cf. 3.13; 6.20), but the description of his suffering – even considering the Colossian description – remains strangely faint and discreet. Other characteristics supplement this perception.

The next element that should be mentioned here concerns the historical situation presupposed or constructed by the letters of Colossians and Ephesians. Where and in what sense does an apologetic or polemical dimension appear? The case of Colossians is instructive, precisely because we can identify a rhetoric that is selectively polemical (for the first time in Col. 2.4, then in 2.16-23). What is striking is that the authority of Paul is in no way questioned or subjected to apologetics but is used without hesitation to immunize the recipient community against an alternative religious movement – the famous 'Colossian philosophy' – which the author of Colossians disqualifies as anachronistic in light of the absolute and liberating supremacy of the exalted Christ. In this line of argumentation, the Christ Hymn of Col. 1.15-20 – a text belonging to the introductory part of the letter and thus reflecting the belief system of the recipient community – plays a crucial role.[8] Ephesians, for its part, once again goes even further. The difficulties in identifying a concrete historical situation which this writing might be addressing or clarifying

6   M. Gese, *Das Vermächtnis des Apostels. Die Rezeption der paulinischen Theologie im Epheserbrief* (WUNT, 2/99; Tübingen: Mohr Siebeck, 1997), pp. 240–49. According to Gese, the entire emphasis in the Ephesian description of Paul is on his understanding, deemed unique, of the 'mystery' of salvation, while he as a person is described with 'discretion': 'If Paul's task is particularly portrayed, one notes a *clear reluctance* to associate sayings to the person of Paul' (p. 241, emphasis mine).

7   On this subject, see in French, for example, P. Nicolet, 'Le concept d'imitation de l'apôtre dans la correspondance paulinienne', in *Paul, une théologie en construction* (ed. A. Dettwiler, J.-D. Kaestli, and D. Marguerat; MdB, 51; Genève: Labor et Fides, 2004), pp. 393–415.

8   In this regard, cf. A. Dettwiler, 'Démystification céleste. La fonction argumentative de l'hymne au Christ (Col 1,15-20) dans la lettre aux Colossiens', in *Les hymnes du Nouveau Testament et leurs fonctions* (ed. D. Gerber and P. Keith; XXIIᵉ congrès de l'ACFEB [Strasbourg 2007]; LD; Paris: Cerf, 2009), pp. 325–40.

are well known. First, the original recipients of Ephesians remain in the shadows of history since the localizing phrase ἐν Ἐφέσῳ in the *adscriptio* of Eph. 1.1 is absent in the oldest and most reliable manuscripts. Second, the relationship between 'Paul' and the recipients is reduced to a bare minimum, as demonstrated by reading the final exhortations and salutation (Eph. 6.10-24) and comparing them with those in Colossians (Col. 4.2-18). Finally, the *auctor ad Ephesios* does not seem to have made any effort to create a strong and convincing 'pseudepigraphical situation'.[9] To borrow a delightful observation from Rainer Kampling: we are dealing here with a pseudepigraphy that lacks real pseudepigraphical elements![10]

Kampling makes the following assessment: 'Ephesians is undoubtedly a post-Pauline letter, but one that takes little account of the methods of pseudepigraphy. It neither constructs an inner-textual situation out of which the letter is to have emerged, nor does it provide any evidence of extra-textual events that might clarify, at least partially, its delayed publication.'[11] Taking up an idea from Michael Wolter,[12] Kampling prefers to speak of 'symbolic pseudonymity'.[13] The primary intention, therefore, does not lie in a concern to 'hide' behind the name of the apostle or to impose upon the recipient community a particular theology by usurping another's authority, but in the obligation to update Pauline theology for a new historical context. The mention of the apostle Paul would then serve the primary function of indicating the place from which the author of Ephesians constructs his theology (his point of reference) as well as providing the criteria for judging the letter's theology.[14]

Rather than stumbling against the historical indeterminacy of Ephesians, exegetes would do better to take seriously this intentional feature of Ephesians and to interpret it. Clearly Ephesians remains in continuity with the thought-world of its older sister (Colossians) while at the same time accomplishing the 'iconization' of the figure of Paul.

What about the Lukan figure of Paul on this subject? It seems that the models that read Luke's Paul as a polemical figure are not very compelling. Several contributions have shown that the Lukan affirmation of Paul's authority – or, conversely, its alleged relativism – is not based on an interest in polemical demarcation.[15] The

---

9   Very well demonstrated by R. Kampling, 'Innewerden des Mysteriums. Theologie als *traditio apostolica* im Epheserbrief', in *Christologie in der Paulus-Schule. Zur Rezeptionsgeschichte des paulinischen Evangeliums* (ed. K. Scholtissek; SBS, 181; Stuttgart: Katholisches Bibelwerk, 2000), pp. 104–23 (108–16).

10   Kampling, 'Innewerden des Mysteriums', p. 110 (formulated as a question).

11   Ibid., p. 112.

12   M. Wolter, 'Pseudonymität II', in *TRE* 27 (1997), pp. 662–70 (663).

13   Kampling, 'Innewerden des Mysteriums', pp. 112–14.

14   Ibid., p. 113: 'In fact, mentioning the apostle Paul is a commitment to the realization of his theology in a new time, identification of the point of reference for the theology of the author of Ephesians, and a criterion for the evaluation of this theology.'

15   Cf., among others, C. Burchard, *Der dreizehnte Zeuge. Traditions- und kompositionsgeschichtliche Untersuchungen zu Lukas' Darstellung der Frühzeit des Paulus* (FRLANT, 103; Göttingen: Vandenhoeck & Ruprecht, 1970). As shown in the programmatic and original designation of the 'thirteenth witness', Burchard places Paul on the same level as the Twelve in his central function as witness. See, for example, the following citation: 'In principle, Luke's intent is not

critical question concerning this issue is, rightly understood, the Lukan conception of the apostolate. The fact that the author of Acts does not use, with two exceptions, the title of *apostle* for Paul in no way implies a relativization of Paul's role in the irresistible expansion of God's Word 'to the ends of the earth' (Acts 1.8). If this were the case – perhaps for specific, polemical circumstances – we could not make sense of the famous 'faux pas' of Acts 14.4, 14.[16] On this point, we tend to follow Andreas Lindemann, according to whom Luke accords no 'fundamental primacy' to the title ἀπόστολος.[17] Also note that the author of the Lukan work does not hesitate to use the verb 'send' (ἀποστέλλειν) to describe the mission that the risen Lord gives to Paul.[18] Nevertheless, the status of authority that Luke attributes to Paul is entirely comparable to the Colossian and Ephesian image of Paul as the missionary to the nations *par excellence*. According to Luke, the authority of Paul is uncontested.[19] The simple fact that Luke gives his hero the privilege of making a programmatic speech, practically a farewell speech (Acts 20.18-35),[20] which is intended to outline

---

to subordinate this one [Paul] to the status of the twelve but rather to rank him as one of thirteen witnesses' (p. 174); A. Lindemann, *Paulus im ältesten Christentum. Das Bild des Apostels und die Rezeption der paulinischen Theologie in der frühchristlichen Literatur bis Marcion* (BHT, 58; Tübingen: Mohr Siebeck, 1979), pp. 66–68; Roloff, 'Die Paulus-Darstellung', p. 519: 'Through the way in which he deals with the traditions concerning Paul, one recognizes that Luke knows nothing more about Paul ever having been a controversial figure in the church'; M. C. de Boer, 'Images of Paul in the Post-Apostolic Period', *CBQ* 42 (1980), pp. 359–80 (365–66): 'Luke [...] certainly did not intend to diminish the stature of Paul [...]. In Luke's notion of *Heilsgeschichte* [...], the fact that Paul's mission is an extension of that of the Jerusalem apostles suggests not that he is a lesser figure than "the apostles" but rather that *his* mission and achievements are *the divinely planned goal of the apostolic period* [...]. This suggests that Paul, though essentially denied the honored title "apostle", is very much an apostle-like figure in Acts.'

16   Rightly Roloff, 'Die Paulus-Darstellung', pp. 519–20: '[Luke retains] the term "apostle" for Paul and Barnabas in the Antiochene traditions seen in 14,4 and 14, [...] although he otherwise reserves the title "apostle" for the twelve. This carelessness would be virtually unexplainable if it were Luke himself who removed the title "apostle" from Paul due to a prevailing polemical circumstance. But obviously the foundational limitation of the apostolate to the twelve was already part of the tradition of his church. It seems that he was no longer aware that at some point this could have been a point of contention.'

17   Cf. Lindemann, *Paulus im ältesten Christentum*, pp. 60–62.

18   Cf. also J. Schröter, 'Paulus als Modell christlicher Zeugenschaft. Apg 9,15f. und 28,30f. als Rahmen der lukanischen Paulusdarstellung und Rezeption des "historischen" Paulus', in D. Marguerat (ed.), *Reception of Paulinism in Acts. Réception du paulinisme dans les Actes des apôtres* (BETL, 229; Leuven: Peeters, 2009), pp. 53–80 (71–72).

19   Let us turn again to Lindemann, *Paulus im ältesten Christentum*, p. 67: '[...] the portrayal of Paul in Acts [conveys] very few polemical elements. Paul appears in Acts as an absolute, unquestioned authority'; and a little farther on: 'One can therefore say that at the time when Acts was composed, the view of Paul in the church was not seriously in danger; on the other hand, however, Luke found it necessary to establish deliberately the portrayal of Paul' (p. 68).

20   The characterization of Acts 20.18-35 as a 'farewell speech' dominates – in our view rightly – the research (G. Ballhorn, 'Die Miletrede – ein Literaturbericht', in *Das Ende des Paulus. Historische, theologische und literaturgeschichtliche Aspekte* [ed. F. W. Horn; BZNW, 106; Berlin: W. de Gruyter, 2001], pp. 37–47 [41–42], provides a brief overview of the issue), but there is not unanimity. See, e.g., the hesitations of A. Lindemann, 'Paulus und die Rede in Milet (Apg 20,17-38)', in D. Marguerat (ed.), *Reception of Paulinism in Acts. Réception du paulinisme*

continuity from one generation to another, is significant in itself. In addition, 'the narrative's increasingly personalized nature at the end of Acts, and its focus on the person of Paul in his role as teacher and martyr'[21] is in direct contrast with an alleged relativization of the Lukan Paul.

The fact that the different receptions of the apostle – epistolary and historiographical – both transform him into a figure of uncontested authority could be paired with a process of idealization or legendarization. We have seen, however, that the author of Ephesians resists this trend. On this point, the Lukan corpus appears more complex. The historiographical genre tends to turn its heroes into paradigmatic figures. The tendency to idealize the central character – especially in Acts 21–28 – seems inevitable, especially since the medium of narrative allows the author to describe the character in all his 'vividness' and present him to the audience as a character with whom to identify. At the same time, the Lukan Paul does not escape suffering and decline. Does the 'theology of suffering' in Luke[22] function to counterbalance the tendency to idealize the hero of a story? Or is it, instead, used in service of this idealization? That brings us to our next point.

b. An Authority Inscribed in the Dialectic between Presence and Absence

The second thesis we wish to develop is that Pauline authority is inscribed in the dialectic between presence and absence. Let us begin again with the epistolary reception. We touch here upon a special feature – one recognized from antiquity – of the literary genre of the letter.[23]

Cicero, for example, defines in passing the 'friendly letter' by referring to its eminently dialogical nature, as 'conversations between absent friends'(*amicorum colloquia absentium*) (*Philippica* 2.7). The passage is worth citing because it shows Cicero's concern for preserving the private sphere, to which the friendly letter testifies. Cicero accuses his opponent of having read one of his letters in public:

> In his hopeless ignorance of civilized conduct and the usages of society, he read it aloud. Has anyone possessing the least acquaintance with the behavior of gentlemen ever produced a letter written to him by a friend with whom he had subsequently had a difference and read it aloud in public? That amounts to robbing life of its social

dans les Actes des apôtres (BETL, 229; Leuven: Peeters, 2009), pp. 175–205.

21   D. Marguerat, 'L'image de Paul dans les Actes des apôtres', in *L'aube du christianisme* (ed. D. Marguerat; MdB, 60; Genève: Labor et Fides, 2008), pp. 469–98 (493). This was first published in M. Berder (ed.), *Les Actes des Apôtres. Histoire, récit, théologie: XXe congrès de l'ACFEB [Angers, 2003]*; LD, 199; Paris, Cerf, 2005), pp. 121–54.

22   Marguerat, 'L'image de Paul', pp. 496–97.

23   For an introduction to letters in Greco-Roman antiquity (in chronological order): K. Thraede, *Grundzüge griechisch-römischer Brieftopik* (Zetemata, 48; München: C. H. Beck, 1970); see, for example, S. K. Stowers, *Letter Writing in Greco-Roman Antiquity* (Library of Early Christianity; Philadelphia: Westminster Press, 1986); idem, 'Letters. Greek and Latin Letters', in *ABD* (vol. 4; 1992), pp. 290–93; the anthology of A. J. Malherbe, *Ancient Epistolary Theorists* (SBLSBS, 19; Atlanta: Scholars Press, 1988); in French, see, for example R. Burnet, *Épîtres et lettres. Ier-IIe siècle. De Paul de Tarse à Polycarpe de Smyrne* (LD, 192; Paris: Cerf, 2003), *passim* (for the letter as a substitute for real presence, cf. pp. 64–70).

foundations, abolishing conversation between absent friends. How many jests find their way into letters which would seem silly if produced in public? (Bailey, LCL)[24]

Cicero repeatedly emphasizes the dialogical nature of the letter. In *Ad Familiares* 12.30.1 (Letter 417), for example, he sees the letter as a substitute for real dialogue: 'Now that I cannot talk to you face to face, what could I like better than writing to you or reading your letters?' (Bailey, LCL).[25] The dialogical dimension is also regularly mentioned in *Ad Atticum*, for example, in 12.39.2 (Letter 280): 'Still it is a comfort to talk to you in absence, and a much greater one to read your letters (*Tamen adlevor cum loquor tecum absens, multo etiam magis cum tuas litteras lego*)' (Bailey, LCL).[26] About a century later, Seneca places himself in this same tradition when he repeatedly emphasizes, in particular in his *Epistulae morales,* the close proximity between letter and dialogue. Hildegard Cancik interprets *Epistulae* 67.2; 38.1; 40.1 and 55.9, 11 in this way.[27] The last of these letters (*Epistula* 55) even suggests that the 'being-together' at a distance that is achieved by means of a letter is of a superior quality to that of real, immediate presence. The traditional notion that the letter is a deficient substitute for real presence is here eclipsed:

'You may hold converse with your friends when they are absent, and indeed as often as you wish and for as long as you wish. For we enjoy this, the greatest of pleasures, all the more when we are absent from one another (*Conversari cum amicis absentibus licet, et quidem quotiens velis, quamdiu velis: magis hac voluptate, quae maxima est, fruimur, dum absumus*) [...]. A friend should be retained in the spirit; such a friend can never be absent (*Amicus animo possidendus est; hic autem numquam abest* (55.11) [... .] I see you, my dear Lucilius, and at this very moment I hear you; I am with you to such an extent that I hesitate whether I should not begin to write you notes instead of letters' (*Video te, mi Lucili; cum maxime audio: adeo tecum sum, ut dubitem, an incipiam non epistulas, sed codicellos tibi scribere*) (ibid.; Basore; LCL).[28]

Finally, Demetrius, Περὶ ἑρμηνείας 223, cites Artemon, the editor of Aristotle's letters, who says that the letter should be written in the same way as a dialogue and

---

24   Cicero, *Philippics* (trans. D. R. Shackleton Bailey; LCL; 2 vols; Cambridge: Harvard University Press, 2010).

25   Cicero, *Letters to Friends* (trans. D. R. Shackleton Bailey; LCL; 3 vols; Cambridge: Harvard University Press, 2001). Though it is letter 12.30.1 in the traditional numbering it is now listed as Letter 417 in the 2001 edition.

26   Cicero, *Letters to Atticus* (trans. D. R. Shackleton Bailey; LCL; 4 vols; Cambridge: Harvard University Press, 1999). A detailed analysis of the letters to Atticus from the point of view of the dialectic between absence and presence is provided by E. Gavoille, 'La relation à l'absent dans les lettres de Cicéron à Atticus', in *Epistulae Antiquae. Actes du Ier colloque 'Le genre épistolaire antique et ses prolongements'*(ed. L. Nadjo and E. Gavoille; Université François-Rabelais, Tours, 18-19 septembre 1998; Leuven and Paris: Peeters, 2000), pp. 153–76.

27   H. Cancik, *Untersuchungen zu Senecas Epistulae morales* (Spudasmata, 18; Hildesheim: Georg Olms Verlagsbuchhandlung, 1967), p. 52.

28   Seneca, *Epistulae morales* (trans. John W. Basore; LCL; 3 vols; Cambridge: Harvard University Press, 1928–1935).

be understood as one half of a dialogue: 'Artemon [...] says that a letter should be written in the same manner as a dialogue; the letter, he says, is like one of the two sides to a dialogue' (... εἶναι γὰρ τὴν ἐπιστολὴν οἷον τὸ ἕτερον μέρος τοῦ διαλόγου). What follows, however, shows that Demetrius agrees only in part with the position of Artemon, stressing the difference between the spoken and the written word: 'There is perhaps some truth in what he says, but not the whole truth. The letter should be a little more formal than the dialogue, since the latter imitates improvised conversation, while the former is written and sent as a kind of gift' (224; Innes, LCL).[29]

As Stanley K. Stowers rightly points out, in an epistle, the presence of the author with the recipient acts as a fictive presence.[30] The letter aims to overcome the geographic distance (or in the Deutero-Pauline letters, a temporal distance) while presupposing and, in a sense, sustaining the experience of absence. Hildegard Cancik, interpreting the first passage of Cicero quoted above, expresses it capably: 'In the paradoxical formulation "conversation between absent friends", the opinion that the absent friend is present in a particular way is an inherent tension implied by the letter; from the constraint of indirect communication, which is part of the situation of the letter, new possibilities of communication can arise.'[31] The same *topos* of 'presence in absence' which appears in various places in Pauline literature (e.g., 1 Cor. 5.3: ἐγὼ μὲν γάρ, ἀπὼν τῷ σώματι παρὼν δὲ τῷ πνεύματι, κτλ.) explicitly asserts this dialectic between absence and presence. It reappears in the Deutero-Pauline material, as evidenced by Col. 2.5a (εἰ γὰρ καὶ τῇ σαρκὶ ἄπειμι, ἀλλὰ τῷ πνεύματι σὺν ὑμῖν εἰμι, κτλ.). In this pronounced context, the dialectic lends itself quite well to indicating the historical place of the letter (i.e. a Deutero-Pauline setting) and to allowing for the resuscitation of 'Paul', at least literarily, in order to offer a 'second presence'.[32] In addition, the element of absence within the (epistolary) presence is accentuated by the fact that 'Paul' is in prison. From a theological point of view, the extreme situation of Paul's imprisonment (Col. 1.24 in connection with 4.3; Eph. 3.1, 13; 6.20) emphasizes his suffering 'on your behalf' and thus inscribes itself within a pronounced ecclesiological and christological conception that understands the unconditional commitment of the apostle to the nations as the culmination or completion of the Christ project. At least this is how we understand the very complex passage of Col. 1.24 ('I am now rejoicing in my sufferings for your sake, and in my flesh I am completing what is lacking in Christ's afflictions for the sake of his body, that is, the church').[33]

What about this dialectic in the Lukan description of Paul? While recognizing the specificities of literary genres – epistolary, on the one hand, historiographical,

29   Demetrius, *On Style* (trans. Doreen C. Innes and W. Rhys Roberts; LCL; Cambridge: Harvard University Press, 1995).

30   Stowers, *Letters*, p. 290: 'The letter "fictionalizes" the personal presence of the sender and receiver. The authorial voice is constructed as if speaking directly to the audience.'

31   Cancik, *Untersuchungen*, p. 51.

32   Cf. H. D. Betz, 'Paul's "Second Presence" in Colossians', in *Texts and Contexts: Biblical Texts in Their Textual and Situational Contexts. Essays in Honor of Lars Hartman* (ed. T. Fornberg and D. Hellholm; Oslo: Scandinavian University Press, 1995), pp. 507–18 (510–17).

33   Quotation from the NRSV.

on the other – we believe we are able to observe an analogous dialectic in Luke. Acts is interested in mediating the narrative presence of Paul. The historiographical genre, while respecting the temporal distance of the events and characters of the past, establishes, by means of the story, a kind of narrative immediacy between the reader and the world of the story, an immediacy that is realized at the moment when the reader finds himself or herself involved or 'entangled'[34] in this narrative device. What we find most interesting, however, is the fact that within this narrative device, Acts progressively inscribes the dimensions of Paul's absence, decline, and his eventual death. This anticipation of the end starts early in the narrative – in fact, with the debut of Paul's new career as announced in the programmatic affirmation of the risen Christ to Ananias in Acts 9.15-16 – and then gradually develops, in a dramatic way, for example, in Paul's speech to the elders of Ephesus at Miletus (Acts 20.18-35), finding its culmination in the last section of the narrative (Acts 21–28), with its end left open as a narrative finale in Acts 28.30-31. Along with Daniel Marguerat[35] we think it is legitimate to see, as the final theological outcome, the decline of the figure of Paul in favour of what carries him or transcends him, namely, the divine Word.

c. A De-centred Authority

When we inquire into the source of Paul's apostolic authority in Colossians and Ephesians, the answer is clear. Certainly Colossians, for example, is concerned with presenting a Paul who 'toils' (1.29) and leads an intense 'struggle' on behalf of the Church universal (θέλω γὰρ ὑμᾶς εἰδέναι ἡλίκον ἀγῶνα ἔχω ὑπὲρ ὑμῶν καὶ τῶν ἐν Λαοδικείᾳ καὶ ὅσοι οὐχ ἑόρακαν τὸ πρόσωπόν μου ἐν σαρκί, 2.1). It is thus a Paul who assumes entirely the task which has been entrusted to him, a task given specifically from God (κατὰ τὴν οἰκονομίαν τοῦ θεοῦ τὴν δοθεῖσάν μοι, 1.25)! His authority does not rest in any human performance, but in God. Even his struggle is ultimately an expression of the divine 'energy' (... ἀγωνιζόμενος κατὰ τὴν ἐνέργειαν αὐτοῦ τὴν ἐνεργουμένην ἐν ἐμοὶ ἐν δυνάμει, 1.29). It is a question of decentralized authority. The two key texts that highlight this aspect of decentralization are the epistolary self-commendation in Col. 1.24–2.5 and its Ephesian redaction in Eph. 3.1-13. The focus is specifically theocentric. It attempts to clarify the role given to Paul – or, if we grant the Deutero-Pauline fiction, the role that Paul gives to himself – in the process of revealing the 'mystery' to the nations. In a helpful contribution, Helmut Merklein points out that in Colossians and Ephesians, the key term μυστήριον – which is materially identical to 'Christ among you' (Χριστὸς ἐν ὑμῖν, 1.27), formally identical to the Word of God (λόγος

---

34 We owe the metaphor to W. Schapp, *In Geschichten verstrickt. Zum Sein von Mensch und Ding* (Frankfurt: Klostermann, 3rd edn, 1985); French translation: *Empêtrés dans des histoires. L'être de l'homme et de la chose* (La nuit surveillée; Paris: Cerf, 1992).

35 Marguerat, 'L'image de Paul', p. 495: 'The Acts of the Apostles is neither an account of apostolic succession […], nor is it an account of an institution […], but rather, the account of what the Word instituted. Paul stands out as the exemplary figure of the witness who effaces himself behind the word that he proclaims. Narratively, this effacement is concretized at the end of Acts, by the absence of any mention of his death'; cf. also pp. 496–97 ('a theology of suffering').

τοῦ θεοῦ, 1.25c), and retrospectively identical to the Gospel (εὐαγγέλιον, 1.5) – means any mediation of Christ that finds its origin in God and is accomplished by Paul's preaching to the nations.[36] The conclusion is clear: the Paul of Colossians and Ephesians is now an integral part of the Gospel. A Christ who does not meet the world through the missionary activity of Paul remains an unfulfilled, disembodied Christ. This integration of Paul into the process of revelation constitutes, therefore, the original attempt to reflect in a systematic way on an articulation which, *de facto*, already exists in the undisputed Pauline literature: the relationship between the revelation of Christ and the apostolic preaching of the historical Paul.

We arrive, therefore, at the following intermediate result. On the one hand, the attribution of authority to Paul in Colossians and Ephesians strives to emphasize the de-centred dimension of this authority. On the other hand, this authority is reinforced to such an extent that Paul, the recipient and bearer of the divine revelation (quite pronounced in Eph. 3.3-7), appears to receive a quasi-soteriological status. Such a development in the figure of Paul at first seems surprising and in discontinuity with the Paul of the authentic Pauline letters. However, 1 Cor. 9.22 and possibly also certain parts of 2 Cor. 2.14–7.4 may reflect a similar self-understanding of Paul and thus allow the relationship between the historical Paul and his subsequent reception to be placed along a line of continuity.[37] We will leave the question open here.

Again we discover that the Lukan image of Paul does not differ fundamentally from the epistolary reception of Paul. The passage to analyze in detail, of course, is the account of Paul's conversion (Acts 9) and its two reprises (Acts 22 and 26) in the guise of autobiographical recounts.[38] Here Paul receives his new identity and consequently his new role as a 'witness' (μάρτυς) *par excellence* (explicitly Acts

---

36   H. Merklein, 'Paulinische Theologie in der Rezeption des Kolosser- und Epheserbriefes', in *Paulus in den neutestamentlichen Spätschriften. Zur Paulusrezeption im Neuen Testament* (ed. K. Kertelge; QD, 89; Freiburg: Herder, 1981), pp. 25–69 (28–29): 'This entire process (Christ— Gospel—Paul—World) is summarized by the epistles to the Colossians and Ephesians in the term "mysterium" [...]. Briefly: The "mysterium" [...] is the missiologically or ecclesiologically shaped "gospel" of the homologumena [...]. Thus, what is constitutive for the portrayal of Paul in the epistles to the Colossians and Ephesians is that "Paul" himself now is part of the content of the proclamation and therefore belongs within the "mysterium"' (29).

37   Concerning 2 Corinthians 2–7, see for example J. Schröter, *Der versöhnte Versöhner. Paulus als unentbehrlicher Mittler im Heilsvorgang zwischen Gott und Gemeinde nach 2 Kor 2,14–7,4* (TANZ, 10; Tübingen: Francke Verlag, 1993). The question of whether Paul is effectively given a soteriological quality, and if so, in what sense and in what literary contexts, however, should be examined critically. See the Catholic exegete (!) K. Backhaus '"Mitteilhaber des Evangeliums" (1 Kor 9,23). Zur christologischen Grundlegung einer "Paulus-Schule" bei Paulus', in *Christologie in der Paulus-Schule. Zur Rezeptionsgeschichte des paulinischen Evangeliums* (ed. K. Scholtissek; SBS, 181; Stuttgart: Katholisches Bibelwerk, 2000), pp. 44–71 (62–64: is at least sceptical on this subject).

38   On the subject of the three versions of Paul's conversion in Acts, one should consult, for example, D. Marguerat, 'La conversion de Saul (Ac 9; 22; 26)', in *La première histoire du christianisme (Les Actes des apôtres)* (LD, 180; Paris: Cerf, 1999), pp. 275–306. ET: *The First Christian Historian: Writing the 'Acts of the Apostles'*, (trans. K. McKinney, G. Laughery, and R. Bauckham; SNTSMS, 121; Cambridge: Cambridge University Press, 2002). *Idem, Les Actes des apôtres (1–12)* (CNT, 5a; Genève: Labor et Fides, 2007), pp. 314–46 (on Acts 9 and its reprises in Acts 22 and 26).

22.15; 26.16) from the risen Christ himself. On this point, Luke and Ephesians occasionally converge, to the extent that the self-commendation of Ephesians 3 picks up and updates the biographical information taken from Galatians and 1 Corinthians (Eph. 3.3 picks up Gal. 1.16, and Eph. 3.8 picks up 1 Cor. 15.8).

But how does the revelation of Christ fit into the world, or more specifically, what are its modes of transmission? Are we dealing with a similar configuration to that of Colossians and Ephesians where Paul, the missionary to the nations *par excellence*, receives a quasi-soteriological status? This seems unlikely, because the general theological tendencies of Colossians (and Ephesians) on the one hand, and the Lukan corpus on the other, are very different: Lukan theology is fundamentally built along a line of continuity – the temporal continuity of the Church and the Spirit, but also the continuity between Judaism and Christianity in so far as Luke understands Christianity to be the finality or the fulfilment of Judaism. The description of Paul as prisoner (Acts 21–28), which continues to assert his Pharisaical identity, can be taken in this way. Colossians, in contrast, does not at all take up the paradigm of salvation-historical continuity. There is continuity, but it is mostly within the (Pauline) Christian tradition! As outrageous as it may seem, the author of Colossians renews a theology of *rupture*, based on the exclusivity of the revelation of Christ, while at the same time linking it to the (Pauline) *tradition*. In Ephesians the situation is slightly more complex. On the one hand, the author takes up and emphasizes the 'pattern of revelation' in Eph. 3.1-13 which, originating from the apocalyptic tradition, puts the entire emphasis on the radical newness of the revelation of Christ.[39] On the other hand, Ephesians also encourages the reader to think within the context of salvation history, with the following main emphases: first, Ephesians links Paul with the foundational age of the 'apostles and (Christian) prophets' (2.20; 3.5) and thus creates a temporal distinction between the apostolic and post-apostolic age. The present age of the letter's recipients, therefore, is recognized as an age *sui generis*.[40] Second, Ephesians conceives of the establishment of the universal Church as a synthesis between Israel and the nations (2.11-22).

d. An Authority Based on Teaching and Argumentation

Our fourth thesis evokes an important rhetorical and hermeneutical dimension that is already fully present in the undisputed Pauline literature. It is important to take the phenomenon of the (apostolic) letter seriously, not only at the technical level (as a means of transmitting knowledge from a distance), nor only at the historical level (which includes the question of pseudepigraphy), but also specifically at the hermeneutical level. Hans Weder has drawn attention to the fact that the letter's form itself, and in particular its dialogical character, includes an intrinsic affinity with

---

39   See for example Berger, *Formgeschichte*, p. 269, or M. Wolter, 'Verborgene Weisheit und Heil für die Heiden. Zur Traditionsgeschichte und Intention des "Revelationsschemas"', *ZTK* 84 (1987), pp. 297–319. For a synthetic analysis of Eph 3:1-13 and a partially critical discussion of Wolter, see Gese, *Vermächtnis*, pp. 228–39.

40   Well noted by ibid., p. 238.

the content of the gospel.[41] Add to this the fact that the Pauline school continued to cultivate a central element of the legacy of the apostle from Tarsus, namely, the development of an argumentative theology. This is not the place to treat the subject in all of its nuances. If we understand correctly, the particular theological reflection advanced by Colossians, and subsequently by Ephesians, is meant to develop a kind of theology of memory (or of reviewing the past). The Paul of the Deutero-Pauline letters does not come across as one who would convey a wholly unknown and new knowledge to the recipient community. On the contrary, the argumentative strategy of Colossians, and also Ephesians, aims to revive a religious knowledge that the author of the letter presumes is known. Accordingly, 'Paul' assumes the role of a competent interpreter of the past in order to clarify the present. It then follows that the (unbelievably enormous!) authority given to the apostle is not an end in itself, but fits rather into a hermeneutical approach that simultaneously presupposes and makes accessible the intelligibility of the tradition and the faith. In other words, the hermeneutical competence of 'Paul' – at the literary level, the epistolary staging of 'Paul' as a competent teacher – is manifested in the concern for a tradition (in this case a Pauline tradition) and a well-argued faith and thus strives for, at the pragmatic level, not blind obedience, but knowledge and consent on the part of the recipient community. To echo the words of the great twentieth-century philosopher of hermeneutics, Hans-Georg Gadamer, authority is not primarily a phenomenon connected to obedience (in its worst form, blind obedience) but is above all a structural element of *knowledge*.[42]

Let us try again to articulate our understanding of Deutero-Paulinism in terms of what we find in Luke. Here the differences seem to be accentuated. It remains a difficult task to understand the Lukan Paul not as a missionary preacher but as an 'authoritative teacher of the Church'.[43] This depends, in large part, on how one addresses the problem and what questions one poses to the Lukan text. We suggest considering, at least, the following three elements.

First, we must consider the simple fact that this historiographical reception places its hero in the earliest phase of his missionary activity, that is, Paul's first appearance is among the various urban centres of the Roman Empire, an appearance described

---

41 H. Weder, *Neutestamentliche Hermeneutik* (Zürcher Grundrisse zur Bibel; Zürich: TVZ, 1986), pp. 314–25; e.g.,: 'an inner affinity between the gospel itself and the form of proclamation in a letter' (314).

42 See H.-G. Gadamer, *Truth and Method* (trans. Joel Weinsheimer and Donald G. Marshall; London: Continuum, 2004), p. 281, concerning the phenomenon of authority: 'Admittedly, it is primarily persons that have authority; but the authority of persons is ultimately based not on the subjection and abdication of reason but on an act of acknowledgment and knowledge—the knowledge, namely, that the other is superior to oneself in judgment and insight and that for this reason his judgment takes precedence—i.e., it has priority over one's own. This is connected with the fact that authority cannot actually be bestowed but is earned, and must be earned if someone is to lay claim to it. It rests on acknowledgment and hence on an act of reason itself which, aware of its own limitations, trusts to the better insight of others. Authority in this sense, properly understood, has nothing to do with blind obedience to commands. Indeed, authority has to do not with obedience but rather with knowledge.'

43 Thus De Boer, *Images*, pp. 378–79, summarizes the problem.

in terms of speeches and miraculous activities and not in terms of epistolary activity.[44] The epistolary correspondence of the undisputed Pauline letters, on the other hand, reflects a later phase of communication in which Paul resumes contact with communities he had founded himself – with the exception of Romans. Pragmatically, Colossians, and without question Ephesians, are similar to Romans to the extent that these two Deutero-Pauline letters presuppose and construct a communicational model analogous to Romans: the author and the recipients do not know one another. This specific example notwithstanding, the differences between the historiographical and the epistolary receptions remain clear, in the following way: Luke wants to present a Paul in the earliest stages of his missionary activity, but this tendency is nowhere present in the Deutero-Pauline literature. Colossians, for example, introduces Epaphras and not Paul as the founder of the community, in order to establish a subtle interplay between the promotion of Epaphras' authority and its assimilation into the authority of 'Paul'.[45]

Second, the question of how Luke presents Paul's teaching authority should not be confused with the question of whether there are authentic Pauline theological elements in the Lukan presentation of Paul. In our view, identifying some passages as having a '(Deutero)-Pauline' tint – the most evident being Acts 13.38-39 and 20.18-35[46] – does not fundamentally change the fact that the theology of 'Paul' is more Lukan than Pauline.[47] Moreover, the question of whether the author of the Lukan work was aware of any of Paul's letters[48] and, if so, why he would not have more clearly used them, is the kind of question that, while continually supplying fodder for scholarship, may not ultimately be of much help due to the lack of sufficiently clear textual evidence. The two aspects that we have just mentioned are not determinative for our problem.

---

44   See for example, Schröter, 'Paulus als Modell', pp. 57–58.

45   See on this subject Müller, *Anfänge der Paulusschule*, p. 297.

46   Methodologically, we find it more interesting to connect these passages with the evolution of Pauline theology as it appears, for example, in Colossians, Ephesians and the Pastoral Epistles than to question the degree of discrepancy between Acts and the proto-Pauline letters. Concerning Acts 20.18-35, see for example C. K. Barrett, *The Acts of the Apostles. Vol. II: Acts XV–XXVIII* (ICC; Edinburgh: T&T Clark, 1998), pp. 964–65, who shows their proximity with the Pastorals; cf. also Ballhorn, 'Die Miletrede', pp. 43–45. Concerning Acts 13.38-39, it is appropriate, for example, to be aware that the language of 'forgiveness of sins' (ἄφεσις ἁμαρτιῶν, Acts 13.38) belongs to the Deutero-Pauline reception (see Col. 1.14b, repeated in Eph. 1.7) rather than the historical Paul.

47   The position of Burchard, *Der dreizehnte Zeuge*, p. 173, is still relevant: 'Luke does not have Paul say anything different than the apostles, although here and there his speech is tinted in distinctive Pauline tones'; or also R. Maddox, *The Purpose of Luke-Acts* (FRLANT, 126; Göttingen: Vandenhoeck & Ruprecht, 1982), pp. 66–90 (67): 'Luke's representation of Paul's theology […] is not, in any case, the most important aspect of Luke's picture of Paul. The theology which Paul preaches and teaches in Acts is Lukan rather than Pauline: or, better, it is not distinctively Pauline but shares the general character of early Christian theology as Luke understands it.'

48   For good recent discussion of the issue, see N. Hyldahl, 'The Reception of Paul in the Acts of the Apostles', in *The New Testament as Reception (Copenhagen International Seminar 11)* (ed. M. Müller and H. Tronier; JSNTSup, 230; Sheffield, Sheffield Academic Press, 2002), pp. 101–19 (101–107).

Third, it seems clear on the other hand that Luke wanted the reader to think of his Paul *also* as a theologian! Andreas Lindemann rightly stressed this point, even if we remain hesitant to accept his emphasis on justification: 'It is true that the image of Paul in Acts is not determined by the theological work of the Apostle himself. But on the other hand, Paul is also portrayed via the Lukan sermons as a theologian, and in his first speech [cf. Acts 13.15-31] still more (and in my opinion programmatically) as a theologian of justification.'[49] Yet the question is what general status Luke accords to the teaching authority of his Paul. Two elements in this regard must suffice here. First, the author *ad Theophilum* is concerned to give the greatest possible intelligibility to the missionary preaching of the Lukan Paul. The discourse of 'Paul' at the Areopagus before cultured Greeks in Acts 17.22-31, with its subtle rhetoric of including the cultural and religious context of his interlocutors, provides an excellent illustration of this despite the fact that the Lukan Paul's attempt leads to a (partial) failure. Furthermore, it is interesting to observe – as Jürgen Roloff has rightly noted – that the Lukan Paul's teaching does not seem to assume a criteriological or normative function: 'He [Paul] is [...] for this church not a theological authority, upon whom one calls for the definition and boundary of one's particular theological position in ongoing theological arguments.'[50] Paul's speech at Miletus (Acts 20.18-35) – a text that plays a central role in the construction of Paul's image as pastor and theologian – in our opinion does not contradict this reading. Admittedly, the speech emphasizes Paul as a model servant and faultless witness. But what will enable the church to live in an age without the apostles and the 'thirteenth witness' is specifically not loyalty to an exclusively Pauline tradition, but the awareness of living by the 'word of grace' (λόγος τῆς χάριτος, Acts 20.32).[51]

e. An Authority That Is Both Unique and Paradigmatic?

Let us return to the beginning of our journey, to our observations on the uncontested nature of Paul's authority. What interests us here is a slightly different problem, which we will formulate as follows: in what sense is 'Paul' perceived as a unique figure and in what sense does he assume a paradigmatic function?

---

49   Lindemann, *Paulus im ältesten Christentum*, p. 67.
50   Roloff, 'Die Paulus-Darstellung', p. 520.
51   See ibid., pp. 521–22, concerning Acts 20: 'What, however, is completely missing is the commitment of the church to a specific form of Pauline teaching' (521). This is also well understood by Marguerat, 'L'image de Paul', p. 149: 'The surprise comes from the fact that the author of Acts does not take advantage of this speech [i.e., Acts 20.18-35] in order to link Christian memory to the person of Paul, or even to Paul's word(s) (which is what the Pastorals will do!). To the contrary, Luke links the farewell to the word, to the Word [...] Paul commits his own to the power of the Word.'

What is the situation in Colossians and Ephesians? It is undeniable that the complex and multidimensional image of Paul in Colossians – and to a lesser degree in Ephesians – includes paradigmatic traits. But the general tendency is rather to assign Paul a unique role in the process of communicating the divine 'mystery'. We have already addressed the key function of the epistolary self-commendations (Col. 1.24–2.5; Eph. 3.1-13) that establish 'Paul' as one who through his teaching, and even more so through his suffering, 'fulfils' the Christ event (Colossians) and who is not only the bearer of the 'mystery' *par excellence* but at the same time its enlightened interpreter (Ephesians). In Ephesians this tendency is further highlighted by the fact that 'Paul' is part of the apostolic generation (Eph. 2.20; 3.5) and is thus temporally separated from the recipients of the writing.

Finally, let us consider briefly Luke's work. How does one reconcile the apparently unique salvation-historical role of the Lukan Paul with our tendency to conceive the same figure in a paradigmatic sense? We see two major axes in the research. One emphasizes Paul's unique role within the conceptual theological framework of salvation history. There is, for example, the question of whether Paul is a 'figure *sui generis*, for which there can be no successor'.[52] The other axis sees Paul as 'representative',[53] 'symbolic' or 'paradigmatic' for the condition of the believer[54] or, more precisely, the condition of the suffering witness.[55] All of the suggestions in the second category prefer to see Paul as a figure with whom to identify. But the conclusions vary and can be understood in different ways. According to Jürgen Roloff, for Luke's church Paul became a figure with whom to identify and through whom to better understand its own situation, in particular the demarcation from the Jewish tradition to a new religious identity.[56] Paul, far from functioning merely as an ethical figure with whom to identify, serves here as a paradigm – at an individual level, but also, and above all, at a communal

---

52   Lindemann, *Paulus im ältesten Christentum*, p. 67: 'In Acts, Paul is not a link in the chain which connects the church and apostolic tradition. Paul is, rather a figure *sui generis*, for which there can be no successor, as the "missing" conclusion shows.' Cf. also Burchard, *Der dreizehnte Zeuge*, p. 176: '[…] Paul's influence [represents] an historical process […], the end of which constitutes an historical caesura […]. As a witness, it is just as unlikely that he can have a successor as the twelve; there is also no one else in another capacity in view. (It is striking that Luke has no interest in recommending any of Paul's coworkers or companions; in this way he does not construct any possible chain of tradition […].'

53   Thus, for example, Maddox, *Purpose*, p. 70: 'There remains the possibility that Paul is important to Luke as a representative or symbol of the whole of Christianity in the generation before Luke's own.'

54   Thus Marguerat, 'L'image de Paul', pp. 485–86, on the second retelling of the narrative of Paul's conversion in Acts 26.

55   Thus Schröter, 'Paulus als Modell', p. 72: the author sees two complementary trends: the first is that Luke highlights the 'salvation-historical' particularity of Paul as the privileged recipient of a vision of the risen Lord that leads to his calling as missionary to the gentiles; the second is the exemplary, 'existential' dimension: 'The exemplary, and what is to be universal, is in the meantime found in the confession, as well as in the situations involving suffering and being persecuted.'

56   Roloff, 'Die Paulus-Darstellung', p. 520.

one – which goes far beyond the ethical dimension.[57] Is this how – by means of a retrospective understanding of his special identity, as reflected in this eminent figure of early Christianity – we can finally reconcile the two aspects, i.e., the unique character and the paradigmatic character of 'Paul'? This question deserves further and deeper study.

---

57   In this sense too, apparently, Marguerat, 'L'image de Paul', p. 486; cf. p. 497: 'The figure of Paul in Acts is the narrative point of deployment for Christian identity; to tell of Paul's mission is consistent with a deployment of the identity of Christianity [itself]. The figure of Paul in Acts has an "identity" function. This [function] permits the author to reveal the bond of continuity with Judaism and the causes of the break, the universality of the new faith, the foundational role of the Word, and the entry of Christianity into the social fabric of the Roman Empire. Here, Paul is emblematic of the future of Christianity.'

Chapter 14

RUMOUR: A CATEGORY FOR ARTICULATING THE SELF-PORTRAITS AND
RECEPTION OF PAUL. 'FOR THEY SAY, "HIS LETTERS ARE WEIGHTY ...
BUT HIS SPEECH IS CONTEMPTIBLE"' (2 CORINTHIANS 10.10)

Claire Clivaz
Trans. Eric Gilchrest and Nicholas J. Zola

I. Introduction

The publication of a volume dedicated to Paulinism in Luke-Acts signals that the
Lukan author is no longer seated at the back of the class of Pauline receptions, a
fact underscored in the research[1] and summarized by Odile Flichy: 'The Paul of
Acts is no longer suspected of treason against the Paul of the letters.'[2] Nonetheless,
Luke should also not be pushed forward to the top spot among the students of
Paul's legacy, as taking, for instance, the position of the *authorized author* of the
beginnings of Christianity so that the Acts represents the normative portrayal. Here
also the shift in research is important if we bear in mind with the historian Carlos
Ginzburg that our sources are always 'distorting mirrors'.[3] From this perspective,
any Pauline reception, whether canonical or non-canonical, is to be considered a
reconfiguration, and more authors and texts of early Christianity can now claim to
participate in the writing of the 'history of Paul of Tarsus'. Mindful of *1 Clement*,
as were Oscar Cullmann and Morton Smith,[4] Gerd Theissen has proposed,

---

1   See J. Schröter, 'Kirche im Anschluss an Paulus. Aspekte der Paulusrezeption in der
Apostelgeschichte und in den Pastoralbriefen', *ZNW* 98/1 (2007), pp. 77–104 (79). For a history
of this change in the research, see O. Flichy, *La figure de Paul dans les Actes des Apôtres. Un phénomène de réception de la tradition paulinienne à la fin du premier siècle* (LD, 214; Paris, Cerf,
2007), pp. 11–34. Flichy pinpoints the work of Jacob Jervell as the fountainhead for this change
in perspective in the research (ibid., p. 27). In French exegesis, the work of Daniel Marguerat particularly has made a contribution, see D. Marguerat, 'L'image de Paul dans les Actes des Apôtres',
in *Les Actes des Apôtres. Histoire, récit, théologie. XXᵉ congrès de l'Association catholique
française pour l'étude de la Bible (Angers, 2003)* (ed. M. Berder; LD, 199; Paris: Cerf, 2005), pp.
121–54; *idem*, 'Paul après Paul: une histoire de réception', *NTS* 54 (2008), pp. 317–37.
2   Flichy, *La figure de Paul*, p. 34.
3   See C. Ginzburg, *History, Rhetoric, and Proof* (The Menahem Stern Jerusalem Lectures;
Hanover: University Press of New England, 1999), p. 25.
4   See O. Cullmann, 'Les causes de la mort de Pierre et de Paul d'après le témoignage de
Clément Romain', *RHPh* 3 (1930), pp. 294–300; M. Smith, 'The Report about Peter in Clement
5, 4', *NTS* 7 (1960–1961), pp. 86–88.

for example, that one consider Paul as an indirect and ill-fated founder of the community at Rome, leading, despite his efforts, to its persecution under Nero.[5] And Helmut Köster, mindful of the Pastorals, is inclined to place the martyrdom of Paul at Philippi, where his tomb has been venerated since the fourth century.[6]

Furthermore, the 'Paul of the letters' is now himself often considered a construct, whether due to the dependence of this figure on the collection of the canonical letters[7] or because of the literary phenomenon of the 'radical constructivity of the Pauline "I"',[8] which in 1 Corinthians, for example, translates as the 'figure of a founder, father and apostle of the community'.[9] Last but not least, Mueller emphasizes that the concept of 'Paulinism', coined in 1836 by Schrader, has been promoted with success by the *Tendenzkritik* and corresponds largely to a confessional construction.[10] Nevertheless, as shown in the title of this volume, current research does not yet wish to discard this notion. But can we continue to use it without challenging it? In my opinion, without a serious challenge to this concept, the quest for 'Paulinism in Luke-Acts' may be reduced to listing the possible points of contact between the Pauline letters and the Lukan literature, with the same energy that Baur or Vielhauer used in seeking contradictions. To avoid simply becoming a quest in reverse, I believe research into the relationships between the self-portraits and receptions of Paul should take 'Paulinism' head-on as a notion that has created and incessantly generates a 'letdown' among exegetes who read the later receptions of Paul (see section II). If it is possible to overcome this feeling of disappointment, then the tasks ahead are, first, to reconsider the notion of authorship in reading Paul's letters with the aid of recent achievements in literary criticism (section III); and second, to honour and ponder the claim of the Lukan author that 'I too decided' to record – and, therefore, record in his *own way*, but one way among others – the story that 'many have undertaken to set down' (Lk. 1.1-4). He is indeed the only gospel writer to give voice to his critical *persona*[11] – albeit briefly – and to claim to tell *accurately* 'the events that have been fulfilled among us' (section IV.1).

---

5   See G. Theissen, 'Paulus - der Unglücksstifter. Paulus und die Verfolgung der Gemeinden in Jerusalem und Rom', in *Biographie und Persönlichkeit des Paulus* (ed. E.-M. Becker and P. Pilhofer; WUNT, 1.187; Tübingen: Mohr Siebeck, 2005), pp. 228–44 (241, 244).

6   See H. Köster, *Paul & His World. Interpreting the New Testament in Its Context* (Minneapolis: Fortress, 2007), pp. 70–79, 86–90; p. 77: 'All information gathered from the books of the New Testament canon would not conflict with the assumption that Paul was martyred in Philippi.'

7   See Flichy, *La figure de Paul*, p. 39.

8   L. Bormann, 'Autobiographische Fiktionalität bei Paulus', in *Biographie und Persönlichkeit des Paulus* (ed. E.-M. Becker and P. Pilhofer; WUNT, 187; Tübingen: Mohr Siebeck, 2005), pp. 106–24 (108).

9   L. Nasrallah, *An Ecstasy of Folly. Prophecy and Authority in Early Christianity* (HTS; Cambridge: Harvard University Press, 2003), p. 199.

10   See P.-G. Müller, 'Der "Paulinismus" in der Apostelgeschichte: Ein forschungsgeschichtlicher Überblick', in *Paulus in den neutestamentlichen Spätschriften* (ed. K. Kertelge; QD, 89; Freiburg: Herder, 1981), pp. 157–201 (160–63, 181–83).

11   See L. Alexander, 'Fact, Fiction and the Genre of Acts', in *NTS* 44 (1998), pp. 380–399 (397).

To illustrate these methodological considerations, I have chosen what appears to be a blatant counter example to 'Paulinism' in the Lukan corpus: the persuasiveness of Paul's oratory (section IV.2). The Paul of the letters mentions a rumour to which he acquiesces: his speech is 'contemptible' (2 Cor. 10.10), and he is 'untrained' with respect to eloquence (ἰδιώτης in 2 Cor. 11.6). But the Paul of Acts does not stop speaking and persuading, and he even quotes Greek poetry (Acts 17.28); the book ends on the image of a man who embodies speaking with 'boldness' (παρρησία, Acts 28.31). Apparently, we have here an obvious point of contradiction, one which I do not intend to minimize. I rather intend to interrogate this tension or contradiction and to draw it out using the notion of 'rumour'. This category will lead me, in conclusion, to emphasize a fundamental point common both to Paul and to the Lukan author: they both wrote in order to (re)assure and comfort their recipients and to redirect their recipients' point of view (section V).

II. 'Remember my chains' (Colossians 4.18) ... and not 'My Theology'. Towards a Pluralized Notion of 'Paulinism'

To address again the notion of 'Paulinism', in order to reformulate it or to move beyond it, we must also bid our farewells: primitive Christianity did not seek *primarily* to remember 'Paul the Theologian', whether modern Protestant exegetes like it or not. The pseudepigraphical letter to the Colossians ends with this invitation: 'Remember my chains!' (Col. 4.18). Many are the scholars who would have preferred to read here, 'Remember my justification by faith!' or at least, 'Remember my letters and my theology, that Christ is the end of the Law!' A similar disappointment awaits them in the last verse of the Acts of the Apostles which emphasizes the image of a prisoner who teaches 'with all boldness and without hindrance' and only alludes to the content of his message (cf. 'the kingdom of God' and 'teaching about the Lord Jesus Christ' in Acts 28.31).[12]

That the memory of Paul's chains initially took precedence over the memory of Paul's theology is something Andreas Lindemann has noted about *1 Clement*, the earliest reception of Paul outside the canon. This text, 'tells us little about the influence of Pauline *theology* in the Roman church in the last years of the first century. But the letter does show that Paul was of great importance for the church of Rome, both as an apostle and as a teacher of the church, even several decades after Paul's death.'[13] We can make the same observation of Luke's Acts of the Apostles, which does not seem to give chief importance to the theology of Paul

---

12 Acts 21–28 is consonant with 2 Timothy on the issue of the image of a suffering Paul, as noted by Jens Schröter (see Schröter, 'Kirche im Anschluss an Paulus', pp. 91, 95).

13 A. Lindemann, 'Paul's Influence on "Clement" and Ignatius', in *The New Testament and the Apostolic Fathers: Volume II – Trajectories through the New Testament and the Apostolic Fathers* (ed. A. F. Gregory and C. M. Tuckett; Oxford: Oxford University Press, 2006), pp. 9–24 (16). In 1979, Lindemann had already noted that even Irenaeus and Valentinus were not concerned to understand Paul's theology for itself (see *idem*, *Paulus im ältesten Christentum: Das Bild des Apostels und die Rezeption der paulinishcen Theologie in der frühchristlichen Literatur bis Marcion* [BHT, 58; Tübingen: Mohr Siebeck, 1979], p. 307).

but seeks to present Paul as a hero. If one finds that in certain places of Pauline reception the memory of his chains outweighs the memory of his theology, which theoretical model accounts for the Pauline reception in the first century? The model of François Bovon – who distinguishes between a 'documentary' Paul (the texts) and a 'monumental' Paul (the figure)[14] – is operational primarily from the second century, in my opinion. In the first century, the documentary Paul is included within the monumental Paul, as Bovon himself notes: 'the epistles are venerated like a jewel in a setting'.[15] It is because these epistles are *by Paul* that they will be preserved, as shown by *1 Clement* and developed below. In other words, one guards the documentary by virtue of the monumental: Paul the document is included within Paul the monument in the first century.

Regarding the end of the first century – after the death of Paul – Daniel Marguerat proposes that one understand the Pauline reception as 'three parallel tracks': the biographical, the documentary (the writings from Paul's hand), and the doctoral (the pseudepigraphical writings).[16] However, *1 Clement*, a writing nearly contemporaneous with Luke-Acts, prevents us from considering an interest in Paul's biography and an interest in his documents as 'parallel' paths. In this writing, attributed to Clement of Rome, the documentary reception of Paul does not constitute an 'individual branch'[17] but is subordinated under the biographical memory of the apostle. On the one hand, *1 Clement* shows a strong devotion on the part of the Church of Rome to the figure of Paul, that is, to his biography, but also to his writings, as we saw with Lindemann. The famous passage of *1 Clem.* 5.5-7 indicates that various stories were circulating about the mission and death of Paul, attributed here to 'jealousy and strife' (5.5) towards this 'good apostle' (5.3) who evangelized as far as Spain (5.7), a tradition also mentioned in the *Muratorian Canon* 38-39.[18] On the other hand, *1 Clement* also reflects a commitment to the letters of Paul, the archiving of which had already begun. *First Clement* 47.1-4 invites the Corinthians to 'take up the epistle of the blessed Paul the apostle' and quotes the beginning of this letter, which implies that the Corinthians and the Romans each had copies. *First Clement* also appears to have known Romans, Galatians, and Philippians.[19] This early devotion to the archiving of Paul's letters is not surprising if one considers that Paul himself was aware of the effect of his letters (2 Cor. 10.9-10) and was already asking that they be reread until they reached all

---

14   See F. Bovon, 'Paul comme Document et Paul comme Monument', in *Chrétiens en conflit. L'Épître de Paul aux Galates* (ed. J. Allaz *et al.*; Essais Bibliques, 13; Genève: Labor et Fides, 1987), pp. 54–65 (54). ET: 'Paul as Document and Paul as Monument', in *New Testament and Christian Apocrypha: Collected Studies II* (ed. F. Bovon and G. Snyder; Tübingen: Mohr Siebeck, 2009), pp. 307–17.

15   Bovon, 'Paul comme document et Paul comme monument', p. 57.

16   See Marguerat, 'Paul après Paul', p. 322.

17   Ibid.

18   For a French translation of this canon, see J.-D. Kaestli, 'Histoire du canon du Nouveau Testament', in *Introduction au Nouveau Testament: Son histoire, son écriture, sa théologie* (ed. D. Marguerat; MdB, 41; Geneva: Labor et Fides, 3rd edn, 2004), pp. 449–74 (471–73).

19   See A. Jaubert (ed.), *Clément de Rome. Epître aux Corinthiens* (SC, 167; Paris: Cerf, 1971), p. 57.

their recipients (1 Thess. 5.27). In Antiquity, the public reading of a text was equivalent to its circulation, making it available to the public domain (πρὸς ἔκδοσιν).[20] The other meaning of ἔκδοσις, in the modern sense of 'edition', generally occurs after the author's death.[21]

In addition, *1 Clement* reinforces the idea of an early archiving of Paul's letters when one also analyzes the way in which this writing refers to the words of Jesus (*1 Clem.* 13.1-4; 14.7-8): certain words of Jesus are cited, but they cannot be clearly linked to a canonical Gospel or another source.[22] The chronology postulated by scholars between the Pauline letters and the final redaction of the canonical Gospels is verified here by Paul's reception. Furthermore, *1 Clement* invites us to relativize the theological objections constructed from the notion of 'Paulinism'. This text, which is tied to the person of Paul *and* the preservation of his letters, is at the same time very close to the epistle to the Hebrews, which it quotes, or with which it shares a common source (cf. *1 Clem.* 36.2-5, for example).[23] *First Clement* is thus an early witness to the logic that places Hebrews just after the epistle to the Romans in Papyrus 46 – copied around 200 in Egypt.[24]

Carefully considering this information from *1 Clement*, I postulate that one of the strongest impulses for the preservation of Paul's letters in the decades after his death was not the fact that they were perceived to contain summaries of his theology, nor was it out of a particular admiration for Paul as a polemical writer as such. In fact, it is precisely this polemical tone that led to difficulties in early Christianity: Tit. 3.9 appeals to 'domestic peace' about the controversy concerning the Law, and 2 Pet. 3.16 directly addresses the question of quarrels arising from conflicting readings of the letters of Paul in the community. I suggest that what led to the *initial* archiving of Paul's letters was the fact that they were from the hand of the one whose memory the community wished to guard, as the founding apostle of the community, and as the one whose 'chains' they were to 'remember'.[25] For Clement of Rome – or the author of *1 Clement* – 1 Corinthians is not a theological treatise nor an interesting polemical writing but a circumstantial letter expressing a bond between Paul and a local community. It is because of the memory of this

20   See T. Dorandi, *Le stylet et la tablette: Dans le secret des auteurs antiques* (Paris: Les Belles Lettres, 2000), pp. 104, 115–16. Dorandi refers to a list of testimonies of these public practices published by E. Rohde, *Der grieschische Roman und seine Vorläufer* (Leipzig: Breitkopf und Härtel, 2nd edn, 1900), p. 327–29, note 1 (see Dorandi, *Le stylet et la tablette*, p. 115, note 49).

21   See Dorandi, *Le stylet et la tablette*, p. 104.

22   See Jaubert (ed.), *Clément de Rome*, p. 53.

23   See ibid., p. 57.

24   See D. Trobisch, *Die Paulusbriefe und die Anfänge der christlichen Publizistik* (Kaiser Taschenbücher, 135; Gütersloh: Chr. Kaiser, 1994), pp. 28, 32.

25   On the question of the collection of Paul's letters in Marcion, a consensus has now been established which is increasingly clear in the research that recognizes that Marcion inherited a collection of Paul's letters, and did not create them (see H. Y. Gamble, 'The New Testament Canon: Recent Research and the Status Quaestionis', in *The Canon Debate* [ed. L. M. McDonald and J. A. Sanders; Peabody: Hendrickson Publishers, 2004], pp. 267–94 [283]). Marcion, moreover, does not indicate in any way that the letters were created apart from a devotion to the figure of Paul – Paul in chains. On the topic of the 'Paul in chains', see also R. J. Cassidy, *Paul in Chains. Roman Imprisonment and the Letters of St. Paul* (New York: Crossroad, 2001).

bond that Clement considers it appropriate to use this letter, and he only uses that which will help in the context of the *current* conflict that the Corinthian community was experiencing, as Lindemann points out.[26] The importance of responding to the *current* situations while referring to the memory of Paul is certainly confirmed in the redaction of the pseudepigraphical works of Paul. Even the *Acts of Paul* has integrated a pseudepigraphical letter of Paul, *3 Corinthians* (*Acts of Paul* 10.4-6; [ET 8.3.1-40]), while it most likely knows 1 Corinthians:[27] here too the interest is in the link that exists between the community and Paul and not in the link between an archived text and a community. There is, therefore, no longer reason to be disappointed in the fact that early on the memory of Paul's 'chains' overtook the memory of Paul's 'theology'. Without the memory of his chains, there might simply be nothing left to remember about the theology of the Paul of the letters, who became the 'good apostle' (*1 Clem.* 5.4).

If one, therefore, wants to retain the notion of 'Paulinism', one must at least use it in the plural in order to include the dimension of the strong (sometimes even excessive) devotion to the figure of Paul. Such a devotion is clearly inserted into the narrative of the *Acts of Paul*, but the narrow definition of 'Paulinism' has made us forget that it is already present in the Pauline letters, as shown by the following three examples. Monika Betz has managed to write an article in which the angelic description of Paul in *Acts of Paul* 3.3 is a central theme without noting what Paul says in Gal. 4.14: '[you] welcomed me as an angel of God, as Christ Jesus'.[28] Secondly, Gal. 4.14 superimposes Paul over 'Christ Jesus', a phenomenon one finds in *Acts of Paul* 3.21: '[Thecla] saw the Lord sitting in the form of Paul.' This parallelism between Gal. 4.14 and *Acts of Paul* 3.21 also escapes Betz. Finally, the Galatians' near-fanatical devotion that the apostle mentions in 4.15 – 'had it been possible, you would have torn out your eyes and given them to me' – has nothing on the devotion that Thecla demonstrates when she rolls upon the ground in the place where Paul had previously been sitting in prison (*Acts of Paul* 3.20). On this type of Paulinism, the classical *Tendenzkritik* has scarcely made comment, and yet even the Acts of the Apostles has retained an echo of it through the 'healing handkerchiefs' of Paul (Acts 19.11-12). Returning to the terminology proposed by Jan Assmann,[29]

---

26 See Lindemann, *Paulus im ältesten Christentum*, p. 298: 'In any case, 1 Corinthians possesses contemporary significance for *1 Clement*. But this relationship also helps to explain why 1 Corinthians 15 in fact plays no role in the discussion of "resurrection" in *1 Clement* 24—26: Because there was no controversy between Rome and Corinth on this issue, the author had no need in this passage to appeal to Paul's authority' (editors' trans.).

27 See *Acts of Paul* 3.5 which is an allusion to 1 Cor. 7.29; see F. Bovon and P. Geoltrain (eds), *Ecrits apocryphes chrétiens 1* (La Pléiade, 442; Paris: Gallimard, 1997), p. 1130. For an English introduction to and translation of *Acts of Paul*, see 'The Acts of Paul', in *New Testament Apocrypha* (ed. E. Hennecke and W. Schneelmelcher; trans. R. Wilson; vol. 2; Atlanta: Westminster John Knox, 1992), pp. 213–70.

28 Betz seeks to explain *Acts of Paul* 3.3 in terms of a Valentinian background (see M. Betz, 'Die betörenden Worte des fremden Mannes: Zur Funktion der Paulusbeschreibung in den Theklaakten', *NTS* 53 [2007], pp. 130–45 [135]).

29 See J. Assmann, *Moïse l'Egyptien: Un essai d'histoire de la mémoire* (trans. L. Bernadi; Paris: Flammarion, 2003), p. 325.

one can say that the extreme devotion that gave rise to the figure of Paul became the victim of a 'cultural amnesia' with the introduction of the category of Paulinism in the nineteenth century. To speak of 'Paulinisms' allows consideration of certain trajectories that have been marginalized in the reception of Paul and in modern research, but which are important in the history of early Christianity. Such is the case with the devotion to the 'good apostle' (*1 Clem.* 5.4), which did not quite reach the magnitude of Gal. 4.14-16, Acts 19.11-12, or the *Acts of Paul* 3, but consistently played a role in the reception of Paul and the preservation of his writings.

III. Readdressing the Notion of Author in the Pauline Letters

a. The Concept of Literary Posture

As noted by Andreas Dettwiler, Pauline scholarship no longer operates in a time in which Paul is considered a 'solitary genius',[30] a unique author with total control over his work; this idea was born in the crucible of Romanticism[31] and has largely fuelled modern exegesis. In his work analyzing the interactions between philosophy, New Testament exegesis, and secularization, Ward Blanton has clearly shown that this kind of romantic image of the author has guided the Pauline exegesis of Alfred Deissmann,[32] which in turn influenced Heidegger's formation of the 'Pauline spirit'.[33] Wishing to take the notion of author beyond its romantic and modern singularity, Jérôme Meizoz, a sociologist of literature, formulated the concept of 'literary postures'.[34] Interested in autobiographies, 'autofictions', correspondences, diaries, and media statements that modern authors make about themselves,[35] Meizoz stresses that an author 'develops a posture or a series of postures over the course of his or her life by drawing on the repertoire provided by

---

30   A. Dettwiler, 'L'école paulinienne: évaluation d'une hypothèse', in *Paul, une théologie en construction* (ed. A. Dettwiler, J. D. Kaestli, and D. Marguerat; MdB, 51; Genève: Labor et Fides, 2004), pp. 419–40 (429).

31   See J. Meizoz, *Postures littéraires: Mises en scène modernes de l'auteur. Essai* (Geneva: Slatkine Erudition, 2007), pp. 24–25: 'Since the era of Romanticism (for art history, the time of the Renaissance), literary history has constructed a fiction of the unique author which was then reinforced by the popularity of genetic criticism in the 1980s. In practice it is a plural authorship that is most often the case.'

32   See A. Deissmann, *Paulus: eine kultur- und religionsgeschichtliche Schule* (Tübingen: Mohr Siebeck, 1911); idem, *Licht vom Osten. Das Neue Testament und die neuentdeckten Texte der hellenistisch-römischen Welt* (Tübingen: Mohr Siebeck, 1923).

33   See W. Blanton, *Displacing Christian Origins. Philosophy, Secularity, and the New Testament* (Chicago: University of Chicago Press, 2007), pp. 112–22.

34   See Meizoz, *Postures littéraires*. A second volume has been recently published: J. Meizoz, *La Fabrique des singularités: Postures littéraires II* (Geneva: Slatkine Erudition, 2011). For an English presentation of the notion of literary posture, see J. Meizoz, 'Modern Posterities of Posture: Jean-Jacques Rousseau', in *Authorship Revisited. Conceptions of Authorship Around 1900 and 2000* (ed. G. Dorleijn, R. Grüttenmeier, and L. Korthals Altes; Leuven: Peeters, 2010), pp. 81–94.

35   See Meizoz, *Postures littéraires*, p. 28.

the [literary] tradition itself';[36] he gives the example of Louis-Ferdinand Céline, who presents himself as the 'doctor of the poor'.[37] Since the Enlightenment, 'the posture is the public face or the *persona* of the would-be writer'; it plays on the *ethos* that 'maintains the self-image which the speaker sets forth in the discourse in order to ensure its impact'.[38] Instead of articulating various aspects of an authorial singularity,[39] the originality of Meizoz's approach is to consider every author a plurality, 'the height of the individual and the collective', inserted in a socio-historical context and comprising author, editor, printer, typographer, and 'the various institutions involved in the writing project'.[40] He goes so far as to say that 'for the public, an author is always the sum of what accumulates and circulates about him in both scholarly circles and on the street'.[41] The modern author is well aware, 'more than at any other time', of entering into the gaze of others after the author's first literary expression, of taking on 'various identities constructed from both the author's text and lifestyle in the public arena'.[42]

As we have seen, Meizoz situates the beginning of 'literary postures' at the time of the Enlightenment because he considers that prior to this 'the author as subject disappears or recedes behind the formal poetic art, the imitation of the ancients'.[43] However, as Blanton has shown through rereading Heidegger and Deissmann, scholarship has largely used the modern notion of author in its readings of Paul because of the strong presence of 'I' in his letters. This usage, however, has not been purely a retrojection of a modern category. I would like to stress that ancient authors also claimed an authorial singularity and were likewise conscious of 'entering into the gaze of others' in their literary expressions. Cicero takes an interest in the publication of his own letters.[44] Galen, in the second century CE, writes a metacritical work on his own way of writing books, *De libris propriis*.[45] Origen takes offence at the fact that the gnostic Candide has forged one of his texts.[46] And the pseudepigrapha, contrary to popular opinion, are far from having provoked indifference.[47] As for the letters of Paul – private letters that slowly but surely became Christian literature – they indicate that their author was already aware of his status as a writer

36   Ibid., p. 189.

37   See ibid., p. 30.

38   Ibid., pp. 27, 22.

39   Jérôme Meizoz considers, for example, the triad inscriber/author/person developed by Dominique Maigueneau for understanding the notion of an author 'to remain very singularizing' (Meizoz, *Postures littéraires*, p. 24).

40   Ibid., p. 25.

41   Ibid., p. 45.

42   Ibid., p. 187.

43   Ibid., p. 27.

44   See Cicero, *Ad Atticum* XVI.5.5; cited by Trobisch, *Die Paulusbriefe*, p. 83.

45   See V. Boudon (ed.), *Galien. Introduction générale; Sur l'ordre de ses propres livres; Sur ses propres livres; Que l'excellent médecin est aussi philosophe* (Paris: Les Belles Lettres, 2007).

46   This episode is narrated in *Letter to Friends in Alexandria* by Origen, transmitted by Rufin (Rufin, *De adultera* 7); thanks to prof. Eric Jonod for this reference.

47   See J.-D. Kaestli, 'Mémoire et pseudépigraphie dans le christianisme de l'âge post-apostolique', *RThPh* 125 (1993), pp. 41–63 (47); cited in Dettwiler, *L'école paulinienne*, p. 431.

and his reputation in the social microcosm of nascent Christianity: by expressly asking that his letters be read (1 Thess. 5.27), Paul repeatedly shows that he is aware of and plays with his role as writer[48] and the response he will receive; he knows that his letters may sadden (2 Cor. 2.4), or shame (1 Cor. 4.14), or test (2 Cor. 2.8) their recipients. Moreover, the fact that Pauline authorship is functionally plural is well known to scholars. Paul dictated his letters, as evidenced by his signatures announcing his autograph (1 Cor. 16.11; Gal. 6.14; Phlm. 9), and perhaps even allowed, in part, for a co-author, as may be suggested by the supplemental note from the secretary Tertius in Rom. 16.22: 'I Tertius, the writer of this letter, greet you in the Lord.' However, 'the place of (a) Tertius in the biblical legacy remains to be fixed [...], and promises a return on an investment in the further analysis of the ancient (and modern) intertwining of religion and writing technologies of all sorts', as noted by Blanton.[49] Methodologically, I would say that the interaction between ancient texts and recent developments in the concept of the author exhibits itself today as a comparative approach that is aware of all of its limitations and potentialities.

b. *Paul's Literary Postures: The Absent Father Who Becomes Divine Prisoner*

How should we think about the notion of 'literary posture' in the microcosm of earliest Christianity, since it rests in large part on the role of the media? Insofar as Meizoz postulates that an author is nothing but 'the sum of what accumulates and circulates about him',[50] I propose to take into account the role of rumour as a factor involved in establishing the posture of an ancient author. As I will develop on this issue, the role of rumour is clearly discernible in the writing of Paul and contributes to the development of two literary postures of him, with the second superimposed over the first: the absent father and the divine prisoner. In section IV, we will see that rumour is also involved in the Lukan reception of Paul and commends itself as a fruitful category for articulating the self-portraits and receptions of Paul.

Ancient sources tell us that rumours could have held considerable weight, for example in Tacitus: 'But neither human help, nor imperial munificence, nor all the modes of placating Heaven, could stifle scandal or dispel the belief that the fire had taken place by order. Therefore, *to scotch the rumour*, Nero substituted as culprits, and punished with the utmost refinements of cruelty, a class of men, loathed for their vices, whom the crowd styled Christians'(Tacitus, *Ann.* XV.44.3-4 [Jackson, LCL]). The sociologist Jean-Noël Kapferer has conducted landmark research on the idea of rumour that has led to the development of several studies on the issue;[51] I will take up some of his findings here. For Kapferer, rumour has its place alongside the media as a source of knowledge and derives a certain authority from being

---

48   See notably 1 Thess. 4.9; 5.9, 27; 1 Cor. 4.14; 9.14-15; 16.21; 2 Cor. 1.12; 2.4, 8; 3.1-4; 7.8-9; 9.1; 10.9-10; Phil. 3.1; Gal. 4.20; 6.11; Rom. 15.14-16; Phlm. 9.

49   Blanton, *Displacing Christian Origins*, p. 127.

50   Meizoz, *Postures littéraires*, p. 45.

51   See J.-N. Kapferer, *Rumeurs. Le plus vieux média du monde* (Paris: Seuil, 2nd edn, 1992). See also P. Froissart, *La rumeur: histoire et fantasmes* (Débats; Paris: Belin, 2002).

anti-establishment.[52] Rumour is not necessarily false, but it remains unofficial and guarantees freedom of expression: 'The negative understanding that associates rumor and falsity is of a technical nature, claiming that the only good communication is controlled communication. Rumor upholds a different value, advocating that the only good communication is free communication, even if reliability has to suffer by it. In other words, "false" rumors are the price we must pay for founded rumors.'[53] In Paul's letters the theme of rumour and its effects occur several times: I note here three examples. First, the rumour about Paul's past as a persecutor turned convert: this rumour precedes him, for example, in the church of Judea which had simply heard that, 'The one who formerly was persecuting us is now proclaiming the faith he once tried to destroy' (Gal. 1.23). Being preceded by such a rumour becomes a difficulty with which Paul must come to terms, for the rumour of being a persecutor is sometimes more tenacious than that of being a convert and remains variously appreciated: Paul says 'I am the least of the apostles, unfit to be called an apostle, because I persecuted the church of God' (1 Cor. 15.9).

A second rumour accompanies Paul, as we find in 2 Cor. 10.9-10, a passage that particularly stresses the interaction between the rumour and the literary posture Paul adopts: 'I do not want to seem as though I am trying to frighten you with my letters. For they say, "His letters are weighty and strong, but his bodily presence is weak, and his speech is contemptible."' A strong pen but a weak presence – this is how the author portrays himself in the letters he writes, concerning the rumour as he perceives it. And this passage is far from an exception. Several times Paul contrasts, on the one hand, the 'bold' (2 Cor. 10.1; Rom. 15.15), even 'frightening' (2 Cor. 10.9) writing with which he asserts his authority (2 Cor. 1.23), with, on the other hand, his presence as 'gentle' (1 Thess. 2.7), 'humble' (2 Cor. 10.1), and at times repulsive (Gal. 4.14). He even admits to being weak in rhetorical eloquence, in which he seems to have little training, in the sense of ἰδιώτης ('untrained') in 2 Cor. 11.6. Against this backdrop, he constructs the literary posture of a father 'absent in body, but present in spirit' through his writings (1 Cor. 5.3; 1 Thess. 2.17), one that continually communicates his desire to see his recipients, a desire deferred (Phil. 1.27; 1 Thess. 2.17; Gal. 4.20; Rom. 15.22-23, 32). Paul also does not hesitate to use emotional pressure in his writing: 'For even if I made you sorry with my letter, I do not regret it (though I did regret it, for I see that I grieved you with that letter, though only briefly). Now I rejoice, not because you were grieved, but because your grief led to repentance' (2 Cor. 7.8-9). Responding to the rumour that highlights the contrast between his writing and his presence, Paul constructs the literary posture of an absent father who is present in his writings.

In the latter part of his life, due to his captivity, Paul transforms this posture by superimposing over it a posture of himself as the divine prisoner, the 'prisoner of Christ Jesus' (Phlm. 9). This theological explanation of his imprisonment may be understood as a literary posture that he builds in response to a third hostile rumour against him, a rumour that interprets his status as a prisoner negatively and is

---

52   See Kapferer, *Rumeurs*, pp. 22, 25.
53   Ibid., p. 311.

perceivable in between the lines of Phil. 1.15-20. Other Christian missionaries are in competition with Paul (Phil. 1.15) and seek to use his imprisonment to gain an advantage over him (1.17); this affirms all the more that he 'will not be put to shame' and that his boldness remains no matter what happens (1.20). This second posture, the divine prisoner, is developed in the receptions of Paul, as seen in Eph. 3.1 ('I Paul am a prisoner for Christ Jesus for the sake of you gentiles') and in Acts 20.22 where Paul is called 'captive to the Spirit'. Second Tim. 1.8 even confirms for us the existence of a rumour hostile to Paul based on his status as prisoner when the pseudepigraphical Paul invites his recipient to 'not be ashamed ... of me [the Lord's] prisoner'; he also emphasizes that Onesiphorus was 'not ashamed of my chain' (2 Tim. 1.16) though 'all who are in Asia have turned away from me' (1.15). Thus my hypothesis on the posture of the divine prisoner and its link to rumour is confirmed in certain receptions of Paul.

To summarize section III.b, we found, in reading Paul's letters, that Paul dealt with a rumour that preceded him concerning his past as a persecutor, then later with a rumour that emphasized the gap between the persuasive force of his letters and his less convincing oral presentation. Such rumours led him to construct his literary posture of an absent father who is present in his writings. Lastly, the latter part of his life spent in captivity forced him to face a challenge to his ministry precisely because of this imprisonment, ultimately leading him to adopt the posture of a divine prisoner, largely reflected in the Deutero-Pauline letters. But how does the rumour about the feebleness of his speech fit into the Lukan corpus? Is not Acts the antithesis of such a rumour, where Paul is so often characterized in the midst of discourse? To address this delicate question I will begin by returning to the compositional project of Luke-Acts; then I will analyze how the concept of παρρησία – 'boldness in speech' – is deployed in Acts.

IV. The Lukan Reception of Paul

a. 'It Seemed Good to Me Also' (Luke 1.3): Writing in the Midst of Rumours

The Lukan author should not be considered free of constraint and all-powerful in the wording of his work any more than Paul is. I have defended elsewhere the idea that the Lukan author did not suppress points of view that differed from his own but made them accessible;[54] I will recall some elements of this argument here. Since the Lukan author claims to draw on common memory – that of 'the events that have been fulfilled among us' (Lk. 1.1) – he cannot say anything he wants nor suppress anything he wants, because it would run against this common memory he shares with his recipient(s). In this realm of common memory, rumour is already present in Luke's preface with the verb κατηχέω. The expression 'the things about which you have been instructed' (Lk. 1.4) may seem ambivalent; as François Bovon notes,

---

54   See, for the demonstration of this thesis, C. Clivaz, *L'ange et la sueur de sang (Lc 22,43-44) ou comment on pourrait bien encore écrire l'histoire* (BiTS, 7; Leuven: Peeters, 2010), pp. 78–82.

the word κατηχέω often refers to Christian teaching (cf. 1 Cor. 14.19; Gal. 6.6; Acts 18.25), but also to 'secular' information being spread (Acts 21.21, 24).[55] The definition, therefore, remains open. I note, however, that the two occurrences in Acts 21.21, 24 concern 'what they have been told' about Paul and, therefore, information circulating among the people who are already aware of current Christian events and are concerned with their implications. Both of these occurrences thus also refer to a context of internal communication, even if κατηχέω is used in its 'secular' sense. Additionally, I believe four other elements link the expression περὶ ὧν κατηχήθης λογών (Lk. 1.4) to an internal communication, which suggests either 'teaching', or 'hearsay', or teaching the author considers as 'hearsay' in need of being reworked.

First, the word λόγος is introduced in Lk. 1.2 with the phrase 'servants of the word', which Pierre Létourneau describes as the 'only clearly theological element' in the prologue.[56] In the context of the preface, therefore, λόγος suggests that this work be understood as an internal communication. Second, Acts 21.34 and 25.26 show two gentiles, first a tribune and then Festus, unable to find or write something 'sure' (ἀσφαλές), whereas the Lukan author considers himself capable of writing to Theophilus so that Theophilus may obtain this same 'assurance' (ἀσφάλεια); the house of Israel itself is even invited to know 'with certainty' (ἀσφαλῶς) in Acts 2.36.[57] Third, the mention of 'us' precedes the mention of the author in the preface (Lk. 1.1) and reveals a domain common to the recipient and the author, a domain that functions as the frame of reference for this act of communication. The 'us' indicates that the 'events that have been fulfilled' are an 'accepted fact' by both author and recipient, to borrow an expression from Theon in the *Progymnasmata*.[58] Fourth, Phil. 3.1 and 1 Thess. 5.1-2 likewise suggest a link between the need to write and the strengthening of the recipients' faith, thus providing a model to imitate.[59] The assumption of an underlying Christian teaching or 'hearsay' that precedes Lk. 1.4 seems clear to me. This analysis reinforces what Loveday Alexander observes: the preface sets up a communication between *insiders*.[60] However, if the author of the prologue considers this 'tradition' or 'hearsay' as valid to the point of strengthening,

---

55   F. Bovon, *L'Evangile selon Luc: Volume I – 1,1-9,50* (CNT, IIIa; Geneva: Labor et Fides, 1991), p. 43. ET: F. Bovon, *Luke 1: A Commentary on Luke 1:1-9:50* (trans. C. M. Thomas; Hermeneia; vol. 1; Minneapolis: Fortress, 2002).

56   P. Létourneau, 'Commencer un Evangile: Luc', in *La Bible en récits: L'exégèse biblique à l'heure du lecteur* (ed. D. Marguerat; Geneva: Labor et Fides, 2003), pp. 326–39 (333).

57   See in the first volume, D. P. Moessner, 'The Appeal and Power of Poetics (Luke 1:1-4)', in *Jesus and the Heritage of Israel: Luke's Narrative Claim upon Israel's Legacy* (vol. 1; Luke the Interpreter of Israel; ed. D. P. Moessner; Harrisburg: Trinity Press, 1999), pp. 84–123 (106); Bovon, *L'Evangile selon Luc*, vol. 1, p. 42.

58   Aélius Théon, *Progymnasmata* 106.5-6. Todd Penner believes that Luke-Acts is similar to the teaching of the *Progymnasmata*, see T. Penner, 'Reconfiguring the Rhetorical study of Acts: Reflections on the Method in and Learning of a Progymnastic Poetics', *PRSt* 30 (2003), pp. 425–39 (431–39).

59   See section V for the development of this point.

60   See L. Alexander, 'Fact, Fiction and the Genre of Acts', p. 399 [n. 11 above].

he immediately presents himself as a critical persona of this same tradition[61] since he must in a precise way consolidate its content. This move is not a simple repetition or affiliation but rather a critical reappropriation.

The challenge, therefore, is to (re)assure Theophilus (Lk.1.4) on account of what he has heard. Amid these rumours, I postulate, was the one about Paul being awkward in public and unable to persuade his hearers at certain key moments. This hypothesis is confirmed by the fact that this rumour about Paul has not completely disappeared in the Acts of the Apostles, though it is certainly not validated. It is present but viewed negatively or as subversive, and it allows us to understand much better the energy employed by the Lukan author to provide evidence linking the concept of παρρησία with the figure of Paul, as our reading of the data from Acts on the vocabulary of 'boldness' in speech will highlight (παρρησία and παρρησιάζομαι).

b. Paul and παρρησία in the Acts of the Apostles

The term παρρησία/παρρησιάζομαι is not present in the first volume of the Lukan corpus because it refers to a problematic not present in Jesus' ministry, but one that will be prominent in the ministry of his witnesses, Paul in particular. An analysis of the scope of παρρησία and παρρησιάζομαι in Acts shows that the concern of this terminology is notably theological for the author: the last verse of Acts points to 'proclaiming the kingdom of God', which Paul does boldly and without hindrance (Acts 28.31). But this theological design is entirely dependent on the conditions of that proclamation. This explains the fundamental ambiguity of the ἐξόν that accompanies the first occurrence of the term παρρησία in Acts 2.29: 'Fellow Israelites, it is permissible/possible (ἐξόν) to say to you confidently... .' Because Peter – who is speaking here – does so with παρρησία, it has become possible to speak the Christian proclamation, which accordingly is also permissible, in keeping with the double meaning of ἐξόν.[62] From the second occurrence on, the semantic field of 'boldness' in Acts clearly moves towards a reflection on the possibility of strong speech in service of the Christian proclamation: 'Now when [the rulers, elders, and scribes] saw the boldness of Peter and John and realized that they were uneducated and ordinary men, they were amazed and recognized them as companions of Jesus' (Acts 4.13). In other words, the Lukan author stresses from the very beginning of his narrative that boldness in speech may have nothing to do with education in rhetoric. The end of ch. 4 shows that παρρησία is given to the witnesses by the Lord, from whom it is appropriate to request it (Acts 4.29); it accompanies the outpouring of the Spirit (Acts 4.31). This boldness, therefore, is presented

---

61   A point also largely emphasized by Alexander (ibid., n. 11).

62   The translation above emphasizes the sense of permission in Acts 2.29, while that of Daniel Marguerat points to the freedom of Peter's speech: 'Let me tell you frankly' (D. Marguerat, *Les Actes des apôtres [1–12]* [CNT, 5a; Genève: Labor et Fides, 2007], p. 82). He chose this translation because of the redundant expression 'Brothers, men' at the beginning of the verse, in which Peter reduces 'the distance between his audience by showing his membership to their religious community' (ibid., p. 92).

as a key part of Christian speech, independent of the rhetorical education of the relevant witnesses.

This introductory framework is especially important because the terminology παρρησία and παρρησιάζομαι is later used almost exclusively[63] to describe Paul's speech (Acts 9.22, 26, 28; 13.46; 14.3; 19.3; 26.26; 28.31). Paul's boldness is introduced in relation to the rumour that precedes him, that of his past as a persecutor (cf. Gal. 1.23), a rumour heard by Ananias (Acts 9.13) and the synagogues of Damascus (Acts 9.21). At this stage in the narrative this rumour is not harmful; on the contrary, 'Saul became increasingly more powerful' (Acts 9.22). This wording links, in a paradoxical way, the rumour about Saul's past and the strength he displays in his speech. This tension between 'past as persecutor / strong in speech' is found in Acts 9.26-28: the apostles begin to fear that Paul is still an enemy, but Barnabas argues using the proof of Paul's boldness as displayed in Damascus. However, when the rumours hostile to Paul later make their return in Jerusalem (Acts 21.21, 24, 27), his past as a persecutor turned convert no longer serves him well, even becoming a threat to him. In fact, Paul recounts having protested in vain before Jesus, who tells him that those in Jerusalem will not welcome his testimony (Acts 22.18). Paul replies, 'Lord, they themselves know that in every synagogue I imprisoned and beat those who believed in you' (Acts 22.19). In response to this hopeful plea, Paul receives the order to leave (Acts 22.21). The unfolding narrative of Acts seems to show that at first – at Damascus and Jerusalem (Acts 9) – the boldness exhibited by Paul allows him to curb the suspicion aroused by the rumour of his past as a former persecutor, but it is not the same thereafter (Acts 21–22). In the end, it is as a prisoner that Paul again demonstrates his boldness, in speaking before Agrippa (Acts 26.26), and under house arrest in Rome in the final scene of the Lukan corpus (Acts 28.31).

Along the way, the notion of παρρησία in Acts comes to a dramatic climax when Paul is put in competition with Apollos regarding their oratorical abilities. Apollos is described in Acts 18.24 as λόγιος and speaks with παρρησία (18.26). This eloquence enables him to succeed where Paul has difficulties, namely, in the synagogue of Ephesus. The Lukan author takes care to give precedence to Paul who speaks first but briefly to the synagogue of Ephesus and then leaves (Acts 18.19-21). When Apollos arrives in Ephesus, he speaks out 'boldly in the synagogue', but he still needs an additional catechism from Priscilla and Aquila (Acts 18.26). When Paul returns – once Apollos has left for Corinth – he [Paul], however, enters into conflict with the synagogue, a conflict that leads to the relocation of his preaching to the lecture hall of Tyrannus (Acts 19.8-10). It is at this point that the short episode about the linens and handkerchiefs touching Paul slips in, a sign of extreme devotion to his person (Acts 19.11-12). The implicit contest between Apollos and Paul is told in several stages: Apollos is well received in the synagogue, but despite his eloquence, the boldness that he demonstrates (Acts 18.26) must be corrected by Priscilla and Aquila. But does he really listen to them? The handful of people whom

---

63   Acts 13.46 and 14.3 concern Paul and Barnabas; Acts 18.26 concerns Apollos who is precisely placed in competition with Paul in relation to the origin of their respective παρρησία, as I elaborate below.

Paul must baptize in the name of Jesus with the laying on of hands (Acts 19.1-7) suggests that Apollos continued to baptize only in the name of John. If Apollos is presented as a λόγιος orator from Alexandria, the Lukan author emphasizes that Paul also knows how to speak 'boldly' in the synagogue of Ephesus (ἐπαρρησιάζετο in Acts 19.8).

A distinction is thus made in Acts 18.24–19.10 between the boldness that comes from Apollos' rhetorical ability and the boldness that Paul exhibits following his conversion (Acts 9.22); this is consistent with the picture of Christian παρρησία as narrated in Acts 4.13, 29, 31. Furthermore, this distinction occurs in a key setting, Ephesus, in the heart of Asia where Paul was twice prevented from going (Acts 16.6; 20.16), preferring to meet the elders of Ephesus at Miletus (Acts 20.17). Asia is also the source of the wave of rumours that lead to Paul's final arrest (Acts 21.27; 24.19). I postulate that the Lukan author knows the rumour that circulates about Paul's untrained speech and weak public presence, and that the tradition of his troubles at Ephesus had to include this rumour. The hypothesis of such a rumour in Ephesus can also draw on the *Acts of Paul* which, for its part, emphasizes Paul's eloquence at Ephesus in the mouth of the governor, who says Paul 'has spoken well I know' (*Acts of Paul* 7.15-16; [Schneelmelcher]). Here we come full circle, for Paul has become λόγιος at Ephesus in the *Acts of Paul*, a dramatic way of trying to end the controversy over this issue. Another source gives us still a further way to discuss Paul's speech: Second Tim. 4.16-17 says that everyone deserted Paul at his defence, but the pseudepigraphical Paul emphasizes that 'the Lord stood by me and gave me strength (ἐνδυνάμωσεν), so that through me the message might be fully proclaimed and all the gentiles might hear it'. This 'strength' that enables Paul to speak is precisely indicated by the Lukan author beginning in the very first speech of the converted Saul (ἐνδυναμοῦτο in Acts 9.22).

Comparison of the Lukan depiction of Paul's speech with, upstream, the Pauline letters and, downstream, the *Acts of Paul* or 2 Timothy, shows, therefore, that there were grounds for discussion on this issue, as Paul himself concedes in 2 Cor. 10.10. Between the self-portraits of Paul and the Lukan reception, one can see a point of agreement about the fact that Paul was presented as 'untrained' in matters of eloquence (ἰδιώτης in 2 Cor. 11.6): this is also the implicit result of the Lukan distinction between Paul and Apollos precisely concerning the training of the λόγιος Alexandrian (Acts 18.24). In Acts, authentic παρρησία is a gift from the Lord not related to one's education (Acts 4.13), and it is offered with the outpouring of the Spirit (Acts 4.31). The self-portraits of Paul and the Lukan reception stand in opposition, however, with respect to the evaluation of the efficacy of Paul's speech. The two authors essentially defend two different literary postures for Paul. Paul relies on his epistles to defend his first literary posture, that of an absent father who is present in his writings. This is the goal throughout all of 1 and 2 Corinthians. But around 80–90 CE, the Lukan author works hard to defend the second literary posture adopted by Paul in the later years of his life, that of divine prisoner (Phlm. 9; Phil. 1.15-20). As we saw in section III.b, this image was taken up and developed in the earliest Pauline reception (Col. 4.18; Eph. 3.1; Acts 20.22), and around it the controversy continued to rage on (2 Tim. 1.8, 16).

Still other sources show that the controversy surrounding Paul, particularly concerning his past as a persecutor, is alive and well at the turn of the first century and continues on into the second. First Timothy 1.13 goes so far as to justify why Paul's past as a persecutor has been forgiven: 'I received mercy because I had acted ignorantly in unbelief.' Moreover, there are four occurrences of an interpretation of Gen. 49.47 as a prophecy about Paul's fate – two in Tertullian and two in Hippolytus.[64] This quadruple attestation highlights the antiquity of such a tradition, according to Moreschini and Braun.[65] For example, in *Adversus Marcionem*:

> Because even the book of Genesis so long ago promised me *the Apostle* Paul. For among the types and prophetic blessings which Jacob pronounced over his sons, when he turned his attention to Benjamin, he exclaimed, 'Benjamin is a ravenous wolf, in the morning devouring the prey, and in the evening distributing it'. He foresaw that Paul would arise out of the tribe of Benjamin, a voracious wolf, devouring his prey in the morning—in other words, in the early period of his life he would devastate the Lord's sheep, as a persecutor of the churches; but in the evening he would give them nourishment, which means that in his declining years he would educate the fold of Christ, as the teacher of the Gentiles.[66]

The fact that it was necessary to invoke a prophecy from Genesis in order to justify Paul's past persecution highlights how sensitive the issue was and how long it had been a subject of controversy. For examples of complete opposition to Paul, we can turn, of course, to the pseudo-Clementine *Recognitions* I.70-71 and *Homilies* XVII.13-19, or to the fact that, according to Epiphanius, the Ebionites knew a story of Paul in which he was a pagan converted to Judaism.[67] The exegesis of Gen. 49.47 possibly came about as a defence against such accusations.

We have found traces of the Lukan author's attempt to subvert three rumours hostile to Paul: his unforgivable past as a persecutor, his feeble speech, and his disgraceful imprisonment. He considers them capable of catching up to Paul even at the very end of the narrative (cf. Acts 28.21). By introducing Paul in accordance with the rumour about his past – Saul the persecutor in Acts 7.56–8.1 – the Lukan author addresses this rumour head-on and defuses it by associating it with Saul's strong speech (Acts 9.22, 26, 28), simultaneously countering the rumour about Paul's feeble speech as well. He continues this effort by distinguishing between the boldness born of eloquence (Acts 18.24-26) and the freedom of Paul's speech, which even becomes the concluding image of Acts (28.31). And if Paul the prisoner speaks with all boldness and without hindrance, it is a sign that he is a divine prisoner, empowered by the παρρησία that comes from the Lord (Acts 4.29-31). In fact, the Lukan author is promoting the second literary posture of Paul – the divine prisoner – and not the posture of his presence through letters. Associated

---

64   See Tertullien, *Contra Marcion* V.1.5; *idem, Sorpiace* XIII.1; Hippolytus, *Comm. Gn* LII; *idem, Benedictions of Isaac and Jacob* XXVIII.

65   See Tertullien, *Contre Marcion. Livre 5* (SC, 483; ed. C. Moreschini and R. Braun; Paris: Cerf, 2004), p. 76, note 2.

66   Tertullian, *Contra Marcion* V.1.5 (*ANF* 3:430, modified).

67   See Epiphanius, *Panarion* XXX.16.8-9.

with the image of the divine prisoner, Paul's παρρησία acquires a semantic range that even incorporates the political dimension into Acts 28.31: whatever his actual circumstances, whatever his qualifications, here the Christian proclamation is permissible and possible, possible and permissible, just as Peter announced in Acts 2.29 (cf. ἐξόν).

V. Gladium stilo mutans: When the Figure of Paul is Standardized

Using Jérôme Meizoz's theory of literary postures allows us, therefore, to identify two successive postures in Paul's letters: that of the absent father who is present in his writings, over which Paul superimposes in the later years of his life the posture of divine prisoner. What is the effect of these postures in the reception of Paul? Or, to put it in literary terms, what is the effect of these postures on the figure of Paul? It is the second posture that will be the most strained in the period following Paul's death, at a time when Christianity is pluriform and not concerned with the theological study of Paul's letters, but rather with the safe-keeping of Paul's memory. The Lukan reception shows knowledge of the various rumours circulating about Paul and, like Col. 4.18, serves to promote the memory of his chains, the memory of the divine prisoner. As the Lukan author himself says, he writes to provide assurance (ἀσφάλεια) to Theophilus. If I were to identify the clearest point of continuity between the Pauline and Lukan writings, without doubt I would place it here, in the act of writing that seeks to strengthen its audience. On this point the Lukan author takes part in the *imitatio Pauli*, as seen in Phil. 3.1: 'Finally, my brothers and sisters, rejoice in the Lord. *To write the same things to you* is not troublesome to me, and for you it is a *safeguard* (ἀσφαλές)'; or even in the litotes of 1 Thess. 5.1-2: 'Now concerning the times and the seasons, brothers and sisters, *you do not need to have anything written to you. For you yourselves know very well* (ἀκριβῶς) that the day of the Lord will come like a thief in the night.'

    In conclusion, the Lukan author seems to have succeeded in reassuring his recipients, that is to say, in convincing them to guard the memory of Paul's chains and in persuading them to recognize him as a divine prisoner. This is attested in the gradual standardization of the figure of Paul during the second century. The Lukan author has certainly not been alone in his persuasive task: the author of *1 Clement* works in the same way, as we saw in section II. The effort of these authors at the turn of the first century will be rewarded by the circulation of collections of Paul's letters even before Marcion,[68] by the support of Irenaeus for the history of Christian origins as told in the Acts of the Apostles, and by the fact that an author such as Tertullian shows us a standardized figure of Paul, where his past as a persecutor, his verve as a writer, and the memory of his chains come together. For Tertullian, Paul is indeed the one who 'transforms the sword into a stylus', *gladium stilo mutans*.[69]

---

68   See note 25 above.
69   Tertullien, *Scorpiace* XIII.1 (ed. G. Azzali Bernardelli). This perception of Paul is made possible by the fact that Tertullian read Paul alongside Acts (see Tertullien, *Contra Marcion* V.1.4).

But to achieve this standardized figure that subverts the rumours hostile to Paul, one indispensable action was necessary: Clement of Rome, Luke, and others were able to subordinate under the memory of the divine prisoner the archive of the letters of one who sought almost to 'lord it over [the] faith' of the community (2 Cor. 1.24). The image of the prisoner who is free to speak in Acts 28.31 has helped to establish narratively the 'memory of his chains' (Col. 4.18).

Chapter 15

'WORKING WITH ONE'S HANDS': ONE MODEL, MANY APPLICATIONS (ACTS 20.33; 1 TIMOTHY 5.17; 2 THESSALONIANS 3.7-10)

Yann Redalié

Trans. Michael D. Thomas, Alexandre Thiltges, and Theresa Varney Kennedy

Concluding his speech in Miletus (Acts 20.33-35), Paul, while demonstrating his leadership over the community, provides his personal example, well known to all – ('You yourselves know', v. 34; 'In all this I have given you an example', v. 35; cf. Acts 18.3) – in order to move from a call to selflessness to exhorting a showing of solidarity with the weak.

Indeed, by working with his hands, Paul managed not only to provide for his own needs but was equally able to supply the needs of his co-workers. Thus, it is by working in this manner (οὕτως κοπιῶντας δεῖ, v. 35) that the Ephesian elders should support the weak. While doing this they will practise the beatitude pronounced by the Lord Jesus himself: 'It is more blessed to give than to receive' (20.28).

How 'Pauline' are these verses? Is it possible to evaluate the degree of Paulinism? Or perhaps even better: how can we situate these statements within the reception of Paul? In fact, when we compare this conclusion of the sermon at Miletus to other texts of the Pauline tradition (1 Tim. 5.17; 2 Tim. 3.7-10), it becomes clear that this same pattern of Paul working with his hands can be used in completely divergent ways.

I. Paul as a Model of Solidarity (Acts 20.33-35)

If some commentators have pointed out that certain manuscripts conclude Acts 20.32 with a clear-cut doxology, thus emphasizing the apparently self-propagating tone of vv. 33-35,[1] the more recent trend is rather to place the emphasis on the integration and the function of these last verses in the general context of his farewell speech at Miletus. Paul is presented as a model in the conclusion of

---

1   As in later recommendations written by Paul's hand at the end of a letter, or like the instructions given to the rich in 1 Tim. 6.17-19 after the doxology in v. 16. See J. Dupont, *Le discours de Milet, testament pastoral de Saint Paul, Ac 20,18-36* (LD, 32; Paris: Cerf, 1962), p. 285.

the exhortation, in which the Ephesian elders are frequently exhorted to imitate the apostle.[2]

Paul's example is presented in three consecutive parts. First there is the selflessness that was already mentioned in v. 24: 'But I do not count my life of any value to myself.' In Ephesus, Paul did not act in order to benefit materially in any way,[3] and he did not covet anyone's possessions.[4] One hears again from Paul's mouth the motifs that can already be found in Samuel's farewell speech (1 Sam. 12.3).[5] In his letters, Paul likewise reminds readers of his selflessness and in 1 Cor. 9.12, 2 Cor. 7.2, 11.7-11, and 1 Thess. 2.5, 9 defends himself against the accusation that he exploited the communities.

There Paul mentions his autonomy in properly taking care of his own needs, which is also a proof of selflessness and of non-covetousness. He works in order to provide for his own needs and not to be a burden on the community. If his behaviour is mentioned on numerous occasions in Paul's letters,[6] it is not so much the case here.

Paul switches immediately to the third stage of the proposed model: the subsistence of his close co-workers is now also assured by the work of the apostle. The model has to be interpreted, motivated, and imitated, based on this last motif, which is absent in Pauline texts: 'In all this I have given you an example that by such work we must support the weak' (Acts 20.35; πάντα ὑπέδειξα ὑμῖν ὅτι οὕτως κοπιῶντας δεῖ ...).[7]

If Acts 20.33 reflects a source for Paul's paranetic example in his refusal to be cared for by the community (cf. 1 Thess. 2.9; 1 Cor. 4.12; 9.12, 15-18; 2 Cor. 11.9; 12.14), it does not preserve the Pauline motivation for denying dependence upon the community (1 Thess. 2.5), namely, the freedom and autonomy to preach the gospel (1 Cor. 9.12). In Acts 20.33-35, it is rather the development of charity

---

2   Paul exhorts them that they may be vigilant as he was (Acts 20.31) and that they may take care of themselves (v. 28) as Paul did. They are to watch over the flocks (v. 28) as Paul cared for them (vv. 20, 26). The word of grace is ready to equip them (v. 32) as it equipped Paul (v. 24).

3   Paul's visit to Ephesus provides us with a good context for the economic questions (19.24-27); note also the contrast between Paul (20.25) and Demetrius (19.24).

4   'Gold, silver, clothing', represents a triad built by traditions. In Gen. 24.53; Exod. 3.21; 11.2 LXX (clothing in Greek only); 12.35-6: 1 Kings 10.24; 2 Kings 5.5; Zech 14.14 'gold, silver and clothing' are riches that are given to elected officials. In other texts they represent rich furnishings, stolen objects, or gifts. The three terms may also become symbols of perishable riches (Jas 5.23), according to Dupont, *Discours*, pp. 286–91. In addition, the denunciation of the desire of riches is widespread in the various ethic and religious traditions of Antiquity (Philostr. *Vita Apol Thyana* 1.34; Dio Chrysostom, *Oratio* 32.9, 11; Stobeo 3.417.5; Pseudo-Phocylides 42; but also Sir. 27.1-2; 31.5-6).

5   See also Num. 16.15 with regards to Moses in the context of the revolt of Korah.

6   Not charging for the minister's services is a qualifying criterion for the 'Pauline' minister in contrast to his rivals or adversaries (1 Thess. 2.3; Gal. 4.17; 2 Cor. 11.8; 12.13; 2 Tim. 3.2, 6-9; Tit. 1.11; 2 Pet. 2.3; *Did.* 11.5; 9.12). For material autonomy see Acts 18.3; 1 Cor. 4.12; 9.15-18; 1 Thess. 4.11.

7   κοπιάω generally refers to the minister's work, but in 1 Cor. 4.12 it has the same meaning as here. κόπος is used for manual labour in 1 Thess. 2.9 and 2 Thess. 3.8 (see also Lk. 5.5; 12.27; 1 Cor. 16.16; Gal. 4.11; 2 Tim. 2.6).

itself that motivates the exhortation for the elders to engage in manual labour. This injunction, which consists of a call to help the weak, is in turn based upon the *macaristic agraphon* of Jesus.[8] The perspective becomes broader. The exhortation then would not be limited to ministers, but be extended to the whole community who are invited to follow Jesus's teachings related to money and to property. This could only happen if, in turn, the elders became the models of this teaching.[9]

Thus the model of Paul, proposed in the conclusion of the speech at Miletus, is articulated within a Lukan perspective of 'beneficent charity', according to Dupont's expression;[10] that is to say, of sharing according to what is needed, which is well represented in Luke's narrative through archetypical characters: the Good Samaritan (Lk. 10.30-37), Zacchaeus, who makes restitution for ill-gotten goods (Lk. 19.8), Tabitha and her works (Acts 9.36-39), Barnabas' act of generosity (Acts 4.37), the centurions who, from the beginning, are generous men, attentive to the needs of the community, and of course, the fraternal sharing of the first community in Acts 2.42, 44; 4.32, 34.

Furthermore in the story of Acts, Paul's material autonomy is expressed not only through his activity as a tent maker in Acts 18.3, but also when he himself pays the expenses incurred by the four Jerusalem pilgrims who take the Nazarite vow in 21.24, 26, or again when he pays his own living expenses in Rome in 28.30.[11]

Mutual material aid is certainly also a preoccupation in Paul's letters, if only in the passages related to the organization of and participation in the Collection (2 Cor. 8 and 9; Rom. 15.25-27). Mutual aid is seen flowing in the opposite direction than Acts 20.33-35 when Paul addresses his thanks to the Philippians (Phil. 4.10-20) for the help when he himself was in need.

Concerning the link between manual labour and mutual aid, it is explicitly formulated and close to Acts 20.35 with reference to the thief in Eph. 4.28: 'Thieves must give up stealing; rather, let them labor and work honestly with their own hands, so as to have something to share with the needy' (... μᾶλλον δὲ κοπιάτω ἐργαζόμενος ταῖς [ἰδίαις] χερσὶν τὸ ἀγαθόν, ἵνα ἔχῃ μεταδιδόναι τῷ χρείαν ἔχοντι). In a sort of anticipation of modern *restorative justice*, the

---

8   Or could it be a common saying, known otherwise, that Acts attributes here to Jesus? The discussion is open to debate (see 1 Thess. 4.15). See Acts 11.16 where Peter evokes as word of the Lord a Greco-Roman proverb, spoken by the mouth of Jesus. Here, there are two distinctives in the teaching of the beatitude in v. 35: it is formulated in the neutral and not relative to a person; it is comparative and not absolute. There are a few possibilities according to Dupont, *Discours*, pp. 327–35: a) The maxim appears to have been widely used among the Greeks – we may cite Thucydides II 97.4; Plutarch, *Mor.* 173 d; Plutarch, *Caes* 16 – and similar to the saying of Jesus; b) Jesus may have used the maxim to illustrate what he was trying to say; c) The beatitude summarizes Gospel teaching and is without a doubt influenced by a proverbial Greek expression. For the Christianizing influence of Lk. 6.20, see Mt. 5.3. The spirit of the citation is captured in Did 1.5 and Shepherd of Hermas, *Mand.* 2.4-6.

9   J. Roloff, 'Themen und Traditionen urchristlicher Amtsträgerparänese', in *Neues Testament und Ethik* (Festschrift R. Schnackenburg; ed. H. Merklein; Freiburg: Herder, 1989), pp. 507–28 (514).

10   Dupont, *Discours*, pp. 313–14.

11   S. Walton, *Leadership and Lifestyle. The Portrait of Paul in the Miletus speech and 1 Thessalonians* (SNTSMS, 108; Cambridge University Press, Cambridge, 2000), p. 89.

motivation for work goes beyond personal subsistence and material autonomy by also helping those who are in need.[12]

Acts sheds light on this helping the needy by stating that Paul took care of his needs and those of his co-workers. In fact, to avoid the risk of being misunderstood, Paul refused to exert his apostolic right of receiving material sustenance from the community (1 Cor. 9.12b, 15-18), although as an apostle – and he is determined to defend his rights – he could have legitimately demanded it (1 Cor. 9.1-12a, 13-14). Did he not accept aid from the churches of Macedonia (Phil. 4.10-20; 2 Cor. 11.18)? And the fact that he stopped working when Silas and Timothy arrived from Macedonia (Acts 18.5) certainly refers to the donation made by the Philippians. In 1 Thess. 2.8, love and total devotion lead the apostle to the voluntary decision to work with his hands so that he does not become a burden to the community.

Acts thus transforms into a valuable principle for all ministers that which was merely a personal and exceptional situation for Paul: not to depend on the community for material well-being (1 Cor. 4.12; 1 Thess. 2.9).

II. An Income for the Elders of Ephesus? (1 Timothy 5.17)

If we trust the information given in 1 Timothy (1 Tim. 1.3), the leadership status of the elders of the community of Ephesus is also the subject of 1 Tim. 5.17-19. Yet the exhortation diverges from the one found in the discourse given in Miletus. It acknowledges some of these elders as worthy of 'double honour' (διπλῆ τιμή), according to their ability to govern well, and is applied to the ministry of the Word and teaching.[13]

A large consensus of criticism has formed that recognizes in the expression 'double honour' a form of income based on the motivation expressed in 5.18. This type of support is viewed as deriving legitimately from the apostle's right to receive material aid according to 1 Cor. 9.9, 14: 'You shall not muzzle an ox while it is treading out the grain' (Deut. 25.4), or again, the dominical 'The labourer deserves to be paid' (cf. Lk. 10.7).[14]

---

12   For Walton, *Leadership*, 170, the exhortation to work 'with one's own hands' in 1 Thess. 4.11 is seen also in the perspective of solidarity with those who are in need. In this sense the togetherness of 4.9-12 is centred around fraternal love. Vv. 9-10a recall the principles and vv. 10b-12 give the concrete application. In this manner one would find a parallel with Acts 20.34 (it concerns in both cases an echo; the term χρεία is used to express one's needs in Acts 20.34 and 1 Thess. 4.12).

13   V. 17: 'Let the elders who rule well (οἱ καλῶς προεστῶτες) be considered worthy of double honour, especially those who labour in preaching and teaching' (μάλιστα οἱ κοπιῶντες ἐν λόγῳ καὶ διδασκαλίᾳ). Meaning of μάλιστα: a) 'above all', 'particularly'; see 4.10; 5.8; Gal. 6.10; Phil. 4.22; Phlm. 16; or b) 'meaning'; see Tit. 1.10. H. P. Towner, *The Letters to Timothy and Titus* (NICNT; Grand Rapids: Eerdmans, 2006), p. 361, presents two hypotheses: a) it concerns elders who rule well, among which the best (μάλιστα) teach and preach, and thus distinguish themselves from those who are mediocre; b) it concerns those who direct the community, meaning the best (μάλιστα) are those who teach and preach, and distinguish themselves from the mediocre.

14   N. Brox, *Die Pastoralbriefe* (RNT, 7.2; Regensburg: F. Pustet, 1969), p. 149; M. Dibelius and H. Conzelmann, *Die Pastoralbriefe* (Hermeneia; Tübingen, Mohr Siebeck, 3rd edn,

The indifference with regard to money is also found in the list of qualities required to exercise authority in the community (1 Tim. 3.3: for the overseer not to be 'a lover of money' [ἀφιλάργυρος]; 1 Tim. 3.8 and Tit. 1.7: deacons and overseers shall not be 'greedy for money' [αἰ σχροκερδεῖς]). It still seems that the minister is to manage certain amounts of money, even if only a fund established to take care of the female widows (1 Tim. 5.3).

Furthermore, the polemic against the opponents also applies to the lure of money, which is their motivation (1 Tim. 1.5; 2 Tim. 3.6-9). The author sets the model of the honest overseer against those who profit from their piety, seeking to make money from their religious activities (1 Tim. 3.8; 6.5; 2 Tim. 3.2; Tit. 1.7, 11). The criterion is αὐτάρκεια (1 Tim. 6.6), namely, what is necessary is sufficient, divulging the motivation of the mandate received by the Lord (1 Tim. 6.12-16).

Certainly part of the response to these problems is the affirmation of the right of the elders who deserve to receive, if not a regular income, at least some form of material compensation. This affirmation also represents an attempt to regulate practice.

Therefore, for 1 Timothy, the exception Paul makes for himself – the refusal to be taken care of by the community – does not modify the primary rules earlier pronounced by Paul and which are therefore still valid. This is why 1 Timothy paraphrases as closely as possible the regulations formulated in 1 Corinthians 9, rules which establish the remuneration of ministers (1 Cor. 9.4, 14; 1 Tim. 5.17). In 1 Tim. 5.18b, the author can take for granted the metaphorical interpretation of Deut. 25.4 already fixed by 1 Cor. 9.9 in order to legitimize the right of the apostle to have material needs met by the community ('Does he [Moses] not speak entirely for our sake?').[15]

1955), p. 61 (ET: M. Dibelius and H. Conzelmann, *The Pastoral Epistles: A Commentary on the Pastoral Epistles* [trans. P. Buttolph and A. Yarbro; Philadelphia: Fortress Press, 1972], p. 78); L. T. Johnson, *The First and Second Letters to Timothy* (AB, 35A; New York: Doubleday, 2001), p. 277; J. Roloff, *Der erste Brief an Timotheus* (EKKNT, 15; Zürich: Benziger, 1988), p. 309; P. Trummer, *Die Paulustradition der Pastoralbriefe* (Frankfurt: Peter Lang, 1978), p. 224. G. Schoellgen, 'Die "diplè time" von 1Tm 5,17', *ZNW* 80 (1989), pp. 232–39, discusses the various interpretations of the expression in 1 Tim. 5.17 'honour' or 'honoraries' apart from that of H. von Lips, *Glaube, Gemeinde, Amt. Zum Verständnis der Ordination in den Pastoralbriefen* (FRLANT, 122; Göttingen: Vandenhoeck u. Ruprecht, 1979), pp. 108–11. Although he also thinks that it concerns here material compensation, he sees too many difficulties (lexical, p. 234; historical, p. 235; socio-economic, ibid.) for us to be able to envision a regular salary. From the associative practices of the time period, he formulates the hypothesis (that, in my opinion, is not even supported by the text in 1 Timothy) that these 'honoraries' consisted in a double 'honorific' portion during community meals (p. 238). For R. F. Collins, *I and II Timothy and Titus* (Louisville: John Knox, 2002), p. 144, it was more than a double salary. It consisted of being held in high esteem by the community and was more than just the fact of being supported by it. This doubly merited privilege, economic subsistence and guarantee of consideration, expressed by the grievances against the elder who exercised leadership, may only be confirmed through the testimony of two witnesses (v. 19).

15   Similarly, the three likenesses spoken in 1 Cor. 9.7 – the army, the vineyard, the sheep – echo those of the army, the athlete, and the harvested field indicated in 2 Tim. 2.3, 6.

The Pastoral Epistles, therefore, preclude as a motivating standard for future ministers the right to refuse remuneration as based on Paul's own example – which Acts 20.34 nonetheless endorses. Thus through the pseudepigraphy of the Pastorals ('fictive self-interpretation'),[16] the interpretive space for a legitimate understanding of 1 Corinthians 9 is fixed and defined.

Finally, if we noted earlier that the exhortation to solidarity with the weakest in Acts 20.35 was motivated by a word of the Lord, we also notice that this word of the Lord stands in contrast to the word stated in 1 Tim. 5.18b which favours remuneration of the elders. '... for the worker deserves a salary,' echoing 1 Cor. 9.14: 'In the same way, the Lord commanded that those who proclaim the gospel should get their living by the gospel' (cf. Lk. 10.7, ἄξιος γὰρ ὁ ἐργάτης τοῦ μισθοῦ αὐτου, in the context of the mission of the Seventy; cf. the mission of the Twelve in Mt. 10.10). Does one find on this particular point a hint of tension between authorial arguments and actual community practice?

III. Not to Be a Burden to the Community (2 Thessalonians 3.7-10)

The instruction in 2 Thess. 3.7-10, often quoted because of its resemblance to Acts 20.33, will use the traditions related to the right of the remuneration of the apostle by the community (ἐξουσία) and his choice not to claim it, in yet another sense. Applied to the members of the community – and not to its leaders – the apostle's material autonomy becomes emblematic of reducing, perhaps even eliminating, the burden on the community of those who are materially dependent upon it. Thus, this exhortation seems to run counter to solidarity with the needy as commended at Miletus.

The only concern is 'not to be a burden to the community'. Compared to 1 Thess. 2.9, of the three incentives given for the work of the apostles – love for the recipients, preaching of the gospel, and self-reliance – only the last motive is maintained in 2 Thess. 3.8. The attitude of the apostles is singled out and treated apart from any relation to preaching. The rationale here in 2 Thessalonians is applied only to the model of imitation which urges restraint from material dependency and thus also from becoming a burden upon the community (v. 9).[17]

This theme is foreshadowed in 1 Thessalonians. Paul's conduct in 1 Thess. 2.9 – the gift of the apostles themselves to their recipients as their motive for choosing manual labour and not wanting to be dependent on anybody – anticipates and implicitly introduces the exhortation to similar behaviour on the part of the Thessalonians (1 Thess. 4.11). In 2 Thess. 3.7-9, this relationship becomes explicit.

16   A. Merz, *Die fiktive Selbstauslegung des Paulus: Intertextuelle Studien zur Intention und Rezeption der Pastoralbriefe* (NTOA, 52; Göttingen: Vandenhoeck und Ruprecht, 2004), pp. 59, 212–13, 132–33.

17   See 1 Thess. 1.6-7, where the Thessalonians imitated Paul and became, in their own way examples to be imitated by the churches of Macedonia. The term 'model' (τύπον) in 1 Thess. 1.7 is applied to the Thessalonians. Here the 'model' is Paul and his co-workers (Phil. 3.17). This didactic finality of the example (see Rom. 5.14; 6.17; 1 Cor. 10.6; Phil. 3.17; Jn. 20.25; Acts 7.43-44; 23.25) may be linked to 2 Thess. 2.15: 'the traditions that you were taught by us' (ἐδιδάχθητε).

Paul is now expecting to be imitated and indicates how this shall be done. After all, the reason the apostles chose this manner of behaviour was for the purpose of eliciting imitation.

The last antithesis of 2 Thess. 3.9, like that in 1 Thess. 2.7, contrasts two ways of exercising apostolic authority: 1) Taking advantage of the right to be cared for, or in other words, imposing oneself on the community, or – and this is where the two letters diverge – 2) resembling the wet-nurse of 1 Thess. 2.8 who, tenderly keeping her infants warm night and day as though they were her own, forms the model to be imitated (2 Thess. 3.7, 9).

'But with toil and labour we worked night and day, so that we might not burden any of you' (2 Thess. 3.8) repeats almost word for word 1 Thess. 2.9. We note the differences in motivation and goal attributed to apostolic behaviour expressed in almost identical terms. In 1 Thess. 2.8 it was the love and complete devotion to the community, the sharing of the gospel and of life, that caused the apostle to do manual labour of his own free will, not only sharing the gospel, but also his own life. Second Thessalonians 3.8 does not mention any of these motives. From the very beginning the purpose is to be a model intended to be imitated. And if the verb 'to give oneself' is once again present, it is because one is supposed to '*give oneself for you as an example to be followed*' (2 Thess. 3.9).

Finally, and in a more significant way, as in Acts 20.35 and 1 Tim. 5.18b the argument is built on a word of authority, and it is no longer the reminder of the word of the Lord, but the reminder of the word of apostles *in vivo* 'when we were with you' (2 Thess. 3.10): 'Anyone unwilling to work should not eat.'

This maxim reflects a mentality common at that time.[18] However, it is not found in the exact same expression, with its distinctive emphasis on volition: 'If a man will not work.'[19] It is not certain that the citation is from a pre-existing maxim. The maxim could have been used by the author of 2 Thessalonians, taken from popular sayings and Pauline texts dedicated to manual labour, or even from Gen. 3.17-19.[20]

---

18   Numerous references in A. J. Malherbe, *The Letters to the Thessalonians* (AB, 32B; New York: Doubleday, 2000), p. 452. A. Deissmann, *Light from the Ancient East: The New Testament Illustrated by Recently Discovered Texts of the Graeco-Roman World* (New York: Harper and Brothers, 1908), p. 314, refers to the 'good old work ethic' according to which, for example, the lazy apprentice should not sit down at the table for dinner. Cf. also Str-B 3.641-42; B. Rigaux, *Saint Paul. Les épîtres aux Thessaloniciens* (EBib; Paris: Lecoffre, 1956), p. 710. The truism 'eat to live' is widely diffused (Ps. 128.2; Prov. 6.6-11; 10.4; 12.11; 28.19; 19.15; Gen Rab 2.2). Psd Phocylides 154 claims that 'every idle man lives from what his hands can steal' (trans. P. W. van der Horst in *The Old Testament Pseudepigrapha* [ed. James H. Charlesworth; Peabody, Mass.: Hendrickson, 2009]. p. 579).

19   οὐ θέλει; Rigaux, *Thessaloniciens*, p. 56, 709; S. Légasse, *Les épîtres de Paul aux Thessaloniciens*, (LD, 7; Paris, Cerf: 1999), p. 432; M. J. J. Menken, *2 Thessalonians* (New Testament Readings; London: Routledge, 1994), p. 135.

20   W. Marxsen, *Der zweite Brief an die Thessaloniker* (ZBK, 11.2; Zürich: TVZ, 1982), p. 101. If the qualification of the apostolic tradition attributed to this sentence surprises W. Trilling, *Der zweite Brief an die Thessalonicher* (EKK, 14; Zürich: Benziger-Neukirchener, 1980), p. 148, then we know that it must be common sense. It is for P. Müller, *Anfänge der Paulusschule, darg-estellt am zweiten Thesslonischerbrief und am Kolosserbrief* (AThANT, 74; Zürich: Theologischer

For many commentators this insistence on some in the community's 'unwillingness' to work is interpreted as a strong argument for withdrawing community support from the 'disorderly' folk of Thessalonica, as a rationale for liberating those who feel obliged to uphold them materially.

IV. Paul, One Model, Many Applications: A Summary

Where does the model of Paul working with his hands stand within the Pauline reception? The model functions in various and almost opposite ways.

In Acts 20.33-35, Paul's refusal to receive support from the community is extended as a model for the whole community by its grounding in Paul's own care for his colleagues' material needs, a rationale not expressly stated in the Pauline letters. Working with one's hands therefore makes Paul himself a model of solidarity with those in need, a norm to which the elders must aspire as they model their leadership by caring for the rest of the community.

In 1 Tim. 5.17, on the contrary, words of scripture and the word of the Lord, though borrowed from the same context as in 1 Corinthians 9, maintain the right of the apostle to be supported by the community. These arguments of Paul are repeated for the purpose of regulating financial questions and for legitimating the right of elders to receive remuneration for their service. Paul's refusal for himself forms an implicit exception, while his right to remuneration provides the rule.

Finally, in 2 Thess. 3.7-10, the Pauline example of the autonomy of the apostles applied to the members of the community possesses a corrective function. Distinguishing itself from the conclusion of the discourse at Miletus, this injunction intends to reduce and perhaps even eliminate those who unduly claim the right to be supported financially by other members of the community.

Verlag Zurich, 1988), p. 165, indicative of an impoverishment of theological reflection, that does not take up, for example, a preoccupation with the society (1 Thess. 4.11).

Chapter 16

'BE IMITATORS OF ME, BROTHERS AND SISTERS' (PHILIPPIANS 3.17): PAUL AS AN EXEMPLARY FIGURE IN THE PAULINE CORPUS AND THE ACTS OF THE APOSTLES

Jean-François Landolt
Trans. Michael D. Thomas, Eric Gilchrest, and Timothy Brookins

I. Introduction

This study examines Paul's 'self-presentation' and, more specifically, the question of his exemplarity. Beginning with an analysis of the way in which Paul presents himself and offers himself as an example in his letters, we want to see whether, via a process of tradition, the same Pauline image can be found in the Acts of the Apostles. If at times Paul presents himself in his letters as an example to imitate, could one say that the Lukan construction of Paul retains the same exemplary dimension? If so, in what way does Paul present himself as an example? And is Luke's version consistent with this same model of exemplarity?

Our analysis will develop in three successive stages. Starting with Paul's letters, we shall limit ourselves to his exhortations to imitate him. We will first consider the instances of exhortation where the term μιμητής ('imitator') is used with reference to emulating Paul and with a verb in the imperative mood. These criteria limit us to 1 Cor. 4.16; 11.1 and Phil. 3.17. That said, if our three criteria are not applied as such, 1 Thess. 1.6 can also be added to the list. This text does not use an imperative, so it is not, strictly speaking, an exhortation. Paul, however, makes reference to the same kind of imitation as that proposed in the first three occurrences considered. Even if it is after the fact – that is, even if imitation has already occurred – Paul's praise of the occurrence implicitly renders it an exhortation. In any case, apart from the application of all our criteria we also have Gal. 4.12. Though the term μιμητής is not found, the imperative and the ἐγώ of the injunction γίνεσθε ὡς ἐγώ ('become as I am') creates an exhortation similar to the first three examples we have noted.

Among the different texts in which these exhortations occur, we will look at Philippians 3 specifically; then we will focus on a passage in Paul's letters in which he expresses himself in the first person singular: chapter 7 of the Epistle to the Romans. After briefly showing how this passage is in our view autobiographical, we will demonstrate how Paul's 'I' also trains with him the believer, even if it is not a question of a direct exhortation to imitation.

In Acts, the question of self-presentation – and more generally the exemplarity of Paul – manifests itself differently. Here, the discourses of Paul are included in the context of a narrative. This narration apparently characterizes Paul in the context of two specific roles. We see Paul as witness (Acts 9.26-27), an instrument in the service of the Lord (Acts 9.15-16); and at the same time, Luke takes care to paint the portrait of Paul as a man of enviable social status (Paul even invokes this status directly in certain discourses; we will examine the function and extent of each instance). We will focus precisely on the three accounts of his conversion (Acts 9.1-19; 22.4-21; 26.9-18).

The third part of our task will be to consider a formulation of the character of Paul as exemplary (whether it is he who presents himself as such or Luke who presents him to us in this way, in the various places that afford us the opportunity to consider such a question).

II. Paul's Self-presentation and Exemplarity in the Pauline Corpus: the Example of Philippians 3 °

a. A Journey of Conversion

In focusing first on the example of Philippians 3, we should say that our goal will not be to propose a detailed exegesis for the whole of the pericope but to draw from relevant parts in order to move our inquiry forward. First and foremost we must justify the choice of this text for our objective: if the whole of the pericope is to be taken into account, two passages contain formal elements which immediately demand our attention, namely vv. 4-6 and v. 17. It will be essential to explain the referent of each of these passages as well as to determine how each functions beginning with an analysis of the immediate context. The first of these two passages (3.4-7) emphasizes Paul's 'Jewish' qualities (περιτομῆ: 'with respect to circumcision'; ἐκ γένου Ἰσραήλ: 'of the race of Israel'), a zealous Pharisee, in order to arrive in v. 6b at his blamelessness with respect to the Law (κατὰ δικαιοσύνην τὴν ἐν νόμῳ γενόμενος ἄμεμπτος: 'as to righteousness under the law, blameless'). This conclusion regarding his irreproachability has a bearing upon what opens this small unit (v. 4), i.e. Paul's reasons to have confidence (πεποίθησις) in the flesh (ἐν σαρκί). The French TOB translation (in view of the context, and interpreting a bit) renders 'confidence in the flesh' as 'confidence in myself', that is, in Paul. If this translation displaces the Greek term σάρξ ('flesh', 'body'), it nevertheless accounts for the following meaning: the confidence here related by Paul is effectively a confidence founded upon himself. However, such a rendering perhaps lacks that which σάρξ most nearly conveys – confidence founded upon himself, but only as one belonging to the chosen people.[1] It is possible to shed some light here on the precise meaning of the words introduced in v. 4 by referring to Peter O'Brien,

---

1   Cf. D. Marguerat, 'Paul et la Loi: Le retournement', in *Paul, une théologie en construction* (ed. A. Dettwiler, J. D. Kaestli, and D. Marguerat; MdB, 51; Genève: Labor et Fides, 2004), pp. 251–75 (267).

who pauses to examine the transition between vv. 3 and 4. He begins by showing the tension between the two formulas that immediately follow one another in this passage – καὶ οὐκ ἐν σαρκὶ πεποιθότες and καίπερ ἐγὼ ἔχων πεποίθησιν καὶ ἐν σαρκί – in order to emphasize the transition from an adversative formula to a concessive (καίπερ + participle), concomitant with a change of person, namely, from ἡμεῖς to a consequently more emphatic ἐγώ. What Paul has to say in vv. 4-14 is deeply personal, and so the plural does not appear again until v. 15.[2]

Before pursuing the function of these passages, they may be situated as playing a key role in restoring 'the Pharisaic conscience that Paul had before his conversion'.[3] Philippians 3.17, the second passage of interest for our purposes, as an exhortation to imitation, represents the principle point of interest in the pericope of which we hope to be able to explain: 'Be imitators of me, brothers and sisters ...'

Based on what we have said with regard to vv. 4-6, we can see what is developed through v. 17 and what will permit us to emphasize the manner in which 'the example' is proposed. Looking ahead a bit, we should say that what is alluded to in this passage is (to use again the language of Daniel Marguerat)[4] Paul's 'reversal' regarding righteousness and its relation to the Law. The sequence of vv. 4-6 is scarcely completed before v. 7, which opens with an ἀλλά ('but on the contrary', clearly an adversative term),[5] announces that what was just said will be refuted; this is soon confirmed by two terms set in opposition: ζημία, 'loss', and κέρδος, 'gain'. We can see at this stage that what was once considered gain is now understood as loss; but moving to v. 8, we notice also an amplification of what we said about v. 7.[6] It is now necessary to ask what the pivot point is; it is from this point that we can elucidate how we ought to understand Paul's exemplarity and his exhortation to imitation (v. 17). The answer is in v. 7 (διὰ τὸν Χριστόν), but it becomes clear in 8b (τῆς γνώσεως Χριστοῦ Ἰησοῦ τοῦ κυρίου μου); it is 'knowing Christ Jesus, my Lord'. The preposition διὰ (in v. 7 as in v. 8) that follows the accusative indicates that Christ is the cause of this change of perspective, an allusion to his conversion.[7] If in our text the reference to his conversion is not explicit, it is

2   P. T. O'Brien, *The Epistle to the Philippians. A Commentary on the Greek Text* (NIGTC; Grand Rapids: Eerdmans, 1991), p. 366–367.

3   Marguerat, 'Paul et la Loi', p. 260.

4   'Paul et la Loi'.

5   On the use of ἀλλά in Philippians, one may refer to J. T. Reed, *A Discourse Analysis of Philippians. Method and Rhetoric in the Debate over Literary Integrity* (JSNTSup, 136; Sheffield: Sheffield Academic Press, 1997), p. 328.

6   One may refer here to J.-B. Édart, *L'Épître aux Philippiens, rhétorique et composition stylistique* (EtB, 45; Paris: Gabalda, 2002), p. 238: Paul 'resumes the second part of the *propositio* (7b) in 8a-8c. The amplifier (πᾶς instead of ταῦτα) enlarges Paul's judgment and unconsciously modifies the object. In the past (connoted by the perfect in v. 7), Paul had treated his Jewish heritage as a loss because of Christ. But now this is no longer the only object he considers a loss. It is *everything*.' Cf. also O'Brien, *The Epistle to the Philippians*, pp. 386–387.

7   Jean-Noël Aletti accounts for this aspect well: 'Repeating the declaration of v. 7 by supplementing and tightening it, the declaration of v. 8 specifies the διὰ τὸν Χριστόν, namely, it provides the Christological reasons for this radical change of perspective', cf. J.-N. Aletti, *Saint Paul. Épître aux Philippiens* (EtB, 55; Paris, Gabalda, 2005), p. 237.

nevertheless evident through the reference to a pivotal moment that produced a radical change ('For his sake I have suffered the loss of all things', v. 8b) and was based on 'knowing Christ'. What is meant here by 'knowledge' (γνῶσις)? Verse 10 reads as follows: τοῦ γνῶναι αὐτὸν καὶ τὴν δύναμιν τῆς ἀναστάσεως αὐτοῦ καὶ [τὴν] κοινωνίαν [τῶν] παθημάτων αὐτοῦ, συμμορφιζόμενος τῷ θανάτῳ αὐτοῦ, that is, 'I want to know Christ and the power of his resurrection and the sharing of his sufferings by becoming like him in his death.' We understand that it does not concern knowledge of an intellectual sort, objective and aloof. It is a knowledge that implies participation of a person's entire being, even his or her corporeality, which in this passage means in life, sufferings and death.[8] Returning to Paul's Pharisaic notion of the self as articulated in Phil. 3.4-6, we can illuminate our understanding of the 'knowledge' mentioned in v. 10 by citing the words of Philipe Nicolet:[9] '[...] Paul lives in a complete renunciation of his past prerogatives, in an austerity, and in a crucifixion of his pharisaic personality, by communing with the judgment apportioned by God in the cross of Christ'.[10] Furthermore, if we look more carefully at the quote from Nicolet, we find the terms that ought to define the nature and significance of this 'knowledge': 'And Paul does not consider this crucifixion a past event: it defines his *present mode of existence.*'[11]

Paul's Pharisaic confidence, predicated firstly upon his being a part of the people of Israel and secondly upon his strict observance of the Law, is rendered bankrupt. To determine the function of vv. 4-6, we must note that the portrait drawn in this regard is meant to be exemplary. The second part of v. 4 clearly creates this impression: εἴ τις δοκεῖ ἄλλος πεποιθέναι ἐν σαρκί, ἐγὼ μᾶλλον ('If anyone else has reason to be confident in the flesh, I have more'). Verse 6 then ends with Paul's blamelessness (from the point of view of the Law). Even if the tenor of the pericope is polemical, as Philippe Nicolet suggests (based on the harsh warning of Phil. 3.2: βλέπετε τοὺς κύνας, βλέπετε τοὺς κακοὺς ἐργάτας, βλέπετε τὴν κατατομήν, 'Beware of the dogs, beware of the evil workers, beware of those who mutilate the flesh!' and on Phil. 3.18 which makes the polemical front explicit: τοὺς ἐχθροὺς τοῦ σταυροῦ τοῦ Χριστοῦ, 'enemies of the cross of Christ'),[12] it is

---

8   On this point one may refer to J. N. Aletti: 'Philippians 3 again symbolically illustrates what the word "to know" denotes, connotes, and implies for the Christian: not primarily truths or values but a person, Jesus Christ. In addition, the knowledge of a believer does not remain external to its object (and vice versa, its object is not external to it), because knowing happens through conforming to the journey of Christ and implies a being with and a becoming like (him), and a progressive transformation of one's being.' Cf. Aletti, *Épître aux Philippiens*, p. 262.

9   P. Nicolet, 'Le concept d'imitation de l'apôtre dans la correspondance paulinienne', in *Paul, une théologie en construction* (ed. A. Dettwiler, J.-D. Kaestli, and D. Marguerat; MdB, 51; Genève: Labor et Fides, 2004), pp. 393–415 (410).

10   P. Nicolet cites here P. Bonnard, *L'Épître de Saint Paul aux Philippiens* (CNT, 10; Neuchâtel, Delachaux et Niestlé, 1950), p. 66.

11   Cf. Nicolet, 'Le concept d'imitation', p. 410 (emphasis mine).

12   For identifying of this polemical front, cf. especially Aletti, *Épître aux Philippiens*, pp. 224–27, who is inclined toward Judeo-Christian missionaries. But also Édart, *Épître aux Philippiens*, p. 222–26, 247–51. Édart draws attention to the difficulty of identifying the enemies of 3.18 and of evaluating their relation to the figures that the Philippians are to beware of in 3.2, though, without being able to settle the question, he is inclined toward 'an allusion to disorderly behavior'.

important to grasp the reality of the portrait Paul paints of himself as one expressing his Pharisaic conscience before his conversion and not as a purely polemical assertion intended only to be contrasted to a second, better portrait, which would radically devalue the first. To be sure, this aspect is present, but its function has much more force when Paul is understood, as he *really* was, passing from one paradigm (at first held in esteem) to another, thereby radically depreciating the first. This real-life Paul is highlighted by Jean-Noël Aletti who shows how Paul does not simply relate a past perspective as an outsider, but rather, speaks from within a Pharisaic point of view.[13] It is only after having accounted for this change of perspective and having explained the nature of his new life – understood, in the context of our inquiry in terms of his new way of understanding himself before God as well as that on which he founds his confidence – that Paul in v. 17 exhorts the Philippians to imitate him: συμμιμηταί μου γίνεσθε, ἀδελφοί (v. 17a), 'Brothers and sisters, join in imitating me'.

b. 'Be imitators of me, brothers and sisters' (Συμμιμηταί μου γίνεσθε, ἀδελφοί) (Philippians 3.17a): To imitate Paul? But in What Way?

At the outset of this section, we shall resume a question of Aletti: 'What about Paul are the Philippians to imitate? Is it not contrary to the attitude of humility, enjoined by Paul himself in Phil. 2.3, to offer himself as an example?'[14] We must address these two questions (the second will be treated more specifically in section IV.c when we address the question of the relationship between Philippians 2 and 3).

We noted earlier the importance that Peter O'Brien gives to the usage of the first person singular in Phil. 3.4-14 before the plural reappears beginning in v. 15 (in quite specific terms, to which we shall return) and continues until the exhortation in v. 17. If we remain on the level of a general observation, we can easily see that this arrangement is not insignificant. In introducing this part of the study, I refer to O'Brien, who makes explicit the link between his first remark about vv. 4-14[15] and v. 17, thereby connecting our two parts: 'The first person singulars ("I") of vv. 8-14 have full paradigmatic force in this appeal to imitation.'[16]

---

13   Aletti, *Épître aux Philippiens*, p. 235. He begins with the phrase κατὰ δικαιοσύνην τὴν ἐν νόμῳ (Phil. 3.6) which creates a tension in Paul's thought: 'If Paul also declares that the (Mosaic) Law cannot justify in Phil. 3.6 and 9, and Rom. 10.5, he seems to say the opposite that the Law renders righteous anyone who obeys it … and we are examining the coherence of the Apostle's claim.' The response is entirely from the Pharisaic stance in which Paul is positioned here; 'obedience to the law makes one righteous'. Finally, the question of his blamelessness (γενό μενος ἄμεμπτος) creates the same sort of tension (cf. Rom. 3.19-20 and 7.7-25; where one cannot fully observe the Law), to which Aletti rejoins with the same response: 'the perspective is that of a Pharisee convinced that one can be blameless before the Law'.

14   Ibid., p. 266.

15   O'Brien, *The Epistle to the Philippians*, p. 366–67.

16   Ibid., p. 444.

Given the presentation of a radically different mode for evaluating one's religiosity, we are no longer to imitate a man who has innate (by birth) and ethical (by relation to the Law) qualities, but rather, a man who has received and continues to receive something. From then on, one is redirected, as it were, beyond Paul toward the one who has done the giving and toward the gift given to him. This gift can be found in vv. 10-11. It is the knowledge of Christ which governs the life of the believer, a life that starts with the cross. Paul, in exhorting the Philippians to imitate him, does not propose specific qualities but rather that existence which ought to constitute the life of the believer (in Christ). Returning earlier in the pericope, we find support for this last assertion in v. 3, as Aletti reads it, if we take this verse in relation to that which is going to occupy our attention later in 3.17. Aletti considers the personal journey related by Paul on the basis of what precedes it in v. 3: ἡμεῖς γάρ ἐσμεν ἡ περιτομή, οἱ πνεύματι θεοῦ λατρεύοντες καὶ καυχώμενοι ἐν Χριστῷ Ἰησοῦ καὶ οὐκ ἐν σαρκὶ πεποιθότες ('For it is we who are the circumcision, who worship in the Spirit of God and boast in Christ Jesus and have no confidence in the flesh'); he remarks that 'if the latter (Paul) seems to be praising himself, it is not out of vanity but because his journey is emblematic of the condition of all who believe in Christ'.[17] This perspective, the importance of which Aletti notes, indeed confers a different tone upon the language that opens the sequence of v. 4 and following, a clue that is not without consequence for the significance of v. 17.

Nonetheless, certain scholars, such as Reumann,[18] see in Phil. 3.17 only an exhortation to imitate Paul and not Christ – or, 'imitation' of Christ whom Paul represents. First, Paul does not speak of imitation of the life and conduct of Christ but rather, as Philippe Nicolet says, of the need to 'continue to bear the judgment of the cross on their lives'.[19] If one can raise an issue such as Reumann has, it is because in Phil. 3.17 – contrary to 1 Cor. 11.1, for instance – Paul does not add to his exhortation that he imitates Christ. Nonetheless, the same process ought to be at work implicitly, given the fact that he has described the foundation of the believer's life (total surrender in the act of being taken hold of by Christ: cf. Phil. 3.8, 12), the only condition out of which he can become an example to imitate (we shall return to this below, cf. the relation between Philippians 2 and 3). Moreover, to avoid too great a focus on the apostle, we note his use of the first person plural (3.16 and 17b) as well as the image of a common journey that he proposes in v. 16: πλὴν εἰς ὃ ἐφθάσαμεν, τῷ αὐτῷ στοιχεῖν ('only let us hold fast to what we have attained'). After referencing the remark of Reumann, Demetrius Williams[20] then reframes the issue using v. 17b: καὶ σκοπεῖτε τοὺς οὕτω περιπατοῦντας καθὼς ἔχετε τύπον ἡμᾶς ('and observe those who live according to the example you have in us'). He makes the following statement: 'It does not call them to only

17   Aletti, *Épître aux Philippiens*, p. 230.
18   Cited by D. K. Williams, *Enemies of the Cross of Christ. The Terminology of the Cross and Conflict in Philippians* (JSNTSup, 223; London, Sheffield Academic Press, 2002), p. 215.
19   Nicolet, 'Le concept d'imitation', p. 410.
20   Cf. note 18.

follow him (Paul), but all who follow should also do so in the example of Christ.'[21] However, looking back a verse to v. 16, we find another 'we' of a scope wider still, in our view, which demonstrates Paul's concern for community and unity. Before exhorting them to imitate him, he employs a formula in which he shows himself bound to the Philippians in the same spiritual journey. Moreover, this remark finds an echo in vv. 12-14 where Paul indicates that he himself has by no means advanced to the point of perfection. In this line of interpretation, we point to J. B. Édart,[22] for whom Paul places himself in this scenario 'emphasizing that he has not completed his journey ... reducing the distance that may exist between him and his auditor while maintaining his function as example'. In doing so, Paul both 'begins to reach the Philippians and makes the model plausible'.

To finish up Philippians 3 – if we may add to our last remarks – we should note a term also in v. 17, συμμιμητής (found only in the Pauline letters),[23] which may be translated 'co-imitator'. More often than not, the interpretation and translation of this term serves to demonstrate Paul's concern to see the Philippians 'together', 'all together', in whatever behaviour he is commending to them. We find in his *parenesis* a concern for community and unity;[24] but in view of his formula(tion) in v. 16, we would not be unjustified in asking whether συμμιμηταί should not also include Paul, even though it is he who does the exhorting.[25] In Philippians 3, by listing autobiographical elements, Paul has demonstrated the bankruptcy of confidence in 'an innate and earned righteousness'[26] (Phil. 3.4-6) vis-à-vis that received in the knowledge of Christ's crucifixion and resurrection. Paul has explained through his journey the significance of life and the understanding of salvation in the knowledge of Christ (suffering, death on the cross, resurrection). Daniel Marguerat speaks of a 'redefinition of the believer's identity for which Paul makes himself the paradigm'[27] – a believing identity in which Paul wants to train the Philippians along with himself.

We have chosen to spend some time on Philippians 3, but other occurrences of the call to imitation in Paul's correspondence would have been possible: 1 Cor. 4.6; 11.1; 1 Thess. 1.6; Gal. 4.12. Now, to conclude regarding what stands out to us in

---

21   Williams, *Enemies of the Cross of Christ*, p. 214. This reading is also corroborated by what Aletti proposes: 'The injunction is interesting, because if Paul is an example to follow, those who behave as he does—and take him as a model or take Christ as a model since he is ultimately the model *princeps*—also become like him', *Épître aux philippiens*, p. 267.

22   Édart, *Épître aux Philippiens*, p. 270.

23   It is necessary to go even further since Aletti writes that 'συμμιμηταί is an absolute *hapax*'. But we should also note – and this could present an interesting possibility to keep in mind in the next part of the study – that he makes mention of the presence of the verb συμμιμέομαι (to imitate together) in Plato. A verb whose 'idea is not that of a slavish copy or exact replica but a creative and original reprisal of the model'. *Épître aux Philippiens*, p. 265.

24   This is the sense that O'Brien ultimately prefers, *Epistle to the Philippians*, p. 445: 'Accordingly we favour (4), namely that the apostle has in mind the unity of the Philippians among themselves: "Imitate me with one accord."'

25   In which case, one is perhaps already pointed beyond Paul to Christ for the model to imitate (cf. below, IV).

26   Marguerat, 'Paul et la Loi', p. 271.

27   Ibid.

this sort of passage, we should further say a few words regarding 1 Thess. 1.6. In his article on the concept of imitation cited above, Philippe Nicolet explains what Paul can do with the theme of imitation. For Paul this theme can serve to '(re)define the nature of the relationships that unite the communities he created', or 'remember how he understands his apostolate', or 'revisit the exposition of a fundamental aspect of his theological reflection'.[28] In our discussion of Philippians 3, which emphasizes that we should not forget the central importance of the question of the Law (revisiting a fundamental aspect of his theological reflection), we have underscored Paul's concern for community and unity, including the basis for the redefinition of the life of the believer. This understood, 1 Thess. 1.6 ought to reinforce the sense of this reading: καὶ ὑμεῖς μιμηταὶ ἡμῶν ἐγενήθητε καὶ τοῦ κυρίου, δεξάμενοι τὸν λόγον ἐν θλίψει πολλῇ μετὰ χαρᾶς πνεύματος ἁγίου ('And you became imitators of us and of the Lord, for in spite of persecution you received the word with joy inspired by the Holy Spirit'). First, the tone, register, or language does not signal exhortation, but rather acknowledgement. Next, we should note the context: 1 Thess. 1.6 is found in a pericope in which we can locate the unity between v. 2 ('we always give thanks to God for all of you and mention you in our prayers') and 10; the unit consists of a prayer of thanksgiving. Here, Paul does not utilize imitation in the context of a parenesis; through usage of the same vocabulary, he lauds the fact that the acceptance of a believing life, to which he exhorts them in Philippians 3, has fully found a place among his addressees.

c. Digression: Possible Illumination from Romans 7

Still tracing the same inquiry, that of Paul's exemplarity and its intersection with autobiography, we should now like to leave the strict context of imitation and focus on one final text from the Pauline corpus: Rom. 7.7-25. Our interest in this text is to demonstrate how Paul, by using the first person singular, trains the believer through the utterance of the 'I'. It is necessary first of all to point out that this issue is not our chief concern, since Romans 7 is less an issue of imitation than it is of Paul's paradigmatic behaviour. The topic, therefore, is related to the present study and will shed light on it, though when we use these verses about Paul and his paradigmatic dimension, we must do so with precision in order to avoid confusion and be mindful of the different contexts.

Let us begin by briefly setting in context the pericope in which the first person singular will emerge. In Romans 6 through 7.6, Paul writes in the first and second persons plural. Romans 7.7 marks a break in the style and, therefore, in the mode of the message's transmission: 'What then should we say? That the law is sin? By no means! Yet, if it had not been for the law, I would not have known sin. I would not have known what it is to covet if the law had not said, "You shall not covet."' To the rhetorical question (v. 7a) asked (still) in the first person plural is given a response using 'I' which thereby acquires a new validity. We will not be able to trace here the whole of the problem of the pericope, but we shall try to provide an interpretation of Paul's usage of the first person singular. One common view tends

---

28   Nicolet, 'Le concept d'imitation', pp. 396–97.

to regard it as a rhetorical convention, but we shall see that this understanding need not be exclusive or restrictive. If v. 7 can be read from the perspective of the person of Paul, this is not directly possible in the verses that follow. An allusion is made to an earlier time, a time without the Law (we shall see later that we can read this as a reference to the accounts of Genesis 2–3) and then a time under the Law. There is, then, beginning in 7.9 a new speaker who is not named and who is not historical.

We shall offer here Jean-Baptiste Édart's proposal,[29] for whom it is a matter of *prosopopoeia* (the speaker or writer attributes speech to a person or thing that is absent, dead, inanimate, or fictive). Along these lines, he adds the possibility that this device would have been incomprehensible to the copyist confronted with it. Such a copyist, through concern for harmonization, would have preferred in 8.2 the first person rather than the second ('For the law of the Spirit of life in Christ Jesus has set me (you) free from the law of sin and of death').[30] For Jean-Baptiste Édart, the second proposal dovetails well with *prosopopoeia*; Paul is speaking to the fictive persona of 7.7-25. Now let us see how, without entirely denying *prosopopoeia* as a solution, we might be able to imagine other possibilities. We should note first of all that, however confusing the 'I' persona may be, it does not lack lucidity on his situation on what he needs (i.e., of a saviour, cf. 7.24b). It is the use of the first person singular – in this *prosopopoeia*, not introduced by the presentation of a persona – that elicits this confusion (is this Paul speaking?). Whether or not this 'I' conveys his personal experiences or is a rhetorical device that mingles the author's lived experiences with a fictive persona, 8.2 may also convey his reality despite the tense situation depicted a few verses earlier (7.7-25). Recourse to to the use of an 'I' (an individual subject, even if in this instance neither identified nor defined) gives to the discourse a global dimension that at the same time draws the individual back into his heart. The Jew is taken to task by the reference to the Law (v. 7, 9) and also the approximate connection or even identification with the narrative of Genesis 2–3, which can be observed at the semantic level: ἀποθνήσκω (Rom. 7.10; Gen. 2.17), ἐξαπατάω / ἀπατάω (Rom. 7.11; Gen. 3.13), ἐντολή (Rom. 7.9-11), which recalls ἐντέλλομαι (Gen. 2.16; 3.11, 17). The Law and the divine injunction to Adam are identified with each other in a widening of the field of reference, moving from a people clearly defined to the origins of the world and humanity at large. The rhetorical function is therefore evident; but what interests us is to see whether we can also find Paul in it. Glenn Holland[31] proposes the following interpretation: if Paul is included in the 'I' that he makes bear witness, we must understand it in the context of the letter. Paul presents himself as an example to his readers/auditors (1 Cor. 11.1; 4.16; Phil. 3.17; 4.9; 1 Thess. 1.6 ; Gal. 4.12) when he is addressing communities that recognize the person and the work of the

---

29   J.-B. Édart, 'De la nécessité d'un sauveur: Rhétorique et théologie de Rm 7,7-25 ', *RB* 105 (1998), pp. 359–96.

30   The TOB opts for με; The French Jerusalem Bible reads *you*, the variant preferred by Nestle-Aland.

31   G. S. Holland, 'The Self against the Self in Romans 7, 7-25a', in *The Rhetorical Interpretation of Scripture. Essays from the 1996 Malibu Conference* (ed. S. E. Porter and D. L. Stamps; JSNTSup, 180; Sheffield: Sheffield Academic Press, 1999), pp. 260–71.

apostle. But when he writes to Rome, he hardly knows how the church regards his apostolic authority, and what sort of impression they have of him. He cannot merely wield his apostolic authority (from a distance). He therefore aims to promote solidarity with the addressees, who will be drawn into the embrace of his first person singular. This (ambiguous) identification is a part of his rhetorical strategy.

The difficulty remains in knowing whether we should include in the scope of the 'I' the 'liberated' Christian in question, as noted in the earlier and later contexts of the pericope. Scholars such as Jean-Noël Aletti and Franz Leenhardt[32] deny an autobiographical dimension and limit the referent to humanity without Christ. Aletti notes that this would weaken the affirmations of these verses, suggesting that nowhere else does Paul place the Christian in such a situation of powerlessness and weakness; in fact, if the Christian lives in the flesh, he is no longer enslaved to it (2 Cor. 10.3). We should conclude by attempting to show how the 'I' can also account for the Christian experience. In the first place, the present tense brings us back to the current reality of the believer. The picture is bleak, and at first blush the abrupt change might even seem inconsistent with what is said of the free Christian. This is why we must look at what the text says on another level and observe the context. We can see that the context concerns a level of reality in which the Christian finds himself or herself, a reality from which no human being can escape. The permanence of sin is experienced also by the Christian (he or she is not exempt), except that the Christian has been taken charge of by the Spirit implying not condemnation (8.1) but, rather, liberation (it is not in any case explicitly a question of condemnation in 7.7-25). Now, this absence of condemnation is not situated in the immediate present at the level of actual existence. In support of my point, I refer to the theme of hope in Rom. 4.18 and 5.2 and to the theme of distress in 5.3. Hope refers to something 'beyond the present'. The current difficulties are not eliminated. Likewise, we note 8.18, which again links distress and hope (despite the pain experienced in the world, we are given hope). We should also note Paul's vocabulary in 6.19. The same people to whom he addresses 6.18 and 22 ('you, having been set free from sin, have become slaves of righteousness'; 'But now that you have been freed from sin and enslaved to God, the advantage you get is sanctification. The end is eternal life'), he speaks of their weakness in 6.19 ('I am speaking in human terms because of your natural limitations. For just as you once presented your members as slaves to impurity and to greater and greater iniquity, so now present your members as slaves to righteousness for sanctification'). In support of this reading we should further note the use of the future tense in 5.9, 10.

The 'I' of Rom. 7.7-25 may therefore be that of our common origin expressed in Genesis 2–3 from which no person can escape. The condition described is experienced universally, a universality expressed in the 'I', from which neither the Jew nor the Christian is excluded; nor does it exclude Paul who has passed through both of these states and even himself cannot escape the reality he articulates. Paul, wanting to guard against the sin that continues to be a threat through his wicked

---

32   J.-N. Aletti, 'Rm 7,7-25 encore une fois: Enjeux et propositions', *NTS* 48 (2002), pp. 358–76; F. J. Leenhardt, *L'épître de saint Paul aux Romains* (CNT, 6; Genève, Labor et Fides, 1981).

nature, uses a first person singular with which the reader at first seeks to identify him before perceiving that it encompasses all people, including the believer. In comparison with the theme of Paul's self-presentation and exemplarity, it is the paradigmatic dimension of Paul's 'I' that is instructive in this passage. If it is not a question of exemplarity in Romans 7, then what concerns us still is Paul's usage of an 'I' which, taken in a strict sense, refers specifically to his own situation, but ultimately refers to the human condition beyond Paul's own specific case.

III. Paul, an 'Exemplary' Figure? What is in the Narrative Tradition of the Acts of the Apostles?

In beginning this section, we should recall what we have already mentioned in the introduction, namely that the speaker has changed. In Acts, we no longer have the 'I' issuing from Paul's own lips, but from a character, Saul/Paul, presented and conveyed through a narrative discourse, whose own speech (the discourses of Paul) is placed in the context of a larger account into which that speech is inserted and by which that speech is conveyed. However reliable or consistent he is in relation to the Paul of his letters, we have here a phenomenon of reception.

Before we look more specifically at certain texts, we should say just a word from a formal point of view regarding the role that Paul plays in Acts. Though the figure of Peter dominates the first twelve chapters, he then disappears from the scene, and in Acts 13–28 Paul becomes the main character.

a. The First Account of the Conversion of Saul/Paul in Acts 9

Our investigation begins with Acts 9.1-30, the first account of Saul's conversion before the two later versions of this event in 22.4-21 and 26.9-18. The pericope of Acts 9.1-30, according to the divisions defended by Daniel Marguerat[33] and Odile Flichy,[34] is to be read in its entirety as an account of the conversion of Saul, that is to say, from his life before conversion (vv. 1-2), through the event on the road to Damascus (vv. 3-9), to the beginning of his preaching in Damascus (vv. 19b-25), before his introduction to the apostles by Barnabas (vv. 26-30) in Jerusalem. We should add that the primary purpose of the episode is almost entirely overshadowed by the recollection of his past activity and fear associated with it. This motif appears in Christ's pronouncement to Ananias concerning his encounter with Saul (vv. 10-14), then, again, among those who heard his preaching in Damascus (vv. 20-21), and finally in Jerusalem where 'they were all afraid of him, for they could not believe that he was a disciple' (v. 26b). At the onset of Paul's missionary circuit, it is necessary to establish what is this 'new' person and how real is what we might call the 'reversal' that he has undergone. The description of Saul and the nature of the

---

33   D. Marguerat, *La première histoire du christianisme (Les Actes des apôtres)* (LD, 180; Paris: Cerf, 2nd edn, 2003), ET p. 147.

34   O. Flichy, *La figure de Paul dans les Actes des Apôtres. Un phénomène de réception de la tradition paulinienne à la fin du premier siècle* (LD, 214; Paris: Cerf, 2007), p. 73.

journey he undertook in vv. 1-2 – underscoring the force of his actions (ἀπειλῆς καὶ φόνου, 'threats and murders') and his determination (he asked 'for letters to the synagogues at Damascus', letters that support and validate the repression that he must carry out) – will better allow us to demonstrate the transforming power of the encounter he had on the road. In examining this text, we note that Saul's effort in vv. 1-2 has halted, that the active and determined traveller has become passive. In v. 8, he is raised up (ἐγέρθη: aorist passive indicative); his eyes having been opened, he nevertheless sees nothing, and it is in greater passivity/fragility that he finishes his journey to Damascus and begins his stay there: χειραγωγοῦντες δὲ αὐτὸν εἰσήγαγον εἰς Δαμασκόν ('they led him by the hand and brought him into Damascus', v. 8b); καὶ ἦν ἡμέρας τρεῖς μὴ βλέπων, καὶ οὐκ ἔφαγεν οὐδὲ ἔπιεν ('for three days he was without sight, and neither ate nor drank', v. 9). At the surface level, we can say that these facts attest to the failure of his initial effort at persecution; at a deeper level, however, this can be understood (and this is how Odile Flichy understands it) as a sort of death. Flichy says at first that he is 'practically dead';[35] then she gives a fuller explanation: 'the light of salvation which has come to him … emphasizes the darkness in which he is immersed through the blindness that strikes him', and 'his not eating or drinking for three days is synonymous with death. The encounter with Christ who introduced Saul to a new life implies the death of his previous existence.'[36]

We began with vv. 1-2 and the fact that the memory of Paul's reputation persistently pervades the whole passage; now it seems that, as in the case we have just seen, this persistence allows the newness of Paul's existence to be recalled and put forth as evidence. This is announced in particularly interesting terms in vv. 15-16, in which Ananias expresses to the Lord his misgivings about Saul when the Lord appears to him 'in a vision' (v. 10) and commands him to go and find him and lay hands upon him. What happened and what is going to happen to Saul is made clear to the reader: in v. 15 he is σκεῦος ἐκλογῆς, 'an instrument chosen' by or for the Lord. Odile Flichy wonders about the proper translation of σκεῦος, which could also be rendered 'vessel' and according to a certain biblical precedent could place Saul/the vessel in a special relationship with God the potter. Be that as it may, we find here an expression of significance for Paul's new life/being. But more interesting still for our question is v. 16: ἐγὼ γὰρ ὑποδείξω αὐτῷ ὅσα δεῖ αὐτὸν ὑπὲρ τοῦ ὀνόματός μου παθεῖν ('I myself will show him how much he must suffer for the sake of my name'). This verse indeed distils different interesting elements that advance the question that has been guiding this study. If we return to the question of the word σκεῦος, it could be said that the translation 'instrument' functions quite well in v. 15b, making Paul an instrument (in the hand of God) for the mission;[37] but the metaphor of a vessel could itself find an echo in

---

35   Ibid., p. 78.

36   Ibid., p.80.

37   If in this occurrence of the term σκεῦος, we prefer the interpretation and translation 'instrument', this should also retain the sense of the Greek term as denoting a 'recipient', 'vessel', 'glass' (whatever thing can be filled); cf. D. Marguerat, *Les Actes des apôtres (1–12)* (CNT, 5a; Genève: Labor et Fides, 2007), p. 334: σκεῦος has a broadly defined meaning: *a recipient, a ves-*

the formula of v. 16. The sufferings associated with the name of the Lord recall the proclamation of Christ as dead and raised; from then on we can understand in the fact that the Lord 'will show' what it is necessary for Paul to suffer, that Paul has been appointed for the journey of Christ. Along these lines, Odile Flichy comes to the following interpretation: speaking of the words of the Lord, she proposes 'In my example he will follow, he will know …',[38] as a rendering of 'I myself will show him'.

This reading can be further supported by recalling the ἐγώ and its position at the beginning of the phrase, a position that gives it emphatic force. The emphasis is placed on me/Christ as the one who 'shows'. This emphasis may also be an echo of Philippians 3, where between vv. 8 and 9 one discovers a similar connection between Paul and Christ in the description of Paul's changed life. In Phil. 3.8c we read δι' ὃν τὰ πάντα ἐζημιώθην, καὶ ἡγοῦμαι σκύβαλα, ἵνα Χριστὸν κερδήσω ('For his sake I have suffered the loss of all things, and I regard them as rubbish, in order that I may gain Christ'). While Paul's change in point of view is attributable to the *cause* (διὰ) of Christ, the verse ends with the formula 'in order that I may gain Christ', which instead places the emphasis on the *effect* of Paul's action. We must therefore be attentive to the beginning of the verse that follows because its formulation will act as a 'corrective' to what precedes in the sense of the Paul-Christ relationship, the interpretation of which was suggested above for Acts 9.16. The formula of Phil. 3.9a is καὶ εὑρεθῶ ἐν αὐτῷ which makes the transition from the active form κερδήσω to a passive form: 'and be found in him'. Paul is passive, in Christ and according to him, the one to whom the initiative is given.[39]

Returning to Acts 9, we should finally address the elements that will attest to the complete reversal of Saul through his identification with Christ. We find these elements in the beginning of his preaching in Damascus (vv. 19b-25) and his arrival in Jerusalem (vv. 26-30). Almost as quickly as Saul has been converted and baptized, he begins to proclaim Jesus as the Son of God. In the face of the difficulty of communicating his message, he strives to bear witness to the truth of his words (v. 22) which ends up working against him by inciting the Jews to plot 'to kill him' (v. 23c). In Jerusalem, after his introduction to the apostles – which once again is necessary proof of his transformation that was required in order to supplant his old reputation as a persecutor of Christians: he has 'seen the Lord, who had spoken to him', and 'he had spoken boldly in the name of Jesus' (v. 27) – he becomes the object of the same sort of plot. Because he travels with the apostles and speaks with boldness (παρρησιάζομαι) in the name of the Lord (v. 28), he arouses against himself a plot from the Hellenistic-Jewish party (cf. v. 29): 'they were trying to kill

---

sel, an instrument, in short, any equipment (*furniture, tool, weapon*). The same term is used for the linen that descends from the sky during Peter's trance: 10.11, 16; 11.5. The two interpretations do not exclude one another but can be linked together.

38   Flichy, *La figure de Paul*, p. 84.

39   Aletti proposes a reading of this passive construction along the same lines, even if he does not speak of a 'corrective' as we do: 'An active desire, effort and struggle (v. 8) is followed by a passive: "to be found" in Christ. Thus is expressed the apostle's desire to not be separated from Christ but to be *incorporated* and assimilated into him.' *Épître aux Philippiens*, p. 241.

him' (v. 29). As I have already said, it was necessary to demonstrate proof of Saul's reversal through some form of identification of his new identity with Christ. This I shall now do. The verses that will be most helpful in achieving this are Acts 9.4-5, specifically v. 5: 'He asked, "Who are you, Lord?" The reply came, "I am Jesus, whom you are persecuting."' It is interesting to compare this situation described by Jesus – that is, Saul/Paul as a Jewish persecutor of Jesus by persecuting Jesus' disciples – with those we have mentioned in which Paul is threatened with death at the hands of the Jews on account of his proclamation of the name of Jesus. The relationship between Saul the persecutor and Jesus the persecuted has been transformed: Saul also is persecuted and for the same reasons as those whom he himself persecuted. We find a similar reading in Daniel Marguerat: 'From being the persecutor with schemes of killing (9.1-2), Saul becomes the persecuted one, threatened with death (9.23-9).'[40]

b. Acts 22 and 26: Retellings and Variations of an Important Event for Christian Identity

Let us now widen our investigation to Acts 22 and 26 where we find the account of the event in Damascus but in the first person singular. In his narrative, Luke has Paul say 'I'. Once again, we should remember that our study will not be able to include the whole scope of the problem contained in the passages we are going to analyze. Rather we shall try to treat the elements that are pertinent to our question. We shall begin, therefore, with three quick remarks that should guide our reading of these texts. First of all, we should consider a point made by John C. Lentz (we shall later treat more carefully his manner of approaching the question of Paul's exemplarity in Acts) from whom, even if we do not accept his conclusions, we are able to maintain this: 'Luke held Paul to be the model Christian. Therefore, the last eight chapters of Acts are encomiastic in nature in that, in praising Paul, Luke offers an example for his readers to respect and imitate.'[41] Second, we should note the relationship between Acts 9 and the same events (with variations) in chs 22 and 26 and the simple fact that Luke transitions to an autobiographical discourse indicating a stronger focus on Paul's character. This development can be corroborated by the fact that in Acts 22, 'for the first time, a discourse in Acts pays more attention to the one doing the speaking than to Christ and his destiny'.[42] Lastly, in ch. 26 after the third account of the Damascus experience, recalling both the events leading up to it and its effects (26.1-23), one finds in v. 29 Paul's exhortation to 'become such as I am' (γενέσθαι τοιούτους ὁποῖος καὶ ἐγώ εἰμι).

40   Marguerat, *The First Christian Historian*, 191.
41   J. C. Lentz, *Luke's Portrait of Paul* (SNTSMS, 77; Cambridge: Cambridge University Press, 1993), p. 63.
42   Aletti, *Quand Luc raconte. Le récit comme théologie* (Lire la Bible, 115; Paris, Cerf, 1998), p. 131.

In Acts 22, Paul's discourse spans vv. 1-22. Paul is in Jerusalem and has been arrested by the tribune and his soldiers (21, 32-33) after being alerted to a great disturbance. Paul has been recognized in the Temple by the Jews as an enemy of Judaism ('… of our people, our law, and this place', 21.28). He is accused also of having brought Greeks into the Temple (that is to say, the impure). He has been dragged from the Temple, and the gates are immediately (εὐθέως) closed behind him; only the intervention of the tribune saves him from certain death, as v. 31 bears witness. These closed gates which we have mentioned confirm the theme of discord and symbolically attest to Paul's exclusion. This theme will guide his speech, presented by him as a 'defence' (ἀπολογία) and proclaimed in the Hebrew tongue (21, 40b), further intensifying the tone and producing a temporary effect (22.2). Paul's concern in this discourse is to show both the lack of contradiction and the continuity of his present calling with Judaism. He, therefore, emphasizes all references to his faithfulness to Judaism while recounting his past and the consequences of what happened on the road to Damascus. In v. 3 he recounts his Jewish upbringing[43] (born in Tarsus) and his education to which he gives solid references: in Jerusalem, 'at the feet of Gamaliel'. In v. 4 following a recounting of his past as a persecutor of the 'way' he again gives solid references: the high priests and the elders are able to bear him witness (v. 5a), a point he then connects to the beginning of what led him to the Damascus road (v. 5b). Having related the road to Damascus event (vv. 6-11), we turn to the introduction of Paul and Ananias and the terms of their encounter (vv. 12-17). In v. 8 Jesus is specifically identified as a Nazarene, a title whose meaning is 'without equivocation'[44] for his Jerusalem auditors. Paul begins with Ananias by validating his remarks with reference to Judaism. Ananias, a disciple (originally Jewish) from Damascus, who in Acts 9.10 is described as 'a disciple', is seen defined in Acts 22 with reference to his Jewish qualities ('a devout man according to the law and well spoken of by all the Jews living there').[45] Then, in the speech that Ananias addresses to Saul, what happened to Saul is validated with a reference to 'the God of our ancestors' (22.14), who has destined/chosen him (προχειρίζω).

These few remarks ought to help show how, through the stories of Paul's conversion, the reader is given a portrait of Paul's Christian identity. We note here a quite simple, but telling, point that the same event is repeated three times. This attests to the importance of the Damascus event for Luke. By repeating the narrative in different places throughout his work, varying the interpretation,

---

43   Cf. Marguerat, *La première histoire du christianisme*, p. 297 [ET p. 197], who speaks of the fact that, for Paul, affirmation of his origin is highly important and newsworthy: 'The formula of v. 3 ἐγώ εἰμι ἀνὴρ Ἰουδαῖος is not only a statement of identity; it constitutes a *theological thesis of his speech, which includes the uninterrupted fidelity of Paul to the Jewish tradition.*'

44   Flichy, *La figure de Paul*, p. 104.

45   In the same sense, cf. D. Marguerat, 'L'image de Paul dans les Actes des Apôtres', in *Les Actes des Apôtres: Histoire, récit, théologie; XXᵉ congrès de l'Association catholique française pour l'étude de la Bible (Angers 2003)* (ed. M. Berder; LD, 199; Paris: Cerf, 2005), pp. 121–154 (139): 'His conversion is received by Ananias who, incidentally, is no longer presented as a "disciple" of the Lord (9.10) but as a "a devout man according to the law and well spoken of by all the Jews living there" (22.12)'.

Luke deploys the widest range of meanings of which he can, to his mind, be a messenger.[46] If Acts 9 places the emphasis on the conversion that the coming of Christ into his life has brought about for Paul, Acts 22 aims to highlight, through the testimony of Paul himself, the continuity of his Christian identity with Judaism. Daniel Marguerat speaks of '… *a profile of Christian identity* in its relation to the continuity and discontinuity with Judaism',[47] a 'profile' defined by means of the journey of the life of Saul/Paul. We have highlighted the continuity that Luke wants to stress, but in following the text, it is necessary to close this section, before moving to our reading of Acts 26, with the abruptness or resistance that closes the episode of this discourse. Paul, backed by the rationale that he has given to his encounter with 'the Lord'/ 'Jesus' as being the will of the God of their forefathers, mentions the inauguration of his mission to the gentiles. In 22.17 he is in Jerusalem praying in the Temple, which again attests to the continuation of his Jewish piety after his conversion and baptism (22.16). It is there that he reports having received in a vision (καὶ ἰδεῖν αὐτὸν ['and (I) saw him']) the order to go to the gentiles (v. 21). If we can imagine his discourse as having been received peacefully to this point, once he roots Christianity in Judaism, we can understand why the Jews cannot accept the specificity here embodied by Paul (22.22-23).

Before tackling Acts 26, and in light of what we have already tried to draw out from these texts, we call for caution with regard to the use of the term *example* or *exemplarity*. This appeal is particularly necessary since this passage of Paul's discourse (26.2-29) places even more emphasis[48] on the apostle than do the others. We note, for example, the disappearance of the intermediary Ananias which, in the words of Daniel Marguerat, 'led to an unmediated struggle between Saul and the Lord'.[49] Acts 9 demonstrated the reversal of Saul's identity, Acts 22 his continuity with Judaism in this new identity, as well as in the end, the resistance of the Jews to accept this continuity and that which it implies (in this case, the opening of the way for the gentiles). What Luke means to convey through these texts, at first by the narrator – though the narrator then hides himself behind his character – is a journey of conversion of which the full details are increasingly made more explicit in their context, in this particular case his relationship to

---

46 Regarding Luke's aim (Zielsetzung), Gerhard Lohfink writes: 'He simultaneously interpreted this conversion, however, and explained its significance for the history of the church.' Cf. G. Lohfink, *Paulus vor Damaskus: Arbeitsweisen der neueren Bibelwissenschaft dargestellt an den Texten Apg. 9,1-19; 22,3-21; 26,9-18* (SBS, 4; Stuttgart: Katholisches Bibelwerk, 1965), pp. 76–78. And more importantly still, he adds: 'At first Luke assigns an unusually significant meaning to the Damascus event for his account. Indeed, he narrates it not less than three times—of course not to take up space, as J. Wellhausen argued. Instead, he does so in order to impress his readers: here you have an especially important event in my book!' (p. 77).

47 Marguerat, *La première histoire du christianisme*, p. 299 [ET p. 197].

48 On the ever-sharpening focus in the course of the three accounts, cf. Lohfink, *Paulus vor Damaskus*, p. 84: 'The climax is not reached until chapter 26: finally, Paul is now truly being commissioned, namely directly through Christ and directly before Damascus. Through this Luke causes Paul's commissioning to become more clearly and directly in view with each subsequent report.'

49 Marguerat, *La première histoire du christianisme*, p. 302 [ET p. 200].

Judaism. The act of walking through the journey of Paul's conversion, a character who holds a dominant place in a book reporting the beginnings of Christianity, demonstrates the exemplarity of this journey. Note, however, that it is not Paul who is set forth as an example to imitate.[50] But the focus on his 'I', accentuated ever more to the point that it has the same effect as the formula of Acts 26.29, attempts to return the reader through a particular character to the journey reported in the first account (Acts 9) and in the two discourses (22 and 26), that is to say, to the identity that is constructed. We find support for this reading in Daniel Marguerat: 'Since the book of Acts uses historiography to convey identity, the figure of Paul should not be isolated but treated as a vehicle through which the identity of Christians, for Luke, arrives at its completion.'[51]

Let us now return to the text of Acts 26. As a result of what has happened in Acts 22, Paul, who is in captivity, again makes an apology, this time before King Agrippa. The thrust of his plea is again continuity with Judaism, which he shows by noting explicitly what has been revealed to him in the context of the promise made to their forefathers; it is 'on account of my hope in the promise made by God to our ancestors' [that he has been placed on trial]. We can make a critical remark here regarding the argumentation of these verses (26.6-8). The one whom Paul has experienced, the one whose name Paul proclaims, this is Jesus Christ who died and was raised (v. 23); now, speaking of his reliance on the promise, and in light of v. 8 ('Why is it thought incredible by any of you that God raises the dead?'), it seems that Paul's discourse reduces the promise, as understood by Judaism to the hope of the resurrection of the dead, of which Christ, 'the first', marked the fulfilment (cf. v. 23). Is it not 'reductionistic' to say that this reference to the resurrection of the dead can sum up for the whole of Judaism what is the substance of the promise (cf. Matt. 22.23-33; Mk 12.18-27; Lk. 20.20-26)? This belief characterizes more specifically the sect of the Pharisees[52] (cf. Acts 23.6-8). This point does not (on the contrary) address the fact that Paul wants to highlight the continuity that we have spoken of, which culminates in vv. 22-23 where what he proclaims is explicitly noted as fulfilling the scriptures: 'saying nothing but what the prophets and Moses said would take place' (26.22b). We must understand Moses and the prophets as references to the first two parts of the Hebrew Bible (*Torah* and *Nevi'im*). We should note once again that in the second discourse, at the same time Paul, having recalled his Jewishness (of the Pharisaic variety), is evoking his past as persecutor

50   Cf. ibid., p. 300.
51   Marguerat, *L'image de Paul*, p. 135.
52   Cf. especially Skinner, *Locating Paul: Places of Custody as Narrative Settings in Acts 21–28* (SBL Academia Biblica, 13; Atlanta: Society of Biblical Literature, 2003), p. 122: 'Paul's invocation of the resurrection becomes a ground of his defence against the accusations from Jewish opponents. In speeches to come he answers the charges against him, no matter how they are articulated, by claiming that the belief at the heart of the gospel is not at odds with Jewish belief, but constitutive of Jewish (or, at least, Pharisaic) hope in the resurrection of the dead', although the reduction is not highlighted as such. More explicitly, Marguerat, *La première histoire du christianisme*, p. 304 [ET p. 202]: 'One cannot help but think that, theologically, Luke presses the issue. Condensing the Jewish faith to one promise … is possible; but that this promise is itself reduced to the resurrection of the dead (26.8) would only be acceptable to Pharisaic piety.'

of Christians, he is already anticipating his change of perspective: 'Indeed, I myself was convinced that I ought to do many things against the name of Jesus of Nazareth' (26.9).

If we return to Paul and the more pronounced focus on his character, one perceives that the explanations that come through the intermediary of Ananias (Acts 9.15-17; 22.14-16) and then through the vision (22.17-21) are in ch. 26 grouped together in the speeches that the Resurrected One addresses to Saul on the road to Damascus (vv. 15b-18). The account of the conversion event and the effect it produced is concentrated in a more restricted space (vv. 12-20). To this immediacy between Saul and Christ corresponds the immediacy of his reaction: v. 19, 'After that, King Agrippa, I was not disobedient to the heavenly vision.' In v. 20, Paul recalls the beginning of his preaching and conveys its contents: it is an appeal to 'repent' (μετανοεῖν), to 'turn to God and do deeds consistent with repentance'. If Paul has reported the circumstances of his own conversion, it is in order to appeal to listeners to recognize the need for conversion, which he does in his preaching, without explicitly making reference to his own conversion but rather by speaking, more generally, of 'repentance' (ἄξια τῆς μετανοίας ἔργα πράσσοντας). When at last, in v. 29 one finds in Paul's mouth the following assertion – 'not only you but also all who are listening to me today might become such as I am – except for these chains' – we need not read it as an appeal to imitate a unique model that they (Paul's listeners, but above all Luke's readers) perceive in his character. This formulation returns us to the journey of Paul's conversion, but in such a way that his journey is representative of the conversion[53] of all believers, as we have attempted to show from vv. 19 and 20. In these last remarks, it is not a matter of minimizing the importance of Paul as a model, as Luke presents him (in this case, a unique, singular example). Our main point is to demonstrate that the example of this converted one who appeals to his conversion looks back to something else, prior to his personal experience.

c. Paul, a Model by Virtue of his Social Status? Another Reading

Before closing our second section on the exemplarity of the character of Paul in the book of Acts, it is fitting to consider briefly a different sort of approach. In the epistles as in the book of Acts, we have the fact of Paul's Jewishness, of his status as a Hebrew and his membership in the sect of the Pharisees; in references to these categories, his qualities and his respectability are more often highlighted, either by Paul himself or by Luke. In Acts, two other qualities will be added in order to define his social status: he is from the city of Tarsus (21.39) and is a Roman citizen (22.25-28). For Jürgen Becker, this multiple membership does not pose a problem, since Paul could be a Pharisee observing the Law in all its rigour while being a

---

53 Regarding the three accounts of the road to Damascus event in Acts 26, Marguerat notes: 'Paul's conversion in Damascus is taken from an autobiographical record, taken from Paul himself to acquire a paradigmatic status; it illustrates the believer's condition as such, and it becomes representative of the Christian experience.... . The event ... becomes an example of one's acceptance into the faith', *L'image de Paul*, p. 140.

citizen of Tarsus, a city at the centre of Hellenistic culture. 'The citizenship that his family, with its Pharisaic orientation, possessed displays an openness toward the Roman Empire, which was certainly characteristic of segments of Judaism in the Diaspora.'[54]

On that note, it behooves us to pause for a moment on the work of John Lentz. Lentz is not of the same view regarding the historical plausibility of these aspects of the portrait of Paul as he is regarding its consistency with the Paul of the letters. Once again, to confine ourselves to the context of the problem of where to begin, what commands our attention is not so much a general question of historical plausibility or the consistency of the Lukan portrait of Paul in comparison to that of the proto-Pauline epistles as it is the fact that John Lentz, after having put his finger on certain difficulties for articulating the differences in the portrait given,[55] wants to show where Luke constructs through these attributes an exemplary image of Paul based upon the recognition of his social status. Although he retains continuity with Judaism and continues to insist upon its value (as we have shown above), John Lentz reckons that what is more important for Luke is, 'Paul the Tarsian and Roman who showed himself to be comfortable in the company of the high and mighty of the first-century Greco-Roman world. ... Paul is always in control. His authority is not only recognized among the Christians. He is also acknowledged as a man not to be taken lightly by the secular leaders as well.'[56] Such an observation can be said to underpin Lentz's work; it is from here that he seeks Luke's intention in the construction of Paul's character. Lentz begins from the importance of 'social stratification'[57] in the Greco-Roman world which according to him explains the care Luke takes to define Paul's status vis-à-vis criteria from the world in which he was reared. Our purpose is not to resume the whole method of Lentz. It is important, however, to point out the basic contours since certain elements will return in the third and final part of our study, where we address again the question of consistency in terms of the whole regarding the question of the 'exemplarity' of the Lukan character of Paul. For the moment, we will be content with picking up some of the main elements which one happens to find in a text on which we have already lingered: Acts 22. There is an element there that captures Lentz's attention: Paul, being beaten by the Jews, is saved by the arrival of the tribune (21.32). Arrested and bound by the tribune and his men, he is taken to their barracks; it is just when he has escaped the immediate danger presented by the Jews that he makes a request to the tribune: 'May I say something to you?' (21.37b). More than the content, it is the form and sequence of this request that I find interesting. Paul has spoken in Greek to the great astonishment of the tribune (21.37c, 'You know Greek?'), who thinks he has arrested an Egyptian, an agitator 'who stirred up a revolt and led the four thousand men of the Assassins out into

---

54   J. Becker, *Paul. L'Apôtre des nations* (Paris, Cerf, 1995), p. 53.

55   Significantly, Lentz remarks that if the possession of two citizenships, Roman and Greek, was indeed possible, it nonetheless would indicate a high degree of hellenization difficult to reconcile with Pharisaic observance of the Law.

56   Lentz, *Luke's Portrait of Paul*, p. 2.

57   Ibid., p. 7.

the wilderness?' (21.38b). The second element to note is Paul's response in v. 39: 'But Paul said, "I am a Jew of Tarsus in Cilicia, a citizen of no insignificant city; and I beg you, allow me to speak to the people."' The surprise of the tribune attests to the effect produced by Paul, who now broaches the topic of social order. Paul is not an Egyptian, a people to whom Lentz, citing Josephus,[58] informs us that Rome denied the civil law. For him, the response Paul makes stems from indignation in the face of this affront; Paul hastens to convey his status and credentials. The way Paul speaks of his city will confirm this interpretation: 'no insignificant city' (39b). Finally, we should note the effect produced (the permission to speak to the people), which Paul seems not to want to doubt when, in the same phrase in which he utters these references, he inserts his claim (21.39).

After Paul's discourse and the threats of the crowd restart, he is taken into the barracks (22.24a); it is there, when he about to be scourged, that he claims his Roman citizenship. By order of the tribune (v. 24), Paul had been bound and was about to be flogged. It is just then that he intervenes with his status of Roman citizenship: 'Is it legal for you to flog a Roman citizen who has not been condemned?' (22.25). In this passage, which stretches from v. 25 to v. 29, for a second time the tribune expresses a misconception concerning Paul (vv. 26 and 29); this leads to an exchange between Paul and the tribune over their respective citizenships, an exchange that suggests the superiority of that of Paul based on how they attained their citizenships. Verse 28 places their respective situations quite clearly on the balance, and in Paul's favour: 'The tribune answered, "It cost me a large sum of money to obtain my citizenship." Paul said, "But I was born a citizen;"' and v. 29 concludes with the effect of this report: those who ought to question him (with the whip) withdraw from him, and the tribune is afraid (ἐφοβήθη). It is from such observations, especially in Acts 21–28, that Lentz understands Paul as having been placed 'on a pedestal above all others'.[59] As far as Acts 26 is concerned, and specifically the understanding that he proposes of Paul's conversion, Lentz follows the same course. He begins with the contrast (26.24-25) between the folly of which Festus accuses Paul – because of what he says – and the σωφροσύνη (wisdom; good sense) that Paul claims for his speeches. Paul says that he is not mad (οὐ μαίνομαι). This exchange between the two characters returns Festus to his folly, to his blindness, since he 'does not have the same φρόνησις (proper knowledge)'.[60] As for Lentz, the question is the meaning that Luke gives to Paul's conversion. According to him, the before and after of conversion are to be evaluated in these terms: 'Paul, before his conversion is not a man of σωφροσύνη; hence, he rages not only against Christians but also against God. The pre-conversion Paul lacks moral virtue, for he resists God';[61] but 'After Paul's conversion he has self-control and is sober and therefore has become virtuous.'[62] Conversion is of the order of 'acquired

---

58   Flavius Josephus, *Contra Apionem* 2,41.
59   Lentz, *Luke's Portrait of Paul*, p. 4.
60   Ibid., p. 88.
61   Ibid., p. 87.
62   Ibid.

knowledge'.[63] Finally, in order to establish a link with the idea of a pedestal that was noted above, we should mention again the tight connection that Lentz sees between the virtues (above all σωφροσύνη) and social status: 'In recognizing Christ, Paul has become a man of true virtue corresponding to his natural advantages of good pedigree, wealth, and high social status, as described by Luke.'[64]

Before concluding this point and passing to the last part of our study, we should note that it remains that the Paul of Acts 21–28 has been arrested and imprisoned (in Jerusalem, then in Caesarea), and that he is briefly placed on trial before at last being taken to Rome.

The third main part of this study will present a critique of Lentz's proposal. Our brief remark regarding Paul standing at the point of judgement and Paul as prisoner should already provide a clue regarding the limits of the point of view of the present author. To see a Paul as having an enviable social status, on a pedestal, should not lead us to minimize the problems he encounters, nor the meaning these problems convey.

IV. From Paul to Acts. In Search of a Basic Uniformity

In the first two parts of this work, we have successively investigated the texts of the Pauline epistles and the Acts of the Apostles, the mode in which the exemplarity of Paul was presented, and whether it was presented explicitly or not. The object of this last stage will be to take up again certain observations related to each of these corpuses in order to make a comparison between them, and chiefly to look beyond the differences so as to uncover their fundamental coherence.

a. The Same Itinerary of Conversion

In Philippians 3, we have noted that Paul, in explaining his conversion caused by his knowledge of Christ, was establishing a definition for the way of Christian existence. Verse 17, which exhorts its hearers to imitation, ought from then on to be understood as beginning from the development that comes from describing Paul, giving him paradigmatic value. We should recall that Paul does not place himself *beneath* those whom he addresses, but rather, as the usage of the first person plural demonstrates (Phil. 3.15-16), *with* them. In this way, Paul does not present his example as a goal to attain, but as a picture of a paradigmatic progress. In v. 12, he expresses his position as a journey. It cannot be a matter of a position already attained: he always progresses, having been laid hold of by Christ. Then, in v. 16, we find a 'we' surrounding Paul, indicating those who are with him and the Philippians, once again understood as a common itinerary to pursue: πλὴν εἰς ὃ ἐφθάσαμεν, τῷ αὐτῷ στοιχεῖν ('Only let us hold fast to what we have attained, by the same rule let us walk').

---

63   Ibid., p. 88.
64   Ibid., p. 83.

In the Acts of the Apostles, we find the same basic contours as regards Paul's exemplarity, even if it is articulated in a different form and with different motifs. In Philippians 3, we have referred to the case of Paul's conversion, speaking of his self-worth and confidence based on the appropriate qualities and prerogatives with respect to righteousness and salvation, that he has passed over to the abandonment of these prerogatives (considering them as refuse) on account of the knowledge of Christ. In the same way, the three accounts of Acts treated above begin by referring to the old Jew and Pharisee in Paul, taking care to accentuate his qualities and punctiliousness. On this point, Acts 9.1-2, 22.3-5, and 26.4-5 find an echo in Phil. 3.4-6, though we should be conscious of the fact that Paul's continuity with Judaism is explicitly upheld by the discourses of Acts 22 and 26, whereas Philippians 3 demonstrates unequivocally the failure of the system connected with vv. 4-6. However, the basic contours are just the same. These four instances which recount Paul's former relation to the Law share the characteristics of the account that refers to the Law's end. Highlighted or not, whatever continuity there may be with Judaism, as well as with the Law (though interpreted differently), Paul's encounter with Christ and his knowledge of him transfer him to another mode of being. If Philippians 3 does not recount 'the history' of his conversion, vv. 7-9 surely recount his change of perspective as regards his understanding of his existence, as well as his understanding of the Law and, ultimately, of salvation, with the knowledge of Christ as the crux (his sufferings, death, and resurrection, cf. v. 10-11). In Acts 9, 22 and then 26, the pivotal moment takes place in the road-to-Damascus event, as we follow the two re-tellings, focusing increasingly on the moment of Paul's conversion and the meaning of his encounter with Christ, (cf. Acts 26.15-18). Compare Phil. 3.9 (καὶ εὑρεθῶ ἐν αὐτῷ, μὴ ἔχων ἐμὴν δικαιοσύνην τὴν ἐκ νόμου ἀλλὰ τὴν διὰ πίστεως Χριστοῦ, τὴν ἐκ θεοῦ δικαιοσύνην ἐπὶ τῇ πίστει, 'and be found in him, not having a righteousness of my own that comes from the law, but one that comes through faith in Christ, the righteousness from God based on faith') and Acts 26.18b (τοῦ λαβεῖν αὐτοὺς ἄφεσιν ἁμαρτιῶν καὶ κλῆρον ἐν τοῖς ἡγιασμένοις πίστει τῇ εἰς ἐμέ, 'in order that they may receive forgiveness of sins and an inheritance among those who have been sanctified by faith in Me'). The mode of expression is different. In Philippians, Paul explains his new position with respect to the Law. In Acts, the speeches by the resurrected Jesus relate the content of the message of Christ's mission to Paul, and thereby also the content of his new identity, which is followed by his immediate obedience in the next verse. Nonetheless the conversion is much the same.

If we continue, we see that in Philippians just as in Acts the transition experienced by the apostle himself is then enlarged, so that his experience is made to signify something for all believers. We referred at the opening of this final section to the 'we' of Phil. 3.16, and earlier, in the second part, to Acts 26.20. We would do well to take from this verse the fact that Paul's preaching makes reference to 'repentance' (τῇ μετανοίᾳ), not to 'a certain repentance', to which is added the practice of works worthy of repentance, an integral part of the journey of every Christian. Despite the particulars that are peculiar to the context, it seems therefore that one could see a consistent outline in the way in which exemplarity is finally presented in the exhortations to imitation found in Phil 3.17 and Acts 26.29.

b. What Continuity with Judaism?

A point that still remains for us to clarify in making the connection between these texts is the question of Paul's continuity with Judaism; if such continuity exists, in what way does it exist? This question does not directly touch the guiding concern of this work, but it is implied nonetheless and is too important to ignore. More importantly, it will lead us back to the text of Rom. 7.7-25, which we addressed in the first part.

In working with Paul's discourses in Acts 22 and 26, we have referred to the common occurrence of his desire to demonstrate the continuity of his preaching with Judaism; now in Philippians 3, the most prominent aspect of Paul's conversion is described with respect to his understanding of the Law, specifically concerning his transition from a righteousness that comes from the Law to that which comes from God by faith. In this text, where is the continuity with Judaism that Luke aims to demonstrate with Paul's discourses in Acts? The text, formally speaking, says nothing about this; the emphasis is clearly placed on the reversal of perspective in relation to the Law. That said, we may note that it is not based on a judgement of the Law as such, but on the relation of the believer to the Law. Now, if we consider two texts of Acts, we will notice that the continuity does not diminish the force of Paul's conversion. In fact, even if Paul appeals to his continuity with Judaism, his brand of Judaism is nonetheless not exactly the same, or even nearly the same, for placing himself in this continuity does not make his message less radically new. If we turn again to Acts 22, we are able to point out the Hebrew language with which Paul expresses himself (21.40b), as well as the assertion ἐγώ εἰμι ἀνὴρ Ἰουδαῖος ('I am a Jew'), and his claim that he had a certain education (παρὰ τοὺς πόδας Γαμαλιὴλ πεπαιδευμένος κατὰ ἀκρίβειαν τοῦ πατρῴου νόμου, 'I had my education at the feet of Gamaliel, instructed to the strict manner of the Law of the Fathers', 22.3). In order to confirm more certainly that these remarks from Paul mean to convey at least a certain measure of continuity, we can further refer to 22.1: Paul makes a defence (ἀπολογία). To conclude, the fact that the continuity does not diminish the novelty of his message and the reality of his conversion is particularly visible in vv. 16 and 17. In 22.16, after the road-to-Damascus event, Paul is baptized; that – we must note – does not prevent him from praying in the Temple (22.17) on his return to Jerusalem, however. Daniel Marguerat, in his work *L'image de Paul dans les Actes des Apôtres*, says of the event on the road to Damascus that 'this violent reversal does not endear Saul to his Jewishness but reorients it'.[65] Then he adds: 'What changes dramatically here is the gaze with which he focuses on Christ.'[66]

---

65   Marguerat, *L'image de Paul*, p. 137.

66   Ibid. We recognize the occurrence of the knowledge of Christ that we treated in Philippians 3 as a central locus of conversion (centred here on the recognition of his divine sonship; Acts 9.20 and Gal. 1.15-16a).

To conclude this question, let us return to the text of Rom. 7.7-25. We have shown how, in this text, Paul's 'I' departs from having a strict autobiographical reference and widens so as to include every person along with him, creating in effect one particular experience which is at the same time the experience of every person. The 'I' of this pericope is that of a man torn by sin; we have mentioned that the liberation from sin of which there is a question earlier and later is here left as if in suspense. As regards the question of the Law, this text speaks of the permanence of sin in spite of the Law, and even refers to how the sin uses the Law to act. In this regard, one could cite Rom. 7.8: ἀφορμὴν δὲ λαβοῦσα ἡ ἁμαρτία διὰ τῆς ἐντολῆς κατειργάσατο ἐν ἐμοὶ πᾶσαν ἐπιθυμίαν· χωρὶς γὰρ νόμου ἁμαρτία νεκρά ('But sin, seizing an opportunity in the commandment, produced in me all kinds of covetousness. Apart from the law sin lies dead'). What has been said strongly regarding the perverse nature of sin is expressed in Rom. 7.13: τὸ οὖν ἀγαθὸν ἐμοὶ ἐγένετο θάνατος; μὴ γένοιτο· ἀλλὰ ἡ ἁμαρτία, ἵνα φανῇ ἁμαρτία διὰ τοῦ ἀγαθοῦ μοι κατεργαζομένη θάνατον, ἵνα γένηται καθ' ὑπερβολὴν ἁμαρτωλὸς ἡ ἁμαρτία διὰ τῆς ἐντολῆς ('Did what is good, then, bring death to me? By no means! It was sin, working death in me through what is good, in order that sin might be shown to be sin, and through the commandment might become sinful beyond measure'). If we have successfully demonstrated in the first part of this study that the condition of the man of Rom. 7.7-25 was also that of the believer, we will note that the permanence of sin and its transmission through the Law and the precept do not condemn the Law as such. It is sin that is the agent; the Law is described as something good, and itself holy (vv. 12-13).

We would like to clarify here a tension in the question of continuity, or lack thereof, with Judaism; in fact it seems that from the question of the validity of the Law, this text partly allows for such an explanation. In this pericope, the Law is validated in spite of its complete failure to prevent man from sin; in this failure, it is not the Law per se that is directly condemned, but its inadequacy vis-à-vis man; cf. Rom. 7.14: οἴδαμεν γὰρ ὅτι ὁ νόμος πνευματικός ἐστιν, ἐγὼ δὲ σάρκινός εἰμι πεπραμένος ὑπὸ τὴν ἁμαρτίαν ('For we know that the law is spiritual; but I am of the flesh, sold into slavery under sin'); there is also 7.22-23. From then on, if in spite of the absolute necessity of a saviour (vv. 24-25), it is maintained to be holy, good, and spiritual, then surely the question is how it is to be understood. The 'I' of Rom. 7.7-25, and therefore the existence that is defined in it, do not empty the Law, but nonetheless cannot be based on it; it has need of a saviour.

c. From Paul to Luke-Acts: Following Jesus, in 'Conformity'. The Limitations of J. C. Lentz's Model

In our remarks on the various texts treated, we have referred both to the important dimension of 'imitation' of Christ that precedes and underlies Paul's appeals and to the progress of Christian existence to which these texts appeal. In Phil. 3.17 we noted that this reference was not explicit, contrary to the other occurrences of this type of appeal, as in 1 Thess. 1.6 or 1 Cor. 11.1. We have tried to show, however, that this sense is no less evident in this text, since, in this case of 'imitation', it is a matter of Paul understanding his existence based on the knowledge of Christ (sufferings, death, resurrection). In the case of Philippians, we have perhaps not mentioned the fact that the pericope we have treated from chapter 3 was preceded with Phil 2.1-11. This passage presents Christ as a paradigm: τοῦτο φρονεῖτε ἐν ὑμῖν ὁ καὶ ἐν Χριστῷ Ἰησοῦ ('Let the same mind be in you that was in Christ Jesus', 2.5). The hymn (2.6-11) tells how he has been exalted (v. 9) in his renunciation, his humility and his weakness, which he has accepted to the point of death on the cross. Christ is therefore glorified in the fashion of the kenosis, in a passage at the heart of which Paul means to impart to his addressees how to comport themselves in Christ (vv. 3-5), before relating, first, his own renunciation in Phil 3.7, and then, in 3.10, his sharing in Christ's sufferings by becoming like him in his death. The relation between Philippians 2 and 3, namely, the understanding of Paul's exemplarity on the basis of conformity to the itinerary of Christ, is highlighted by Jean-Noël Aletti, among others, in his commentary cited above: he notes that 'the function of the exemplum is identical in the first and second parts of Philippians, what is said about Paul in Philippians 3 refers to what is said about Christ in Philippians 2'.[67] Philippians 3, according to him, takes its full force only from its allusions to Philippians 2.[68]

As for Acts, we will perceive the consistency in what we have referred to (cf. III.a), regarding the change from persecutor to persecuted. Saul was persecuting the Christians, and as such was in fact persecuting Christ, who identified himself with them (Acts 9.5; 22.8; 26.15); now Saul, having been converted, himself persecuted[69] for the same reasons that he was persecuting Christians, is likewise to be identified with Christ. One therefore discovers in the character of Paul presented by Luke the same sufferings in and for the name of Christ. One notes in Acts 9.15-16, where Jesus declares that Paul will have to suffer on account of his name, that the word used in v. 16 is πάσχω. This is the same word that is used in Luke-Acts to speak of Christ's passion. The use of this word specifically (which suggests something beyond mere rejection or opposition) allows us to affirm that v. 16 supports the sense of continuity between the ministries of Jesus and Paul.[70]

---

67   Aletti, *Épître aux Philippiens*, p. 215, note 1. O'Brien speaks along these lines: '... the apostle has already reminded his readers that Christ Jesus is the example par excellence (2.5-8) and that their attitude and behaviour should be like his, whether or not the συν- in συμμιμηταί signifies "(be) fellow imitators *with me* (of Christ)"'; O'Brien, *The Epistle to the Philippians*, p. 447. He does not formally confirm our proposition regarding συμμιμηταί, but at the heart of it, what he says of imitation and the place that Paul gives it does dovetail with my point (cf. II.a).

68   Let us simply observe the parallels: μορφή (2.7) // συμμορφιζόμενος (3.10); ἡγέομαι (2.6 // 3.7-8); γενόμενος (2.7-8 // 3.6); εὑρεθείς (2.7) // εὑρεθῶ (3.9); θάνατος (2.8 // 3.10).

69   Cf. Acts 9.23-24, 29-30; 14.2-5, 19; 16.19; 17.5-14; 18.12-13. Then from 21.30-33 he is arrested and stands under judgement.

70   Cf. especially Skinner, *Locating Paul*, pp. 96–97. In the same sense, also W. S. Kurz, 'Narrative Models for Imitation in Luke–Acts', in *Greeks, Romans and Christians. Essays in Honor of Abraham J. Malherbe* (ed. D. L. Balch, E. Ferguson and W. A. Meeks; Minneapolis: Fortress, 1990), pp. 171–89 (174–75): 'The farewell addresses in Acts 20:17-38 and Luke 22:14-38 draw explicit attention to Paul and Jesus as models to be imitated'; and M.-E. Rosenblatt, *Paul the Accused. His Portrait in the Acts of the Apostles* (Zacchaeus Studies. NT; Collegeville, Minn.: Liturgical Press, 1995), p. 11: 'Within Acts, the technique of doubling also establishes a harmonious relationship between Peter and Paul. Several advantages for Paul result. His actions match

At this point, we can return to an observation of Jean-Noël Aletti. Aletti, whose work draws attention to parallels found in the Lukan corpus, goes so far as to show what parallels there are between the Paul of Acts and the Jesus of the third Gospel; in this regard, such verses as Luke 9.23 or 14.27 in the first part of Luke's work prefigure what will appear later the following as regards the character of Paul in Acts. Finally, if we pause for a moment on this last verse, in which there is the question of each person's 'cross' (τὸν σταυρὸν αὐτοῦ: 'his own cross'), we understand that, in following/imitation, it is more a matter of having a certain attitude in the face of trials[71] that come on account of Christ than it is of imitation of Christ in the strict sense (i.e., imitation of the same trial). These last remarks will assist us in discerning the basic consistency that we seek regarding the exemplarity of Paul and his imitation such as we have found it in his letters.

Based on these last remarks, we shall end with a critical evaluation of the work of John Lentz. We had concluded the second part of this work by noting a certain tension that made us wonder whether Paul may be constructed as an exemplary character in Acts 21–28 in terms of the value of his personal qualities (notably his social rank), placing him on a 'pedestal', then even whether this sequence sees him as bound, in the instance of judgement (when he is arrested by authorities), and transferred from one place of imprisonment to another. The movement that leads Paul to Rome under judgement, according to John Lentz, comes into play with this same purpose of demonstrating his credentials: 'Paul's arrival in Rome was important for Luke for, at last, his hero was where he belonged: in the captial, the center of power and prestige.'[72] Without denying the importance of the fact that Acts ends in Rome, it should be said that the interpretation that John Lentz here proposes deviates a good deal from the fact that he who arrives in Rome is a prisoner: in 28.20 he always carries a chain, and is watched under 'house arrest' (28.16, 30). Paul's freedom of speech in Acts 28, stated in vv. 30-31, could perhaps legitimate a reading of the sort that John Lentz proposes; but it does not seem to us that this reading is the most judicious one. Paul, a prisoner in Rome on account of Christ, could easily have been presented as unhindered (as far as his speech was concerned), since his captivity is registered in continuity with what his calling implies in Acts 9.15-16.[73] Having set forth a certain understanding of Paul's

---

those of Peter. As Peter's sufferings mirror those of Jesus, so Paul's mission is a continuation of the work of Jesus. Paul's mission is legitimated within the Church on two counts: he is like Jesus and he is like Peter. If Paul resembles Jesus and Peter, then Paul's leadership and his convictions as a missionary have validity. The narrative strategy of doubling serves Luke's theological and pastoral purpose as they are personified in Paul.'

71   Rosenblatt, *Paul the Accused*, p. 94, says this in the following terms: 'Rather, the pastoral perspective calls attention to Paul as model for community members who face struggles similar to those Paul endured as a missionary faithful to his preaching vocation.'

72   Lentz, *Luke's Portrait of Paul*, 4.

73   The article from C. Clivaz (*La rumeur, une catégorie pour articuler autoportraits et réceptions de Paul. 'Car ses lettres, dit-on, ont du poids ... et sa parole est nulle' [2 Cor. 10.10]*), pp. 239–59 [cf. pp. 264–281 in the present volume]), may be illuminating both for our understanding of the consistency between Paul's captivity and his calling, and, in the same way, in the fact that she does not imply a weakness of speech. What especially interests me in her work is that

exemplarity, from Paul to Acts, it is important to show the limits of an exemplary model of the Paul of Acts such as is proposed by John Lentz. Lentz, to my mind, does not entirely take into account the status of Paul the prisoner in Rome, a prisoner whose status, we have found, coheres with that in his letters.

V. Conclusion

As we close this study, we summarize what it seems to us that we have drawn from the different texts we have examined. We began with the Pauline letters, first seeking out what image of Paul could be conveyed from the passages that spoke autobiographically, and then seeking what mode was used (by him) to present his exemplarity. In doing this, we focused specifically on the meaning of exhortation to imitation in Phil. 3.17; we then widened our scope to a passage that does not explicitly treat imitation (Romans 7), but in which the particular function of the autobiographical language clarified our earlier conclusions, albeit from a slightly different perspective.

Passing to the texts from the Acts of the Apostles, we had to be conscious of the fact that we were dealing with a *reception* of Paul. Linking certain pieces of data from the texts of Paul's letters with those of Acts, at first blush, created tension as to the elaboration of a 'portrait of Paul'. The author who has made us more attentive to the difficulty of reconciling the image given there with the Paul of the letters is John Lentz. Having briefly called attention to the inconsistencies he found between the Pauline corpus and Acts regarding the character of Paul, and, as a consequence, the historical implausibility of certain aspects of the Paul of Acts, we have pointed out the intention that John Lentz discerns in the Lukan construction of Paul: to construct a Paul of enviable social status, one sitting on a pedestal. In that regard, however, our object was not the question of the historical plausibility of the portrait of Paul in Acts, nor the consistency of the portrait of Paul in the Pauline corpus and Acts. In what we have highlighted from the Pauline corpus and Acts with respect to the question of the character of Paul as 'exemplary', it was our concern to show the limits of a reading that does not take into account the trials associated with the way of Paul in Acts.

We opened this study with a series of questions that could be reformulated as follows: does the exemplary aspect of Paul, in exhorting others to imitation in

---

she sees Paul as a 'divine prisoner'. In the reception of the Paul of the Deutero-Pauline epistles and pastorals, we find the following assertions: Eph 3.1 ('This is the reason that I Paul am a prisoner for Christ Jesus for the sake of you Gentiles') and 2 Tim 1.8, where 'the pseudepigraphical Paul invites his recipient to "not be ashamed ... of me [The Lord's] prisoner"; he also emphasizes that Onesiphorus, "was not ashamed of my chain".' Claire Clivaz understands in these assertions the attestation of a response, the attestation of an echo that his reception would make a 'rumour hostile to Paul based on his status as prisoner', a report that finds an original attestation in Phil. 1.15-20, which was received as if Paul wrote it in captivity: 'Other Christian missionaries are in competition with Paul (1.15) and seek to use his imprisonment to gain an advantage over him (1.17); this affirms all the more that he "will not be put to shame" and that his boldness remains no matter what happens (1.20).'

his letters, continue in Acts? If so, in what way does Paul present himself as an example, and is Luke's representation of this fact consistent with Paul's way of being an example?

We have said that the place Luke gives to Paul in Acts tends to show that he makes of him an exemplary figure for the identity of a believer. Returning to our questions, what chief points of convergence have we been able to demonstrate between the two exemplary figures of Paul?

In Acts (9, 22, and 26) as well as in the example of Philippians 3, our study has demonstrated that Paul is inscribed into the same journey of conversion. In Philippians 3 as in the three repeated accounts of the Damascus-road event in Acts, the particular experience of Paul ultimately refers beyond himself. Paul's experience thus becomes that of every believer. In that regard, there are the uses of the first person plural in Phil. 3.15-16 and the interpretation of 'repentance' in Acts 26.20 as referring to the repentance of every believer, which fact allows us to speak of a certain homogeneity. Finally, we have shown the homogeneity between the one figure of Paul and the other with respect to his relation to Christ. On account of the knowledge of Christ, Paul's example refers beyond himself, through his own imitation of Christ or his conformity with him. For Philippians, we have relied on the relation between Philippians 2 and 3 and on the interpretation, in Philippians 3, of the 'knowledge of Christ' as a participatory knowledge. In Acts, we have shown that there is a uniform relation between the character of Paul and Christ. We were chiefly concerned with the interpretation of Christ as Paul's example in Acts 9.16, and the meaning of the reversal of his status from persecutor to persecuted (cf. Acts 9.5; 22.8; 26.15 read in connection with the trials of Paul on account of his preaching).

The Paul of Acts is presented in connection with following/imitation of Christ. On this basis, we can at last return to his trials in Acts so as to attest to the convergence between the two exemplary figures of Paul that we have studied. In the epistles just as in Acts, the example of Paul is not a fixed goal to be attained, but a paradigmatic way. As one moves along this path, Paul's example constitutes a noteworthy attitude in the face of trials.

MEDIATOR, MIRACLE-WORKER, DOCTOR OF THE CHURCH? THE
CONTINUING MYSTERY OF PAUL IN THE NEW TESTAMENT AND IN
EARLY CHRISTIANITY

David P. Moessner, with D. Marguerat, M. C. Parsons, and M. Wolter

This is a great mystery. But I take it to mean Christ and the church. (Eph. 5.32)

Apart from Jesus of Nazareth himself, no one in the story of the early Christian movement has evoked such curiosity, not to mention contempt, as Paul the apostle. As the pages of this volume illustrate again, it is impossible to fit Paul into any 'straightjacket' of historical and theological significance whether in the New Testament or other literature of the early church. He is not only a powerful proclaimer but also a mediator of the mysteries of Christ. He is not only a charismatic evangel of the Spirit but also a worker of miracles that heal and save. And to say that he is a tenacious rhētor of the wisdom of the faith does not in the slightest diminish his role as prophet who receives and expounds oracles from God. Even as Paul utters mysteries of this faith, he himself remains much of a mystery.

But this manifold embrace of Paul only serves to make a study of his 'reception' all the more fascinating. Is it possible to capture the 'essence' of the man, the character of one whose stature in Christian history quickly became and has continued to be so great? Is it possible to make rhyme or reason of the wide swath of the progression and diffusion of his influence? It is of course impossible to encapsulate all the new insights and answers to these questions that unfold in these essays. We can attempt here only a few salient features.

Perhaps what is most striking in *Paul and the Heritage of Israel* is the very different terms of the debate.

I. The Dissolution of Tendenzkritik *through Multi-faceted Approaches to the 'Thought' of Paul and of Luke*

The rapid decline of the influence of the 'Tübingen School's' profile of Luke's relation to Paul is due in large measure to the proliferation of newer analyses and strategies for discerning the 'mind' and 'intent' of Paul and of Luke in their own writings. Probably the two 'modes' that have changed the landscape of interpretation the most, while overlapping significantly, are 'rhetoric' and 'narratology'. In tandem, these two methods have significantly shaped the overall approach of 'reception history'.

1. *Rhetoric*. The postmodern period has witnessed a flurry of studies of the rhetorical handbooks to see how ancient writers designed the shape of their persuasion. The application of rhetoric both to the discursive arguments of the Pauline letters and to the narrative-rhetorical strategies of the Lukan narrative have yielded dramatic results. Whereas with *Tendenzkritik* it was Luke who 'tended' to write out of his specific ecclesiastical *Sitz im Leben* in order to promote or defend the integrity of the consolidating church, now Paul is also 'read' as persuading audiences in light of his concrete historical and ecclesiastical situations. If Luke wrote out of his ecclesiastical convictions, so did Paul. This levelling of the 'minds' of the authors like Luke and Paul by virtue of their intended audience impact has probably contributed more to the demise of Tübingen's influence than any other 'approach'. Now from the varying social and ecclesiastical contexts identified by the diverging audiences and social worlds of the text, 'trajectories' can be traced through different literatures to delineate specific traditions of influence. The contributions particularly of S. Butticaz, O. Flichy, D. Marguerat, and G. Sterling provide ample illustrations of this paradigm shift in the interpretation of both Paul and Luke in the last thirty or so years. Whether from within the Pauline corpus (e.g., from 1 Corinthians to 2 Corinthians or from the Corinthian letters to the Deutero-Paulines, etc.) or by traversing the boundaries of other literatures such as Luke or Clement of Rome or the *Acts of Paul*, etc., the older dichotomy between Paul's reliable intent or thought versus the tendentious construals of him in 'later' literature disappears. F. C. Baur's elevation of the undisputed Paulines as the norm for all things 'Paul', no longer holds validity.

To be sure, 'levelling' of authorial intent is anything but a 'harmonizing'of thought or purpose. This differentiation is demonstrated most ably in the variety of narrative interpretations.

2. *Narrative*. Both modern and ancient hermeneutical discussions of narrative meaning reveal the considerable expanse and versatility of narrative/diēgēsis to incorporate and nuance multiple levels of 'thought' and 'point of view' into a new ensemble of relationships and understandings of the world. Rather than 'dumb down' the pure *logos* of discursive thought, narrative enables great subtleties of thought to be expressed in equally if not even more complex ways of enlightenment. Luke's use of narrative (Lk. 1.1-4) to confirm 'certain' things about the Christian movement is not therefore *de facto* inferior to Paul's suasive rhetoric. In fact, the subtleties of generic and sub-generic differences are maximized in narrative interpretation. If Vielhauer's distinctions between Paul and Luke now seem skewed, it is largely because of the very different valuation of narrative as a means of communication in the clime of postmodern hermeneutics (see esp. S. Butticaz, D. Moessner, M. Parsons).

Both rhetorical and diēgētic categories in combination are especially deft in highlighting the peculiarities as well as the commonalities among and between the manifold socio-rhetorical worlds of the Greco-Roman milieu. Rather than categorize narrative as primarily 'historical' or 'ideological', or Luke as essentially historian or theologian, narrative rhetoric divulges how closely fused historical 'thought' and authorial intent are through the narrative-rhetorical identifications of targeted audiences in discrete socio-historical contexts. The main conclusions of volume one of *Jesus and the Heritage of Israel* are thus re-confirmed. Luke configures both history and theology through the rhetoric of the narrative. His Acts is no less theological than Paul's letters, though it will differ from Paul and presumably for most, not match the brilliance of Paul's theological elucidations and formulations. Conversely, Paul's letters, whether disputed as genuine utterances of Paul or not, are neither more nor less historical than the biographical-narrative descriptions of Paul in Acts or the traditions of Paul in the *Acts of Paul*. For both rhetorical and narrative interpretation take into full account the differences between first-person 'disposition' and third-person narration, between first-hand persuasion and second-hand re-counting, between eyewitness claims to authenticity and stereotyped abstractions and apocopated recapitulations, between convergences with similar generic texts and similarities between texts of diverging genres, between texts of canonical status and those of contested origin.

3. *Reception History*. For these and other factors that could be mentioned, narrative-rhetorical interpretation is particularly well suited to sort out the various ways Paul was 'utilized' and 'remembered' in succeeding texts that draw in some fashion upon what is known to be *from* or *about* Paul. *Paul and the Heritage of Israel* documents on nearly every page the importance of re-defining 'Paulinism' through a developing method of interpretation best described as 'reception history'. As evidenced in these essays, the history of the reception of a text is becoming an eclectic combining of 'reader-reception' theories (U. Eco's 'cultural encyclopedia' of knowledge has become prominent) and evolving forms of an earlier emphasis on the history of the impact of a particular text or *Wirkungsgeschichte* (such as J. C. Beker's 'legacy'). Perhaps even more 'typical' of this emerging access to textual meaning is the mixing of 'intertextual' ingredients into the basic reception 'recipe'. 'Transtextuality' or the 'trans-narrativizing' of Pauline phrases and conceptions into a new assembly of relationships inscribed in various genres and sub-genres is becoming characteristic of the process of tagging and appraising Pauline influence. These and other intertextual 'sensors' have become instrumental in discerning resonances and echoes between successor and precursor texts, between derivative hypertextual rereadings and hypo-texts re-read [Genette] (see esp. the chapters by Butticaz, Clivaz, Dettwiler, Hays, Landolt, Marguerat, Pervo, Redalié, Schröter, Wolter). In *Paul and the Heritage of Israel* this dynamic understanding of tradition and its intricate intertextuality combined with socio-anthropological analyses has generated new models for understanding the relation of Paul in Acts to the Pauline letters: e.g., Luke's portrayal of Paul in Acts is an organic development from within a Pauline symbolic world (R. Hays); the Deutero-Paulines and Pastorals present a (new) 'religion of tradition' developing out of a 'religion of conversion' from traditions of Judaism as presented by Paul in his undisputed letters (M. Wolter); three main forms of transtextuality (documentary, biographical, 'doctoral') comprehend Paul and his legacies (D. Marguerat); or, Paul as a *persona* of the NT

letters becomes fixed only in the second century when Irenaeus trans-narrativizes Paul by juxtaposing his letters with the narratives of Acts and the Four Gospels (C. Mount).

Consequently one of the real advances that *Paul and the Heritage of Israel* offers in interpreting Paul *and* Luke is the application of more sophisticated under-standings of the ways tradition grows and is received by differing groups with differing impacts resulting in a diverging array of literatures. In this burgeoning influence of Paul, 'displacement' of a characteristic 'conceptualization' is a normal phenomenon of reappropriation rather than a necessary perversion or betrayal of authenticity (see Butticaz, Flichy, Schröter). Whether or not one accepts the post-Pauline writing of the Deutero-Paulines and the Pastorals of the NT,[1] what becomes manifest is the authoritative influence that Paul commands as his words and ideas are resituated in diverging *Sitze im Leben* such that precursor texts exhibit both continuity and displacement, consistency and change, in successor texts (see Clivaz, Dettwiler, Landolt, Marguerat, Redalié). Paul and Paulinism proceed hand in hand.

II. The Continuing 'Sea Change' of Luke as Promoter rather than Archiver of Israel's History and Heritage in the Messiah Jesus

Even if the disposition of *Tendenzkritik* no longer prevails in evaluating the Paul of Acts, it is clear nevertheless from our analysis above that the Tübingen School's influence cannot simply be dismissed. A. J. Mattill's assessment over thirty years ago would seem still to be accurate, that we have no choice but to 'begin with its [Tübingen School's] conclusions and proceed to build upon, modify, or reject them'.[2] One of the enduring legacies of that approach was the marginalization of Judaism as the preparatory religion of Jesus to be superseded through his resur-rection and worldwide mission with its super-apostle Paul into the new (and by implication, superior) universal religion. *Paul and the Heritage of Israel* demon-strates how widespread and pervasive this view of Judaism as prospective only in value for Luke or for Paul has been rejected. On the contrary, study after study in the past thirty years or so has argued – to use a phrase from *Jesus and the Heritage of Israel* – that 'Luke's "Hellenistic" Gospel' is 'alive to the thoroughly Jewish question of Jesus and Israel', arguing consistently throughout the two volumes that 'Jesus of Nazareth is Israel's true heritage and enduring legacy to the world' (p. 3).

---

1   See, e.g., B. Reicke, *Re-examining Paul's Letters. The History of the Pauline Correspondence* (ed. D. P. Moessner and I. Reicke; Harrisburg, Pa.: Trinity Press International, 2001), who envisions a 'writing team' within Paul's cohorts to explain the very different style and idioms and emphases of the 'Deutero-Paulines' and Pastorals as due to the diversity, versatility, and adaptability of this group of composers whom Paul encouraged as interpreter-theologians and authorized to write on his behalf – whether through dictation or general directions – while Paul was still alive.

2   'The Value of Acts as a Source for the Study of Paul', in ed. C. H. Talbert, *Perspectives on Luke-Acts* [Danville, VA: Association of Baptist Professors of Religion, 1978], pp. 76–98 (98).

While not all of the essays treat the relation of Paul to Israel directly, all of the contributors agree that the basic profile of Paul and Paulinisms within the NT literature exhibit a basic continuity with at least certain of the themes and emphases of Israel's scriptures, particularly the role of Paul in Acts to preach the gospel concerning Israel's Messiah to the gentile peoples of the nations. Wherever one places the dating of Acts, it is curious that in the second century both Jesus and Paul are perforce linked in the emerging Christian history that is written *alongside* apostolic tradition (e.g., Irenaeus) in order to distinguish or even separate Christianity from Judaism and other syntheses such as the scheme of Marcion (see Mount, Pervo). It would appear that Paul's legacy can not be easily extricated from the incipient 'orthodox' construals of Jesus the Christ in the second century (see Clivaz).

Accordingly one of the intriguing results of several of the essays is the paradoxical role that Paul is assigned or assumes in Acts or the Deutero-Paulines and Pastorals in relation to the God of the Jewish scriptures and the history of Israel that is being played out in the Jesus messianic movement. On the one hand, Paul is the last of those called in the apostolic summons because he is in essence the 'least of the apostles' (e.g., 1 Cor. 15.3-11) as the 'first' or 'foremost of sinners' against Messiah Jesus (e.g., 1 Tim. 1.15-16). On the other hand, this one who is 'last' is 'first' in receiving the mystery at the end of the age of the revelation of Messiah Jesus who unites both Jew and gentile as one people of God (Sterling). Precisely as *successor* of the apostles Paul becomes the *originator* of the mission to the nations as he himself has become an integral part of the mystery as the herald of the new solidarity of Christ in both Jews and gentiles (Marguerat). Whether Paul and Luke share a wider intertextual, messianic hermeneutical discourse (Hays) or Paul's teaching on justification spawns a distinctly Christian cultural encyclo-pedia of new Christian tradition spanning the human *being* both Jew and gentile in a new creation (Wolter) or Paul's witness serves as guarantee of the authentic messianic fulfilment of Israel's scriptures in a universal mission, including within it an ongoing disbelieving Israel of the eschatological 'people of God' (Moessner), Paul and a variety of Paulinisms court and consummate an abiding ambivalence in the mystery that is Paul. In sum, through both Acts (Butticaz, Flichy, Landolt, Parsons, Pervo) and the Deutero-Paulines (Clivaz, Dettwiler, Redalié, Schröter, Sterling) Paul is placed at the very centre of the traditions of a growing catholic network of churches that will in time ensconce this role at the heart of the New Testament writings.

Paul and the Heritage of Israel thus opens up lanes of discovery on the new sea scape that is Luke and Acts and sets up plumb lines for those still-large patches of uncharted terrain of Paul's influence in the Mediterranean basin of the late first and second centuries. If these essays have 'proven' anything, they show that the more recent advances in narrative rhetoric and reception history now offer even more opportunity for future readers of the Lukan and Pauline writings to reflect on the meaning of truth in history that the narrative and discursive arguments put forward and the kinds of audiences that 'heard' within the force fields of Roman Empire. New breakthroughs of knowledge are to be expected in this new atmosphere of multi-pronged, interactive approaches to meanings of texts, new appreciations of the intertextual gravitas of scriptural arguments, new syntheses of hermeneutics and social-scientific methods, and new suspicions of older dichotomies that try inexorably to pit tradition against history. Whoever Luke was, *Paul and the Heritage of Israel* demonstrates that he is intent on showing how the Christian movement, represented iconically (and ironically!) by Paul, is organically tied to the history and scriptures of Israel and claims its heritage as the legitimate growth and flowering of God's election of a special people.

BIBLIOGRAPHY

Achtemeier, P. J., *1 Peter* (Hermeneia; Minneapolis: Fortress, 1996).

Aland, K., and B. Aland, *The Text of the New Testament: An Introduction to the Critical Editions and to the Theory and Practice of Modern Textual Criticism* (trans. E. F. Rhodes; Leiden: Brill, 2nd edn, 1989).

Aletti, J.-N., *Quand Luc raconte: Le récit comme théologie* (Lire la Bible, 115; Paris: Cerf, 1998).

———, 'Rm 7,7-25 encore une fois: Enjeux et propositions', *NTS* 48 (2002), pp. 358–76.

———, *Saint Paul. Épître aux Colossiens* (EtB, 55; Paris: Gabalda, 2005).

———, *Saint Paul. Épître aux Philippiens* (EtB, 55; Paris, Gabalda, 2005).

Alexander, L., 'Fact, Fiction and the Genre of Acts', *NTS* 44 (1998), pp. 380–99.

———, 'The Preface to Acts and the Historians', in *Acts in its Ancient Literary Context. A Classicist Looks at the Acts of the Apostles* (LNTS, 298; London: T&T Clark, 2005), pp. 21–42.

Alter, R., *The Art of Biblical Narrative* (New York: Basic Books, 1981).

Ashton, J., *The Religion of Paul the Apostle* (New Haven: Yale University Press, 2000).

Assmann, J., 'Kollektives Gedächtnis und kulturelle Identität', in *Kultur und Gedächtnis* (ed. J. Assmann and T. Hölscher; Frankfurt am Main: Suhrkamp, 1988), pp. 9–19.

———, *Das kulturelle Gedächtnis* (München: Beck, 1999).

———, *Moïse l'Egyptien: Un essai d'histoire de la mémoire* (trans. L. Bernadi; Paris: Flammarion, 2003).

Aubineau, M., 'Le panégyrique de Thècle, attribué à Jean Chrysostome (BHG 1720): la fin retrouvée d'un texte motile', *Analecta Bollandiana* 93 (1975), pp. 349–62.

Backhaus, K., '"Mitteilhaber des Evangeliums" (1 Kor 9,23). Zur christologischen Grundlegung einer "Paulus-Schule" bei Paulus', in *Christologie in der Paulus-Schule. Zur Rezeptionsgeschichte des paulinischen Evangeliums* (ed. K. Scholtissek; SBS, 181; Stuttgart: Katholisches Bibelwerk, 2000), pp. 44–71.

Ballhorn, G., 'Die Miletrede – ein Literaturbericht', in *Das Ende des Paulus. Historische, theologische und literaturgeschichtliche Aspekte* (ed. F. W. Horn; BZNW, 106; Berlin: W. de Gruyter, 2001), pp. 37–47.

Barbi, A., 'Il Paolinismo degli Atti', *RivBib* 48 (1986), pp. 471–518.

Barnes, T. D., *Early Christian Hagiography and Roman History* (Tübingen: Mohr Siebeck, 2010).

Barrett, C. K., 'Acts and the Pauline Corpus', *ET* 78 (1976), pp. 2–5.

———, *The Acts of the Apostles. Vol. II: Acts XV-XXVIII* (ICC; Edinburgh: T&T Clark, 1998).

———, 'The Historicity of Acts', *JTS* 50 (1995), pp. 515–34.

———, *Luke the Historian in Recent Study* (London: Epworth Press, 1961).

Barth, K., *Nein! Antwort an Emil Brunner* (TEH, 14; München: C. Kaiser, 1934). ET: Brunner, E., and K. Barth, *Natural Theology: Comprising 'Nature and Grace'* (trans. P. Fraenkel; London: The Centenary Press, 1946).

Bassler, J. M., *Divine Impartiality: Paul and a Theological Axiom* (SBLDS, 59; Chico, Calif.: Scholars Press, 1982).

Bauer, W., *Orthodoxy and Heresy in Earliest Christianity* (trans. Philadelphia Seminar on Christian Origins; Philadelphia: Fortress, 1971).

Bauernfeind, O. *Die Apostelgeschichte des Lukas* (THKNT, 5; Leipzig: A. Deichert, 1939).

Baur, F. C., *Das Christentum und die christliche Kirche der drei ersten Jahrhunderte* (Tübingen: Fues, 2nd edn, 1860).

———, 'Die Christuspartei in der korinthische Gemeinde, der Gegensatz des petrinischen und paulinischen Christentums in der ältesten Kirche', *TZTh* 5/4 (1831), pp. 61–206.

———, *Paulus, der Apostel Jesu Christi: Sein Leben und Wirken, seine Briefe und seine Lehre: Ein Beitrag zu einer kritischen Geschichte des Urchristenthums* (Stuttgart: Becher & Müller, 1845). ET: *Paul: The Apostle of Jesus Christ, His Life and Work, His Epistles and Doctrine, A Contribution to a Critical History of Primitive Christianity* (2 vols; London: Williams and Norgate, 2nd edn, 1875–1876).

———, *Über der Ursprung des Episcopats* (Tübingen: 1838).

Becker, J., *Paul: L'Apôtre des nations* (Paris: Cerf, 1995).

Beker, J. C., *Heirs of Paul: Paul's Legacy in the New Testament and in the Church Today* (Minneapolis: Fortress, 1991).

Benoit, P., 'Ephesians (Épître aux)', *DBS* 7 (1966), pp. 195–211.

Berger, K., *Formgeschichte des Neuen Testaments* (Heidelberg: Quelle und Meyer, 1984).

———, 'Hellenistische Gattungen im Neuen Testament', in *ANRW* II.25.2 (1984), pp. 1031–1432, 1831–85.

Berger, P. L. and T. Luckmann, *The Social Construction of Reality* (Garden City, N.Y.: Doubleday, 1966).

Best, E., *Ephesians* (ICC; Edinburgh: T&T Clark, 1998).

———, 'Ephesians 1.1 Again', in *Paul and Paulinism* (Festschrift C. K. Barrett; ed. M. D. Hooker; London: SPCK, 1982), pp. 273–79.

———, 'The Revelation to Evangelize the Gentiles', *JTS* 35 (1984), pp. 1–31.

———, 'Who used Whom? The Relationship of Ephesians and Colossians', *NTS* 43 (1997), pp. 72–96.

Betz, H. D., 'Paul's "Second Presence" in Colossians', in *Texts and Contexts. Biblical Texts in Their Textual and Situational Contexts* (Festschrift

L. Hartman; ed. T. Fornberg and D. Hellholm; Oslo: Scandinavian University Press, 1995), pp. 507–18.

Betz, M., 'Die betörenden Worte des fremden Mannes: Zur Funktion der Paulusbeschreibung in den Theklaakten', *NTS* 53 (2007), pp. 130–45.

Billings, B. S., '"At the Age of 12": The Boy Jesus in the Temple (Luke 2:41-52), the Emperor Augustus, and the Social Setting of the Third Gospel', *JTS* 60 (2009), pp. 70–89.

Blanton, W., *Displacing Christian Origins. Philosophy, Secularity, and the New Testament* (Chicago: University of Chicago Press, 2007).

Blasi, J., *Making Charisma: The Social Construction of Paul's Public Image* (New Brunswick: Transaction, 1991).

Boismard, M.-É., *L'Enigme de la letter aux Éphésians* (EtB, 39; Paris: J. Gabalda, 1999).

Bolyki, J., 'Events after the Martyrdom: Missionary Transformation of an Apocalyptical Metaphor in Martyrium Pauli', in *The Apocryphal Acts of Paul and Thecla* (ed. Jan Bremer; SECA, 2; Kampen: Kok Pharos, 1996), pp. 92–106.

Bonnard, P., *L'Épître de Saint Paul aux Philippiens* (CNT, 10; Neuchâtel, Delachaux et Niestlé, 1950).

Bonner, S. F., *The Literary Treatises of Dionysius of Halicarnassus. A Study in the Development of Critical Method* (Cambridge Classical Studies, V; Cambridge: Cambridge University, 1939).

Bonz, M. P., 'Luke's Revision of Paul's Reflection in Romans 9–11', in *Early Christian Voices in Texts, Traditions and Symbols* (Festschrift S. F. Bovon; ed. D. H. Warren *et al.*; BIS, 66; Leiden: Brill, 2003), pp. 143–51.

Bormann, L., 'Autobiographische Fiktionalität bei Paulus', in *Biographie und Persönlichkeit des Paulus* (ed. E.-M. Becker and P. Pilhofer; WUNT, 187; Tübingen: Mohr Siebeck, 2005), pp. 106–24.

Boudon, V. (ed.), *Galien. Introduction générale; Sur l'ordre de ses propres livres; Sur ses propres livres; Que l'excellent médecin est aussi philosophe* (Paris: Les Belles Lettres, 2007).

Bovon, F., *L'Evangile selon Luc: Volume I – 1,1-9,50* (CNT, IIIa; Geneva: Labor et Fides, 1991). ET: *Luke 1: A Commentary on Luke 1:1-9:50* (trans. C. M. Thomas; Hermeneia; vol. 1; Minneapolis: Fortress, 2002).

———, '"Il a bien parlé à vos pères, le Saint-Esprit, par le prophète Esaïe" (Actes 28,25)', in *L'œuvre de Luc* (LD, 130; Paris: Cerf, 1987), pp. 145–53.

———, *Luc le théologien* (MdB, 5; Geneva: Labor et Fides, 3rd edn, 2006). ET: *Luke the Theologian: Fifty-Five Years of Research (1950-2005)* (Waco: Baylor University Press, 2006).

———, 'La mort de Jésus en Luc-Actes. La perspective sotériologique', in *'Christ est mort pour nous.' Études sémiotiques, féministes et sotériologiques en l'honneur d'Olivette Genest* (ed. A. Gignac and A. Fortin; Sciences bibliques - Études/Instruments, 14; Montréal: Médiaspaul, 2005), pp. 359–74.

————, 'Paul comme Document et Paul comme Monument', in *Chrétiens en conflit. L'Épître de Paul aux Galates* (ed. J. Allaz *et al.*; Essais Bibliques, 13; Genève: Labor et Fides, 1987), pp. 54–65. ET: 'Paul as Document and Paul as Monument', in *New Testament and Christian Apocrypha: Collected Studies II* (ed. F. Bovon and G. Snyder; Tübingen: Mohr Siebeck, 2009), pp. 307–17.

————, *Studies in Early Christianity* (WUNT, 161; Tübingen: Mohr Siebeck, 2003).

————, 'La vie des Apôtres: traditions bibliques et narrations apocryphes', in *Les Actes des apôtres: christianisme et monde païen* (ed. F. Bovon; Geneva: Labor et Fi'des, 1981), 141–48.

Bovon, F. and P. Geoltrain (eds), *Ecrits apocryphes chrétiens 1* (La Pléiade, 442; Paris: Gallimard, 1997).

Boyarin, D., *Dying for God. Martyrdom and the Making of Christianity and Judaism* (Stanford: Stanford University Press, 1999).

Brawley, R. L., *Luke-Acts and the Jews: Conflict, Apology, Conciliation* (SBLMS, 33; Atlanta: Scholars Press, 1987).

————, 'Paul in Acts: Aspects of Structure and Characterization', in *SBL Seminar Papers, 1988* (SBLSP, 27; Chico, Calif.: Scholars Press, 1988), pp. 90–105.

Brock, A. G., 'Political Authority and Cultural Accommodation: Social Diversity in the *Acts of Paul* and the *Acts of Peter*', in *The Apocryphal Acts of the Apostles* (ed. F. Bovon, A. G. Brock, and C. R. Matthews; Cambridge: Harvard University Press, 1999), pp. 145–69.

Bromiley, G. W. (ed.), *Theological Dictionary of the New Testament* (10 vols; Grand Rapids: Eerdmans, 1888–1948).

Brown, R. E., *The Birth of the Messiah* (ABRL; New York: Doubleday, 2nd edn, 1993).

Brox, N., *Die Pastoralbriefe* (RNT, 7.2; Regensburg: F. Pustet, 1969).

————, 'Zum Problemstand in der Erforschung der altchristlichen Pseudepigraphie', in *Pseudepigraphie in der heidnischen und jüdisch-christlichen Antike* (ed. N. Brox; WdF, 484; Darmstadt: Wiss. Buchgesellschaft, 1977), pp. 311–34.

Bruce, F. F., *The Acts of the Apostles: The Greek Text with Introduction and Commentary* (Grand Rapids: Eerdmans, 3rd edn, 1990).

————, 'Is the Paul of Acts the Real Paul?', *BJRL* 58 (1976), pp. 282–305.

Brunner, E., *Natur und Gnade* (Tübingen: Mohr, 1934).

Buckwalter, H. D., *The Character and Purpose of Luke's Christology* (SNTSMS, 89; Cambridge: Cambridge University Press, 1996).

Bultmann, R., 'Anknüpfung und Widerspruch: Zur Frage nach der Anknüpfung der neutestamentlichen Verkündigung an die natürliche Theologie der Stoa, die hellenistischen Mysterienreligionen und die Gnosis', *ThZ* 2 (1946), pp. 401–18.

————, *Primitive Christianity in Its Contemporary Setting* (trans. R. H. Fuller; New York: Meridian Books, 1956).

————, *Theology of the New Testament* (trans. K. Grobel; New York: Scribner, 1951).

Burchard, C., *Der Dreizehnte Zeuge: Traditions- und compositions-geschicht- liche Untersuchungen zu Lukas' Darstellung der Frühzeit des Paulus* (FRLANT, 103; Göttingen: Vandenhoeck & Ruprecht, 1970).

————, 'Paulus in der Apostelgeschichte', *TLZ* 100 (1975), pp. 880–95.

Burnet, R., *Épîtres et lettres. Iᵉʳ-IIᵉ siècle. De Paul de Tarse à Polycarpe de Smyrne* (LD, 192; Paris, Cerf, 2003).

Butticaz, S., '"Dieu a-t-il rejeté son peuple?" (Rm 11,1): Le destin d'Israël de Paul aux Actes des Apôtres; Gestion narrative d'un héritage théologique', in *Reception of Paulinism in Acts (Réception du pau- linisme dans les Actes des Apôtres)* (ed. D. Marguerat; BETL, 229; Leuven: Peeters, 2009), pp. 207–25.

————, 'La figure de Paul en fondateur de colonie', in *Et vous, qui dites-vous que je suis? La gestion des personnages dans les récits bibliques* (ed. P. Létourneau and M. Talbot; Montréal: Mediaspaul, 2006), pp. 173–88.

————, *La finale des Actes entre parole et silence [Ac 28, 16-31]. Récits de fondation, mimèsis littéraire et rhétorique du silence* (Lausanne: n.p., 2005).

————, 'La relecture des *lapsi* pauliniens chez Luc: Esquisse d'une typolo- gie', in *Écriture et réécritures, 5ᵉ colloque international du RRENAB* (ed. C. Clivaz *et al.*; BETL; Geneva: Peeters, 2011 [forthcoming]).

Cadbury, H. J., *The Making of Luke-Acts* (London: Macmillan, 1927; Peabody, Mass.: Hendrickson, 2nd edn, 1999).

————, *The Style and Literary Method of Luke* (HThS, 6; Cambridge: Harvard University Press, 1920).

Cadoux, E. J., *The Early Christian Attitude to War* (New York: Gordon, 1919; repr. 1975).

Campenhausen, H. von, *Aus der Frühzeit des Christentums: Studien zur Kirchengeschichte des ersten und zweiten Jahrhunderts* (Tübingen: Mohr Siebeck, 1963).

————, *The Formation of the Christian Bible* (trans. J. A. Baker; Philadelphia: Fortress, 1972).

Cancik, H., 'The History of Culture, Religion, and Institutions in Ancient Historiography: Philological Observations concerning Luke's History', *JBL* 116 (1997), pp. 673–95.

————, *Untersuchungen zu Senecas Epistulae morales* (Spudasmata, 18; Hildesheim: Georg Olms Verlagsbuchhandlung, 1967).

Caragounis, C., *The Ephesian Mysterion: Meaning and Content* (ConBNT, 8; Lund: G. C. K. Gleerup, 1977).

Cassidy, R. J., *Paul in Chains. Roman Imprisonment and the Letters of St. Paul* (New York: Crossroad, 2001).

————, *Society and Politics in the Acts of the Apostles* (Maryknoll, N.Y.: Orbis, 1987).

Cassidy, R. J., and P. J. Sharper, eds., *Political Issues in Luke-Acts* (Maryknoll, N.Y.: Orbis, 1983).

Certeau (de), M., *L'écriture de l'histoire* (NRF; Paris: Gallimard, 1975).

Charlesworth, J. H. (ed.), *The Old Testament Pseudepigrapha* (Peabody, Mass.: Hendrickson, 2009).

Chester, S. J., *Conversion at Corinth. Perspectives on Conversion in Paul's Theology and the Corinthian Church* (London: T&T Clark, 2003).

Clarke, G. W., *The Octavius of Marcus Minucius Felix* (ACW, 39; New York: Newman Press, 1974).

Clivaz, C., *L'ange et la sueur de sang (Lc 22,43-44) ou comment on pourrait bien encore écrire l'histoire* (BiTS, 7; Leuven: Peeters, 2010).

———, 'La rumeur, une catégorie pour articuler autoportraits et réceptions de Paul. "Car ses lettres, dit-on, ont du poids… et sa parole est nulle" (2 Co 10,10)', in *Reception of Paulinism in Acts (Réception du paulinisme dans les Actes des apôtres)* (ed. D. Marguerat; BETL, 229; Leuven: Peeters, 2009), pp. 239–59.

Coady, C. A. J., *Testimony. A Philosophical Study* (Oxford: Clarendon Press, 1992).

Cobet, J., *Herodots Exkurse und die Frage der Einheit seines Werkes* (Historia Einzelschriften, 17; Wiesbaden: Steiner, 1971).

Collins, A. Y., *The Beginnings of the Gospel: Probings of Mark in Context* (Minneapolis: Fortress, 1992).

Collins, R. F., *I and II Timothy and Titus* (Louisville: John Knox, 2002).

Conzelmann, H., *Acts of the Apostles* (trans. J. Liburg, A. T. Kraabel, and D. H. Juel; Hermeneia; Philadelphia: Fortress, 1987).

———, *Die Mitte der Zeit: Studien zur Theologie des Lukas* (BHT, 17; Tübingen: Mohr, 5th edn, 1964). ET: *The Theology of St. Luke* (trans. G. Buswell; Philadelphia: Fortress, 1961).

Cramer, J. A. (ed.), *Catenae Graecorum Patrum in Novum Testamentum* (8 vols; Hildesheim: Goerg Olms Verlagsbuchhandlung, 1969).

Cranfield, C. E. B., *The Epistle to the Romans* (ICC; 2 vols; Edinburgh: T&T Clark, 1979).

Cullmann, O., 'Les causes de la mort de Pierre et de Paul d'après le témoignage de Clément Romain', *RHPh* 3 (1930), pp. 294–300.

Cumont, F., *Oriental Religions in Roman Paganism* (London: G. Routledge & Sons, 2nd edn, 1911).

Dahl, N. A., 'Formgeschichte Beobactungen zur Christusverkündigung in der Gemeindepredigt', in *Neutestamentliche Studien für Rudolf Bultmann zu seinem 70. Geburtstag am 20. August 1954* (BZNW, 21; Berlin: Walter de Gruyter, 1954).

———, *Studies in Ephesians: Introductory Questions, Text- & Edition-Critical Issues, Interpretations of Texts and Themes* (ed. D. Hellholm, V. Blombvist, and T. Rornberg; WUNT, 131; Tübingen: Mohr Siebeck, 2000).

Dassmann, E., *Der Stachel im Fleisch. Paulus in der frühchristlichen Literatur bis Irenäus* (Münster: Aschendorff, 1978).

Davies, L., 'I Wrote Afore in Few Words (Eph 3,3)', *ET* 46 (1934–1935), p. 568.

Davies, S. L., *Jesus the Healer: Possession, Trance, and the Origins of Christianity* (New York: Continuum, 1995).

De Boer, M. C., 'Images of Paul in the Post-Apostolic Period', *CBQ* 42 (1980), pp. 359–80.

De Wette, W. M. L., *Lehrbuch der historischen-kritischen Einleitung in die Bibel Alten und Neuen Testaments. Zweiter Teil: Die Einleitung in das Neue Testament enthaltend* (Berlin: G. Reimer, 1826).

Deissmann, A., *Licht vom Osten. Das Neue Testament und die neuentdeckten Texte der hellenistisch-römischen Welt* (Tübingen: Mohr Siebeck, 1908). ET: *Light from the Ancient East: The New Testament Illustrated by Recently Discovered Texts of the Graeco-Roman World* (trans. L. R. M. Strachan; London: Hodder & Stoughton, 1910).

——, *Paulus: eine kultur- und religionsgeschichtliche Schule* (Tübingen: Mohr Siebeck, 1911).

Dettwiler, A., 'Démystification céleste. La fonction argumentative de l'hymne au Christ (Col 1,15-20) dans la lettre aux Colossiens', in *Les hymnes du Nouveau Testament et leurs fonctions* (ed. D. Gerber and P. Keith; XXIIe congrès de l'ACFEB, Strasbourg 2007; LD; Paris: Cerf, 2009), pp. 325–40.

——, 'L'école paulinienne: évaluation d'une hypothèse', in *Paul, une théologie en construction* (ed. A. Dettwiler, J. D. Kaestli, and D. Marguerat; MdB, 51; Genève: Labor et Fides, 2004), pp. 419–40.

——, 'L'épître aux Colossiens', in *Introduction au Nouveau Testament. Son histoire, son écriture, sa théologie* (ed. D. Marguerat; MdB 41; Genève: Labor et Fides, 2000), pp. 287–300.

Deutschmann, A., *Synagoge und Gemeindebildung. Christliche Gemeinde und Israel am Beispiel von Apg 13, 42-52* (BU, 30; Regensburg: Pustet, 2001).

Devine, A. M., 'Manuscripts of John Chrysostom's "Commentary on the Acts of the Apostles": A Preliminary Study for a Critical Edition', *Ancient World* 20 (1989), pp. 111–25.

Devreese, R., 'Chaines exégétiques grecques', in *DBSup* (ed. F. Vigouroux; vol.1; Paris: Librairie Letouzey et Ané, 1928), col. 1083–1233.

Dibelius, M., *An die Kolosser Epheser. An Philemon* (HNT, 12; Tübingen: Mohr Siebeck, 2nd edn, 1927).

——, 'The Apostolic Council', in *Studies in the Acts of the Apostles* (ed. H. Greeven; trans. M. Ling; New York: C. Scribner's Sons, 1956), pp. 93–101.

——, *Aufsätze zur Apostelgeschichte* (FRLANT, 60; Göttingen: Vandenhoeck & Ruprecht, 5th edn, 1968). ETs: *Studies in the Acts of the Apostles* (ed. H. Greeven; trans. M. Ling; London: SCM, 1956); *The Books of Acts: Form, Style, and Theology* (ed. K. C. Hanson; Fortress Classics in Biblical Studies; Minneapolis: Fortress, 2004).

——, *Botschaft und Geschichte. II. Zum Urchristentum und zur hellenistischen Religionsgeschichte* (Tübingen: Mohr Siebeck, 1956).

————, *Die formgeschichte des evangeliums* (Tübingen: Mohr Siebeck,1933). ET: *From Tradition to Gospel* (trans. B. L. Wolf; London: Ivor Nicholson and Watson, 1934).

————, *A Fresh Approach to the New Testament and Early Christian Literature* (New York: Scribner, 1936).

————, 'Paul on the Areopagus', in *Studies in the Acts of the Apostles* (ed. H. Greeven; trans. M. Ling; New York: C. Scribner's Sons, 1956), pp. 27–77.

————, 'The Speeches in Acts and Ancient Historiography', in *Studies in the Acts of the Apostles* (ed. H. Greeven; trans. M. Ling; New York: C. Scribner's Sons, 1956), pp. 138–85.

————, 'Style Criticism of the Book of Acts', in *Studies in the Acts of the Apostles* (ed. H. Greeven; trans. M. Ling; New York: C. Scribner's Sons, 1956), pp. 1–25.

Dibelius, M., and H. Conzelmann, *Die Pastoralbriefe* (Hermeneia; Tübingen: Mohr Siebeck, 3rd edn, 1955). ET: *The Pastoral Epistles* (trans. P. Buttolph and A. Yarbro; Hermeneia; Philadelphia: Fortress, 1972).

Dorandi, T., *Le stylet et la tablette: Dans le secret des auteurs antiques* (Paris: Les Belles Lettres, 2000).

Droge, A. J., *Homer or Moses? Early Christian Interpretations of the History of Culture* (HUT, 26; Tübingen: Mohr Siebeck, 1989).

Dumais, M., 'Les Actes des Apôtres, bilan et orientations', in *De bien des manières: La recherche biblique aux abords du XXIe siècle* (ed. M. Gourgues and L. Laberge; LD, 163; Montreal: Fides, 1995), pp. 307–64.

————, *Le langage de l'évangélisation: L'annonce missionnaire en milieu juif [Ac 13,16–41]* (Recherches, 16; Tournai: Desclée, 1976).

Dunn, J. D. G., *Beginning from Jerusalem Vol. 2: Christianity in the Making* (Grand Rapids: Eerdmans, 2009).

————, *Romans 9-16* (Word, 38b; Dallas: Word, 1988).

Dupont, J., *Le discours de Milet. Testament pastoral de saint Paul (Actes 20,18-36)* (LD, 32; Paris: Cerf, 1962).

————, *Études sur les Actes des Apôtres* (Paris: Cerf, 1967).

————, *Nouvelles études sur les Actes des Apôtres* (Paris: Cerf, 1984).

Édart, J.-B., 'De la nécessité d'un sauveur: Rhétorique et théologie de Rm 7,7-25', *RB* 105 (1998), pp. 359–96.

————, *L'Épître aux Philippiens, rhétorique et composition stylistique* (EtB, 45; Paris: Gabalda, 2002).

Eden, K., *Poetic and Legal Fiction in the Aristotelian Tradition* (Princeton: Princeton University Press, 1986).

Ehrman, B., *Didymus the Blind and the Text of the Gospels* (The New Testament in the Greek Fathers, 1; Atlanta: Scholars Press, 1986).

Eichhorn, J. G., *Einleitung in das Neue Testament* (Leipzig: Weidmannischen Buchhandlung, 1810).

Eissfeldt, O., 'The Promises of Grace to David in Isaiah 55:1-5', in *Israel's Prophetic Heritage* (Festschrift S. J. Muilenburg; ed. B. W. Anderson and W. Harrelson; New York: Harper & Brothers, 1962), pp. 196–207.

Elliott, J. H., *A Home for the Homeless* (London: SCM Press, 1981).

Else, G. F., *Plato and Aristotle on Poetry* (ed. P. Burian; Chapel Hill: University of North Carolina Press, 1986).

Enos, R. L., *Greek Rhetoric Before Aristotle* (Prospect Heights, Ill.: Waveland Press, 1993).

Esler, P. F., 'Glossolalia and the Admission of Gentiles into the Early Christian Community', *BTB* 22 (1992), pp. 136–42.

Feldman, L. H., *Josephus' Interpretation of the Bible* (Hellenistic Culture and Society, 27; Berkeley: University of California Press, 1998).

———, *Studies in Josephus' Rewritten Bible* (JSJSup, 58; Leiden: Brill, 1998).

Fischer, K. M., *Tendenz und Absicht des Epheserbrief* (FRLANT, 111; Göttingen: Vandenhoeck & Ruprecht, 1973).

Fitzmyer, J. A., *The Acts of the Apostles* (AB, 31; New York: Doubleday, 1998).

———, *The Gospel according to Luke* (AB 28; vol. 1; Garden City, N.Y.: Doubleday, 1981).

Flichy, O., 'État des recherches actuelles sur les Actes des Apôtres', *Les Actes des Apôtres: Histoire, récit, théologie: XXe congrès de l'Association Catholique Française pour l'Étude de la Bible (Angers, 2003)* (ed. M. Berder; LD, 199; Paris: Cerf, 2005), pp. 13–42.

———, *La figure de Paul dans les Actes des Apôtres. Un phénomène de réception de la tradition paulinienne à la fin du premier siècle* (LD, 214; Paris: Cerf, 2007).

Foakes-Jackson, F. J., and K. Lake (eds), *The Beginnings of Christianity* (vol. 1 of *The Acts of the Apostles*; London: Macmillan, 1920–1933).

Frei, H., *The Eclipse of Biblical Narrative: A Study in Eighteenth and Nineteenth Century Hermeneutics* (New Haven: Yale University Press, 1974).

Frey, J., C. K. Rothschild, and J. Schröter (eds), *Die Apostelgeschichte im Kontext antiker und frühchristlicher Historiographie* (BZNW, 162; Berlin: de Gruyter, 2009).

Froissart, P., *La rumeur: histoire et fantasmes* (Débats; Paris: Belin, 2002).

Fusco, V., 'Luke-Acts and the Future of Israel', *NovT* 38 (1996), pp. 10–15.

———, '"Point of View" and "Implicit Reader" in two Eschatological Texts. Lk 19,11-28; Acts 1,6-8', in *The Four Gospels 1992* (Festschrift F. Neirynck; ed. F. van Segbroeck *et al.*; BETL, 100; vol. 2; Leuven: Leuven University Press, 1992), pp. 1677–1696.

Gabba, E., *Dionysius and the History of Archaic Rome* (Berkeley: University of California Press, 1991).

Gadamer, H.-G., *Truth and Method* (trans. J. Weinsheimer and D. G. Marshall; London: Continuum, 2004).

Gamble, H. Y., 'The New Testament Canon: Recent Research and the Status Quaestionis', in *The Canon Debate* (ed. L. M. McDonald and J. A. Sanders, Peabody: Hendrickson Publishers, 2004), pp. 267–94.

334   Bibliography

Gasque, W. W., *A History of the Criticism of the Acts of the Apostles* (Grand
      Rapids: Eerdmans, 1975).
————, *A History of the Interpretation of the Acts of the Apostles* (Peabody, Mass.:
      Hendrickson, 1989).
Gaventa, B. R., 'The Overthrown Enemy: Luke's Portrait of Paul', in *SBL Seminar
      Papers, 1985* (ed. K. H. Richards; SBLSP, 24; Atlanta: Scholars Press,
      1985), pp. 439–49.
————, 'Theology and Ecclesiology in the Miletus Speech: Reflections on
      Content and Context', *NTS* 50 (2004), pp. 36–52.
————, 'Toward a Theology of Acts. Reading and Rereading', *Int* 42 (1988),
      pp. 146–57.
Gavoille, E., 'La relation à l'absent dans les lettres de Cicéron à Atticus', in
      *Epistulae Antiquae. Actes du Ier colloque 'Le genre épistolaire antique et
      ses prolongements'* (ed. L. Nadjo and E. Gavoille; Université François-
      Rabelais, Tours, 18-19 septembre 1998; Leuven: Peeters, 2000), pp.
      153–76.
Gebhardt, W., 'Charisma und Ordnung. Formen des institutionalisierten Charisma
      - Überlegungen im Anschluß an Max Weber', in *Charisma. Theorie -
      Religion - Politik* (ed. W. Gebhardt, A. Zingerle, and M. N. Ebertz; Berlin:
      W. de Gruyter, 1993), pp. 47–68.
Geerard, M. (ed.), *Clavis Patrum Graecorum* (Turnhout: Brepols, 1974–1983).
Genette, G., *Narrative Discourse Revisited* (Ithaca, N.Y.: Cornell University Press,
      1988).
————, *Palimpsestes. La littérature au second degré* (Poétique; Paris: Seuil,
      1982).
Gerber, C., *Paulus und seine 'Kinder'. Studien zur Beziehungsmetaphorik der
      paulinischen Briefe* (BZNW, 136; Berlin: W. de Gruyter, 2005).
Gese, M., *Das Vermächtnis des Apostels. Die Rezeption der paulinischen Theologie
      im Epheserbrief* (WUNT, 2.99; Tübingen: Mohr Siebeck, 1997).
Ginzburg, C., *History, Rhetoric, and Proof* (The Menahem Stern Jerusalem
      Lectures; Hanover: University Press of New England, 1999).
Gnilka, J., *Der Epheserbrief* (HThK, 10.2; Freiburg: Herder, 1971).
————, 'Das Paulusbild im Kolosser- und Epheserbrief', in *Kontinuität und
      Einheit* (Festschrift F. Mußner; ed. P-G. Müller and W. Stenger; Freiburg:
      Herder, 1981), pp. 179–93.
————, *Die Verstockung Israels. Isaias 6,9-10 in der Theologie der Synoptiker*
      (SANT, 3; München: Kösel-Verlag, 1961).
Golden, L., *Aristotle on Tragic and Comic Mimesis* (American Philological
      Association American Classical Studies, 29; Atlanta: Scholars Press,
      1992).
Goodspeed, E. J., *The Meaning of Ephesians* (Chicago: University of Chicago
      Press, 1933).
————, *New Solutions of New Testament Problems* (Chicago: University of
      Chicago Press, 1927).

Grube, G. M. A., 'Dionysius of Halicarnassus on Thucydides', *The Phoenix* 4 (1950), pp. 95–110.

Haacker, K., 'Das Bekenntnis des Paulus zur Hoffnung Israels nach der Apostelgeschichte des Lukas', *NTS* 31 (1985), pp. 437–51.

Haenchen, E., *Die Apostelgeschichte* (KEK, 3; Göttingen: Vandenhoeck & Ruprecht, 13th edn, 1961; 16th edn, 1977). ET: *The Acts of the Apostles: A Commentary* (trans. B. Noble *et al.*; Oxford: Blackwell, 1971).

Hahn, F., *Studien zum Neuen Testament. II. Bekenntnisbildung und Theologie in urchristlicher Zeit* (WUNT, 192; Tübingen: Mohr, 2006).

Harnack, A. von, *Militia Christi, The Christian Religion and the Military in the First Three Centuries* (trans. D. M. Gracie; Philadelphia: Fortress, 1981).

———, *The Mission and Expansion of Christianity in the First Three Centuries* (trans. J. Moffatt; 2 vols; New York: G. P. Putnam's Sons, 1908).

———, *Neue Untersuchungen zur Apostelgeschichte und zur Abfassungszeit der synoptischen Evangelien* (Leipzig: Hinrich, 1911).

Hay, D. M., *Glory at the Right Hand: Psalm 110 in Early Christianity* (SBLMS, 18; New York: Abingdon Press, 1973).

Hays, R. B., *The Conversion of the Imagination: Paul as Interpreter of Israel's Scripture* (Grand Rapids: Eerdmans, 2005).

Hays, R. B., S. Alkier and L. A. Huizenga (eds), *Reading the Bible Intertextually* (Waco: Baylor University Press, 2009).

Heath, M., *Unity in Greek Poetics* (Oxford: Clarendon, 1989).

Helgeland, J., 'Christians and the Roman Army from Marcus Aurelius to Constantine', in *ANRW* II.23.1 (1979), pp. 724–834.

Hemer, C. J., *The Book of Acts in the Setting of Hellenistic History* (ed. C. J. Gempf; Winona Lake, Ind.: Eisenbrauns, 1990).

———, *The Book of Acts in the Setting of Hellenistic History* (WUNT, 49; Tübingen: Mohr, 1989).

Hengel, M., *The Four Gospels and the One Gospel of Jesus Christ: An Investigation of the Collection and Origin of the Canonical Gospels* (trans. J. Bowden; Harrisburg: Trinity Press International, 2000).

Hengel, M., and A. Schwemer, *Paulus zwischen Damaskus und Antiochien* (WUNT, 108; Tübingen: Mohr, 1998). ET: *Paul between Damascus and Antioch* (trans. J. Bowden; London: SCM, 1997).

Hennecke E., and W. Schneelmelcher (eds), *New Testament Apocrypha* (trans. R. Wilson; vol. 2; Atlanta: Westminster John Knox, 1992).

Hillard, T., A. Nobbs, and B. Winter, 'Acts and the Pauline Corpus I; Ancient Literary Parallels', in *The Book of Acts in Its First Century Setting* (ed. B. W. Winter and A. D. Clarke; vol. 1; Grand Rapids: Eerdmans, 1993), pp. 183–213.

Hoehner, H., *Ephesians: An Exegetical Commentary* (Grand Rapids: Baker Academic, 2002).

Holland, G. S., 'The Self against the Self in Romans 7, 7-25a', in *The Rhetorical Interpretation of Scripture. Essays from the 1996 Malibu Conference* (ed. S. E. Porter and D. L. Stamps; JSNTSup, 180; Sheffield: Sheffield Academic Press, 1999), pp. 260–71.

Holmes, M. W. (trans.), *The Apostolic Fathers. Greek Texts and English Translations* (Grand Rapids: Baker, 3rd edn, 2007).

Horst, P. W. van der, *Philo's Flaccus. The First Pogrom* (Atlanta: Society of Biblical Literature, 2003).

Howell, J. 'The Imperial Authority and Benefaction of Centurions and Acts 10.34-43', *JSNT* 31 (2008), pp. 25–51.

Humphrey, E. M., 'Collision of Modes?–Vision and Determining Argument in Acts 10:1-11:18', *Semeia* 71 (1995), pp. 65–84.

Hyldahl, N., 'The Reception of Paul in the Acts of the Apostles', in *The New Testament as Reception (Copenhagen International Seminar 11)* (ed. M. Müller and H. Tronier; JSNTSup, 230; Sheffield, Sheffield Academic Press, 2002).

Jaubert, A. (ed.), *Clément de Rome. Epître aux Corinthiens* (SC, 167; Paris: Cerf, 1971).

Jenkins, C., 'The Origen-Citations in Cramer's Catena on 1 Corinthians', *JTS* 6 (1904), pp. 113–16.

———, 'Origen on I Corinthians', *JTS* 9 (1908), pp. 231–247; 353–372; 500–514.

———, 'Origen on I Corinthians', *JTS* 10 (1909), pp. 29–51.

Jeremias, J. *The Eucharistic Words of Jesus* (trans. A. Ehrhardt; New York: Macmillan, 1955).

———, 'Untersuchungen zum Quellenproblem der Apostelgeschichte', *ZNW* 36 (1937), pp. 205–21.

Jervell, J., *Die Apostelgeschichte* (KEK, 3; Göttingen: Vandenhoeck & Ruprecht, 17th edn, 1998).

———, 'The Church of Jews and God-Fearers', in *Luke-Acts and the Jewish People: Eight Critical Perspectives* (ed. J. B. Tyson; Minneapolis: Augsburg, 1988), pp. 11–20.

———, *Luke and the People of God: A New Look at Luke-Acts* (Minneapolis: Augsburg, 1972).

———, 'Paul in the Acts of the Apostles: Tradition, History, Theology', in *Les Actes des Apôtres: Traditions, redactions, théologie* (ed. J. Kremer; BETL, 48; Leuven: Leuven University Press, 1979), pp. 299–306.

———, 'Paulus – der Lehrer Israels: Zu den apologetischen Paulusreden in der Apostelgeschichte', *NovT* 10 (1968), pp. 164–90.

———, 'Paulus in der Apostelgeschichte und die Geschichte des Urchristentums', *NTS* 32 (1986), pp. 378–92.

———, 'Der unbekannte Paulus', in *Die paulinische Literatur und Theologie/The Pauline Literature and Theology* (ed. S. Pedersen; Århus: Forlaget Aros; 1980), pp. 29–49.

———, *The Unknown Paul: Essays on Luke-Acts and Early Christian History* (Minneapolis: Augsburg, 1984).

Jewett, R., *Romans* (Hermeneia; Minneapolis: Fortress, 2007).

Johnson, L. T., *The Acts of the Apostles* (SP, 5; Collegeville, Minn.: Liturgical Press/Michael Glazier, 1992).

———, *The First and Second Letters to Timothy* (AB, 35A; New York: Doubleday, 2001).

Jones, P. R., *The Epistle of Jude as Expounded by the Fathers—Clement of Alexandria, Didymus of Alexandria, the Scholia of Cramer's Catena, Pseudo-Oecumenius, and Bede* (Lewiston: The Edwin Mellen Press, 2001).

Jong, I. de, 'Metalepsis in Ancient Greek Literature', in *Narratology and Interpretation. The Content of Narrative Form in Ancient Literature* (ed. J. Grethlein and A. Rengakos; Trends in Classics—Supplementary Volumes, 4; Berlin: de Gruyter, 2009), pp. 87–115.

Jüngel, E., *God as the Mystery of the World. On the Foundation of the Theology of the Crucified One in the Dispute between Theism and Atheism* (trans. D. L. Guder; Edinburgh: T&T Clark, 1983).

Kaestli, J.-D., 'Histoire du canon du Nouveau Testament', in *Introduction au Nouveau Testament: Son histoire, son écriture, sa théologie* (ed. D. Marguerat; MdB, 41; Geneva: Labor et Fides, 3rd edn, 2004), pp. 449–74.

———, 'Mémoire et pseudépigraphie dans le christianisme de l'âge post-apostolique', *RThPh* 125 (1993), pp. 41–63.

Kampling, R., 'Innewerden des Mysteriums. Theologie als *traditio apostolica* im Epheserbrief', in *Christologie in der Paulus-Schule. Zur Rezeptionsgeschichte des paulinischen Evangeliums* (ed. Scholtissek, K.; SBS, 181; Stuttgart: Katholisches Bibelwerk, 2000), pp. 104–23.

Kapferer, J.-N., *Rumeurs. Le plus vieux média du monde* (Paris: Seuil, 2nd edn, 1992).

Karakolis, C., '"A Mystery Hidden to be Revealed?" Philological and Theological Correlations between Eph 3 and 1', in *Ethik als angewandte Ekklesiologie. Der Brief an die Epheser* (ed. M. Wolter; Monographische Reihe von 'Benedictina'. Bibl.-Ökumen, 17; Rome: Benedictina, 2005), pp. 65–108.

Karrer, M., '"Und ich werde sie heilen". Das Verstockungsmotiv aus Jes 6,9f. in Apg 28,26f.', in *Kirche und Volk Gottes* (Festschrift J. Roloff; Neukirchen-Vluyn: Neukirchener, 2000), pp. 255–71.

Käsemann, E., *An Die Römer* (HNT, 8a; Tübingen: Mohr Siebeck, 1973).

———, 'Ephesians and Acts', in *Studies in Luke-Acts* (ed. L. E. Keck and J. L. Martin; Philadelphia: Fortress, 1980), pp. 288–97.

———, 'Paul and Nascent Catholicism', *JTC* 3 (1967), pp. 14–27.

Keck, L. E. and J. L. Martyn (eds), *Studies in Luke-Acts* (Nashville: Abingdon, 1966).

Kittel, G. *Theologisches Wörterbuch zum Neuen Testament* (10 vols; Stuttgart, W. Kohlhammer: 1932).

Klauck, H-J., *Magic and Paganism in Early Christianity: The World of the Acts of the Apostles* (trans. B. McNeil; Edinburgh: T&T Clark, 2000).

Koester, H., 'GNOMAI DIAPHOROI: The Origin and Nature of Diversification in the History of Early Christianity', in *Trajectories through Early Christianity* (ed. H. Koester and J. M. Robinson; Philadelphia: Fortress, 1971), pp. 114–57.

Köster, H., *Paul & His World. Interpreting the New Testament in Its Context* (Minneapolis: Fortress, 2007).

Kurz, W. S., 'Hellenistic Rhetoric in the Christological Proof of Luke-Acts', *CBQ* 42 (1980), pp. 171–95.

———, 'Narrative Models for Imitation in Luke–Acts', in *Greeks, Romans and Christians. Essays in Honor of Abraham J. Malherbe* (ed. D. L. Balch, E. Ferguson and W. A. Meeks; Minneapolis: Fortress, 1990), pp. 171–89.

Lake, K., 'The Conversion of Paul and the Events Immediately Following It', in *The Beginnings of Christianity* (eds. F. J. Foakes Jackson and K. Lake; 5 vols; repr., Grand Rapids: Baker, 1979), 5:188–95.

Lamari, A. A., 'Knowing a Story's End: Future Reflexive in the Tragic Narrative of the Argive Expedition Against Thebes', in *Narratology and Interpretation. The Content of Narrative Form in Ancient Literature* (Trends in Classics—Supplementary Volumes, 4; eds J. Grethlein, A. Rengakos; Berlin: W. de Gruyter, 2009), pp. 399–419.

Leenhardt, F. J., *L'épître de saint Paul aux Romains* (CNT, 6; Genève: Labor et Fides, 1981).

Légasse, S., *Les épîtres de Paul aux Thessaloniciens* (LD, 7; Paris, Cerf: 1999).

Lentz, J. C., *Luke's Portrait of Paul* (SNTSMS, 77; Cambridge: Cambridge University Press, 1993). FT: *Le portrait de Paul selon Luc dans les Actes des Apôtres* (LD, 172; Paris, Cerf, 1998).

Létourneau, P., 'Commencer un Evangile: Luc', in *La Bible en récits: L'exégèse biblique à l'heure du lecteur* (ed. D. Marguerat; Geneva: Labor et Fides, 2003), pp. 326–39.

Lewis, I. M., *Ecstatic Religion: A Study of Shamanism and Spirit Possession*, (London: Routledge, 3rd edn, 2003).

Lietzmann, H. *An die Korinther I-II* (HNT, 9; Tübingen: Mohr Siebeck, 1931).

Lightfoot, J. B., *The Apostolic Fathers* (5 vols; New York: Macmillan, 1889–1890).

Lincoln, A. T., *Ephesians* (WBC, 42; Nashville: Thomas Nelson, 1990).

Lindemann, A., *Die Clemensbriefe* (HNT, 17; Tübingen: Mohr/Siebeck, 1992).

———, 'Paul's Influence on "Clement" and Ignatius', in *The New Testament and the Apostolic Fathers: Volume II – Trajectories through the New Testament and the Apostolic Fathers* (ed. A. F. Gregory and C. M. Tuckett Oxford: Oxford University Press, 2006), pp. 9–24.

———, *Paulus, Apostel und Lehrer der Kirche: Studien zu Paulus und zum frühen Paulusverständnis* (Tübingen: Mohr Siebeck, 1999).

———, *Paulus im ältesten Christentum: Das Bild des Apostels und die Rezeption der paulinishcen Theologie in der frühchristlichen Literatur bis Marcion* (BHT, 58; Tübingen: Mohr Siebeck, 1979).

————, 'Paulus und die Rede in Milet (Apg 20,17-38)', in *Reception of Paulinism in Acts (Réception du paulinisme dans les Actes des apôtres)* (ed. D. Marguerat; BETL, 229; Leuven: Peeters, 2009), pp. 175–205.

Lips, H. von, *Glaube, Gemeinde, Amt. Zum Verständnis der Ordination in den Pastoralbriefen* (FRLANT, 122; Göttingen: Vandenhoeck u. Ruprecht, 1979).

Loening, K., 'Das Evangelium und die Kulturen. Heilsgeschichtliche und kulturelle Aspekte kirchlicher Realität in der Apostelgeschichte', in *ANRW* II.25.3 (1985), pp. 2604–46.

Lohfink, G., 'Paulinische Theologie in der Rezeption der Pastoralbriefe', in *Paulus in den neutestamentlichen Spätschriften* (ed. K. Kertelge; QD, 89; Freiburg: Herder, 1981), pp. 70–121.

————, *Paulus vor Damaskus: Arbeitsweisen der neueren Bibelwissenschaft dargestellt an den Texten Apg. 9,1-19; 22,3-21; 26,9-18* (SBS, 4; Stuttgart: Katholisches Bibelwerk, 1965).

————, 'Die Vermittlung des Paulinismus zu den Pastoralbriefen', in *Studien zum Neuen Testament* (SBAB, 5; Stuttgart: Katholisches Bibelwerk, 1989), pp. 267–89.

Lohse, E., *Colossians and Philemon* (trans. W. R. Poehlmann and R. J. Karris; Hermeneia; Philadelphia: Fortress, 1971).

Lona, H. E., *Die Eschatologie im Kolosser- und Epheserbrief* (FB, 48; Würzburg: Echter Verlag, 1984).

Löning, K., 'Paulinismus in der Apostelgeschichte', in *Paulus in den neutestamentlichen Spätschriften. Zur Paulusrezeption im Neuen Testament* (ed. K. Kertelge; QD, 89; Freiburg: Herder, 1981), pp. 202–34

————, *Die Saulustradition in der Apostelgeschichte* (NTA, 9; Munster: Aschendorff, 1973).

Lührmann, D., *Das Offenbarungs-Verständnis bei Paulus und in paulinisschen Gemeinden* (WMANT, 16; Neukirchen-Vlyn: Neukirchener Verlag, 1965).

Luz, U., 'Rechtfertigung bei den Paulusschülern', in *Rechtfertigung. Festschrift E. Käsemann* (Göttingen: Vandenhoeck und Ruprecht, 1976), pp. 365–83.

MacDonald, D. R., *The Legend and the Apostle: The Battle for Paul in Story and Canon* (Philadelphia: Westminster Press, 1983).

————, 'Luke's Eutychus and Homer's Elpenor: Acts 20:7-12 and *Odyssey*, 10-12', *JHC* 1 (1994), pp. 5–24.

MacDonald, D. R., and A. D. Scrimgeour, 'Pseudo-Chrysostom's *Panegyric to Thecla*: The Heroine of the *Acts of Paul* in Homily and Art', *Semeia* 38 (1986), pp. 151–50.

MacMullen, R., *Enemies of the Roman Order* (Cambridge: Harvard University Press, 1966).

Maddox, R., *The Purpose of Luke-Acts* (FRLANT, 126; Göttingen: Vandenhoeck & Ruprecht, 1982).

Malherbe, A. J., *Ancient Epistolary Theorists* (SBLSBS, 19; Atlanta: Scholars Press, 1988).

————, *The Letters to the Thessalonians* (AB, 32B; New York: Doubleday, 2000).

Marguerat, D., *Les Actes des apôtres (1–12)* (CNT, 5a; Genève: Labor et Fides, 2007).

————, 'Les Actes des Apôtres', in *Introduction au Nouveau Testament: Son histoire, son écriture, sa théologie* (ed. D. Marguerat; MdB, 41; Geneva: Labor et Fides, 2000), pp. 105–28.

————, 'The Enigma of the Silent Closing of Acts (28:16-31)', in *Jesus and the Heritage of Israel: Luke's Narrative Claim upon Israel's Legacy* (vol. 1 of *Luke the Interpreter of Israel*; ed. D. Moessner; Harrisburg: Trinity Press International, 1999), pp. 284–304.

————, 'L'image de Paul dans les Actes des Apôtres', in *Les Actes des Apôtres: Histoire, récit, théologie; XXe congrès de l'Association catholique française pour l'étude de la Bible (Angers 2003)* (ed. M. Berder; LD, 199; Paris: Cerf, 2005), pp. 121–54.

————, 'L'image de Paul dans les Actes des apôtres', in *L'aube du christianisme* (ed. D. Marguerat; MdB, 60; Genève: Labor et Fides, 2008), pp. 469–98.

————, 'Juifs et chrétiens selon Luc-Actes', in *Le Déchirement: Juifs et chrétiens au premier siècle* (ed. D. Marguerat and M. C. de Boer; MdB, 32; Geneva: Labor et Fides, 1996), pp. 151–78.

————, 'Luc-Actes: une unité à construire', in *The Unity of Luke-Acts* (ed. J. Verheyden; BETL, 142; Leuven: Leuven University Press, 1999), pp. 57–81.

————, 'Paul après Paul: Une histoire de réception', *NTS* 54 (2008), pp. 317–37.

————, *Paul de Tarse. Un homme aux prises avec Dieu* (Poliez-le-Grand: Ed. du Moulin, 1999).

————, 'Paul et la Loi: Le retournement', in *Paul, une théologie en construction* (ed. A. Dettwiler, J. D. Kaestli, and D. Marguerat; MdB, 51; Genève: Labor et Fides, 2004), pp. 251–75.

————, 'Paul et la Torah dans les Actes des Apôtres', in *Reception of Paulinism in Acts (Réception du paulinisme dans les Actes des apôtres)* (ed. D. Marguerat; BETL, 229; Leuven: Peeters, 2009), pp. 81–100.

————, *La première histoire du christianisme (Les Actes des apôtres)* (LD, 180; Paris: Cerf, 1999; 2nd end, 2003). ET: *The First Christian Historian: Writing the 'Acts of the Apostles'* (trans. K. McKinney, G. Laughery, and R. Bauckham; SNTSMS, 121; Cambridge: Cambridge University Press, 2002).

Marguerat, D. (ed.), *L'aube du christianisme* (MdB, 60; Genève: Labor et Fides, 2008).

————, *Reception of Paulinism in Acts (Réception du paulinisme dans les Actes des Apôtres)* (BETL, 229; Leuven: Peeters, 2009).

Marrou, H.-I., *De la connaissance historique* (Points histoire, 21; Paris: Seuil, 1954; 2nd edn, 1975).

Marshall, I. H., *The Acts of the Apostles* (ICC; Edinburgh: T&T Clark, 1994–1998).

Martin, R. P., 'An Epistle in Search of a Life-Setting', *ET* 79 (1968), pp. 296–302.

————, *New Testament Foundations: A Guide for Christian Students* (Grand Rapids: Eerdmans, 1975–1978).

Marxsen, W., *Der zweite Brief an die Thessaloniker* (ZBK, 11.2; Zürich: TVZ, 1982).

Mason, S., *Josephus and the New Testament* (Peabody, Mass.: Hendrickson Publishers, 2nd edn, 2003).

Meizoz, J., *La Fabrique des singularités: Postures littéraires II* (Geneva: Slatkine Erudition, 2011).

————, 'Modern Posterities of Posture: Jean-Jacques Rousseau', in *Authorship Revisited. Conceptions of Authorship Around 1900 and 2000* (ed. G. Dorleijn, R. Grüttenmeier, and L. Korthals Altes; Leuven: Peeters, 2010), pp. 81–94.

————, *Postures littéraires: Mises en scène modernes de l'auteur. Essai* (Geneva: Slatkine Erudition, 2007).

Menken, M. J. J., *2 Thessalonians* (New Testament Readings; London: Routledge, 1994).

Merkel, H., 'Der Epheserbrief in der neueren exegetischen Diskussion', in *ANRW* II.25.4 (1987), pp. 3156–246.

Merklein, H., *Christus und die Kirche. Die theologische Grundstruktur des Epheserbriefes nach Eph. 2.11-18* (SBS, 66; Stuttgart: Kath. Bibelwerk, 1973).

————, *Das kirchliche Amt nach dem Epheserbrief* (StANT, 33; München: Kösel, 1973).

————, 'Paulinische Theologie in der Rezeption des Kolosser- und Epheser-briefes', in *Paulus in den neutestamentlichen Spätschriften. Zur Paulusrezeption im Neuen Testament* (ed. K. Kertelge; QD, 89; Freiburg: Herder, 1981), pp. 25–69.

Merz, A., *Die fiktive Selbstauslegung des Paulus. Intertextuelle Studien zur Intention und Rezeption der Pastoralbriefe* (NTOA, 52; Göttingen: Vandenhoeck und Ruprecht, 2004).

Metzger, B. M., *A Textual Commentary on the Greek New Testament* (Stuttgart: United Bible Societies, 2nd edn, 2000).

Meyer, E., *Ursprung und Anfänge des Christentums* (3 vols; Stuttgart: J. G. Cotta, 1921).

Michaelis, J. D., *Introduction to the New Testament* (London: Rivington, 4th edn, 1823).

Miller, J. B., *Convinced That God Had Called Us: Dreams, Visions, and the Perception of God's Will in Luke-Acts* (BIS, 85; Leiden: Brill, 2007).

Mittelstaedt, A., *Lukas als Historiker. Zur Datierung des lukanischen Doppelwerkes* (TANZ, 43; Tübingen: Franke, 2006).

Mitton, C. L., *The Epistle to the Ephesians: Its Authorship, Origin and Purpose* (Oxford: Clarendon, 1951).

Moessner, D. P., 'The Appeal and Power of Poetics (Luke 1:1-4)', in *Jesus and the Heritage of Israel: Luke's Narrative Claim upon Israel's*

342   *Bibliography*

   Legacy (vol. 1 of *Luke the Interpreter of Israel*; ed. D. Moessner;
   Harrisburg: Trinity Press International, 1999), pp. 84–123.

———, '"Completed End(s)ings" of Historiographical Narrative: Diodorus
   Siculus and the End(ing) of Acts', in *Die Apostelgeschichte und hel-*
   lenistische Geschichtsschreibung. Festschrift für Dr. Plümacher (ed.
   C. Breytenbach and J. Schröter; AGAJU, 57; Leiden: Brill, 2004), pp.
   193–221.

———, *Lord of the Banquet. The Literary and Theological Significance of the*
   Lukan Travel Narrative (Minneapolis: Fortress, 1989; Harrisburg, Pa.:
   Trinity Press International, pb. edn, 1998).

———, 'Luke's "Plan of God" from the Greek Psalter: The Rhetorical Thrust
   of "The Prophets and the Psalms" in Peter's Speech at Pentecost', in
   Scripture and Traditions: Essays on Early Judaism and Christianity in
   Honor of Carl R. Holladay (ed. P. Gray and G. R. O'Day; NovTSup, 129;
   Leiden: Brill, 2008), pp. 223–38.

———, '"Managing the Audience". The Rhetoric of Authorial Intent and
   Audience Comprehension in the Narrative Epistemology of Polybius of
   Megalopolis, Diodorus Siculus, and Luke the Evangelist', in *The Word*
   Leaps the Gap: Essays on Scripture and Theology in Honor of Richard
   B. Hays (ed. J. R. Wagner, C. K. Rowe, and A. K. Grieb; Grand Rapids:
   Eerdmans, 2008), pp. 179–97.

———, 'The "script" of the Scriptures in Acts: suffering as God's "plan" (βουλή)
   for the world for the "release of sins"' in *History, Literature, and Society*
   in the Book of Acts (ed. B. Witherington; Cambridge: Cambridge
   University Press, 1996), pp. 218–50.

———, 'The triadic synergy of Hellenistic poetics in the narrative epistemology
   of Dionysius of Halicarnassus and the authorial intent of the evangelist
   Luke (Luke 1:1-4; Acts 1:1-8)', *Neot* 42 (2008), pp. 289–303.

———, '*Two* Lords "at the Right Hand"? The Psalms and an Intertextual Reading
   of Peter's Pentecost Speech (Acts 2:14-36)', in *Literary Studies in Luke-*
   Acts: Essays in Honor of Joseph B. Tyson (ed. R. P. Thompson and T. E.
   Phillips; Macon, Ga.: Mercer University Press, 1998), pp. 15–32.

Moessner, D. P. (ed.), *Jesus and the Heritage of Israel, Luke's Narrative Claim*
   Upon Israel's Legacy (vol. 1 of *Luke the Interpreter of Israel*; Harrisburg:
   Trinity Press International, 1999).

Morrison, C., *The Powers that Be: Earthly Rulers and Demonic Powers in*
   Romans 13.1-7 (SBT, 29. Naperville, Ill.: Allenson, 1960).

Mount, C., '1 Corinthians 11:3-16: Spirit Possession and Authority in a Non-
   Pauline Interpolation', *JBL* (2005), pp. 313–40.

———, 'Luke-Acts and the Investigation of Apostolic Tradition: From a Life of
   Jesus to a History of Christianity', in *Apostelgeschichte im Kontext* (ed.
   J. Frey, *et al.*; BZNW, 162; Berlin: Walter de Gruyter, 2009), pp. 380–92.

———, *Pauline Christianity: Luke-Acts and the Legacy of Paul* (NovTSup, 104;
   Leiden: Brill, 2002).

————, 'Religious Experience, the Religion of Paul, and Women in Pauline Churches', in *Women and Gender in Ancient Religions: Interdisciplinary Approaches* (ed. Stephen P. Ahearne-Kroll, Paul A. Holloway, and James A. Kelhoffer; WUNT, 263; Tübingen: Mohr Siebeck, 2010), pp. 323–47.

————, Review of Steve Walton, *Leadership and Lifestyle: The Portrait of Paul in the Miletus Speech and 1 Thessalonians, JR* 82 (2002), pp. 100–101.

Müller, P., *Anfänge der Paulusschule. Dargestellt am zweiten Thessalonicherbrief und am Kolosserbrief* (ATANT, 74; Zürich: TVZ, 1988).

Müller, P. G., 'Der "Paulinismus" in der Apostelgeschichte: Ein forschungs-geschichtlicher Überblick', in *Paulus in den neutestamentlichen Spätschriften* (ed. K. Kertelge; QD, 89; Freiburg: Herder, 1981), pp. 157–201.

Munck, J., *The Acts of the Apostles* (AB, 31; Garden City: Doubleday, 1967).

Mussner, F., 'Die Idee der Apokatastasis in der Apostelgeschichte', in *Lex Tua Veritas* (Festschrift H. Junker; Trier: Paulinus, 1961), pp. 293–306.

Musurillo, H., *The Acts of the Christian Martyrs* (Oxford: Clarendon, 1972).

————, *The Acts of the Pagan Martyrs* (Oxford: Clarendon Press, 1954).

Nasrallah, L., *An Ecstasy of Folly. Prophecy and Authority in Early Christianity* (HTS; Cambridge: Harvard University Press, 2003).

Neagoe, A., *The Trial of the Gospel: An Apologetic Reading of Luke's Trial Narratives* (SNTSMS, 116; Cambridge: Cambridge University Press, 2002).

Nicolet, P., 'Le concept d'imitation de l'apôtre dans la correspondance paulinienne', in *Paul, une théologie en construction* (ed. A. Dettwiler, J.-D. Kaestli, and D. Marguerat; MdB, 51; Genève: Labor et Fides, 2004), pp. 393–415.

Nigg, W., *Die Kirchengeschichtsschreibung* (München: C. H. Beck, 1934).

Noormann, R., *Irenäus als Paulusinterpret: Zur Rezeption und Wirkung der paulinischen und deuteropaulinischen Briefe im Werk des Irenäus von Lyon* (WUNT, 2.66; Tübingen: Mohr Siebeck, 1994).

O'Brien, P. T., *Colossians, Philemon* (WBC, 44; Waco: Word, 1982).

————, *The Epistle to the Philippians. A Commentary on the Greek Text* (NIGTC; Grand Rapids: Eerdmans, 1991).

O'Neill, J. C., *Paul's Letter to the Romans* (Hammondsworth: Penguin, 1975).

Overbeck, F., *Christentum und Kultur. Gedanken und Anmerkungen zur modernen Theologie* (Basel: Benno Schwabe, 1919; Darmstadt: Wissenschaftliche Buchgesellschaft, 2nd edn, 1963).

————, 'Ueber das Verhältnis Justins des Märtyrers zur Apostelgeschichte', *ZWT* 15 (1872), pp. 305–49.

Overbeck, F., and W. M. de Wette, *Erklärung der Apostelgeschichte* (Leipzig: S. Hirzel, 4th rev. edn, 1870).

Parsons, M. C., *Acts* (Paideia Commentaries on the NT; Grand Rapids: Baker Academic, 2008).

————, *Luke. Storyteller, Interpreter, Evangelist* (Peabody, Mass.: Hendrickson, 2007).

Penner, T., 'Reconfiguring the Rhetorical Study of Acts. Reflections on the Method
    in and Learning of a Progymnastic Poetics', *PRSt* 30 (2003), pp. 425–39.
Percy, E., *Die Probleme der Kolosser- und Epheserbriefe* (Acta reg. societatis
    humaniorum litterarum Lundensis, 39; Lund: G. C. K. Gleerup, 1946).
Pervo, R. I., *Acts. A Commentary* (Hermeneia; Minneapolis: Fortress, 2009).
———, *Dating Acts: Between the Evangelists and the Apologist* (Santa Rosa,
    Calif.: Polebridge, 2006).
———, 'A Hard Act to Follow: *The Acts of Paul* and the Canonical Acts', *JHC*
    2 (1995), pp. 3–32.
———, *The Making of Paul: Constructions of the Apostle in Early Christianity*
    (Minneapolis: Fortress, 2010).
———, *Profit with Delight: The Literary Genre of the Acts of the Apostles*
    (Philadelphia: Fortress, 1987).
Pichler, J., *Paulusrezeption in der Apostelgeschichte: Untersuchungen zur Rede im
    pisidischen Antiochien* (Innsbrucker Theologische Studien, 50; Innsbruck:
    Tyrolia-Verlag, 1997).
———, 'Das theologische Anliegen der Paulusrezeption im lukanischen Werk', in
    The Unity of Luke-Acts (ed. J. Verheyden; BETL, 142; Leuven: Leuven
    University Press, 1999), pp. 731–33.
Pilch, J. J., *Visions and Healing in the Acts of the Apostles: How the Early
    Believers Experienced God* (Collegeville, Minn.: Liturgical Press, 2004).
Pilhofer, P., *ΠΡΕΣΒΥΤΕΡΟΝ ΚΡΕΙΤΤΟΝ* (WUNT, 2.39; Tübingen: Mohr,
    1990).
Plümacher, E., 'Rom in der Apostelgeschichte', in *Geschichte und Geschichten.
    Aufsätze zur Apostelgeschichte und zu den Johannesakten* (ed. J. Schröter
    and R. Brucker; WUNT, 170; Tübingen: Mohr Siebeck, 2004).
Pohlenz, M., 'Paulus und die Stoa', *ZNW* 42 (1949), pp. 69–104.
Pokorny, P., *Der Brief des Paulus an die Epheser* (ThHK, 10.2; Leipsig:
    Evangelische Verlagsanstalt, 1992).
Popkes, W., *Paränese und Neues Testament* (SBS, 168; Stuttgart: Kath. Bibelwerk,
    1996).
Porter, S. E., *The Paul of Acts: Essays in Literary Criticism, Rhetoric, and
    Theology* (WUNT, 115; Tübingen: Mohr Siebeck, 1999).
Radl, W, *Paulus und Jesus im lukanischen Doppelwerk: Untersuchungen zu
    Parallelmotiven im Lukasevangelium und in der Apostelgeschichte*
    (Bern: Herbert Lang; 1975).
Rahner, H., 'Ammonios v. Alexandrien', in *Lexicon für Theologie und Kirche* (ed.
    M. Buchberger; Freiburg: Herder, 1957–1965), p. 441.
Reasoner, M., *Romans in Full Circle: A History of Interpretation* (Louisville:
    Westminster, 2005).
———, 'The Theme of Acts: Institutional History or Divine Necessity in
    History?', *JBL* 118 (1999), pp. 635–59.
Redalié, Y., *Paul après Paul: Le temps, le salut, la morale selon les épîtres à
    Timothée et à Tite* (MdB, 31; Geneva: Labor et Fides, 1994).

Reed, J. T., *A Discourse Analysis of Philippians: Method and Rhetoric in the Debate over Literary Integrity* (JSNTSup, 136; Sheffield: Sheffield Academic Press, 1997).

Reicke, B., *Re-examining Paul's Letters. The History of the Pauline Correspondence* (ed. D. P. Moessner and I. Reicke; Harrisburg, Pa.: Trinity Press International, 2001).

Reis, D. M., 'Following in Paul's Footstep: Mimèsis and Power in Ignatius of Antioch', in *Trajectories through the New Testament and the Apostolic Fathers* (ed. A. F. Gregory and C. M. Tuckett; Oxford: Oxford University Press, 2005), pp. 287–305.

Reynier, C., *Évangile et mystère: Les enjeux théologiques de l'épître aux Ephesians* (LD, 149; Paris: Éditions du Cerf, 1992).

Rice, G., 'Western Non-Interpolations: A Defense of the Apostolate', in *Luke-Acts: New Perspectives from the Society of Biblical Literature Seminar* (ed. C. Talbert; New York: Crossroad, 1983), pp. 1–16.

Ricoeur, P., *Temps et Récit* (vol. 1; Paris: Seuil, 1983). ET: *Time and Narrative* (trans. by K. McLaughlin and D. Pellauer; Chicago: University of Chicago Press, 1984).

Rigaux, B., *Saint Paul. Les épîtres aux Thessaloniciens* (EBib; Paris: Lecoffre, 1956).

Robbins, V. K., 'The Claims of the Prologues and Greco-Roman Rhetoric: The Prefaces to Luke and Acts in Light of Greco-Roman Rhetorical Strategies', in *Jesus and the Heritage of Israel. Luke's Narrative Claim upon Israel's Legacy* (vol. 1 of *Luke the Interpreter of Israel*; ed. D. Moessner; Harrisburg: Trinity Press International, 1999), pp. 63–83.

———, 'Prefaces in Greco-Roman Biography and Luke-Acts', *PRSt* 6 (1979), pp. 94–108; repr. in *Society of Biblical Literature Seminar Papers, 1978* (vol. 2; Missoula, Mont.: Scholars Press, 1978), pp. 193–207.

Robinson J. R., and H. Koester, *Trajectories through Early Christianity* (Philadelphia, Fortress, 1971).

Rohde, E., *Der grieschische Roman und seine Vorläufer* (Leipzig: Breitkopf und Härtel, 2nd edn, 1900).

Roloff, J., *Die Apostelgeschichte* (NTD, 5; Göttingen: Vandenhoeck & Ruprecht, 1981).

———, *Der erste Brief an Timotheus* (EKKNT, 15; Zürich: Benziger, 1988).

———, *Die Kirche im Neuen Testament* (GNT, 10; Göttingen: Vandenhoeck & Ruprecht, 1993).

———, 'Die Paulus-Darstellung des Lukas. Ihre geschichtlichen Voraussetzungen und ihr theologisches Ziel', *EvTh* 39 (1979), pp. 510–31.

———, 'Themen und Traditionen urchristlicher Amtsträgerparänese', in *Neues Testament und Ethik* (Festschrift R. Schnackenburg; ed. H. Merklein; Freiburg: Herder, 1989), pp. 507–28.

Rordorf, W., 'Die neronische Christenverfolgung im Spiegel der Apokryphen Paulusakten', *NTS* 28 (1981–1982), pp. 365–74; repr. in idem, *Lex*

Orandi—Lex Credendi. Gesammelte Aufsätze zum 60. Geburtstag
(Paradosis, 36; Fribourg: Universtitätsverlag, 1993), pp. 368–77.

————, 'Tertullians Beurteilung des Soldatenstandes', in *Lex orandi, lex credenda: gesammelte Aufsätze zum 60. Geburtstag* (Freiburg: Universitätsverlag, 1993), pp. 263–299.

Roscher, W. H., 'Ganymedes', in *Ausführliches Lexicon der Griechischen und Römischen Mythologie* (ed. T. Birth and W. H. Roscher; 13 vols; Leipzig: Teubner, 1886-1890), pp. 1:1595–1603.

Rosenblatt, M.-E., *Paul the Accused: His Portrait in the Acts of the Apostles* (Zacchaeus Studies, NT; Collegeville, Minn.: Liturgical Press, 1995).

Rousseau, A., and L. Doutreleau, *Irénée de Lyon. Contre les hérésies. Livre III* (Sources Chrétiennes; 2 vols; Paris: Les Éditions du Cerf, 1974).

Rowe, C. K., *Early Narrative Christology: The Lord in the Gospel of Luke* (BZNW, 139; Berlin: W. de Gruyter, 2006).

————, 'The Grammar of Life: The Areopagus Speech and Pagan Tradition'. Paper presented at the annual meeting of the Society of Biblical Literature. Atlanta, Ga., November 21, 2010.

————, 'Luke-Acts and the Imperial Cult: A Way through the Conundrum?', *JSNT* 27 (2005), pp. 279–300.

————, 'Romans 10.13: What is the Name of the Lord?', *HBT* 22.2 (2000), pp. 135–73.

————, *World Upside Down: Reading Acts in the Graeco-Roman Age* (Oxford: Oxford University Press, 2009).

Russell, D. A., *Criticism in Antiquity* (Berkeley: University of California Press, 1981).

Sacks, K. S., *Diodorus Siculus and the First Century* (Princeton: Princeton University, 1990).

Scafuro, A. C., 'Universal History and the Genres of Greek Historiography' (unpublished doctoral dissertation, Yale University, 1983).

Schaff, P., *Nicene and Post-Nicene Fathers* (First Series, 11; repr., Buffalo, N.Y.: Christian Literature, 1999).

Schapp, W., *In Geschichten verstrickt. Zum Sein von Mensch und Ding* (Frankfurt: Klostermann, 3rd edn, 1985).

Schluchter, W., 'Einleitung. Max Webers Analyse des antiken Christentums. Grundzüge eines unvollendeten Projekts', in *Max Webers Sicht des antiken Christentums* (ed. W. Schluchter; Frankfurt am Main: Suhrkamp, 1985), pp. 11–71.

————, 'Umbildungen des Charismas. Überlegungen zur Herrschaftssoziologie', in *Religion und Lebensführung. Studien zu Max Webers Kultur- und Werttheorie II* (ed. W. Schluchter; Frankfurt am Main: Suhrkamp, 1988), pp. 535–54.

Schmeller, T., *Schulen im Neuen Testament? Zur Stellung des Urchristentums in der Bildungswelt seiner Zeit. Mit einem Beitrag von Christian Cebuli zur johanneischen Schule* (HBS, 30; Freiburg: Herder, 2001).

Schmid, W., 'Die Rede des Apostels Paulus vor den Philosophen und Areopagiten in Athen', *Philologus* 95 (1942), pp. 79–120.

Schmitals, W., *The Office of the Apostle in the Early Church* (trans. J. E. Steely; Nashville: Abingdon, 1969).

Schnackenburg, R., *Ephesians: A Commentary* (Edinburgh: T&T Clark, 1991).

Schneider, G., *Die Apostelgeschichte* (HThK, 5.1-2; Freiburg: Herder, 1980–82).

Schnelle, U., *Theologie des Neuen Testaments* (UTB, 2917; Göttingen: Vandenhoeck & Ruprecht, 2007).

Schnider, F., and W. Stenger, *Studien zum neutestamentliochen Briefformular* (NTTS, 11; Leiden: Brill, 1987).

Schoellgen, G., 'Die "diplè time" von 1 Tm 5,17', *ZNW* 80 (1989), pp. 232–39.

Schrader, K., *Der Apostel Paulus* (5 vols; Leipzig: Christian Ernst Kollmann, 1830–1836).

Schröter, J., 'Kirche im Anschluss an Paulus: Aspekte der Paulusrezeption in der Apostelgeschichte und in den Pastoralbriefen', *ZNW* 98 (2007), pp. 77–104.

———, 'Paulus als Modell christlicher Zeugenschaft. Apg 9,15f. und 28,30f. als Rahmen der lukanischen Paulusdarstellung und Rezeption des "historischen" Paulus', in *Reception of Paulinism in Acts (Réception du paulinisme dans les Actes des apôtres)* (ed. D. Marguerat; BETL, 229; Leuven: Peeters, 2009), pp. 53–80.

———, *Der versöhnte Versöhner. Paulus als unentbehrlicher Mittler im Heilsvorgang zwischen Gott und Gemeinde nach 2 Kor 2,14–7,4* (TANZ, 10; Tübingen: Francke Verlag, 1993).

———, 'Zur Stellung der Apostelgeschichte im Kontext der antiken Historiographie', in *Apostelgeschichte im Kontext* (ed. J. Frey, *et al.*; BZNW, 162; Berlin: Walter de Gruyter, 2009), pp. 27–47.

Schulze, G., 'Das Paulusbgild des Lukas. Ein historisch-exegetischer Versuch als Beitrag zur Erforschung der lukanischen Theologie' (unpublished dissertation, Kiel, 1960).

Schürer, E., *A History of the Jewish People in the Time of Jesus Christ.* (Rev. and ed. G. Vermes, F. Millar, *et al.*; 3 vols; Edinburgh: T&T Clark, 1973–1987).

Seeberg, B. 'Zur Geschichtstheologie Justins des Märtyrers', *ZKG* LVIII (1939), pp. 1–81.

Segal, A. F., *Paul the Convert: The Apostolate and Apostasy of Saul the Pharisee* (New Haven: Yale University Press, 1990).

Sellin, G., 'Adresse und Intention des Epheserbriefes', in *Paulus, Apostel Jesu Christi* (Festschrift G. Klein; ed. M. Trowitzsch; Tübingen: Mohr, 1998), pp. 171–86.

———, *Der Brief an die Epheser* (KEK, 8; Göttingen: Vandenhoeck & Ruprecht, 2008).

Selwyn, E. G., *The First Epistle of St. Peter* (London: Macmillan, 2nd edn, 1947).

Shantz, C., *Paul in Ecstasy: The Neurobiology of the Apostle's Life and Thought* (Cambridge: Cambridge University Press, 2009).

Ska, J.-L., 'La "nouvelle critique" et l'exégèse anglo-saxonne', *RSR* 80 (1992), pp. 29–53.

Skinner, M. L., *Locating Paul: Places of Custody as Narrative Settings in Acts 21–28* (SBL Academia Biblica, 13; Atlanta: Society of Biblical Literature, 2003).

Smith, J. Z., *Drudgery Divine: On the Comparison of Early Christianities and the Religions of Late Antiquity* (Chicago: University of Chicago Press, 1990).

———, *Map Is Not Territory: Studies in the History of Religions* (SJLA, 23; Leiden: Brill, 1978).

Smith, M., *Jesus the Magician* (San Francisco: Harper & Row, 1978).

———, 'The Report about Peter in Clement 5, 4', *NTS* 7 (1960–1961), pp. 86–88.

Snyder, G. E., 'Remembering the *Acts of Paul*', (unpublished dissertation, Harvard, 2010).

Sobrino, J., *No Salvation Outside the Poor: Utopian-Prophetic Essays* (Maryknoll, N.Y.: Orbis, 2008).

Soden, H. von., 'Sakrament und Ethik bei Paulus', in *Marburger Theologische Studien* (Festschrift R. Otto; Gotha: Leopold Klotz Verlag, 1931).

Spicq, C., *Les épitres pastorales* (EB; 2 vols; Paris: Galbalda, 4th edn, 1969).

Squires, J. T., *The Plan of God in Luke-Acts* (SNTSMS, 76; Cambridge: Cambridge University Press, 1993).

Staab, K., 'Die griechischen Katenenkommentare zu den katholischen Briefen', *Bib* 5 (1924), pp. 296–353.

Stadter, P., 'Biography and History', in *A Companion to Greek and Roman Historiography* (ed. J. Marincola; Blackwell Companions to the Ancient World; 2 vols; Oxford: Blackwell, 2007), 2:528–40.

Sterling, G. E., 'From Apostle to the Gentiles to Apostle of the Church: Images of Paul at the End of the First Century', *ZNW* 99 (2008), pp. 74–98.

———, *Historiography and Self-Definition: Josephos, Luke-Acts and Apologetic Historiography* (NovTSup, 64; Leiden: Brill, 1992).

———, '"Opening the Scriptures": The Legitimation of the Jewish Diaspora and the Early Christian Mission', in *Jesus and the Heritage of Israel: Luke's Narrative Claim upon Israel's Legacy* (vol. 1 of *Luke the Interpreter of Israel*; ed. D. Moessner; Harrisburg: Trinity Press International, 1999), pp. 199–225.

Stolle V., *Der Zeuge als Angeklagter: Untersuchungen zum Paulusbild des Lukas* (BWANT, 102; Stuttgart: Kohlhammer, 1973).

Stowers, S. K., *Letter Writing in Greco-Roman Antiquity* (LEC; Philadelphia: Westminster Press, 1986).

———, 'Letters. Greek and Latin Letters', in *Anchor Bible Dictionary* (6 vols; New York: Doubleday, 1992), pp. 290–93.

Strobel, A., 'Furcht, wem Furcht gebührt. Zum profangriechischen Hintergrund von Röm 13, 1-7', *ZNW* 55 (1964), pp. 58–62.

———, 'Zum Verständnis von Röm 13', *ZNW* 47 (1956), pp. 67–93.

Stuehrenberg, P. F., 'The Study of Acts before the Reformation: A Bibliographic Introduction', *NovT* 29 (1987), pp.100–36.

Swain, S., *Hellenism and Empire. Language, Classicism, and Power in the Greek World, AD 50-250* (Oxford: Clarendon, 1996).

Tajra, H. W., *The Martyrdom of St. Paul: Historical and Judicial Context, Traditions, and Legends* (WUNT, 67. Tübingen: Mohr Siebeck, 1994).

Talbert, C. H., *Literary Patterns, Theological Themes and the Genre of Luke-Acts* (SBLMS, 20; Missoula, Mont.: Scholars Press, 1974).

———, *Reading Luke-A Literary and Theological Commentary on the Third Gospel* (New York: Crossroad, 1982).

Tannehill R. C., *The Narrative Unity of Luke-Acts: A Literary Interpretation* (2 vols; Minneapolis: Fortress, 1986–1990).

Theissen, G., 'Paulus - der Unglücksstifter: Paulus und die Verfolgung der Gemeinden in Jerusalem und Rom', in *Biographie und Persönlichkeit des Paulus* (ed. E.-M. Becker and P. Pilhofer; WUNT, 187; Tübingen: Mohr & Siebeck, 2005), pp. 228–44.

Theobald, M., 'Der Kanon von der Rechtfertigung (Gal. 2.16; Rom. 3.28) - Eigentum des Paulus oder Gemeingut der Kirche?', in *Worum geht es in der Rechtfertigungslehre?* (ed. Th. Söding; QD, 180; Freiburg: Herder, 1999), pp. 131–92.

Thompson, A. J., *One Lord, One People: The Unity of the Church in Acts in its Literary Setting* (LNTS, 359; London: T&T Clark, 2008).

Thompson, G. H. P., 'Eph 3,3 and 2 Tim 2,10 in Light of Col 1,24', *ET* 71 (1959–60), pp. 187–89.

Thompson, R. P. and T. E. Phillips (eds), *Literary Studies in Luke-Acts: Essays in Honor of Joseph B. Tyson* (Macon, Ga.: Mercer University Press, 1998).

Thornton, C-J., *Der Zeuge des Zeugen: Lukas als Historiker der Paulusreisen* (WUNT, 56; Tübingen: Mohr Siebeck, 1991).

Thraede, K., *Grundzüge griechisch-römischer Brieftopik* (Zetemata, 48; München: C. H. Beck, 1970).

Towner, H. P., *The Letters to Timothy and Titus* (NICNT; Grand Rapids: Eerdmans, 2006).

Trilling, W., *Der zweite Brief an die Thessalonicher* (EKK, 14; Zürich: Benziger-Neukirchener, 1980).

Trimpi, W., *Muses of One Mind. The Literary Analysis of Experience and Its Continuity* (Princeton: Princeton University Press, 1983).

Trites, A., *The New Testament Concept of Witness* (SNTSMS, 31; Cambridge: Cambridge University Press, 1977).

Trobisch, D., *Die Paulusbriefe und die Anfänge der christlichen Publizistik* (Kaiser Taschenbücher, 135; Gütersloh: Chr. Kaiser, 1994).

Trummer, P., *Die Paulustradition der Pastoralbriefe* (Frankfurt: Peter Lang, 1978).

Turner, V. W., 'Betwixt and Between: The Liminal Period in Rites de Passage', in *Symposium on New Approaches to the Study of Religion: Proceedings of the 1964 Annual Spring Meeting of the American Ethnological Society* (ed. J. Helm; Seattle: American Ethnological Society, 1964), pp. 4–20.

———, *The Ritual Process: Structure and Anti-structure* (London: Routledge & Kegan, 1969).

Tyson, J. B., *Marcion and Luke-Acts: A Defining Struggle* (Columbia: University of South Carolina Press, 2006).

Tyson, J. B. (ed.), *Luke-Acts and the Jewish People. Eight Critical Perspectives* (Minneapolis: Augsburg, 1988).

Veyne, P., *Comment on écrit l'histoire: Essai d'épistémologie* (L'univers historique; Paris: Seuil, 1971). ET: *Writing History: Essay on Epistemology* (trans. M. Moore-Rinvolucri; Middletown, Conn.: Wesleyan University Press, 1984).

Vielhauer, P., *Geschichte der urchristlichen Literatur: Einleitung in das Neue Testament, die Apokryphen und die Apostolischen Väter* (Berlin: Walter de Gruyter, 1975).

———, 'Zum "Paulinismus" der Apostelgeschichte', *EvTh* 10 (1950–1951), pp. 1–15; repr. in P. Vielhauer, *Aufsätze zum Neuen Testament* (TB, 31; München: Kaiser, 1965), pp. 9–27. ET: 'On the "Paulinism" of Acts', in *Studies in Luke-Acts* (ed. L. Keck and J. Louis Martyn; trans. W. C. Robinson and V. P. Furnish; Philadelphia: Fortress, 1980), pp. 33–50.

Vollenweider, S., 'Paul entre exégèse et histoire de la réception', in *Paul, une théologie en construction* (ed. A. Dettwiler, J.-D. Kaestli, and D. Marguerat; MdB 51; Genève: Labor et Fides, 2004), pp. 441–59.

Wagner, J. R., *Heralds of the Good News: Isaiah and Paul 'In Concert' in the Letter to the Romans* (NovTSup, 101; Leiden: Brill, 2002).

Walker, W. O., 'Acts and the Pauline Corpus Reconsidered', *JSNT* 24 (1985), pp. 3–23; repr. in *The Pauline Writings* (eds. S. E. Porter and C. E. Evans; The Biblical Seminar, 34; Sheffield: Sheffield Academic Press, 1995), pp. 55–74.

———, *Interpolations in the Pauline Letters* (JSNTS, 213; London: Sheffield Academic Press, 2001).

Walton, S., *Leadership and Lifestyle: The Portrait of Paul in the Miletus Speech and 1 Thessalonians* (SNTSMS, 108; Cambridge: Cambridge University Press, 2000).

———, 'The State They Were In: Luke's View of the Roman Empire', in *Rome in the Bible and the Early Church* (ed. Peter Oakes; Grand Rapids: Baker, 2002), pp. 1–41.

Waters, K. H., *Herodotus the Historian: His Problems, Methods and Originality* (Norman: University of Oklahoma Press, 1985).

Weber, M., *Economy and Society* (London: Routledge, 2008).

Weder, H., *Neutestamentliche Hermeneutik* (Zürcher Grundrisse zur Bibel; Zürich: Theologischer Verlag Zürich, 1986).

Wenham, D., 'Acts and the Pauline Corpus: II. The Evidence of Parallels', in *The Book of Acts in Its Ancient Literary Setting* (ed. B. W. Winter and A. D. Clarke; Grand Rapids: Eerdmans, 1993), pp. 215–58.

Wilken, R. L., *The Christians As the Romans Saw Them* (New Haven: Yale University Press, 1984).

Williams, D. K., *Enemies of the Cross of Christ: The Terminology of the Cross and Conflict in Philippians* (JSNTSup, 223; London: Sheffield Academic Press, 2002).

Williamson, G. A., and A. Louth, *Eusebius. The History of the Church from Christ to Constantine* (London: Penguin Books, rev. edn, 1989).

Wilson, B. R., *Magic and the Millennium. A Sociological Study of Religious Movements of Protest among Tribal and Third-World Peoples* (New York: Harper & Row, 1973).

Winston, D., *The Wisdom of Solomon* (AB, 43. Garden City, N.Y.: Doubleday, 1979).

Wirth, G., *Diodor und das Ende des Hellenismus. Mutmassungen zu einem fast unbekannten Historiker* (Oesterreichische Akademie der Wissenschaften, 600; Wien: Verlag der Oestereichischen Akademie der Wissenschaften, 1993).

Witherington III, B., *Grace in Galatia. A Commentary on St Paul's Letter to the Galatians* (Grand Rapids: Eerdmans 1998).

———, 'Why the "Lost Gospels" Lost Out', *Christianity Today* 48 (June 2004), pp. 26–32.

Witulski, Th., 'Gegenwart und Zukunft in den eschatologischen Konzeptionen des Kolosser- und des Epheserbriefes', *ZNW* 96 (2005), pp. 211–42.

Wolter, M., 'Der Apostel und seine Gemeinden als Teilhaber am Leidensgeschick Jesu Christi: Beobachtungen zur paulinischen Theologie', *NTS* 36 (1990), pp. 535–57.

———, *Der Brief an die Kolosser. Der Brief an Philemon* (ÖTBK, 12; Gütersloh: Gütersloher Verlag, 1993).

———, 'Jesu Tod und Sündenvergebung bei Lukas und Paulus', in *Reception of Paulinism in Acts (Réception du paulinisme dans les Actes des apôtres)* (ed. D. Marguerat; BETL, 229; Leuven: Peeters, 2009), pp. 15–35.

———, *Das Lukasevangelium* (HNT, 5; Tübingen: Mohr, 2008).

———, *Die Pastoralbriefe als Paulustradition* (FRLANT, 146; Göttingen: Vandenhoeck und Ruprecht, 1988).

———, 'Die Proömien des lukanischen Doppelwerks (Lk1,1-4 und Apg 1,1-2)', in *Die Apostelgeschichte im Kontext* (ed. J. Frey, *et al.*; BZNW, 162; Berlin: Walter de Gruyter, 2009), pp. 476–94.

———, 'Pseudonymität II', in *Theologische Realenzyklopädie* (ed. G. Krause and S. M. Schwertner; vol. 27; Berlin: de Gruyter, 1997), pp. 662–70.

———, *Theologie und Ethos im frühen Christentum* (WUNT, 236; Tübingen: Mohr, 2009).

———, 'Verborgene Weisheit und Heil für die Heiden. Zur Traditionsgeschichte und Intention des "Revelationsschemas"', *ZTK* 84 (1987), pp. 297–319.

Yamazaki-Ransom, K. *The Roman Empire in Luke's Narrative* (LNTS, 404; New York: T&T Clark, 2010).

Yee, T. L. N., *Jews, Gentile and Ethnic Reconciliation: Paul's Jewish Identity and Ephesians* (SNTSMS, 130; Cambridge: Cambridge University Press, 2005).

INDEX OF ANCIENT SOURCES

INDEX OF MODERN AUTHORS

Lightning Source UK Ltd.
Milton Keynes UK
UKOW04f1804260914

239222UK00005B/69/P